Critical Acclaim for Robin
The Demon Lover: The Roots of Terrorism

Robin Morgan, an award-winning writer, feminist leader, political theorist, journalist, and editor, has published seventeen books, including the best-selling *The Demon Lover* (Washington Square Press), and the now-classic anthologies *Sisterhood Is Powerful* (1970), and *Sisterhood Is Global* (1984/1996). A founder of contemporary U.S. feminism, she has also been a leader in the international Women's Movement for decades. Her latest books include *A Hot January: Poems 1996–1999*, and *Saturday's Child: A Memoir* (2000). A recipient of the National Endowment for the Arts Prize (Poetry), the Front Page Award for Distinguished Journalism, the Feminist Majority Foundation Award, and numerous other honors, she lives in New York City.

ALSO BY ROBIN MORGAN

POETRY
A Hot January: Poems 1996–1999
Upstairs in the Garden: Selected and New Poems
Depth Perception
Death Benefits
Lady of the Beasts
Monster

FICTION
Dry Your Smile
The Mer Child

NONFICTION
Saturday's Child: A Memoir
The Word of a Woman
A Woman's Creed
The Demon Lover
The Anatomy of Freedom
Going Too Far
Sisterhood Is Global (ed.)
Sisterhood Is Powerful (ed.)
The New Woman (co-ed.)

SISTERHOOD IS FOREVER

THE WOMEN'S ANTHOLOGY
FOR A NEW MILLENNIUM

Compiled, Edited, and with an Introduction by

ROBIN MORGAN

WSP

WASHINGTON SQUARE PRESS

New York   London   Toronto   Sydney   Singapore

A WASHINGTON SQUARE PRESS *Original* Publication

 WSP Washington Square Press
1230 Avenue of the Americas,
New York, NY 10020

ISBN: 0-7434-6627-6

First Washington Square Press trade paperback printing March 2003

10 9 8 7 6 5 4 3 2 1

WASHINGTON SQUARE PRESS and colophon are
registered trademarks of Simon & Schuster, Inc.

For information regarding special discounts for bulk purchases,
please contact Simon & Schuster Special Sales at 1-800-456-6798
or business@simonandschuster.com

Printed in the U.S.A.

Copyright Acknowledgments

"Biologically Correct" is Copyright © 2003 by Natalie Angier; "Landscape of
the Ordinary: Violence Against Women" is Copyright © 2003 by Andrea
Dworkin; "Theater: A Sacred Home for Women" is Copyright © 2003 by Eve
Ensler; "Women in Sports: What's the Score?" is Copyright © 2003 by Barbara
Findlen; "Poverty Wears a Female Face" is Copyright © 2003 by Theresa
Funiciello; "The Proper Study of Womankind: Women's Studies" is Copy-
right © 2003 by Florence Howe; "Outer Space: The Worldly Frontier" is
Copyright © 2003 by Mae C. Jemison; "Parenting: A New Social Contract"
is Copyright © 2003 by Suzanne Braun Levine; "The Politics of Aging" is
Copyright © 2002, 2003 by Cynthia Rich; "Women and Law: The Power
to Change" is Copyright © 2003 by Catharine A. MacKinnon; "Notes of a
Feminist Long Distance Runner" is Copyright © 2003 by Eleanor Holmes
Norton; "The Media and the Movement: A User's Guide" is Copyright © 2003
by Gloria Steinem; "Unfinished Agenda: Reproductive Rights" is Copyright
© 2003 by Faye Wattleton.

ACKNOWLEDGMENTS

SPECIAL THANKS GO to the following people, who helped nurture this anthology to fruition with many different gestures of practical and emotional support and advice: Eve Abzug, Liz Abzug, Malaika Adero, Gloria Anzaldúa, Jeri Baldwin, Mary Kay Blakeley, Kathy Bonk, Cori Chertoff, Esther Cohen (Bread and Roses), Judith Curr, Linda Dingler, Joanne Edgar, Helen French, Marcia Ann Gillespie, Lesley Gore, Rayna Green, Nancy Gruver (*New Moon*), Rebecca Hart, Jennifer Jackman, Gloria Jacobs, Karla Jay, Veronica Jordan, Shelley Kolton, Edite Kroll, Vivienne Labatier, Helen Ann Lally, Ursula K. Le Guin, Suzanne Braun Levine, Deborah Ann Light, Diedre Lovell, Jane Manning, Gail Maynor, Doxie A. McCoy, Michelle Mulbauer, Blake Morgan, Marysa Navarro, Jessica Neuwirth, Joanne Omang, Eleanor Pam, Joyce Patterson, Jan Peterson, Charlotte Phillips, Amy Richards, Isel Rivero, Cheryl Rogers, Kate Rounds, Virginia Sanchez-Korral, Lois Sasson, Claire Serling, Pamela Shifman, Jane Stanicki, Gloria Steinem, Mary Thom, Lily Tomlin, Urvashi Vaid, Genevieve Vaughan, and Jane Wagner. Particular gratitude goes to Rosemary Ahern, former Vice President and Director of Washington Square Press; her Executive Assistant, Jennifer Thompson; and Senior Production Editor Linda Roberts.

For
Bella Savitsky Abzug
(1920–1998)

whose legacy endures:

"Never underestimate
the importance
of what we are doing here,
never hesitate to tell the truth,
and never, ever give in—or give up."

CONTENTS

PART III. JUGGLING JEOPARDIES

PART IV. BODIES POLITIC

PERSONAL POSTSCRIPTS

INTRODUCTION: NEW WORLD WOMEN

ROBIN MORGAN

THIS IS A TRULY American book—in the oldest sense and the newest, the broadest sense and the deepest.

It's American in the oldest sense because it gleams with the vision of a New World, but one based on genuinely democratic, holistic values, following Native American models: as Cherokee feminist Rayna Green wrote in her article representing the United States in *Sisterhood Is Global,* "A feminist revolution here would simply honor American tradition, not overthrow it."

It's American in the newest sense because we've crossed the threshold into a (Common Era) fresh century and millennium. More new knowledge has been acquired in the past forty years than in the previous 5,000. That knowledge—whether about DNA, contraceptives, computers, the environment, our human and animal neighbors on this shrinking planet, the neighboring planets in this galaxy, or anything else—affects us all, including the numerical majority of the human species: women.

It's American in the broadest sense because the United States, with its many faults, is still the most multiracial, multiethnic, multicultural nation in the world, a microcosm *of* the world, a still-fragile experiment with enormous potential—and because the U.S. Women's Movement, with all *its* imperfections, is still the most inclusive social justice movement in history.

Last, this book is American in the deepest sense because it proudly sings feminism, which—far from being a "special interest group" phenomenon—represents the well-being of the U.S. majority (women), *and* the sanity and humanity of the minority (men), and because feminism affects every aspect of society in an ultimately transformative manner. We might as well grasp the enormity of our own endeavor: the U.S. Women's Movement is tactically situated to change Earth's now-sole superpower from acting like the bullying scourge of the planet into actually living up to its rhetoric as the hope of the world.

I write this at a time of crisis, fourteen months after the September 11, 2001 attacks. The nation teeters on the brink of initiating an aggressive war no one but oil magnates and politicians seem to want. Across the country, ordinary good people express anxiety, depression, mistrust, helplessness, and anger at major institutions of American life that are imploding in layers of hypocrisy and betrayal. Disillusion has not yet healed from wounds to the electoral process and judicial autonomy— our democracy's twin pride—in the 2000 presidential race, given Florida's disenfranchisement of voters and the Supreme Court's descent into partisan politics. Disillusion grows over a cruelly imbalanced economy (the most unequal distribution of wealth in the industrialized world), whose leaders prate "family values" but practice support for CEOs, not kids—and that disillusion is aggravated by corruption the business community can no longer conceal, with scandals devastating at least six major corporations to date. Disillusion and fear deepen about the intensifying erosion of our prized civil liberties, while disillusion and rage mount over the callousness of U.S. foreign policy and the ineffectiveness of domestic security. Disillusion and bitterness spread against religious institutions for covering up sexual abuse by clergymen—most dramatically, though certainly not exclusively, of children by Roman Catholic priests protected by the Church hierarchy. It could all be stated this way: "With the moral chaos that surrounds us on every side, the corruption in the state, the dissensions in the church, the jealousies in the home, what thinking mind does not feel that we need something new and revolutionary in every department of life?" That was written by Elizabeth Cady Stanton and Susan B. Anthony for the first issue of the newspaper they published from 1868 to 1870, defiantly titled *The Revolution*. They then answered their own question: "The name speaks its purpose. It is to revolutionize. It is radicalism practical, not theoretical. It is to effect changes through abolitions, reconstructions, and restorations. It is to realize ancient visions, answer long-uttered prayers, and fulfill old prophecies."

Radicalism practical. The Women's Movement.

A Tale of Three Sisterhoods . . .

The U.S. Women's Movement is in a sense the victim of its own success: our accomplishments, while almost never credited to feminism, are construed as negating the *need* for feminism. In our young country, American women (and men) often suffer from ahistoric unawareness, find ourselves vulnerable to superficial media interpretation, and risk becoming more reactive than proactive because of too little strategizing about the future. Partly, that's traceable to the lack of an accessible recent history, insightful perspectives on the present, and the articulation of visionary yet pragmatic strategies. We enjoy a renaissance in feminist writing: literature, political theory, scholarly research. But with *Sisterhood Is Powerful* now available only in hard-to-find copies, there's no "entry" book, no "primer," no composite mural of the vastness that now comprises U.S. feminism(s). And there's no single, trustworthy, populist, portable resource that offers women—and men of conscience—the multifaceted truths about where we've been, are now, and are going. This book aims to meet that need.

The year 2000 marked the thirtieth anniversary of *Sisterhood Is Powerful*'s publication.[1] Thirty years steadily in print is quite a record— a particularly delicious one since, as I was compiling that anthology, publishing colleagues urged me to hurry the deadline, fearing that if we didn't *rush* into print, "this women's lib thing" would vanish in six months. Yet *SIP* soon became a classic, the personal ticket to feminist consciousness for millions of women. Other feminist anthologies came and went—but the famous chunky book with the red-on-white cover and feminist symbol kept going: serving as the basic primer of women's studies in thousands of high-school, college, and graduate courses, becoming indispensable to libraries, researchers, and classes in sociology, political science, psychology, sexuality, gender studies, men's studies, lesbian/gay studies, American studies, black studies,[2] etc. *Sisterhood Is*

---

1. *Sisterhood Is Powerful: An Anthology of Writings from the Women's Liberation Movement*, compiled, edited, and with an introduction by Robin Morgan (New York: Random House and Vintage Books, 1970). *SIP* finally went out of print in 2001.

2. It's a source of pride that distinguished feminist educator Beverly Guy-Sheftall, in her essay here on the legacy of black feminism, notes how Frances Beale's article, "Double Jeopardy: To Be Black and Female," in *Sisterhood Is Powerful* influenced her and other younger African American women toward their own feminism.

Powerful inspired the first feminist grant-giving organization in U.S. history, The Sisterhood Is Powerful Fund, which I established with the royalties.[3] Authoritarian regimes of the Right and Left—South Africa's apartheid administration, the Chinese government, the Chilean military junta—banned the menacing little anthology, but the American Librarians' Association listed *Sisterhood Is Powerful* among The 100 Most Influential Books of the Twentieth Century, alongside the works of Marx, Freud, and Einstein. I can't count the number of women who, over these decades, have kindly come up to me—after speeches, on picket lines, in airports, even at the grocery checkout—simply to say, "*Sisterhood Is Powerful* changed my life. Thanks."

It changed mine, too. So right back at you: *Thanks.*

In 1984, my second *Sisterhood* anthology, *Sisterhood Is Global*—fourteen years in the making and covering more than eighty countries—came out,[4] inviting critical praise and even more academic course adoption (in addition to the disciplines mentioned above: international affairs, development studies, law, anthropology, environmental studies, and diplomacy). Alice Walker called *Sisterhood Is Global* "one of the most important human rights documents of the century." Contributors included major figures like the late Simone de Beauvoir (with her final statement on feminism), and introduced to Western readers various writers who subsequently found U.S. audiences for their own books. *SIG* spun off into activism, inspiring the first international feminist think tank, The Sisterhood Is Global Institute *(www.SIGI.org)*. It was published in a United Kingdom Commonwealth edition (London: Penguin, 1985), and a Spanish edition, *Mujeres del Mundo* (Barcelona: Editions Hacer, 1993). Despite major political shifts in Eastern Europe,

---

3. In its lifetime, the Fund made history, set a precedent, and gave money to hundreds of women's groups across the country. Grants helped to establish the alternative feminist media—newspapers, magazines, and book publishers—as well as the first rape crisis center, the first shelters for battered wives and incest survivors, and many of the first constituency-focused feminist organizations: African American, Latina, Asian American, Native American, lesbian, and welfare-advocacy groups. For details, see *Saturday's Child: A Memoir*, by Robin Morgan (New York: W. W. Norton, 2000).

4. *Sisterhood Is Global: The International Women's Movement Anthology*, compiled, edited, and introduced by Robin Morgan (New York: Doubleday and Anchor Books, 1984; 2d, updated ed., New York: The Feminist Press at CUNY, 1996).

South Africa, and South America, the statistics on women's status ironically stayed virtually the same, so *SIG* remained timely and stayed in print for twelve years. When the rights reverted to me in 1996, I readily agreed to The Feminist Press's request to bring the book back into print immediately. That edition—for which I wrote a new, updating preface—thrives to this day.

I've been asked about the so-called secret of these anthologies, what fosters their popularity and unusual longevity, why many regard them as "definitive." The question is flattering, but there's no secret—or if there is, the components are simple: (1) commissioning brand-new articles from a deliberately audacious mix of voices: famous through moderately known to virtually unknown contributors; (2) being broadly inclusive so as to be representative, while honestly acknowledging the impossibility of ever being exhaustive; (3) respecting—in fact celebrating—the *personal* voice and experience of each contributor: her humor, passion, anger, and the integrity of her unique perspective; (4) nurturing each piece via the editing process to forge its information and energy into a bridge between the contributor's reality and the reader's, toward an electrifying moment of recognition—what elsewhere I've termed the "You, *too?!*" Epiphany. The process isn't easy. But it's worth it.

Like *Sisterhood Is Powerful*, this collection focuses on the U.S. Women's Movement and its multiple constituencies—for two reasons. First, *Sisterhood Is Global* remains in print and relevant; second, the U.S. movement has grown exponentially during the past three decades, so a mere updating of *Sisterhood Is Powerful* couldn't possibly suffice. A new, American *Sisterhood*, for today and the future, was needed. And it *is* needed, because contemporary feminism is here to *stay*. Hence the title of this book. *We ain't goin' backward, crazy, under, or away.*

We've spent almost forty years building a vital, alternate feminist "establishment"—visionaries, theorists, organizers, leaders, and activists who've created and solidified concepts and institutions that have profoundly transformed the ways Americans live, how we perceive ourselves and the world. The contents page lists many of these well-known women, addressing and updating specific subjects with which they're most associated through years of activism. But fresh feminist definitions are also bursting forth from younger women, teenagers, and girls; these voices—enthusiastic, determined, sometimes surprising—are proudly featured here. The energy of dialogue hums across these pages, a communication spanning not only race, ethnicity, age, class, and sexual-preference/orientation differences, but among such previously ignored, silenced, or marginalized constituencies as disabled women, old women, women on welfare, women in prison, and prostituted women fighting sexual slavery.

This is what I call *multidimensional feminism*, or "a multiplicity of feminism*s*."[5]

Why Here? Why Now?

Some may wonder: Why a new anthology specific to the United States? Isn't feminism old-hat here, having already triumphed? (I must've been in the shower and missed it.) Haven't American women "got it made," especially when our situation is compared with women's circumstances in many other countries? Shouldn't we aim our activism only outward at, say, the plight of Afghan women? Such questions expose a triple ignorance: about women's current status in the United States, about the dynamism of international feminism, and about the impact that activism here has abroad.

Wherever women are, we constitute, in effect, a colony: low on (controlling) technology, intensive on labor, and often "mined for our natural resources"—e.g., sexuality and offspring.[6] Still, a few specifics never hurt. So here are some signs of progress hard-won by American women. Here, too, is some evidence of why we'll be "post-feminist" only when we're "post-patriarchy."

• In 1970, when *Sisterhood Is Powerful* was published, one woman was in the Senate and 12 were in the House of Representatives.

---

5. See *The Anatomy of Freedom: Feminism in Four Dimensions*, by Robin Morgan, 2d ed. (New York: W. W. Norton, 1994).

6. If that statement strikes you as "extreme," see the articles by Gail Dines (p. 306) and Vednita Carter (p. 315), on the economics of, respectively, the pornography and prostitution industries.

At this writing, a record 13 women[7] sit in the Senate (out of 100) and a record 60 sit in the House (out of 435); not one committee in the 107th Congress is headed by a woman. There are 12 African American women in the House (plus one delegate and one Caribbean American delegate), and 6 Latinas; in September 2002, we mourned the death of Representative Patsy Mink, a feminist leader, an Asian American, and the first woman of color ever to be elected to Congress. Currently, there are no women (or men) of color in the Senate. Women account for only 13 percent of the world's parliamentarians, and the U.S. ranks 45th in representation of women in national legislatures or parliaments worldwide.[8] Women now comprise approximately 20 percent of state legislators in the U.S., also a record. There have been only 19 women state governors in U.S. history (a record high of 5 currently sitting) with a record 10 women having won their state primaries now poised for the November 2002 elections.[9] (As Pat Schroeder urges here in her sharp-witted article on electoral politics, this is a job category *lots* of women should be seeking.)

• In 1970, the number of women Supreme Court justices was zero; currently it's two out of nine. (As Catharine MacKinnon makes clear in her essay, law has the power to revolutionize our lives—but not until we clasp the power to revolutionize law.)

• In 1970, women earned 59.4 cents to every dollar men earned; today, overall, women earn 76 percent of what men earn (though the narrowing gap is partly due to a drop in *men's* earnings, and mostly affects single employed women). Three quarters of U.S.

---

7. One senator, Hillary Rodham Clinton, broke historical precedent. There had been politically active "First Ladies" before—most notably Edith Wilson and Eleanor Roosevelt—but never had a First Lady dared run for a seat in the U.S. Senate. This would have been unthinkable if not for three decades of contemporary feminism.

8. The highest participation is in the Nordic countries—running between 35 percent of the parliament in Iceland to 42 percent in Sweden—as compared with 13 percent in the United States.

9. See The Center for the American Woman in Politics website *(www.cawp. rutgers.edu)* and that of The White House Project *(www.thewhitehouseproject.org)*.

women working fulltime still make less than $25,000 a year; more than a third of all employed U.S. women earn less than $10,000. The "Workplaces" section of this anthology brims with the figures, and the "Juggling Jeopardies" section disaggregates still more workforce statistics by race, ethnicity, immigration status, disability, and prison labor. But here's a taste: women in executive, administrative, and managerial positions earn 68 percent of what their male counterparts earn;[10] women pharmacists get 86 percent of what male colleagues earn, women college professors 77 percent, women surgeons 76 percent, women lawyers 70 percent. Women have made progress breaking into traditionally male-dominated fields though, of course, they earn less: women engineers earn 82 percent of what men do, women construction workers 74 percent, women truckdrivers 71 percent; the number of women veterinarians increased 22-fold from 1989 to 2001 (this is the fastest gaining occupation for women, who are now almost 43 percent of vets), but they earn 15 percent less than male vets.[11] And here's a shock: in traditionally *female* fields, women also earn less than men: nurses 94 percent, social workers 93 percent, elementary-school teachers 90 percent, food-preparation service workers 89 percent. Half the workforce isn't covered by the Family and Medical Leave Act, and 80 percent of working-poor mothers have less than one week of sick leave per year.

• Unionized women earn 31 percent more than non-union women, but while women constitute almost 40 percent of trade-union members worldwide, only one percent of trade-union

---

10. The difference in managerial salaries between women and men *increased* from 1995 to 2000, according to a report by the U.S. Congress General Accounting Office. Women comprise half the U.S. workforce but only 12 percent of the managers. As of 2002, of the chief executives who run Fortune 500 companies, only six are women.

11. This phenomenon—a job version of "block busting"—wherein women finally break into a field and then "drive the property values down," crops up in a number of articles. For instance, Ellen Bravo reveals the history of how secretarial/clerical work originally was prestigious and highly paid—*until* women entered the field.

leaders are women.[12] Women holding jobs particularly vulnerable to exploitation—housecleaners, maids, nannies, home-aid caregivers, etc.—are attempting to union-organize.[13] Over 90 percent of those who care for children and/or a disabled, frail, ailing, or dying adult in the home are women; 43 percent of caregivers report incomes under $30,000; *76 percent* of caregivers are *un*paid—yet the estimated value of family care of adults alone is more than $200 billion per year.[14] (Theresa Funiciello's cogent, demystifying article on how poor women are kept poor—and how that's connected to the unvalued caregiving of *all* women—offers specifics and solutions.) *An American woman is five times more likely to die in poverty than an American man.*

• Even in the nonprofit world, inequity persists. Over half of all personal wealth in the United States is now held under women's names (attempts to *control* their own wealth are another story); but less than 7 percent of grants from traditional funding sources go to programs for women and girls—a percentage that's barely changed since 1995. Women in the nonprofit sector earn less than their male counterparts, and look *where* they are: women are the chief executives at organizations with annual budgets of $500,000 or less, but men hold 76 percent of those jobs at organizations with budgets of more than $5 million, and *88 percent* of top jobs at organizations with budgets over $50 million.[15] That's called *systemic power*—even over the cash necessary to try to *change* the system.

• Visibility itself remains an issue. Approximately 90 percent of lead characters in educational TV are male—as are 87 percent

---

12. "ILO Director-General Takes Aim at 'Glass Ceiling,' Commits Organisation to Gender Equality in Workplace" (press release, International Labour Organisation, 8 March 2001).

13. One such effort is the United Domestic Workers of America *(www.udwa.org)*.

14. Social Agenda (The Women's Think Tank and Advisory Group): the Caregiver Credit Campaign *(www.caregivercredit.org)*.

15. 2001 study by GuideStar, national database on nonprofit organizations.

of experts cited on public affairs and news programs, and 80 percent of the decision-making characters in top films.

• There's been major progress in sports, thanks to feminist agitation, an athlete named Billie Jean King, and a little law called Title IX (currently under assault by conservatives). In 1974, there were 107 female pro tennis players, 18 tournaments and $1 million in prize money; by the late 1990s there were more than 1,100 pro players, 54 tournaments, and $38 million in prize money. In 1970, one in 27 girls participated in high-school sports; by 2000, it was *one in less than three girls*. Barbara Findlen's spirited report celebrates the progress, but sounds the alarm about current threats—including backlash, persistent homophobia, and exploitative commercial marketing.

• Attitudinal and "lifestyle" change has been dramatic—and the too-modest Women's Movement should claim credit from the rooftops. In 1972, almost 43 percent of women said sex before marriage was wrong; by 1996, it had fallen to 27 percent.[16] Demographics reflect women marrying later, having kids later, having fewer kids, deciding to have kids without marrying at all, and deciding to live full lives without having any kids. As definitions of "family" broaden, by 2001, traditional "nuclear" families for the first time constituted less than 25 percent of American households. Bible Belt couples are among the high marriage casualties: the divorce rate in Arkansas, Oklahoma, Tennessee, etc., is roughly 50 percent above the national average, and happens to coincide with areas that have the highest rates of domestic violence.[17] (No wonder the Bush II administration and its Right-wing religious-fundamentalist base push legislation to promote marriage!) We've made great gains in liberating language: nonsexist terminology is now largely mandated in government usage, as well as at most business, media, religious, and

---

16. Because, as Faye Wattleton aptly notes (p. 17), fear of and conflict over female sexuality underlie the entire reproductive rights debate, this demographic statistic is even more important than it looks.

17. "Bible Belt Couples 'Put Asunder' More, Despite Concerted Efforts," by Blaine Harden (*New York Times*, 21 May 2001).

other institutions—all of which change slowly, only under pressure. Because the struggles of one generation tend to provoke the next generation's yawns, it's naturally hard for younger women fully to comprehend that their mothers (or older sisters), if married, could not get bank accounts of their own; that an accidental pregnancy meant bearing an unwanted child or risking likely death in an illegal back-alley abortion; that it was normal to call a secretary "Cutie" but unheard of to call a secretary of state "Her Excellency"; that it was impossible to take a course in women's history, much less major in women's studies—since neither existed.

- Science itself, ostensibly unbiased, is being freed from embedded male bias by contemporary feminism. Natalie Angier's witty, informative article on biology is fine evidence of that. More evidence is provided by Carol Gilligan, reporting on how psychology is experiencing a "quiet revolution" by including women's presence, values, and realities (back in 1970, Freud still reigned supreme). Only since 1995 has the federal government, after decades of movement agitation, mandated broad representation of both sexes in agency-funded medically relevant research grants (see Pat Schroeder's behind-the-scenes story on how *that* happened). One result among many: in March 2002 (in a study published in the *Psychological Review* of the American Psychological Association), UCLA researchers identified key biobehavioral patterns used by women to manage stress. They named the patterns "tend and befriend," noting that women, like the females of many species, respond to stressful conditions by protecting and nurturing their young (tend) and seeking contact and support from others, especially other females (befriend). This is in contrast, say the researchers, to the "fight or flight" behavior (aggressive response or withdrawal) men show under stress, which had been assumed to be the norm for men *and* women.[18] This finding means a re-evaluation of all stress-management studies—one example of how scientific findings

---

18. Women's reaction may be based on the release of oxytocin. Men release it too, but its effects appear to get reduced by male hormones.

vital to everyone are enhanced when not based on less than half the population.

- Internationally, a brief status report is heartening—and heart-breaking. Over the years, attendance at international women's conferences has grown exponentially. International, regional, and national women's NGOs (non-governmental organizations) have been networking and litigating, using the hard-won 1998 landmark decision of the UN that finally recognized rape as a war crime.[19] Similarly, we've been building precedent, using UN Security Council Resolution 1325 (passed in 2000 after intense feminist lobbying), which recognizes the crucial role of women in conflict prevention, resolution, and management, as well as in peace building. In 2001, after three decades of Women's Movement pressure, Amnesty International became the first human-rights organization to define circumstances of private violence against women as torture. Feminists have even forced the World Bank to concede the centrality of women's activism to sustainable development. In the spring of 2002, international demographers expressed shock that what feminists have been saying for decades is actually *true:* when women—no matter how poor or illiterate—gain control over their reproductive lives, population declines (in India, for example, by 2100 there may be 600 million fewer people than demographers had predicted). Furthermore, once choice—not imposed "population control"—is available, women start pushing for greater decision-making roles in families and society, more literacy training, more economic independence.[20]

But wait. Contrast the above with the Bush administration's July 2002 decision to cut off all $34 million in funds for the United Nations Population Fund (UNFPA)—in every one of the 142 countries where it operates. The rationale? Protest at China's coercive-contraception population policy, even though

---

19. This of course begs the question, *If rape in war is a crime against humanity, then what is it in peacetime?* But, as feminists know, we take it one step at a time.

20. "Population Estimates Fall as Poor Women Assert Control," by Barbara Crossette (*New York Times,* 10 March 2002).

the State Department found no evidence that U.S. dollars have ever been channeled into such programs. (A secondary excuse cited was lack of funds—ironic, considering the priorities.[21]) The administration even insisted the phrase "reproductive health services" be deleted from documents of the UN Earth Summit in South Africa, as their anti-choice voter base feels such a phrase connotes abortion. Let's forget for a moment that the U.S. has the highest teen pregnancy and infant death rates of any industrialized nation; let's focus on the *global* effect of such a vicious policy—on health, life expectancy, population. Pregnancy is the leading cause of death among girls age 15 to 19 in most poor countries, many of them child brides in forced marriages or children caught in the sex-trafficking industry; 99 percent of the 500,000 deaths from maternal mortality each year are in developing countries. The U.S. policy claims to target China, but means no emergency obstetric care in Bangladesh or Mali, higher rates of maternal and infant mortality in Burundi, less emergency medical aid for survivors of female genital mutilation in Sudan, less attention to the more than 300 million cases of STIs (sexually transmitted infections) diagnosed annually worldwide—afflicting one in 20 adolescents and five times more women than men—and less medicine for the record 33.4 million people infected with HIV/AIDS globally (half of them now women), with 16,000 new cases every day.

In 2000, UNFPA and Unicef (UN Children's Fund) updated their international statistics on women's status. A few examples suffice. Given approximately 80 million unwanted pregnancies a year and 20 million unsafe abortions, one woman a minute dies of pregnancy-related causes. Two thirds of the 300 million children lacking access to education are girls, and two thirds of the 880 million illiterate adults are women. Unicef reported a rise in violence against women; 100 million women and girls are "missing" globally—victims of sex-selection abortion, female infanti-

---

21. In 2000, the U.S. spent $281 billion on our military, more than the next 11 nations *combined*. By 2003, our military expenditures will have risen to $378 billion. Meanwhile, the Bush II administration has allotted $100 million to "promote marriage."

cide, and sex-based denial of food and medical attention. Meanwhile, because of arm-twisting by the United States, the UN announced budget cuts: the deepest in administrative services—including programs to fight poverty and enhance women's status.

So to those who'd ask "Why an American-focused women's anthology now?" I'd answer, "Because American women are nowhere near finished with *our* revolution, for *ourselves.* Because what happens here is also critical to the entire world. Because like it or not, this is now the sole superpower, and every U.S. policy has global ripple effects. Because the world comes *to* us: approximately one million immigrants arrive in the United States each year, 52 percent from Latin America, 30 percent from Asia, 13 percent from Europe.[22] Because such realizations should inspire *not* guilt—a paralyzing, counterproductive emotion—but *action.* Because *what you and I do here matters.*"

How we do it means understanding what we have (and haven't) done so far.

Some History . . .

Just as the multifaceted U.S. population reflects the world's people, so U.S. feminism is in some ways a microcosm of international feminism. They share many refrains—a basic one being that women have initiated or volunteered for virtually every progressive cause, only to be excluded as the goal nears realization, then to become radicalized about their own oppression. But U.S. feminism has also been influenced by issues specific to its context. Primary among them is a scar of racism left on the national psyche by the wound of institutionalized slavery. Another is the bigotry innocently aroused and painfully suffered by waves of immigrant populations lured by promises of opportunity but met by discriminations from which the only escape seemed (implicitly forced) assimilation.

---

22. Statistics in the above three paragraphs drawn from the World Health Organization, Unicef, UNFPA, UNAIDS, UN Development Programme, The Population Council, the U.S. Census Bureau, and the U.S. Immigration and Naturalization Services.

Feminism as an evolving movement in the United States has been partly or wholly responsible for extraordinary social progress—for which, maddeningly, it is rarely credited. Women's entrance into the educational system was the direct result of feminist organizing, as were women's attempts to unionize; the emergence of women into the professions in the late nineteenth and early twentieth centuries; the fight for reproductive freedom; the battle for women's property, inheritance, credit, divorce, and custody rights; the diminishing size of the family and its redefinition in broader terms; the struggle for the rights of lesbian women, disabled women, girls, and old women; and women's continuing efforts to become full citizens with equal civil and political rights under the Constitution. That's a *sampling* of feminist accomplishment.

Interestingly, feminists seem to have understood from the beginning that *all* issues are "women's issues," so it's not coincidental that they were also founders and organizers in the earliest stages of (only a partial list): anti-poverty work, abolition of slavery, child-welfare crusades, penal reform, public-health campaigns, peace movements (regarding every violent conflict, including the Civil War), and environmental activism—often overtly identifying a problem as a symptom of the underlying malady: patriarchy. Women's activism in the temperance movement, for instance, was based on their precocious analysis that a correlation existed between male alcoholism and wife battery; more than a century later, scientific data would confirm the experience-based hypothesis of these "crazy" women.

Given such pervasive activism, it's seriously misleading to term the nineteenth-century women's rights movement "the first wave," then call the contemporary movement begun in the 1960s "the second wave," and name younger feminists "third wavers."[23] These misnomers are accurate only if we define feminism narrowly: polite organizing done in the U.S. by primarily white, middle-class women, for a limited number of equal rights (however important) attainable under the social, economic, and political status quo. And "wave" terminology makes *no* sense internationally. There were twelfth-century harem revolts in what is

23. "Wave" terminology got started with a well-meant, off-hand remark in the late 1960s by Kate Millett; it was picked up by the media and thereafter institutionalized—along with "bra burning," a media invention of an act that never took place (see *Saturday's Child*, op. cit.).

now Turkey; Christine de Pisan penned her furious feminist tracts in thirteenth-century France; all-female armies fought for women's rights in China during the 1790s White Lotus Rebellion, the 1851 Taiping Rebellion, *and* the 1899 Boxer Rebellion; Gandhi acknowledged that he copied his nonviolent resistance tactics from the Indian women's rights movement; Argentina's Feminist Party was founded as early as 1918—you get the point.[24] "Wave" oversimplification makes no sense domestically, either. Beverly Guy-Sheftall's essay on black feminism is a superb example of the buried history of activism by U.S. women of color, from colonial times through slavery, westward expansion, and immigration, to the present. Clara Sue Kidwell (on Native American women), Edna Acosta-Belén and Christine Bose (on multi-faceted Latina organizing), and Helen Zia (on the many faces of Asian American and Pacific Islander feminism), further expand feminist history—*if* we *hear* them. "Waving," however well-intentioned, collaborates in the erasure of that history, and its implicit definition of "the F word" seems all the more shallow when contrasted with a definition of feminism as "aiming at nothing less than an entire subversion of the present order of society, a dissolution of the whole existing social compact." So declared Elizabeth Oakes Smith—in 1852. Actually, today's Women's Movement is more like "the ten thousandth wave"—a *tidal* wave—that keeps on rolling.

Any summary of U.S. feminism hazarded in such limited space will be unavoidably superficial. Fortunately, there's no lack of excellent histories available;[25] some are Internet-accessible on-line, for free.[26]

---

24. See *Sisterhood Is Global*, op. cit.

25. See, for example, *The Reader's Companion to U.S. Women's History*, Wilma Mankiller et al., eds. (New York: Houghton Mifflin, 1998); *Words on Fire: An Anthology of African American Feminist Thought*, B. Guy-Sheftall, ed. (New York: New Press, 1995); *Feminism: The Essential Historical Writings*, Miriam Schneir, ed. (New York: Vintage, 1972); *The Vintage Book of Feminism*, M. Schneir, ed. (New York: Vintage, 1994); *Feminism in Our Time*, M. Schneir, ed. (New York: Vintage, 1994); and *The Creation of Feminist Consciousness*, by Gerda Lerner (New York: Oxford University Press, 1993).

26. See "Women in American History (1600s through the 1990s)" at the Encyclopaedia Britannica On-Line *(www.women.eb.com)*, and "The Feminist Chronicles" (1953–1993) at the website of the Feminist Majority Foundation *(www.feminist.org)*. The National Women's History Project *(www.nwhp.org)* has hyperlinks to women's history websites; see also the National Women's History Museum's CyberMuseum at *www.nwhm.org*.

Nevertheless, even a synopsis must properly begin with the indigenous women of North America, many of whom were *sachems* (chiefs) enjoying an equality and authority destroyed by the European invasion.[27] Depending on the Native nation—e.g., the Cherokee, Hopi, or Iroquois—women could and did hold and exercise secular as well as spiritual power. When European men undermined female governance by negotiating treaties with Native men unauthorized to do so, Native women did not take it lightly. It could be said that "New World feminism" was born at that moment.

Those European men, many in flight from political or religious persecution, didn't extend the search for liberty to their European sisters. Instead, they established a Colonial America reflecting Old World values, including its (dis)regard for female people. The women—whether they arrived as rare gentry or, more commonly, as indentured servants, as slaves, or in bride ships—may have had to endure the hardships of colonial life,[28] but they were not docilely resigned to a familiar, proscribed, female existence. Poet Anne Bradstreet, intellectual Ann Hopkins, political agitator Margaret Brent, theologian Anne Hutchinson, and Quaker martyr Mary Dyer are five of many known examples of explicit female rebellion. Women traders in then-New Amsterdam were notorious for their boldness, and numerous women—usually feisty widows and "spinsters"[29]—lodged lawsuits for property denied them because of their sex. Women pushed for a proposal granting them an equal portion of colonial lands in Virginia as early as 1619; the Virginia House of Burgesses rejected it.

Later, not content with a support role, some women would successfully disguise themselves as men to fight in the revolutionary war of in-

---

27. The Americas that Columbus "discovered" were already home to between 72 and 75 million people—a population approximately that of sixteenth-century Europe. North America alone (including what is now Canada, Alaska, and the contiguous United States) was inhabited by an estimated 7 million people of more than 1,000 nations ("Indigenous Peoples—1492 and 1992," *Ms.*, September/October 1992).

28. For example, due to onerous labor, disease, and requirements to "populate" the colonies, of the 144 women of marriageable age who arrived on one of the bride ships to Virginia in 1619, only 35 were still alive six years later.

29. So named for single women who earned their livelihoods, literally, by spinning and weaving.

dependence, as Deborah Sampson did. Small wonder that by 1776, while in Philadelphia at the drafting of the Declaration of Independence, John Adams would receive from his wife, Abigail Smith Adams, the epistolary prophecy warning him that "If particular care and attention is not paid to the ladies, we are determined to foment a rebellion, and will not hold ourselves bound by any laws in which we have no voice or representation." Unfortunately, Adams heeded her advice no more than Thomas Jefferson heeded that of his de facto wife, Sally Hemmings, on denouncing slavery.[30] Nor would this be the last betrayal of female citizens by a revolution that would set an example for worldwide "democracy." Westward expansion, for instance, relied on female labor and sacrifice. As one anonymous Iowan woman wrote at the time, such life "was mighty easy for the men and horses, but death on cattle and women." There were a few roles that broke free from the presumptive one of wife/mother (schoolteacher, solo farmer, businesswoman, even brothel-madam or missionary), but roles enjoying such relative freedom were unattainable for most women.

The same refrain—capitalizing on women's ideas and labor, then forsaking women's rights—surfaces in the history of resistance to slavery. Enslaved women fought back, by stealth or open defiance; they hid fugitive slaves and worked sabotage, managing somehow to keep alive spiritual and cultural values—and, where possible, their families. It was women who organized and sustained the underground railroad for people escaping slavery; it was women who focused the black community's energy on education. The revolt of Nat Turner is deservedly honored. But why don't we equally praise the inherently rebellious work of Lucy Terry and of Phillis Wheatley—both eighteenth-century African slaves, both scholars, both poets? Or the impassioned testimony of Linda Brent who, like most women in bondage, survived sexual slavery in addition to labor slavery, and escaped to become an abolitionist crusader? Or such early women's rights leaders as lecturer Maria Miller Stewart,

---

30. Sally Hemmings, a black woman owned by Jefferson, was his longtime companion and mother to a number of his children. See *Thomas Jefferson: An Intimate History*, by Fawn Brodie (New York: Bantam Books, 1974); *Sally Hemmings*, by Barbara Chase-Riboud (New York: Viking Press, 1979; Avon Press, 1980). See also "Blood Types: An Anatomy of Kin," in *The Anatomy of Freedom: Feminism in Four Dimensions*, op. cit.

suffragist Frances Watkins Harper, and author Anna Julia Cooper, who published the first black feminist book, *A Voice from the South*, in 1892? Women's studies and African American studies have raised the profiles of such titans as Harriet Tubman, the military genius who used the code name "Moses" in her work shepherding hundreds of escaped slaves to freedom, and the stubbornly feminist Sojourner Truth, who fought enslavement in every form and worked actively for women's suffrage. But how many thousands of other such names still go unsung? Why was it that sexism (of black *and* white men) and racism (of white women) was allowed to tear apart the suffrage movement, so that black men gained full national enfranchisement in 1870 with the Fifteenth Amendment, but black women had to wait until 1920 and the Nineteenth?[31] The Abolitionist movement against slavery was itself energized largely by women, in some cases European American women (like the feminist Grimké sisters, Sarah and Angelina) in mutiny against their own white group's privileges.

It was from that Abolitionist movement that the "formal" women's rights movement in the United States was born. Most women present at the historic Seneca Falls Convention in 1848 had been, like the conveners, Lucretia Mott and Elizabeth Cady Stanton, anti-slavery activists for decades. (This pattern would repeat itself in the 1960s, when the more radical wing of the contemporary feminist movement was begun by young veterans—black and white—of the civil-rights struggle.)[32]

Popular belief has it that the nineteenth-century movement focused solely on suffrage, but that became true only in the movement's later, diluted form. At Seneca Falls, the demand for suffrage was almost an afterthought, a last-minute item Stanton tacked on to the list—the only resolution not unanimously supported. In fact, at its inception, this movement was radical and multi-issued. It named male power over women "absolute tyranny." It demanded women's economic and property rights, and denounced slavery, educational discrimination, and the

---

31. Native American women, along with Native American men of federally recognized tribes, were not enfranchised until 1924.

32. See *But Some of Us Are Brave*, Barbara Smith, Gloria Hull, and Patricia Bell Scott, eds. (New York: The Feminist Press, 1982). See also *The Word of a Woman*, by Robin Morgan, 2d ed. (New York: W. W. Norton, 1991), and *Saturday's Child*, op. cit.

exploitation of women as cheap labor in the workforce. It attacked male-supremacist morals and ethics, and identified marriage and the patriarchal family (along with divorce and child-custody laws of the day) as institutions perpetuating women's oppression. It even dared confront organized religion as a primary propagator of misogyny, and called for redefining a woman's sense of self. Pretty modern for a passel of hoop-skirted ladies.

Decades of opposition would be required to wear such radicalism down into a reform movement. But in time even Anthony—who consistently took the position that "When this platform is too narrow for all to stand on, I shall not be on it"—was persuaded that the key for unlocking women's freedom was the vote. It's possible that without that single-issue emphasis, the struggle for women's suffrage might have taken even longer than 75 years. Yet the price was tragically high: relinquishing female solidarity across the divides of race and class, and abandoning positions that had confronted patriarchal power not just at the ballot box.

That process, by which original, complex, radical approaches to critical societal change become simplified, diffused, and weakened—what I call political entropy—is usually justified by the rationale that ideas must be tamed to be "popularized." But hindsight teaches that such dilution often was unnecessary; populists frequently underestimate their own constituencies' readiness, even hunger, for change. Still, factions of the nineteenth-century movement striving for acceptability were eager to distance themselves from its "incendiaries." Consequently, many creative propositions (and sometimes the women who'd conceived them) suffered marginalization or outright denunciation. Among them: Lucy Stone's refusal to bear her husband's name; Maria Stewart's tenacity about women's right to speak publicly (and before racially mixed audiences) and her critique linking racism and sexism; the startling renunciation of marriage as "legalized [economic] prostitution" by Victoria Woodhull; Margaret Fuller's endorsement of communal living; Mary Shadd Cary's insistence on the need for women to be economically self-reliant; the iconoclastic economic theories of Charlotte Perkins Gilman; and Stanton's radical pronouncements on everything from religion to childraising to female sexuality. Settling for a single-issue focus meant that all these concerns have had to be re-engaged by later feminist generations.

One such issue has been the task of fortifying feminism among women in the labor force. Industrialization had a major impact on women's lives. At first it isolated women's work, as men went to the factories. Later, with the advent of the power loom, it swept thousands of women into the paid workforce. While this meant some financial independence, it also meant exploitation—and established what became a sex-segregated labor market. In her *Sisterhood* article, noted labor scholar Alice Kessler-Harris explains how the "pink collar ghetto" came about, *and* how and why it's still with us. The 1840s and '50s saw strikes for better wages and working conditions for "the mill girls," inspiring a movement rallying cry that employed women should join unions and "together say Equal Pay for Equal Work." Many sweatshops and approximately a century later, the Coalition of Labor Union Women (CLUW) would form to address the betrayal of women's interests by male-dominated unions, and to continue the fight.

Twentieth-century feminism had to deal with much of this unfinished business, as well as with new issues continually surfacing—for instance, the *faux* sexual liberation of the 1920s "flapper," and yo-yo attitudes toward employed women—welcomed in the workforce during both World Wars, then castigated for not staying home as fulltime homemakers once the men returned.

The 1960s saw two streams of the contemporary Women's Movement emerge: a reform-oriented "equality feminism," represented by such dues-paying, formal-membership groups as the National Organization for Women (NOW); and a "women's liberation" feminism represented by somewhat younger women activists seasoned in the civil-rights and anti-war movements. At its inception, the moderate or reform-oriented wing was composed largely of European American, heterosexual, middle-class, and politically middle-ground members (NOW invites male membership)—although city and state chapters were often bolder in their positions and actions than the national headquarters. Fortunately, by the mid-1970s, NOW would become much more risk-taking (for example, by 1979, NOW was promulgating a Homemaker's Bill of Rights), and it persists in that direction today. Meanwhile, the looser "revolutionary" wing of the movement was a mix of races, ethnicities, sexual preferences/orientations, and classes. Despite the media myth that "only white women are interested in feminism," this urban-based wing from the onset celebrated participation by women of color. Despite the campus-centered activism of the 1960s and 1970s, this wing embraced neighborhood groups and welfare-rights organizations. Despite the blatant homophobia of the time, lesbian feminists were at the forefront of these early groups—though, deplorably, not always with the freedom to be "out." (One who *was* proudly out was Karla Jay, author of the lesbian-feminist overview here, an essay managing at once to be informative, hilarious, radical, and wise.) Secretaries, pink collar and blue collar employees, household workers, disabled women, older women, and institutionalized women all became part of this eclectic, energetic wing of the movement.

To the more "mainstream"[33] groups fell the unglamorous but crucial job of tackling legislative reforms (including what is, at this writing, the ongoing crusade to establish the Equal Rights Amendment as part of the Constitution). To this part of the movement also fell the tasks of helping women integrate male preserves and nontraditional jobs, bettering the lot of employed women in general and professional women (assumed to "have it all") in particular, trying to absorb the thousands of women clamoring to "join" the Women's Movement, and racing to deal with each new issue as it arose. That could mean fighting discrimination against females as police officers, newspaper reporters, or Little League baseball players one day and as clergy, flight attendants, or domestic workers the next. Furthermore, this wing had the foresight to draft legislation and to urge more women to run for public office, and created support systems for those candidates—groups like the bipartisan National Women's Political Caucus. Generally, through the mid-1970s, the moderates avoided "controversial sexual politics": lesbian custody rights, or pornography and prostitution, or even domestic abuse (nervously considered a "privacy" problem). But what the moderates may have lacked in audacity they compensated for in organizational skills: most of the institutions these women forged *lasted*. Moreover, they've grown in influence and, happily, in political inclusiveness—of constituents as well as of issues.

The same could not be said of the more dramatic revolutionaries, of

---

33. I put "mainstream" in quotes, because, difficult as it may be to believe or remember, in the 1960s and '70s, the fight for a married woman's right to have a driver's license or credit card in her own (e.g., "maiden," that is, father's) name was regarded as radical.

whom I decidedly was one. We were women who braved tear-gas, beatings, and jail—but seemed unwilling to risk any established order. Nonrigidity may be admirable, but some of our groups formed, split, disbanded, and resurrected within weeks, making it difficult for movement newcomers even to *find* us. Furthermore, this "women's liberation" wing was fervently divided into two general camps. There were the "politicos," socialist feminists who operated from a loosely Marxian political analysis and felt loyal to the New Left (even when its priorities were male-defined—e.g., fighting the military draft was revolutionary; fighting for childcare centers was bourgeois). Then there were the "radical feminists," who made women's rights their priority, viewing that as central to *all* progressive social change. In 1968, at the first Miss America Pageant Protest in Atlantic City, both factions of this wing went public, with the first mass demonstration of contemporary feminism.[34] From then on, separately or together, the radicals—both politicos and feminists—created a high-energy friction of activism: consciousness-raising (CR) groups, pickets, marches, and guerrilla-theater "zap" actions (like publicly hexing the Stock Exchange to close, while privately pouring glue into its front-door locks). We organized women's caucuses in New Left organizations but then, weary of Leftist ladies' auxiliaries, founded autonomous groups—Radical Women, WITCH, the National Black Feminist Organization (NBFO), Redstockings, the Combahee River Collective, the Lavender Menace, Cell 16, Mujeres, Radicalesbians, Asian Women United, First Mothers Native Women, OWL (Older Women's Liberation), and others. We marched in the "Jeanette Rankin Brigade"[35] against the Vietnam War. We demonstrated against the forced sterilization of poor women and women of color—while also providing underground abortion referrals at a time when both counseling and performing the procedure were felonies. We led building seizures and occupations denouncing pornography as violent sexist

---

34. For the organizer's personal, behind-the-scenes story of how this demonstration got started, what really happened there, and the aftermath, see *Saturday's Child*, op. cit., and *The Word of a Woman*, op. cit.

35. So named for the first woman to enter the House of Representatives (in 1917). Rankin voted against U.S. entry into World War I, lost her seat, regained it, and later cast the sole vote (even after Pearl Harbor) against U.S. entry into World War II.

propaganda (as early as 1970), and protested advertising's objectified images of women. We organized women's groups at all mainstream media, and founded what would become a massive alternative media. We worked with women arrested for prostitution, redefining them as political prisoners; and we turned experience into political theory, conceiving such terms as "battered woman," "sexual harassment," and "date rape," voicing what had been the subjects of whispers or shrugs. We established storefront women's centers, childcare groups, and health clinics; founded the first crisis shelters for rape survivors, brutalized wives, and incest victims; and produced the first self-defense courses devised for women. We created a "women's culture" in music, visual and performing arts, literature, even spirituality (and established festivals, museums, galleries, theaters, record companies). We were women who meant to leave no battle unjoined.[36]

Overall, however, we put precious little energy into legislative reforms (at least until the late 1970s), and ignored or dismissed the moderates' push for more women in public office or positions of institutional power. A self-righteous purity at times infected our part of the movement with contempt for those "working inside the system" (as if anyone could manage to work totally *out*side it). This more-radical-than-thou scorn turned in on itself, with frequent periods of infighting between, for instance, feminists who considered themselves "separatist" (which had at least seven different definitions) and those who didn't, between mothers and child-free women, and along already stressed fault lines: race, class, and sexuality differences.

The larger estrangement went both ways: exasperation felt by radicals toward moderates was reciprocated—with the moderates (their wing suffering its own versions of similar schisms) characterizing us radicals as hairy-legged and wild-eyed. In part, the gap was generational. It

---

36. See *Saturday's Child*, op. cit., and *Going Too Far: The Personal Chronicle of a Feminist*, by Robin Morgan (New York: Random House, 1977). For other recollections of this high-spirited period, see, for example, *In Our Time: Memoir of a Revolution*, by Susan Brownmiller (New York: The Dial Press, 1999); *Dear Sisters: Dispatches from the Women's Liberation Movement*, Rosalyn Baxendall and Linda Gordon, eds. (New York: Basic Books, 2000); *The Black Woman: An Anthology*, Toni Cade, ed. (New York: NAL/Signet, 1970); and *Tales of the Lavender Menace: A Memoir of Liberation*, by Karla Jay (New York: Basic Books, 1999).

also echoed the split in the nineteenth-century movement—but few of us in either wing knew enough women's history to recognize that.

. . . and Some Herstory[37]

It's taken almost forty years of feminist activism for the Women's Movement to outgrow these rancorous categorizations, and it's taken courageous work by many "long-distance runner" feminists on both sides of the divide to bridge the chasm and further the maturation process. Simplistic compartmentalizations just don't work anymore. Feminism itself—certainly in the Elizabeth Oakes Smith definition above—is implicitly, potentially so radical that moderates continue to astonish themselves and radical feminists may eventually find the adjective redundant. There have been too many moderates willing to risk everything and too many radicals rethinking purity and running for office not to notice that the boundaries have become permeable. Besides, backlash ignores such fine distinctions—and backlash has tried to flatten us, starting in the late '70s, escalating through the '80s and '90s, and today developed to a fine art by the well-heeled, media-savvy, highly organized, religious ultra-Right.[38]

One creative strategy developed by the contemporary movement to deal with disagreement over priorities—and to keep from falling into the single-issue trap of the nineteenth-century movement—has been to *spawn other movements*, which become autonomous yet simultaneously remain part of the extended family. More than one contributor to this anthology refers to this phenomenon. Wendy Chavkin (in her article on women physicians and women's health), Judy Norsigian (on health activism), and Laura Hershey (on disabled women's activism) all address the impact of the *women's health movement*. Florence Howe (in her impressive overview of women's studies) and Beverly Guy-Sheftall both as-

---

37. I coined this word half jokingly in 1968 and endured the consequential slings and arrows from semanticists. Now that the United Nations and NASA have adopted the use of "herstory" in official documents, it's probably time to reclaim it (smiling).

38. See *Backlash: The Undeclared War Against American Women*, by Susan Faludi (New York: Crown, 1991).

sess their work in the context of the *women's studies movement*. Helen Zia (discussing her activism as an Asian American feminist) and Andrea Dworkin (in her impassioned essay on violence against women) are among the contributors who refer to the *women's anti-violence movement*; Margot Adler (writing on women, religion, and spirituality) examines the *women's spirituality movement*; and Gloria Steinem calls for the creation of a *women's media movement*. For some, the specialized focus is pivotal: a particular issue galvanizes their experience, emotions, and expertise, and they're reluctant to dilute their energies in other feminist areas, however significant. For others (we might term them "generalists"), the vision and energy of feminism resides precisely in making the connections *between* issues. It's a sign of movement maturation that both approaches can now be equally respected as effective, and can even nourish each other.

After all, *the best organizing starts from where you are*. In that sense, it's encouraging to watch expanding definitions of activism emerge as a pattern in these pages. We might expect Howe, as an educator, to view teaching as an agent of change, and we may be familiar with The Guerrilla Girls' irrepressible activist antics in confronting the art world. But how interesting to read Marie Wilson defining fundraising as a form of organizing, or Eve Ensler regarding her work in the theater as political, or Sara Gould charting the growth of women-owned small businesses as potentially revolutionary, or rock-star Kathleen Hanna deliberately positioning her songs *as* her feminist activism.

Still, organized feminism has had to endure being ahead of its time on many issues—not least, sexual harassment and violence against women. Since the late '60s, we've been hammering at both issues—but neither fully entered public consciousness until the early 1990s, and it then fell to the movement to channel women's rage into constructive action. Anita Hill's contribution to this anthology, about the subject on which she innocently galvanized American women, offers a trenchant analysis of how far she and we have come on the issue of sexual harassment (covering the economic as well as psychological impact), but how far we still have to go. Dworkin's overview on violence against women is even more sobering. So is Vednita Carter's justifiably enraged article revealing what prostituted women suffer. So is Gail Dines's exposé on the staggering growth of the pornography industry with its propaganda promulgating violence against women. In their searing article on women in prison, Roslyn Smith and Kathy Boudin write that most incarcerated women have endured so much violence throughout their daily lives that prison actually feels *safer* for them. Since the United Nations considers the killing of 15,000 people in one year in a country an indicator of war, it's past time to *say* it: *There's a war against women going on*—all the more lethal for being private, informal, and undeclared.

While welcoming mainstream attention to familiar issues and fielding new ones, the Women's Movement has been forced (with a straight face) to cope with media announcements of "post-feminism" because "younger women aren't political." Those of us who speak frequently at colleges and universities around the country must be hallucinating the thousands of young women (and lots of young men) who come to listen, laugh, applaud, and vent against sexism. It's a continual source of wonder: the consistency with which feminism has been wishfully declared dead at least once a month since 1968. Gloria Steinem, in her smart, humorous essay on the media, offers ways to combat this, and to develop and enhance vital communication skills and tools.

By the mid-1990s, the Women's Movement had grown enormous in numbers, inclusive in constituencies, encyclopedic in issues, and sophisticated in tactics. It was local, regional, national—and networked, in itself and to the world. More than 60 percent of U.S. women said they identified as feminists or as part of the Women's Movement. Women were becoming visible (sometimes actually powerful) on previously male-only turf—though nowhere near proportional to being more than half the population (yes, tokenism lives). Additional concerns kept surfacing: reproductive technology and so-called surrogacy, the "feminization of poverty," the graying of the population (primarily women, who tend to outlive men), rising hate crimes (racial, ethnic, and homophobic), intensifying religious-fundamentalist (Christian/Jewish/Hindu/Muslim) crusades targeting women, the growing militancy of disabled women, the linking of domestic prostitution with global sexual slavery, the struggle to count women's unpaid labor in the GDP, educational campaigns about environmental toxicity and breast cancer, and the rising HIV/AIDS toll on women—these are only a few such issues.

Simultaneously, backlash kept on coming, sometimes in subtle forms from unanticipated directions. A movement so huge (and, all things being relative, "successful") tempted some toward careerism, creating a growing concern over the professionalization of NGOs. The matter is complicated, because nobody wants women to return to stereotypical, self-sacrificial volunteerism, or to be poor. But as some women's groups develop bigger budgets (good news), and more hierarchical staff structures (problematic news), they sometimes adopt what others feel are questionable corporate values (*not* good news). Concurrently, an academic fad of deconstructionist, post-modernist, and post-structuralist theory, while a serious endeavor for some scholars, has proven reactionary in practice. Some previously coherent academics found themselves proclaiming the end of history (coincidentally, *just* when all women, men of color, and other have-nots were entering it?); they pronounced sexism, racism, etc. illusory; and they announced that authentic feminist or anti-racist theory must emanate only from the academy—and be "above" politics. As Florence Howe notes, many feminists have been highly critical of this development, because of its implicit denial of activist concerns and because the French-inspired theoretical models were white, Western, middle-class, and male—unaware of (or indifferent to) the realities of the world's women.[39] The *experiential basis* of feminist political theory—the idea that *every woman is the expert on her own life*—has always blessed feminism with its ethical, grassroots power: "radicalism practical, not theoretical." Furthermore, unlike political theory issuing from an academic ivory tower (or any other central committee), theory based on real experience is inherently *democratic*. That leads to desmystification—so that ordinary folks get involved.[40] It also leads to sharing, which tends to seek validation through similarity but be curious about difference, always a sign of intellectual health.

Most important, the 1980s and '90s witnessed a growing consciousness about the place of U.S. feminism in the global Women's Movement. In the 1970s, an embarrassing number of U.S. women had behaved like

---

39. Another suspect gift from post-structuralists has been the trendy use of "gender studies" to edge out women's studies, in a curriculum that already, as Jane Roland Martin writes, "continues to give far more space and attention to the study of men than women." (The sheer *creativity* of backlash is awesome. No wonder feminists have, contrary to stereotype, a sharp sense of humor. Without it, we'd be suicidal.)

40. A lovely leitmotif in these articles is that welcoming tone. For instance, Natalie Angier and Donna Hughes plead that science isn't just for scientists but for everyone, and Catharine MacKinnon urges the same thing regarding law.

"keepers of the feminist flame"—missionaries, as it were, to the unenlightened rest of the world. This exposed their unfamiliarity with the history of international feminism (and with that of the U.S. women's rights/suffrage movement—which considered itself part of a global campaign). Such ignorance, compounded by characteristic American arrogance, didn't endear U.S. women to our sisters abroad. But American women didn't *want* to be the world's only, lonely feminists, and were hungry for information.[41] Fortunately, by the late 1990s, U.S. women seemed to have realized that our feminism is one tile—albeit a significant one—in the vast mosaic of the global Women's Movement.

As the new century and millennium unfold, U.S. feminism is more influential and varied than ever before. A relatively high literacy rate plus technology making available instant worldwide communications mean that the legacy of contemporary feminism here cannot be as effectively buried as that of its predecessors, hopefully avoiding perpetual reinvention of the political wheel. But we're making sure of that *ourselves* (see Eleanor Smeal's article on building feminist institutions to *last*). We intend to plant herstory audaciously in history—and not budge until it's *our* story.

Sisterhood Is Forever: Between the Covers and Behind the Scenes

We were a little over halfway through this project when 9/11 struck. So much has changed since then, and so little. But women's concepts of "security" still differ considerably from men's,[42] and that consciousness

---

41. *Sisterhood Is Global* was conceived in part to address this hunger. When it came out in 1984, some publishing experts told me that the anthology would fail, because "American women aren't interested in international issues." In the early 1990s, when I was editor in chief of *Ms.* and we introduced greater international news coverage and features on women abroad, I was told the same thing. *Sisterhood Is Global* is still comfortably in print, almost twenty years later, and polls of *Ms.* readers consistently named the international news coverage as their favorite part of the magazine. Moral: If you listen to the women, not the pundits, you get to say "I told you so."

42. A June 2000 study by the Aspen Institute found U.S. women far more likely than U.S. men to "frame their foreign policy concerns around global social issues like health, poverty, and human rights." Men are more likely "to favor military solutions or put a higher priority on trade." Of the women polled in the Aspen study, 69 percent urged the U.S. to work more closely with the UN and other international

pervades this book. Pat Schroeder warns of critically endangered democracy at home, while Jessica Neuwirth revisions what *feminist* globalization could be. Carol Gilligan and Eleanor Holmes Norton address intimacy, and Andrea Dworkin addresses the violation of intimacy. Faye Wattleton writes about the frightening, increasing erosion of reproductive rights, and Paula DiPerna grounds security in a nontoxic environment. Retired General Claudia Kennedy calls for a total redefinition of the military (this alone would have a revolutionary effect on the country), while Grace Paley gives us a poignant prose poem on why women are now *the* key to peace. Listen for the refrain. It's present throughout.

Structure. Originally, each contributor was asked to conceive her article in roughly three parts: where we're coming from on the relevant issue, where we are now, and where we're going (or unfortunately are *not* going, or *should* be going . . .). This was to provide past context and present clarity, while suggesting personal and public strategies not just for surviving into the future but transforming it. Most contributors opted to follow this vague structure (after all, we're talking about more than 60 wonderfully strong, stubborn women). The Suggested Further Reading list following each piece has usually been chosen by the contributor; it's there for greater exploration of the subject, once the article whets your thirst.

The sections are self-evident, but a little explanation is in order.

"Some Basics" is simply that—*some*, not all. Without question, Wattleton's powerful article belongs here, because reproductive rights are as basic as it gets. Similarly, how to cope if one *has* a child or children still falls largely and literally into a woman's lap, so Suzanne Braun Levine's warm, creative vision of a genuinely child-and-parent-friendly society

---

organizations; 39 percent said they wanted the government to pay greater attention to foreign affairs. Women consistently placed higher priorities on disease-prevention programs, equal education for girls, promoting fair labor practices, and making contraceptives available. In a heartening narrowing of the gender gap, only 4 percent of U.S. women and 5 percent of U.S. men want to see our country be the world's policeman; 67 percent of the women (and 56 percent of the men) said international cooperation was crucial to the well-being of future generations. But the women ranked in order as deserving of U.S. support: first, poor countries, then countries important to U.S. security, last, trading partners; the men ranked security first, then trading partners, with poor countries last.

belongs here. And there is no real Women's Movement unless *all* women define and energize it—hence Kimberlé Crenshaw's challenging essay on how discriminations intersect, and what to *do* about that. I could argue that the articles on law, health, lesbian rights, spirituality, environment, poverty, peace, sexual harassment, and other subjects are just as basic. In feminism, *everything's* basic. So I admit to a seemingly arbitrary structure—yet there's method in my madness.

"A Movement for All Seasons" is a section that gives me vengeful glee. The "young women aren't interested in feminism" myth always struck me as doubly ironic, since in the 1960s we were warned that the movement would never get going because it was "too filled with young women," and that "older women never will be interested in feminism." [43] It's *so* satisfying to flaunt these articles, by contributors ranging in age from 14 to 86. I love the sense of entitlement in Ana Grossman and Emma Peters-Axtell's declaration of what girls want (and do *not* want). Jasmine Victoria's rejection of the Gen Y category is as unexpected as her analysis of her contemporaries' feminism is refreshing—and the dedication that the 9/11 Twin Towers attack forced her to add at the end of her essay is very moving. Kathleen Hanna's funny, honest lament about surviving rock-star Riot Grrrl status (while trying to locate feminist history so she wouldn't have to invent it) is as intelligent as it is entertaining. "Stealth Feminists"—thirtysomething women—is Debra Michals's pithy, reassuring term for an integrated-into-daily-life mode of activism, enthusiastically described by her. As if in response, Eleanor Holmes Norton—the voice of "baby boomers" here—insightfully sees younger women as *"functional* feminists," where her contemporaries were *"catalytic* feminists." [44] And the importance of the "Politics of Aging" by Barbara Macdonald, with Cynthia Rich's foreword, should

---

43. During the Cold War, similar patriarchal nonlogic smeared U.S. feminists as communists—while in the USSR, feminists were accused of being CIA agents. You can't win. So you just keep on until you *do*.

44. It's personally gratifying to have this new piece by Eleanor—currently in her sixth Congressional term—in the anthology. We've known one another since the 1960s and the Civil Rights Movement, and she contributed one of the three essays on black feminism in *Sisterhood Is Powerful*. She is the only contributor to appear in both anthologies—so it's fitting that hers is the essay on "long-distance-runner" feminism.

be obvious—if for no other reason than that old women will soon constitute a demographic bulge of historic proportions.[45] Macdonald's unflinching analysis of ageism *as a form of sexism* brings home why ending age discrimination should concern *every* woman—especially because (with dubious luck) she'll eventually face it.

Above, I've discussed various pieces in the "Juggling Jeopardies" section. A special word, though, about Laura Hershey's fierce, enlightening report on the issues and activism of women with disabilities. This constituency was not present in *Sisterhood Is Powerful*—an omission that's haunted me for years. I'm grateful for a chance to correct the mistake. Simply put, we can none of us move forward until we each understand how *every* article in this section—on race, ethnicity, poverty, sexual preference, (dis)ability, *and* incarceration (due usually to some combination of the previous factors)—"intersects," in Crenshaw's concept, with each other, feminism, and our own lives.

"Bodies Politic" is yet another "basics" section. How could it not be? Issues like body image (updated in Judy Norsigian's health activism overview) are still being engaged by young women in the "Movement for All Seasons" section. Generally, the breadth of issues (wins *and* losses) covered by Norsigian and her *Our Bodies Ourselves* colleagues, plus Barbara Findlen's reflection on sports, might tempt you to raise a glass of champagne, gazing backward at how far we've come. If so, the articles by Anita Hill, Gail Dines, and Vednita Carter will firmly set you facing forward on the path.

"Workplaces" could be a book, or library, in itself. It's the largest section, reflecting the fact that most women now have jobs, comprising half the (paid) workforce and virtually *all* the *un*paid workforce. Because feminists have said for years that housekeeping and childraising are *work*, Helen Drusine's piece on being a housewife and mother belongs here. Because rural women are too often overlooked (yet they're organizing), Carolyn Sach's piece was much needed. Between them, Ellen Bravo's report on "the clerical proletariat" and Alice Kessler-Harris's on pink collar and blue collar workers, cover the jobs at which most employed women in the U.S. work—for little money and less respect. Yet profes-

---

45. See the statistics in the essay, and see also "A Personal Postscript to Vintage Feminists," p. 571.

sional women can hardly relax. Wendy Chavkin traces the struggles of women physicians, and analyzes how that impacts on women's health. Donna Hughes takes on the masculinist, pornocratic culture in science, engineering, and technology, while Jane Roland Martin exposes how "estrangement from women" is a basic tenet of academia and calls for women to reconceive *that* culture, from curriculum through professoriate to academic values. This struggle—to *redefine terms and claim turf*—has emerged as a major refrain, about everything from Darwinism to globalization. Claudia Kennedy wants to redefine the military. Ellen Appel-Bronstein explores the difference between "careers" and "jobs," amusingly relating her trek through campuses and corporations, where women "leak" out of the pipelines leading to power. Carol Jenkins, writing about broadcast media in an article guaranteed to raise your indignation level, explains how news gets dumbed down into entertainment, and how women's lack of clout in front of (*and* behind) the camera is ultimately due to lack of female *ownership* of major media—those pipelines again. In fact, Appel-Bronstein (and later, Sara Gould, writing on women-owned small businesses) also address ownership as one necessary way of changing the system. *But.* In "Six Personal Testimonies," Sandy Lerner's is a cautionary tale: she *did* own her own company—Cisco Systems—yet reveals here what happens to women when venture capital controls things offstage. All six "Testimonies" address this need to redefine terms and claim turf. These women love their work, but in the Transforming Traditions section, Mary Foley (nurses), Patricia Silverthorn (teachers), and Patricia Friend (flight attendants) note that their traditionally "women's fields" are in crisis, in part because women still lack sufficient power *in* those fields. In the Breaking Barriers section, Brenda Berkman (firefighters), Mary Baird (hard hats), and Sandy Lerner (computer programming), divulge the personal cost of integrating all-male preserves, since such acts constitute a de facto redefinition of the job itself. Two voices from the arts (workplaces, after all) close this section.[46]

---

46. My original, overly ambitious plan was to organize a series of taped conversations transcribed for what would be a separate section in this book, conversations between women representing every creative and performing art—dance (ballet, modern, folk, etc.), music (symphonic through rap), fiction, poetry, painting, sculpture, film, you name it. That proved logistically ridiculous. It also would have made each copy of this book cost over $300 and weigh more than any reader could

Eve Ensler, in a piece that will make you tear up and giggle at the same time, relates how her play *The Vagina Monologues*—and the political phenomenon it became—changed the way she regards her workplace, the theater. And the Guerrilla Girls—Feminist Masked Avengers and scourge of the art world—employ their inimitable mischief in confronting what happens to women artists, with a what-the-hell-why-not sideswipe at Hollywood, for good measure.

"Tactics and Trends" might seem the most arbitrary category, since *every* contributor offers strategies. For instance, elsewhere both Smeal and Steinem call for a trained media component in all women's groups. The potential for boycott power—time-honored tactic honed with twenty-first century techniques—crops up in Dines's piece on pornography, Neuwirth's on globalization, Steinem's on media, Boudin and Smith's on women in prison. In other sections, you can find out how to form a voting group, make air travel safer, hold a press conference, change legislation, start a business, or survive as the first woman in an all-male workplace; you can learn why we should buy cable stations, run for office, play sports, become engineers, file lawsuits, or go to Mars. Still, Catharine MacKinnon elevates tactics to a new level as she charts previous feminist struggles with the law and envisions what a truly *just* legal system might be. Sara Gould reports a strategic trend already in motion: women who form the fastest growing segment of the U.S. economy, entrepreneurs who own small businesses—*and* humanize the workplace. Cecile Richards, drawing on her experience in organizing creatively against the religious Right, puts tools into our hands for the escalating struggle with this politically powerful, home-grown Christian Taliban. Frances Kissling, leading the feminist charge against the Vatican's positions on women, analyzes the current policies (and scandals) of the Roman Catholic Church and suggests ways to hurry along its epiphany. Marie Wilson's alphabet of how-to's on fundraising is surely tactical. Carol Adams, who's written persuasively on the connections between the causes of women's oppression and that of animals, here condenses her finest thinking on the subject. And Paula DiPerna

---

lift. Suffice it to say that, yes, we now have a National Museum of Women in the Arts, and we can relish Toni Morrison's well-deserved Nobel Prize. But no, the struggle, in every art, is nowhere *near* over for women.

reminds us how feminism and environmentalism are inseparable, and sets forth a new, pragmatic strategy linking them.

"Politics for the New Millennium" contains old verities all the more acutely relevant today—like Paley's tragicomic contribution on war, peace, men, and women, and Margot Adler's thoughtful overview on religion and spirituality. But essential as it is not to forget the past, it's just as essential to remember the future—and there are new truths, too. If you think you already comprehend the political potential of the Internet, read Amy Richards and Marianne Schnall's piece on cyberfeminism, and think again. If you believe you know enough about globalization to settle for demonizing it (instead of trying to co-opt, change, and use it), brace yourself for Jessica Neuwirth's tactically sophisticated article on why this is a twenty-first-century opportunity for women. The future simply isn't the future without space exploration, and astronaut Mae Jemison—the first woman of color in space—makes clear that such exploration damned well better include not just half the human species but all of it. To ensure that, Eleanor Smeal writes on the art of building feminist institutions to *last*; Ellie's is a core contribution to *Sisterhood Is Forever*, one of the first pieces I commissioned.

Last come two personal postscripts—one to "vintage" feminists, one to younger women. Sometimes there's a bit of generational huffing and glaring back and forth, so I hope these PS's might help. All I ask is that *each* of you in *both* groups peek at the other's PS. You might be surprised.

Footnotes. There are quite a few. Ignore them if you find them interruptive, but they're not unimportant. Some are scholarly references. Most are to squeeze in more background information; to put more statistics, websites, and facts at your disposal. There's generous cross-referencing, when other pieces throughout the book resonate with or extrapolate on points a contributor makes—because, frankly, the synchronicity between authors who hadn't read each other's pieces fascinated me.

Terminology. Language reflects and defines attitudes and thus behavior, so it's no nit-picky thing. You won't find the phrase "working women," since homemakers work; *employed* women is the term for those in the formal labor force. You won't find "women's issues," since all issues are on the feminist agenda (lack of a national health care system is decried in the pieces on nurses, physicians, health activism, disability, poverty, aging, politics, and *farming*, among others). "Second (or first or third) wave" terminology is critiqued above. European American is used interchangeably with "white," just as African American is with "black"; it's insufficient to write/say Native American, Asian American, and so on, if you don't also write/say "European American"—otherwise "white" becomes the generic. But you *will* encounter here invigorating new concepts like "the right to bodily integrity," a neat short-hand phrase uniting issues rooted in the flesh: skin color, age, sexual and reproductive choice, disability rights, beauty standards, violence against women, etc. "Feminism" is used throughout. If you feel itchy about the word but believe in everything it stands for—"I'm no feminist, but . . ."—don't let this throw you (though you might just ponder that odd disconnect). The women writing here profess feminism; I'm one. We know its history and the life-affirming social progress it has forged. On the other hand, if you choose to call yourself a term more familiar from your own culture ("womanist," "mujerista," etc.), or if you reject all political identification yet still feel committed to saving yourself (and maybe other women, men, and the planet)—*go* for it. Call yourself "squirrel" if you want—but get out there and make healthy mayhem. Then there's that word: *"sisterhood."* Some think sisterhood doesn't exist. Some think it doesn't exist *yet*. Some think it's sappy anyway, reminiscent of nuns or union-organizing. In a way, I agree with all three. Still, I *know* it exists. I've felt its power—in a dusty Oklahoma town, a West Bank refugee camp, a jail cell, a boardroom, these pages. I also know that sisterhood isn't yet as vivid, reliable, and representative as I want it to be, but if it isn't called into reality by the *naming* of it—the power of language—it never *will* exist. As for sappiness, well, I know some pretty plucky feminist nuns (and union organizers), so I see nothing wrong with those semantic resonances. As Boudin and Smith write, "Although the word 'sisterhood' is not part of our common language [in prison] and women might even laugh cynically if someone said 'sister,' we slowly become that for one another." If they can do it, we can.

Apologia. An aside about what you *won't* find in this book. There's no piece on or by men. I considered it, but decided that one token piece couldn't fairly represent the progressive views of anti-sexist men of conscience, but that more than one piece would begin to eat up air in a collection focused on and by women. Furthermore, due to space limitations, only the major "minority groups"[47] are represented here.[48] (And only a woman would worry about what's *not* in a book this gigantic and multidimensional.)

What Is It Women Really Want?

Freud asked that silly question and some guys still actually wonder. So here are the answers yet again—plus new ones. Three major themes emerge in this book.

1. *Time to Change the Institutions.* Sexism, like other bigotries, is *systemic.* Patriarchy doesn't need "plotters"—six pale male billionaires sitting around conspiring (though they often do)—because it's structured to work by itself. It has its own nonlogic, like the myth that progressive solutions "cost too much"—which gets applied to breast-feeding, prison-education programs, and clean water, though all these are actually *cheaper* than the alternatives (see Norsigian, Boudin and Smith, and DiPerna). So far, the contemporary Women's Movement has voiced the problems, organized ourselves, and integrated where we could, knowing that we needed to enter fields closed to us as a first step. Now we need to *restructure* those (and other) fields. Perhaps it was to be expected that the deepest changes have been in how we actually live our lives—sexual and childbearing patterns, relationships, family demographics—because we have at least a modicum of control in those areas. But in the larger societal structure, having boldly gone where we weren't supposed to, we're now back to basics: who

---

47. Quotes intended sarcastically: people of color actually constitute the *majority* of the human species.

48. I would have liked to commission an essay by one of many Arab American feminists I know, but in these times that would have necessitated a balancing article on Jewish American feminism—and then we'd be off into the confusion about whether we're talking race, ethnicity, or religion. No religious constituencies per se are represented here, though Adler covers the field generally. However, the Kissling and Richards essays are imperative because they address religious groups deliberately and disastrously influencing policies that have a direct effect on women's lives.

wants a piece of the pie when the pie is poisonous and needs rebaking? Partly this involves *redefining* . . . well, everything (see above), including power. That requires asking: *Who* defines—"news," "family," "work," "security"? *Who* decides—how the decoded genome will be used, whether "sex-work" is "groovy" or not, does job-sharing help or hurt the employee, how will transnationalism play out, what rights do you have over your own body? Essay after essay presents the need to *change the institutions drastically*, and—get ready, politicians—to revolutionize *policy*. Since most women still juggle two jobs (work and home), and women's labor remains undervalued and *un*valued, it's not surprising that when Suzanne Braun Levine calls for "a new social contract" to support families, there's an echoing roar from women writing on homemaking, poverty, pink and blue collar and clerical work, health (practitioners *and* consumers), the military, and more. When academics, scientists, and lawyers decry the *male climate/male culture* saturating their disciplines, they set a new goal: to *change the disciplines* themselves. You can't do that alone; you'll go crazy. Such transformation happens because of a strong Women's Movement. In Hughes's words, "Women's gains and losses in science, engineering, and technology run parallel to the rise and fall of feminism's strength as a social force." *Dismantling systemic patriarchy and replacing it with humane values, policies, and practices is the task for twenty-first-century feminism.*

2. *Time for Multifeminism.* That task will require every one of us, each in her own way, and will need originality, vision, and leadership, which will come from unexpected sources. Our strength as a movement—as a nation—has always lain in our diversity, though appallingly large amounts of energy are still spent ignoring or denying that. The writers here affirm everyone's right to work on her own priorities, but know that the need to build, strengthen, expand, and act from coalitions is the basis for moving forward. Margot Adler, writing on women's spirituality, expresses it beautifully: "The spiritual world is like the natural world: only diversity will save it." Only (more) diversity will save feminism, too. This means *not* looking around to

pluck a token or two from a different racial, age, sexuality, etc. constituency *after* having set priorities and strategies; it means building those priorities and strategies *together*, from the ground up—because analyses, tactics, and solutions reflect those who evolved them. Besides, it's simply more enriching, more *fun* to see the world in dimensional depth. Think what it does to your perception of Harriet Tubman, Civil War leader of the underground railroad, to learn that she was disabled—as was Elizabeth Blackwell, the first American woman to earn a medical degree. In a sense, as Kimberlé Crenshaw points out, the key is to reject both the "difference" and "sameness" arguments that try to shape the struggle for equality. (Back to Angier and biology 101: of *course* we're different—and of *course* we're the same. *Enough* bifurcated either/or thinking, already! It's time for both/and.) People deserve to be free, whether they resemble the folks who hold power or not—that simple. Welcoming this into our thinking and organizing will change the system *inside* us.

3. *Time to Stop Settling.* This is a natural outgrowth of points 1 and 2. We can't afford to dwindle down into tepid reforms this time. We need to go for the gold, and that requires, as much as diversity and strategy, *passion.* We need to *hear* our own justifiable fury—expressed, for instance, by Barbara Macdonald about the way old women are patronized, or Vednita Carter about how prostituted women are considered dispensable. We need to let ourselves feel our own outrage again (we're beautiful when we're angry). We need to push at *all* the boundaries—push, in Ellie Smeal's phrase, "for what we want, not just what we can get." That means daring to work not merely for the absence of war but for the presence of peace, not merely to stop poverty but to reconceptualize wealth. The vision and passion *are* there—though not always recognized across generational or cultural gaps. Wattleton and Schroeder both express fear that younger women don't *care* sufficiently to become actively involved. (Their respective subjects, reproductive rights and electoral politics, are both crucial, and have suffered serious erosion after women had made great visible gains; hence the danger that later generations might buy into the propaganda that "it's all

been taken care of.") Yet Jasmine Victoria, still an undergraduate, calls her generation to arms, and vows that "abortion is one issue we will not let get lost in the shuffle." And Schroeder's despair about too-few women running for office is addressed by fourteen-year-old Ana Grossman's flat-out self-assertive plans to run for president. There's another reason for passion: the "other side"—the fundamentalists, arch conservatives, racists, sexists, and homophobes, the people who want to deregulate industries and decontrol guns but regulate your spirituality and control your womb—*they* have passion. They're a minority—but they're dedicated, and very hungry to win. It may come down to *who wants it more*, and *who shows up*. As Jemison writes: "who participates determines what opportunities are seen, developed, and exploited." So it's time to get involved, and to get confrontative again. It's easier now: there's more of us, and we've learned a *lot*. The fate of real democracy is worthy of passion. Look how women, with many men of conscience, have steadily been inventing the democratic home; the family is still the core of the state, and, as the late internationalist Perdita Huston wrote, "The democratization of the family has had far reaching effects."[49] Gilligan sees feminism as being, at its heart, the movement to free democracy from patriarchy. Besides, it's patriarchy that's unnatural; *our* societal vision is *organic*. Angier reminds us that biology shows ours is a remarkably plastic species; our egalitarian impulses are part of human nature: "feminism is an evolved trait." The scientists are telling us that *we're genetically wired for democracy and cooperation*. Our own genome is whispering, *"This time, go all the way!"*

For years, I declined flattering requests from publishers to consider compiling a third *Sisterhood* anthology. Between writing priorities of my own plus activism, such a project seemed out of the question. These anthologies are jealous goddesses, demanding sacrifice on their altars. From the challenge of imagining the perfect person to write on a partic-

---

49. *Families As We Are: Conversations from Around the World*, by Perdita Huston (New York: The Feminist Press at CUNY, 2001).

ular subject or collaborating long-distance on revisions with authors in prison, through that of nagging activists about their deadlines, editing and protecting work entrusted by contributors to one's care, and never forgetting one's responsibility to the reader—it's rather intensive. Now, I'm happy to have done it. I'm especially glad to dedicate the book to Bella Abzug, former U.S. Congresswoman, international stateswoman, feminist leader of vision, audacity, laughter, rage, and tactical virtuosity. We loved her. We miss her every day.

My introduction to *Sisterhood Is Powerful* began with the words, "This book is an action." It was. As is this anthology. My motto for *Sisterhood Is Global* was "Only she who attempts the absurd can achieve the impossible." I still believe that, too. The book that rests in your hands is a tool for the future—a future that also rests in your hands.

So here it is. No matter how they try to marginalize it, trivialize it, stereotype it, mourn it, or demonize it: the U.S. Women's Movement. *Still here*—and further reinventing itself. Not for nothing does the refrain *"it's up to us"* ring through these essays. Sisterhood *is* powerful, global, "forever"—and also complex, hilarious, stubborn, elastic, tender, furious, sophisticated, dynamic, a work in progress. Feminism is reborn every time a woman sits alone at her kitchen table with a damp wad of tissues and a cup of tea at four A.M., thinking *I have to change my life*. She—and you and I—together can free ourselves and also profoundly affect society, becoming agents of evolution who help our human species past its painful, perilous adolescence. This is why *feminism is the politics of the twenty-first century*.

In that sense, New World women have just begun.

Robin Morgan
November 2002
New York City

PART I.

Some Basics

Biologically Correct

NATALIE ANGIER

IN ALL MY YEARS as a science writer, I've sought to encourage friends, relatives, and other members of the laity not to be so afraid of science. Science doesn't belong only to scientists, I've exhorted, any more than art belongs only to artists, or politics to the Eeyores and Dumbos of Washington, D.C. Science is the property of the human race. It's one of our greatest achievements, and it doesn't take nearly as much effort as nonscientists believe to become reasonably literate in a particular discipline, to the point where you may even venture an opinion on, say, the rights of a U.S. consumer to drive an SUV, global warming be damned, versus the rights of a citizen of Bangladesh to continue living above sea level.

But I'm afraid that when it comes to my most cherished of subjects, evolutionary biology, the concept of scientific populism has been taken too far. It seems practically everybody is now an amateur Darwinist, willing to speculate grandly on the deep Plio-Pleistocene origins of all modern vices known to man, woman, or Tony Soprano. Lawyers bring evolutionary reasoning into the courtroom. Psychologists discuss the evolutionary basis of depression, neuroticism, anorexia, alcoholism, a wicked sweet tooth. Theologians insist the human brain evolved to believe in god, who may or may not return the favor by believing in evolution.

Now, I don't believe evolution is a "theory," any more than I believe gravity and the second law of thermodynamics are theories. I consider myself a Darwinist right down to my DNA, which I'm happy to share 98.5 percent of with our cousins, the chimpanzees. But it's one thing to revel in Darwin's magnificent, overarching theory of evolution by natural selection, and another to play Spin-the-HMS *Beagle* of a Saturday night and call the results "science." Yet to my disgust and occasionally

3

crippling sense of despair, many of the slap-happy, data-free Darwinesque theory-ettes to emerge in recent years have been widely dispensed and accepted, to the point where they, too, are considered the biological equivalents of E=MC². And nowhere has the acceptance of evolution-tinged notions been greater, more credulous, and more insidious than for those purporting to explain the supposed differences between the sexes. Darwinophiles, particularly the subspecies who label themselves "evolutionary psychologists," love to talk about the gulf that separates men and women. Everywhere I turn, there they are: thematic variations of the dreary old ditty, "Higgamus hoggamus/women are monogamous; hoggamus, higgamus/men are polygamous." Or, in another mildewed rendering: men are ardent, women coy. Or how about: men want quantity, women quality. Or take that: men want sex, women want love. Evolutionary psychology has newly proved old verities to be true. Not necessarily with data, mind you—how much data do you need to prove the obvious?—but with nifty new theoretical constructs and sufficiently high jargon-wattage terminology to lend a spangle of rigor to the field.

For example, evolutionary psychologists (evo psychos) love to talk about "mental modules," little cerebral fiefdoms that supposedly operate independently and subliminally to prevent us from behaving in the rational, integrated, thoughtful manner that we deluded femi-Nazi types might strive to accomplish. As a result of these finely honed modules, which evo psychos liken to the separate tools in a Swiss army knife, we will do things that may seem illogical and even counterproductive to our lives overall—say, by choosing a dumb mate just because he's tall or she has big breasts and our "mate-finding" module sees the person as a bearer of good genes or a fecund womb, thus the best tool for the job of reproducing. So what if our intellectual or kinship-bonding modules disapprove of what our mate-finding module brought home? And so what if there is as yet no evidence for the *existence* of these mental modules? Evo psychos also emphasize the "differential reproductive potential" between men and women, transmutating the numeric discrepancy between a man's sperm cells and a woman's egg cells into any and all sex-linked inequities you care to mention: the rarity of female CEOs or Nobel laureates; the spareness of the average female's salary; the disparity in gumption, motion, get-up-and-go-tion.

No longer are the "evolved" differences between men and women presumed hypothetical until proven actual, as they might have been as recently as the early 1990s; now they are pretty much post-factual. For example, in his essay "The End of Courtship," bioethicist Leon Kass (chosen by President George W. Bush to head a national bioethics advisory panel), quotes the tired hoggamus doggerel, declaring—without apology, footnote, or citation—that "Ogden Nash had it right." (Memo to Kass: the verse was written by William James.) This keeper of the nation's moral compass asserts that a "natural obstacle" to courtship and marriage is "the deeply ingrained, natural waywardness and unruliness of the human male." One can make a "good case," Kass continues, "that biblical religion is, not least, an attempt to domesticate male sexuality and male erotic longings," although how good a case depends on whether you consider an Old Testament hero like King Solomon, who had 700 wives and 300 concubines, to be an exemplar of domesticated masculinity. As for modern women, Kass pities us as we hop unnaturally from bed to uncommitted bed, "living their most fertile years neither in the homes of their fathers nor their husbands." Far from enjoying "sexual liberation," he says, we are awash in quiet desperation, "unprotected, lonely, and out of sync with their inborn nature."

Apart from the general yuckiness of Kass's aspartame-tainted nostalgia, I wouldn't mind terribly if such self-styled neo-Darwinists restricted their pontificating to insisting that men are, on average, more sexually rapacious and prone to philandering than women. I don't believe that claim, and in fact some evidence indicates otherwise: while performing routine prenatal screening tests for the presence of disease genes, genetic counselors have found incidentally that anywhere from 5 to 15 percent of babies are fathered by somebody other than the mother's husband—and surely not all these women were forced against their "inborn nature" into adulterous copulations.

Nevertheless, I can keep my erotic longings to myself, and if it makes a fellow feel better to insist that his are bigger and more unruly than mine, he can insist away. What is far more disturbing, and what I cannot accept without mounting my soapbox for a lusty rant, is the tendency of the evo-psycho crowd to attribute to men not only greater sexual ardor, but greater ardor for *life*. Kass writes that men are not only innate sexual "predators," but are also "naturally more restless and ambitious than women; lacking women's powerful and immediate link to life's generative answer to mortality, men flee from the fear of death into heroic deed, great quests, or sheer distraction after distraction."

Others are even more presumptuous. On a computer list populated by academic sex researchers, one member recently asked for commentary about the following quote from an unnamed source:

> As a consequence of differential evolutionary histories, human genetic males, on average, differ from genetic females in fundamental behavioral ways. Males are more competitive, aggressive, creative, and inquisitive than females. These behavioral characteristics are evident throughout human societies to one degree or the other, and in aggregate are irrefutable. These average differences are clearly reflected in the dominance and achievements of males over the course of human history in politics, architecture, science, technology, philosophy, and literature, among other areas of human activity and intellectual concentration. It is reasonable to posit that these average differences between human males and females are functions of the differential environmental demands human males encountered over tens of thousands of years in human evolution. Today these differences are founded in the genetic and hormonal constitution of the human male.

My reaction on reading this was, *Huh? Are you joking?* Men by their "genetic and hormonal constitution," are more "creative" and "inquisitive" than women? Sez who? Sez *what* data? To my dismay, other members of the list were unperturbed. "It is pretty standard evolutionary psychology of sex differences," shrugged one professor, referring to various popular books about evolutionary psychology, including the bluntly titled, *Why Men Rule: A Theory of Male Dominance.* Woe to this professor's female students if he conveys to them his settled opinion that males have a hardwired advantage in exactly those traits necessary to excel in his class. Well, every trait except cleavage.

I don't mean to be flip and sarcastic. OK, I do. But I also want to express my frustration at how readily and arrogantly so much evolutionary blather can be bandied about, with hardly a whimper of complaint or an attempt at alternative interpretation. Remember, I'm a big fan of Darwinism, convinced that by considering the deep roots of our past we can enrich our lives now, if only because understanding always trumps ignorance and denial. I also believe that evolutionary biology is a growth industry, and that we will be seeing ever more effort, inside and outside of academia, to examine contemporary human behavior from a Darwinian perspective. Fine. But maybe we shouldn't leave the analysis to a small, self-referential cabal of evolutionary psychologists, who attempt to reify the status quo with a few sweeping, simplistic, binary formulations.

Maybe we should seek to use Darwinian principles to our own nefarious ends—beginning with a fresh understanding of feminist impulses. Many mainstream neo-Darwinists try to dismiss feminism: "We're scientists! We seek the truth about human nature, however unpleasant," they self-righteously maintain. "We must resist the forces of 'political correctness' and get at the truth."

But what this smug dismissal fails to address is the fact that *feminism and its attendant egalitarian impulses are very much part of human nature.* Hence, any system that purports to explain the primal origins of our desires must also explain why any of us want to be feminists in the first place. I would argue that *feminism is an evolved trait*—part of the puzzle to be solved, not a distraction from it. If it takes evolutionary biologists who double as feminists to tackle this particular puzzle piece, they can fairly be said to be at their most "scientific" just when evo-psycho critics are pooh-poohing them for being driven by "political" motives.

Some scientists do see the need to move beyond clichés toward a more nuanced picture of human motivation, a recognition of the suppleness of human nature, the capacity for men and women to adjust their social and reproductive strategies as conditions around them change. Male as well as female scientists lately have argued for broadening the field of evolutionary psychology to incorporate the notion that our psychology does in fact evolve, is designed to evolve, even in the absence of genetic evolution.[1] There is a reason why we have managed, for better or worse, to colonize virtually every habitat on the earth's surface,

---

1. See "Sisterhood Is Pleasurable: A Quiet Revolution in Psychology," by Carol Gilligan, p. 94.—Ed.

and to turn the planet and its glorious diversity into a vast playground for Homo sapiens. It's because we are omnivores in every sense of the word—nutritionally, culturally, behaviorally. Any theoretical framework that slights our plasticity, that declares all or most men to be like this, and all or most women to be like that, is a framework fit only for kindling.

Here's an example of rigid absolutism, again from Sexnet, which made me run for my matchbook. A hard-core evolutionary psychologist presented his little gedanken, then kindly told us just how to gedank about it: "There is a contest," he wrote. "If you win you get either of two prizes: unlimited store credit at Saks Fifth Avenue for a 10-day period— that is, you can have anything you can walk away with—or have 10 extremely attractive total strangers of the preferred sex, a different one each night, come to your room, rip your clothes off, and have mad sex with you. I guarantee you that close to 100 percent of young men will choose the latter, and close to 100 percent (or literally 100 percent) of women, young or older, will choose the former."

The old Sex vs. Saks dilemma. When I read this, I thought, "*Neither* of the above, sir." I won't go into what my fantasy prize might be—or might have been in the days when I was a single woman without kids— but these boxes don't hold me and never did. Nor do they hold a lot of people, including a lot of good evolutionary scientists. I expressed my annoyance to David Sloan Wilson of the State University of New York at Binghamton, a scientist I mostly adore (with the exception of his occasional fits of didacticism that seem endemic to the scientific trade). Wilson has criticized much of the current evo-psycho literature while still considering himself an evolutionary psychologist, so I knew he'd sympathize with my desire for a more inclusive, expansive approach to understanding the evolution of human nature. I sent him the gedanken, and described my surly feelings about it. Darwin bless him for his delicious reply: "Your 'Neither of the above' answer can be given a serious scientific formulation. The evolutionary psychology view assumes that *all* resources for women flow through men, leaving only the 'strategies' of 'find the best husband' or 'maximize your returns from sexual favors.' The option that is not listed is 'self-determination,' or calling one's own shots. With this simple addition, feminism finds an evolutionary voice capable of silencing the evolutionary psychology voice on its own turf."

Wilson then paused for a pious commercial break, warning me that whenever I sought to argue against "the narrow evolutionary psychology view, or any other objectionable evolutionary theory of human behavior," I must do so from an evolutionary perspective of my own, lest I "leave the opposition holding the banner of Darwinism," crowing about the stupidity of their critics for rejecting evolution altogether. "As an aside," Wilson went on, "even in its shriveled form the Sex vs. Saks experiment wouldn't work. Any guy with a brain (an oxymoron in most cases) would choose the Saks option and amass so much stuff over 10 days that he could have more than 10 women long enough to actually impregnate them. If he could choose Abercrombie & Fitch instead of Saks, he'd probably throw it all away for a single fishing pole. The boneheads who chose the women would probably have second thoughts by night 5 and would beg numbers 8, 9, and 10 to watch TV instead of having sex." In the words of George Bernard Shaw, Wilson concluded, " 'They are barbarians who mistake their own customs for human nature.' "

What can we do to reclaim the blessed turf of Darwinism? How can we think afresh about our contemporary selves in the light of several million years of thrashing around in the grim and shank of nature? Let me toss out a few ideas I feel have been neglected in most pop renditions of neo-evo. Let me try, to the best of my ability as a serious if not officially credentialed Darwin hobbyist, to present an ancestral Eve who had greater or at least more complex aims in life than a Stone Age shopping spree.

I'll start with the answer I give whenever anybody asks me what I think the real, primal, non-negotiable differences between men and women may be. I preface my response by claiming the ignorance we all suffer under in any discussion of the roots of something as intangible and free of fossil evidence as human nature. But there is one big difference—which amounts to an amusing similarity, with profound consequences. A woman, like any female primate, has two core desires. First, access to resources, which means food, shelter, and—ever since we were so rudely and coldly depilated—clothing, for herself and her young. Second, control over her sex life and her reproduction. What are a man's core desires? He, too, wants access to resources and control over the means of reproduction, which, in the absence of male parthenogenesis, means control over women. There's nothing *inherently* wrong with this desire. But the fact that women and men are tussling over the same piece of valuable real estate—the female body—means that the tedious, endlessly vivisected "war between the sexes" is pretty much built into the system. I'm by no means arguing that men and women can never get along. The best of friends and allies are often cunning competitors. Consider the Greek warriors in the *Iliad* who, during intermissions in the Trojan War, could think of no zestier way to spend their leisure than holding mini-Olympics to see who could run the fastest, throw the farthest, jump the highest—all in the nude, no less. Recall as well that even the most seemingly like-minded, bodily bonded of dyads, mother and infant, engage in subtle conflicts. The fetus wants to grow very big very fast, while the mother wants to keep its dimensions compact and manageable to preserve her body for future trials, which is why some fetus-specific genes are designed to enhance the growth of the placenta, and the maternal equivalents of those genes help suppress placental ambitions. The child wants to stay on the breast year after year, the better to forestall births of rival siblings through the ovulatory suppression that nursing imparts; the mother wants to wean her greedy suckler and maybe have a few more kids without depleting her calcium stores and risking every osteocyte in her body.

Yet such subconscious clashes of interest do not mean that mother and young are "really" enemies rather than the great lovers they often appear to be.[2] Instead, they are living creatures, bound together by fourteen-carat compromise, trading up Paradise Lost for Paradox Found, and relishing the match. So, too, can men and women love each other wildly without necessarily, or even desirably, seeing eye to eye—provided everyone's eyes are wide and gimlet.

What the inherent dialectic of the sexes does mean is that men and women may have differing definitions of freedom. Evo psychos, opining from their standard masculinist perspective, emphasize the clash between a man's "restlessness" and a woman's desire for "commitment," as exemplified by the Leon Kass passage quoted above—the assumption being that men need freedom and women do not. But if you take a more female-primate point of view, you see that quite often it is the woman

---

2. See Gilligan, op. cit.—Ed.

who wants her freedom, and the man, or men collectively, who are de-termined to circumscribe her. A woman may want freedom to walk by herself down the street, just as a female chimpanzee may have the urge to move from denuded bush *A* to bursting berry patch *B*; but if the way-farer happens to be a young urban Homo sapien, she will be harassed en route more mercilessly than any free-ranging ape. A woman may also want the opportunity to exercise that old gift of Mother Nature known as female choice—to socialize, flirt, and, if the chemistry fits, to mate with the men she likes while avoiding those she does not.

But think of how many women are abused and beaten, sometimes hunted down and killed, by men who have either fallen off the women's *A* list, often because they were too aggressively possessive, or never made it to the chosen column in the first place.[3] Many men play within the bounds of female choice and seek to please the women they find pleasing, just as women usually strive to please the men by whom they themselves hope to be chosen. But sometimes a man has little patience for the strictures of female choice; he wants access to the means of per-sonal perpetuity that only a female body can give him, so whack smack get over here bitch! Who, in these cases, is seeking to "domesticate" whom, and who most fearful of being barred from connubial bliss?

Evo psychos are well aware of the potential ferocity of male sexual jealousy; they incorporate the power of that jealousy into many of their theories about differing male and female strategies. But they fail to admit that male jealousy exists because women are, whether they take the tag or spurn it, born feminists. Women, like men, want the freedom to roam, explore, experiment—all desires to be expected in a highly in-telligent, inquisitive, shrewd, opportunistic, social species. It's not "out of sync" with our "nature" to want autonomy. The individual is the re-productive unit. Through the fantastic efforts of eons of evolution, the individual is born to like its particular genome, to want to get as much of that genome into the population as possible. The individual does not like being pushed around, deprived of choice, enslaved. The individual tends to chafe against excessive oppression. This is not "political cor-

---

3. See "Landscape of the Ordinary: Violence Against Women," by Andrea Dworkin, p. 58, and "The Nature of the Beast: Sexual Harassment," by Anita Hill, p. 296.—Ed.

rectness." This is common sense, Darwinian sense; our past, present, and future sense.

Then there is the bracing sense of dollars and cents. Not only do women yearn for the plain old primate liberty to come and go, pick and choose. Protestations of Kass and company notwithstanding, women are also born ambitious: they want social power, respect, admiration. Such desires are not the invention of the modern feminist movement. They are our birthright, or burden, as a profoundly social species, in which personal power translates into all the goodies of life. Nor is the lust for acclaim and high rank in contradistinction to a woman's more familiar "nurturing" side. The two impulses—to succeed in society, and to care for your children—are expressions of the same drive. A good mother is a powerful mother. A good mother can accrue resources for her young, and a really good mother can outcompete other mothers in the neighborhood, thereby ensuring that her children will do really well, while the children of less ambitious stock skulk around the back forest smoking acanthus leaves before getting picked off by a leopard.

The inherent ambitiousness of women can be seen in any country where women are not confined to home or *burqa*. At the slightest opportunity, women flock to schools, so much so that university officials in the United States bemoan the comparative lack of male faces in the classroom. Women take to the professions with astonishing ease: ever since the contemporary feminist movement helped open heretofore forbidden trades to women, the number of female doctors and lawyers has jumped from a few percent to nearly 50 percent, and woman-owned businesses are the fastest growing sector of our society.[4] Despite media gloatographies about the women who yearn to stay at home and be supported by a man, surveys repeatedly show that most employed women like earning a paycheck.

Yet despite the evidence, evo-bloviators have ignored or denied the existence of women's ambition. Behind this neglect are a couple of conceptual chestnuts in serious need of roasting.

First is the idea that males and females have wildly different repro-

---

4. See "Diagnosis and Prognosis: Women Physicians and Women's Health," by Wendy Chavkin, M.D., p. 378; "Women and Law: The Power to Change," by Catherine MacKinnon, p. 447; and "Owning the Future: Women Entrepreneurs," by Sara K. Gould, p. 456.—Ed.

ductive prospects. By this notion, males tend to fall on either end of the reproductive scale, as "zeroes" or "heroes," with most failing utterly to reproduce, and a minority of lucky stiffs monopolizing most of the females and siring most of the young. In contrast, females have been viewed as interchangeable, bearing more or less the same number of offspring and being more or less similarly talented in mothering skills. Hence, males had a strong spur to be hyperambitious and competitive, while females supposedly did best by keeping a low profile, busying themselves with a predictable number of bairns.

Recent research, including extensive paternity studies using DNA fingerprinting techniques, has skewered this folklore. As it turns out, the alpha males in many species breed fewer young than presumed, and the supposed duds sometimes prove spermic studs. Among females, on the other hand, the discrepancy in fruitfulness is far greater than previously believed. Some females are much better at bearing and rearing young than others, and those supermoms, as it happens, are the powerhouses of their societies. For example, Flo, a member of the Gombe chimpanzee troop long studied by Jane Goodall, was the most prolific female chimp of all time. She reared all but one of her nine infants to adulthood, a success rate at least twice that for the average chimpanzee mother. Flo also happened to be the most powerful female chimpanzee any researcher has ever observed. She could displace virtually any other chimpanzee—save the highest ranking, much larger males—from a prize feeding site, and her subordinates competed for the chance to groom her. So powerful was Flo that her daughters managed to stay in their birthplace rather than being forced to migrate at puberty as female chimps usually are; those daughters in turn became powerful, prolific matriarchs.

"Mother chimps like Flo were not simply doting nurturers but entrepreneurial dynasts as well," writes the primatologist Sarah Blaffer Hrdy in her marvelous book, *Mother Nature: Maternal Instincts and How They Shape the Human Species* (Pantheon, 1999). "A female's quest for status— her ambition, if you will—has become inseparable from her ability to keep her offspring and grand-offspring alive."[5] As Hrdy sees it, a gener-

---

5. See "Bitch, Chick, Cow: Women's and (Other) Animals' Rights," by Carol J. Adams, p. 494.—Ed.

alized striving for local clout was programmed into the primate female's psyche long ago, the result of a convergence between high status and successful motherhood.

Another reason why the evo psychos have shortchanged female striving stems from their assumption that whatever status and power women have sought they sought secondhand, by coupling with strong, ambitious, powerful men. This supposition is part of the larger tenet that women have a much greater need for men than any other female primate has for her male counterpart. The prolonged helplessness of the human infant (the story goes) means that a woman can't rear it alone; hence the evolution of love, romance, and committed fathers. It's true that women need help to rear their young, much more help than any other female ape requires. But the most recent anthropological evidence strongly suggests that women get such help from many quarters: from men, from relatives, from their older children. In some traditional cultures, senior females are indispensable to the welfare of their young kin; in others, women rely more on the assistance of brothers, uncles, and male cousins than on the take-home prey of their mates; elsewhere, women accept contributions from a number of different consorts. As anthropologist Meredith F. Small notes in *Kids: How Biology and Culture Shape the Way We Raise Our Children* (Doubleday, 2001), about 90 percent of childcare in the world is performed by older siblings.

In sum, women through the ages and across the world's stages have been remarkably creative and adaptable when seeking solutions to the childcare crisis.[6] We have always lived in a nanny state of one sort or another. For their part, men do not always display the hallmarks of devoted fatherhood. As Geoffrey F. Miller has described in *The Mating Mind: How Sexual Choice Shaped the Evolution of Human Nature* (Doubleday, 2000), much of the behavior we view as paternal may be a courtship display, a way of pleasing one's current mate and perhaps attracting the attention of other females in the vicinity. If good fathering conduct were driven by the same thing as is maternal behavior—a desire to improve one's offspring's chances of survival—why, Miller asks, would so many fathers end up as deadbeat dads who invest virtually nothing in the children of women they have divorced or abandoned? After all, DNA pater-

---

6. See "Parenting: A New Social Contract," by Suzanne Braun Levine, p. 85.—Ed.

nity testing is a ridiculously recent invention, and the grim male fears synopsized by the couplet, "Mother's baby/Father's maybe" are not to be dismissed out of hand.

If paternity uncertainty bred waffling fathers prone to bolting from their responsibilities, we would expect as a corollary women who likewise waffled about pinning their future and their children's welfare to one man, however alpha. How foolish a woman would be to forsake any attempt at gaining a degree of personal power or cultivating a reliable route to resources, simply for the opportunity to marry an ambitious man who could easily abandon her, be killed while out hunting, or simply prove to be a fraud. It's tempting to think that women have indeed "evolved" to hook their prospects to their mates, because we see as much in the annals of history—not to mention the pages of Jane Austen—but in fact the condition of extreme female dependency on husbands is very recent, and depends for its maintenance on a strong set of laws making divorce difficult and punishing deadbeatism. As we've seen in recent decades of loosened divorce laws, women who cling to the model of complete economic reliance on a husband suffer terrible financial hardship when the marriage breaks up, and they and their children are all too likely to be cast into poverty. That such a risky "my man is my meal ticket" strategy could have arisen and persisted in prehistory, in the absence of a legal system and in the face of chronic threats of famine, seems to me frankly laughable. Better to be ambitious, cunning, and, yes, creative, competitive, and aggressive. Better to earn your degree, learn a trade, get a paycheck, kiss it, and sock it away. If you're going to bank on anything, it might as well be a bank.

NATALIE ANGIER is a best-selling author and Pulitzer Prize–winning science writer for *The New York Times*. Previously, she has been senior science writer for *Time* magazine, an editor at the women's business magazine, *Savvy*, and a professor at New York University's Graduate Program in Science and Environmental Reporting. Her first book, *Natural Obsessions* (Houghton Mifflin), an inside look at the world of cancer research, was named a notable book of the year by *The New York Times* and the American Association for the Advancement of Science (AAAS). In 1990, she began working for *The New York Times;* the following year, she won a Pulitzer in the category of beat reporting, for a series of articles on a wide array of scientific topics, from the biology of scorpions, to the astonishing prevalence of infidelity in the animal kingdom. Among her other awards are the AAAS-Westinghouse award for excellence in science journalism, and the Lewis Thomas Award for distinguished writing in the life sciences. Her second book, *The Beauty of the Beastly* (Houghton Mifflin), has been translated into eight languages. Her latest, *Woman: An Intimate Geography* (Houghton Mifflin, 1999; Anchor Vintage paperback, 2000), was a bestseller, a National Book Award finalist, winner of a Maggie Award from the Planned Parenthood Federation, and named one of the best books of the year by the *Los Angeles Times*, the *Chicago Tribune*, and other major media. She is the editor of *The Best American Science and Nature Writing 2002* (Houghton Mifflin). Her writing has appeared in numerous periodicals ranging from the *Atlantic Monthly* to *Natural History*, from *Cosmopolitan* to *Ms.*

Suggested Further Reading

Ehrlich, Paul R. *Human Natures: Genes, Cultures, and Human Prospects.* Washington, D.C.: Island Press, 2000.

Hrdy, Sarah Blaffer. *The Woman That Never Evolved.* Boston: Harvard University Press, 1981; reissued with a new Preface in 1999.

Jolly, Alison. *Lucy's Legacy: Sex and Intelligence in Human Evolution.* Cambridge, Massachusetts: Harvard University Press, 1999.

Rose, Hilary, and Steven Rose, eds. *Alas, Poor Darwin: Arguments Against Evolutionary Psychology.* New York: Random House, 2000.

Small, Meredith F. *What's Love Got to Do with It? The Evolution of Human Mating.* New York: Anchor Books, 1995.

Unfinished Agenda: Reproductive Rights

FAYE WATTLETON

"Sisters, I'm not clear what you be after. If women want any rights more than they've got, why don't they just take them and not be talking about it."
—Sojourner Truth, First National Women's Rights Convention, October 1850

As WE ENTER the twenty-first century, the need has never been greater for women to assert the power of our leadership, framed within a global community. Triumphs won and hardships faced by women of all nations are now shared across borders, and our increasing global consciousness helps us recognize that the economic, political, and social progress made by some are still being sought by others. There *is* progress, but if we rest on our laurels or abandon our vigilance, we must hold ourselves accountable for whatever freedoms are lost due to our neglect.

Protecting the fundamental rights of women over our bodies remains a long, arduous struggle. Those who refuse to accept the Supreme Court's constitutional recognition of reproductive rights in *Roe v. Wade* have waged an effective, incremental battle. They've weathered opposition, employed semantics and imagery, and never lost sight of their goal. Facing their determination to erode and eventually eradicate women's fundamental rights, the first question before us is basic: *Do we, as women of the twenty-first century, have a vision of who we are, and of the value of our bodily integrity?*

Sexual behavior and reproductive rights continue to be at the core of the struggle for women's equality, because vested in these rights is enormous power—to control the entry of life itself. Embedded in this debate is a fundamental, unresolved conflict over female sexuality. Some progress has been made: we're openly (arguably) more tolerant of women making nontraditional choices regarding sexuality. But make no mistake. The rudiments of women's sexual oppression lurk dangerously close to the surface. They infuse the reproductive-rights discussion, using the fetus as proxy for a larger purpose. Nor is fear of women's power restricted to men; women fear claiming it for themselves and allowing it to other women. It's threatening to change the balance of human relationships, and reassuring to have defined boundaries—especially when what's at stake is handing authority to those who've traditionally been denied it. But if women of the early twenty-first century claim not to be "feminists," they should wake to reality: they are *beneficiaries of feminism*—who stand to lose what they take for granted.[1]

Yet women seem to have lost our sense of *the centrality of these rights to the foundation on which all our other choices rest.* Our judgment has been corrupted by a temptation to minimize the seriousness of unwanted pregnancy—precisely because fewer women face the prospect of being forced to carry a pregnancy to term against their will, or to settle for a dangerous alternative that could injure or kill them. But though we may distance ourselves from such circumstances, our opposition persists in creating conditions that gradually restore the humiliation and desperation from which women were liberated. The questions then become: *How much destruction can they do to the perception of what fundamental rights mean to women?* And: *Are we worthy of total ownership of our bodies without regulation by the state?*

These days, it's fashionable to shrink from calling for courage, to crouch on "common ground," to condition rights "payment" with "appropriate responsibility." What *is* "appropriate?" Who decides? And why are such qualifiers as "appropriate" and "responsible" uniquely attached to a woman's situation? Interestingly, U.S. citizens weathered the controversial 2000 presidential election in which we exercised our right to vote—yet never heard any companion obligation to "vote responsibly." Why does a value-judgment obligation lurk only in the exer-

---

1. See "Generation 'Why?': A Call to Arms," by Jasmine Victoria, p. 126, and "Gen X Survivor: From Riot Grrrl Rock Star to Feminist Artist," by Kathleen Hanna, p. 131.—Ed.

cise of *women's* behavior and choices? Most Americans have succumbed to intimidation, to the seduction of the seemingly benign notion of "common ground" for the sake of peace. *Authentic* common ground is the recognition that women must be protected from a government that would force a woman to bear a child against her will—*and* force a woman *not* to bear a child against her will. Wisely, the Supreme Court already established common ground on January 22, 1973, when it created a framework for the exercise of *the most fundamental human right: the right to procreate in a civil society*. The Court did *not* enable states to require a woman to undergo an abortion under certain conditions, and it ruled that the state—unless it showed compelling interest in protecting the life of the fetus—could *not* interfere in a woman's decision to end an unwanted pregnancy. Even in later stages of a pregnancy (when the state may attempt to protect the life of a viable fetus), the woman's life or health would never be compromised as a condition for preserving the fetus. Yet the foundation of the Court's reasoning has been assiduously challenged, as though the Court had never defined or clarified the meaning of a constitutionally protected right.

Complacency ambushes revolutions. Throughout history, failure to learn lessons of the past weakens the benefits of revolutions.[2] The fight to restore and protect the reproductive revolution is as urgent today as it was when it began at the beginning of the twentieth century. In 1976, only three years after *Roe v. Wade*—and in the midst of relentless clinic violence—the first national legislative attack was mounted. By discriminating against poor women, the Hyde Amendment banned federal funding of abortions under Medicaid except in cases of rape or incest or to save the life of the woman. Though poor women suffered first (and have always borne the heaviest burden of social and political struggles[3]), *no* woman is as free now as the courts liberated her to be only one generation ago. Women in many states must now wait for a prescribed period after requesting an abortion. Women must now travel great distances, often hundreds of miles, to gain access to a clinic. Once there, women now likely face humiliation by walking through phalanxes of

2. See "The Art of Building Feminist Institutions to Last," by Eleanor Smeal, p. 541.—Ed.

3. See "Poverty Wears a Female Face," by Theresa Funiciello, p. 222.—Ed.

abuse from screaming strangers whose rhetoric incites violence. Once inside, women are subjected to state-ordered scrutiny, state-ordered messages, and state-ordered invasion of the most private aspect of their lives. Sexuality education in schools is viciously attacked. Contraceptive programs are being undermined worldwide. It may be difficult for some readers to accept, but *the issue is broader than abortion.* In this struggle, when we cede *any* principle—much less such a fundamental one—we concede defeat in what is a war of attrition. And aren't we allowing ourselves to be consigned to the backwaters of the reform movement of thirty years ago, by codifying a woman's fundamental reproductive rights on a state-by-state basis?

The loss of our rights is neither an act of God nor a testament to any justice in our adversaries' causes. Rather, without effective opposition, graphic and rhetorical assassination have found their mark. In certain areas, the revolution has succumbed to anti-choice bombast. Incendiary rhetoric depicting late-term abortion was concocted as a tactical diversion—yet even our strongest pro-choice advocates have seemed unwilling to confront it. The late-term-abortion flank of the attack was opened as an incremental campaign with the release of the film, *The Silent Scream,* in the early 1980s. With inverse reasoning (but effective propaganda), opponents of legal abortion calculated that the fetus could be humanized and women *de*humanized (by being ignored outright or, in the case of teens, infantilized). Thus the status of the fetus could compete with women for legal protection. Anti-choicers also argue for advancing adoption, with the not-so-subtle message that if adoption is readily available, a woman has no legitimate reason to terminate a pregnancy. *But if we value women as worthy of the protections of fundamental rights, we must value their power not to be forced to bear a child for another's purposes.* Adoption is a legitimate option for a woman who *chooses* to carry her pregnancy to term. But adoption is an *alternative—not a substitute*—for the right to make a different decision. Similarly, the availability of a medical alternative (RU486, for example) is another alternative to surgical abortion, *not* a solution for all abortions: 90 percent of abortions are performed in the first trimester of pregnancy, when the medical alternative is effective—but what about the real needs of the real women who are not candidates for this method, and what about those who comprise that other 10 percent?

Opponents of a woman's fundamental right to control her fertility falsely accuse pro-choice advocates of failing to recognize the moral conflict inherent in terminating developing life. The fact is that abortion does kill developing life; abortion is unpleasant at any stage of pregnancy; unwanted pregnancy is a predicament in which no woman *wants* to find herself. But what gets lost in the rhetoric is the fact that most *anti-choice* advocates can find some point at which abortion is, from their moral vantage, permissible.[4] So the question becomes not *whether* but *when*. At which point on the spectrum between ovulation and birth must a woman sacrifice *her* right to that of the fetus? Under whose rules and by what authority must she subject her body to pregnancy and its attendant perils against her will?

Over the years, some people have assumed that, given my activism, I must be rebelling against my childhood's strict religious upbringing. Actually, my chosen profession of nursing—based on acceptance of people without regard for lifestyle or religious affiliation—took me farther from my background's Christian fundamentalist teachings than any act of political defiance could. Not so paradoxically, I remained close to the values of service. Nursing meant *caring* for people—kindness, patience, and compassion—regardless of others' personal conduct or moral and religious values. I saw the devastating effects of failed abortions early in my career, when I trained as a nurse midwife at New York's Harlem Hospital. Women arrived with objects jammed into their uteri beyond their reach, objects that tore surrounding tissue. Unsterile witch-hazel sticks, bought over the counter, had been inserted into the cervix—to gather moisture, expand, and dilate the opening until contractions started. Soft rubber catheters, made to empty the bladder, had been pushed into the pregnant womb and left for days, until the tissue became sufficiently inflamed so the muscle would violently contract, emptying its contents. Whether the objects were catheters, witch-hazel sticks, or coat hangers, dangerous infection was virtually inevitable. Even if medical attention came quickly, there was a high risk of ending any potential for future pregnancies. With especially unlucky women, invading organisms reached the Fallopian tubes and spread to the ab-

4. See, for example, the changing position of the Roman Catholic Church on this issue, down through history, in "Dancing Against the Vatican," by Frances Kissling, p. 474.—Ed.

domen and blood vessels, so death from a fulminating infection occurred quickly, despite massive doses of antibiotics. The odor of abortion infections and the feeling of hopeless helplessness to save dying women are unforgettable for anyone who can remember "how it was." But although women are constitutionally sheltered from such dangers, in a recent national survey of women, only 34 percent were in favor of abortions being generally available to those who want them.[5]

The sight of a pregnant girl in her early teens summons powerful emotions in most people, including the professionals caring for her. Oddly, the public finds the notion of a sexually active or pregnant teenager, appearing in a clinic without her parents' knowledge or consent, more disturbing. For teenage girls, pregnancy is a searing experience, regardless of any coping strategies. Though rates show an encouraging decline, the U.S. still has, at this writing, the highest teenage pregnancy rate in the "developed" world. Pregnant teenage girls in any family situation face the second trauma of parental disappointment and retribution; furthermore, far too many teens live in dysfunctional families. But disadvantage, dysfunction, or parental approval are not prerequisites for sexual intercourse without protection. Despite little evidence that laws forcing a family chat engender family cohesion, 32 states have joined the political herd requiring parental consent or notification unless a judge determines that the woman is "mature." Whose needs are being met when a judge has to decide if a teenager is mature enough to make her own decisions? If luck is not in her favor, a girl presumed too immature for an abortion is somehow mature enough to continue through pregnancy to motherhood? Are the needs being met those of the teenage girl, or of voting blocs of the politically ambitious? Why not admit that teenage pregnancy is actually more an adult problem than a teen problem?

Nor does this battle stop at teenage abortion rights. The lines between abortion and contraception itself have dissolved under the agenda of the ultra Right.[6] In 1984, at the UN World Conference on Population in Mexico City, a little over a decade after *Roe v. Wade*, the

---

5. *Possibilities and Perils: How Gender Issues Unite and Divide Women*, Princeton Survey Research Associates, Inc. (2001): 11.

6. See "Combating the Religious Right," by Cecile Richards, p. 464.—Ed.

U.S. announced funding prohibitions on organizations that, *with their own funds* (*not* U.S. aid), provided counseling and referral for abortion, or worked for legal reform. It didn't matter that the World Health Organization had estimated that 200,000 women died annually from illegal, botched abortions. The U.S. government, to appease the Vatican's objections to abortion and family-planning policies in the U.S. and abroad, was using its purse strings to impose restrictions on *other* countries—restrictions that neither the Constitution nor U.S. women would tolerate.[7] It was a rule with the force of law, an exploitation of court-sanctioned authority of the president to "conduct foreign policy." Appallingly, there was little public outrage about this assault on the world's poorest women.

Earlier, in 1982, the Reagan administration had attacked the federal family-planning program and attempted to attach regulations requiring clinics to inform parents of minor girls who received prescription contraception. Such regulations would have required minors to *surrender established constitutional rights of confidentiality*, for no compelling state interest, as a condition of receiving benefits to which they would otherwise be *entitled*.

By 1987, the forces against reproductive rights reached critical mass. President Reagan introduced the domestic "gag rule," which decreed that any *mention* of abortion cease in all clinics receiving Title X federal family-planning funding. This coup was the domestic version of the Mexico City policy. It should have been a wake-up call to any who had trivialized the earlier rules as being just a government measure to discourage abortion. This wasn't about funding organizations in distant lands; these were our clinics in U.S. cities being ordered to remain silent—even if a woman specifically asked for abortion information or requested an abortion referral.[8]

During the twelve years of the Reagan/Bush administration(s), the federal judiciary was realigned with jurists who ostensibly will divine and impose the intentions of the original constitutional Framers—from

---

7. See Kissling, op. cit.—Ed.

8. For data on women in the U.S. military being denied this reproductive right, see "Redefining the Warrior Mentality: Women in the Military," by Claudia J. Kennedy, p. 409.—Ed.

back when women couldn't vote and blacks were slaves.[9] Then, in 1991, a politically restructured Supreme Court voted five to four (*Rust v. Sullivan*) to uphold the ban on free speech in women's clinics. Ultimately, the domestic gag rule did fail—not because the Court ruled that the president couldn't censor speech, but because President Clinton came to power before the Bush administration could figure out how to impose such censorship.

Ironically, the later restoration of some of the damage done to reproductive rights during the Reagan/Bush era was not the work of a united pro-choice offensive. When the Clinton administration came into office, the rules (but not the legislation) were overturned by a sweep of the presidential pen. Eight years later, in one of his first acts as president, George W. Bush *re*imposed the international gag rule, upheld by the Court. Why have we allowed reproductive rights to become a political football? If women determined that this issue be taken off the playing field of politics and returned to the privacy of our lives—as the Supreme Court intended in *Roe v. Wade*—the struggle would end.

Meanwhile, though abortion is still (restrictively) legal, it's becoming de facto unavailable for far too many women.[10] Where have all the doctors gone?[11] Encouragingly, women constitute a growing proportion of physicians, but the availability of those willing to provide safe preg-

---

9. See "Women and Law: The Power to Change," by Catharine A. MacKinnon, p. 447.—Ed.

10. See "Our Bodies, Our Future: Women's Health Activism Overview," by Judy Norsigian et al., p. 269, and "Diagnosis and Prognosis: Women Physicians and Women's Health," by Wendy Chavkin, M.D., p. 378.—Ed.

11. Although only about half the residency programs in the U.S. now teach ob-gyns in training how to perform abortions, more are—as of 2002—adding the training to their programs. In July 2002, New York became the first U.S. city to require abortion techniques as standard part of training for ob-gyn residents at public hospitals (one of seven doctors in the U.S. does a New York City residency). The National Abortion and Reproductive Rights Action League (NARAL) hopes to duplicate the New York City model in other cities, attempting to reverse a downturn in the number of doctors who perform the procedure. But more training in itself won't solve the problem, since other factors discourage physicians from performing this medical service: violence, harassment, restrictions that vary state-by-state, difficulty obtaining malpractice coverage, and contracts doctors must sign that explicitly forbid abortions when they affiliate with certain hospitals or join certain group practices. (See "Newest Skill for Future Ob-Gyns: Abortion," by Linda Villarosa, *The New York Times*, 11 June 2002.)—Ed.

nancy termination is inverse: 86 percent of all U.S. counties have no abortion provider; in 44 states, the number of physicians performing abortions *declined* between 1992 and 1996.[12]

There are no easy panaceas in the struggle for justice, no evading the hard work earlier reformers passionately engaged. We must ask ourselves how we allowed our lack of vigilance to collaborate with adversaries of progressive change; how we allowed our opponents to regain ground that had been won by the ultimate sacrifice; how we permitted the erasure from memory of suffering, injured, and dead women. Are they to be consigned to historical oblivion by women who are the very beneficiaries of their lives, lives sacrificed by atrocities of government coercion over women's bodies—whether through forced sterilization[13] *or* forced childbirth? Women, more than 50 percent of the U.S. population, have sufficient power—not to protect (as hand-wringing fencesitters put it) "one moral position against another," but to protect the right of *all* women to make their *own* moral decisions.

I have never believed in the impossible. My mother is a preacher, herself the daughter of a preacher. My roots are in a family of doers, independent thinkers with strong wills and convictions. Rooted in this heritage, I've never accepted the idea that some things can't be done, or will never change. I've always believed it's just a matter of figuring out *how*.

Leadership is required to shift the tide of regression—not just the leadership of courage but the leadership of *will*. Today's women are a diverse generation of doers; they too are independent thinkers with strong wills and convictions. The political and social progress won during the twentieth century make it possible for our daughters to grow up believing implicitly that there is nothing they can't do, given desire, will, and perseverance. My daughter Felicia, now a young woman, forges her own path of struggle and accomplishment. As her generation carries the

---

12. Stanley K. Henshaw, "Abortion Incidence and Services in the United States, 1995–96," *Family Planning Perspectives*, vol. 30, no. 6 (Nov./Dec. 1998): 263, 266, 267, table 5.

13. See "Native Americans: Restoring the Power of Thought Woman," by Clara Sue Kidwell, p. 165, and "African American Women: The Legacy of Black Feminism," by Beverly Guy-Sheftall, p. 176.—Ed.

torch alongside (and eventually beyond) us, we must ask them the questions we ask ourselves:

Who will have the power to decide the most intimate aspects of your body and your life force?

By whose moral and religious values will you live?

Who will make the decisions about your *daughter's body and the choices in* her *life?*

The preservation and exercise of our rights must continue—in fact, *expand.* Until women decide that our rights are not negotiable, our future's choices will never rest secure. Until women's bodies are no longer politicized and our privacy no longer contested, our struggle must continue. The irony is that *if women in our country and across our planet united to end injustice, it would be ended.* The direction of women's lives in the twenty-first century rests on our shoulders. It will be defined by the quality of our vision and the courage of our leadership.

FAYE WATTLETON holds a Bachelor of Science degree in nursing from Ohio State University and a Master of Science in maternal and infant care, with certification as a nurse-midwife from Columbia University. From 1978 to 1992, she played a major role in defining the national debate over reproductive rights and health, and in shaping family-planning policies and programs around the world, during her tenure as the first woman president (since founder Margaret Sanger) of Planned Parenthood Federation of America. In additional to numerous awards (including the American Public Health Association's Award of Excellence, the Congressional Black Caucus Foundation Humanitarian Award, and the Women's Honors in Public Service from the American Nurses Association), she was inducted in 1993 into the National Women's Hall of Fame. She holds twelve honorary degrees and is currently president of the New York-based Center for Gender Equality, a social science research, education, and advocacy institution founded in 1995 to advance women's equality and full participation in society. She lectures widely on women's rights and is the author of numerous articles, as well as of a memoir, *Life on the Line* (Ballantine Books, 1996).

Suggested Further Reading

Chesler, Ellen. *Woman of Valor: Margaret Sanger and the Birth Control Movement in America*. New York: Simon & Schuster, 1992.

Gordon, Linda. *Woman's Body, Woman's Right: A Social History of Birth Control in America*. New York: Penguin Books, 1976, 1990.

Kennedy, David. *Birth Control in America: The Career of Margaret Sanger*. New Haven and London: Yale University Press, 1970.

Mohr, James C. *Abortion in America: The Origins and Evolutions of National Policy, 1800–1900*. New York: Oxford University Press, 1978.

Risen, James, and Judy L. Thomas. *Wrath of Angels: The American Abortion War*. New York: Basic Books, 1997.

Running for Our Lives: Electoral Politics

PAT SCHROEDER

WHEN ARE YOU running for public office?

I'm serious.

Our country is suffering from an epidemic of cynicism about electoral politics, and tasting a real fear that democracy is being eroded—especially given Attorney General John Ashcroft's alarming surveillance strategies post 9/11. The public doesn't trust the institutions of American life anymore—politics, Wall Street, even the churches—but the public *does* notice, poll after poll, that women seem to have a different value system. Women were the whistle-blowers at Enron and other imploding corporations. Women were protesting the secretive, arrogant hierarchy of the Roman Catholic Church long before the pedophilia scandals. The voting gender gap persists, with women being more consistently anti-war and pro-environment.

So there *is* hope. Never before have there been so many well-educated young women who could grab the controls, stop this nonsense, *take over.* Why are so many of them sitting in the bleachers and wringing their hands?

You can't wring your hands and roll up your shirtsleeves at the same time. Pick one.

You think you lack skills? Oh, please. Look at the men already elected! Too young? No experience, staff, money, backers, party support? Let me tell you a story.

There I was, a young activist in the social-justice movements of the 1960s and early '70s. I'd been a lawyer for the National Labor Relations Board (NLRB) in Colorado, done pro bono work for fair housing and

Rocky Mountain Planned Parenthood; Jim (my husband) and I were active in anti-Vietnam war stuff. In 1972, Denver's Republican incumbent congressman held political positions somewhere to the Right of Attila the Hun. Worse, the Democrat set to oppose him—the minority leader in the state senate—planned to run to the *Right* of the Republican. Jim was involved with a group of young activists desperate for an alternative, begging anybody with political credentials, "Run! We'll back you!" But everyone laughed, "Even if we won the primary, we'd never beat the other guy!" The Republican was the best-known politician in the state, and McGovern—heading the Democratic ticket—had no rideable coattails.

One night, Jim came home from a meeting of this young activist group. I had *just* finally put the two-year-old and the six-year-old to bed (which, as any mother knows, is when you realize you feel you've been hit by a truck). "Guess what?" he chuckled. Then he told me that the group, despairing, had sat around realizing they'd have to give up, when someone said, "How about your wife, Schroeder?" I stared at Jim. "Were you guys drinking at this meeting?" I asked. I then announced that I wasn't running for *anything.* "Well, you'd never *win,*" he acknowledged, "but it's so important to *stake out the issues.*" (See, there's the hook.) Then the group arrived: "Pat, you can take on everything from South Africa's apartheid"—which I'd worked on back in college— "through busing. Every issue you care about. We at least have to *articulate* these issues; we can't let the Democrats be silent! Besides, *it'll all be over in September.*" I had two great part-time jobs I didn't want to give up—teaching at the university and working on hearings for the state— plus, of course, the kids. So I refused. Then Jim used guilt: "But you tell your students that each one of us *has* to get out there and *do* something." Adding, of course: *"Besides, it'll all end in September."*

So we opened up a room in the basement. We had no campaign headquarters. My friends and I—we called ourselves "kitchen table media"— did everything. We had no money. I said, "I am *not* going into debt for this," because everybody knew it was a losing campaign. Of course, the freedom of thinking "It's a losing campaign" is interesting: it meant we could be honest, be ourselves. We were living examples of that Janis Joplin line, "Freedom's just another word for nothing left to lose."

We had only three posters. One was a picture of Denver's military cemetery, with a bird flying over the tombstones and a quote from Nixon: "Yes, many of our troops have already been withdrawn"—and on the back, my position on Vietnam. The second was about a possible Denver Olympics (which was also on the ballot). Being an environmentalist who'd seen through the Chamber of Commerce spiel, I knew these guys didn't have the money, anyway. So our poster had a picture of an old woman with a cane, and the line, "Cheer up! The Olympics are coming!" On the back was our statement: the Olympics were a noble idea, but there wasn't enough funding or infrastructure, and Denver taxpayers would get stuck with the bill. The third poster was a migrant child squatting on a dirt floor beneath a crucifix (Coloradans never liked to admit we had migrant kids there), with the message: "This radical troublemaker is out to get something from you. Hope." Our kitchen media posters actually won awards. We printed them on bright colored paper because we got the sheets for a penny apiece—pink, orange, yellow—colors you apparently *never* use in politics. We violated all the rules, because we knew none. But people got excited by the posters— plastering them on windows, walls, streetlamps—because a political campaign was actually taking *stands.*

Meanwhile, our little dirt-cheap campaign was getting outspent five to one by the other guy. *No one in our state Democratic party—except for the elected African Americans—endorsed me;* they all backed the state senator. The party wouldn't even give me a map of my district. But the saddest moment involved women. I'd helped found the Colorado Women's Political Caucus, so I went to see them, thinking, "*Finally*, I'll have some support." But they announced, "We're not endorsing you. It's too early for a woman to run. You should have tried for city council or school board." They felt I was bound to lose, and for the next 20 years people would say, "We ran a woman once, and she lost." Which would be my fault. These were *friends,* so it felt like I'd been hit with a hammer. I thought, "Ha, I'm a viable candidate? I can't even get the Women's Caucus to endorse me!"

September came. I still hadn't given up my two jobs.

Primary day.

I *won.*

Oops. Suddenly, we're in the big time. *Now* where will the support come from? Back then, there was no Emily's List,[1] no anything. So I thought, the *unions!* After all, I'd been representing them for years. Besides, in Salt Lake City and Iowa City guys as young as I were running— with *no* labor ties—who were getting thousands of dollars from labor. But I wasn't a guy. The AFL-CIO sent me 50 bucks. I sent it back.

This was a nightmare. We were still running the campaign out of the basement, I was still keeping my jobs, and of course the kids were still being the kids. I went to Washington to see the Democratic National Committee (DNC). They wouldn't even make fundraising appointments for me. When I showed them my stuff (See? I'm so proud, *look* what we've done!) they gasped, "These posters went *out?!*" They were horrified. I got on a plane and went home. From then on, all my money came from people in the district; *the average campaign contribution was seven dollars and fifty cents.* We did no polls. We had no *money* to do polls. We did one black-and-white TV spot that cost us $1,500—kitchen table media again.

I was waiting for election night so life could return to normal.

November came.

I won again.

There I am. The Colorado party is embarrassed. The DNC is embarrassed. Nobody wants to talk to me. I'm 32 years old. I'm in Congress.

I remember even Bella Abzug[2] worrying, "Your children are still little. I don't know how you're going to do this." No women in Congress had small children, and two and six—that's really *little*. Also, 32 is really *young*. Totally unprepared for everything, I arrived in Washington for the briefing. Almost everyone in the party regarded me with "Oh, *her!*" expressions. I remember saying to the senior woman (a Democrat), "Hi, I'm Pat Schroeder. I know who you are, but what should I call you?" And she huffed, "My name is Mrs. John Sullivan." So I smiled, "Oh, I

---

1. Emily's List was founded in 1985 to provide financial and political resources for pro-choice Democratic women candidates. The name comes from the acronym and slogan "Early Money Is Like Yeast: It makes the dough rise."—Ed.

2. Democratic congresswoman from New York City. See the Introduction to this anthology, and the dedication page.—Ed.

know *that*. I mean, what should I *call* you?" *"My name is Mrs. John Sullivan."* Wow, I thought, *we've* got a lot in common. At the time, about half the women had inherited their seats and were carrying their husband's flags. We did have Bella standing tall, and Shirley Chisholm, Barbara Jordan, Patsy Mink. But they were older, and they'd raised their children.

We were a long way from anything like a real women's caucus. Still, sometime between '72 and '74, Peggy Heckler (a Massachusetts Republican) tried to form one. But it fell flat. Then, in '74, with the Watergate crisis, we got quite a few more women elected. So we tried again. There was much *angst*—"we can only take positions if we're unanimous"—and pontificating: "Oh, *I* never had any trouble as a *woman*." Yeah, sure, because you ran as Mrs. John Sullivan! (Which of course I couldn't say out loud.) So we actually started the Congressional Caucus on Women's Issues in '75—but it was feeble. Peggy and Liz Holtzman[3] were the first co-chairs. When Liz left, I took it over. I said, "Look, we were voted in—and if this caucus can't decide anything by our *own* majority vote, we look silly. Also, we need to spend some money getting research behind what we're doing. We can donate that out of our legislative kitties. And we should have a Men's Auxiliary. Men always hide behind our skirts on 'women's issues,' so we might as well let them pay to join and help us with our causes." We juiced it up nicely, and things went pretty well for years. Until Newt Gingrich rose to power, riding on the Right-wing seizure of the Republican Party and the House in 1994.[4] As Speaker of the House, he made life hell for all the caucuses—especially the Black Caucus and us. Still, in our time, we managed to get some important things done.

For example, women's health.[5] Nowadays, we're upset over the latest

3. Elizabeth Holtzman, former Democratic congresswoman from New York City, who came to national prominence during the Congressional hearings on Watergate.—Ed.

4. Gingrich, Speaker of the U.S. House of Representatives from 1995 to 1999, resigned from Congress in 1999 in the face of personal and political scandals.—Ed.

5. See "Our Bodies, Our Future: Women's Health Activism Overview," by Judy Norsigian et al., for The Boston Women's Health Book Collective, p. 269, and "Diagnosis and Prognosis: Women Physicians and Women's Health," by Wendy Chavkin, M.D., p. 378.—Ed.

test results on hormone replacement therapy's effects—but at least now there *are* tests! Back then, without a clue, they were shoving HRT at every menopausal woman. All of us who *knew* there'd been no tests were screaming, "*Wait* a minute!" There'd been no research on osteoporosis, on bladder incontinence, even on *breast cancer.* The National Institutes of Health had run the breast cancer research on *men.* It was enough to make you crazy. This was federal money, and they weren't putting women into any of the tests, trials, or studies. Our bipartisan women's caucus made a real difference on those issues. Still, our solidarity was always under assault.

Some women in politics long to be part of the boys' "gang." When Gerry Ferraro ran for vice president,[6] I saw many a woman attack her, thinking that would be an entry ticket into the gang—but no way. Such a woman accomplishes nothing except selling out another woman. Every time so-called liberal women want something—day care, pay equity—the gang sends one of "their" women out on attack. On TV it looks as if one woman says it's a great idea, another says it's not, so women haven't made up their minds—therefore we needn't do anything about it. Unfortunately, Republicans have developed this tactic into an art. On the Democratic side, there are women hesitant to push the guys as hard as some of us did, because these men weep all over you, whining, "You don't *understand!* If I vote pro-choice, ooooh, what will they say!" Then there are the women who are "trying to move things along." It's not that they lack vision, but they want to remain players. Whereas I arrived realizing I would *never* be a player—so I would play the outsider game.

When I first came onto the Armed Services Committee, the chairman had a fit. He insisted I *share* a seat with Ron Dellums—he didn't want any women *or* black men—so each of us would be half a committee member. Traditionally, if that happened to a new member, the poor soul would be traumatized. You *dare* not get on the outs with your chairman; you need *goodies* from your chairman; you *placate* your chairman. But I marched right to the press, saying, "Look what this guy's done to me." It ended up with that chairman being overruled by the whole Democratic caucus.

---

6. Walter Mondale and Geraldine Ferraro were the Democratic candidates for president and vice president in 1984.—Ed.

True, I had an ace up my sleeve: I didn't care if I didn't get re-elected, because then I'd go back home and have a saner life. That willingness to take a risk made all the difference—plus the fact that nobody had invested in me (except people who gave seven dollars and fifty cents), so I had no big donors pressuring me to chill out.

Congress was a pretty un-family-friendly workplace in those days—and juggling family along with the job was, to say the least, challenging. I know it's been said this contributes to our attrition problem: why, even when we get more women into national office, they soon quit. But things have changed. Today, serving in Congress is probably the highest-paid *hourly* job in the U.S. a woman can get. When I left in '96, and Diana DeGette (a good friend) replaced me, I warned her to move her family to Washington or else she'd never see them. But in 2001 she told me, "I'm moving my family back to Denver. You wouldn't believe this place now. I can take my kids to school Tuesday morning, fly to Washington, and not miss one vote—because they don't vote before 6:30 P.M. on Tuesdays! *And* I can be home for dinner in Denver by Thursday." Talk about a "do-nothing Congress"! They vote names for post offices. They don't do committee work intensely—the full hearing process, deep research. I believe the current [2002] House leadership [Republican] doesn't *want* things to happen. But at least I'd say to any woman who's considering *not* running because of the workload and time constraints: *think again*.

There's a kind of "settling" for whatever crumbs can be had, these days. Where is the intensity, the passion? What about the magic moment during the Hill/Thomas hearings in 1991,[7] when we congresswomen marched over to the Senate—which *just isn't done*—pounding on the doors and demanding that Hill be heard? Are we sliding backwards? If so, how do we turn it around?

Some days I worry that we did *too* good a job. Young women today can do many things my generation couldn't. So when I go to a campus and urge them to get involved, I know they're thinking, "Oh, you're one of those tired old feminists like my mother." A few years later, by their mid-twenties, they're in my office screaming, "Do you *know* what *happened* to me?" But by then it's much harder to organize them, because

---

7. See "The Nature of the Beast: Sexual Harassment," by Anita Hill, p. 296.—Ed.

they're dispersed.[8] Right now, there isn't as strong a grassroots movement as there should be—on campuses *and* off. The National Women's Political Caucus is a shadow of its former self. People seem to have retrenched. I don't know how *any* women can be complacent when we've lost ground on pay equity and job advancement; when the steady erosion of reproductive rights is terrifying; when the UN has graded the U.S. with an "F" for having moved more women into poverty.[9] I know some people feel that you can't make an impact on "Them" anymore, that the system is too corrupt, remote, closed. But dammit, you can still try to *become* "Them"—the ones in power—and *change* things.

After leaving Congress, I taught at the Woodrow Wilson School of Public and International Affairs at Princeton University. The first day, I asked, "How many of you are considering running for office?" About two-thirds of the class were women, some of the best and brightest in the country, interested in public service. *No hands went up.* I thought maybe I was in the wrong place. "This *is* the graduate school of public service, right? Are we just being shy?" A pause. Then someone replied, "Oh, I wouldn't do that with *my* life." (I thought, Oh, so *I'm* the dumb one?) Stunned, I asked, "Well, what *do* you want to do?" "We want to write the memos for the guys in power, to be advisors, like George Stephanopolous." *Omigod*, I thought. Holding public office, they shrugged, intrudes on your private life—and a bunch of other excuses. I could knock down every one of those excuses (and did). But this was alarming.

We've come so far—and not far at all. Case in point: Nancy Pelosi (D., California). Nancy understands the political machines and games, yet she's one of the most ethical people I know. Her district was trying to make nice with China over trade—yet Pelosi went there and held a demonstration in Tiananmen Square. She's Catholic, but strong on

8. See "Generation 'Why?': A Call to Arms," by Jasmine Victoria, p. 126; "Gen X Survivor: From Riot Grrrl Rock Star to Feminist Artist," by Kathleen Hanna, p. 131; and "Stealth Feminists: The Thirtysomething Revolution," by Debra Michals, p. 138. See also "Notes of a Feminist Long Distance Runner," by Eleanor Holmes Norton, p. 145.—Ed.

9. See the Workplaces section, p. 323; see also "Unfinished Agenda: Reproductive Rights," by Faye Wattleton, p. 17, and "Poverty Wears a Female Face," by Theresa Funiciello, p. 222.—Ed.

choice—though that's pained her down to her toes. I was delighted when she became Democratic Whip. She was the perfect candidate, raising lots of money for the party, gracious to everyone (she's got that "lady" thing I never had). Had she been a man, *no* one would have run against her, and now it's happening again: Dick Gephardt (D., Missouri)—House Democratic Leader—might step aside to run for president in 2004; normally, whoever is Whip moves up, becoming Leader. But the boys are *already* lining up to run against Nancy. That's how far we still have to go.

Frankly, *neither* party is very good on women. To some extent, the Republicans are better at showcasing their women. Furthermore, the Democrats have known for a long time that on the *issues*, women—like most minority men—are closer to them than to the Republicans. So they take us for granted.

I'm often asked what would it take to make the process friendlier to women—what about the women's political action committees (PACs), what kinds of campaign-finance reform would be most effective, would free airtime regulations help, what about proportional representation. If PACs exist, I guess women should have ours. But while I see nothing wrong with saying, "These candidates are good; send them money if you want," why not do it directly? Why bundle it through a PAC? PACs make the people who run them more powerful in the political parties, but if those people aren't using that power to lobby for *issues*, what's the point? As for campaign financing, simple. *If every woman in a district would write a check for what her last outfit cost, that would do it.* Those who buy designer outfits would pay more than those who buy from JCPenney. *Women are not a minority! We can out-fundraise all the guys if we do this!* Whenever I ran for office, I'd get money from the same kind of folks Gary Hart[10] did (we had similar voting records). But his checks would come from men and be for $1,000; mine from women, for $50 to $100—and those were probably the first checks for a candidate they'd ever written. That's exciting, and I would never demean it. But the costs of my campaign didn't get a 90 percent discount. I watch my husband in the male culture call a friend and say, "I'm raising money for Princeton," and the other guy says, "I'm raising money for the symphony." And

---

10. Former Democratic senator from Colorado.

they'll exchange checks. They don't even ask! But call a woman, and she says, "Hmmm. Well . . . tell me about it." With women, it's still retail, there's no wholesale. So reform can help, but what would really do it is women supporting women candidates with words, action, *and* cash.

I'm encouraged by some developments. Every year, polls show the number of people saying they won't vote for a woman is declining. (But the same people say, "Oh, *I* would vote for a woman, but *my friends* wouldn't." So you wonder . . .) I'm glad more women are running for governor. Those are executive positions—pipelines to the presidential level, which will still take time to crack. Women now constitute approximately 20 percent of all state legislatures. So we do make progress. But if anyone in 1972 had told me that 30 years later I'd be saying isn't it terrific that we have 13 women in the Senate (out of *100!*) and 50-some-odd in the House (out of *435!*), I'd have scoffed.

Backlash hit us, for one thing. Maybe underestimating the resistance we face—even from some women—for another. For example, when in office, I got more mail about my hair than *any* other subject. Sorry to say, these writers would be women.

"I saw you on television."

"Fine, what'd you think (about what I'd said on the economy, or foreign policy, or health care)?"

"Well, to be perfectly honest, I didn't like you in green."

They're still doing this to Hillary Rodham Clinton, even as a senator. Nobody ever told Gingrich to go thin his hair. *Until we see women as other than geisha girls or Barbies, this will keep happening.* It comes from centuries of defining women by how we look, not what we do. Sure, feminists have *said* all this. But whole industries—beauty, fashion, entertainment, magazines—are built on the other message. And they promote their message better than we do ours.

The relatively few women who have power—and principles—need to raise their national profiles much higher. Bella had a high profile, as did Shirley. That inspires younger women. Legislative vision inspires, too, and stubbornness. I introduced the Family and Medical Leave Act. I was the only sponsor. No one would get on it. It took *nine years.* But though it had no power or money behind it, it had *press* sizzling. We need to get on the air and *keep talking.*

But that means *not* arriving on Tuesday and leaving by Thursday.

You've got to *work* it; otherwise, you're not leading. Which is fine with the Republicans, who wouldn't want to be led where women want to go anyway. If I were heading the caucus now, I'd ask all the women to stay on Friday so we could hold a hearing on pay equity. If they wouldn't give us a room, we'd set up in the yard under a tent and say, "Isn't it too bad the leadership won't let us have a room!" You just *do* it. You don't get all the way, but you get somewhere. And audacity is *fun.*

In Colorado, feminists used satire. We formed Ladies Against Women, wore hats, gloves, and "I'd Rather Be Ironing" buttons, and loudly denounced the ERA.[11] When a nutcake (like today's Ashcroft) showed up, we'd go *support* him. Everyone knew it was a gag—but since we weren't protesting, they couldn't arrest us. They didn't know *what* to do. We had a ball. Now we wring our hands over an Ashcroft instead of making him look as ridiculous as he really is.

We need to take ourselves more seriously, and take the men in power less seriously.

We also need to be more knowledgeable. For instance, local book clubs are very popular with women, which is great. Now we need *voting* clubs. If every woman reading this got together with five or six friends and talked about local candidates—who's worth it, who isn't—presto! You're a voting group. Look at the Hollywood Women's Political Caucus: *there* was a powerful bunch of women. They would *audition* candidates. You might not be in Hollywood, but if you've got a pissed-off group of women anywhere—friends, work colleagues, mothers from your kids' playgroup or school, whatever—just set yourself up. Read, talk, *act.*

We need to be creative, too. A small group of women can figure out how to make life hell for the men in power. You can go to a copy shop, make 500 copies of something—*"Did you know Senator X voted against the Civil Rights Act!?!"*—or whatever. Then mail one to Senator X: "Dear Sir, We just made 500 copies of this. We're putting them in bathrooms, sticking them in menus at restaurants, leaving them in laundry rooms, and so forth. Have a nice day." They *hate* that! What they want you to do is write them a long, thoughtful letter. (Personally, I think let-

---

11. For more on the Equal Rights Amendment, see "Women and Law: The Power to Change," by Catharine A. MacKinnon, p. 447.—Ed.

ter writing can be a waste of time. Ditto those enormously expensive page ads in *The New York Times* or *The Washington Post*. The money for one *New York Times* ad could pay a lot of campaign costs for a decent candidate. The ads make *no* difference—except that people like to read their names in the newspaper.) Politicians know they don't have to answer your thoughtful letter at all, or they can get away with a form reply. They know you'll then get mad at them, so *your* normal response will be, "I wrote Senator X a letter and he didn't answer. I'll show him. I won't even vote." *Which is exactly what he wants you to do, because then he's done away with one negative vote.*

The conservatives have become very sophisticated. They hide behind international issues, even though they can't connect the dots between overpopulation, family planning, and terrorism. Suddenly, after 9/11, they cared passionately about Afghan women—but if any Afghan woman wants an abortion, forget it. They claim concern for women in the Middle East while kowtowing to Saudi Arabia! But if women organize more effectively *here*, we can *do* something about all that. Women all over the world have told us clearly: we'd be doing something for them if we clean up our own act.

When I left Congress, I'd been there almost a quarter of a century— yes, 24 years of housework, and the place is *still* a mess—12 terms in a career I'd never planned in the first place. Suddenly, I was 55. Ageism is alive and well.[12] Also, Gingrich was running the place. Miserable as my life had been when Democrats controlled it, this was worse. It felt like being in a food fight all day, every day. True, I was an effective food fighter—and being Irish, loved every food fight I was in. But that's hardly a satisfactory way to legislate. Furthermore, depressingly, I saw Democrats caving in. When we first lost, I understood that they were in shock. But after three months, six months, nine months? There was a hard core—six to ten of us—who'd pound away, but our *own* party wouldn't let us move. Or else they'd urge me, "Go at 'em on this, get 'em on that"—and I'd look around and say, "Hey, why am I the only food fighter? It'd be really nice if the rest of you joined in." It reminded me of when men would ask, "How come you have all these 'women's is-

---

12. See "The Politics of Aging," by Barbara Macdonald with Cynthia Rich, p. 152.—Ed.

sues'?" and I'd answer, "You know what? I don't need them all. Which ones would *you* like to carry?" They'd turned pale: "Oh, no, we don't want to be the prime sponsor of *that*." And I'd think, Well, that may be why I'm carrying them all.

No one generation should have to deliver everything (which is why I'm standing here waving my torch, yelling, "Come get it! It's burning my hand!"). But it makes me crazy when we don't insist on getting credit for what we *did* deliver. Women never brag, "We're the folks who brought you—Family Leave, Title IX, whatever." Men give each other medals! During World War II commemorations they celebrate every beach, building, ship. The day Elvis died gets more press than the day women won the right to vote!

Not that we haven't made mistakes. We never bought cable television stations. The Right-wing religious guys did, and they blanket the air-waves. The far Right's also shrewd at setting up think tanks and getting young, thin, blond, female creatures, stuffing them with propaganda, and sending them out on the air, 24–7. We need more strong spokes-women, especially younger ones. When we get those voting clubs going, each one should have a media element (kitchen table media lives!). It's impossible to overestimate the influence of broadcast media.[13] Newspapers no longer affect communities as they once did. That's troubling, because taking time to digest the written word is cru-cial. The best thing that could happen to Americans would be to sit down and *read*—which requires paying attention. When something like 9/11 comes at us, everyone has to scramble to figure out even the basics, because of dumbed-down reporting and public ignorance. Ready or not, the world did come at us, reminding us we're part of it. If that's not a wake-up call, I don't know what is.

Meanwhile, they haven't taken your vote away—*yet*. But they're close. The 2000 presidential election, with the Florida scandal and the Supreme Court interference—was *real* close.

So. Are you wringing your hands? Or are you rolling up your sleeves?

---

13. See "The Media and the Movement: A User's Guide," by Gloria Steinem, p. 103, and "Standing By: Women in Broadcast Media," by Carol Jenkins, p. 418.—Ed.

Former Congresswoman PATRICIA SCOTT SCHROEDER graduated the University of Minnesota magna cum laude in 1961 (working as an insurance-claims adjuster to put herself through college); went to Harvard Law School, one of 15 women in a class of more than 500 men; earned her J.D. in 1964, and moved to Colorado with her husband James. In 1996, she left Congress undefeated after serving 24 years, during which time she became the Dean of Congressional Women, co-chaired the Congressional Caucus on Women's Issues (for 10 years), and served on the House Judiciary Committee, the Post Office and Civil Service Committee, and (the first woman) the House Armed Services Committee. As chair of the House Select Committee on Children, Youth, and Families (1991–1993), she saw the Family and Medical Leave Act and the National Institutes of Health Revitalization Act to fruition. She was an early supporter of legalized abortion, and sponsored legislation making it a federal crime to obstruct access to abortion clinics. She was also active in military issues, expediting the National Security Committee's vote to allow women to fly combat missions (1991), and working to improve the situation of military families through passage of her Military Family Act in 1985. A leader in education issues, as Ranking Member of the House Judiciary Subcommittee on Courts and Intellectual Property, she was one of the most knowledgeable members of Congress on copyright and intellectual property rights issues. Pat Schroeder currently leads New Century/New Solutions, an outside-the-box think tank, for the Institute for Civil Society in Newton, Massachusetts, and co-chairs Democracy Online Project's National Task Force. Since 1997, she has been president and CEO of the Association of American Publishers (AAP), the national trade organization of the U.S. book publishing industry. She herself is the author of two books: *Champion of the Great American Family* (New York: Random House, 1989) and *24 Years of House Work . . . and the Place Is Still a Mess* (Kansas City, Mo.: Andrews McMeel, 1998).

Suggested Further Reading

Asbell, Bernard. *The Pill: A Biography of the Drug that Changed the World.* New York: Random House, 1995.

DePauw, Linda Grant, and K. Conover Hunt. *Remember the Ladies: Women in America 1750–1815*. New York: Viking Press, 1976.

Sidel, Ruth. *Women and Children Last: The Plight of Poor Women in Affluent America*. New York: Viking Penguin, 1986.

McCaffery, Edward. *Taxing Women*. Chicago, Illinois: The University of Chicago Press, 1996.

Morgan, Robin, ed. *Sisterhood Is Global: The International Women's Movement Anthology*. New York: Doubleday and Anchor Books, 1984; updated edition, The Feminist Press at CUNY, 1996.

Whitney, Catherine. *Nine and Counting: The Women of the Senate*. New York: William Morrow, 2000; HarperCollins paperback, 2001.

Traffic at the Crossroads: Multiple Oppressions

KIMBERLÉ CRENSHAW

THERE IS GROWING RECOGNITION that racism and sexism are not mutually exclusive, nor are other forms of discrimination separate and distinct. Yet both mainstream feminism and anti-racist activism (as well as other liberation movements) have sometimes stopped short of including all aspects of the types of discrimination they address. With the provisional framework below, I hope to inspire greater attention to the *interactive effects of discrimination.* (My focus on the intersection of race and gender is merely illustrative; I don't mean to imply that the framework is exclusive to race and gender, or that race and gender are the exclusive intersections that illumine conditions faced by women of color.)

A paradox of U.S. equality law is that it's least effective where most needed.[1] It promises protection against race and gender discrimination, but the protection unravels when encountering the reality of group and intergroup difference. Not only is the law unsure of what to do with difference, it's often contradictory in its approach to difference.

For example, in the context of race discrimination, there's a growing impatience with any assertion of racial difference (especially when difference is used to justify affirmative action and other programs designed to correct for inequalities). Recognition of difference is now regarded as if recognition itself were racial stereotyping, a relic of the past in our supposedly post-civil-rights society. Equality law now promulgates the concept of "color-blindness"—*ignoring* racial difference—as the key to

---

1. See "Women and Law: The Power to Change," by Catharine A. MacKinnon, p. 447.—Ed.

achieving race equality, regardless of whether or not this *reinforces* historical inequalities.

By contrast, conventional sex-equality debates appear *preoccupied* with difference. They are almost entirely absorbed in measuring the "difference between men and women," to determine whether women are "enough like men" to be treated the same, or "too different" from men to expect equitable treatment. When women demand equality notwithstanding their differences from men, this is often heard as a demand for "special treatment or preference."[2]

As a whole, U.S. equality discourse is contradictory in its attitude toward difference, yet ironically consistent in its conclusions: Racial inequalities can be ignored, because the races are essentially the *same*. Gender inequalities can also be ignored, because the sexes are essentially *different*.

This Catch 22 has not gone uncriticized.

In fact, much of the work by feminists and race theorists has been to re-articulate a vision of justice that transcends the narrow confines of equality debate. Feminists have argued that *women should enjoy privileges and opportunities denied them, whether or not women are similar to men.* Race theorists have similarly argued that *"color-blindness" illegitimately anchors racial justice to "norms" of whiteness and forecloses possibilities for racial transformation.*[3] The key to both is a rejection of "difference" as the beginning and end to equality.

Given that the discourse is already limited in its ability to find equality when faced with difference, it's not surprising that assertions of difference *within* difference can stress equality's operating system beyond its conceptual capacity. Thus, when the law encounters *racial difference in the context of gender discrimination*, or *gender difference in the context of race discrimination*, efforts to process these claims wreak havoc. There are large gaps between the conceptual world of law and policy—where gender and race discrimination(s) are sometimes framed as separate,

---

2. See Catharine A. MacKinnon, *Feminism Unmodified* (Cambridge, Massachusetts: Harvard University Press, 1987).

3. See *Critical Race Theory: The Key Writings That Shaped the Movement,* Kimberlé Crenshaw et al., eds. (New York: The New Press, 1995).

mutually exclusive occurrences—and the real world, where experiences of oppression(s) overlap in many complex ways.

There are gaps, too, between the inclusive aspirations of resistance movements and their ability to meet such aspirations. Even as the Women's Movement (domestically and globally) struggles to ensure that women's differences from men should not be used against women's well-being, differences *between* women have posed political and theoretical challenges. Similar challenges have also arisen in various racial liberation movements and, recently, in organizing efforts around the issues of sexuality, (dis)ability, and age.[4]

Women of color have been especially vocal in demanding recognition of race and class differences in the politics and practices of feminism.[5] Clearly, if the Women's Movement is to include all women, feminism must be grounded in the diversity of women's experience. Yet the demand for inclusion is often easier said than done. The mere recognition that women are different from each other doesn't determine the *significance* of these differences, nor *how* they should ground a re-articulation of feminism. Practically speaking, any successful effort to incorporate differences among women into feminism—and into other resistance movements—needs tools with which to analyze *what difference difference really makes.*

Oddly, it's sometimes assumed that members of two or more discriminated-against groups somehow benefit from this precarious position. Women of color can be thought to have an advantage over men of color, or over white women, based on their "two-fer" status. Similarly, the claim that legal protections against racism and sexism are separate, noncombinable causes of action gets justified by the contention that allow-

---

4. See, for example, "Confessions of a Worrywart: Ruminations on a Lesbian Feminist Overview," by Karla Jay, p. 212; "Rights, Realities, and Issues of Women with Disabilities," by Laura Hershey, p. 233; and "The Politics of Aging," by Barbara Macdonald with Cynthia Rich, p. 152.—Ed.

5. See, for example, "Native Americans: Restoring the Power of Thought Woman," by Clara Sue Kidwell, p. 165; "African American Women: The Legacy of Black Feminism," by Beverly Guy-Sheftall, p. 176; "Reclaiming the Past, Redefining the Future: Asian American and Pacific Islander Women," by Helen Zia, p. 188; and "U.S. Latinas: Active at the Intersections of Gender, Nationality, Race, and Class," by Edna Acosta-Belén and Christine E. Bose, p. 198.—Ed.

ing women of color to combine remedies gives them the advantage of being a "super class" of workers with powers to advance their claims over workers subject to single-form discrimination. On the contrary, groups subject to multiple, intersecting discrimination(s) not only face forms of oppression others in their class might not, but these forms are frequently marginalized, distorted, or wholly erased by the resistance politics of the very groups claiming them as constituents. Women of color, for example, are obviously members of at least two, and possibly more, identity groups[6] in which there are organized efforts to mobilize resources on the group's behalf. But their *simultaneous vulnerability* to more than one form of discrimination is not necessarily anticipated by conventional group-based politics, which tend to acknowledge the familiar form but render invisible any/all other(s).

Intersectionality: The Metaphor

The common cause of these invisibilities is inattention to the *interactive effects of discrimination*. This has variously been described as compound discrimination, interlinked forms of discrimination, multiple burdens, or double or triple oppressions.[7] Intersectionality is a means of capturing both the *structural* and *dynamic* (e.g., *active*) aspects of multiple discrimination, thus affecting both theory and practice. It addresses the manner in which racism, sexism, and other discriminatory *systems* create background inequalities that define the relative positions of women, races, etc. It also addresses the *dynamics:* ways that specific acts and policies create burdens constituting the *active* aspects of disempowerment. In other words: how discrimination is *structured,* and also how it *works.*

---

6. A woman may, for instance, be of both African American and Latina descent, (with Native, Asian, and European ancestry as well) at the same time that she is a lesbian, a single mother, poor, disabled, incarcerated, and old, etc. See the "Juggling Jeopardies" section of this anthology, p. 163.—Ed.

7. See Deborah K. King, "Multiple Jeopardy, Multiple Consciousness: The Context of a Black Feminist Ideology," in *Signs: A Journal of Women in Culture & Society,* Autumn 1988. [See also, for example, "Double Jeopardy: To Be Black and Female," by Frances Beale, in *Sisterhood Is Powerful,* R. Morgan, ed. (New York: Random House and Vintage Books, 1970).—Ed.]

To use the metaphor of an intersection, we first analogize various routes of power—gender, race, age, class, etc.—as the thoroughfares that map the social, economic, or political terrain. These thoroughfares are generally perceived as mutually exclusive. In fact, the systems are never fully distinct, and always affect people who are also trapped in other systems. Intersectionality frames these convergences as a series of *multiple intersections* that often cross each other, creating complex crossroads where two, three, or more of these routes may meet in overlapping dimensions.

The *traffic is the activity of discrimination:* the decisions and policies that flow along these thoroughfares, converging and colliding at various intersections. Groups located at these intersections by virtue of their specific identities must negotiate that traffic. Heavily traveled intersections are collision prone, so occupying these crossroads is particularly dangerous—especially since traffic flows simultaneously from many directions. In sum, the roads reflect the systemic patterns/hierarchies of power that intersect; the traffic is composed of the everyday decisions moving along those roads, decisions that collide with those who stand at the intersection.

Targeted Discrimination

Targeted discrimination is an intersectional collision that is simultaneous, direct, and intentional: traffic seeking the precise crossroads where certain women are located. Hideous examples would include the ethnic- or race-based violence against women suffered during armed conflict, military occupation, and apartheid-like circumstances. The racism and sexism manifested in these rapes reflect the *race or ethnic-based targeting* of women *in an explicitly gender-based violation.*

Targeted discrimination is also reflected in sexualized racial propaganda against certain women, propaganda that often precedes outright violence.[8] The propaganda itself is sometimes regarded as a human-

---

8. For more on race- and ethnic-based anti-woman propaganda, see "From Fantasy to Reality: Unmasking the Pornography Industry," by Gail Dines, p. 306. See also "Landscape of the Ordinary: Violence Against Women," by Andrea Dworkin, p. 58.—Ed.

rights abuse. In Rwanda, Hutu propaganda represented Tutsi women as highly sexualized temptresses, loose women who had no honor (and therefore "invited" sexual attack).

Even where sexualized propaganda doesn't culminate in mass-scale sexual violence, it's damaging in a host of other ways. Propaganda against poor and racialized women not only renders them likely targets of sexualized violence; it also contributes to the tendency of many people to doubt these victims' truthfulness when they seek the protection of authorities.[9] In the U.S., African American and Latina women are least likely to see men accused of raping them prosecuted and incarcerated.[10] Studies suggest that the victim's racial identity plays a significant role in determining such outcomes; there is evidence that jurors may be influenced by sexualized propaganda, thus believing that these women were more likely to consent to sex in circumstances jurors would find unlikely if the victim were European American.[11]

Targeted discrimination can also affect policies designed to curtail the reproductive rights of women from selective groups, promoting stereotypes of these women as being more sexual, irresponsible, and likely to bear children in circumstances threatening the majority's well-being. The propaganda is an intersectional abuse both because only women are subject to certain constraints ("highly sexualized women are in need of control") and because these gender-based sanctions intersect with race-based stereotypes ("certain races are more likely to be sexually undisciplined than others").

Compound Discrimination

Compound discrimination occurs where women of color are excluded—because of gender—from jobs reserved for men, and also

9. See "Prostitution = Slavery," by Vednita Carter, p. 315.—Ed.

10. Crenshaw, "Mapping the Margins: Intersectionality, Identity Politics, and Violence Against Women of Color," 43 *Stanford Law Review*, 1241 (1992), citing statistics supporting the claim that women of color are less likely to have their cases pursued in the criminal justice system.

11. Ibid., 1275–82, discussing and critiquing Gary LaFree's *Rape and Criminal Justice: The Social Construction of Sexual Assault* (Belmont, California: Wadsworth Publications, 1989).

excluded—because of race—from so-called women's jobs.[12] For instance, nonwhite women may encounter compound discrimination when only women are hired for office jobs, and when only racial or ethnic minorities are hired for industrial or other forms of gender-segregated work. The women's work is racialized (no nonwhites need apply) and the racialized work is gendered (no women need apply.)[13] This kind of discrimination potentially affects everyone who is gendered and everyone who is raced, but especially affects women who are raced *and* gendered. Men might also experience compound discrimination, when work available to women is deemed not appropriate for men,[14] and work available to more privileged men is not procurable by racially subordinate men.[15]

Structural Subordination

In this type of intersectional injury (unlike previous examples), there is no *dynamic or active* discrimination directed toward women. But some women can be affected by policies that impact differently on them because of their *structural* position. When governments fail to provide certain services (or retract them), women wind up bearing the weight of caregiving and other support services.[16] Moreover, while these respon-

---

12. See, for example, "The Clerical Proletariat," by Ellen Bravo, p. 349, and "Pink Collar Ghetto, Blue Collar Token," by Alice Kessler-Harris, p. 358; see also the "Transforming Traditions" section of "Transforming Traditions and Breaking Barriers," p. 325.—Ed.

13. See, for example, *DeGraffenreid v. General Motors Assembly Division*, St. Louis, 413 F. Supp. 142 (E.D. Mo. 1976).

14. See M. Patricia Fernandez Kelly, "Underclass and Immigrant Women as Economic Actors: Rethinking Citizenship in a Changing Global Economy," 9 *American University Journal of International Law & Policy* 150, 159–64 (1993), explaining the California electronics industry's preference for women workers. [For more on this subject, see Zia, op. cit., and Acosta-Belén and Bose, op. cit.; see also Kessler-Harris, op. cit., and Bravo, op. cit.—Ed.]

15. See, for example, *Wards Cove Packing Co., Inc. v. Atonio*, 490 U.S. 642 (1989): cannery jobs are filled predominantly by nonwhites, Filipinos, and Native Alaskans, while noncannery jobs—which pay more—are filled almost exclusively by whites. [See also Zia, op. cit.—Ed.]

16. For more on the economics and politics of caregiving, see "Poverty Wears a Female Face," by Theresa Funiciello, p. 222, and Kessler-Harris, op. cit.—Ed.

sibilities might also fall on elite women (given their gender identities), their class advantage may allow them to shift these duties to working-class or poor women by purchasing their services. Such policies may hit working-class and poor women especially hard, driving them to work more hours to cover their own increased expenses for childcare and other needs. But because these are largely "women's jobs"—domestic work, care of the young and infirm, and other service jobs—the wages are low and the benefits often nonexistent.[17] Women who take on these gender-based tasks comprise a large percentage of the working poor, and these jobs, in turn, are highly populated by women of color, who are locked out of other professions and have few alternate resources.

Staying with our metaphor of intersections and traffic, it's crucial to understand that the "ambulances" and "EMS personnel" necessary to aid victims of these collisions—constituent communities, liberation movements, progressive activists—often don't reach the collision victims in time, or at all, or may be insufficiently equipped to make the right diagnoses for full rescue and remedy. Some examples of this are:

Over Inclusion

This occurs where a condition disproportionately affecting women of color is characterized as a gender problem, while contributing factors—race and/or class—aren't acknowledged. These circumstances are "over included," *absorbed* into a gender framework with no attempt to acknowledge the role another form of discrimination may have played in creating the problem. Consequently, interventions based on gender alone won't be sufficient, because they don't address all aspects of the problem.

An example would be efforts to mobilize against the prostituting and trafficking of women for sexual and other abusive purposes. This is sometimes cast as solely a gender problem—yet there are hierarchies among women in the United States and all over the world that contribute to a woman being prostituted or trafficked.[18] Ethnically and socially marginal women have fewer economic options and are more

---

17. See Kessler-Harris, op. cit.; see also Hershey, op. cit.—Ed.

18. For data on the race and class aspects of this, see Carter, op. cit.—Ed.

vulnerable to traffickers and pimps; they may also be powerless to demand governmental intervention on their behalf, either in their communities or in their countries of origin.

Under Inclusion

This occurs where a condition affects a subset of women, but the issue
isn't widely regarded as a "women's issue" because it generally doesn't
affect women from the society's dominant groups—e.g., the general silence of organized women's groups on the dramatic increase in women's
incarceration rates, which have far outpaced those of men.[19] Women
represent the fastest-growing group of incarcerated Americans, increasing by more than 800 percent between 1984 and 1994. This is a social
crisis of tremendous magnitude, not only for the incarcerated women,
but also for their families—yet this problem is seldom framed as a critical "gender issue," because it primarily affects a racially defined subgroup of women (specifically, African Americans and Latinas) and thus
gets framed as a "race issue." Yet the circumstances that land women in
prison, and women's incarceration itself, are as thoroughly "gendered"
experiences[20] as are those in "traditional" feminist issues (reproductive
rights, childcare, the glass ceiling, etc.).

The same could be said about the issue of women's health care.
HIV/AIDS is the leading cause of death for African American women
between the ages of 25 and 44; black women are now more likely to die
of AIDS than are gay white men. Their vulnerability to the epidemic reflects a convergence of gender, race, age, and class factors.[21] Yet AIDS is
seldom framed as a critical *women's* health issue.[22] Fundraising and

---

19. See "Alive Behind the Labels: Women in Prison," by Kathy Boudin and Roslyn
D. Smith, p. 244.—Ed.

20. Ibid.—Ed.

21. It also reflects sexual preference/orientation, since among African American
women heterosexual contact is currently [2002] the greatest risk factor/mode of
transmission (National Black Women's Health Project: *www.blackwomenshealth.org*).
See also Guy-Sheftall, op. cit., and Boudin and Smith, op. cit.—Ed.

22. See "Our Bodies, Our Future: Women's Health Activism Overview," by Judy
Norsigian et al., p. 269.—Ed.

awareness campaigns tend to focus primarily on breast cancer. But more black women die of AIDS than of any other cause—though awareness of this has barely reached the consciousness of black women themselves, much less the broader women's community. (This actually points to a problem of *dual under inclusion:* attention to AIDS has been resisted in the African American community even as the epidemic has moved squarely into it.)[23] Obviously, black women are also vulnerable to breast cancer; given their higher mortality rate,[24] attention to that issue should benefit them, too.[25]

Anti-racism agendas often marginalize the issues of women of color, too. For example, the reproductive freedom of some women of color has been brutally controlled through forced sterilization.[26] These practices persisted late into the twentieth century; vestiges remain in court-ordered use of Norplant on certain would-be mothers.[27] Furthermore, punitive provisions designed to control the reproductive capacities of select groups of women were contained in such policy shifts as the abolition of AFDC [welfare].[28] Such efforts traditionally have been linked

---

23. For a cogent critique of the deadly consequences of narrowly conceived black community politics in the face of AIDS, see *The Boundaries of Blackness: Aids and the Breakdown of Black Politics,* by Cathy J. Cohen (Chicago, Illinois: University of Chicago Press, 1999).

24. African American women are 28 percent more likely to die from breast cancer than are European American women. See Guy-Sheftall, op. cit.; see also Norsigian et al., op. cit.—Ed.

25. Even this assumption is questionable. Several studies have found profound racial disparities in the delivery of health services, even when controlling for access to health insurance and information. Moreover, though breast cancer affects all women, images designed to raise awareness of this risk are not always integrated. One major magazine published a portrait of nearly a dozen high-profile women in a campaign to raise awareness of breast cancer; all the women in the portrait were white.

26. See Kidwell, op. cit., and Guy-Sheftall, op. cit. See also "Unfinished Agenda: Reproductive Rights," by Faye Wattleton, p. 17, and the Introduction, p. *xv.*—Ed.

27. See, for example, "Crime, Race and Reproduction," by Dorothy Roberts (tracing the history of involuntary sterilizations of African American women from the 1930s to the 1990s), in her book *Killing the Black Body* (see Suggested Further Reading, below). See also Rebecca Tsosie's essay, "Changing Women: The Crosscurrents of American Indian Feminine Identity," in *Unequal Sisters: A Multicultural Reader in U.S. Women's History,* Ellen Carol DuBois et al., eds. (New York: Routledge, 1990).

28. See Funiciello, op. cit.—Ed.

to racially explicit concerns about "population control" of "suspect" communities, but neither the historical problem nor its contemporary analogues are grasped as central "race issues"; they don't appear beside such readily identifiable race issues as profiling, for instance. One inference might be that sterilization affects *women*—not African Americans, Latinos, or Native Americans per se—which makes it a "women's concern" rather than a "race concern." Although the racial dimension of sterilization abuse is well-known by anti-racist leaders, if one were to conduct a survey on core racial abuses suffered by people of color in the United States, it's doubtful that reproductive abuses (or *anything* experienced primarily by *women*) would be among them.

Misappropriation

Here is, metaphorically, another ambulance that got waylaid en route to a collision site. One might argue that genocide has long been a concern of Native Americans and African Americans, and that under this rubric, sterilization is recognized as an assault on *people* of color. But that would be a problematic illustration of another way women of color are rendered invisible—misappropriation: *when an injury or oppression suffered by women is acknowledged, but the injury is recognized primarily as an injury to the community at large rather than to women themselves.* For instance, the sexual assault of women by men of other races is often politicized as an assault on the integrity of the *community*, even specifically an attack on the *men* of the community. The horrors of slavery's sexual abuses are sometimes still deplored as examples of the "emasculating" dimensions of racism. Black victims of *inter-racial* rape can expect their stories to be believed by their communities more readily than victims of *intra-racial* rape—because the injury is often framed as an assault against the collectivized *male* ego of the community. One well-regarded African American professor was known to dramatize slavery by exhorting his students to place themselves in the shoes of a father, husband, son, or brother of a woman who was sexually assaulted by their owner. Framing a woman's suffering through the gaze of her male relatives was meant to render the helplessness of the *men* palpable—but in fact it demonstrates that the horror experienced by the woman was considered less significant than the inability of men in her family to prevent it.

The problem with misappropriation is that the appropriated experience usually never gets returned, accompanied by resources and support, to address the immediate victim's (in this case, the woman's) recovery. This pattern is replicated internationally. Women raped during the genocidal campaigns in Bosnia and Rwanda were often ostracized by the very communities that claimed these rapes as an assault against *them*.[29] Tragically, concern about what their rape meant to "the community" did not translate into efforts to heal and reintegrate the women survivors themselves.[30]

Structural-Dynamic Discrimination

At times, the intersectional nature of subordination goes unnoticed because some contributing aspect of a problem—economic, cultural, or social—forms the backdrop. I call this "The Invisible Hand." *Such background forces are often rendered invisible because they're so common they seem to constitute a natural—or at least unchangeable—fact of life.* In such cases, only the most immediate aspect of the discrimination gets noticed, while the background structure making women vulnerable in the first place stays obscured. As a result, the discriminatory process in question might be seen solely as sexist (if a racial structure forms the backdrop) or solely as racist (if a gendered structure forms the backdrop).

---

29. For information about the ethnically motivated sexual violence perpetrated in Rwanda, see "Report of the Special Rapporteur on Violence Against Women, Its Causes and Consequences," Radhika Coomaraswamy, Addendum, *Report of the Mission to Rwanda on the Issues of Violence Against Women in Situations of Armed Conflict*, U.N. ESCOR, 54th Sess., U.N. Doc. E/CN.4/1998; see also Internationale des Ligues des Droits de L'Homme, "Shattered Lives: Sexual Violence During the Rwandan Genocide and Its Aftermath" (1996). For similar information about Bosnia, see Alexandra Stiglmayer, "The Rapes in Bosnia-Herzegovina," in *Mass Rape: The War Against Women in Bosnia-Herzegovina*, Alexandra Stiglmayer, ed. (Lincoln, Nebraska: University of Nebraska, 1994); and Catharine A. MacKinnon, "Rape, Genocide, and Women's Human Rights," *Harvard Women's Law Journal* (1994): 5–16.

30. In the Balkans, "most of the rape victims have been cast out of their homes and left to fend for themselves . . . in battle zones without food, warm clothing, or shelter" ("Balkan War Rape Victims: Traumatized and Ignored," by Carol J. Williams, *Los Angeles Times*, 30 November 1992). Similarly, in Rwanda, those who survived the genocide have had to deal with social isolation and ostracization as victims of sexual violence (see *Shattered Lives*, op. cit.).

For example, immigration law requires non-resident spouses of U.S. citizens to stay married for two years in order to receive permanent resident status. That puts women who are victims of domestic violence in the position of having to choose between serious injury (even death) at the hands of abusive husbands, or deportation at the hands of the government. This might be seen as a clear case of gender subordination: a woman facing physical abuse by her male spouse. But it's also an intersectional problem: the background has been shaped by an immigration policy infused with anti-immigrant sensibilities. Still more hierarchies lurk in the immigration context—some dictating different procedures for those seeking to become permanent residents depending on their status; others reflecting varying levels of social and cultural integration into U.S. society.[31]

Obviously, if the nature of an injury isn't fully understood, interventions intended to remedy the problem will likely be ineffective. Domestic-violence activists generally didn't anticipate that tougher immigration policies would excacerbate the vulnerability of some immigrant women to domestic violence, because this legislation was framed as an *immigration* matter.[32] Therefore, it wouldn't be surprising if women's groups weren't significantly involved in debating immigration policy, since it wasn't perceived as a significant *gender* issue. Yet even after activists and legislators became aware of the problem, the reform designed to address it wasn't sufficiently targeted to overcome specific barriers faced by the most isolated, socially marginal women. New legislation was passed to provide abused women with a waiver of the two-year rule—but to *obtain* the waiver, a woman would have to prove (through narrowly proscribed means) that she was a victim of abuse—including submitting psychiatric evidence or some other public record. The waiver was a step in the right direction; doubtless some women were able to benefit from it. But there were no provisions to ensure that

31. For a further critique, along with a broader discussion of the failure of some domestic-violence shelters to address the needs of non-English-proficient women, see Kimberlé Crenshaw, "Mapping the Margins: Intersectionality, Identity Politics, and Violence Against Women of Color," op. cit. [See also Zia, op. cit.; for data on comparable inaccessibility of shelters to disabled women, see Hershey, op. cit.—Ed.]

32. See Zia, op. cit., and Acosta-Belén and Bose, op. cit.—Ed.

information about the waiver was broadly available in various languages, and no provisions to provide women with access to mechanisms that could produce the waiver. Had the reformers considered these matters in intersectional terms, they might have framed a more successful intervention.

Why does all this matter? It matters because we don't want difference to *make* a difference when injustices and human suffering need to be acknowledged and addressed. *Without a lens focused on the interactive nature of subordination, we function with a partial view of what sexism, racism, homophobia, etc. really look like—as if we were squinting at the world with one eye closed.* That way of viewing—literally and figuratively a lack of depth perception—has been created and normalized by those who are relatively privileged. But in order to expand and deepen liberation politics, our basic conceptions of discrimination have to broaden—as does our basic practice. Rather than settling for top-down analytical strategies, we need to listen to ground-level experts—the marginalized women themselves—and examine *their* experience and actual conditions, exploring how these reflect overlapping systems of discrimination.

Above all, we should always dare ask the "other" questions. As Mari Matsuda[33] urges, when we see sex (or another) discrimination, we often end the analysis there. But we can always go further, asking "What is the element of racism in this?" and "What is the heterosexism in this?" and "Is there an age element—or a class, or (dis)ability bias, etc.—operating here?"

If we really want to begin noticing more intersectionalities, we must train our eyes to look for them. We truly *are* at a crossroads, in more ways than one.

KIMBERLÉ WILLIAMS CRENSHAW (J.D. Harvard; L.L.M. University of Wisconsin, B.A. Cornell) is a professor of law at UCLA and at Columbia Law School. Writing in the area of civil rights, black feminist legal theory, and race, racism and the law, she has published in the *Har-*

---

33. A law professor at Georgetown University known for her distinguished work on Constitutional law and jurisprudence issues, including hate speech, feminist theory, and affirmative action.—Ed.

vard Law Review, National Black Law Journal, Stanford Law Review and *Southern California Law Review*. She is the founding coordinator of the Critical Race Theory Workshop, and coeditor of *Critical Race Theory: The Key Writings That Shaped the Movement* (New Press, 1995). She has lectured nationally and internationally, and her work on race and gender was influential in drafting the equality clause for the new South African Constitution. She has served on the National Science Foundation's committee to research violence against women, and assisted the legal team representing Anita Hill. In 1996, she co-founded the African American Policy Forum, to highlight the centrality of gender in racial-justice discourses. A founding member of the Women's Media Initiative, she is a regular commentator on National Public Radio. In 2001, she authored the background paper on "Race and Gender Discrimination" for the U.N. World Conference on Racism, Xenophobia, and Related Intolerances, and helped facilitate the inclusion of gender in the conference declaration. [This essay is adapted from that paper; the author wishes to acknowledge several contributions: Luke Charles Harris provided critical editorial assistance and support; Radhika Balakrishnan, Anita Nayar, Uma Narayan, Terri James, Devon Carbado, and Veena Vasista offered valuable comments on earlier drafts; and Silke Sahl provided reference support.]

Suggested Further Reading

Cohen, Cathy. *The Boundaries of Blackness: Aids and the Breakdown of Black Politics*. Chicago, Illinois: University of Chicago Press, 1999.

hooks, bell. *Feminist Theory from Margin to Center*. Cambridge, Massachusetts: South End Press, 1984, 2000.

Narayan, Uma. *Dislocating Cultures: Identities, Traditions and Third World Feminisms*. London and New York: Routledge, 1997.

Dorothy Roberts. *Killing the Black Body: Race, Reproduction and the Meaning of Liberty*. New York: Vintage, 1997.

Landscape of the Ordinary:
Violence Against Women

ANDREA DWORKIN

A WOMAN SITS in her living room reading. A woman makes her way to her bed. A woman works, eats, sleeps. She walks along the street. She does the work of the house even if she is not a housewife. Then somewhere, sometime, somehow, in the landscape of the ordinary, she is battered or assaulted or raped or molested; she is hit or punched or touched without her desire or consent. Some of the crimes are repetitive—for instance, battery may not happen every day but it happens often and it creates an ongoing environment of threat and hostility. Some crimes happen once—for instance, the rapist who is a stranger rips apart a woman's life, shreds it with his bare hands, a penis, a knife, the poison of an amnesiac drug, and after that every shadow has the possibility of a rapist folded into it. Nothing about being raped by a stranger guarantees that she will not be raped again: by a stranger or an acquaintance or a friend or a husband or a lover.

To understand the enormity of the crimes against women, one must first accept that women are human beings and like all human beings have an intrinsic value that need not be earned. No special pleading is required to say that an assault against a woman is anti-human, that it distresses the flesh and wreaks havoc on the mind. The boundaries of a woman's body are the boundaries the perpetrator violates. Usually he believes that he has a right to transgress against those boundaries. Until the Women's Movement challenged that belief, law and social policy supported it.[1]

---

1. See "Women and Law: The Power to Change," by Catharine A. MacKinnon, p. 447.—Ed.

Through political activism, the culture has changed enough to stigmatize rape and battery as crimes against women. Over the past three decades, rape crisis centers, sexual abuse and battery shelters, sexual assault laws, marital rape laws, third-person battery intervention laws, laws forbidding convicted batterers (including police officers) to carry guns, date and acquaintance rape prosecutions, police precinct and emergency room special training for dealing with survivors, and passage of the 1994 Violence Against Women Act—all these changes and more have been won by feminist activism.

Nevertheless, there is still a war going on against women, and the violence of that war is overwhelming. In the United States, four women a day are killed as a result of domestic violence.[2] Among same-sex couples, men remain the principal aggressors; even women in same-sex couples who have been assaulted have been assaulted more frequently by men.[3] Approximately 4.8 million women are raped and assaulted annually.[4] It is estimated that more than 350 rapes per year occur on col-

---

2. "Violence Against Women: A National Crime Victimization Survey Report," U.S. Department of Justice, Washington, D.C., January 1994. A 2000 report (publication #NCJ 167237) produced by the Justice Department's Bureau of Justice Statistics (BJS)—a compilation of data from the above-mentioned survey report and the FBI's Uniform Crime Reporting Program—also noted that each year, approximately 30 percent of all women killed in the U.S. die at the hands of a former or current intimate partner, as compared with 6 percent of men (*www.ojp.usdoj.gov/bjs*, or 1-800-732-3277).

3. "Extent, Nature, and Consequence of Intimate Partner Violence Research Report: Findings from the National Violence Against Women Survey," by Patricia Tjaden and Nancy Thoennes, U.S. Department of Justice, Office of Justice Programs, published by the National Institute of Justice and the Centers for Disease Control and Prevention, 2000. The study also found that 30.4 percent of same-sex cohabiting women reported being victimized by a male partner, whereas 11.4 percent reported being victimized by a female partner. Same-sex cohabiting men were nearly twice as likely to report being victimized by a male partner than were opposite-sex cohabiting men by a female partner (15.4 percent and 7.7 percent). The study concluded that these findings suggest that intimate partner violence is perpetrated primarily by men, whether against male or female partners. [For data on homicide emerging as the most common cause of maternal mortality, see "Our Bodies, Our Future: Women's Health Activism Overview," by Judy Norsigian, et al., p. 269.—Ed.]

4. "Extent, Nature, and Consequence of Intimate Partner Violence: Findings from the National Violence Against Women Survey," U.S. Department of Justice, Office of Justice Programs, 2000. The 1999 National Crime Victimization Survey (NCVS)

lege campuses of 10,000 students; 22.8 percent of the victims have been multiply raped[5]; 27.7 percent of college women reported a sexual experience that met the legal definition of rape, these events occurring since age fourteen.[6] An estimated 503,485 women are stalked by an intimate partner each year.[7] Only one-fifth of all rapes, one-quarter of all physical assaults, and one-half of all stalkings are ever even reported to the police.[8] Women are ten times more likely than men to be victimized by an intimate.[9] Rape is the most underreported violent crime.[10]

---

noted that although total violent crime had dropped by approximately 10 percent nationwide since 1995, sexual assault was *up* by 60 percent, and the combined total of attempted and completed rapes and sexual assaults had risen by 21 percent; 89 percent of victims were female; young women and poor women continued to be at far more risk than any other demographic group; African American women were more likely to be raped than European American women (2.6 per 1,000 people versus 1.6 per 1,000, respectively). [See also "African American Women: The Legacy of Black Feminism," by Beverly Guy-Sheftall, p. 176.—Ed.]

5. "The Sexual Victimization of College Women," by Bonnie S. Fisher, Francis T. Cullen, and Michael G. Turner, U.S. Department of Justice, Office of Justice Programs, National Institute of Justice, Bureau of Justice Statistics, 2000.

6. "Predictors of Sexual Aggression Among a National Sample of Male College Students," by M. P. Koss and T. E. Dinero, Annals of the New York Academy of Science, 1989.

7. "Extent, Nature, and Consequence of Intimate Partner Violence: Findings from the National Violence Against Women Survey," U.S. Department of Justice, Office of Justice Programs, 2000. Furthermore, the National Violence Against Women Survey found that one out of every 12 U.S. women (8.2 million) has been stalked at some time in her life, as opposed to one out of every 45 U.S. men (2 million); 78 percent of stalking victims were women, i.e., 4 out of 5. Overall, 94 percent of the stalkers identified by female victims and 60 percent of stalkers identified by male victims were male. Although the NVAW Survey showed little or no difference in stalking prevalence between white women and women of color generally, it did show that American Indian/Alaskan Native women report significantly more stalking victimization than women of other racial and ethnic backgrounds—underscoring the need for specificity while comparing rates among women of different ethnic or racial backgrounds. [See "Native Americans: Restoring the Power of Thought Woman," by Clara Sue Kidwell, p. 165. See also "Traffic at the Crossroads: Multiple Oppressions," by Kimberlé Crenshaw, p. 43.—Ed.]

8. "Extent, Nature, and Consequence of Intimate Partner Violence: Findings from the National Violence Against Women Survey," U.S. Department of Justice, Office of Justice Programs, 2000.

9. "Violence Against Women: A National Crime Victimization Survey Report," op. cit.

10. RAINN: The Rape, Abuse & Incest National Network. RAINN is a nonprofit organization based in Washington, D.C. that operates the only national hotline for

These are all conservative statistics.

The husband batters; the uncle molests; the father rapes; strangers attack with words and fists or hunt through stalking. The girl is molested, the sister is forced to take a penis into her mouth, the wife is hit repeatedly until fear is all she knows. The prostitute is made to enact particularly degraded sex.[11] Pornography is the story, in words and pictures, of violent conquest and petty hate.[12] In pornography, the real woman, to whom the acts are done in real time, is the woman as stranger alienated from the human. Violence against women is both systematic and random.

The Characteristics of Each Crime

Battery. A man is the head of the household; he is the centerpiece of the couple. He seeks control. He can be charming and charismatic. He can be any age or race or class. He can be a financier or a porter. She may even be the breadwinner. He often begins with violence against objects. He destroys chairs or kicks in doors. He takes the woman as an accomplice; at first, he may be violent against others, and she is on his side. He expects her loyalty to be absolute. If she poses a question, the question itself may be betrayal, since his word is law. Society gives him implicit rights over her, and when law fails, habit reigns.

Because she must support him without criticism or query, she is slowly isolated by him: his enemies are her enemies; she has no friends not vetted by him; she has no sovereignty, no boundaries; her body is his.

The degradation is a slow process of overcoming her separate will and behavior. When he destroys inanimate objects and she calms him down, consoles him in his anger, she does not see that she is moving her body and will into the sphere of his anger so that his anger overshadows

---

victims of sexual assault. The hotline—1-800-656-HOPE—offers free, confidential counseling and support 24 hours a day, from anywhere in the country. RAINN's website—*www.rainn.org*—also offers statistical archives and news updates.

11. See "Prostitution = Slavery," by Vednita Carter, p. 315.—Ed.

12. See "From Fantasy to Reality: Unmasking the Pornography Industry," by Gail Dines, p. 306.—Ed.

her. Eventually he will turn his anger directly against her without benefit of any intermediary. Eventually his shadow battens on her, and there is no place for her that is not his place. She quivers under the threat of his oncoming storm. She cannot know when exactly there will be thunder or lightning or a tornado will raise her up and pitch her body far away.

She will try to stop the storm from coming and it is in this process that she will find herself increasingly absent from herself. She must be his valiant companion no matter what the cost. Even after he has beaten her she will defend him. Especially, she will protect him from the police. When he hurts someone else, even a child, she will experience a relief that she will never dare acknowledge. That and her complicity with him, her protection of him, are the roots of her shame. She wants to live; that is her crime. We now know that she is afraid to flee, or that she has nowhere to go. Many batterers track their victims to shelters.[13] More women are killed after they run than when they stay.[14] Diane Rosenfeld—formerly in the Violence Against Women Office of the Clinton administration's Justice Department—proposes the creation of detention centers for the batterer, so that the woman will not have to be homeless. This would make the woman a full citizen, emphasizing her rights to safety and freedom of movement. Currently, too many convicted batterers are merely sentenced to do community service. The crime needs to be punished by significant jail time. When the batterer

---

13. For additional factors regarding violence affecting women with disabilities—and the lack of wheelchair access to most shelters—see "Rights, Realities, and Issues of Women with Disabilities," by Laura Hershey, p. 233; see also Crenshaw, op. cit., for data on shelter unavailability to non-English-proficient women.—Ed.

14. In addition, studies have shown that, even when a woman expresses the desire for a separation, violence is likely to occur—and nowhere is this more true than in the U.S. military. The Task Force on Domestic Violence of the Department of Defense admits that a series of studies have shown the rate of domestic violence in the military to be *double* that in the civilian population. The Miles Foundation, an advocacy group for victims of military domestic violence, puts the figure higher—at two to *five times greater* than that of the general population. The Miles Foundation notes that the DOD only counts cases involving married couples, not those involving former spouses or girlfriends. "Wife Killings at Fort [Bragg] Reflect Growing Problem in Military," by Fox Butterfield (*The New York Times*, 29 July 2002). See also "Redefining the Warrior Mentality: Women in the Military," by Claudia J. Kennedy, p. 409.—Ed.

serves time for a felony absent parole, the woman becomes a citizen with rights. In the Violence Against Women Act, both battery and rape were defined as civil-rights violations of women, and women were given legal standing to sue; the Supreme Court struck down this part of the bill in 2000.

Marital Rape. Inside the battery there will be rape. She cannot say no. If she does say no, the word will be met with his fist or with an angrier punishment. Each rape will become part of the marriage, a flash freeze frame behind her smile. Because she wants to live, she will keep the rape secret. Other people might see the bruises; they don't get to see the rape unless he films it. (Often, such men film it.) Marriage gives this kind of rape a sanctity that guarantees privacy.

There is the threat, the fist, and then the rape. Sometimes sex is initiated by the victim: she anticipates the violence and wants to forestall it; she wants to placate him. If there is sex, she figures, the violence will stop; he will sleep afterward; the tension will be released. She will prove to him that she does not hold against him the violence that has already occurred. She has only herself to blame, she thinks, and so she cannot tell anyone. She did more than consent, she thinks; she encouraged. This makes her responsible for the outcome. This means she cannot accuse him either then or later. This means that if she tries to act against the battery, the larger world will find her guilty, someone who asked for what she got. Initiating sex is a way of trying to survive what she alone can recognize as inevitable violence.

Women hate reporting rape in marriage even to sympathetic listeners or researchers. There is no way to explain that once the terror has been established there *is* no more "consensual sex." On the good days the sex is as inherently coerced as on the bad days when he slams her across the room. She cannot face it herself or let anyone else in on her dirty secret.

Prosecutors have had a terrible time trying to prosecute marital rape. Juries line up with the offender. What matters here is public education that is clear and absolute about the existence and reality of this crime. People also need to be educated about the moral failure involved in blaming the victim. Prosecutors, rather than giving up, have to continue prosecuting. Zero tolerance for marital rape should be public policy.

Rape. Defined differently in different states in the U.S., rape is essentially sexual assault or forced intercourse. There are various charges of sexual abuse to account for anomalies; for instance, rape with an object instead of a penis. Law has more kinks than rape does. Defense lawyers have more kinks than either. The reason that so many women think they have not been raped when they have been is that they think about the law and the defense lawyer rather than the crime itself. Any woman can cross-examine herself in her own mind and find herself guilty of having "provoked" an assault. Her sense of being the one responsible transforms rape into something shameful that *she* did. Once she finds herself guilty she finds him innocent.

In the ancient, androcentric view of rape, the female person's mere existence is a concrete provocation; she is the daughter or she is the wife and the rape is a crime against her father or husband; the law is based on punishing the one who aggresses against her owner. The rapist contaminates the woman so that she no longer is clean—so that the husband or father will suffer from the pollution of his injured property. Rape is a way of vengeance and revenge, a retaliation. As recently as 1970 the girl or woman was rarely seen as the victim of the rape. From 1970 on, the Women's Movement fought to make visible the woman or girl as the actual victim of the assault against her. This opened the way to having rape in marriage understood as rape per se, even if it remains almost impossible to prosecute successfully.

The fact is that one infers stranger-rape from the word "rape." Hard as it is to accept, stranger-rape is the least likely[15] but the oldest rape insofar as cultural or historical acknowledgement goes. The rapist is presumed to be a stranger because otherwise one must acknowledge that this is a rape culture. It is impossible to comprehend how much rape there is; to add in all the husbands as rapists and lovers as rapists and fathers and acquaintances and relatives and neighbors as rapists is grotesque—and so the term "forcible rape" implies someone unknown, a stone-cold rapist who may pick and stalk the victim but has no other relationship with her.

Still, stranger-rape is hell on earth: it includes the psychotic rapist, the serial rapist-killer, gang rape, Internet-initiated rape, and drug rape.

---

15. The 1999 National Crime Victimization Survey (available on the RAINN website) found that 69 percent of rape and sexual assault victims knew their assailant.

These are paradigms of impersonal rage, an impersonal hatred against woman. Stranger-rape brings with it fear and horror for the victim. The legal system, reformed as it has been by feminists, is still only able to prosecute stranger-rapes with any success at all—and for that reason, too, "rape" means stranger-rape in the public mind.

The power of prosecution, its ability to make rape real to a larger public, cannot be overstated. But the victim is still on trial. The laws of evidence need to be changed, especially in admitting prior rapes, assaults, attempts at rape, and homicide into the trial. Rape needs to be treated as an abrogation of a citizen's (woman's) liberty.

Stalking. This is a kind of violence named and defined by feminists; it denotes the connection between how he picks her, studies her. Like most sexual abuse, stalking can be done by acquaintances—especially former husbands or boyfriends—or by strangers. The motivation is to cause fear in the woman, to shrink her life. The stalking can lead to rape or assault or murder.[16]

Stalking might be the poor man's version of mimicking the Marquis de Sade. Like Sade in the madhouse, the stalker creates a theater piece. He watches. As he watches, he designs a drama in which he is the monster-king, she the victim, the object of his imagination. His eye is on her. Eventually he lets her know that he's watching. He creeps her out, especially by following her or by writing her letters or by taking pictures of her. He gets closer to her by increments. Is he there or not? Was he the noise or not? Is he the guy in the car or not? Is he the guy behind her or not? The threat is in the slowness of the chase, its stubborn persistence. He writes romantic letters or threatening letters. He builds a grand mental picture for himself of them together, then tries to impose it on her by the way in which he watches her.

This is a horror movie—but acted out in real time, in real life. Since the law typically punishes what has already happened, not what will happen, the woman is left to convulse with the threat. He and she know what he means by the slow chase but the law, until stalking laws were en-

16. The NVAW Survey provides compelling evidence of the link between stalking and other forms of violence in intimate relationships; 81 percent of the women who were stalked by a current or former husband or cohabiting partner were also physically assaulted by the same partner, and 31 percent were also sexually assaulted by that partner.

acted, knew nothing. Thanks to stalking laws, a court can issue an order allowing him to come no closer to her than 500 or so feet. A court can issue an order forbidding him from harassing her. But his freedom is still paramount. Since our democracy prides itself on individual freedom, even the stalker brought before the court must be allowed to walk where he wants, behind her, beside her.

The truth is that he can be told to be reticent. Courts don't take the stalker too seriously: it's just a crush; it's not a serious threat. Because the law is benign with respect to the stalker, stalking more often than not ends in her having to hide inside a new identity, to move, change names, change jobs, change every detail of her public and private life so that she is unrecognizable. Since the court is not willing to consider what will happen to her if the court does nothing or nearly nothing, the stalker has the law on his side. Feminists have named the crime and persuaded the legal system that a crime does exist, but stalking is still considered minor, even though the outcome can mean that a woman loses her life, either by being killed or terrorized or having to change every aspect of her existence. (Stalkers of celebrities, especially male celebrities, are, however, taken seriously.) There are those in the legal community who are outraged that any boundaries are put on the stalker at all: how can one find a man guilty when his crime is one of devotion?

The crime needs to be a felony, not a misdemeanor. These cases, like rape and battery, should be treated as serious violations of a citizen's (woman's) freedom.

Incest. The child is inside, a prisoner in a bed. Daddy or stepdaddy or brother or uncle or the mother's lover is the rapist who assaults the child. There is a commonplace narrative to incest. The perpetrator seduces so that the child feels guilty; the perpetrator gives a reward to the child for sexual access. The home provides privacy and protection for the perpetrator. The girl is trained to be the lover Daddy wants, his shining thing, his perfect object. The girl is strained and drained. The girl essentially becomes a prostituted child, ready to give sex for his consideration. He will reward her flat-out with money or special affection or bartered gifts or love, sweet love.

Teachers can identify an incested child, but too rarely act on it. A burden should be put on schools to identify the incested child so that the perpetrator can be taken out of the home and jailed. Special victims' units need to be trained in interviewing incested children and building cases with good evidence, especially forensic evidence. Media asserting that children are manipulated into lying must be challenged until the child per se is regarded as a truth-teller.

Child Sexual Abuse. There is the stranger who will molest the child. Some abusers molest hundreds of children before or without being caught: witness the Roman Catholic Church scandals and cover-ups. The child has a dirty secret. There is shame because there is fear that the child brought it on herself/himself. (Girls are victimized more than boys.) There is confusion because there is certainty that the child did something bad, but what could it have been? There is the chance that play will bring on molestation again. There is the belief that the perpetrator's threats will come true: if you tell anyone, I'll come and get you; if you tell anyone, I'll hurt your baby sister; if you tell anyone, I'll tell your mommy the bad things you did.

The stranger molester requires the full force of law to put him away. Since, so far as we now know, he is at high risk of recidivism, committing him to psychiatric institutions after he has served time is the only way to keep him from molesting again.

Prostitution. Incest and child sexual abuse in particular lead to prostitution. Incest is the training ground for the child who learns to barter sex for money or toys or other rewards; child sexual abuse is the boot camp of the child prostitute. Most prostitution actually begins in childhood. The child is abused in the home, runs away, thinks the streets will be kinder than the house, finds they are not. The pimps seek out lonely, homeless, poor girls, already raped.[17]

The act of prostituting should be decriminalized.[18] But pimping and consuming should be criminalized. Pimps and johns should be seen as robbers and rapists; their acts should be prosecuted as felonies, not misdemeanors. Prostituted women need safe shelter, peer counseling, job training, and often drug rehabilitation (many are addicted because of

---

17. See Carter, op. cit., and Crenshaw, op. cit.—Ed.

18. Decriminalization is very different from legalization. In the latter, prostitution becomes societally affirmed and formally institutionalized, with the state functioning as the pimp, the johns repositioned as consumers, and the women still left powerless, exploited, and abused.

the pain of prostituting, not—as stereotype would have it—prostituting for the sake of drugs).

Pornography. Take a girl, put her in any scenario of sexual abuse, and you have the hard-core artifact, the girl used, the girl who can be bought, sold, and re-sold a hundred times, a million times. From child to adult, in the pages of pornography magazines, in the videos, on the Internet, pornography is proof that the abuse happens. Any woman can wind up as the pornographic object, but usually the dispossessed do. This dispossession should be ended by use of the RICO statute against pornographers and the corporations that shield them. (RICO—the Racketeer Influenced and Corrupt Organizations Act— would permit prosecutors to freeze assets and convict pornographers of racketeering.) An anti-pornography civil ordinance should be passed that will allow any person hurt by pornographers to sue for damages.[19] Pornography should be defined as the sexually explicit subordination of women in scenarios ranging from sexually objectifying a woman to raping or murdering her for sexual pleasure. If the material is used to plan or perpetrate a rape, or in sexual harassment on the job or in school, or to defame someone, or if it is forced on a person, that person should have the right to sue purveyors.[20] A woman should be able to sue on behalf of all women, since pornography is a civil liability creating and promulgating second-class citizenship. It would be the plaintiff's burden to make the case—a burden less deadly than having to bear the pornography itself.

Each woman has a life and in that life there is the probability—not just the possibility—of sexual abuse. Crimes of violence against women are the norm, not the exception. Each day requires strategies for taking the victim out of her isolation. It's up to all of us.

---

19. Andrea Dworkin and Catharine MacKinnon pioneered draft legislation in the form of a local ordinance permitting civil—not criminal—action toward obtaining relief from pornography's violent effects. The ordinance was attacked and ultimately defeated, despite its potential to afford legal recourse for defending one's civil rights, which is, as a number of Constitutional scholars noted, *not* "censorship." See also Dines, op. cit.—Ed.

20. See "The Nature of the Beast: Sexual Harassment," by Anita Hill, p. 296.—Ed.

ANDREA DWORKIN is the author of fourteen books, including *Woman Hating* (Dutton, 1974), *Pornography: Men Possessing Women* (Putnam Perigee, 1981), *Right-wing Women* (Coward McCann, 1983), *Intercourse* (Free Press, 1985), and *Scapegoat: The Jews, Israel, and Women's Liberation* (Free Press, 2000), which won an American Book Award. She has also published the novels *Ice and Fire* (Secker & Warburg, 1986) and *Mercy* (Secker & Warburg, 1990). Her most recent book is *Heartbreak: The Political Memoir of a Feminist Militant* (Basic Books, 2002). She and Catharine MacKinnon coauthored legislation recognizing pornography as a violation of women's civil rights.

Suggested Further Reading

Barry, Kathleen. *The Prostitution of Sexuality: The Global Exploitation of Women.* New York: New York University Press, 1995.

Jeffreys, Sheila. *Anticlimax: A Feminist Perspective on the Sexual Revolution.* New York: New York University Press, 1990.

MacKinnon, Catharine A. *Only Words.* Cambridge, Massachusetts: Harvard University Press, 1993.

Morgan, Robin. *The Demon Lover: The Roots of Terrorism.* New York: W. W. Norton, 1989; updated 2nd edition, New York: Washington Square Press, 2001.

Russell, Diana E. H. *Sexual Exploitation: Rape, Child Sexual Abuse, and Workplace Harassment.* Beverly Hills: Sage Library of Social Research, 1984.

The Proper Study of Womankind: Women's Studies

FLORENCE HOWE

THE 1960S BIRTHED WOMEN'S STUDIES, though the phenomenon was nameless until the 1970s. The period was a time of awakening, not just for the young but for those who, like me, had come to adulthood without asking sufficient questions about race, class, or gender; many women's studies pioneers honed their political consciousness and organizing skills in the civil-rights and anti-war movements.[1]

By 1969, the Women's Movement had hit the campuses with full force. Unknown to each other, a handful of faculty women were teaching courses focused on the literature or history of women. I was one of those who, in 1964, returned from teaching in Mississippi's Freedom Schools,[2] aware that all education was political and that education might be a pow-

---

1. On campuses where students were activists on their own behalf, some scholars were also concerned about the university's mission. In 1962, various prestigious academics as well as the Students for a Democratic Society (SDS) declared the American university intellectually, morally, and politically in desperate need of reform. By mid-decade, several hundred "free university" and "experimental colleges" had been organized on as many campuses, some of which helped to establish black studies programs and departments. But in all this, there was *one* course in women's history, at the University of Washington's free university in Seattle. See "Service on Campus: The Free University Movement and Educational Reform," in *The Conspiracy of the Young*, Paul Lauter and Florence Howe (New York: World Publishing Company, 1970).

2. Freedom schools, taught by volunteers (both local and from "up north"), were part of the Civil Rights Movement, organized as educational alternatives to the numerous then-still-segregated schools in the U.S. South.—Ed.

erful strategy for teaching the possibilities of change.[3] African American women students I'd taught in Mississippi had written moving poems about freedom and blackness.[4] What themes might rouse white, middle-class women to write with power and consciousness? For five years, I taught composition classes using fiction and memoir by such writers as Mary McCarthy and Kate Chopin, urging my students to think about themselves in relation to "their brothers."[5] But in 1969, when some of these same students—touched by the burgeoning Women's Movement—entered my eighteenth-century literature courses and asked why no women writers appeared on the syllabus, I was shocked into understanding the deficiency of my own education. (I could hear my undergraduate professor of eighteenth- and nineteenth-century literature lecturing a classroom of women students: "The only poets worth reading are men." Hadn't I shaped my studying and teaching life around that sentence?)

Though other faculty were asking similar questions, we wouldn't have known about each other but for Malcolm Scully—then an intrepid reporter for the newly founded *Chronicle of Higher Education*—who visited my class and then wrote a story about my "teaching consciousness." The mail that followed that article's publication (February 9, 1970) provided the first women's studies network. This was because an equally intrepid work-study student, Carol Ahlum, typed up a list of names and addresses of some fifty people who wrote to me about *their* "teaching consciousness"—and we sent that list to all of them.

---

3. See Florence Howe, "Mississippi's Freedom Schools: The Politics of Education," first published in *Harvard Educational Review* in 1965, reprinted several times and also by the author in *Myths of Coeducation* (see Suggested Further Reading, below). [For a moving example of "education as a powerful strategy for teaching the possibilities of change," see "Alive Behind the Labels: Women in Prison," by Kathy Boudin and Roslyn D. Smith, p. 244.—Ed.]

4. See "African American Women: The Legacy of Black Feminism," by Beverly Guy-Sheftall, p. 176.—Ed.

5. See "Identity and Expression: A Writing Course for Women," first mimeographed in 1970, published in *College English* (1971), reprinted frequently, and collected in *Myths of Coeducation: Selected Essays* by Florence Howe (see Suggested Further Reading, below).

Two other fortuitous events quickly doubled and quadrupled that still-in-formation network. In 1969, appointed Chair of the Commission on the Status and Education of Women for the Modern Language Association (MLA), I was charged with studying the status of women in 5,000 departments of English and the modern languages. In addition, I distributed the Ahlum list at the 1969 MLA annual meeting, afterward receiving not only names of people teaching about women, but their actual course syllabi. Then, in 1970, historian Sheila Tobias asked KNOW, Inc., a small feminist press in Pittsburgh,[6] to print *Female Studies I*, a collection of seventeen course syllabi. Tobias sold some 200 of these at the annual meeting of The American Psychological Association, and arrived triumphantly at the first East Coast women's studies conference (at the University of Pittsburgh in October 1970), announcing that she had titled the volume "one" so that there could be a "two"— and more. Several hundred copies of *Female Studies II*, containing *sixty* course syllabi, appeared only two months later, at the December 1970 meeting of the MLA—and sold out. Eight more volumes followed, some with essays suggesting new feminist teaching strategies; today, all are collectors' items. Two factors were thus essential to the rapid spread of this phenomenon: Tobias's brilliant idea to begin publishing course syllabi, and the willingness of pioneering feminists to cast aside the traditional secrecy in academic teaching, and to *share* their syllabi.

Movements do not simply happen. They need strategic institutional assistance as well as numbers primed for action. By 1975, all ten *Female Studies* volumes had been distributed at scores of professional associations' annual meetings. By then, feminists in these associations had formed caucuses within them or independent organizations outside, each of which issued newsletters and/or journals while sharing mailing lists and course syllabi. Many of these groups organized studies on the status of women *in* their profession, the shocking results of which further energized work on curricular change, and on research to support that change.[7]

---

6. For more about KNOW, see "The Art of Building Feminist Institutions to Last," by Eleanor Smeal, p. 541.—Ed.

7. See "Women's Groups in Professional Associations" in *Women in Academe: Progress and Prospects*, Mariam K. Chamberlain, ed. (New York: Russell Sage Foun-

Study of the status of women—even in literature, to take an example from a strongly typed "female discipline"—convincingly demonstrated the latent malice inherent in the male-centered curriculum.[8] What made women students with better grades than their male peers choose *not* to enter doctoral programs? One couldn't blame discrimination when 33 percent of male undergraduates in English became 66 percent of doctoral candidates while most women chose to go only so far as a Master's degree.[9] How could one explain why women didn't aspire to be college professors despite grades superior to their male peers? Reviews of collegiate texts (and elementary-school readers and other school-books) documented messages teaching girls and boys they were made of different material for different purposes: despite their brains, girls needed to become mommies, or maybe part-time teachers or secretaries—and females who didn't conform could be regarded as peculiar, ill, even dangerous. Research on college curriculum and texts consistently revealed women's inferiority and invisibility, men's superiority and dominance. The message in teaching chiefly male poets is that there are few (or no) worthy female poets. The message of "great" male novelists, from the eighteenth through the mid-twentieth century, could be summarized in one sentence: women die or marry—or sometimes marry, then die.

Through the 1970s, '80s, and '90s, feminists counted, measured, labeled, and recorded layers of sexist behavior and belief documented in the canon used to teach children and adults. The excitement of discovery drove these pioneers past the jeers of those who declared the movement a fad or a communist plot; we spoke and wrote about feeling *ourselves* changed by this study of women, and we heard students exult that they, too, felt transformed.

---

dation, 1988). [See also "Climbing the Ivory Walls: Women in Academia," by Jane Roland Martin, p. 401; "Up the Down Labyrinth: Ins and Outs of Women's Corporate and Campus Careers," by Ellen Appel-Bronstein, p. 387; and "Changing a Masculinist Culture: Women in Science, Engineering, and Technology," by Donna M. Hughes, p. 393.—Ed.]

8. See Martin, op. cit., on the continuing need for a "co-curriculum" as well as for a "co-professoriate."—Ed.

9. See Florence Howe, Laura Morlock, and Richard Berk, "The Status of Women in Modern Language Departments: A Report," PMLA, May 1971; and Florence Howe, "A Report on Women and the Professions," *College English*, May 1971.

In the 1960s, some feminists had studied black history and/or the history of Vietnam. *Why was there no history of women in the curriculum?* What would happen, we thought, to the generation of women at college during the next decades if we were to teach women about their history, make it possible for them to read women writers, hear the music of women composers, view women artists' paintings (then stored in museum basements or mislabeled as work by men)? [10] What would become of women familiar with the terms "sexism" and "patriarchy," women who could compare what had been promised in 1920 with the winning of suffrage with what had actually occurred since then? What if hundreds of women went into politics? [11] What if more women went into medicine, and discovered that experiments claiming "human" findings were based only on male subjects? [12] What if women went into law and began to see that "law" for men was different than for women, that men were ruled by law and women were ruled by men? [13] What might these students of the '70s and '80s become in the '90s—and in the new century?

At first, faculty used the male curriculum (as well as print and other media) to demonstrate sexist ideology. Some of us used such fugitive materials in newsprint as the first pamphlet of *Our Bodies, Ourselves.* By 1970, we also had a few books, notably inclusive of black women: *Sisterhood Is Powerful,* edited by Robin Morgan (Random House/Vintage Books); *The Black Woman,* edited by Toni Cade Bambara (NAL/Signet); *Sexual Politics* by Kate Millett (Doubleday); *The Dialectic of Sex* by Shulamith Firestone (Morrow); and *Woman Power* by Celestine Ware (Tower Books).

Not surprisingly, publishing was to be a significant part of women's studies: the curriculum needed texts from which to teach. Until the

10. See "Women and the Art World: Diary of the Feminist Masked Avengers," by The Guerrilla Girls, p. 437.—Ed.

11. See "Running for Our Lives: Electoral Politics," by Pat Schroeder, p. 28.—Ed.

12. See "Diagnosis and Prognosis: Women Physicians and Women's Health," by Wendy Chavkin, M.D., p. 378, and "Our Bodies, Our Future: Women's Health Activism Overview," by Judy Norsigian et al., p. 269.—Ed.

13. See "Women and Law: The Power to Change," by Catharine A. MacKinnon, p. 447.—Ed.

early 1980s, The Feminist Press (founded 1970) was the only publisher focused on restoring "lost" gems of women's literature; by 1973, two of its first three reprints had raised the question of class (*Life in the Iron Mills* by Rebecca Harding Davis and *Daughter of Earth* by Agnes Smedley); the third, *The Yellow Wallpaper* by Charlotte Perkins Gilman, would attain iconic status in the curriculum of women's studies courses in psychology, sociology, medicine, literature, and history. In 1979, The Feminist Press[14] was first to begin the long-overdue publishing of African American women writers with Zora Neale Hurston's *I Love Myself When I Am Laughing, and Then Again When I Am Looking Mean and Impressive*, edited by Alice Walker; followed (in the early 1980s) by then-out-of-print novels by Sarah T. Wright, Louise Meriwether, and Paule Marshall. The use of these books in women's studies courses makes clear that, at least by the mid-1980s, race had become as important a theme as sex and gender. Through these two decades—beginning in 1972 with *Feminist Studies, Women's Studies*, and *Women's Studies Newsletter* (later *Women's Studies Quarterly*)—scores of feminist newsletters and journals were founded, including *Ms.* (1972) and *Signs* (1975).[15] By the 1980s, university presses and mainstream trade publishers—impressed by a growing market—were reissuing the work of women writers and beginning to publish new feminist scholarship.

The rapidity of women's studies' growth—in research and publishing, as well as curricular and institutional development—is a remarkable story. In 1972, Mariam Chamberlain, then at The Ford Foundation, was curious about the size of this burgeoning area of study, and asked The Feminist Press to conduct a survey. The results, published in 1974, listed 4,658 courses and 112 programs, taught by 2,964 faculty (female and male) at 885 institutions.[16] While the initial appearance of women's studies courses in 1970 and 1971 followed the energy and visibility of the Women's Movement up the East Coast from Baltimore to New England and down the West Coast from Seattle to San Diego (with rela-

---

14. For the backlist and current catalog, see *www.feministpress.org.*—Ed.

15. See "The Media and the Movement: A User's Guide," by Gloria Steinem, p. 103.—Ed.

16. Tamar Berkowitz, Jean Mangi, and Jane Williamson, eds., *Who's Who and Where in Women's Studies* (Old Westbury, New York: The Feminist Press, 1974).

tively few courses in the Midwest), as early as 1974 no area of the country was without women's studies. Initially these courses were in departments of English, history, psychology, and sociology, but by '74, these departments had hundreds of listings; in addition, most other areas of the curriculum—for example, library science, industrial and labor relations, human biology, *la raza* studies, law, nursing, peace science, and public administration—had at least one listing.[17]

Where were these courses and programs? Not in elite, private universities, where women faculty were few and usually powerless. They were chiefly at public land-grant universities and urban universities, where women faculty and students were numerous and the Women's Movement was vibrant. They flourished where feminist faculty and students were willing to work together—even without budgets, offices, or formal recognition. On many campuses, feminist faculty, librarians, and students (with the help of a friendly dean) gained the attention of an administration beset by its own financial problems. The early 1970s were not flush years for academe; they were years of falling enrollments and falling budgets. A few feminist faculty in a variety of departments—perhaps several of them tenured, with others risking loss of tenure by placing their names on the roster of women's studies—taught new courses of their own invention. Usually, a voluntary coordinator worked out of her own faculty office in her own department to hold together the swiftly growing group of disparate courses, and to try to devise an introductory interdisciplinary course suitable for interested students.

I've called this period "creative anarchy." Most early women's studies programs had to pass through it if they were to survive and enter "phase two": a designated office and small budget; a named coordinator who might have some hours released from teaching as payment rather than salary; a more stable staff (perhaps with joint appointments, or, rarely, an actual appointment in women's studies). In this stage, a faculty-student committee might spend years moving through administrative hurdles toward establishing a program offering a major, minor, or certificate, and possibly some graduate courses. None of this was quick to

---

17. Florence Howe and Carol Ahlum, "Women's Studies and Social Change," in *Academic Women on the Move*, Alice S. Rossi and Ann Calderwood, eds. (New York: Russell Sage Foundation, 1973).

happen, since university budgets remained tight. But in cities like New York and Philadelphia, unemployed doctorates could be hired part-time as needed, while at large universities, graduate students wanted the experience and often had fresh expertise to offer in undergraduate courses.[18]

Despite relentless opposition, skepticism, and Right-wing harrass-ment through the 1970s and '80s, undergraduate enrollments soared. Faculty regarded teaching women's studies with delight, because stu-dents were highly motivated. An unusual proportion of them, especially in urban universities, were returning students who had dropped out to have families or had never gone to college at all. Stimulated by the Women's Movement, many were angry about what they'd been taught in high school or by the culture at large. They were working out not only their identities as women of a certain age, class, race, sexuality, reli-gion, ethnicity, politics, and ability. They were also seriously consider-ing how to live their lives, what kind of work to choose, what sort of personal relationships. Not surprisingly, students became far more am-bitious than I'd found them back in the 1960s. Statistics confirm the sea-change in today's academe: in the "female-typed" professions, women Ph.D.s today far outnumber men; in the male-dominated fields, women have gained visibility as a strong minority.[19]

Who were the faculty? In a 1977 study, I reported that one-third of the women faculty in fifteen women's studies programs were re-entry scholars.[20] The Women's Movement had inspired them to return to school for graduate work, and they had chosen to teach in women's studies. These were heady times. Learning was exciting, and led directly to the creation of new curriculum and thence new publications. If tenured, these women could decide to teach a course called "Images of

18. Florence Howe, *Seven Years Later: Women's Studies Programs in 1976*, Washing-ton, D.C.: A Report of the National Advisory Council on Women's Educational Programs, H.U.D., 1977.

19. Mariam Chamberlain, "Women and Leadership in Higher Education," in *The American Woman, 2001–2002: Getting to the Top*, Cynthia B. Costello and Anne J. Stone, eds. (New York: W. W. Norton & Co., 2001). [See also Martin, op. cit., and Hughes, op. cit.—Ed.]

20. *Seven Years Later*, op. cit.

Women in British Literature" in the English department or "History of Women in the U.S." in the history department. They were also activists, engaged on the campus in conducting studies of pay scales for women faculty and clerical and other workers, or establishing rape-crisis centers, day-care centers, and women's centers. At the same time, they were productive scholars. When surveyed in 1985, more than 80 percent of women's studies faculty had published one or more books and was about to publish another.[21]

What were the goals of the new women's studies curriculum? Introductory courses focused on raising consciousness about sexism and the sex-role stereotyping that permeated society. In addition, at some colleges and universities—including SUNY's campuses at Old Westbury and Buffalo, CUNY's Brooklyn College, Chicago's University of Illinois campus, and San Francisco State University—issues of race and class bias were also prominent in women's studies courses. Meanwhile, courses titled "The Sociology of Women" or "The Psychology of Women"[22]—as well as women's history courses and courses on women writers—aimed to compensate for the absence of women from the general curriculum.

The growth continued. By 1984, there were 482 programs; by 1997, 620 (a figure that doesn't account for campuses where women's studies courses are offered in departments, without a formal program). By the mid-1980s, women's studies could be found in the most elite institutions, many of which, like Princeton and Yale, had become coeducational. By then, African American women's studies had become a field of its own, especially (but not only) on historically black campuses, with Spelman College leading the way.[23] Faculty who pioneered lesbian studies in the early 1980s have had to decide in the 1990s whether to stay in-

---

21. Florence Howe, "Women's Studies and Curricular Change," in *Women in Academe*, op. cit.

22. Such courses were the seeds for, in time, astonishing fruit. See, for example, "Sisterhood Is Pleasurable: A Quiet Revolution in Psychology," by Carol Gilligan, p. 94.—Ed.

23. See Guy-Sheftall, op. cit.—Ed.

side women's studies programs or join separate gay and lesbian studies programs, themselves recently giving way to queer studies.[24]

By the mid-1980s, women's studies had two major organizations: the National Association of Women's Studies (NWSA, formed 1977) and the National Council for Research on Women (NCRW, formed 1982). But neither could offer women's studies a unified direction. No organization or group has controlled what's been described (by both friends and enemies) as a political phenomenon: a social and educational movement without visible leadership. Indeed, women's studies faculty continue to be discipline-based, attend their own professional meetings, and direct their own graduate students, who are earning doctorates usually in traditional departments, though sometimes with women's studies perspectives.

What then holds women's studies together so that we can call it a "phenomenon" or a "movement"? I propose two chief factors: *conflict* and *vision*.

From the first, women's studies had to battle the university to establish courses and programs. When those struggles eased, other pressures—some internal, some external—established new battlegrounds. When, for example, hundreds of programs burst into existence in the 1980s and 1990s (without having to pass through a decade of struggle), they entered into contested intellectual space. By 1980, the word "woman" was under attack as "essentialist"—as though founders of women's studies programs had been unaware of "difference." Many feminists, struck by the timing of this attack—*just* as women were gaining the right to construct histories, rediscover cultural roots, and claim human rights—struck back. The battle, engaged at conferences and in print, is ongoing, and lends a certain edginess to women's studies today.

Some take the position that feminist theory can emanate only from academe, and must be pure and above politics. Others deride this as cowardly or as opportunistic careerism, the professionalization of women's studies. Many recall that feminist theory originally gained its power from being experientially based (as in "the personal is political")

---

24. See "Confessions of a Worrywart: Ruminations on a Lesbian Feminist Overview," by Karla Jay, p. 212.—Ed.

and rooted in real life. "We are *all* theorists," Janet Zandy once quietly remarked to me—adding that some of us recognize the material world in need of change.[25] Early on, Gayatri Spiwak helpfully enunciated the concept of "strategic essentialism" in defense of a movement that needed to continue making gains on behalf of women's education and equality. One effect of this debate has been the renaming of some programs as "gender studies" or "women and gender studies."[26]

As (or more) important has been the effect of post-structuralist theories on women's studies, which the late Barbara Christian addressed in "A Race to Theory," a groundbreaking essay first published in *Cultural Critique* (Spring 1987). Christian and other women of color were especially critical of this development, not only because of its inherent abandonment of activist concerns, but also because the dominant, French-inspired, theoretical models—Lacan, Derrida, etc.—were totally Western in origin, with complete ignorance of (or indifference to) the intellectual and cultural realities and lives of women across the world. Simultaneously, radical feminists critiqued those same models as being white, Western, middle-class, and *male*.[27]

Still, despite such internal conflict, the vision persists. In the 1980s and '90s, women's studies took on still other responsibilities within the university: to change the overall collegiate curriculum. Some eighty curriculum-integration projects were in process by the mid-1980s, when, between 1986 and 1991, The Ford Foundation funded thirteen campuses to "mainstream minority women's studies"—not only into

25. See Janet Zandy, ed., *Calling Home: Working-Class Women's Writings* (New Brunswick, New Jersey: Rutgers University Press, 1990); and *Liberating Memory: Our Work and Our Working-Class Consciousness* (Rutgers University Press, 1995). For summaries of positions and quarrels regarding "theorists," see "The Quest for Theory" in *When Women Ask the Questions* (see Suggested Further Reading, below). See also "Institutionalizing and Intellectualizing Feminist Studies," by Ellen Messer-Davidow, in *Disciplining Feminism: From Social Activism to Academic Discourse* (Durham, North Carolina: Duke University Press, 2002).

26. See the Introduction, p. *xv*.—Ed.

27. For witty, internationalist, feminist critiques of postmodernism, see *Nothing Mat(t)ers*, by Somer Brodribb (New York: New York University Press, 1992; reissued Melbourne, Australia: Spinifex Press, 1998); and *Radically Speaking: Feminism Reclaimed*, Diane Bell and Renate Klein, eds. (Melbourne: Spinifex Press, 1996).—Ed.

women's studies courses, but also into as much of the collegiate curriculum as could be reached. By the early 1990s, another set of women's studies programs and research centers was devising methods of "internationalizing" women's studies and urging area-studies faculty to add women and gender to their teaching.[28] Not surprisingly, women of color took center stage in curricular development and in theory.[29]

What are the issues today, near the end of three decades of women's studies? Conferences and publications reveal many different voices in disagreement.[30] None are uncritical. Some proclaim the field "messy," too complex even in a single disciplinary area—history, literature, or anthropology, for example—for any faculty to master. Others insist that the field requires the complexity of a global vision, that the U.S. needs to be de-centered in the women's studies classroom.[31] Though some deplore the separation of theory from action and research from practice, others bemoan a loss of critical (read theoretical?) energy to such newer interdisciplinary fields as cultural studies and queer studies. Are we the victims of our own success? "How did it happen," Ellen Messer-Davidow asks, "that a bold venture launched thirty years ago to transform academic and social institutions was itself transformed by them?"[32]

Meanwhile, others are engaged in an old struggle for the re-visioning

---

28. For more on this trend, see "U.S. Latinas: Active at the Intersections of Gender, Nationality, Race, and Class," by Edna Acosta-Belén and Christine E. Bose, p. 198.—Ed.

29. These were two projects of the National Council for Research on Women. See pamphlets by Mariam Chamberlain, "Mainstreaming Minority Women's Studies Programs" (1991); and "Women's Studies, Area & International Studies Curriculum Integration Project" (1996). See also two volumes that emerged from these projects: *Women of Color and the Multicultural Curriculum: Transforming the College Classroom*, Liza Fiol-Matta and Mariam K. Chamberlain, eds. (New York: The Feminist Press at CUNY, 1994); and *Encompassing Gender: Integrating International Studies and Women's Studies*, Mary M. Lay, Janice Monk, and Deborah S. Rosenfelt, eds. (New York: The Feminist Press at CUNY, 2002).

30. For a lively mélange of views, see the 1997 issue of *differences: A Journal of Feminist Cultural Studies*. See also the various summaries offered by Marilyn Boxer and Ellen Messer-Davidow in their important books (Suggested Further Reading, below).

31. See Acosta-Belén and Bose, op. cit.—Ed.

32. Messer-Davidow, op. cit.

of women's studies: form and substance. Should women's studies be re-conceived as a discipline rather than an interdisciplinary area of knowledge responsible for changing all the other disciplines? This is not an abstract question. It has immediate practical consequences: hundreds of programs might easily become departments, stabilize their curriculum, budgets, and faculties; and university programs might offer the doctorate as confirmation of their formal admission as full members of the university. To see women's studies as a discipline (albeit an interdisciplinary discipline) may be essential to establishing a doctorate in women's studies as intellectually viable and useful to graduates. But what might be the effect? Won't this potential success blunt the most important goal of women's studies: to change the minds and hearts of undergraduates, who still enter higher education schooled by a sexist curriculum? Will the cost be measured in the loss of women's studies' original vision as change agent for the *whole* university? Will the doctorate signify that women's studies has now joined Virginia Woolf's "procession of educated men?" Will women's studies rest contentedly yoked to that enterprise?

Or will some way be found—given the creative energies of feminists—to have it all ways? It's encouraging to scan the websites of major university programs. For instance, along with a prospectus announcing the soon-to-be-ratified doctorate, Ohio State posts the twenty-five-year history of its program, each segment written by one of the program's pioneers. Such histories provide perspective and specificity. They don't mask conflict, but they do celebrate real achievements. The vast curriculum—some courses offered by women's studies, others in collaboration with departments—testifies to the continuing vitality, ambivalence, and just plain *inclusiveness* of the field.

Women—feminists in particular—need to know their own history, especially if they are to sustain the vision and vigilance needed to maintain programs and continue reforming the curriculum (if not the entire university). Not even the most naive of the pioneers thirty years ago believed that women's studies could change academe in several decades. What we've learned has come hard. Still, despite internal and external strife, the vision persists. *Now there are thousands who can teach this knowledge and consciousness.* They and their students can read narratives about the power of women organized into collective action by the urgency of that shared vision. Defiantly risking their academic careers, unafraid to be called "political," these women forged real change.[33]

Sometimes I worry that students today take their access to a feminist curriculum for granted, enjoying—sometimes even complaining about—the difficulties of studying this new, complex area of knowledge. We wanted our daughters to be advantaged in precisely this way. But we'd also like them to understand that anything built in thirty years can be dismantled even more quickly, and that the history of educational change is, at best, very slow. The conservative forces now attacking women's studies don't appear in the form of unregenerate old male academics, but as stylish, media-hungry, female academics presenting themselves as "feminists" in order to denounce the Women's Movement (thus earning the wry nickname, "faux feminists").

What keeps me optimistic is still the vision—and the realization that *we have been the very first women ever able to write, publish, and teach women's history for generations to come.* We have been able to publish— and *keep* in print—literature by women. Misogynists would now have to burn down entire libraries to erase women's history and literature. Unlike previous feminist waves, we have institutionalized ourselves.[34]

Although this essay and anthology are focused on U.S. women, it and we exist as part of the world.[35] Women's studies has been from the start an international movement, though only in the last decade has scholarship generated in the global South begun to move "north."[36] Hopefully, exchange programs beyond the Fulbrights will increase such dynamic connections. The energy and vision in women's studies is now coming from *outside* the U.S. and Europe—from the majority of the world's

---

33. See *The Politics of Women's Studies: Testimony from 30 Founding Mothers.* Florence Howe, ed. (Suggested Further Reading, below).

34. See "Notes of a Feminist Long Distance Runner," by Eleanor Holmes Norton, p. 145; and "The Art of Building Feminist Institutions to Last," by Eleanor Smeal, p. 541.—Ed.

35. See "Globalization: A Strategic Advance for Feminism?" by Jessica Neuwirth, p. 526, and the Introduction, op. cit.—Ed.

36. Some of this movement has depended on the ability of research universities with large women's studies programs, like the University of Maryland, to bring to its campus feminist scholars from Africa, Asia, and Latin America.

population, from countries where research is still valued for its ability to change real lives (of women *and* men), from where theory and practice are still inseparable.

FLORENCE HOWE has been called by many people across the globe "the mother of women's studies." Also the mother of The Feminist Press *(www.feministpress.org)*, itself a major Women's Movement institution, she regards herself as "a teacher/scholar/activist trying to become a writer." Her first love was poetry; she began teaching at the University of Wisconsin in 1951, founded The Feminist Press in 1970, and stopped teaching in the mid-1980s to devote full time to the Press—by then in residence at the City University of New York, where Howe held a professorship in the English department. She retired from directing The Feminist Press and from CUNY in 2000. Howe has written or edited more than a dozen books and more than 100 essays. She is probably best known as the compiler/editor of *No More Masks! An Anthology of Poems by American Women Poets* (Doubleday/Anchor 1973; expanded edition HarperCollins, 1993). Currently, she is co-director of a massive project, "Women Writing Africa," which will produce four regional anthologies, the first in the fall of 2002. When not in Africa or working on African texts, she is writing a memoir.

Suggested Further Reading

Boxer, Marilyn. *When Women Ask the Questions*. Baltimore, Maryland: Johns Hopkins University Press, 1998.

Helly, Dorothy, and Elaine R. Hedges, eds. *Looking Back, Moving Forward: 25 Years of Women's Studies History, Women's Studies Quarterly*, Vol. xxv, numbers 1 & 2, Spring/Summer 1997.

Howe, Florence. *Myths of Coeducation: Selected Essays, 1964–1983*. Bloomington, Indiana: Indiana University Press, 1984.

Howe, Florence, ed. *The Politics of Women's Studies: Testimony from 30 Founding Mothers*. New York: The Feminist Press at CUNY, 2000.

Messer-Davidow, Ellen. *Disciplining Feminism: From Social Activism to Academic Discourse*. Durham, North Carolina: Duke University Press, 2002.

Parenting:
A New Social Contract

SUZANNE BRAUN LEVINE

PARENTING USED to be considered a Mom and Pop operation with a clear division of labor: Mom was the nurturer, Pop the disciplinarian. The trouble was Pop got to impose his will on everyone, while Mom couldn't impose her will on anything, even her own circumstances. Parenting used to be considered the result of a precise event, sex between a man and a woman. The trouble was that if the "sanctity" of marriage was lacking, so was protection of the offspring, unless Pop chose to claim his property; Mom, needless to say, had no choice at all.

Today, family life is much more egalitarian. The designated "head of household" is no more, women are no longer defined by childbearing, and men are increasingly breaking free of the limitations of a paterfamilias role to discover the joys of nurturing their children. Today, men and women mix and match in a wide array of combinations, or go solo, and bring children into their lives in a range of ways made possible by scientific breakthroughs and social circumstances—adoption, in vitro fertilization, insemination, blending families. And marriage, the mainstay of tradition, is becoming a minority model. According to the millennium U.S. Census, the number of classic nuclear families has dropped for the first time to below 25 percent of all households, while the number of single mothers *and* single fathers has shot up, along with the number of cohabiting-parents and same-sex-parents family units.

One thing all these parents have in common is that they are dancing as fast as they can to support their children. In the majority of two-parent families, both are working outside the home. Overall, the vast majority of women with children in school are employed in the workforce.[1] But most jobs require longer hours—the equivalent of a month more a year than people worked in the 1960s—for barely more pay; the average median income has remained almost static since 1980, while income for the bottom 20 percent of the population has actually fallen in, as they say, "real terms." At the same time, according to the U.S. Department of Agriculture annual accounting, the dollar cost of providing the necessities of life to raise a child to age eighteen keeps going up—to $165,630, or over $9,000 per year!

These hard-working parents want desperately to do right by their children and would trade almost anything to do so. According to a Radcliffe Public Policy Center study released in 2000, 70 percent of women *and* men put "spending more time with my family" at the top of their wish list—ahead of success, power, and even more money. Across the country men and women are showing their willingness to trade raises for flexibility and to respond to family-friendly policies with loyalty and hard work, qualities that redound to their employers' bottom line. Yet all too few employers are taking them up on it.

The miracle is that despite their anxiety, parents are *not* spending less time with their children than previous generations (about 21 hours a week for single moms—as much as stay-at-home moms in 1981—and up for two-parent families to 31 hours for women and 23 for men). To accomplish this, they play a constant game of trade-offs, with time for themselves—particularly sleep—and for each other falling by the wayside.

Then why, pray tell, does school let out at three o'clock?

This is not a facetious question. It goes to the heart of the American hypocrisy about families. We know that parents spend an average of 8 percent of their annual income on children; we can assume that much of that goes to coverage during the after-school hours between three and six. Studies show that most teenage crime takes place and most teenage pregnancies originate between the hours of three and six; that many workplaces show a drop in efficiency as parents try to track their kids' after-school activities between three and six; that most kids are parked in front of the TV in an empty house—*if* their worried parents are lucky—between three and six. There seems to be a pattern here. . . .

---

1. See the "Workplaces" section, p. 323.—Ed.

If this were an assembly-line glitch or a Martian enigma, the best minds would be on the case. Why, then, doesn't someone fix an outdated system that was set up to accommodate the needs of an agricultural society with chores every afternoon and a long summer harvest season? Because we don't want to. We (some of us more than others) have too much invested in the American Dream—the American Fantasy, really—that grew from that real farm-family model to a much less real one based on an ethos both sentimental and heartless.

Ozzie and Harriet and Ricky and David were a TV institution of the 1950s, a nuclear family in which Father went out into the world and came back with a paycheck, and Mother waited at home for him and their two children to bound into "her" cozy kitchen for a dose of maternal indulgence. The Ozzie-and-Harriet fiction has become an ideal—unattainable and guilt-producing, but promoted as the best environment for children. Behind that pastel stage set, though, are the crude bricks of a "rugged individualism" that presumes those who can't build it on their own just didn't try hard enough. This has become the excuse for doing so little to help real families.

The mixed message of an unattainable ideal and a punitive reality has led to a bad case of double-speak. We can glance at just a few examples. While pundits deplore violence in the schools, at this writing, twenty-three states permit "paddling" of schoolchildren. Although activists succeeded, after seven long years, in winning family- and medical-leave legislation, Congress refused to require that the leave be *paid*—putting it out of reach of those who need it most, and leaving the United States lagging behind other industrialized countries. Parents are blamed when they don't provide adequate childcare, but are not offered the public alternative of universal and government-subsidized availability common in most European countries. Furthermore, Americans tolerate a childcare system that is haphazard, lacking in standards, and expensive—*and* one that pays the people who take care of our children less than those who take care of our cars. Then, when a study shows that a percentage of children in day care are slightly more aggressive than kids at home, mothers are blamed for not staying home with their children!

It isn't as though the facts of family life go totally unacknowledged in our culture. Marketers, for example, promote the works—from fast-food products to life-management services to one-stop everything for busy parents—because it makes sound economic sense to cater to their needs. Our policy makers, on the other hand, are reluctant to put their (our!) money where their mouths are. If our national budget is, as many have suggested, our only true statement of values, we don't yet value families—no matter how much hot air is expended on promoting "family values."

Understanding that families do not fall under a singular definition and that they do not need "values" *imposed* on them but value *accorded* them has been the agenda of the U.S. Feminist Movement for 150 years. "Feminists are not concerned with maintaining the 'sanctity of the family,' a pleasant enough phrase that has been used to cover an awful lot of damage . . . ," wrote Barbara Katz Rothman in *Recreating Motherhood* (W. W. Norton & Company, 1989); "As feminists we are concerned not with the control and ownership and kinship issues of the traditional family, but with the *relationships* people establish with one another, with adults and with children."

Generations of feminists have made a great deal of progress in moving public consciousness and policy in that direction since Elizabeth Cady Stanton, writing in 1854, deplored the power inequities within the family: "If [a woman] have a worthless husband, a confirmed drunkard, a villain, or a vagrant, he has still all the rights of a man, a husband, and a father. Though the whole support of the family be thrown upon the wife, if the wages she earns be paid to her by an employer, the husband can receive them again. . . . The father can apprentice his child, bind him out to a trade, without the mother's consent—yea, in direct opposition to her most earnest entreaties, prayers and tears. . . . He may bind his daughter to the owner of a brothel, and by the degradation of his child, supply his daily wants."[2]

A century later, the form of women's lives had changed dramatically, but less so the content. By 1970, women "had most of the legal freedoms, the literal assurance that they were considered full political citizens of society—and yet they had no power," wrote Shulamith Fire-

---

2. "Address to the Legislature of New York on Women's Rights," February 14, 1854. *History of Women's Suffrage*, Vol. I, eds. E. C. Stanton, S. B. Anthony, and Matilda J. Gage (Rochester: Susan B. Anthony, 1881); collected in *Elizabeth Cady Stanton and Susan B. Anthony: Correspondence, Writings, Speeches*, Ellen Carol DuBois, ed. (New York: Schocken Books, 1981).

stone in *The Dialectic of Sex* (William Morrow and Company, 1970), at the time. Even more so within the family, where a woman's economic, social, and parental rights were tightly bound to her husband's will. Indeed, a woman who tried to earn a living could not find a job with a salary equal to a man's in the sex-segregated "help wanted—female" listings, and a woman who cared for her children at home and depended on the support of her husband was, as the saying went, "one man away from welfare." Ironically, if she was receiving welfare, the reverse was true; the discovery of a man sharing her home would cut her *off* from benefits.

Today, family life is more supportive of both parents' independence, and most women feel less terror at the prospect of managing on their own. But one assumption is holding families hostage to the Ozzie-and-Harriet model: women are still expected to be the caregivers of first and last resort.[3] Even back when that seemed to be true, women had the support of a wide safety net of extended family and community institutions to fall back on. Today, parents are operating on their own to a heart-breaking degree, and even two parents can't do it all. Until that piece of fantasy is replaced with social policy that reflects and addresses reality, the stress parents are experiencing is going to intensify.

"When families cannot provide the various kinds of care that their children or elders or others may need, and when public supports are not available because families are *supposed* to take care of themselves, the unmet need for care has to go somewhere," wrote political scientist Mona Harrington, in *Care and Equality* (see Suggested Further Reading below), "Generally it spills over onto public institutions that were not designed—and are not funded—to handle it."

"The fact is," Harrington concluded, "the old formulas cannot yield both care and equality. They are bankrupt. And they are generating a social crisis that cannot be addressed realistically until we can remove the blinders of traditional thinking. . . . "

The most important blinder that must go is the notion that each family can take care of itself. On that count, the 2000 Census has two very sobering messages. First, the number of children living in poverty has reached 12.1 million, one in six pre-voting citizens. Second, the percentage of the population living alone is increasing (due to extended life

---

3. See "*Just* a Housewife?!" by Helen Drusine, p. 342.—Ed.

expectancy and more independent lifestyles); as their votes are weighed against families with children, it will be harder than ever to promote policies that support families—unless we change the mindset about whose responsibility it is to foster the next generation. (In fact, there's a growing anti-child movement among people who don't want to live in neighborhoods or eat in restaurants that cater to children. A group called No Kidding! arranges child-free social events. In five years it has grown from five to forty-seven chapters.)

The parenting issue of the future is nothing less than a mandate to rewrite the American Dream. And if anyone tries to sell the idea of going back to the traditional ways, let them consider the fact that while divorce is leveling off throughout the general population, it has risen 125 percent among the most conservative groups. "Bible Belt" women, in particular, are increasingly unwilling to accept the idea that they must grin and bear a life not of their own design: "I had this vision that this is just what people do: get married, have kids, and Christ comes back," an Oklahoma divorcee with a young daughter told *The New York Times*. "No one asked me, 'Are you sure this is what you want?' "[4] And if anyone thinks that "fathers first" groups like the Promise Keepers can keep their promise of a groundswell of men making everything all right by reclaiming their patriarchal thrones, most American men will tell you, as they told me when I wrote a book about fatherhood, that their role model for the good father they want to be is "not like my father."

Furthermore, if you ask the children whether they long for the Ozzie-and-Harriet family model, they will tell you, as they told Ellen Galinsky in 1999 for her study *Ask the Children* [see below], they don't resent their parents working. In fact, they're proud of them and grateful for the material advantages provided. But they are concerned about the stress that the work/family tension puts on their parents—and the consequences for themselves. They know their parents need relief, but they buy into the same you-must-solve-your-problems-on-your-own ethic that their parents are too busy to question: "Don't work too hard. Know when to quit, because if you don't you'll get all stressed out and take it out on us," was the advice of a fifteen-year-old girl. Since American par-

---

4. Quoted in *The New York Times*, 21 May 2001.

ents are running faster and faster just to stay in the same place economically, it would take not a parental decision, but a wholehearted commitment to the concept of a living wage and a living workweek, to implement her advice.

As Sylvia Ann Hewlett and Cornel West pointed out in *The War Against Parents* [see below], what's needed is a lobbying powerhouse the size of the American Association of Retired Persons plus a national commitment the size of the G.I. Bill of Rights, which helped returning World War II vets get an education, start a business, and buy a house.

A new American Dream requires a new social contract based on the premise that support for caregivers is a right of citizenship, not a handout to the certified needy. And that our national public service system, not our beleaguered families, is the caregiver of last resort, and in some cases—particularly education and health care—of first resort. A good example of creative thinking in this area is the Caregiver Credit campaign, a project of Social Agenda, which is gaining national momentum. It modifies the current tax code with a modest proposal: to convert the child tax credit—currently $600 per child—to a "caregiver tax credit to cover the care of adults and children—anyone who gives care to everyone who needs it in families of blood or choice." And in order to cover those who care and give but earn so little they don't pay taxes, the legislation would make the credit refundable—in cash.[5]

In the same vein, here is a vision of what could be happening at three o'clock in school buildings across the country (and all day long during the summer). As the children are dismissed from their last classes, a fresh crew of teachers and other qualified adults arrive and begin sorting out sports equipment and setting up a variety of clubs, library projects, and quiet homework rooms. Some take up their positions as monitors in areas where kids can just hang out and listen to music or putter with computers. A public-health nurse opens her office for business, which includes keeping inoculations up-to-date and handling minor medical problems. A social worker has regular hours that run into the evening so that she's available to counsel kids and make sure families get any help

---

5. For more on the Caregiver Credit Campaign, see "Poverty Wears a Female Face," by Theresa Funiciello, p. 222.—Ed.

they need dealing with the system. Throughout the year other special-ists show up—a tax advisor in the spring, a continuing education coun-selor, a nutritionist—to brief parents when they pick up their kids.

Neighbors get to know one another as they show up after work or put in the requisite one or two days a year of volunteering with the program. On those days they organize a range of off-campus activities such as (this idea is my personal favorite) taking some of the older kids grocery shopping for the family dinner. Imagine what a relief it would be for an exhausted parent not to have to stop for last-minute items, and how proud their teenagers would feel, doing their share.

Somewhere around 8:00 P.M., things quiet down and the doors are fi-nally locked.

With all this activity, elected officials would surely begin showing up, too, and their interest could generate political action. In other words, the school—the most extensive facility in most communities and the one with which most people have contact—could become the Town Well that was. In recent years, communities have lost their gathering places: libraries have had to cut back on hours; houses of worship have trouble getting people to give up part of their errand-crowded or second-job-filled weekends; people will do anything to avoid entering a municipal building, regarded as a nightmare of red tape and frustration. The pulse of a dynamic, continuing, school day could generate a revival of civic life.

If you think that's visionary, it's only as visionary as it was when Eliz-abeth Cady Stanton, herself the mother of seven, wrote in 1872: "In ed-ucation woman should demand an extension of our common school system at both ends, to infant schools and public colleges. The children of women dependent on daily labor should be cared for during the hours of labor, including the noon intermission. They should be ac-counted as little cadets of the state and should be furnished with ginger snaps, milk, etc. . . . "[6] I don't know about the "cadets," but the ginger snaps sound awfully homey.

When all is said and done, every mother and father knows that milk and ginger snaps at school can't replace parental love and attention. But

---

6. "Proposal to Form a New Party," May 1872. Library of Congress, E. C. Stanton Papers. Collected in DuBois, op. cit.

we also know that all the devotion we shower on our children can't make up for a national mindset that doesn't consider parenting a public good. After all, depending on how they grow up, "other people's children" will be the ones writing our laws, curing our diseases, and making us laugh— or not.

SUZANNE BRAUN LEVINE was chief editor of *Ms.* magazine (1972–1988), as well as chief editor of the *Columbia Journalism Review*. She produced the Peabody Award-winning television special *She's Nobody's Baby: A History of American Women in the Twentieth Century*, and is the author of *Father Courage: What Happens When Men Put Family First* (Harcourt, 2000), and of the forthcoming *A Woman's Guide to Second Adulthood* (Viking, 2004). She has written and spoken widely about journalism, feminism, and family life, and she and her husband, Robert Levine, have two teenage children.

Suggested Further Reading

Dinnerstein, Dorothy. *The Mermaid and the Minotaur: Sexual Arrangements and Human Malaise.* New York: HarperCollins, 1977.

Galinsky, Ellen. *Ask the Children: The Breakthrough Study That Reveals How to Succeed at Work and Parenting.* New York: William Morrow and Quill paperback, 1999.

Harrington, Mona. *Care and Equality: Inventing a New Family Politics.* New York: Knopf, 1999.

Hewlett, Sylvia Ann, and Cornel West. *The War Against Parents: What We Can Do for America's Beleaguered Moms and Dads.* New York: Houghton Mifflin, 1998.

Huston, Perdita. *Families As We Are: Conversations from Around the World.* New York: The Feminist Press at CUNY, 2001.

Sisterhood Is Pleasurable:
A Quiet Revolution
in Psychology

CAROL GILLIGAN

IN A RECENT [2002] issue of the journal *Neuron*, scientists using magnetic resonance to study neural activity in women reported what seemed to be a startling discovery: sisterhood is pleasurable. Among women playing Prisoner's Dilemma, a game in which they could choose cooperative or competitive strategies, the brain lit up most brightly when women chose cooperation. Natalie Angier reported on the findings in *The New York Times:* "the small, brave act of cooperating with another person, of choosing trust over cynicism, generosity over selfishness, makes the brain light up with quiet joy." [1]

These findings join a growing convergence of evidence across the human sciences leading to a revolutionary shift in consciousness. Primed to explain competitive behavior, the scientists had expected the biggest response in cases where one woman cooperated and another woman sought to gain personal advantage at the other's expense. They were surprised to discover that the brightest brain signals arose in cooperative alliances and the response grew stronger the longer cooperation lasted. Even more startling, the areas of the brain lit up by cooperation were those that respond to "chocolate, pretty faces, money, cocaine, and a range of licit and illicit delights." [2] The researchers said there is every

---

1. "Why We're So Nice: We're Wired to Cooperate," by Natalie Angier, *The New York Times*, 23 July 2002.

2. Ibid.

reason to assume that this is true for men as well as women. If cooperation, typically associated with altruism and self-sacrifice, sets off the
same signals of delight as pleasures commonly associated with hedo-
nism and self-indulgence; if the opposition between selfish and selfless,
self vs. relationship neurologically makes no sense, then a new paradigm
is necessary to reframe the very terms of the conversation. Scientists are
discovering that we are hard-wired for relationship.

It is hard to resist the impression that psychology is catching up with
feminism, and with a long line of artists and writers. More than 30 years
ago, writing "*Kinder, Kuche, Kirche* As Scientific Law: Psychology Constructs the Female,"[3] Naomi Weisstein deconstructed a psychology that
had construed patriarchy as nature. In a devastating critique, she exposed the fallacy of turning a patriarchal "is" into a psychological
"ought," and underscored the dangers of bestowing scientific authority
on patriarchal norms and values.[4]

Throughout the 1970s, the feminist analysis of the field cleared the
way for a new psychology. In *Toward a New Psychology of Women* (Boston:
Beacon Press, 1976), Jean Baker Miller observed that for many women,
the sense of self is invested more in maintaining relationships than in establishing hierarchy; she saw in this psychic organization the basis for a
new way of living and functioning. In the research leading to writing *In
a Different Voice*,[5] I found that women's voices, when heard in their own
right and with their own integrity, change the voice of psychology. The
sense of self, the experience of relationship, morality, and development
itself all appear in a different light when starting from a premise of connectedness rather than separateness, when imagining relationships not
as hierarchies but as webs. The hierarchical constructions of a patriarchal psychology (divorcing thought from emotion, mind from body, self
from relationships, culture from nature, and men from women) then

---

3. Robin Morgan, ed., *Sisterhood Is Powerful* (New York: Random House and Vintage Books, 1970).

4. See "Biologically Correct," by Natalie Angier, p. 3.—Ed.

5. Carol Gilligan, "In a Different Voice: Women's Conceptions of Self and of
Morality" (*Harvard Education Review*, Fall 1977); and *In a Different Voice: Psychological Theory and Women's Development* (Cambridge, Massachusetts: Harvard University Press, 1982).

stand out, paradoxically, as constructions in *tension* with human psychology. The nature of this tension and the ways it plays out over the course of development have been clarified during the past twenty years, in particular by two moves made by psychologists doing research: bringing mothers into the study of infants, and bringing girls into the study of adolescence.

When researchers studying infants brought mothers into their laboratories and filmed mothers and babies playing, they saw a world of relationship they had not imagined.[6] Babies, previously described as living in a state of primary narcissism unable to differentiate other from self, were seen actively initiating and participating in responsive relationship. A change in the angle of observation led to a finding that, once seen, appeared obvious: the baby has a voice and thus the ability to communicate with others. If our maps start from a place of relationship, it is the loss or the stunting of relationship that has to be explained. If two-month-old babies (and their mothers) can tell the difference between the *experience of relationship* (being in synchrony with another person) and the *appearance of relationship*, if they know when they are (and are not) in connection, the human world is more transparent than has previously been assumed.[7]

When the mother-baby films were slowed down and analyzed frame by frame, the tidal rhythm of human connection came into view: finding and losing and finding again, turning to, turning away, turning back again, moving in and out of touch. It is the music of love, the play of relationships, the games that delight babies and young children. But the researchers' films also pinpointed moments in the cycle when vulnerability is heightened and relationships are at risk—when losing is not followed by finding; when turning away does not result in turning back. Trust, the researchers discovered, does not depend on the mother sus-

---

6. Daniel Stern, *The Interpersonal World of the Infant* (New York: Basic Books, 1985); see also E. Z. Tronick, "Emotions and Emotional Communication in Infants," *American Psychologist* 44 (2) 1989, 112–119.

7. Lynne Murray and Colwyn Trevarthen, "Emotional Regulation of Interactions Between Two-month-olds and Their Mothers," in T. M. Fields and N. A. Fox, eds. *Social Perception in Infants* (Norwood, New Jersey: Ablex Publishing, 1985); see also Murray and Trevarthen, "The Infant's Role in Mother-Infant Communication," *Journal of Child Language* 13 (1987), 15–29.

taining a perfectly unbroken connection with her baby, but rather on the ability of mother (or father or caregiver) and baby together to establish that they can find one another again after the inevitable moments of losing touch.[8] *The continuation of relationship hinges on the process of repair,* the ability to *mend* breaks in connection.

Here the research with adolescent girls becomes critical, because it illuminates how a process that otherwise can be conceived in purely psychological terms has a political dimension.[9] In adolescence, girls may discover that precisely those abilities they rely on to repair relationships (articulating feelings, being honest) are societally unacceptable. At a time when girls often voice an intense desire for relationship, they are thus in danger of losing relationships—which may explain the intensity of their desire.[10] Listening to adolescent girls, I hear over and over again their desire for honesty in relationships, and the intensity of this desire suggests that they are encountering a dishonesty they had neither expected nor imagined.[11] *They are describing a process of initiation, culturally scripted and enforced.*

The backdrop to my understanding girls' experiences in adolescence

8. E. Z. Tronick and A. Gianino, "Interactive Mismatch and Repair Challenges in the Coping Infant: Zero to Three." *Bulletin of the Center for Clinical Infant Programs* 6 (3) 1986, 1–6; and E. Z. Tronick and M. K. Weinberg, "Depressed Mothers and Infants: Failure to Form Dyadic States of Consciousness," in L. Murray and P. J. Cooper, eds., *Postpartum Depression and Child Development* (New York: Guilford Press, 1997).

9. Carol Gilligan, "Joining the Resistance: Psychology, Politics, Girls and Women," *Michigan Quarterly Review*, Fall 1990; collected in *The Female Body*, Laurence A. Goldstein, ed. (Ann Arbor, Michigan: University of Michigan Press, 1991).

10. Carol Gilligan, "Remembering Iphigenia: Voice, Resonance, and a Talking Cure," in E. Shapiro, ed., *The Inner World in the Outer World* (New Haven: Yale University Press, 1997).

11. Carol Gilligan, Annie G. Rogers, and Deborah Tolman, eds., *Women, Girls, and Psychotherapy: Reframing Resistance* (Binghamton, New York: Haworth Press, 1991); Lyn Mikel Brown and Carol Gilligan, *Meeting at the Crossroads: Women's Psychology and Girls' Development* (Cambridge: Harvard University Press, 1992; New York: Balantine Books, 1993); Jill McLean Taylor, Carol Gilligan, and Amy Sullivan, *Between Voice and Silence: Women and Girls, Race and Relationship* (Cambridge: Harvard University Press, 1996); and Carol Gilligan, Nona P. Lyons, and Trudy Hanmer, *Making Connections: the Relational Worlds of Adolescent Girls at Emma Willard School* (Cambridge: Harvard University Press, 1990).

comes from research with younger girls. That research took place in public and private schools and after-school programs, and the girls came from a range of different social classes, different cultural and family backgrounds—all of which affect the way a girl's initiation is scripted. But one generalization that spans class and cultural differences is that preadolescent girls show remarkable acuity in reading the human world around them; they tune in to the emotional weather and follow the train of people's thoughts and feelings. These skills are so much part of the everyday that they tend to go unnoticed until they surface in surprising ways. In a family therapy session at the Tavistock Institute in London where each member of the family was asked in turn to say what the others were feeling and thinking, I observed that the mother's subjective experience was barely represented by her or any other family member— until it became the eleven-year-old girl's turn. I listened as she named her mother's thoughts and feelings, then watched her mother burst into tears. She had not imagined that anyone knew what she was experiencing.

I see this scenario repeated again and again with slight variations in families and schools as well as family therapy sessions. In dramatic skits where one girl stands behind another and plays "her thoughts," it's apparent how closely girls listen to the conversation beneath the conversation. Judy, age nine, points to her stomach when asked where her mind is; she relies on her gut feeling, her sense of emotional true north. At age eleven, she knows the fight that broke out at the dinner table when her brother refused to eat his carrots "wasn't about the carrots." But she also is aware of a difference between what she knows in her gut and what she calls "the brain knowledge."

Girls at adolescence thus may find themselves caught between a knowledge they trust through experience and a knowledge that is culturally sanctioned. The edge of disparity surfaces in a heightened awareness of the difference between how things are and how things are said to be, as if girls were trying to hold on to their sense of reality. Asking adolescent girls about their experiences of relationship, I was prepared to explain the growth of their emotional and cognitive capacities and their encounter with a new range of experiences, including new experiences of themselves. What surprised me were girls' descriptions of encountering impediments to repairing relationship, suddenly finding their relational skills ineffective. Over and over, I heard girls speak of startling betrayals. It was as if they were in danger of losing their relational footing, their sense of truth. Relational knowing, embodied knowing, connectedness, empathy, and emotional intelligence—the very grounds of relationship—were called into question. Girls' relational intelligence was manifest in their ability to describe clearly what was happening:

- Seeta, age twelve: "If I go up to my friends and say, 'Why are you mad at me?' they will just get madder and it will be like them ten and me one, lone."
- Shiela, sixteen, used a wry, witty image to capture the impasse between herself and her boyfriend: "We were standing in a relationship that was sinking, and I didn't want to say anything because it would upset him and he didn't want to say anything because it would upset me and we were just standing in water about up to our ankles, watching it rise."
- Iris, seventeen, reflecting on the outspokenness of younger girls: "If I were to say what I was feeling and thinking, no one would want to be with me, my voice would be too loud." Then adding, "But you have to have relationships."

Paradoxically, girls are discovering that *in order to have relationships they have to give up relationship.*

Thirteen-year-old Tracy and her classmates participated in a research project for five years. When I asked how they wanted to be involved now that we would be presenting the research at conferences and in a book, a hand shot up without hesitation: "We want you to tell them everything we said and we want our names in the book." Then Tracy added, "When we were nine we were stupid." I said it would never have occurred to me to use the word "stupid" to describe them when they were nine, because what had struck me most about them when they were nine was how much they knew. "I mean," Tracy explained, "when we were nine, we were honest."

I watch girls resisting the loss of honest voices and honesty in relationships—a culturally enforced loss often confused by girls themselves with rudeness, or selfishness, or insensitivity to people's feelings. I am surprised by how often girls are told not to speak, or at least not in public; how often they are reminded that people will not appreciate what they have to say. Eleven-year-old Elissa commented: "My house is wall-papered with lies." I see a healthy resistance to losses that are psychologically costly—the healthy psyche like the healthy body fighting off disease. Girls are resisting an initiation that takes the form of breaking relationship and establishing hierarchy, an initiation that imposes loss and then impedes the process of repair: losing without finding again. I see girls *resisting patriarchy:* the subordination of women to men, the division of women into Good and Bad, the sacrifice of love for "honor," the splitting of reason from emotion, the dividing of themselves from their relationships.

Girls' healthy resistance to psychologically costly loss turns into a political resistance when they confront impediments to their desire for honesty in relationships. In the process, girls may develop a refined double-consciousness, simultaneously holding the contradictions between how they see themselves and how others see them, how they perceive the world and how the world is represented. They want to be present rather than absent, to speak for themselves and to know what they know, to disagree openly rather than bury conflict. These relational skills are vital to love—and, interestingly, to citizenship in a democratic society.

When girls' political resistance becomes embattled or seems too risky, too costly, or futile, the impulse to take action goes underground or turns inward. The division girls feel between themselves and others becomes a division inside themselves. Then they may dissociate themselves from parts of themselves, so that whatever happens is not happening to *them.*

Research with adolescent girls thus uncovers paths otherwise difficult to trace: the path of *initiation* into patriarchy (breaking relationship, imposing loss, impeding the process of repair) and also the path of *resistance* (healthy resistance, political resistance, dissociation). Once dissociation sets in—once girls divide themselves from themselves and begin not to know what they really do know—the conditions for patriarchy have been established within the psyche. Once girls bury the honest voices in themselves, they can readily take on the voices of fathers (or those who speak in the name of the father) and eventually confuse these voices with their own—for as long as the dissociation continues.

Psychological research with adolescent girls—and also young boys—has recovered voices from a time that for many women and men had been lost. These were voices they did not remember, voices they found at once familiar and surprising. Recent research with very young boys shows a parallel in the broadest sense to the research with adolescent girls; it charts a similar route into initiation and a similar path of resistance. But there is a significant difference: four- and five-year-old boys are less articulate and less self-reflective than eleven- and twelve-year-old girls, and are less able to see the broader picture; they have less experience of relationship than girls do at adolescence, and they are also silenced by codes of masculinity.

The quiet revolution in the human sciences is a change in paradigm. The old paradigm, guided by images of hierarchy and compartmentalization, cannot encompass growing evidence of connectedness, and with such evidence the realization that these separations and hierarchies are fundamentally misconceived. Their explanatory value and power are overshadowed by the realization that *they stand in the way of our knowing what we know.*

Patriarchy, although frequently misunderstood to mean the oppression of women by men, literally means a hierarchy, a rule of priests, in which the priest—the *hieros*—is a father. It defines an order of living that elevates fathers, separating fathers from sons (the men from the boys), and men from women, and placing both sons and women (wives and daughters) under a father's authority. By establishing hierarchy in the heart of intimacy (fathers over sons, men over women), patriarchy is in tension with love. *The sacrifice of love becomes the hallmark of patriarchy:* Abraham's willingness to sacrifice Isaac, Jephthah's sacrifice of his daughter, Agamemnon's sacrifice of Iphigenia. Love becomes linked with sacrifice, shadowed by loss, bound by tragedy.

Sisterhood is emerging and alternative—and it *is* powerful, global, and forever. The inherent contradiction between democracy and patriarchy surfaced in the liberation movements of the late twentieth century: civil-rights struggles, anti-Vietnam-war mobilizations, women's liberation, lesbian and gay liberation, student uprisings, anti-imperialism organizing. *Feminism is, at its heart, the movement to free democracy from patriarchy.* This is the battle at the center of our current culture wars.

Until the 1970s, psychology was blindly aligned with patriarchy. That is why psychology needed feminism. And feminism needs psychology because psychology makes it clear that the codes of patriarchy are *not* written into our psyche; the divisions between good and bad guys (*and* good and bad women) and the hierarchies of fathers over sons and men over women are *written over an original, censored, natural, relational script about pleasure*.[12] A quiet revolution in the human sciences has led to the creation of a new paradigm, still in the making, encompassing evidence that we are hard-wired for love and democracy, for pleasure and cooperation.

CAROL GILLIGAN is the author, most recently, of *The Birth of Pleasure* (New York: Knopf, 2002; Vintage paperback 2003). Her 1982 book, *In a Different Voice* (see above), has been translated into 17 languages. With her students, she coauthored and co-edited five books on women's psychology and girls' development (see footnotes above). Now University Professor at New York University, she received her doctorate in psychology from Harvard and was a Harvard faculty member for 34 years, the first holder of the Patricia Albjerg Graham Professorship in Gender Studies, and a founding member of the Harvard Project on Women's Psychology and Girls' Development, a research collaborative she established with her students. The Harvard Center for Gender and Education was created in 2001 to honor and continue her research on the cultural shaping of psychological development. She dedicates this essay to her sisters in feminism—and to her granddaughter, Nora.

Suggested Further Reading

Herman, Judith. *Trauma and Recovery: The Aftermath of Violence—from Domestic Abuse to Political Terror.* New York: Basic Books, 1993.

Miller, Jean Baker, and Irene Stiver. *The Healing Connection: How Women Form Relationships and in Life* (Boston: Beacon Press, 1997).

Goldberger, Nancy, Jill Tarule, Blythe Clinchy, and Mary Belenky, eds. *Knowledge, Difference and Power: Essays on Women's Ways of Knowing.* New York: Basic Books, 1996.

Ward, Janie Victoria. *The Skin We're In.* New York: Free Press, 2000.

Way, Niobe. *Everyday Courage: The Lives and Stories of Urban Teenagers.* New York: New York University Press, 1998.

---

12. Carol Gilligan, *The Birth of Pleasure* (New York: Alfred A Knopf, 2002).

The Media and the Movement:
A User's Guide

GLORIA STEINEM

DICTATORS KNOW what they're doing when they seize control of the media even before seizing control of land or people. Image and narrative are the organizing principles on which our brains work, and the media deliver them with such power and speed that they may overwhelm our experience, actually make us feel less real than the people whose images we see. But media are not reality; reality is reality. After thirty-plus years of traveling as an organizer, I've learned that nothing replaces the experience of being there. Social justice movements (lived experience) will probably always be struggling with the media (derived impressions), and vice versa, yet neither can be credible for long without the other.

Two notes: I've defined "media" here as everything that represents reality, from newspapers and talk shows to the Internet. Movies, novels, poetry, ads, and other works of the imagination are crucial, too, but that's a different story. Second, I've used past examples that might offer ideas for the future. After all, if we don't learn to use the media, mainstream and alternate, global and local—and by "use" I mean monitor, infiltrate, replace, protest, teach with, create our own, whatever the situation demands—we will not only be invisible in the present, but absent from history's first draft.

Lesson 1: How the Movement Changed the Media

In the 1960s, on the cusp of feminism, women were identified in print as "Miss" or "Mrs.," "divorcee" or "widow," "blonde" or "brunette," not to

mention by what we wore. "Women's Pages" in newspapers featured social notes often written to please advertisers—a level of journalism that
would have been a scandal on the (male) news pages. Radio and television refused to hire women to read the news, on the premise that nothing
spoken in a female voice would be taken seriously.[1] Classified ads were
divided into "Help Wanted—Male" and "Help Wanted—Female."
Marriage-announcement pages in newspapers looked like meat markets,
with photos of brides only. The rare woman who made news in men's
terms still might get a headline like, "Grandmother Wins Nobel Prize."
At *Time* magazine, where men wrote and women researched, the most
frequent female cover subject was the Virgin Mary. "Lesbian," "gay," or
"homosexual" were words rarely used to describe anybody, partly because they could be considered libelous. On NBC's *Today Show*, Barbara
Walters was still off-camera writing a script for men to speak, beauty-
contest winners served coffee, and the only female host was a trained
chimp. Rape was described only by such euphemisms as "attacked"
or "interfered with." When African American women were raped and
murdered by European Americans, they were not counted as victims
of racially motivated crimes. Even counterculture, Left-wing, anti-
Vietnam-war kinds of media exempted women from their radical
change: "chicks," staff positions, and sexual service to draft resisters (as
in "Girls Say Yes to Men Who Say No") symbolized our role. Meanwhile, women's magazines enshrined the "feminine" role, and often ran
by formula: every marriage could be saved, only white women could be
on the cover, and, except for Helen Gurley Brown's *Cosmopolitan*, women
who had sex outside marriage were doomed to suffer a sad end.

I offer all that as a reminder of how far we've come—and therefore
how far we can go. However, the idea that the media change as reality
does is a myth. They need the same prodding tactics we've directed at,
say, academia, government, or big business (which, of course, the media
are).[2] The myth of automatic change persists for at least three reasons:

1. See "Standing By: Women in Broadcast Media," by Carol Jenkins, p. 418.—Ed.

2. See "Climbing the Ivory Walls: Women in Academia," by Jane Roland Martin,
p. 401; "Running for Our Lives: Electoral Politics," by Pat Schroeder, p. 28;
"Women and Law: The Power to Change," by Catharine A. MacKinnon, p. 447;
and "Up the Down Labyrinth: Ins and Outs of Women's Corporate and Campus
Careers," by Ellen Appel-Bronstein, p. 387.—Ed.

the media rarely report on their own inner workings; the Women's Movement is as bad as are women in general at taking credit for success; and the mainstream distorts what movements do anyway, so that others will be less likely to follow. Thus, suffragists were depicted as cigar-smoking harridans in the newspapers of their day, only to become impossibly saintly in history. Civil-rights advocates now are portrayed as seeking special privilege, and only in retrospect are viewed as righteous. My generation of feminists was first ridiculed as oversexed "women's libbers," then opposed as "anti-male," "anti-family," and even "anti-sex."[3] We haven't yet reached the safe and saintly stage. No wonder feminists get less approval than do the issues we support; as in, "I'm not a feminist, but . . ."[4]

The plain truth is that nothing changes without change-makers. Media problems like those listed above yielded to tactics like these:

- Employment ads were sex segregated until the National Organization for Women (NOW) petitioned the Equal Employment Opportunity Commission in 1966, picketed *The New York Times* in 1967, and joined such pioneers as Joanne Evans Gardner of Pittsburgh in pressuring local newspapers. Stylebooks began to change only after feminist writers suggested alternatives to sexist language, and more women journalists invaded newsrooms and unions. Grooms turned out to have faces—and brides to have occupations—after feminists complained to newspapers and picketed Bridal Fairs. "Interfered with" and other obscurantisms began to disappear once rape survivors held speak-outs,

3. "Women's liberation" was confused with 1960s "sexual liberation," but once we were seen as being serious about equality per se, a deep cultural assumption took over: sex is so presumed to be passive/dominant that feminists must therefore be anti-sex. Such an attitude won't end until equality is eroticized.

4. In public opinion polls, about a third of U.S. women identify as feminists, roughly the same proportion as identify as Republicans. When polls include a definition of feminism—"the belief in the social, economic, and political equality of males and females"—this rises to over 60 percent. (If pollsters included such multicultural equivalents as "womanist" or "*mujerista*," that number would be even higher.) Given the Right-wing demonization of feminists—including "femi-Nazi," the word popularized by radio talk-show host Rush Limbaugh—this could be seen as a major victory.

feminist legal scholars changed the laws to reflect degrees of sexual assault, rape-crisis centers pressed for media guidelines that protected a survivor's privacy, and rape came to be understood as a criminal act of violence, racial or otherwise, not of sex.[5] Indeed, the pages of *The New York Times* allowed "Ms." as a form of address only in 1986, fourteen years after Congress had passed Bella Abzug's "Ms. Bill" that forbade the federal government from using prefixes indicating marital status, and after an equal number of years of petitions and protests from women inside and outside the *Times*.

• High-spirited feminist sit-ins riveted the attention of the almost totally male editors at *Newsweek* and *The Ladies' Home Journal*, resulting in major coverage and *Journal* articles by and about the Women's Movement. A feminist seizure and occupation at *Rat*, the counterculture newspaper, first yielded an entire issue written by women, then permanent control of the paper by women. Sex-discrimination suits were brought against the Associated Press, *Newsweek, Life, Time, Fortune, Sports Illustrated,* and *The New York Times*. Media actions across the country included lunchtime demonstrations in Chicago's Loop, the invasion of a San Francisco newspaper by seventy-five women from Berkeley Women's Liberation, and a demonstration by women from the United Auto Workers that caused a Detroit TV station to cancel a show in which secretaries and wives competed to see who knew more about the wishes of their bosses/husbands.

• The Women's Movement became a change agent in itself, by creating and redefining news. In 1968, the Miss America Pageant Protest in Atlantic City, New Jersey, was the first time feminists announced they would recognize only news*women*, explaining that this was not to elicit more sympathetic coverage (on the contrary, they knew that some women reporters would bend over backward not to seem sympathetic), but rather to pressure editors to hire women reporters and to assign women to stories other than fashion, society, and flower shows. This

---

5. See "Landscape of the Ordinary: Violence Against Women," by Andrea Dworkin, p. 58.—Ed.

tactic of closing some press conferences to male reporters—despite cries of reverse discrimination—had its effect. (Neither side seemed aware that Eleanor Roosevelt had closed her White House press conferences to male reporters for the same reason: to force the media to employ women.) Coverage of issues like welfare and the Equal Rights Amendment (ERA) expanded when women's groups briefed editorial boards on their importance. New subjects and women leaders got covered when activists arrived with lists of newsworthy story ideas. Some feminist groups issued press releases with no individual names, to keep the media from designating leaders and creating stars. Others recognized the media's need for someone to quote, but rotated spokeswomen. A surprising number of women founded new media, from volunteer-run newspapers and public-access TV to radio shows, news services, and book-publishing houses. Between 1968 and 1975, more than 500 feminist publications began, including *off our backs* in Washington, D.C., *Ain't I a Woman* in Iowa City, Iowa, *It Ain't Me, Babe* in Berkeley, California, *Sojourner* in Boston, Massachusetts, and *Ms.* in New York City, the largest feminist magazine and the only one available on national newsstands. More than thirty years later, *off our backs* and *Ms.* are still publishing. So is The Feminist Press, founded in 1970 to publish new and classic books by women, a harbinger of smaller, women-owned presses that have been cropping up ever since. But whatever their duration, all were testimonies to how hard it is—and how necessary—for a movement to have media of its own, both as independent sources of information and as ways of changing the mainstream.

Lesson 2: Surviving a Backlash

By the 1980s and '90s, this is what success looked like: "Women's Pages" had turned into lifestyle sections, newswomen were visible on local and national television,[6] and Phil Donahue had demonstrated that daytime

---

6. They are still required to be better-looking and younger (by an average of fifteen years) than their male counterparts, and a woman anchor still is almost always "bal-

women viewers were interested in subjects other than food and fashion, a discovery that helped pave the way for Oprah.[7] Female reporters could finally enter locker rooms to interview male athletes, and coverage of female athletes and women's sports had improved.[8] Women journalists were allowed to attend the roasts and banquets of their own profession. Unemployment rates were no longer only taken seriously if they were for white male heads of household, and childcare was covered as an issue of social policy. Though women's magazines had very few pages left after all those praising fashion and beauty products in order to obey advertisers—such are the rules in a publishing industry that treats women's magazines like product catalogues—they did expand health and fitness coverage, and concede that women were sexual beings. After President Reagan's call to overturn *Roe v. Wade* in 1985,[9] *People* magazine featured well-known women who told their abortion stories, a feature modeled on the *Ms.* pre-*Roe v. Wade* petition signed by women declaring they had had (then illegal) abortions, and demanding that abortion be decriminalized; in 1992, *Glamour* won a National Magazine Award for its abortion coverage.[10] By 1994, the editor-in-chief positions at all the major women's magazines were held by women (a first), though such magazines were still male-owned. Naming such hitherto invisible problems as "domestic violence," "homophobia," "date rape," and "sexual harassment"—and such new goals as "reproductive freedom" and "women in development"—honored women's experiences in the 1970s and '80s. By the 1990s, such subjects were entering into general coverage of crime, economics, human rights, and foreign policy.

---

anced" by a male; how often have you seen two *women* as a team? [See Jenkins, op. cit.—Ed.]

7. *The Donahue Show* was often the first place viewers saw feminists being interviewed, and learned that they were not alone in their experiences as women. By the 1990s, Oprah was a multimedia phenomenon, with TV shows, feature films, a book club, and a national magazine.

8. See "Women in Sports: What's the Score?" by Barbara Findlen, p. 285.—Ed.

9. See "Unfinished Agenda: Reproductive Rights," by Faye Wattleton, p. 17.—Ed.

10. The 1972 *Ms.* petition was itself modeled on a published declaration signed by women in France, which led to the founding of the group Choisir, championed by Simone de Beauvoir.

The media were beginning—just beginning—to look at the world as if women mattered.

But backlash follows success as night follows day. Remembering that is the key to surviving. Employers want to retain women as the biggest source of underpaid labor (or, in the case of homemakers, as unpaid workers and full-time consumers). The religious and secular Right wants to control women's bodies as the means of reproduction, which is why they punish anything that allows the individual to separate sexuality from reproduction.[11] (This helps to explain why the same Right-wing groups pressure the media not to publicize contraception *and* lesbianism, abortion *and* sex education.)[12] Together, economic and cultural forces make a potent lobby, in and out of the media, that normalizes inequality. For insight and detail of this backlash that began in the 1980s (and is still with us at this writing), read Susan Faludi's *Backlash* (see Suggested Further Reading, below), then update it by turning on Rupert Murdoch's Fox News (the *Pravda* of the Republican Party[13]), or other TV news and magazine shows, network and cable, that are to the right of majority opinion. Even CNN, which under Ted Turner had a just-the-facts attitude and employed a higher than usual proportion of female executives, is giving way to the macho culture of AOL, owner of Time Warner and now CNN.

Backlash tactics are often so surreal that just naming them can go a long way toward defeating them. Here are some examples:

- *Declaring feminism dead.* In 1998, Erica Jong reported in *The New York Observer* that *Time* magazine had pronounced feminism

---

11. See "Combating the Religious Right," by Cecile Richards, p. 464, and "Dancing Against the Vatican," by Frances Kissling, p. 474.—Ed.

12. Also why many anti-abortion, "pro-life" groups have supported coerced sterilization (usually of women on welfare), or the death penalty. As with any authoritarianism, who has the power to decide is more important than what gets decided.

13. That is, the current Republican Party. Extremists who took it over were often former Democrats—think of Jesse Helms and Ronald Reagan—who left when the Democratic Party became more inclusive. The current Republican Party platform doesn't reflect the views of most Republicans, who are, for example, pro-choice and pro-environment in public-opinion polls.

dead at least 119 times since 1969. The occasion was yet another *Time* cover story asking, "Is Feminism Dead?"[14]

- *Accusing the media of being "liberal."* Journalists have been made to overreport Right-wing views and leaders by long, loud, strategic accusations of underreporting them. In fact, many content analyses show that center-to-progressive views are the ones underrepresented.[15]

- *Inventing Orwellian phrases.* "Right to work" is actually anti-union; "right to life" applies to the fetus but not the woman; "preferential treatment" distorts affirmative action[16]; "family values" is a code phrase that reflects traditional definitions and only a minority of contemporary families; "partial birth abortion" means the late-term removal of a fetus that is not viable; and "homosexual preference" refers merely to ending discrimination against lesbian women and gay men.

- *Training anti-feminist spokeswomen, and demanding equal time for*

---

14. For a spirited response, see "Feminists Want to Know: Is the Media Dead?" in *Manifesta: Young Women, Feminism, and the Future,* by Jennifer Baumgartner and Amy Richards (New York: Farrar, Straus and Giroux, 2000).

15. Media Tenor International, a nonpartisan, Germany-based media analysis firm, surveyed the three major U.S. TV networks throughout 2001 and concluded that "Network news demonstrated a clear tendency to showcase the opinions of the most powerful political and economic actors, while giving limited access to those voices that would be most likely to challenge them." Of news sources, 75 percent were Republicans, 24 percent Democrats, and 1 percent Independents. Women were 15 percent of all sources, African Americans 7 percent, Latinos and Arab Americans 0.6 percent each, Asian Americans 0.2 percent, and Native Americans 0.008 (exactly one person). As with women of all races, men from racial minorities were more likely to be presented as citizens than experts. Union representatives comprised less than 0.2 percent of sources, while corporate spokespersons were 35 times more likely to be heard. Of partisan sources on labor issues, 89 percent were Republicans, 11 percent Democrats. (For additional data in this report, contact *i.howard. mediatenor.com*.)

16. Despite twenty years of allegations that affirmative action lowers standards (it generally raises them), or requires quotas (it's mainly about assuring an open process), a 1995 Harris Poll found that 68 percent of Americans still supported it. By contrast, only 11 percent supported "preferential treatment." Therefore, Right-wing media spokespeople—and anti-affirmative action referenda—just switched phrases. "Racial preference" also concealed the fact that affirmative action benefits white women as well as racial minorities.

their views.[17] An issue may be supported by a majority of women, 60/40 or even 70/30, but confining its discussion to two women arguing will give the impression that women are divided 50/50, also that two women can't get along. Meanwhile, the media have been relieved of doing independent reporting.[18]

- *Flat-out lying.* The Bible makes very clear that abortion is not murder, as those who would criminalize it contend.[19] Similarly, comparative international studies show that sex education and contraception do not cause young people to have more sex, nor do they cause people to have first sexual contact at a younger age.

Fortunately, the numbers of groups practicing such tactics are small. The larger problem is the basic conservatism of corporately owned, advertising-driven media, which provide fertile ground for their seeds.[20]

---

17. To get an idea of the sophistication and money that goes into this training, consider The Leadership Institute. Founded in 1979 by Morton C. Blackwell, former head of Youth for Reagan, this multimillion-dollar facility in Arlington, Virginia, features state-of-the-art TV and radio studios, briefings on issues, a job-placement bank, and dormitories that keep its trainees isolated for maximum influence. With its $8 million annual budget, the Institute, as its website explains, "identifies, recruits, trains and places" conservative leadership that is "unwavering in its commitment to free enterprise, limited government, and traditional values." To "pave the way for a new generation of conservative leadership," the Institute also conducts a "Boot Camp of Politics" on campuses, where students are taught to "stop liberals in their tracks." With 30,000 graduates, including a brigade of anti-feminist women, and such Right-wing stars as the Christian Coalition's Ralph Reed, who now teaches there, the results are probably on your evening news.

18. This is what happened to the ERA. Surveys showed that coverage of it in the media increased confusion. No major media ever did an independent report on what the ERA actually would and wouldn't do. Many articles didn't even include its wording: "Equality of rights under the law shall not be denied or abridged by the United States or by any State on account of sex."

19. Exodus, Chapter 21, Verse XXII. In all versions, a man who strikes a woman and causes her to abort has not committed murder, and is required only to pay a fine set by her husband.

20. Control of the media by an ever-diminishing number of corporate owners also means that content is cross-marketed, creating a kind of monoculture. Blockbuster movies are hyped by exposure on a TV network, both owned by the same company; a book is promoted into a best-seller by exposure on a TV network that owns the

For example, it wasn't the Right wing that invented *Newsweek*'s infamous (June 2, 1986) report that a single woman in her thirties had more chance of getting killed by a terrorist than finding a husband. This bit of misinformation spread like wildfire apparently because many in the media favored evidence that uppity women get punished. On the other hand, Right-wing groups had always opposed sexual-harassment law, and tried to distort and get rid of it—just as they had affirmative-action law—but the media didn't report this background. Instead, they often accepted the later Right-wing contention that sexual-harassment law forbade *all* sex in the workplace, or *all* sex between unequals, even though this interpretation was invented only in an attempt to impeach President Clinton. (In fact, sexual-harassment law addresses *unwelcome* sex and the creation of a hostile environment in school or in the workplace.[21])

Nonetheless, a combination of well-financed anti-feminist activism, the pressure of advertising, increased concentration of media ownership in a few corporations, and garden-variety sexism and racism have combined to make getting coverage for the full range of women's concerns, news, and leaders very difficult. They also have slowed or stopped the progress made in absorbing the female half of the world's concerns and leadership into such areas as science, politics, and international trade.[22] As Pippa Norris noted, this is true even for women in the U.S. Congress, who are more likely to be covered for their work on health and welfare than on foreign policy or military appropriations.[23] Media stud-

---

publishing house; radio stations become unpopulated studios with whirring computer discs that spew out the same news and music nationwide, eliminating the expense of local reporting and disc jockeys who might discover new artists. For a report and chart of who owns what, see "Big Media," a special issue of *The Nation*, 7/14, January 2002.

21. See "The Nature of the Beast: Sexual Harassment," by Anita Hill, p. 296, and "Women and Law: The Power to Change," by Catharine A. MacKinnon, p. 447.—Ed.

22. See "Changing a Masculinist Culture: Women in Science, Engineering, and Technology," by Donna M. Hughes, p. 393; "Running for Our Lives: Electoral Politics," by Pat Schroeder, p. 28; and "Globalization: A Strategic Advance for Feminism?" by Jessica Neuwirth, p. 526.—Ed.

23. "Women Leaders Worldwide: A Splash of Color in the Photo Op," by Pippa Norris, in *Women, Media, and Politics*, edited by Pippa Norris (New York: Oxford University Press, 1997).

ies agree: in the absence of specific knowledge to the contrary, stereotypes prevail.

Lesson 3: New Media and the Future

With the Internet, it's almost as if media themselves had been atomized, so that each of us now has our own TV network/radio station/newspaper. You only have to listen to young girls talk about a home page for their website and publishing their own 'zine, or discover for yourself a community of shared experience in cyberspace, to know that the Internet has subversive potential. Women who once tried unsuccessfully to look up "feminism" in the phone book can now go to dozens of websites to connect to the Women's Movement.[24]

But the Internet also has a downside. We have become even more economically polarized by who has access to technology and who doesn't, and women who rely mainly on the Internet may cocoon—seek out the like-minded—while ceding to others control of mainstream media that still elect candidates and frame social policy. Furthermore, there is no such thing as a virtual movement. Our actual lives either change or they don't.

For example, I felt comforted after the September 2001 attacks on New York and Washington when I found women on the worldwide web who were condemning terrorism yet calling for a response that wasn't confined to bombing, retribution, and more terrorism. We networked and created a joint statement—Afghan and U.S. women, Jewish and Muslim women: definitely a good thing. But with hindsight, I'm reasonably sure we had no impact at all on the U.S. bombing of Afghanistan that may have killed more victims of the Taliban and Al Qaeda than members of both groups, not to mention killing some allied peacekeepers. On the Sunday political talk shows that shape issues and establish experts, the number of women guests dropped by 40 percent in the same period—from one in nine to one in thirteen—so sure were the powers-that-be that war and peace were a male affair.[25] In retrospect, we would

---

24. See "Cyberfeminism: Networking the Net," by Amy Richards and Marianne Schnall, p. 517.—Ed.

25. "Who's Talking, An Analysis of Sunday Morning Talk Shows," a 2001 survey conducted by The White House Project, noted that all three of the principal U.S.

have been better off spending less time networking with each other and more time getting women's protests into mainstream media.

As in the past, the answer lies in *surrounding* our goals, not just approaching them from one direction, whether that's using the Internet, writing a book, holding a press conference, or campaigning for a presidential candidate who will again appoint a Federal Communications Commission that limits media ownership in the public interest. While strategizing to get coverage in the mainstream media, we must also expose its Right-wing slant. While using the Internet for all it's worth, we need to make sure that women in remote areas have hand-cranked radios that require no electricity, much less high-tech expertise, or even literacy. While we fight for the education of women and girls, who are two-thirds of the world's illiterates, we must also remember that oral traditions hold libraries full of wisdom, encouragement, health information, and history. The question isn't: which media to use? The question is: how to use them all?

What we need is a Women's Media Movement that is at least as important as the Women's Health Movement or as efforts to get women elected. It should be coordinated with other progressive movements directed at the media, and be as much a part of our consciousness and daily actions as feminism itself. To that end, I offer some guidelines, from small to large, that I've gathered over the years as a media worker. Each of you will add to them:

- If you're introducing a new idea that's open to misinterpretation, better to use TV or radio first. In print, you and your message will be filtered through the minds, adjectives, and editing of writers, perhaps even advertisers. On radio, your own words will be heard. On TV, the viewer will also see you and get some sense of intent and sincerity.
- When false charges are made against you—and they will be— think twice before answering in public. You may just republicize the false charges.

Senate subcommittees on terrorism are headed by women—Senators Boxer, Feinstein, and Landrieu—yet not one of them showed up as an expert in the way that male senators and retired military leaders did.

- Media deal in the unexpected. They report the exception, not the rule. You will greatly increase the chance of getting a general truth or experience covered if you find a surprising person or a coalition of unexpected groups to espouse it at the press conference. For example, homemakers and women on welfare who join together because both want to value work done in the home, or the relative of a murder victim who opposes capital punishment for the murderer, or an admired celebrity willing to highlight an issue felt by the poor and obscure.

- Remember, language is half the battle. The feminist term "reproductive freedom" was more true to what we had in mind than "population control." The struggle against religious fascism in Afghanistan wasn't expressed by "discrimination against women," but took a leap forward with the phrase, "gender apartheid."

- Go back and reread the footnote about the Leadership Institute. Now ask yourself: what kind of media training are we doing? The point is not to imitate the adversary, but to help create experienced, well-informed, diverse spokespeople. Some may have turned up by accident in the early years of the movement, but we can no longer count on on-the-job learning. Every feminist group needs a media-training component.

- Journalism schools should be recruiting feminist faculty. What better place to help a generation of journalists remove the patriarchal lens from their vision than a school that trains reporters, editors, and TV producers to look at the world as if *everyone* mattered?

- Become the change you wish to see in the media. If you are well-known, try not to speak to the media without bringing along a woman who isn't well-known, preferably one of a race, occupation, or ethnicity different from yours. If you're not well-known, go to an experienced spokeswoman you admire and ask if you can assist her while learning.

- Organize some creative demonstrations; bring an imaginative lawsuit. Whether or not you win right away, both can raise public consciousness and become stepping-stones to eventual victory.

- Advertising, the most ubiquitous censor of all, will become less of an influence only as we protest its power over editorial content and/or pay more for our own media. There is always the tactic of consumer boycott. We could stop buying products that own or sponsor biased media, magazines that are really catalogues, on-line services that litter the screen with ads and sell personal subscriber information, and—well, you get the idea. Remember, we have body power, dollar power, and vote power. Use them all.

Lesson 4: If They Could Do It . . .

When you get discouraged at the contrast between the media and the movement, in imagery or in power, think about women in the abolitionist and suffragist era. They rarely owned property, much less a press, because they *were* property. Learning to read was against the law for slaves, and for all females it was thought to endanger fertility by sending blood to the brain and away from the reproductive organs. Women who spoke in public were breaking the law. The names of upper-class women were supposed to appear in print only when they were born, married, or buried.

Yet suffragists and abolitionists of all races organized "shadow" events wherever reporters were gathered for some official one, marched uninvited at the end of official parades, and otherwise made sure they were visible to the media of their day.[26] They circulated diaries and letters among themselves and wrote essays and novels for any available publication. From Sojourner Truth, a freed slave, to the Grimké sisters, who were white southerners, many traveled and gave speeches that were media events in themselves. They even started such subversive periodicals as *The Women's Advocate for the Female Industrial Classes*, Elizabeth Cady Stanton and Susan B. Anthony's *The Revolution*, and Matilda Joslyn Gage's newspaper supporting the Native American cause and documenting the high status of women in Native cultures as an argument for the equality of all women. Ida B. Wells-Barnett reported

---

26. See "African American Women: The Legacy of Black Feminism," by Beverly Guy-Sheftall, p. 176.—Ed.

lynchings when she herself might have been lynched for doing so, and journalist Nellie Bly risked permanent incarceration by committing herself to an asylum in order to interview wives who had been wrongfully committed.

I could go on and on with such examples of women's historical struggles to be seen and heard. With this inspiration, and with all the world now only seconds away, can we fail to seize the moment—*and* the media?

GLORIA STEINEM is a writer, lecturer, and organizer whose books include *Outrageous Acts and Everyday Rebellions* (Holt, Rhinehart and Winston, 1983), *Revolution from Within* (Little, Brown, 1992), and *Moving Beyond Words* (Simon & Schuster, 1994). She co-founded *Ms.* magazine, the National Women's Political Caucus, Voters for Choice, and the Ms. Foundation for Women.

Suggested Further Reading

Faludi, Susan. *Backlash: The Undeclared War Against American Women.* New York: Crown, 1991; Anchor Paperback, 1992.

Russo, Ann, and Cheris Kramarae. *The Radical Women's Press of the 1850s.* New York: Women's Resource Library/Routledge (Routledge, Chapman, and Hall, Inc.), 1991.

Steinem, Gloria. "Sex, Lies, and Advertising," in G. Steinem, *Moving Beyond Words.* New York: Simon & Schuster, 1994.

Activist resources: The Annenberg Public Policy Center (Washington, D.C.) monitors the state of women as reported on, decision-makers in, and gaining ownership of, the media: *appcdc@appcpenn.org.*; Fairness and Accuracy in Reporting, a national monitoring/watchdog group, issues special reports on women: *www.fair.org*; The International Women's Media Foundation (Washington, D.C.) seeks to strengthen women's role in media through education, forums, and networking women journalists internationally: *www.iwmf.org*; The Women's Institute for Freedom of the Press, a national and international network, seeks to democratize the media by expanding freedom of the press, and publishes a Directory of Women's Media: *www.wifp.org.* See also Women's E-News *(www.womensenews.org).*

PART II.

A Movement for All Seasons

Girls: "We Are the Ones Who Can Make a Change!"

ANA GROSSMAN AND
EMMA PETERS-AXTELL

WHAT IS THE GIRLS' MOVEMENT? Well, we're girls. But we—and most other girls—don't talk about a "Girls' Movement." We just think life should be fair, and things should be equal between girls and guys. And we still have a long way to go to reach that goal.

So, who are we? And who are we to tell you what the Girls' Movement is to girls? We're Ana and Emma; we're both fourteen years old as we write this; and we've been friends since—forever! We're also both editors for *New Moon: The Magazine for Girls and Their Dreams.* That means we hear from a lot of girls. We hear about what girls are doing and thinking. We hear girls' opinions on what they find unfair, and on what they do to change things in their daily life.

We don't actually *call* ourselves "The Girls' Movement," because we just don't feel there is a large organized girls' movement going on, like there is with adult feminism. Also, even though we know there's a long way to go, we feel we've already come a long way, *because* of feminism. Compared to how things were thirty years ago, we feel very lucky to be girls *now.*

We define feminism in terms of our everyday actions: how we react to unfair situations and what we do to change them.

Here are a few stories from girls we are in touch with. These stories show why we still need feminism and how it helps us.

- *"I love sports and play baseball, but since I'm a girl, I always play out-field. I'm pretty good. There are a lot of other girls who play outfield, too. But the boys play infield—where the ball goes."—Kay, from Brussels, Belgium.*

Sports is one area where things have really gotten better for girls (because of Title IX). But there's still unfairness.[1] Last year, Emma's soccer team was discriminated against because they're girls. Her school has one good playing field and the girls weren't allowed to scrimmage there—while boys' teams *were* allowed. The female coach didn't fight the decision because she was worried about retaliation later from the Director of Athletics. Even though we were inspired by our country's huge excitement about the U.S. Women's Soccer Team triumphs in 2000, when it comes closer to home, we're still struggling.

- *"I think things are pretty equal right now, but some aspects of equality need work."—Olya, 14, from Duluth, Minnesota.*

One thing that is still unequal is how people think about "women's jobs" and "men's jobs." Ana's goal is to be a lawyer and one day run for president of the United States. Right now there really are too few women leaders in politics.[2] But when Ana tells people her goals, they sort of laugh and say "Ohhhh . . ." But in their voices it sounds like they are really saying, "She's just a kid, and she doesn't know what she wants, and that goal is *way* too high." In fact, Ana has thought a lot about the process of getting there (lawyer and later president) and she knows what it involves to reach the goal. Also, many people automatically assume that she wants to be the *first* woman president—which she doesn't. She says, "It will be twenty-three years before it is even *possible* for me to run for president, and that is *way* too long for this country to wait for a woman president!!!"

- *"Recently, a girl in my class was assaulted. She didn't want the adults to find out. But I told a teacher and he got her some help from the school nurse."—Molly, 13, from Compton, Rhode Island.*

It's terrible that many girls experience harassment, assault, or date

---

1. See "Women in Sports: What's the Score?" by Barbara Findlen, p. 285. —Ed.

2. See "Running for Our Lives: Electoral Politics," by Pat Schroeder, p. 28.—Ed.

rape.[3] But we can help each other deal with these things. A friend of Emma's was being verbally harassed at school. The things that were said to her made her suffer a great deal. She became self-conscious and withdrawn. But her friends helped her, and with their extra encouragement she felt courageous enough to take the problem to the principal.

- *"I wish the media would realize that girls should be recognized for being talented and healthy-looking."—Justine, 12, from Chicago, Illinois.*

Media image—that's a *huge* issue for girls.[4] When we see unrealistic, "perfect" images over and over, telling us that looking *that* way will make us popular, we start to think those images are the "right" ones. And if that isn't enough, the faces and bodies of models and celebrities are airbrushed to make them even *more* perfect! Many girls then see these impossible images, and strive to be just like them. This creates self-consciousness and low self-esteem. Some girls even end up hurting their bodies, trying to become thinner or look different, in order to fit those images.

We think that's awful—and at *New Moon*, we're *doing* something about it. In 2000, we created the international "Turn Beauty Inside Out" (TBIO) Campaign. Thousands of people have joined it. TBIO protests the narrow way media portrays girls and women. We put the focus on Inner Beauty instead. In 2001, we went to New York to meet with advertising executives. We told them what we thought was good *and* bad in ads, and we developed the "Best Practices for Advertising and Girls." In 2002, we went to Los Angeles, California, to protest Hollywood's images of girls and women. We should not be treated as objects and should not be judged based on our appearance! We should be seen for who we are as *people*!

These stories show what feminism means to us—and that we still

---

3. See "The Nature of the Beast: Sexual Harassment," by Anita Hill, p. 296, and "Landscape of the Ordinary: Violence Against Women," by Andrea Dworkin, p. 58.—Ed.

4. See "The Media and the Movement: A User's Guide," by Gloria Steinem, p. 103, and "Standing By: Women in Broadcast Media," by Carol Jenkins, p. 418.—Ed.

need it. But things are better for girls and women than they were, and we thank feminism for that. It shows that real change *can* happen—*and that women and girls can make it happen.*

In the future, we want women and girls to be treated equally with men and boys; to get the respect men and boys get. We want girls to be encouraged to become scientists and mathematicians. We want girls to be allowed to play any sport a guy can. We want equality in the workplace, at school, and in sports. We want equal opportunity and equal pay. We also want equal representation. Women should be expected and encouraged to take political positions. We want to walk down the halls at school and the streets of our city and feel safe from violence against us. We want to end stereotypes against girls and women.

Equality will not only improve society's view of girls and women; equality will also help us speak up—for ourselves *and* for other people.

We have great dreams for how the world can be a better place. Together, we can make these dreams real.

As Catlyn, 13, of Seattle, Washington, says, "The world would be a better place if girls understood that *we are the ones who can make a change!*"

ANA GROSSMAN (born 1987) loves to read and chat with friends. She wants to be a defense attorney and someday run for president. Ana joined the *New Moon* Girls Editorial Board (GEB) when she was 11.

EMMA PETERS-AXTELL (born 1987) joined *New Moon's* GEB when she was eight. She loves to write poetry and draw. Emma has many dreams for the future, like becoming a politician, lawyer, social worker, or teacher.

The Duluth, Minnesota-based *New Moon: The Magazine for Girls and Their Dreams* was founded in 1992 by Nancy Gruver, Nia Kelly, Mavis Gruver, and Joe Kelly. Its unique editorial board puts girls (ages 8–14) in charge of the award-winning magazine's content (*http://www. newmoon.org*).

Suggested Further Reading

Bolden, Tonya, ed. *33 Things Every Girl Should Know About Women's History*. New York: Alfred A. Knopf, 2002.

Dee, Catherine. *The Girls' Guide to Life*. New York: Little, Brown & Co., 1997.

Girls Know Best Series (three books). Hillsboro, Oregon: Beyond Words Publishing, 1997, 1998, 1999.

Johnston, Andrea. *Girls Speak Out: Finding Your True Self*. New York: Scholastic Press, 1997.

New Moon Books Girls Editorial Board. New Moon book series (four titles: *Friendship; Sports; Money; Writing*). New York: Crown Publishers, 1999, 2000.

Generation "Why?":
A Call to Arms

JASMINE VICTORIA

I'M NOT SURE who decides what the age group is for so-called generations like Gen X or Gen Y, or who gets to name them—but I definitely think that young people need to break out of this mold being set for us. The idea that a generation full of bright, motivated, young individuals can be defined by a randomly chosen letter of the alphabet seems to me not only ridiculous but insulting. I'd prefer to call my generation of women "Generation 'Why?' " in honor of the first question many of us asked as young children—and in honor of the question we must never forget to *keep* asking.

I've asked a lot of questions during my so-far nineteen years of life. Once, when I was six, I asked my uncle, "Isn't racism disgusting?" Thinking someone had said something to me, he asked me what had happened, to which I replied, "Nothing. I was just thinking. . . ." Starting at age eight, I became a reporter for a children's news service called Children's Express. Although I was very young at the time, I was conscientious regarding the types of stories I signed up for—mainly politically affiliated or women's news stories. On one particular assignment, when I was about eleven, I went to cover the first Town Hall Meeting for Girls, sponsored by the Ms. Foundation for Women. This turned out to be the occasion for a formal announcement of the first ever "Take Our Daughters to Work Day." That day I met many prominent women, including Carol Jenkins, then an anchor for New York NBC television news.[1] At the end of the meeting, I had a chance to ask some questions.

---

1. See "Standing By: Women in Broadcast Media," by Carol Jenkins, p. 418.—Ed.

When I'd finished my interviews, my mother prodded me to do some private investigating of my own, so I asked Carol if she had any plans for Take Our Daughters to Work Day. She told me she was going to bring several girls along on a few reporting assignments, and I asked if I could join her for the day. Thus began my induction into the world of feminism.

After spending a day as an NBC News reporter (and making several cameos for the evening news), I found myself chosen as the new "poster child" for Take Our Daughters to Work Day. I co-hosted several events, and made some appearances on radio and TV talk shows with other girl activists, to discuss issues that were then pertinent to girls' lives. Not long after, there I was, presenting at press conferences to announce other new events of special importance to girls (like the YWCA/YMCA's Week Without Violence), and assisting at such functions as the first ever Girls' United Nations Conference.

Many of the issues we dealt with at that time had to do with self-esteem and with peer-pressure problems. These are concerns I'm sure girls still have today, though I couldn't *pretend* to know what problems middle-school girls deal with now.[2] Times have changed drastically, but I can imagine that certain difficulties we had back then have only intensified. I can, however, speak from experience about changes I've seen as I've grown older. A major positive one concerns anorexia/bulimia. I won't claim this is no longer a problem, because it's obvious to anyone who has picked up a fashion magazine recently that things haven't changed *that* much. But at least young women are no longer afraid to *talk* about this issue now. Once upon a time, anorexia was only whispered about. That silence was something we, as young women, felt was our responsibility to change. I remember an incident during my senior year in high school, when a group of tenth graders came up to me and my friends during lunch, to express concerns about one of their classmates' eating habits. This sparked a discussion among us about what steps to take: should we approach her? or involve an authority figure? In the end, a couple of us spoke with the girl and convinced her that she needed to talk with a couple of faculty advisers. Once things were

---

2. See "Girls: 'We Are the Ones Who Can Make a Change!'" by Ana Grossman and Emma Peters-Axtell, p. 121.—Ed.

brought to their attention, her parents became involved, and the girl was able to get some therapy for her problem. The fact that those tenth graders felt comfortable enough to speak up on behalf of their friend showed courage, and was a tremendous step in the right direction. When I was a tenth grader, there were girls in my class we secretly suspected had eating disorders, but we just hoped the problem would correct itself. We would never have thought to utter a word about it to anyone outside the class.

I think one of the biggest issues facing women my age today is the debate over abortion rights. The rate of teenage pregnancies is dropping, but is still too high. In my first year at college, I knew of at least three first-year women and several sophomores (not to mention the girls I had known of in high school) who found themselves faced with the difficult task of choosing education over motherhood.

Although sometimes I think that we as young women take for granted a lot of the freedoms we have today (failing to realize that the struggle is an *ongoing* process), I do feel renewed hope when I see on-campus groups protesting anti-choice proposals to ban abortions.[3] If I worry at times that we young women have become too comfortable with our present situation, that we forget to keep asking "why?" and instead settle for what we have, I can (gratefully) say that *abortion is one issue we will not let get lost in the shuffle, because we know the importance of freedom of choice—and we value it.*

There are, of course, other issues where young women are making their voices heard.[4] Where body-image is concerned, now more than ever we're challenging conventional ideas of beauty, and making the advertising and fashion worlds question their practices of hawking too-perfect, too-thin women's bodies. And the list goes on. In one study,[5] 97 percent of so-called Gen Y women believe in equal pay for equal work, 92 percent think that one's gender should not limit one's lifestyle choices, a surprising 89 percent say they think a woman can be success-

3. See "Unfinished Agenda: Reproductive Rights," by Faye Wattleton, p. 17.—Ed.

4. See *www.thirdwavefoundation.org.*—Ed.

5. Exclusive study conducted for *American Demographics* magazine by Element, a New York City-based youth-market-research firm. See "Granddaughters of Feminism: Gen Y Girls," by Rebecca Gardin, *American Demographics*, April 2001.

ful without either a man or children, and yet 57 percent say they intend to have it all—career, husband, and kids. Only 34 percent of us actually label ourselves "feminist"—yet overwhelmingly we share feminism's goals and values, *and* show its influence: for instance, we expect to achieve higher educational goals and get higher degrees than guys our age do. In 2000, many young women responded to an on-line survey at *ChickClick.com*, to identify our three most crucial issues in the 2000 elections: education (17 percent of respondents), abortion (11 percent), and school violence (8 percent).[6]

I suppose in some ways this article could be read as a call to arms: a reminder to all young women not to forget to ask that ever so important question. After all, where would we be if women like Elizabeth Cady Stanton, Susan B. Anthony, and Sojourner Truth hadn't asked such questions as "*Why* can't women vote?" and "*Why* don't women have property rights?" If they hadn't asked *why*, we would be *completely* powerless in what is already a male-dominated society. But if we keep asking questions, keep standing up for our beliefs, and promise ourselves that we won't ever shrug and turn our backs on any injustice, no matter how large or small—then I believe that Generation "Why" will ensure the continuation of feminism into the next era, and that it will be the key to unlock more freedom for everyone.

JASMINE VICTORIA was born in 1981 to Celeste Torres-Victoria and Bruce Winfield. She lives in New York City, but is currently [2002] a student and University Scholar at Duke University, where she continues to be active fighting racism and sexism and working to promote cultural awareness through various school organizations and projects. A Comparative Area Studies major and Markets and Managements Certificate minor, she hopes to pursue a career in international business and investment banking. She wishes to dedicate her article as follows:

For Celeste Torres-Victoria,
February 21, 1960–September 11, 2001
The strongest, most beautiful woman I have ever known.
I live to make you proud, Mom. I love you.

---

6. Rebecca Gardin article, op. cit.

Suggested Further Reading

Baumgardner, Jennifer, and Amy Richards. *Manifesta: Young Women, Feminism, and the Future.* New York: Farrar, Straus and Giroux, 2000.

Findlen, Barbara, ed. *Listen Up: Voices from the Next Feminist Generation.* Seattle, Washington: Seal Press, 1995.

Morgan, Robin, ed. *Sisterhood Is Global: The International Women's Movement Anthology.* New York: Doubleday/Anchor, 1984; reissued with updated introduction, New York: The Feminist Press at CUNY, 1996.

Walker, Alice. *In Search of Our Mothers' Gardens.* New York: Harcourt, 1983.

Gen X Survivor: From Riot Grrrl Rock Star to Feminist Artist

KATHLEEN HANNA

ON THE DAY that woulda been my graduation from college I was probably in some smelly club singing with my band, Viva Knieval. I'm sure I spoke out against rape that night (I almost always did), heckled back at the men who were heckling me, and smiled at the two or three girls I could see pushing toward the front. Volunteer work at a rape crisis/domestic violence shelter had prepared me for the outpourings of emotion many women would express after the punk shows I played—and college had taught me the postmodernist, deconstructive theories that would later inform my art and fuel its critique of mainstream culture. But feminist history (or "herstory") was still just a footnote to a footnote in my mind, illustrated by some blurry picture of a suffragette holding an illegible sign.

Because of this, I lacked the knowledge to situate my own agenda in the history of the Women's Movement, and especially in radical feminist organizing. The press-hyped construction of the Riot Grrrl movement that gained widespread notoriety in the 1990s—and my role in the media narrative of that phenomenon—were further obstacles to my gaining any historical context. Encouraged to regard our priorities and political style as atypical, antagonistic, and unique to our own generation, we consigned ourselves to reinventing the wheel (as if that were our personal affliction).

I began calling myself a feminist in 1988, the same year some friends and I started a women's art gallery in Olympia, Washington. I gained my chops at that place: put out press releases; negotiated decisions with eight other women; questioned my feelings on pornography, censorship, and art; and wondered how to reach out to a community beyond my immediate peers. That same year I started volunteering at Safeplace, the local shelter—where I got an education beyond my wildest expectations.

Back at the gallery, money was tight (Olympia wasn't the hottest market for feminist photography), so we started putting on rock shows. While several great girl bands were around (Scrawl, Babes in Toyland, and the greatest singer ever, Monica from The Obituaries), most bands we booked were dudes singing the standard "that girl is a real bitch and I hate her" fare over not-so-tight rockbeats. But I wanted to hear songs about what I was learning at the shelter! Songs about how to undo centuries of white-skin privilege, songs about the connections between class and gender, songs about being sexual that didn't cast me as a babe in a tight ZZTop dress. I also wanted to be onstage so I could tell girls about the new teen sexual-assault group we were starting. Since I knew that this would sound better coming from the mouth of a girl in a cool band than coming from plain old me, I decided to *become* the girl in the cool band. I didn't even know that I was really becoming an organizer.

Reading Kathy Acker on the bus. Singing a cappella at a cabaret we staged. Starting my first band. Answering crisis phones. Giving Babes in Toyland directions to the club. I had so much energy, anger, and fear coursing through me! But I still knew almost nothing about feminism. So, as I began to invent my own brand of rebellious-woman panache, I did it with the same biases against feminism most kids of my generation had absorbed: feminists hated any woman who wore lipstick; feminists were anti-sex prudes; feminists liked folk music but dismissed rock 'n' roll as too male. Of course, my solution to everything back then was just to pick up a bass and sing real loud. Little did I know.

By 1990, I was touring with my new band, Bikini Kill. I'd grown more confident onstage, often demanding that women stand up front while we played (for our safety *and* theirs). My bandmates Tobi and Kathi were influencing me on everything from film theory to Marxism, while we rushed around collecting addresses from women who might attend our future shows, in hopes of building a base of female fans who would support and critique our work. Though detractors claimed our music suffered, being "too political," I considered the points of contact between feminist art theory, grassroots activism, and punk rock as the *success* of our art. And we discovered that girls across the country were as hungry as we were to reimagine feminism for themselves, and to change the landscape of a masculinist punk scene that left them sitting on the sidelines. Meanwhile, I was strengthening my range as an artist, singing songs as male and female characters struggling inside one body, for instance, which made our performances pretty memorable. After three years of hard work, our shows were selling out. And people were actually paying *attention* to what I had to say.

But as the newly confident-feminist-self-I-was-trying-to-be confronted sexual politics at every turn, my insides slid around, about as stable as a doe on ice. Nothing in my upbringing or my experience with the "outside world" had taught me what it was like to be *listened* to. As a result, I often overshot my goals. Being silenced for years had bottled up a Molotov cocktail inside me, and suddenly coming to speech meant that I was bound to throw that cocktail through some of the wrong windows.

Coming of age as an artist during the media heyday of ACT UP, Queer Nation, The Guerrilla Girls,[1] and WAC (Women's Action Coalition), allowed me to romanticize the confrontational, theatrical tactics I associated with such groups. In my anger at both big corporations *and* the many assholes in my scene, I sometimes failed to make distinctions between their relative power. Naively, I often refused smart, compassionate dialogue in favor of publicly humiliating my "opponents." Had I known more about the rich repertoire of tactical approaches used by feminists before me, I might have learned earlier how to apply strategies wisely instead of settling for a lazy, instant, one-size-fits-all approach.

By 1991, when my band moved to Washington, D.C., I was tired of scattered conversations in backstage alleys after shows, and I was ready to seek out a real feminist community. Some friends and I handed out flyers to other girls in the punk scene, saying we wanted to start a women's group. Lo and behold: women showed up. Of course, since I still knew so little about the history of contemporary feminism—what some have called "the second wave"—I had no idea that what we really ended up having was a consciousness-raising meeting: a CR group.

---

1. See "Women and the Art World: Diary of the Feminist Masked Avengers," by the Guerrilla Girls, p. 437.—Ed.

I remember the shock-filled relief many of us felt, just being in a room together without men. We talked a lot about sexism and homophobia; we shared skills and we formed bands; we came out as bisexuals, lesbians, and/or sexual-abuse survivors who needed each other. We planned benefit shows (even a bake sale). We organized a convention—attended by more than 100 women from all over the country—that included workshops on body image, rape, and racism, followed by musical events featuring female performers. We helped each other produce 'zines, and created these new, politically based forms of writing along with a distribution plan to get women's writing out to the world. These activities, along with the informal group of female musicians, agitators, and activists who supported and critiqued us, melded into an anti-sexist/pro-girl underground that's still around today.

After the Riot Grrrl convention (August 1992), I became somewhat distanced from the group. I went back out on a chaotic tour that seemed to go on forever, and I wasn't around for a lot of what Riot Grrrl would become. I do know that after the convention the media went crazy on us. *USA Today* did a huge article and everyone, from *Newsweek* to *Cosmopolitan*, followed. As the perceived frontwoman for my band, Bikini Kill, and an original member of the RG group, I was easily mislabeled Queen Riot Grrrl. My peers, who knew that Riot Grrrl was much more than a scheme hatched from my individual brain, were rightfully frustrated at the media portrayal of me as the leading lady. Unfortunately, this frustration was often directed at *me*—though I too was hurt by the attention. I referred to this sudden fame as "poison candy," that is, when I felt safe enough to refer to it at all. Because many grrrls in the group became resentful, there was little feminist support for me as a woman. Meanwhile, article after article appeared, demonizing me as a sexually abused, man-hating stripper on a mission to corrupt teenaged minds. This devastated me personally. It also robbed me of the anonymity I needed at my job (yeah, yeah, I was a stripper).

The Riot Grrrl phenomenon I knew in the '90s wasn't ever really the cohesive political movement many reporters claimed it to be. It was more like a music scene, one that used politics as a way to shape itself. It created feminist songs and 'zines, benefit concerts and parties; it raised consciousness. But it didn't formulate policy, or even protest much outside the parameters of underground music. This led to a self-referential insularity that often confused personality conflicts and petty intrigues with serious dialogues about race, class, and power dynamics as they played out in our collective activities.

During this period, I watched many white, middle-class grrrls publicly wallow in guilt and self-hate, even to the exclusion of proactive anti-racist and anti-classist work. 'Zines by European American women intent on confessing their racism seemed to pop up everywhere. Many of the writers shifted the responsibility to end racism from themselves to the few people of color they knew who might personally "forgive" them. Other white and/or middle-class women mounted bizarre accusatory competitions over who was more racist and classist—all this at the expense of coalition-building in real diversity. Other RG participants simply *left*.

While the press frenzy contributed to a lack of productive political discussion inside Riot Grrrl, it at least replaced the media myth of a "post-feminist era" with the message that young feminists did exist— and were alive and well. As a result, RG groups began cropping up all over. Refusing central leadership, many of these groups wrote their own "Riot Grrrl is . . ." statements, as a way to define themselves. Concurrently, most grrrls refused to speak to the press—and more important, many still refuse to say "It's over." This legacy continues to surface: I was interviewed not long ago by Riot Grrrl Ontario, and recently received mail from a group called Riot Grrrl Malaysia. Like other forms of feminism, Riot Grrrl is still growing, changing, and being redefined by each new participant. I only hope the mistakes some of us made won't be repeated.

By 1998 I was pretty sick of being in a band heavily associated with what's now called "The Riot Grrrl Movement." I'd been celebrated and denounced. I'd been boycotted, punched, shook, spit at, pulled offstage, and nearly arrested. I'd been called everything from a fat slut to "too radical" to "not radical enough." On top of that, I'd lost a lot of friends to HIV/AIDS, heroin addiction, and suicide.

I was tired.

So I quit Bikini Kill and headed to North Carolina to be with my best friend, Tammy Rae. She and her girlfriend Kaia had moved to Durham and were talking about starting a lesbian-feminist record label that I just had to be a part of.

By the time I arrived at their house, I was emotionally (and artistically) debilitated. I'd seen too much horizontal hostility, backbiting, and just plain lazy fake activism. I'd seen too much jealousy and competitiveness masquerading as political disagreement while fruitful discussions were being abandoned. I'd watched too many women pretend that slandering each other on the Internet had anything to do with serious politics or real change. I'd heard too many times words that feminists had fought hard to haul into mainstream consciousness—words like rape, racism, battery—being thrown around in totally reckless ways: whites claiming to be victimized by "reverse racism," or women equating being criticized with being raped or battered. I'd just seen too much trashing. And, ironically, just as I'd once misdirected my anger against the wrong folks while trying to forge an identity in opposition to what I had scorned as "old school feminism," I—still in my twenties—was already being called "old school" myself.

Then I got my hands on some books.

Books like *The Feminist Memoir Project, Daring to Be Bad, Lesbian Ethics*, and yes, *Sisterhood Is Powerful.* I began to see all the crazy twists and turns that activism can take when it's trying to function inside a messed-up, patriarchal, capitalist framework. I began to realize that my problems were historical ones, not just by-products of me and my fucked-up friends. It was then that I began to roll with the punches life offered—more like the skilled basketball-playing ballerina I am, and less like the crotchety, depressed chain-smoker I had started to become.

Had I found my own heritage earlier, had I sought out feminist mentors (and offered myself to help with and learn from their schemes, projects, and ideas) earlier, I might not have felt so alone and freaked out. I could've learned from history and from others' experiences. And now, here I am at the end of writing this, feeling incredibly thankful for the feminists and for the anti-racist activists who have, with much love and labor, painstakingly recorded their own stories so that I/we will not *have* to reinvent the wheel, not have to relive the same wretched silence time and again. Their work pulled me up from what felt like a huge, nameless sadness. Their work welcomed me back to the world of language—where it's actually possible for me to express these emotions, tell this story, and write these ideas down. And while I am, as a musician, still more of a cultural activist than a political one, I can only hope that my small contribution will help another woman re-find her own voice, or at least pick up a pen and try.

KATHLEEN HANNA is a musician who lives in New York City. In 2001, her multimedia band Le Tigre released their third record, *Feminist Sweepstakes*, with the help of their lesbian-feminist record label, Mr. Lady.

Suggested Further Reading

Brown, Elaine. *A Taste of Power: A Black Woman's Story*. Garden City: Doubleday, 1992.

Brownmiller, Susan. *In Our Time: Memoir of a Revolution*. New York: The Dial Press, 1999.

Eagleton, Terry. *The Illusions of Postmodernism*. London: Blackwell Publishers, Ltd., 1996.

Russ, Joanna. *What Are We Fighting For? (Sex, Race, Class, and the Future of Feminism)*. New York: St. Martin's Press, 1998.

Segrest, Mab. *Memoir of a Race Traitor*. Boston: South End Press, 1994.

Stealth Feminists:
The Thirtysomething Revolution

DEBRA MICHALS

WHEN I CLOSE MY EYES, I still see her there, this eighteen-year-old version of myself,[1] gazing out my college-dorm window at protestors on the street below. It was 1981, my first year at Boston University, where I'd gone to study journalism with the goal of "exposing injustice," hoping to make my debut as a campus radical. But as I looked out at the ragtag assembly of demonstrators, I thought, "How passé. Why do we have to copy the '60s and '70s to make a difference?"

I was not alone. Those of us born in the 1960s grew up with Kent State, the anti-Vietnam-war movement, Black Power, and Women's Liberation as the background music of our lives. Heady notions about making a difference seeped into our collective consciousness, embodied in national figures like Bella Abzug and everyday heroes like nine-year-old Maria Pepe of Hoboken, New Jersey, who integrated Little League baseball in 1974. Teachers assigned homework based on TV news or asked where we stood on the Equal Rights Amendment (ERA). We listened to the "Free to Be You and Me" record and watched TV characters from Mary Richards to Maude challenging sexism. We saw a president disgraced over Watergate and we mastered the art of questioning *everything*. We ingested two basic messages: that we could change our world, and that (for those lucky enough to have access) college might be a good place to start.

---

1. I was born in 1962. To make the case that a distinct cohort of thirtysomething "Stealth Feminists" (my term) exists, I have included the birth years of myself and the women quoted in this article.

But when we got there, we found the party was over, or what remained wasn't what we had in mind. Instead of struggles for women's equality and social justice in the USA, we found Anti-Apartheid, No Nukes, El Salvador. Worthwhile causes all—and evidence of emerging global activism—but to many a young mind it felt distant, dated. Again we stood in the shadow of former greatness—first as 1970s teens hearing about the peace-and-love Woodstock generation, then in the 1980s when it seemed activism was dead or wheezing its last breath.

Fast forward to the 1990s and 2000s. While the media claimed feminism was on the lam, the real picture was more complicated. Beyond endless accounts of young women from so-called Generations X, Y, and Z renouncing feminism with the oft-repeated, "I'm not a feminist, *but . . .* ," lay another reality: countless thirtysomething women not only embracing the label but defining our lives as torchbearers for feminism. In our careers, relationships, childraising strategies (or decisions *not* to have children)—in all our choices—"Stealth Feminists" have been quietly, invisibly, and sometimes even subconsciously continuing the work of the Women's Movement.[2]

So how did we slip under the radar? Pop-culture theorists couldn't see these thirtysomethings in part because of false demographic categories lumping the first half of us with Baby Boomers and the second half with Gen Xers.[3] Unconvinced that these labels adequately described my generation and its politics, in 2001 I conducted an Internet survey of women born between 1961 and 1969.[4] The result: *most respon-*

---

2. For more on younger women as "functional feminists," see "Notes of a Feminist Long Distance Runner," by Eleanor Holmes Norton, p. 145.—Ed.

3. Demographers define Baby Boomers as those born between 1946 and 1964, and Gen Xers as born between 1965 and 1978. See "The Baby Boom at Mid-Decade," by Patricia Braus, *American Demographics*, April 1995, and "The Generation X Difference," by Nicholas Zill and John Robinson, *American Demographics*, April 1995.

4. Special thanks to the women who participated in my survey, and to the women's Internet networks that posted my query, among them: *www.ivillage.com, www.systers.org, www.moonlady.com, www.bbwm.com*, Amy Richards and Marianne Schnall at *www.feminist.com*, Irene Stuber at *www.undelete.org/abreb.html* and the list-serv H-Women. My initial query asked if women born between 1961 and 1969 identified with either demographic category of Baby Boomers or Generation Xers, and included questions on the experience of growing up in the politically conscious decades of the 1960s and 1970s. More than seventy women nationwide filled out questionnaires or took part in interviews.

dents identified with neither category. Instead, they defined Baby Boomers as at least ten years older (movers and shakers of the '60s and '70s), and Gen Xers as five to ten years younger (unappreciative, label-shunning beneficiaries of social-justice movements). Others have begun to question these categories; in *Generation Jones* (Vanguard Press, 1999), Jonathan Pontell argued for a group of in-betweeners born 1954 to 1965.[5]

For thirtysomething women, the lack of a unifying generational label intensified our sense of disconnectedness, sending us searching for other ways to define ourselves. For many, feminism filled the void: "I remember thinking we could never measure up, that we had failed as a decade because the '60s was where it was at," recalled Tomi-Ann Roberts (b. 1963), a psychology professor at Colorado College and a respondent to my survey, "It matters that we don't have a label. This sense of being cast adrift is why I take the label 'feminist' so seriously." Without an identifiable movement of their own, Stealth Feminists say they turned their activism into daily life. Another respondent, a network-systems engineer in Kansas City, Missouri (b. 1963), wrote: "I just live and work as a 'practicing feminist' . . . breaking small barriers . . . hopefully changing some minds by example."

Contrary to stereotype, thirtysomething Stealths eagerly self-identify as feminists.[6] *"Absolutely, I'm a feminist!"* was the refrain in Internet and telephone interviews, stressing a belief in equal rights regardless of sex or race. Some define that to mean "humanism" or anticapitalism; all recognize the necessity for *action*, particularly given Right-wing political agendas and anti-woman backlash. "I define feminism as: 1) the understanding that there is inequality between men and

---

5. Others use varying start and end dates for this group of in-betweeners, beginning in the late 1950s and reaching into the latter '60s. There's also an active Internet community for those who fall between the Boomers and Gen Xers at *www. generationjones.com*. For information on the myth of the homogeneous Baby Boom, see "The Four Baby Booms," by Campbell Gibson, *American Demographics*, November 1993.

6. Only two of the women who responded to my survey said they did not identify as feminists. One self-identified as a religious fundamentalist and the other as a member of the military—yet both expressed support for gender equality.

women, and 2) the responsibility of acting upon that knowledge," explained an academic skills specialist in Allegheny, New York (b. 1965).

Ironically, Stealths' invisibility has been the source of our power. While no one was looking, this virtual army of feminists has acted on the lessons of our childhoods. As conservatives urged creationist theories on U.S. classrooms,[7] such Stealth-Feminist educators as Carolyn Eichner (b. 1961), an assistant history professor at the University of South Florida, and Katino Manko (b. 1966), an adjunct professor at the University of Delaware, have introduced new generations to literature from the late-twentieth-century feminist renaissance. Most academics who responded to my survey noted their efforts to teach feminist history and politics, including professors/instructors at Western Michigan University (b. 1963) and Smith College (b. 1965). Others, like Lewis-Clark State College English professor Carman C. Curton (b. 1962)— who traces her awakening to a copy of Germaine Greer's *The Female Eunuch* she discovered in seventh-grade study hall—have made sure their university libraries offer feminist works. Thirtysomething scholars are continuing research inspired by earlier feminists, such as projects studying the intersection of body image, self-surveillance, and media representations emphasizing youth and beauty.[8]

Similarly, Stealth Feminists have infiltrated the worlds of government (working on election campaigns for pro-choice candidates) and business (hiring qualified women, battling management for equal pay). Promoting and training women, particularly in male-dominated sci-tech fields, topped priority lists for many respondents, including an information-technology project manager in Nashville, Tennessee (b. 1968) and a manager of artificial-intelligence programs from Cherry Hill, New Jersey (b. 1961). Others, like a computer scientist at NASA

---

7. See "Combating the Religious Right," by Cecile Richards, p. 464.—Ed.

8. Tomi-Ann Roberts, for example, explored issues of self-surveillance in a study of women's test scores executed while the women were wearing sweaters vs. bathing suits. The women took the tests in rooms alone, yet still their scores plummeted in the swimwear (unlike the scores of their male counterparts, which were roughly the same regardless of the men's apparel), and the women described themselves in bathing suits by using shame words like "disgusting." (The men, on the other hand, described themselves as "silly.")

(b. 1966), report encouraging girls to study science through mentoring and educational demonstrations. Entrepreneurs use their independence to merge business and politics: *www.focusonstyle.com* updates visitors to this fashion website with news on women's rights. In childrearing, Stealths reject gender-biased stories outright, or else explain what's wrong with them—like the title character in Disney's *The Little Mermaid* film becoming voiceless.[9] When her toddler announced that there are no female "firemen," Amy Bowles Reyer (b. 1967) took him to her local Bethesda, Maryland, engine company so he could meet women firefighters. Another survey respondent, a University of Arkansas programmer (b. 1963) proves gender-neutral childrearing works: "As my son was growing, I kept 'girl' toys in the house—dollhouse, shopping cart, baby doll. He played with them some, and grew up very sensitized. . . . [Now seventeen] he sees no conflict between cooking and caring for babies or mowing the lawn and building a deck."

In large part, we Stealths regard ourselves as the first beneficiaries of 1970s feminist sociopolitical victories, and consider it our duty to continue the fight: "My politics are after the same goals of the '60s: equal pay for equal work, adequate childcare, the removal of the glass ceiling, women's right to choose," wrote a Ph.D. candidate at Johns Hopkins University (b. 1965). Militance that seemed passé in the 1980s is getting a second look: Stealths say they would take to the streets over any effort to subjugate women, especially the reversal of *Roe v. Wade*. Our concerns include poverty, the environment, and the exploitation of women and children in the global South by multinational factories. Some Stealths are formulating political agendas around the unrealized promise of Title IX, including lawsuits to contest unequal representation of women in public institutions receiving federal funds.[10]

Parents, teachers, and the culture of our youth sparked this consciousness. Tomi-Ann Roberts flashed back on the memory of her dad

---

9. Several respondents mentioned Disney's *The Little Mermaid* and the problems of women characters being denied the power of speech. See also "Honey, Disney Shrunk the Kids," by Carolyn Mackler, *Ms.*, April/May 2001.

10. Title IX of the 1972 Education Act Amendment protects women from gender discrimination in education by requiring all educational institutions receiving federal funds to provide equal access to female and male students for all available programs, including athletics and vocational education.

mowing their lawn in a conservative suburban neighborhood while wearing a pro-ERA t-shirt. Others had powerful recollections they recognized as key to their awareness: the woman (b. 1965) whose family wasn't shocked when, at age seven, she announced she was marrying her best friend Molly; the information-systems manager (b. 1968) who memorized Helen Reddy's feminist anthem "I Am Woman" while her Mexican American immigrant mother fought for ethnic and gender access to "the American dream"; the Ph.D. candidate (b. 1965) who felt empowered watching Billie Jean King trounce Bobby Riggs in the 1972 "Battle of the Sexes" tennis match; the welfare-rights activist (b. 1963) whose youth was spent reading "all the feminist classics"; the graduate student (b. 1966) whose mother shifted the housework to her spouse while earning a Ph.D. in 1974; the educator (b. 1963) who will never forget her mother voting for Shirley Chisholm in the 1972 presidential election.

Many scholars, reporters, and even some Baby Boomers who engaged in '60s and '70s activism claim that as a unique moment in U.S. history, one with little precedent and few signs of antecedents. Opponents take comfort in what they (want to) believe is the exceptionalism of those decades; some participants preen themselves on having been a rare breed. Both overlook the generation nurtured on that activism. It's a failure of the modern media, victim of its own anti-feminist bias, to have missed perhaps the biggest story of the last decade: the '60s and '70s legacy is alive and well in the consciousness of Stealth Feminists, who are not only passing these politics on to future generations but adding our own spin to yesterday's legacy and today's action. As we age, we will, like our predecessors, gain increasing authority to influence the broader culture with our values. Our existence proves that generations of women activists are *not* cut off from each other. Rather, we *do* stand on each other's shoulders. We are building a bridge from the past through the present to the future.

And, most important, we are *everywhere*.

DEBRA MICHALS is a feminist journalist and scholar who completed her Ph.D. in U.S. history at New York University in 2001. Her dissertation focused on the rise of women's entrepreneurship in the post–World War II decades. She traces the moment of her feminist awakening to her seventh-grade English class, where a male teacher labeled her the class "women's libber" for requesting more readings by female authors. Her journalism has appeared in *Ms.*, *Working Woman*, *American Heritage*, *Self*, and *Harper's Bazaar*. She spent two years as acting associate director of the undergraduate program in women's studies at NYU, where she founded a student-run publication on gender issues, entitled *revolution/ evolution*.

Suggested Further Reading

(There isn't any on Stealth Feminists. That's the point of writing this essay. That's also why I'm writing a book on the Stealth Feminist generation. Meanwhile, the following are sure to inspire the Stealth generation—and beyond. —D.M.)

Baxandall, Roz, and Linda Gordon, eds. *Dear Sisters: Dispatches from the Women's Liberation Movement*. New York: Basic Books, 2000.

DuPlessis, Rachel Blau, and Ann Snitow, eds. *The Feminist Memoir Project: Voices from Women's Liberation*. New York: Three Rivers Press, 1998.

Faludi, Susan. *Backlash: The Undeclared War Against American Women*. New York: Crown, 1991.

Schneir, Miriam. *Feminism in Our Time: The Essential Writings, World War II to the Present*. New York: Vintage Books, 1994.

Walker, Alice. *In Search of Our Mothers' Gardens*. New York: Harcourt, 1983.

Notes of a Feminist Long Distance Runner

ELEANOR HOLMES NORTON

I AM NOT EVERYWOMAN, especially considering that I am a black woman. I am, however, many women of every background and color who crossed into forbidden territory to begin the modern feminist movement in the 1960s. Nearly forty years later, women are not what they were. Even the bit parts I have played tell much about how the great feminist awakening opened a new world for women: law student, activist in the then-new Civil Rights and Feminist Movements, constitutional lawyer, professor of law, local public official, chair of the U.S. Equal Employment Opportunity Commission, member of Congress. At the same time, of course, most of us also were intent on playing the irresistible roles in which women had always been cast. Like most, I was a wife. I am a mother. Very little of the rest of what we have done with our lives was possible for our mothers. Young and daring, we were the first women in any numbers who insisted that we were entitled to try for it all. We did it, running all the way, sometimes stumbling or falling down, yet running still.

No one can doubt that we have shaken to its foundation the great wall that the ages have built around women. This wall, the oldest in human time, had been impenetrable for most women, and invisible to many. For all its different manifestations, the wall has had similar effects on women living in vastly different societies throughout the world. The origins are elusive. In the beginning, men everywhere probably used their physical strength to claim and enforce dominance when physicality was what mattered most for survival. Once male dominance was achieved physically, the rest was not difficult to maintain—until now.

We were not the first women who sought to be as free as men. We were the first who brought a combination of insistence and tactics fit for a wall that stood on the firmest foundation. Our insistence, of course, was aided and abetted by forces larger than our will. Our society had finally achieved control over certain forces that had controlled people in all societies, especially women—ranging from the consequences of fertility, childbirth, and children to changes in the economy and in the nature of work.

My generation's insight was that finally the proverbial wall that divided the sexes, enforcing male superiority in human endeavors, could be taken down. Like all great insights, this one drew its power from the refusal to allow distraction from a potent idea. We demurred to the argument that the wall sometimes had the appearance—and for some women, even the characteristics—of a protective shield. Our goal was to make a revolution, and revolutions are not made by yielding to distractions. A generation later, as we carry forward a revolution that cannot be contained, the complexity of the feminist quest is more easily acknowledged. Today we confront the consequences of the extraordinary changes we have made. Inevitably, the progress that has transformed the lives of millions of American women also has been accompanied by its share of confusion and opposition. Moreover, as it developed, feminism itself helped foster new challenges. New insights are necessary to help meet new issues facing a new generation of women.

The kaleidoscopic quality of the wall that both denied and protected women helps to explain why we were the first generation to insist that the wall, all of it, should come down—and also explains why we are still going at it, and why the generations after us sometimes appear less intense about the feminist mission. Not surprisingly, there are efforts to fortify the wall in the name of marriage, children, and family. Such attempts have some currency because unlike other "inferior" beings, women have always had a uniquely intimate relationship with the men who claimed superiority and dominion over them. This bond remains one of the great mysteries of life. Happily, love and sex always survive revolutions. We wanted women to have more of both. It is no accident that the sexual revolution and the feminist revolution began at the same time or that such profound departures would draw strong reactions. The inevitable questions have been raised. Foremost among them, of course, is how much can the wall be challenged without endangering one of the closest and most important relationships in human existence? Feminists of my generation believe this was a false challenge, then as now. In the process of bringing down the wall, however, such questions cannot simply be shunted aside. They help explain much about the difference between the era of those who made the revolution and the period of those who have inherited it.

The relationship between men and women also casts light on why the subordination of women in the relationship was not systematically challenged earlier.[1] The complicated bond between men and women—one of the permanent wonders of the world—always asserts itself and often obscures the structural defects in the wall. Patriarchy gets confused with fatherhood, manliness with male supremacy. But it is male bias we are after, not males. Without feminist consciousness, this confusion can overwhelm the separation between sex and sexism that my generation finally exposed.

The Women's Movement is not the first to be threatened by the resurgence of an old order. The difference is in the difficulty that comes from banishing part of the unique relationship between the sexes, clinging to the rest, and distinguishing between the two. Should the goal now be to plow ahead against the mountain of remaining gender bias or to concentrate on family, marriage, love, and sex? Have we come this far only to have our choices come down to these?

My generation walked up to the wall and saw unadulterated, unconquered gender bias for what it was. The new generation in the United States sees less of it because we have eliminated much of it. The difference between our generation and our daughters' is less important than it may seem, because the daughters grew up in a world where feminist aspirations were accepted as the way the world operates. That some women have not embraced what we call feminism or do not use the feminist label has had no effect on the pace of feminist change. We were *catalytic feminists*. Younger women are *functional feminists*. The new generation has taken up our issues, changing the world more than we dared,

1. Only the more radical of the nineteenth-century U.S. suffragists engaged this issue, among them Elizabeth Cady Stanton, Lucy Stone, Anna Julia Cooper, and Charlotte Perkins Gillman. Internationally, however, women seem to have confronted the issue as far back as recorded history (see the Introduction).—Ed.

opening many more doors for women, and making demands that did not cross our minds. Their remarkable pluralism defies one language, even the explicit language of feminism. Like every revolutionary vanguard, we were a smaller, more cohesive and homogeneous group. We needed to speak the language of feminism to be understood and to spread the revolution. The new generation says it in many ways, and moves still more women to feminist ideas and feminist modes.[2]

The proof lies not in what they say but in how they act. Today's women think nothing of working on factory floors, driving buses, or building things. They believe it is their prerogative to walk into law firms, corporate boardrooms, surgical operating rooms, congressional hearing rooms, and presidential cabinet rooms. They thrill crowds who have never seen women as players in major sports until now. They have raised the quality of recruits in the armed services, who then rise through the ranks and serve in posts formerly reserved for men only. They do not hesitate to vote their issues as women. They are forging new personal and equal relationships with men.[3]

Even traditional women and families act on a revised view of who a woman is. The average American may not call herself a feminist, yet the substance of the feminist revolution is a potent guide to the way she lives her life. The housewife lifestyle that defined a norm for many women when Betty Friedan wrote *The Feminine Mystique* is no more. The average woman is in the labor force. There is mass approval for work, even for women with young children, and even without universal, educational childcare—an urgent necessity that the new generation must win.

---

2. See, for example, "Girls: 'We Are the Ones Who Can Make a Change!'" by Ana Grossman and Emma Peters-Axtell, p. 121; "Generation 'Why?': A Call to Arms," by Jasmine Victoria, p. 126; "Gen X Survivor: From Riot Grrrl Rock Star to Feminist Artist," by Kathleen Hanna, p. 131; and "Stealth Feminists: The Thirtysomething Revolution," by Debra Michals, p. 138.—Ed.

3. See, for example, "Transforming Traditions and Breaking Barriers: Six Personal Testimonies," p. 325; "Women and Law: The Power to Change," by Catharine A. MacKinnon, p. 447; "Diagnosis and Prognosis: Women Physicians and Women's Health," by Wendy Chavkin, M.D., p. 378; "Running for Our Lives: Electoral Politics," by Pat Schroeder, p. 28; "Women in Sports: What's the Score?" by Barbara Findlen, p. 285; "Redefining the Warrior Mentality: Women in the Military," by Claudia J. Kennedy, p. 409; and "Parenting: A New Social Contract," by Suzanne Braun Levine, p. 85.—Ed.

Contraception, forbidden to be discussed or supported by government until feminists won that vital victory, is no longer controversial; abortion, one of the most important and controversial feminist goals, has the support of an American majority.[4] Segregated education and sports, among the most entrenched of gender traditions, have met their match in federal law. These monumental barriers that helped solidify the wall throughout human history have fallen away in our country—but it's not over yet. The feminist revolution grows and spreads as women here, and in every corner of the earth, pursue their own versions of feminist progress.

In spite of manifest changes, there are some who look past the enlargement of rights, the personal egalitarianism emerging between men and women, and the relaxation of resistance to feminist goals. Despite a new, assertive generation of our descendants, some skeptics fail to recognize the feminism of this generation because the daughters are not carbon copies of their mothers. In the reaction to feminism, many see the "end of feminism."

I do not underestimate the reactionaries, or the pressure on young women to revert to old traditions. There is much to learn, from the fight for women's suffrage in particular.[5] That struggle took longer and was more laborious than ours has been in achieving far more for women. Suffrage released feminist ideas and changes beyond the vote, but that single-minded quest did not bequeath wholesale societal changes similar to those we see today. The reasons are complicated. However, it is clear that the sustained focus that proved necessary to achieve the vote ceased germinating other issues once that great victory was finally achieved. In contrast, the modern feminist agenda was crowded from the outset, and new issues have only multiplied. The work of feminism goes on, with countless women and men, consciously and not, moving it forward. Beyond our own country, the global spread of feminism and the changes pressed by the transformation of women have become an irreversible force that is changing the entire world.

---

4. See "Unfinished Agenda: Reproductive Rights," by Faye Wattleton p. 17.—Ed.

5. See "The Art of Building Feminist Institutions to Last," by Eleanor Smeal, p. 541, "The Media and the Movement: A User's Guide," by Gloria Steinem, p. 103, and the Introduction, p. *xv*.—Ed.

As my generation continues to struggle in our way, the new generation is finding its own way. Our "vanguard generation," of course, could become so intoxicated by the certainty that we have made history that it would be too easy to regard those who follow as insufficiently attentive to the revolution. But the descendants do not need to make the revolution; they are its first beneficiaries. The work of a new generation is both the same and different. It is the same to the extent that our revolution is unfinished. Yet it also is as different as today is from yesterday. To live, a revolution must build on the past, not relive it.

My generation cannot afford to become infatuated with the progress of the last forty years. We need only be confident that women cannot be turned back. Still, it is one thing to believe that our progress will continue; it is another to think that feminist advances are inevitable. To ask men to move over is to ask them to give up a monopoly on everything—power, jobs, athletics, and primacy in the family. Even so, the pace we set yesterday has only quickened.

There are two possible courses for great movements. They fire up, blaze, bring change, glow down into embers, and die—or they mature and keep growing.

Look around. Women are on course.

ELEANOR HOLMES NORTON is, as of 2002, in her sixth term as the U.S. Congresswoman from the District of Columbia. Named by President Jimmy Carter as the first woman to chair the Equal Employment Opportunity Commission, she came to Congress as a national figure who had been a Civil Rights Movement leader and a feminist leader, a tenured professor of law (at Georgetown University), and board member of three Fortune 500 companies. She has been named one of the 100 most important American women in one survey and one of the most powerful women in Washington in another. Her work for full congressional voting representation for the people of the District of Columbia continues her lifelong struggle for universal human rights. She has served in the Democratic House leadership group and as the Democratic chair of the Women's Caucus, and her success in writing bills and getting them enacted has made her one of the most effective legislative leaders in the House, where she serves on the Government Reform Committee and the Transportation and Infrastructure Committee. Her accomplishments for her district include historic breakthroughs (the first vote on D.C. statehood), and major economic and development initiatives and bills. After receiving her bachelor's degree from Antioch College, Norton simultaneously earned her law degree and a master's degree in American Studies from Yale. A fourth-generation Washingtonian, she is the mother of John Holmes Norton and Katherine Felicia Norton.

Suggested Further Reading

Baxendall, Rosalyn, and Linda Gordon, eds. *Dear Sisters: Dispatches from the Women's Liberation Movement.* New York: Basic Books, 2000.

Guy-Sheftall, Beverly, ed., with Johnnetta Cole. *Words of Fire: An Anthology of African American Feminist Thought.* New York: New Press, 1995.

Morgan, Robin, ed. *Sisterhood Is Global: The International Women's Movement Anthology.* New York: Doubleday/Anchor Books, 1984; updated edition, The Feminist Press at CUNY, 1996.

Schneir, Miriam, ed. *Feminism: The Essential Historical Writings.* New York: Vintage Books, 1972.

Schneir, Miriam, ed. *Feminism in Our Time: The Essential Writings, World War II to the Present.* New York: Vintage Books, 1994.

The Politics of Aging

BARBARA MACDONALD

Foreword by Cynthia Rich

"We planned the study of women with an entire piece omitted—age and the oppression of ageism. We cannot now patch up . . . to cover the gaps of our ignorance. We have no choice but to go back . . . and rebuild with a wholeness that includes all women, and all the years of our lives."

That was Barbara Macdonald's challenge to the National Women's Studies Association (NWSA) in 1985, two years after the publication of her groundbreaking work, *Look Me in the Eye: Old Women, Aging and Ageism* (reissued Denver, Colorado: Spinsters, 2001).

Her work on a feminist theory of ageism as a form of sexism—as the oppression of old women (with very powerless, very old men viewed by other men as if they were women)—is now widely read in Women's Studies,[1] and in 1995 NWSA devoted its entire conference to the issue.

Still, today, as the women who were activists in the 1960s and '70s move toward old age, there remains an extraordinary resistance to naming and challenging the erasure that waits just ahead of them. I hear little of the clear anger, the energy required to make deep change. Barbara saw that the consciousness entering feminism around other issues—class, race, anti-Semitism, for example—had been introduced earlier by other progressive movements.

---

1. See "The Proper Study of Womankind: Women's Studies," by Florence Howe, p. 70.—Ed.

Those movements reflected men's interests and concerns. The politics of ageism *as a form of sexism*—like the politics of women's health or violence against women—could develop only during a period of radical feminist thought. But old women were "outside the sisterhood" of the predominantly young women of the 1970s, and awareness of old women's very existence came late to the scene.

Nevertheless, I'm hopeful. I'm hopeful because a generation of women who were ageist in the '70s were also political in the '70s, and—from the Civil Rights Movement and their struggles as women—they learned a language of equality and an ability to identify and analyze oppression. I'm hopeful they haven't lost their edge—that as they find themselves segregated, treated with contempt, erased, they won't tolerate that.

In particular, lesbian women and women of color will, as they age, quickly identify those signs of Otherness: invisibility, stereotyping, a recoil from one's physical presence, the struggle not to internalize society's distortion of your reality, the temptations to pass or be tokenized, and always the arrogant assumption that you would rather be someone else.

I'm hopeful that a new generation of old women will, like Barbara, claim the word "old" as a statement of fact, even of pride, knowing that as long as it's shameful to be called old, it will be shameful to be old.

I was Barbara's partner and sometime coauthor for twenty-six years, until her death in 2000 at age eighty-six. Twenty years her junior, my anger was for her, at the ageism she faced and the ways that loomed at the edge of our relationship. Today I am sixty-nine, and I stand where she stood. I feel the deep, unexpected joys of aging she spoke of—and now my anger rises for myself.

Barbara's work lights a path for me. It can help us all meet the challenge of transforming the way we understand women's aging.—C.R.

•   •   •

[*Editor's note:* The following essay is based on Barbara Macdonald's article "The Politics of Aging: I'm Not Your Mother," in *Ms.* (July/August

1990), and on her writings in the 1991 first expanded edition of *Look Me in the Eye;* statistics have been updated by Cynthia Rich.]

AGEISM PERMEATES ALL our relationships. It affects the decisions made by every woman reading this: your decision whether or not to have a child, your relationship to your children, to your parents and their parents, to older women you meet (or don't), what you wear, the products you buy. At a much deeper level, you are made to dread the last half of your life. Feminism has no choice but to examine ageism as a form of disempowerment of all women.

Has it never occurred to younger women activists organizing around "women's issues" that old women are raped, battered, poor, perform unpaid work in and out of the home, are exploited by male medical practitioners, are in jail, are political prisoners; have to deal with racism, classism, homophobia, anti-Semitism?[2] I read feminist publications and not once have I come across any group of younger women enraged, marching, or organizing legal support because of anything that happened to an old woman. I have to read the *Los Angeles Times* or *Ageing International* to learn what's happening to the women of my generation—and the news is not good.

Worldwide, old women are the poorest of the poor; *two-thirds of impoverished Americans over age fifty-five are women—and the number rises with every year we live.*[3] Almost 40 percent of all widowed women—70 percent of widowed African American women, 76 percent of widowed Latina women—live near or below the poverty line.[4] Conditions in public housing for the elderly—where most residents are women—are

---

2. According to the American Association of Retired Persons (AARP), age discrimination is now the fastest-growing type of complaint received by the Equal Employment Opportunity Commission (the second fastest-growing complaint category is discrimination based on disability; see "Rights, Realities, and Issues of Women with Disabilities," by Laura Hershey, p. 233).—Ed.

3. U.S. Census Bureau data quoted in *The San Diego Union Tribune,* 1 November 2000.—C.R.

4. OWL (Older Women's Liberation), *The State of Older Women in America, 2001;* facts derived from the Social Security Administration, Office of Policy, *Income of the Population 55 or Older,* 1998.—C.R.

scandalous.[5] Though it's illegal, old women in nursing homes are still used as guinea pigs for experimental drugs, a practice eradicated years ago in prisons.[6]

Activists aren't alone in their ageism. Has it never occurred to those in Women's Studies, as they ignore the meaning and politics of women's lives beyond our reproductive years, that this is male-centered thinking? Has it never occurred to feminist theorists that *ageism is a central feminist issue?* Read the books used in Women's Studies as an old woman reads them. They discuss the socialization of little girls from infancy, the struggles of women through adulthood—then it turns out that "adulthood" ends with menopause, or perhaps a woman in her fifties who's a displaced homemaker. Well, try being an eighty-year-old woman in an L.A. shantytown, just trying to cross the street, when a government economic index has valued your life at $2,311 in the courts (in contrast to $717,630 for a thirty-one-year-old man).

Meanwhile, as the numbers of old women rapidly increase, the young women students of five years ago now show up as geriatricians and social workers, because that's where the jobs are. They may call themselves feminists, but lacking a political analysis of women's aging, they define old women as needy, simpleminded, helpless—definitions that correlate conveniently with their services and salaries.

But it's worse than that. Professionals and academicians don't hesitate to exploit us. They come to us for "oral histories," for their own agendas, to learn their feminist (or lesbian or working-class or ethnic) histories, without the slightest interest in our present struggles. They come to fill in much-needed data for a thesis, or to justify a grant for some "service" for old women that imitates the mainstream (and that they plan to direct), or they come to get material for biographies of our

---

5. Poverty for old women is actually what happens to us when we are not in the immediate presence of a man, sharing his life. Despite glossy images of old (European American) couples on the golf course, the reality for most women is harsh: when they finish nursing their husbands through final illnesses, they face a sharp decline in income.—C.R.

6. "Federal health officials have concluded that most nursing homes are understaffed to the point that patients may be endangered." (*The San Diego Union Tribune,* 23 July 2000.)—C.R.

friends and lovers. But they come not as equals, not with any knowledge of what our issues may be. They come to old women who have been serving young women for a lifetime and ask to be served one more time—and then conceal their embarrassment as they depart by saying that they felt as though we were their grandmothers, mothers, aunts.

Let me say it clearly: we are not your mothers, grandmothers, or aunts. We will never build a true Women's Movement until we can organize as equals, woman to woman, without the masks of family roles.

It should come as no surprise that ageism has its roots in the patriarchal family. But in the years it took to get the Women's Movement to address ageism, feminism moved from a position in which we recognized the family as a crucial building block of patriarchy—the place where hierarchical roles are learned, where basic sexist socialization takes place,[7] the structure through which women are colonized, manipulated, controlled, and punished for infractions—back to a position of reaffirming family. Mainstream feminists buy the notion that so long as a woman has a career, family is a safe, wholesome place to be. Radical feminists affirm family as a cultural source—a way of understanding our strengths and oppressions as Native American, African American, Latina, Asian American, Arab or Jewish or working-class women. This return to family is reflected in our writings, where the father is seen less as the oppressor and more as another family member, oppressed by white male imperialism. (And believe me, he is.)

It will be for future feminist historians to explain why, in our reaffirmation of "the family," we never questioned the contradiction with our earlier feminist theory. Nor can history fail to note that our return to family coincides with a reactionary trend back to "traditional family values" engineered by the religious Right—any more than it can ignore our "lesbian baby boom" happening to have coincided with Ronald Reagan's baby boom to save the Gross Domestic Product.[8]

---

7. See, for example, "Parenting: A New Social Contract," by Suzanne Braun Levine, p. 85; "Sisterhood Is Pleasurable: A Quiet Revolution in Psychology," by Carol Gilligan, p. 94; "Poverty Wears a Female Face," by Theresa Funiciello, p. 222; and "Landscape of the Ordinary: Violence Against Women," by Andrea Dworkin, p. 58.—Ed.

8. See "Confessions of a Worrywart: Ruminations on a Lesbian Feminist Overview," by Karla Jay, p. 212.—Ed.

Unfortunately, the challenge of ageism came late in this wave of U.S. feminism. It came at a time when professionalism was on the rise and beginning to co-opt the Women's Movement. The "therapizing" of the personal at the cost of the political was devastating: there we were again, trying to change ourselves rather than working to change society. Obviously, this wasn't a time when feminism could integrate a radical new analysis. Yet "the personal *is* political," and if we are to understand ageism, we have no choice but to bring family again under the lens of a feminist politic. In the past, we examined the father as oppressor, and the mother as oppressor/socializer of daughters, but what has never come under the feminist lens is the daughters' oppression of the mother—that woman who by definition is older than we are.

The source of your ageism, the reason you see older women as there to serve you, comes from the patriarchal family. It was there you learned that your mother exists to serve you, that serving you is her purpose in life. This is not woman's definition of motherhood. This is man's definition, a masculinist myth enforced in family that you still believe—to your peril and mine. It infantilizes you. It erases me.

The old woman stands at the other end of that motherhood myth. She is not supposed to fight for her own issues; if she fights at all it must be for "future generations." Her greatest joy is perceived as giving all to her grandchildren. And to the extent that she no longer directly serves a man—produces his children or is sexually desirable to him—she is erased more completely than she was as a mother.

I'm often asked whether or not I see progress since I first addressed ageism. Sometimes, when I read about feminists wanting to "honor their elders"—extolling old "crones" for our "wisdom and experience" (while offering us professional advice on how to grow old), but never soliciting our input, appointing us to their boards, or offering us any piece of the action—I can't stomach the sentimentality and hypocrisy. Then I'll get a letter or a phone call and I'll realize that some feminists really have heard me, and I'm filled with enthusiasm and hope again. Communities of women make changes slowly, but the individual woman's change is often rapid. It's that "click" of insight, and we're permanently changed, re-examining everything from a new perspective. (I must admit—in case anybody thinks old women are full of wisdom—that I expected the whole feminist community simultaneously to make a great political leap on this issue. I think they heard "invisibility." They didn't hear "equality.") On my best days, I feel the larger hope—that feminism has begun to open up to all the diverse voices in this country and around the globe, and that we *are* changing, in deep ways.

Reports on aging populations worldwide suggest that ageism is as widespread as the patriarchal family, and that it is about women. This division of generations is fostered by the multinational corporations for profit: something reportedly in excess of $50 million was spent on a soft-drink "New Generation" advertising theme. Youth has been so empowered that a product need only be associated with the young, and a disempowered adult world will buy it, wear it, drive it, and (even if it kills them) eat it.

This glorification of youth is a false power. But as images from multinationals bombard us, they widen the division between women on the basis of age. No wonder that your power as a younger woman—even as you move into middle age—is measured by the distance you can keep between yourself and me.

Still, it's terribly exciting to be growing old at this time. I'm part of a generation of women who have never before existed. Never in history have there been 35.5 million Americans over age sixty-five, 25 million of us over seventy-five [in the year 2000], and with every year we grow older we find that our age group is made up more and more of women— women who are outside of "family," women society would like to silence.[9] In so many ways, growing old contradicts the stereotype of the woman hunched over. It's a time for raising your head and looking at the view from the top of the hill, a view of the whole scene you never could see before.

But when I talk about the exhilaration of growing old now, much of my feeling is sobered by what's becoming increasingly apparent. Certainly achievements in controlling epidemics, tuberculosis, syphilis, and

---

9. By the year 2050, people over age 65 will constitute 22.9 percent of the population (up from 12.5 percent in 1990). In 1998, women represented 60 percent of the 32 million Americans age 65 and over. Women on average live seven years longer than men; in 2000, there were 65 men per 100 women over age 65, and 38 men per 100 women over age 85. For Native American, African American, Latina, and Asian/Pacific women, the gender imbalance is even more extreme ["Aging," by Ruth Harriet Jacobs, in *The Reader's Companion to U.S. Women's History,* Wilma Mankiller et al., eds. (New York: Houghton Mifflin, 1998)].—Ed.

pneumonia have changed our lives—and our life expectancy—immeasurably. But a woman of color has every right to ask, "What do you mean, '*our*' lives?"[10] The average life expectancy of European Americans is 77; it is 71 for African Americans.[11] (A major cause of these deaths is said to be homicides—which is another way of blaming the victims.) Longevity has a lot to do with privilege, with how much society values your life, with how expendable you are.[12]

Old women meet yet another obstacle in organizing to end our invisibility. For we too come from patriarchal families, where we too learned a dread of old women. We have become the old women we dreaded to be, and every old woman knows how odd that experience is. We are the women we once saw as boring. We are the women we didn't want to look at. We are the women we expected would sit on the sidelines always loving and admiring us. And we are the women we were once told we must have "respect" for, this admonition to prevent our taunting jeers, our contempt. So long as we hold to this legacy of our own ageism into our sixties, seventies, and eighties, we oppress ourselves from within.

But I believe that every one of us can separate ourselves from our internalized ageism, can know that we are not ugly, only old. We watch our bodies change with a sense of wonder, and know we are in step with life. We see that young women expect us to give them unconditional love, to step aside and acknowledge their lives as more important than

---

10. See "Traffic at the Crossroads: Multiple Oppressions," by Kimberlé Crenshaw, p. 43.—Ed.

11. "Life Expectancy at Selected Ages, 1998," National Center for Health Statistics, U.S. Department of Health and Human Services.—C.R.

12. European American women have a life expectancy on average of 79.4 years, while African American women's life expectancy is 73.6 years. Women in general comprise 71 percent of the elderly poor—but African American women comprise 23 percent of the female elderly poor (disproportionally, since they are only 9 percent of elderly women). More than 40 percent of elderly Latinas are poor. In general, fewer women receive pensions than men, and when they do, the pensions tend to be lower than those men receive (Jacobs, op. cit.). See also "African American Women: The Legacy of Black Feminism," by Beverly Guy-Sheftall, p. 176, "U.S. Latinas: Active at the Intersections of Gender, Nationality, Race, and Class," by Edna Acosta-Belén and Christine E. Bose, p. 198, and "Reclaiming the Past, Redefining the Future: Asian American and Pacific Islander Women," by Helen Zia, p. 188.—Ed.

our own. We hear a young woman speak patronizingly or dismissively to us, and we know she would say she has respect for old women—but we know we will not settle for honor or respect. *We will not settle for less than equality.*

When confronted about their ageism, younger women frequently reply, "But we too experience ageism—at fifty, forty, even thirty." It's true that all women experience the stigma of age (as defined by patriarchy) from girlhood to very old age—but the degree of ageism a younger woman feels is always determined by her distance from that ultimate "old." Unless you eliminate that stigma at the extreme end of life where it derives, you permit the image makers to apply it throughout all of women's lives. First, old women are devalued and marginalized. "Old" then moves down from sixty to fifty; then women grow uneasy at forty, then thirty, as the image makers make ten- and twelve-year-old girls into whores and madonnas. Now we're seeing a kind of "child worship," with politicians telling us that what happens in our lives *now* isn't important: what's important is that "the children are our future." When this kind of obsession with discarding the old for the new is pushed along the continuum to the ultimate, we have "fetus worship." And when the fetus is more important than the woman who carries it, feminism is in deep trouble.

BARBARA MACDONALD (1913–2000) was a lesbian feminist activist, author, and lecturer. *Look Me in the Eye: Old Women, Aging and Ageism* (Spinsters, 1983; expanded editions 1991, 2001), coauthored with her life partner, Cynthia Rich, has been widely anthologized for Women's Studies courses, and was translated into Japanese in 1995. Barbara was a frequently invited speaker at universities, to organizations of social workers, and to lesbian and feminist audiences. She spoke at several international panels on aging at the Non-governmental Organization (NGO) Forum of the 1995 UN World Conference on Women in Beijing and was an invited speaker at the Japan Society on Aging in Tokyo. Her work inspired the formation of Old Lesbians Organizing for Change, a national U.S. organization that combats ageism. The latest expanded edition of *Look Me in the Eye* (Denver, Colorado: Spinsters, 2001) contains two of her previously unpublished speeches.

CYNTHIA RICH (b. 1933) is a lesbian feminist author and lifelong activist for social justice. Coauthor, with Barbara Macdonald, of *Look Me in the Eye: Old Women, Aging and Ageism* (see above), her other works include *Desert Years: Undreaming the American Dream* (Spinsters, 1989), and *Beyond My Mother's House* (Spinsters, 2002), which combines a memoir of Barbara Macdonald's with an account of their last years together. She is co-founder of the San Diego, California based Old Women's Project (*mannieag@pacbell.net*), which works to "raise awareness of old-women's issues, make visible our stake in issues of social justice, and combat the ageist attitudes that ignore, trivialize, or demean us."

Suggested Further Reading

Alexander, Jo, et al., eds. *Women and Aging: An Anthology by Women.* Corvallis, Oregon: Calyx Books, 1986.

Doress-Worters, Paula B. and Diana Laskin Siegal, eds. (for the Boston Women's Health Book Collective). *The New Ourselves, Growing Older: Women Aging with Knowledge and Power.* New York: Simon & Schuster, 1994.

"Women and Aging," *Women's Studies Quarterly,* Spring/Summer 1989. New York: The Feminist Press at CUNY.

PART III.

Juggling Jeopardies

Native Americans: Restoring the Power of Thought Woman

CLARA SUE KIDWELL

IN 1901, JOSEPH GILFILLAN, an Episcopalian minister in Minnesota, published a description of Chippewa customs. He described the Chippewa male as tall and graceful, bounding through the forest unburdened except for bow and arrow—while behind him plodded the short, stodgy Chippewa female, bearing tremendous burdens on her back. According to Gilfillan, she had become squashed down by generations of burden-bearing.

Stereotypes of Indian women in European and American literature and history—the voluptuous princess, as in Pocahontas, or the subservient squaw[1]—emerged from European preconceptions of gender roles embedded in a Judeo-Christian patriarchal tradition of male dominance and female subservience. In reality, men's and women's roles differed across the highly diverse Native cultures of North America. Linguists estimate there were roughly 400 to 500 distinct languages spoken among these peoples. Cultural adaptation took place in regions as harsh as the interior deserts of what is now central Nevada and as lush as the coastal piedmont of contemporary North Carolina.[2] Buffalo

1. "Squaw" is a phonetic rendering of an Algonquian word expressing respect for a woman, which the European invaders debased into a pejorative term. There were *sunksquaws* (hereditary female heads of state) in the mid-Atlantic region during the seventeenth and eighteenth centuries. See *The Sacred Hoop: Recovering the Feminine in American Indian Tradition*, by Paula Gunn Allen (Boston: Beacon Press, 1986; revised edition 1992).—Ed.

2. The "New World" Americas Columbus "discovered" were already home to between 72 and 75 million people—a population approximately as large as that of six-

hunters (men) dominated the Great Plains, while farmers (women) in the eastern woodlands tended crops of corn, beans, squash, sunflowers, and chenopodium (spinach, beets, orach). Even where men provided the bulk of the food supply—large game—women prepared and distributed the meat, and gathered nuts, berries, roots, and wild vegetable foods. In many of the Southwest's Pueblos, men and women worked together to farm and maintain irrigation systems.

Their roles were complementary, demarking women's sphere of influence (childbearing, food provision, hide-tanning, pottery making), and men's (hunting, ceremonial activities, warfare, and public decision-making). Men might assume women's roles and the reverse, in a recognized, sanctioned reciprocity—but rarely. Men and women generally carried out their activities in separate groups, but one realm in which both could participate was exercising the spiritual and medicinal powers of healing—though women mostly functioned as healers later in life, after their childbearing years.[3]

The Cherokee story of Kanati and Selu is a complex metaphor demonstrating women's relationship to spiritual and social power. Kanati, the hunter, confines all the game in the world in a cave. Selu, his wife, feeds her family a delicious grain, but they don't know where she gets it until the sons discover her rubbing skin from parts of her body— skin that turns into corn and beans. They accuse her of witchcraft, and as they kill her, she tells them to drag her body around the fields. The next spring, corn springs from wherever her blood fell. The story is a metaphor about female fertility, the earth's fertility, human sexuality, seasonal food production, and social organization.

The association of female blood with corn demonstrates another aspect of women's traditional power among Native peoples: the menstrual cycle. In Plains societies—Lakota (Sioux), Cheyenne, Crow, for example—men sought visionary experiences of spiritual power, which fre-

---

teenth century Europe. North America alone (including what is now Canada, Alaska, and the contiguous United States) was inhabited by an estimated 7 million people of more than 1,000 nations ("Indigenous Peoples—1492 and 1992," *Ms.*, Vol. III, Number 2, September/October 1992).—Ed.

3. See "The Politics of Aging," by Barbara Macdonald with Cynthia Rich, p. 152.—Ed.

quently involved offering small parts of their own flesh and blood. But where men had to seek such power, it occurred for women naturally, through menstruation, which—as a sign of the power of birthing—was considered greater than the power of spiritual guardians of men's experience. Because men had no control over menstrual blood, they feared it, believing it could destroy their powers in war and hunting. Consequently, in many tribes, women segregated themselves from their communities during their menstrual periods, living in special dwellings for four days.

The power of women's sexuality also has a fearsome aspect for men. Black Elk, a Lakota holy man born in the mid-1800s, compared love to a sickness from which people would recover. Marriage was not a matter of love but a mutual economic arrangement between two families. The male fear of losing control in sex—as well as men's fear of women being instigators of sexual relationships (especially in societies where women enjoy social status and control property) is apparent in tales of the woman with the toothed vagina. These are told in tribes from the northwest coast to the Mississippi valley.[4]

The power of childbirth is still acknowledged in some traditional Pueblo communities where the mother and her newborn are secluded for twenty days, and the child is ceremonially exposed to the sun, who is considered its real father. Navajo tradition relates that Changing Woman was impregnated by water and sunlight, giving birth to twin sons who devoted themselves to ridding the world of monsters born of women who had fornicated with plants and animals. Changing Woman also created the Navajo clans by rubbing skin from her body and shaping it into small figures. When a girl reaches puberty, her first menstrual cycle is still celebrated in the *Kinaaldá* ceremony, re-creating Changing Woman's first menses.

Female power is further evident in the matrilineal descent that was generally the rule in Native communities, especially agricultural societies. The Navajo, the Iroquois (Northeast), and the Choctaw, Chicka-

---

4. Variants of the "vagina dentata" myth can be found on every continent, in virtually every culture. Some scholars have attributed it to male fear of female power not only in childbearing but in sex itself—e.g., the female capacity for multiple orgasms. Certainly the archetype is as old as patriarchy.—Ed.

saw, Cherokee, and Creek (Southeast) were nations with social structures based on clans or moiety divisions where descent—identity itself—was traced through the female line. In these social systems, the family core was the woman, her daughters and their husbands, and her sons. Men married into a lineage, but remained peripheral to their wives' households. As with many indigenous peoples globally, maternal uncles were the central male figures in a child's upbringing, not the biological father.

Individuals who crossed gender lines were recognized in many tribes. Their behavior was generally associated with visions that conveyed special spiritual powers. The Lakota *winkte* has this meaning. Today, a national organization, Gay American Indians (GAI), celebrates this tradition and is an advocacy group for Native American lesbian and gay rights.[5]

Although men played major roles in ceremonial activities, the creative powers of women—and the association of women with knowledge—are apparent. At Laguna Pueblo, Tse che nako, Thought Woman, created everything by thinking about all things and their names. The Lakota on the Plains learned their sacred rituals from White Buffalo Calf Woman, who appeared to two hunters as a beautiful maiden. One stared at her lustfully—and a cloud descended, reducing him to a maggot-ridden corpse; the other gazed at her respectfully, so to him she gave the sacred pipe and knowledge of Seven Rituals, before turning into a buffalo calf and trotting off. The Iroquois origin story

---

5. GAI was founded by the late Barbara May Cameron. See *Two-Spirited People*, Sue-Ellen Jacobs, Wesley Thomas, and Sabine Lang, eds. (Urbana, Illinois: University of Illinois Press, 1997), and *Changing Ones: Third and Fourth Genders in Native North America* by Will Roscoe (New York: Griffin/St. Martin's Press, 2000). The Maricopa believed that a girl who "thought too much" grew into a *kwiraxame;* the Mojave thought that a *hwame* dreamed herself into such a state in her mother's womb. See the chapter "*Hwame, Koshkalaka*, and the Rest: Lesbians in American Indian Cultures," in Paula Gunn Allen, op. cit.; and "Native American Lesbians," by Janice Gould, in *The Reader's Companion to U.S. Women's History*, Wilma Mankiller, et al., eds. (New York: Houghton Mifflin Company, 1998). See also the works of Chrystos and Beth Brant, well-known Native American lesbian poets and activists. Two Spirited People of First Nations is a group that addresses homophobia and racism as well as HIV/AIDS prevention and services; based in Canada, it also works with U.S. activists (see *www.cdn-domain.comtpfn/advocate.html* and/or *www.harmreduction.ca/services;* email to *2spirited@usa.net*).—Ed.

tells of the first being, Sky Woman, who bore twin sons—one good and the other evil—who burst through her side and killed her.[6]

Men operated in the public political spheres as leaders, but their power often derived from women. Among the Iroquois, the matrilineage—a group of persons tracing descent from a common mother—was the basic social unit. These were grouped into clans, which were grouped in moieties representing the father side of the tribe and the mother side—resolving the dichotomy of male and female in a union forming the tribe's overall structure. Among powers exercised by the women of the matrilineage were owning property (personal possessions and land rights), choosing from family members men to fill hereditary clan chieftainships, and initiating procedures to *remove* those men from office if, in the women's opinion, they failed in their duties as defined by the Great Law of Peace of the Iroquois Confederacy.[7] A woman also had the power to forbid her male relatives from going on the warpath. In the political realm, then, the male chiefs ruled at the pleasure of the women.[8] Furthermore, a woman exercised the exclusive right to adopt aliens—usually war captives—into her family, which generally meant the power of life or death over prisoners who would be killed if not adopted. This is a key to the story of Pocahontas and John Smith which, as codified by European Americans, glorifies sentimentalized, romantic

---

6. Virtually all creation myths, cross-culturally, acknowledge a female Creatrix, and mythographers generally "date" the myth approximately to pre- or post-patriarchal societal structure according to whether the Creatrix survives and presides over the world or is destroyed by sons/brothers/husbands after birthing it. See, for example, *The Great Cosmic Mother: Rediscovering the Religion of the Earth*, by Monica Sjöö and Barbara Mor (San Francisco: HarperSanFrancisco, 1987); *The White Goddess: A Historical Grammar of Poetic Myth*, by Robert Graves (London, 1948; New York: Noonday Press 1997); and *The Language of the Goddess*, by Marija Gimbutas with Joseph Campbell (London: Thames & Hudson, 2001).—Ed.

7. The Iroquois Confederacy laws addressed resource sharing, the rights of all people, the need for unity, and the centrality of national alliances; these laws had a profound influence on the framers of the U.S. Constitution (sadly, not regarding women's rights). See "Iroquois Confederacy," by Wilma Mankiller, in *The Reader's Companion to U.S. Women's History*, op. cit.—Ed.

8. In her book *Indian Women Chiefs* (Washington: Zenger Publishers, 1976), Carolyn Foreman quotes one John Adair in the late eighteenth century as deploring the "petticoat government" of the Cherokee and praising their recent emergence "like all of the Iroquoian Indians, from the matriarchal period."—Ed.

love. If indeed it happened at all, Pocahontas, a chief's daughter, probably saved John Smith to demonstrate her power as an emerging woman in Powhatan society—by adopting him. Clan Matrons (Mothers of the Longhouses) are still powerful individuals in Iroquois communities on upstate New York reservations.

Women could also be recognized as leaders in their own right. "Queens" were recognized among some Algonquian tribes on the east coast.[9] The Cherokee in the southeast recognized "Beloved Women" who had gained special status by brave deeds or unusual wisdom. The most famous was Nancy Ward, a Cherokee with a reputation for bravery in battle against the Creeks in 1755. Ward spoke in favor of peace at the negotiation of a treaty with the new U.S. government in 1785, but in 1817 she wrote to Cherokee leaders opposing the cession of Cherokee land to the government. In the twentieth century, another Cherokee woman emerged as a major leader, when Wilma Mankiller was elected principal chief of the Cherokee Nation in an historic 1987 vote.[10] She is one of the most visible members of a generation of women who have served as elected tribal officials in the twentieth century (by 1981, *The Albuquerque Journal* reported that 67 American Indian tribes had women heads of state).

The power of women in their societies eroded under pressures from European contact: Indian men bargained away land that, by rights, in many cases had been inherited by matrilineal descent and traditionally fell under the control of women. Some women chose or were forced to act as cultural intermediaries—for instance, Sacajewea (Shoshone) who, married to a French trader, led the Lewis and Clark expedition west—but most women tried to protect their cultures from the incursion. The fur trade commodified their labor, since it was women who prepared the hides. Diseases decimated Indian populations and disrupted social relationships: in the Roman Catholic missions of California, smallpox and syphilis were rampant, the latter spread by priests and Spanish soldiers

---

9. For an impressive list of female *sachems* (chiefs), *sunksquaws*, and leaders of Women's Councils, see Foreman, op. cit., and Allen, op. cit.—Ed.

10. When asked about the origins of her name (originally WhiteMankiller, an honorific title later changed to Mankiller), Wilma usually smiles wryly and replies, "I earned it."—Ed.

having (usually forced) sexual contact with Indian women. Birth rates in Native populations plummeted; death rates in some missions approached 80 percent. Christian missionaries insisted that Indian girls learn to spin, weave, and keep house, while they made the boys raise cattle and work the fields. Thus, women's roles as farmers and men's as hunters were undermined. In the late nineteenth and early twentieth centuries, some Indian reservations were broken up and the land distributed to individual tribal members, but many Indian families lost land.[11] Unable to survive by traditional subsistence farming, they were forced into a cash economy reliant on wage labor. Commissioner of Indian Affairs John Collier instituted a policy in 1934 to recognize the integrity of tribes as political and cultural groups, but the post-war 1940s saw attempts to complete the assimilation of Indians into American society.

The political foment of the late 1960s and 1970s raised the consciousness of U.S. society on many fronts. Feminism was one. But the issues of the feminist movement (as represented by the media) had little significance for Indian women. Equal work for equal pay felt meaningless in communities where unemployment rates ran as high as 90 percent. Childcare facilities seemed irrelevant when alarming numbers of American Indian children were being taken from their families and placed in non-Indian foster homes. And the right of women to choose whether to bear children appeared less immediate than the sterilization of Indian women without their informed consent—procedures carried out in Indian Health Service hospitals by doctors who'd decided Native women were incapable of caring for children they already had.[12]

In 1968, Indian activists in Minneapolis founded the American Indian

---

11. See "Rural Women: Sustaining Farms, Feeding People," by Carolyn Sachs, p. 368.—Ed.

12. Since the mid-1960s, Women's Movement leaders have consistently named forced sterilization alongside abortion as two of the most basic reproductive-rights concerns, although the press coverage rarely reflected that (see "Unfinished Agenda: Reproductive Rights," by Faye Wattleton, p. 17). The common feminist chant of the late 1960s–early 1970s was: "Free abortion on demand! No forced sterilization!" and the first phrase was never used without the second accompanying it. Forced sterilization has usually been practiced on poor women and women of color, including African Americans and Latinas—but Native women have suffered these procedures in far greater numbers than any other group: approximately one quarter of all Native women in the United States have been sterilized without their consent.—Ed.

Movement (AIM). In 1969, a group of Indians—men, women, and children—occupied the abandoned federal prison on Alcatraz Island in San Francisco Bay, to demonstrate that Indian communities had survived and to demand recognition of their existence. In 1970, the North American Indian Women's Association was founded, and in 1972, AIM's takeover of the village of Wounded Knee on the Pine Ridge (Lakota Sioux) reservation in South Dakota again brought women and men together, protesting an autocratic tribal government backed by the Bureau of Indian Affairs (BIA). A new group, Women of All Red Nations (WARN), emerged, calling attention to sterilization; their report was followed by a government study documenting Indian Health Service hospitals procedures where women were not properly informed about sterilizations they underwent.[13] In 1979, Owanah Andersen founded OHOYO ("sister" in Choctaw), a major resource center; the OHOYO Resource Guide is still available *(www.nativepubs.com)*. Since then, numerous Native women's groups have formed, active on a variety of issues—from land-rights struggles through health and violence to challenging federal deference toward tribal governments that deny certain property rights to women—rights that are their due under ancient tribal law.[14]

---

13. WARN has since extended its concerns to include education, general health issues, violence against women, land rights, and environmental issues (see *http:// manila.cet.middlebury.edu/rzheng*; see also *www.angelfire.com/art/hoganview/WARN. html*).—Ed.

14. For links to such groups, see the website of Native American Women on the Web *(www.library.wisc.edu/libraries/WomensStudies/Native.htm)*, as well as *www. nativeculture.com*, and *www.nativeweb.org/resources/society-culture/women*. Internationally, the World Indigenous Women's Foundation *(www.sixkiller.com)* has been active at international feminist and UN conferences. The Indigenous Women's Environmental Network *(www.indians.org/library/iwen)* is based in Canada but works with Alaskan Native and women of all Indian Nations, focusing on environmental issues. Many Native women's organizations are subject-specific in their focus. The Seventh Generation Fund has since 1977 been the major national funding source for Native and indigenous issues *(www.7genfund.org)*; The First Nations Financial Project *(www.FirstNations.org.)*, founded and directed by Rebecca Adamson, promotes openly stated feminist values. Grandmothers' Wisdom Keepers *(www. wisdomkeepers.org)* aims to teach girls under age 18 skills and values passed on by older women. Native American Women in Military Service seeks recognition for Indian women's contributions in the armed services *(www.indiantrailonline.com/nan. htm)*. For information on Native lesbian women, see resources in footnote 5.—Ed.

Poverty and family violence are the unfortunate legacy of colonialism for contemporary Indian communities. By the early 1990s, the infant mortality rate for Native Americans was three times greater than the national average, the life expectancy was only 47 years, and rates of alcoholism, HIV/AIDS, and suicide were spiraling upward, well above the national average. The Department of Justice reported that violent crime was 2.5 times higher and the rate of sexual assault and rape 3.5 times higher among Native Americans than in the U.S. population as a whole.[15] According to Beverly Wilkins of Peaceful Nations (a consulting firm that educates on violence in tribal communities) and a representative of the Sacred Circle National Resource Center to End Violence Against Native Women, "Lack of funding and of interest on the part of the tribal governments is a major problem."[16] Native women's organizations are taking these issues into their own hands.[17]

Indian women have also been active in Washington, D.C. As a Congresswoman, Ada Deer (Menominee) fought termination of federal recognition of and services to her reservation in northern Wisconsin. In 1993, she was appointed Assistant Secretary for Indian Affairs in the Clinton administration's Department of the Interior—the first woman to hold the highest ranking federal office responsible for governmental relations with Native tribes. LaDonna Harris (Comanche), wife of Oklahoma Senator Fred Harris, became highly visible as an advocate for Indian causes and for women's concerns in general.

Native American women today [2002] serve as tribal chairpersons,

---

15. "Indigenous Peoples—1492 and 1992," *Ms.*, September/October 1992.

16. See report by Caryn Newsmith, *WomensEnews (www.womensenews.org)*, August 3, 2001.

17. Groups focused on actively confronting violence against women include the Minnesota Indian Women's Resource Center *(www.miwrc.org)*; Violence Against American Indian, Alaskan Native, and First Nations Women *(http://home.earthlink. net/~deers/ native)*; Mending the Sacred Hoop: Technical Assistance Project to Stop Violence Against Women *(www.msh-ta.org)*; and the Native American Women's Health Education Resource Center *(www.nativeshop.org/nawherc.html)*, which addresses domestic violence, alcoholism, fetal alcohol syndrome, and HIV/AIDS prevention. See also data in "Landscape of the Ordinary: Violence Against Women," by Andrea Dworkin, p. 58, and "Rights, Realities, and Issues of Women with Disabilities," by Laura Hershey, p. 233.—Ed.

council members, and leaders of such national organizations as the National Congress of American Indians. They constitute approximately 60 percent of the enrollment of the tribally controlled community colleges that serve their communities, and serve as presidents of many of those institutions. In urban areas, where approximately 70 percent of American Indians now live, women run Indian centers, teach in schools for Indian children, manage businesses, and work in the labor force. Their lives are similar to those of their non-Indian counterparts. Native women have also made enriching contributions to the arts. In literature, such notable writers as Louise Erdrich, Joy Harjo, and Leslie Marmon Silko are only a few examples.[18]

There are more than 450 Native nations in the U.S. today, with tribal populations ranging from over 250,000 (Navajo) to less than 100. Despite their diversity, the ultimate value for Indian communities lies in our children and the metaphor of the seventh generation: all decisions being made must be judged by their effects on the seventh generation to come. This sense of responsibility to the future rests significantly on women as bearers of those generations. On these and other issues, Native American women today are reclaiming our power.

CLARA SUE KIDWELL received her Ph.D. in the history of science from the University of Oklahoma, where she is now director of the Native American studies program. She has taught at Haskell Indian Junior College, the University of Minnesota, the University of California at Berkeley, and was visiting assistant professor in Native American studies at Dartmouth. From 1993 to 1995, she was assistant director for Cultural Resources at the National Museum of the American Indian, Smithsonian Institution. She is the author of *Choctaws and Missionaries in Mississippi 1818–1918* (Norman, Oklahoma: University of Oklahoma Press, 1995). Her tribal affiliations are Chippewa and Choctaw.

---

18. See the anthologies *That's What She Said*, Rayna Green, ed. (Bloomington, Indiana: University of Indiana Press, 1984) and *A Gathering of Spirit: A Collection by North American Indian Women*, Beth Brant, ed. (Sinister Wisdom Books, 1984; Firebrand Books 1990).—Ed.

Suggested Further Reading

Bataille, Gretchen M., and Kathleen Mullen Sands. *American Indian Women: Telling Their Lives.* Lincoln, Nebraska: University of Nebraska Press, 1984.

Green, Rayna. *Women in American Indian Society.* New York: Chelsea House, 1992.

Lurie, Nancy Oestreich, ed. *Mountain Wolf Woman, Sister of Crashing Thunder: The Autobiography of a Winnebago Indian.* Ann Arbor, Michigan: University of Michigan Press, 1961.

Mankiller, Wilma, and Michael Wallis. *Mankiller: A Chief and Her People.* New York: St. Martin's Press, 1993.

Perdue, Theda, ed. *Sifters: Native American Women's Lives.* Oxford: Oxford University Press, 2001.

African American Women: The Legacy of Black Feminism

BEVERLY GUY-SHEFTALL

> Black women both shape the world and are shaped by it. . . .
> [They] create their own black feminist theory. They come to
> feminist theory and practice out of the oppression they expe-
> rience as people who are poor and black and women . . .
> black feminism has evolved historically over centuries, out-
> side traditional white feminine roles, white social institu-
> tions, and white feminist cultural theory.
> —Kesho Yvonne Scott, *The Habit of Surviving*, 1991

THE BLACK FEMINIST MOVEMENT, which began to emerge in the mid-
1960s, is a continuation of an intellectual and activist tradition that
began more than a century and a half earlier. I use the term "feminist" to
capture the emancipatory vision and acts of resistance among a diverse
group of black women (and some black men) who articulate their understanding of the complex nature of black womanhood, the interlocking nature of the oppressions black women suffer, and the necessity of
sustained struggle in their quest for self-definition, the liberation of
black people, and gender justice.[1]

The argument that African American women confronted both a

---

1. As a committed feminist educator/activist, I have been making visible in my writing and teaching the largely buried history of African American feminist thought
and praxis. This essay is a condensed version of work that began with my first essay
on the topic, "Remembering Sojourner Truth: On Black Feminism" (*Catalyst*, Fall
1986), and culminated in the publication of a ten-year excavation project, *Words of
Fire: An Anthology of African American Feminist Thought* [see contributor's biography
below]. My more recent interest in global black feminism has resulted in several essays on feminist thought in Africa and the African diaspora.

"woman question" and a "race problem" captured the essence of black feminist thought at the turn of the twentieth century and would reverberate among intellectuals, academics, activists, writers, artists, politicians, and community leaders—both female and male—for generations. While feminist perspectives have in fact been a persistent and important component of the African American literary and intellectual tradition since slavery, scholars until recently have focused primarily on the black community's relentless efforts to dismantle white supremacy. This tendency—which ignored long years of political struggle aimed at eradicating the multiple oppressions black women experience—resulted in erroneous notions about the relevance of feminism to the black community, especially during the contemporary wave of the Women's Movement over the past almost four decades.

Kimberly Springer's compelling chronicle[2] of The Third World Women's Alliance (1968), the National Black Feminist Organization [NBFO] (1973), Black Women Organized for Action (1973), the Combahee River Collective (1974), and the National Alliance of Black Feminists (1976) should put to rest forever the myth of feminism's irrelevance as a resistance strategy for African American women in their struggles for empowerment both within and without their communities during the 1960s and '70s. Similarly, *Words of Fire: An Anthology of African American Feminist Thought*[3] documents the presence of a continuous feminist intellectual tradition among black women going back to the early nineteenth century, when abolition and suffrage were urgent political issues. It is a corrective to the familiar history of U.S. feminism that ignores women of color or marginalizes them in grand narratives about the heroic deeds of political or revolutionary women in the United States.

While black feminism is not a monolithic, static ideology, and while there has been considerable diversity of thought among African Americans with feminist consciousness going back to the 1800s, certain premises characterize what came to be labeled "black feminism" in the 1960s:

---

2. Kimberly Springer, *Living for the Revolution: Black Feminist Organizations, 1968–1980* (Durham, North Carolina: Duke University Press, 2003).

3. Guy-Sheftall, ed., op. cit.

1. Black women experience a special kind of oppression in this country, one that is both racist and sexist, because of their dual racial and gender identities.

2. This "double jeopardy" has meant that the problems, concerns, and needs of black women are different in many ways from those of both white women and black men.

3. Black women must struggle for gender equality *and* black liberation, and have done so throughout their history in the United States.

4. There is no inherent contradiction in the struggle to eradicate sexism and racism, as well as such other "isms" as classism and heterosexism.

5. Black women's unique struggles with respect to racial and sexual politics, their poverty,[4] and their marginalized status have given them a particular view of the world.[5]

---

4. See "Poverty Wears a Female Face," by Theresa Funiciello, p. 222.—Ed.

5. Despite their historically higher labor force participation rates, African American women are nearly three times as likely to live in poverty and twice as likely to be unemployed as European American women. More than half of all black families are headed by females, and 45 percent of these single-parent households are living in poverty. Median family income for black families is only 61 percent of what white families earn. Black women are eight times as likely to go to prison as white women, mainly for drug-related offenses—as is the case for most imprisoned women of any race/ethnicity. HIV/AIDS is the leading cause of death among black women between the ages of 25 and 44. One in 160 black women is infected with HIV, and they are 10 times more likely than whites to be diagnosed with AIDS and 10 times more likely to die from it. African American women are 28 percent more likely to die from breast cancer—the most common type of malignancy among women in the U.S.—than European American women, and more likely to die from all the leading causes of death for women, with the exception of lung disease and suicide. Black women report high rates of partner violence. Rates of severe partner violence are higher for low-income black women as compared to higher-income black women. Black women with unemployed husbands suffer particularly high rates of severe violence. [For more statistics on African American women, see "The Politics of Aging," by Barbara Macdonald with Cynthia Rich, p. 152; "Landscape of the Ordinary: Violence Against Women," by Andrea Dworkin, p. 58; "Alive Behind the Labels: Women in Prison," by Kathy Boudin and Roslyn D. Smith, p. 244; "Prostitution = Slavery," by Vednita Carter, p. 315; "Our Bodies, Our Future: Women's Health Activism Overview," by Judy Norsigian et al., p. 269; and "Rights, Realities, and Issues of Women with Disabilites," by Laura Hershey, p. 233, among other essays in this anthology.—Ed.]

An historical perspective on the evolution of feminist consciousness among African American women is usually thought to have begun with abolition, since the catalyst for the emergence of the women's rights movement in the mid-nineteenth century was the movement to abolish slavery.[6] However, for 200 years enslaved African females had already been struggling for their freedom: protesting beatings, involuntary breeding, sexual exploitation by white masters, having to bring slave children they couldn't protect into the world, family separation, debilitating work schedules, substandard living conditions, and demeaning stereotypes—the most persistent being that they were immoral and sexually insatiable. However, covert use of contraceptives, the practice of abortion, and daring attempts to control the fate of their children—including the desperate act of infanticide—provided slave women some measure of control over their bodies and their reproductive capacity. The best-documented case of infanticide concerns Margaret Garner, who escaped slavery in Kentucky in 1856; during her capture in Cincinnati she killed her baby daughter rather than have the child returned to her master. This event was the inspiration for Toni Morrison's award-winning novel, *Beloved* (New York: Knopf, 1987).

In 1832, Maria W. Stewart, a free black woman from Connecticut with abolitionist and feminist impulses, delivered four public lectures in Boston, the first at the Afric-American Female Intelligence Society. She was probably the first black woman to speak publicly in defense of women's rights, though she is remembered primarily as the first American-born woman of *any* race who lectured publicly to racially mixed audiences of women and men. She spoke on a variety of issues relevant to the black community—literacy, self-determination, abolition, economic empowerment, and racial unity—but she admonished black women in particular to break free from stifling gender definitions and reach their fullest potential by pursuing formal education and careers outside the home, especially teaching. She was also adamant in her belief that black women should assume leadership roles within their communities—all of which are familiar themes in what we now would

---

6. History repeated itself in the twentieth century, since the contemporary Women's Movement—or at least the more radical-feminist wing of it—was born, in no small part, out of the Civil Rights Movement. See the Introduction to this anthology, p. *xv.*—Ed.

identify as a black feminist agenda. Furthermore, she warned against a paradoxical problem—what contemporary black feminists call an internal critique—that would plague the black community for generations: preaching against prejudice in the white community but being discriminatory in their own backyards.

The black women's club movement, which emerged on a national level in the 1890s and has been analyzed mainly in the context of racial uplift, is clearly a manifestation of resistance to both racism *and* sexism. When the First National Conference of Colored Women convened in Boston on July 29, 1895, the agenda included temperance, higher education, morality, vindicating the honor of black women, and education for girls and boys. A pivotal moment in black women's political history had been the founding, a year earlier in 1894, of *Women's Era*, eventually the official organ of the National Association of Colored Women. Since it was founded, edited, and published by Josephine St. Pierre Ruffin, who had initiated the New Era Club in Boston and was active in the Massachusetts women's suffrage movement, it isn't surprising that *Women's Era* advocated strongly for the right of women to vote. Black women were also encouraged to enter the public arena in order to solve their unique problems. In 1892, club woman Anna Julia Cooper published *A Voice from the South by a Black Woman of the South*, an enlightened, progressive discussion of the oppressed status of black women that we would now label pro-feminist. Not content with describing the plight of black females, she argued that they needed to speak out for themselves and stop allowing others, including black men, to speak for them. She criticized both black male sexism and the racism of white women, which links her to contemporary black feminists.

Black women's struggles against both racial and gender oppression would continue throughout the twentieth century, despite the winning of suffrage by women in 1920. The explicitly feminist, visionary writing of Amy Jacques Garvey (Marcus Garvey's second wife) is particularly important in this regard, because of her impact on thousands of working-class urban blacks involved with the Universal Negro Improvement Association (UNIA), which her husband organized in 1914. As editor of the women's page of the *Negro World*, UNIA's weekly newspaper, Amy wrote passionately in her column, "Our Women and What They Think," about the evils of imperialism, materialism, racism, capitalism, and the interlocking race, class, and gender oppression that black and other women experienced globally, particularly in colonial contexts. She believed that the Women's Movement was one of the most significant struggles in human history and that the emancipation of women was imperative. Echoing the legendary Sojourner Truth and Anna Julia Cooper, she espoused a revolutionary feminist vision of the world in which women would set things right because of their more humane inclinations: "You [men] had your day at the helm of the world, and a pretty mess you have made of it . . . and perhaps women's rule will usher in the era of real brotherhood, when national and racial lines will disappear, leaving mankind in peace and harmony with one another." Advocating for birth control was another item of the black feminist agenda during the 1920s and '30s, though it would remain controversial, given the black community's concern about genocide.

In the 1960s, black feminist struggle came to the forefront in a much more explicit manner. It coalesced mainly as a result of the successive failures of the civil rights, black nationalist, and women's rights organizations to address the particular needs and concerns of black women— and also because of heightened consciousness about sexism experienced during the Civil Rights Movement, especially in the Black Power phase, with its pervasive masculinist, cultural-nationalist ideologies. The simultaneous publication in 1970 of Toni Cade's anthology *The Black Woman* (New York: New American Library/Signet), Shirley Chisholm's autobiography *Unbought and Unbossed* (New York: Houghton Mifflin), Toni Morrison's novel *The Bluest Eye* (New York: Holt, Rinehart and Winston), and Audre Lorde's poetry in *Cables to Rage* (London: Paul Breman) signaled a literary awakening among black women. It also signaled the beginning of a clearly defined black women's liberation movement that would have different priorities from those of white feminists and would generate considerable debate, even hostility, within black communities. Toni Cade's anti-racist, anti-sexist, anti-imperialist agenda captures the essence of progressive black feminism in the aftermath of the Civil Rights Movement. She advocated a radical agenda for the Women's Movement that, had it been taken seriously (or even noticed

much), would have altered the course of so-called second-wave feminism:

> [S]et up a comparative study of the woman's role as she saw it
> in all the Third World nations; examine the public school
> system and blueprint some viable alternatives; explore our-
> selves and set the record straight on the matriarch and the
> evil Black bitch; delve into history and pay tribute to all our
> warriors from the ancient times to the slave trade to Harriet
> Tubman to Fannie Lou Hamer to the woman of this morn-
> ing; . . . interview the migrant workers, the quilting bee
> mothers, the grandmothers of the UNIA; analyze the Free-
> dom Budget and design ways to implement it; outline the
> work that has been done in the area of consumer education
> and cooperative economics; . . . provide a forum of opinion
> from the YWCA to the Black Women Enraged; get into the
> whole area of sensuality, sex; chart the steps necessary for
> forming a working alliance with all nonwhite women of the
> world for the formation of, among other things, a clearing-
> house for the exchange of information.[7]

Toni Cade's groundbreaking anthology, which includes a reprint of former Student Nonviolent Coordinating Committee (SNCC) activist
Frances Beale's now classic essay on the "double jeopardy" of black
women,[8] would have a profound impact on a younger generation of
women, such as bell hooks, Farah Griffin, and myself. When I interviewed Toni at her home in Atlanta, Georgia, for my first book, *Sturdy
Black Bridges*, I asked her whether it was a dilemma for her to be both a
feminist and a warrior in race struggle, since for some black folks that
was an oxymoron. She replied unequivocally, "I don't find any basic
contradiction or any tension between being a feminist, being a pan-

---

7. Toni Cade, ed. *The Black Woman: An Anthology* (New York: New American Li-
brary/Signet, 1970).

8. Frances Beale's essay "Double Jeopardy: To Be Black and Female"—first published in *Sisterhood Is Powerful*, Robin Morgan, ed. (New York: Random House/Vin-
tage Paperbacks, 1970)—became the most anthologized essay in the early years of
women's liberation publications.

Africanist, being a black nationalist, being an internationalist, being a socialist, and being a woman in North America."[9] This was precisely the message many of us young black feminists needed, as we found ourselves increasingly under suspicion with respect to our race loyalty.

In 1973, the NBFO would emerge in part as a reminder to the black liberation movement that there shouldn't be liberation for half a race. In their statement of purpose, they objected to the perception of the Women's Movement as solely white and their involvement in it as being disloyal to the race. A year after the founding meeting, NBFO's Boston chapter decided to form a more radical organization and in 1975 named itself The Combahee River Collective (named after Harriet Tubman's 1863 military campaign in South Carolina, which freed nearly 800 enslaved people—the only military campaign in U.S. history planned and led by a woman). In 1977, the Collective issued its now classic manifesto, "The Black Feminist Statement," which asserted that "sexual politics under patriarchy is as pervasive in black women's lives as the politics of class and race."[10] Emphasizing the "simultaneity" of racial, gender, heterosexual, and class oppression[11] in the lives of black women and other women of color, they affirmed their connection to an activist tradition among black women dating back to the nineteenth century, as well as to black liberation struggles of the 1960s. Despite the difficulty of sustaining a radical, socialist, black feminist organization with lesbian

---

9. Interview with Toni Cade Bambara, *Sturdy Black Bridges: Visions of Black Women in Literature*, Roseann P. Bell, Bettye J. Parker, and Beverly Guy-Sheftall, eds. (New York: Doubleday, 1979).

10. *The Combahee River Collective Statement: Black Feminist Organizing in the Seventies and Eighties*, by Demita Frazier, Beverly Smith, and Barbara Smith for The Combahee River Collective, with a foreword by Barbara Smith (Albany, New York: Kitchen Table Women of Color Press, 1985). The Statement has also appeared in the anthologies *All the Women Are White, All the Blacks Are Men, But Some of Us Are Brave: Black Women's Studies*, Barbara Smith, Gloria Hull, and Patricia Bell Scott, eds. (New York: The Feminist Press at CUNY, 1982); *This Bridge Called My Back: Writings by Radical Women of Color*, Cherríe Moraga and Gloria Anzaldúa, eds. (Albany, New York: Kitchen Table Women of Color Press, 1983); *Home Girls: A Black Feminist Anthology*, Barbara Smith, ed. (Albany, New York: Kitchen Table, 1983; reissued New Brunswick, New Jersey: Rutgers University Press, 1999), and *Words of Fire*, Beverly Guy-Sheftall, ed., op. cit.).—Ed.

11. See "Traffic at the Crossroads: Multiple Oppressions," by Kimberlé Crenshaw, p. 43.—Ed.

leadership for six years, they worked tirelessly on a variety of "revolutionary" issues—pro-choice, rape, prison reform, sterilization abuse, violence against women, health care, and racism within the white movement.[12] Just as important was their breaking silence about homophobia in the black community, and their providing opportunities for black women with different sexual preferences/orientations to work together.

Despite their commitment to the ideals of feminism and even their own activism, some black women continued to be alienated by the word "feminist." As an alternative, the term "womanist" came to be preferred by many in the early 1980s, following its introduction in Alice Walker's *In Search of Our Mothers' Gardens: Womanist Prose* (New York: Harcourt, 1983) as a more culturally appropriate way to refer to black feminists.

Nearly a decade later, President George Bush's 1991 nomination of Judge Clarence Thomas to the Supreme Court and Professor Anita Hill's subsequent allegations of sexual harassment sparked perhaps the most profound intraracial tensions around sexual politics that the modern African American community had ever experienced.[13]

Although the Hill/Thomas saga provoked unprecedented anger in the black community, perhaps its most significant outcome, according to feminist historian Paula Giddings, is that a mandate on gender—particularly a "sexual discourse unmediated by the question of racism"—occurred for the first time among the black population at large.[14] Hill's public disclosure of a black-on-black sexual crime provided the catalyst

---

12. See "Unfinished Agenda: Reproductive Rights," by Faye Wattleton, p. 17; "Confessions of a Worrywart: Ruminations on a Lesbian Feminist Overview," by Karla Jay, p. 212; and essays by Dworkin, Boudin and Smith, Hershey, and Norsigian, op. cit. For more on racism, see "U.S. Latinas: Active at the Intersections of Gender, Nationality, Race, and Class," by Edna Acosta-Belén and Christine E. Bose, p. 198; "Reclaiming the Past, Redefining the Future: Asian American and Pacific Islander Women," by Helen Zia, p. 188; and the Introduction, p. *xv*. For more on racist sterilization abuse, see "Native Americans: Restoring the Power of Thought Woman," by Clara Sue Kidwell, p. 165.—Ed.

13. See "The Nature of the Beast: Sexual Harassment," by Anita Hill, p. 296.—Ed.

14. Paula Giddings, "The Last Taboo," in *Race-ing Justice, En-gendering Power: Essays on Anita Hill, Clarence Thomas, and the Construction of Social Reality*, Toni Morrison, ed. (New York: Pantheon, 1992).

for a broad-based, enlightened discussion of gender issues that had enormous potential for resolving a number of problems relating to sexual politics, male privilege, and unequal power relations within black communities. Hill's example was also a challenge to black women to remain silent no longer, under the guise of racial solidarity, about the abuse they suffer from black men.

Black feminism, though still controversial, would emerge from the shadows in the 1990s. It would also move from the margins to the center of mainstream feminist discourse, just as Anita Hill had unwittingly provided a shot in the arm for the entire Women's Movement. Young black feminists and hip-hop generationers (sometimes called "third wavers") would articulate their own brand of feminism, often unrecognizable by "second wavers." [15]

As far as the future of black feminism is concerned, its challenges in the twenty-first century are enormous: improving the lives of black people, especially women and children in poor and working-class communities; convincing young women and men—particularly the thousands who've had no exposure to progressive gender politics—that feminism is useful in struggles for the liberation of black America; making more effective connections between feminist theory and activism or transformative social change around the world, forging linkages with feminists (including gender-progressive men wherever they live), especially feminist activists in Africa and the African Diaspora. In the words of a committed black feminist activist and writer who has become disappointed with the evolution of the contemporary Women's Movement over the course of her 30-year-long involvement: "to restore relevance, significance, and resonance to black feminist theorizing, feminists will need to position their theories much closer to the lived experiences of black women." [16] This wake-up call for *all* feminists is not intended to immo-

---

15. See "Girls: 'We Are the Ones Who Can Make a Change!' " by Ana Grossman and Emma Peters-Axtell, p. 121; "Generation 'Why?': A Call to Arms," by Jasmine Victoria, p. 126; "Stealth Feminists: The Thirtysomething Revolution," by Debra Michals, p. 138; "Notes of a Feminist Long Distance Runner," by Eleanor Holmes Norton, p. 145; and "The Politics of Aging," by Macdonald with Rich, op. cit.—Ed.

16. Sheila Radford-Hill, *Further to Fly: Black Women and the Politics of Empowerment* (Minneapolis, Minnesota: University of Minnesota Press, 2000).

bilize, but rather to recharge our batteries so that we will recommit ourselves to radical social change in a world urgently needing our values and insights, our political strategies, and our visions of social justice. The struggle continues.

BEVERLY GUY-SHEFTALL is founding director of the Women's Research and Resource Center and the Anna Julia Cooper Professor of Women's Studies at Spelman College. She also teaches in the doctoral program in women's studies at Emory University. She has published a number of texts within feminist studies, including her dissertation, *Daughters of Sorrow: Attitudes Toward Black Women, 1880–1920* (New York: Carlson Publishing Company, 1991); *Words of Fire: An Anthology of African American Feminist Thought* (New York: The New Press, 1995); and *Gender Talk*, with Johnnetta B. Cole (New York: Random House, 2003). She has been involved with the national women's studies movement since its inception and provided the leadership for the establishment of the first women's studies major at an historically black college. Beyond the academy, she has been involved in numerous advocacy and activist organizations, including the National Black Women's Health Project, the National Council for Research on Women, and the National Coalition of 100 Black Women. She continues to be active in the international Women's Movement, and teaches courses on global feminism, women of African descent, and feminist theory.

Suggested Further Reading

Byrd, Rudolph P., and Beverly Guy-Sheftall, eds. *Traps: African American Men on Gender and Sexuality*. Bloomington, Indiana: Indiana University Press, 2001.

Collins, Patricia Hill. *Fighting Words: Black Women & the Search for Justice*. Minneapolis, Minnesota: University of Minnesota Press, 1998.

Hine, Darlene Clark, ed. *Black Women in America: An Historical Encyclopedia*. Two volumes. Brooklyn, New York: Carlson Publishing Company, 1993.

James, Joy, T. Denean Sharpley-Whiting, and Tracey T. Sharpley-

Whiting, eds. *The Black Feminist Reader.* Malden, Massachusetts: Blackwell Publishers, Inc., 2000.

James, Stanlie M., and Abena P. A. Busia, eds. *Theorizing Black Feminisms: The Visionary Pragmatism of Black Women.* New York: Routledge, 1993.

Reclaiming the Past, Redefining the Future: Asian American and Pacific Islander Women

HELEN ZIA

IN 1972, I JOINED MY FIRST consciousness-raising group—an Asian American women's study group, an electrifying gathering of young college women. We even succeeded in persuading the university to give us course credit. All of us were of Chinese or Japanese descent (then typical of Asian American demographics), with only a thin slice of Asian American and Pacific Islander (AAPI) diversity. We modeled our studies after other Asian American women's groups, mainly from the West Coast. Our primary textbook was *Roots: An Asian American Reader*,[1] the first compiled writings of the new Asian American movement that linked our many ethnicities together in the struggle against racism and sexism at home with imperialism abroad. Alongside *Roots* was *Sisterhood Is Powerful*,[2] our connection to the women's liberation movement.

To speak of our lives as Asian women was radical, subversive, and thrilling. We "talked story" about our foremothers, how they escaped oppressive feudal family structures by making the transpacific migration to an unfamiliar, often unwelcome place in the United States, where most worked as stoop labor on segregated plantations or in ghetto sweatshops; many had endured war and turmoil in Asia, or had suffered imprisonment in U.S. concentration camps. My group also examined

---

1. Amy Tachiki, Eddie Wong, and Franklin Oda, eds. (Los Angeles: UCLA Asian American Studies Center, 1971).

2. Robin Morgan, ed. (New York: Random House and Vintage Books, 1970).

the Confucian moral codes that governed a woman's place in the patriarchy: the Three Obediences, whereby the daughter obeys the father, the wife obeys the husband, and the widow obeys the son. Our Asian American generation wanted no part of this cultural pattern—and we rebelled.

Asian American feminists at Berkeley and San Francisco State organized International Women's Day celebrations in San Francisco's Chinatown. Women in Los Angeles, San Francisco, Honolulu, Seattle, New York, and Boston led community efforts to resist plans by bureaucrats and real-estate developers to demolish Asian American communities in the name of urban renewal. Second- and third-generation Japanese American women began to reopen painful family memories of their parents' internment during World War II. Asian American women went to Canada to express solidarity with leading women freedom fighters from North Vietnam, who had come to North America to speak of their resistance against U.S. imperialism.

Many Asian American women were active in the New Left of the 1970s, going to Chinatown to build health clinics or organize sweatshop workers, or joining the industrial labor movement on assembly lines. In 1975, I became one of the first women construction workers in Boston, as part of a Third World workers' movement to integrate the nearly all-white and male construction trades. I was proud to call myself a feminist, though many Asian American women activists preferred the term "womanist," or wished simply to be seen as a sister in the struggle. The label was ultimately unimportant; our desire to make the lives of women and girls count was/is the spirit we share with women around the world.

Some of us joined the movement against gender violence, in conjunction with yet independent from mainstream feminist organizing against domestic violence and sexual assault. The first culturally specific domestic violence program for AAPI women was founded in Los Angeles in 1981, soon followed by the New York Asian Women's Center (*www.nyawc.org*) and the San Francisco-based Asian Women's Shelter. In the electoral arena, Representative Patsy Mink of Hawaii was the first woman of color elected to Congress (1965), and Irene Natividad, a Filipina-American, became the first woman of color to head the National Women's Political Caucus (1985–89).

In those days, we expected that our new-found connection to U.S.

history and social struggles would soon become general knowledge, accepted as part of the common heritage—but this still has not happened. Few people beyond ourselves seem to know of the enslavement, bondage, and sexual objectification of Asian American women, or of the genocidal treatment of Pacific Islanders, or how racial and ethnic stratification was a conscious policy employed by government and industry against Asian Americans and Pacific Islanders—all of which are events deeply imbedded in the history of the United States. Not knowing any of this, even fewer people have an inkling of Asian America's impact on contemporary U.S. dynamics.

The very existence of Asian and Pacific Islander women in America was an act of survival and courage. Those pioneering women had to counter overtly racist immigration laws that led to a near-absence of Chinese, Filipina, and South Asian Indian women until the mid-1900s; for example, between 1848 and 1854, only *16* Chinese women were admitted to the U.S.—compared to *45,000* Chinese men. The Page Law of 1875 was the first federal anti-Asian exclusion act—and it was aimed specifically at barring Chinese women. At the same time, European and American imperial powers wreaked economic disaster on the Pacific Islands, and their sexually transmitted diseases reduced the indigenous Native Hawaiian population from thriving communities of 400,000 to 40,000 in only three generations. Today, demographers predict that there will not be a single "full-blooded" Native Hawaiian left in the next generation—just one indicator of why Native Hawaiian sovereignty rights are a great priority.[3]

A Chinese woman named Afong Moy was the first Asian American woman of record, when in 1834 she became a living curio—a literal ex-

---

3. Native Hawaiians had a constitutional monarchy and a governmental structure that ruled the islands long before Captain James Cook brought European interests in 1778. Many Hawaiian rulers had been women, and the tradition of strong female leaders lives on in such legendary figures as Pele, the goddess of fire and the creatrix of the Islands. In 1893, the U.S. military, together with sugar-plantation owners and other mainland capitalists, seized control of Hawaii by overthrowing its constitutional monarchy, then headed by Queen Lili'uokalani. Her goal had been to preserve Hawaii for its native people. She was imprisoned and held under house arrest for more than a year, while Native Hawaiians called in vain for a restoration of their government. Today, more than 100 years later, Native Hawaiians continue to organize against the illegal seizure of their nation, and persist in pressing for self-determination.

hibit among the inanimate Asian artifacts at the American Museum (and other New York exhibition halls). From the beginning, Asian women in America were exploited as exotic, alien commodities—whether they were captured and enslaved in brothels or put on display by Phineas T. Barnum. The image of graceful, voluptuous, compliant Pacific Islander maidens is still heavily marketed as a tourist lure for Hawaii and elsewhere—a soft-core version of the sex tourism that booms in Asia and the Pacific, contributing to the misery and early death of hundreds of thousands of women and girls. Among the many Asian American women who have documented these hardships are Shamita Das DasGupta, Phoebe Eng, Maxine Hong Kingston, Jessica Hagedorn, Elaine Kim, Miriam Ching Louie, Ruthanne Lum McCunn, Janice Mirikitani, and Judy Yung, to name but a few nonfiction writers and essayists. The roster of Asian American women novelists is, happily, too long to attempt here.

U.S. immigration law held a place of special ignominy for the "depraved" and "amoral" Asian woman, because Asian women represented an undesired family stability for Asian immigrant men, a stability many politicians were determined to prevent, since it threatened the status quo with unwanted future generations of "heathens." There were only three Asian Indian wives in the United States by 1910, in contrast to several thousand Indian male emigrés; when a fourth Indian woman arrived, headlines blared, "Hindu Women Next Swarm to California."[4] Japanese American women were the only Asian females permitted to immigrate in any numbers; Japan's military strength impressed Teddy Roosevelt at the dawn of the twentieth century, so the women arrived as picture brides to be used as chattel labor on plantations and farms in Hawaii and California—that is, until the United States shut down all immigration from Japan and Korea in 1907, just as it had excluded Chinese immigration in 1882. Kayo Hatta's 1995 film *Picture Bride* poignantly captures the saga of those foremothers.

Asian women began to immigrate again in the years after World War II, as brides for Asian American (as well as non-Asian) GIs. The racist federal laws that excluded all "Asiatics" from becoming naturalized citi-

---

4. Sucheta Mazumdar, "Asian Pacific Women," in *The Reader's Companion to U.S. Women's History*, Wilma Mankiller et al. (New York: Houghton Mifflin, 1998).

zens weren't removed until 1952. But the biggest changes in community and family came in the decades following the 1965 Immigration Act and the end of the war in Vietnam. New immigrants came from China, the Philippines, India, Korea, Pakistan, Bangladesh, and elsewhere in Asia, in numbers that had not been seen since the 1800s, while nearly a million impoverished refugees from Vietnam, Cambodia, and Laos arrived at relocation communities throughout the country. U.S. military bases and nuclear-bomb-testing sites in the Pacific massively displaced Samoans, Chamorrans, and other indigenous island peoples; nearly as many Samoans now live in California as do in Samoa. The destruction of Pacific Island cultures by U.S., French, Japanese, and multinational business interests is an imminent danger.

As the population of Asian Americans and Pacific Islanders surged in the last decades of the twentieth century, Asian American women have contributed fresh voices and activism. On the issue of domestic violence, for example, the 1990s began with merely four programs in the entire United States that addressed the particular needs of AAPI women. By 2000, there were seven Asian women's shelters across the country and more than a dozen outreach, education, and hotline programs with services for numerous Asian American ethnicities, including South Asian, Hmong, and Korean American communities. The pioneering San Francisco–based Asian Women's Shelter not only provides culturally sensitive services in multiple Asian languages, but also offers a Queer Asian Pacific Islander domestic violence program that reaches out to AAPI lesbian women and educates heterosexual shelter residents about homophobia. These domestic violence activists used the 1994 federal Violence Against Women Act[5] to secure protections for battered immigrant women who previously had risked deportation if they dared to leave abusive relationships. In 2001, these programs were linked together through the Asian and Pacific Islander Domestic Violence Institute (APIDV)[6] a national collaboration between AAPI feminists and

---

5. This Act was later (in 2000) largely invalidated as "a violation of states' rights" in a decision by the conservative majority of the Supreme Court. See "Landscape of the the Ordinary: Violence Against Women," by Andrea Dworkin, p. 58, and "Women and Law: The Power to Change," by Catharine A. MacKinnon, p. 447.—Ed.

6. Reachable at: *www.apiahf.org*, the website of the Asian and Pacific Islander American Health Forum.

other leading domestic violence organizations. APIDV's goal is to make culturally specific issues visible, and to strengthen community models of prevention and intervention—for example, dealing with cultural attitudes in the Hmong and South Asian communities on the issue of forced marriages and marriages of underage girls.

In recent years there have been several national and regional initiatives by and on behalf of AAPI women. These have been examined in a 2002 groundbreaking report to The Ford Foundation by Lora Jo Foo, a longtime AAPI women's advocate. The study, "Asian American Women: Issues, Concerns, and Responsive Human and Civil Rights Advocacy," which also examined health issues, reproductive rights, environmental health, and domestic violence,[7] included the following:

- Asian American women have suffered a double blow since the passage of welfare "reform" in 1996, because a disproportionate burden of budget cuts fall on immigrant women.[8] Asian American women are often denied public benefits because of language barriers, mandatory reporting requirements to the Immigration and Naturalization Service, fear that accessing public benefits might make them perceivable as undesirable public charges, confusion about eligibility, and hostile caseworkers. A high number of Asian women are pushed into dead-end "workfare" jobs where they learn no skills and are denied English-language training as an option. Many immigrant welfare recipients lost or were denied benefits because the state failed to provide interpreters or to translate documents. The results: increases in hunger and illness among Asian immigrant women and their families.
- Each year, approximately 30,000 women from the most impoverished countries of Asia are brought to the United States and held in servitude, forced into prostitution, bonded sweatshop

---

7. See "Our Bodies, Our Future: Women's Health Activism Overview," by Judy Norsigian, et al., p. 269; "Unfinished Agenda: Reproductive Rights," by Faye Wattleton, p. 17; "Update: Feminism and the Environment," by Paula DiPerna, p. 503; and Dworkin, op. cit.—Ed.

8. See "Poverty Wears a Female Face" by Theresa Funiciello, p. 222, and "Traffic at the Crossroads: Multiple Oppressions," by Kimberlé Crenshaw, p. 43.—Ed.

labor, and domestic servitude. Criminal groups lure women to the United States with false promises of high-wage, good-working-conditions jobs as models, nannies, waitresses, and factory workers. These groups front money for the women's travel, charging from $25,000 to $40,000. Once in the United States, the women are forced into prostitution or other servitude and kept there under threats (and acts) of violence until their debts are repaid.[9] Wealthy emigrés—corporate executives, diplomats, and international bureaucrats at the United Nations, the World Bank, and the IMF—also traffick Asian women to the U.S., to work as their domestic help. In addition, 4,000 to 6,000 women, mostly Filipina, are purchased every year by white men and brought to the U.S. as "mail-order brides"; there have been high-profile cases of such women being battered and murdered by their husbands. Until the Trafficking Victims Protection Act was passed in October 2000, law enforcement treated these victims as criminals, prosecuting them as prostitutes or deporting them. To assist trafficked people and end such human rights violations, the Coalition Against Slavery and Trafficking in Women (CAST; *www.trafficked-women.org*) was founded in 1998 in Los Angeles; it started as a result of the infamous El Monte sweatshop case, wherein women were imprisoned and chained to sewing machines.

- Over 60,000 Asian immigrant women work in the Los Angeles, New York, and San Francisco garment industries, the vast majority non-English speakers. Ten- to twelve-hour days, six to seven days a week are the norm these garment workers toil. On piece rate, they earn from $2 an hour to the federal minimum wage of $5.15 per hour—without any overtime pay. They work under hazardous conditions that include blocked fire exits, unsanitary bathrooms, and poor ventilation; they also suffer from repetitive stress injuries. Undocumented workers, particularly those who were smuggled in by traffickers, work under conditions of forced servitude and are subject to beatings, harassment, even death.

---

9. See "Prostitution = Slavery," by Vednita Carter, p. 315.—Ed.

- California's Silicon Valley is famed for its "green," environmentally "safe" products, but the truth is that the women-of-color workers—who labor at the bottom of the highly segregated semiconductor industry—are exposed to toxic chemical agents and atrocious working conditions, with few protections. The job heirarchy adheres to strict race, class, and gender lines: high-paid, stock-optioned professionals are overwhelmingly white European American males; women, especially European American women, comprise nearly 80 percent of the secretarial workforce. Women of color, primarily from Latin America and Asia, are clustered at the bottom of the wage ladder in production jobs, fabrication, and assembly.[10] A 1988 study found that 38 percent of pregnant women in the supposedly "clean" rooms suffered spontaneous abortions; seven chemical agents used by fabrication workers have been linked to spontaneous abortions. Of the 58 chemicals used in the construction of chips, circuits, and monitors, 15 are suspected carcinogens.

Foo's research[11] underscores the conclusions of the National Asian Pacific American Women's Forum *(www.napawf.org)*, which has organized

---

10. See Crenshaw, op. cit., and "U.S. Latinas: Active at the Intersections of Gender, Nationality, Race, and Class," by Edna Acosta-Belén and Christine E. Bose, p. 198.—Ed.

11. The Foo report identified several AAPI women's organizations that address the above and other issues, including the following: Asian Pacific Environmental Network (APEN) works with Laotian girls in Richmond, California (where large oil refineries are concentrated), to develop environmental justice leaders among the girls and raise their knowledge of reproductive health matters *(www.apen4ej.org)*. Asians and Pacific Islanders for Reproductive Health (APIRH), in Oakland, California, is the only organization whose focus is organizing and advocating to ensure reproductive freedom for Asian American women and girls *(www.apirh.org)*. Asian Immigrant Women Advocates (AIWA), based in Oakland, California, since 1983, seeks to foster empowerment of low-income, limited-English-speaking Asian immigrant women who work as seamstresses, hotel-room cleaners, workers, and janitors (e-mail: *Aiwa@igc.apc.org*). The Asian Pacific Islander Lesbian Bisexual Network (APLBN) was founded in 1987 to bridge the Asian lesbian, bisexual, and transgender communities throughout the U.S. and abroad (P. O. Box 210698 San Francisco, California, 94121; *http://expage.com/page/aplbn*). The New York City-based Committee Against Anti-Asian Violence (CAAAV) has a comprehensive ongoing welfare-rights program that includes advocacy for children who are pulled out of school to translate at

grassroots discussion groups in five cities to formulate a national strategy on behalf of Asian American and Pacific Islander women. NAPAWF was founded in 1996 by AAPI feminists after the United Nations Fourth World Congress on Women (Beijing, 1995), for the purpose of founding a grassroots movement for social and economic justice and the political empowerment of AAPI women and girls. These feminists are attempting to bring a national, progressive women's voice to such issues as health care, reproductive rights, economic justice for immigrant women workers, *real* welfare reform, trafficking of women, battered immigrant women, etc.

Despite the serious needs documented by Asian American feminists, a study conducted in 2000 by the Asian Pacific American Women's Leadership Institute *(www.apawli.org)* found that AAPI women are consistently underrepresented at leadership levels of government, education, nonprofit organizations, and corporations. APAWLI noted that race- and gender-based perceptions of AAPI women continue to pose significant barriers. The harmful stereotype of Asian Americans as the "model minority" has hindered grassroots organizers in obtaining support for domestic violence programs; for example—because Asian Americans are not perceived to have social problems or to experience racism. Even in the hierarchies of some feminist organizations, Asian American women experience being relegated to subordinate positions and not being seen as potential leadership, because racial stereotypes of passivity and subservience are so prevalent.

Today, Asian American and Pacific Islander women are on the cutting edge of change in many areas. We are in a state of dynamic transformation—from organizing by multiracial Asian Americans to critiques of transracial adoption as viewed by Korean American women (who are among the 100,000 Korean adoptees raised in mainly non-Asian families); from international networking by Asian American lesbians, bisexual, and transgendered women to South Asian American perspectives on arranged marriages and domestic abuse. On all these fronts and

---

welfare offices for their moms (e-mail: *justice@caaav.org*). Sweatshop Watch, a coalition of 24 organizations formed in 1995, engages in anti-sweatshop work *(www. sweatshopwatch.org)*. Workers Awaaz organizes South Asian workers in New York City, with the primary focus on domestic workers *(Workersawaaz@yahoo.com)*.

more, Asian American women, strong and loud, are not just reclaiming our history; we are defining our present—*and* shaping our future.

HELEN ZIA, a second-generation Chinese American, authored *Asian American Dreams: The Emergence of an American People* (Farrar, Straus and Giroux, 2000), and coauthored *My Country Versus Me* (Hyperion Books, 2002) with Dr. Wen Ho Lee, the Los Alamos scientist falsely accused of spying for China. Zia is an award-winning journalist and a contributing editor to *Ms.* magazine, where she was formerly executive editor, and her articles, essays, and reviews have appeared in numerous publications. In 1999 and 2000, she was named one of the most influential Asian Americans of the decade by *A. Magazine.* A longtime activist for social justice on issues ranging from civil rights and peace to women's rights and countering hate violence, her work on the landmark civil rights case of anti-Asian violence is documented in the Academy Award–nominated film, *Who Killed Vincent Chin?* A graduate of Princeton University's Woodrow Wilson School of Public and International Affairs, Zia was in the university's first graduating class of women. She attended medical school for two years, then quit and found work as a construction laborer, an autoworker, and a community organizer, after which she discovered her life's work as a writer.

Suggested Further Reading

Eng, David L., and Alice Y. Hom, eds. *Q & A: Queer in Asian America.* Philadelphia: Temple University Press, 1998.

Eng, Phoebe. *Warrior Lessons: An Asian American Woman's Journey into Power.* New York: Pocket Books, 1999.

Kim, Elaine, et al. *Making More Waves: New Writing by Asian American Women.* Boston: Beacon Press, 1997.

Nam, Vickie, *Yell-Oh Girls: Emerging Voices Explore Culture, Identity, and Growing Up Asian American.* New York: HarperCollins, 2001.

Shah, Sonia, ed. *Dragon Ladies: Asian American Feminists Breathe Fire.* Boston: South End Press, 1997.

U.S. Latinas: Active at the Intersections of Gender, Nationality, Race, and Class

EDNA ACOSTA-BELÉN AND
CHRISTINE E. BOSE

Historical Background and Demographics

Any discussion about U.S. Latinas or the Hispanic population as a whole implies a recognition of the twenty different nationalities currently classified by the U.S. Census and other government agencies under only one label. This official practice tends to eclipse the many different national origins, races, social and cultural experiences, and histories of the various individual Latino groups. Thus the adequacy of a label that tends to homogenize such a diverse conglomerate of individual nationalities is still strongly contested.

The Hispanic or Latino category includes descendants of early Spanish settlers of North America during the colonial period, as well as newcomers in our time. Many were born in territories once part of Spain and then Mexico; others have arrived in the United States from almost every country in Latin America and the Caribbean, for economic and political reasons, as immigrants or migrants, refugees or undocumented workers. Historically, Latino migratory waves tend to respond to adverse socioeconomic and political conditions in the countries of origin, to displacements and conditions driven by U.S. policies and economic/military interventions in the countries of the hemisphere, and to specific needs of the U.S. economy for low-wage labor during certain periods. Thus every Latino group has its own historical migratory relationship with the United States. Many Mexicans/Chicanos were original settlers of the Southwest before the birth of the U.S. nation, and they lost their land as a result of Texas independence (1836) and the Mexican-American War (1846–1848). Other Latino groups were recruited at different times during the nineteenth and twentieth centuries to work as contract laborers in railroad construction, mining, agricultural, and factory work, while a smaller group ventures into the U.S. as undocumented workers.

There has been an established Cuban and Puerto Rican presence in the United States since the second half of the nineteenth century, when the islands were still under Spanish control, and Antillean emigré communities emerged in cities like New York, Philadelphia, Tampa, New Orleans, and Key West. During this period, the islands of Cuba and Puerto Rico were also important trade partners of the United States and, because of their geographic strategic location, were coveted territories in U.S. designs to establish its hegemony over the American hemisphere. This relationship brought island entrepreneurs, professionals, students, political exiles, and workers to the United States. The Spanish-Cuban-American War of 1898 led to the initial annexation of Cuba and Puerto Rico by the United States, and although Cuba was granted independence in 1903, it was subject to U.S. economic and military intervention until the 1959 Cuban Revolution. Although some Cubans came before the Revolution, after 1959, major waves of Cuban exiles settled in the United States, especially in Florida, New York, and New Jersey. To this day, Puerto Rico remains an unincorporated territory of the United States, and U.S. citizenship was decreed for all Puerto Ricans in 1917. Thus this colonial relationship fostered increased migration of Puerto Ricans, initially to cities like New York, Chicago, and Philadelphia and, in later years, to several cities in the states of Connecticut, Massachusetts, New Jersey, and Florida. In the particular case of Puerto Ricans, their U.S. citizenship allows them to move freely between the island and the continent, which has created a commuter pattern and an unusual demographic reality for a Latin American nation: in the year 2000, the population of Puerto Rico was 3.8 million—compared to the 3.4 million Puerto Ricans residing in the United States.

Latino population growth in the United States since the 1970s has been both unprecedented and ongoing. With a total population in the year 2000 of slightly over 35 million (the equivalent of the combined population of several Latin American countries), this is the largest minority group in U.S. society, which—according to demographic projections—will constitute 25 percent of the total U.S. population by the middle of the twenty-first century. Two major factors explain this significant population growth: when compared to other groups, they have higher immigration and fertility rates, with the birth rate largely due to their young median age of 26 years; at least one third of all Latinos are under age 18. A large majority of Latinas are Roman Catholic—but this has not deterred the emergence of organizations defending the reproductive rights and health of Latinas[1] (there are also significant numbers of the Latino population affiliated with different Protestant denominations and sects, as well as such religious practices as *Espiritismo* and *Santeria*). The majority of the Latino population is concentrated in nine states: California, Texas, New York, New Jersey, Florida, Illinois, Colorado, Arizona, and New Mexico.[2] At least 39.1 percent of the total population is foreign-born. Because some immigration streams have been more male-dominated than others, particularly among Mexicans and Cubans, there are 105.9 Latino men for every 100 Latina women, in comparison to 96.3 men per 100 women in the total U.S. population.

The largest individual Latino groups are Mexicans/Chicanos, Puerto Ricans, Cubans, Dominicans, and Central Americans. Mexicans/Chicanos represent 58.5 percent of all Latinos, followed by Puerto Ricans (9.6 percent), Cubans (3.5 percent), and Dominicans (2.2 percent). Central and South Americans collectively represent 14.5 percent of the total and are largely concentrated in the Washington, D.C. area, and also in New York, California, and Florida.[3]

---

1. See "Dancing Against the Vatican," by Frances Kissling, p. 474.—Ed.

2. A study released in July 2002—a joint project by the Pew Hispanic Center and the Brookings Institution Center on Urban and Metropolitan Policy—confirms that the Hispanic population continues to spread across the U.S. faster and farther than any previous immigrant waves, with the population concentration in large metropolitan cities increasing, but also with a fast-growing dispersal rate to smaller cities and to suburbs ("Latino Population Growth Is Widespread, Study Says," by Lynette Clemetson, *New York Times*, 31 July 2002).—Ed.

3. "The Hispanic Population of the United States," Current Population Reports, U.S. Bureau of the Census, March 2000; and U.S. Census Bureau, Census 2000 Summary File 1.

There are notable differences in the socioeconomic status of each Latino group, but collectively they still fare lower than the white non-Hispanic population in income and employment levels, and in educational achievement.[4] Their present collective poverty rate of 22.8 percent is almost three times higher than for the non-Hispanic white population (7.7 percent); 41 percent of Latino homes with children under age 18 are headed by women and 38.8 percent of Latina heads of households live below the poverty line,[5] resulting in fewer economic resources for these children. The most common occupations among Latinas are in the service sector (26 percent), technical sales (38 percent), managerial (18 percent), and operators and laborers (13 percent).[6]

Another important factor in the lives of Latinas in the United States is their racially mixed profile. A long history of miscegenation in their countries of origin between white European, black, and Indian groups endows each Latino nationality with its own racial categories and definitions that do not fit the generalized white/black racial dichotomy prevalent in U.S. society. For some Latino groups, the black or Indian racial and cultural heritage is more obvious than for others. In this sense, the widespread *mestizaje* (racial mixture) of the Latino population is forcing a redefinition of U.S. racial categories by introducing a broader multiracial optic.

When compared to other immigrant groups in U.S. society, a large portion of the Latino population maintains strong transnational connections and bidirectional exchanges with their countries of origin.

---

4. A 2002 study by the Pew Hispanic Center reported that Latino/Latina high school graduates enroll in college at a *higher* rate than non-Hispanic European Americans, by some measures, but are *less* likely to earn a four-year degree—not because of a lack of interest but due to financial pressures. Furthermore, Latino/Latina college students were far more likely to be enrolled in two-year programs and community colleges than their non-Hispanic white counterparts ("Education Study Finds Hispanics Both Gaining and Lagging," by Diana Jean Schemo, *New York Times*, 8 September 2002).—Ed.

5. See "Poverty Wears a Female Face," by Theresa Funiciello, p. 222; for statistics on older and widowed Latinas, see "The Politics of Aging," by Barbara Macdonald with Cynthia Rich, p. 152.—Ed.

6. "The Hispanic Population of the United States: March 1997," Current Population Survey, U.S. Bureau of the Census, March 1997, Table 9.3. [See also "Pink Collar Ghetto, Blue Collar Token," by Alice Kessler-Harris, p. 358.—Ed.]

More rapidly than ever before, the Latino worlds of the North and South are converging and transcending spurious geographic, cultural, and linguistic borders, particularly in view of current (im)migration patterns, demographic trends, and future projections. What has been termed a *transnational socio-cultural system* keeps many Latinos/Latinas closely linked to their native countries and, at the same time, makes the process of Latinization and Caribbeanization of the United States more apparent, particularly in cities with large Latino populations. This also means that such issues as dual citizenship and money remittances to relatives in the home country are central to the lives of certain Latino groups, particularly Dominicans and Central Americans.

Women's Organizing and the Emergence of a Latina Consciousness

Recognizing the many differences in the historical, cultural, and socio-economic factors that shape the lives of U.S. Latinas helps us to develop a better understanding of their ways of organizing and the issues that have rallied them to promote social change.

The ethnic and women's liberation movements of the 1960s and '70s were crucial in rescuing and reconstructing previously ignored histories of the various Latino groups as active contributors to the development of U.S. society.[7] The then new fields of ethnic studies and women's studies engaged in a sustained critique of the biases of traditional paradigms in interpreting the realities of these groups and their experiences of racism and marginality. Women's studies challenged patriarchal structures and androcentric constructs and behaviors, as well as the canonical practices of the Western intellectual tradition that tended to ignore or exclude women's agency.[8] New knowledge was produced from the process of recovering such hidden or undermined historical experiences; nonetheless, the field was initially dominated by a focus on the

---

7. See, for example, "Colonized Women in the U.S.," by Elizabeth Sutherland Martinez and "The Mexican American Women of La Raza," by Enriqueta Longauex y Vasquez, in *Sisterhood Is Powerful*, R. Morgan, ed. (New York: Random House and Vintage Books, 1970).—Ed.

8. See "The Proper Study of Womankind: Women's Studies," by Florence Howe, p. 70.—Ed.

experiences of white, middle-class women. At the same time, ethnic studies were focusing on issues of ethnic, racial, and class oppression, and on cultural nationalism, without paying due attention to the sexism, heterosexism, and racism found *within* their own groups. Collectively, Latinas felt initially excluded from a white-dominated women's movement and a male-dominated ethnic movement. Consequently, they began to articulate and forge a feminist consciousness and sense of struggle based on their own experiences as members of diverse nationalities, as well as on a collective pan-ethnic and on cross-border identities as Latinas and women of color.[9] This wider identity was based on recognition of multiple layers of oppression shared by Latinas throughout the hemisphere, and by other Third World women in the United States and around the world.[10]

The 1981 pioneering anthology, *This Bridge Called My Back: Writings by Radical Women of Color,* coedited by Chicana feminists Cherríe Moraga and Gloria Anzaldúa (see Suggested Further Reading, below), made clear that the process of constructing new, emancipatory knowledge required consideration of the many interacting sources of marginality and oppression that help explain women's conditions. Writers, artists, academics, and grassroots activists often came together at conferences and *encuentros* organized in the United States and abroad; despite tensions and disagreements sometimes resulting from these activities, there was a great deal of consciousness-raising, and a general sense of solidarity and empowerment.[11]

The collective ethnic consciousness and cultural nationalism of the 1960s and '70s is best reflected in the work of Chicano/Chicana and Puerto Rican writers and artists. The former developed the unifying ideology of *Chicanismo,* which described the experiences of this group as a form of "internal colonialism" and "emphasized cultural pride as a source of political unity and strength capable of mobilizing Chicanos

---

9. Edna Acosta-Belén and Christine E. Bose, "U.S. Latinas and Latin American Feminisms," *Signs* 25 (4): 1113–1119, 2000.

10. See "Traffic at the Crossroads: Multiple Oppressions," by Kimberlé Crenshaw, p. 43.—Ed.

11. Lavrin, Asunción, "Creating Bonds and Respecting Differences Among Women," *Latino(a) Research Review* 4 (3): 37–50, 2002.

and Chicanas into an oppositional political group within the dominant landscape of the United States" (*Chicana Feminist Thought: The Basic Historical Writings*, Alma Garcia, ed.; see Suggested Further Reading, below). Such writers as Ana Castillo, Gloria Anzaldúa, and Cherríe Moraga contributed to engendering this ideology. Castillo introduced the term *Xicanisma* to draw attention to the specific plight and agency of Chicanas in a male-dominated Chicano movement.[12] Anzaldúa in turn, referred to the emergence of

> . . . a new *mestiza* consciousness, *una conciencia de mujer*. It is a consciousness of the Borderlands. . . . *[L]a mestiza* is a product of the transfer of the cultural and spiritual values of one group to another . . . and in a state of perpetual transition, the *mestiza* faces the dilemma of the mixed breed: which collectivity does the daughter of a dark-skinned mother listen to? . . . Cradled in one culture, sandwiched between two cultures, straddling all three cultures and their value systems, *la mestiza* undergoes a struggle of flesh, a struggle of borders, an inner war. . . . At some point in our way to a new consciousness, we will have to leave the opposite bank, the split between two mortal combatants somehow healed so that we are on both shores at once and, at once, see through serpent and eagle eyes. Or perhaps we will decide to disengage from the dominant culture, write it off altogether as a lost cause, and cross the border into a wholly new separate territory. . . . The possibilities are numerous once we decide to act and not react.[13]

The sense of straddling different cultural, racial, and linguistic worlds and contesting the dominant Anglo-American cultural model is also present in the work of Puerto Rican feminists. For them, denouncing

---

12. *Massacre of Dreamers: Essays on Xicanisma* by Ana Castillo (Albuquerque, New Mexico: University of New Mexico Press, 1994).

13. "*La consciencia de la mestiza:* Towards a New Consciousness," in *Making Face, Making Soul: Haciendo Caras: Creative and Cultural Perspectives by Women of Color,* Anzaldúa, Gloria, ed. (San Francisco: Aunt Lute, 1990).

the diverse manifestations of sexist oppression ingrained in the patriarchal concept of *machismo*—which glorifies their role as devoted mothers
and faithful, obedient wives, while limiting their access to the public
sphere—was as important as for other Latinas. U.S. colonialism of the
homeland and the affirmation of a Puerto Rican national identity separate from the United States were central issues among feminists and
within the wider Puerto Rican civil-rights movement—along with combating racism, inequality, and the overall political disenfranchisement of
Puerto Ricans living in the U.S. At inner-city community levels, Puerto
Rican professionals, activists, parents, and students came together to
face official agencies and local governments over such concerns as bilin-
gual education, Puerto Rican studies, better health services, housing,
childcare facilities, widespread sterilization practices, and domestic violence.[14] For Latinas/Latinos from Central America—many of them political refugees from civil war-torn countries who came to the United
States during the 1980s, such issues as political sanctuary and changes in
U.S. immigration policies—as well as the need to create international
awareness about human rights abuses and the need for democratization
of their homeland governments—were central to their organizing
efforts.

Issues of heterosexism and sexual orientation among Latinos finally
came out of the intellectual closet in the 1990s, after being largely considered a taboo subject in Latin American societies. In this sense, the influence of U.S. and international lesbian and gay liberation organizing,[15]
and the Women's Movement, created a welcome space for shattering
stereotypes, as well as for analyzing the contingent nature of sexualities,
how these identities are negotiated, and how constructions of femininity

---

14. See Funiciello, op. cit. For more on sterilization practices against poor women
and women of color in the U.S., see "Native Americans: Restoring the Power of
Thought Woman," by Clara Sue Kidwell, p. 165, and "African American Women:
The Legacy of Black Feminism," by Beverly Guy-Sheftall, p. 176. For data on in-
carcerated Latinas, see "Alive Behind the Labels: Women in Prison," by Kathy
Boudin and Roslyn D. Smith, p. 244. See also "Landscape of the Ordinary: Violence
Against Women," by Andrea Dworkin, p. 58; "The Nature of the Beast: Sexual
Harassment," by Anita Hill, p. 296; and "Prostitution = Slavery," by Vednita Carter,
p. 315.—Ed.

15. See "Confessions of a Worrywart: Ruminations on a Lesbian Feminist Overview," by Karla Jay, p. 212.—Ed.

and masculinity are shaped by sociocultural and historical contexts. The pioneering anthology *Compañeras: Latina Lesbians* (see Suggested Further Reading, below) included narratives and testimonies of self-discovery and affirmation by Latinas of many different nationalities.

In our own work [see both contributors' biographies, below], we have emphasized the importance of the historical effects of colonialism and neocolonial relations in analyzing conditions faced by U.S. Latinas and those in their countries of origin, particularly given current globalization and economic restructuring processes.[16] The concept of *women as a last colony*—which stresses the convergence of race, class, *and* gender for understanding Third World women's conditions and their colonizing experience—has proved useful in this analysis.[17] Both women and colonies are viewed as low-wage and non-wage producers, sharing structural subordination and dependency, and being overwhelmingly poor.[18] We have argued that striving for a *decolonization of gender* requires an analysis of the historical role of colonialism, current neo-colonial practices, and unequal relationships among developed and developing nations, as well as internal colonialism among migrant women and men in metropolitan countries. This process entails the examination of layers of oppression women of color must confront regarding the patriarchal, white-dominant, capitalist society, as well as regarding power relations within their own groups. For the most part, cultural nationalism and national liberation movements still tend to see Latina issues as divisive and a detracting self-indulgence rather than as attempts to challenge oppressive social structures and gender power relations.[19]

---

16. See "Globalization: A Strategic Advance for Feminism?" by Jessica Neuwirth, p. 526.—Ed.

17. See *Women: The Last Colony*, by Maria Mies, Veronika Bencholdt-Thomsen, and Claudia von Werlhof (London: Zen Books, 1988). [See also "On Women as a Colonized People," by Robin Morgan (*Circle One*, 1974) collected in *Going Too Far*, R. Morgan, Random House, 1977, and in *The Word of a Woman*, R. Morgan, W. W. Norton, 1993.—Ed.]

18. See Funiciello, op. cit.; see also the Introduction, p. *xv*.—Ed.

19. For more on internal group dynamics and the by-now-classic patriarchal dismissal of women's activism as "divisive," see Crenshaw, op. cit.; Guy-Sheftall, op. cit.; and the Introduction, op. cit.; see also "Reclaiming the Past, Redefining the Future: Asian American and Pacific Islander Women," by Helen Zia, p. 188.—Ed.

Academics in Latin American, U.S. Latino, and women's or gender studies are increasingly engaged in analyzing the compelling realities of hemispheric integration and globalization processes. These are dictated by the continuing international labor migration flows from developing countries to the leading capitalist nations, by the expanding presence and projected demographic growth of the Latino population, and by complex economic, social, and cultural forms of transnationalism occurring within the Americas and on a global scale.

Collectively, U.S. Latinas at various historical periods have been active in organizing around different issues, at both grassroots and professional levels. As a largely working-class population, Latinas have shown their activism in labor unions, education, health, and housing advocacy groups, voter-registration campaigns, and in combating violence against women and the civil-rights abuses of some of the authoritarian regimes in their countries of origin. They also played major roles in the democratization processes in countries like Chile, Brazil, Argentina, Guatemala, and El Salvador during the 1970s and '80s,[20] and in supporting political refugees from these countries seeking sanctuary in the United States.

As early as the late 1930s, such women as Guatemalan Luisa Moreno, a labor organizer in the garment and tobacco industries, participated in the founding of the Spanish-Speaking Peoples' Congress. Decades later, in the 1960s and '70s, Chicana Dolores Huerta was a leading organizer in Cesar Chavez's farmworkers union. In the 1960s, Puerto Rican migrant Antonia Pantoja brought together a group of young professionals to establish the Puerto Rican Forum and ASPIRA in New York City, institutions that still play key roles in the educational and professional advancement of Puerto Ricans and other Latinos. Pantoja was also a leading force in the founding of such institutions as New York City's Boricua College, and is one of several Latinos to receive the Presidential Medal of Freedom for contributions to her community. On health issues, Puerto Rican physicians Helen Rodríguez-Trías and Antonia Novello have been visible, effective spokespersons; Rodríguez-

---

20. For data on women's leadership and activism in these and other countries, see *Sisterhood Is Global: The International Women's Movement Anthology*, R. Morgan, ed. (New York: Doubleday/Anchor, 1984; updated edition: New York: The Feminist Press at CUNY, 1996).—Ed.

Trías denounced widespread sterilization practices against poor women and the sexual abuse of children and women, and also defended reproductive rights.[21] Novello served as U.S. Surgeon General and is currently Health Commissioner for the State of New York; from these positions, she has been a forceful speaker for HIV/AIDS education.[22]

The concerns of U.S. Latinas vary considerably. Working-class women are more focused on daily survival struggles, the welfare of their families, and a better future for their children. Professional women strive for increased political participation and socioeconomic equality. Both groups often face women's familiar double burden: working outside the home yet still bearing primary responsibility for family caregiving and housework.

Since the 1980s, as a result of ongoing efforts to be more inclusive, it's become clear to Latin Americanists, Caribbeanists, and other area, ethnic, and women's or gender studies specialists that these fields are no longer centered in the United States. Instead, more scholars and activists from the countries and peoples studied are participating and contributing to these efforts. The parochialism of the early years is being replaced by an expanding sense of hemispheric community in which we pay much more attention to the scholarship, policy-making, and activism of Latinas from these regions *and* those residing in the U.S.

However, the convergence of minds and goals among U.S. Latinas—and other women in the hemisphere representing different nationalities, races, and classes—is more an unfinished project than an accomplished fact. The second edition of *This Bridge Called My Back* (see below) has a sobering new foreword by Cherríe Moraga that refers to the state of unity among feminists of color as still posing a major challenge:

---

21. See "Unfinished Agenda: Reproductive Rights," by Faye Wattleton, p. 17; see also "Our Bodies, Our Future: Women's Health Activism Overview," by Judy Norsigian, et al., p. 269.—Ed.

22. Any list of additional distinguished, activist, U.S. Latina feminists would be too lengthy for space limitations—but particularly worth citing are Carmen Delgado-Votaw, who co-chaired (with Bella Abzug) President Jimmy Carter's National Advisory Committee for Women and later served as president of the Inter-America Commission of Women; Aileen Hernandez, co-founder and second president of the National Organization for Women (NOW); and Olga Vives, elected NOW's Action Vice President in 2001.—Ed.

> Third World feminism does not provide the kind of easy po-
> litical framework that women of color are running to in
> droves. We are not so much a "natural" affinity group, as
> women who have come together out of political necessity.
> The idea of Third World feminism has proved to be much
> easier between the covers of a book than between real live
> women.

It is only by addressing the class, national, and racial differences among
Latinas that we can grasp their realities, continue fostering bonds, and
explore the potential for effective coalitions. Our views on strengthening these collaborations among Third World and other women are
shaped by more than thirty years' involvement in promoting feminist
scholarship, and advocating the internationalization and incorporation
of Latinas and other women of color into U.S. women's studies.[23] We
have had numerous opportunities to connect with feminists from many
"developing" countries, and to gain a deeper understanding of their
daily survival struggles, as well as of the obstacles they must overcome to
make even modest inroads regarding their demands for increased participation and better opportunities. Yet even lacking a supportive environment—in ideological and financial terms—Latinas and other
women of color from diverse nationalities, races, and social strata continue to create organizations, academic programs, and research institutes, the better to pursue a feminist agenda for social change.

EDNA ACOSTA-BELÉN is distinguished service professor of Latin
American and Caribbean studies and women's studies at the University
at Albany, SUNY. She is also co-editor of the *Latino(a) Research Review*
and director of the Center for Latino, Latin American, and Caribbean
Studies (CELAC) [*www.albany.edu/celac/*]. She publishes in the areas of
U.S. Latino and Hispanic Caribbean Cultural Studies, and cultural and
literary history. Her books include: *The Puerto Rican Woman: Perspectives
on Culture, History, and Society* (see Suggested Further Reading, below),
The Hispanic Experience in the United States, B. R. Sjostrom, co-ed.

---

23. See Howe, op. cit.; see also Crenshaw, op. cit.; Guy-Sheftall, op. cit.; Kidwell,
op. cit.; Zia, op. cit., and Jay, op. cit.—Ed.

(Westport, Connecticut: Greenwood Publishing Group, 1986), *Researching Women in Latin America and the Caribbean*, with C. E. Bose (Boulder, Colorado: Westview Press, 1993), *Women in the Latin American Development Process*, C. E. Bose, co-ed. (Philadelphia: Temple University Press, 1995), and *"Adios, Borinquen querida": The Puerto Rican Diaspora, Its History, and Contributions*, with M. Benitez, et al. (Albany, New York: Center for Latino, Latin American, and Caribbean Studies, 2000). She is the current president of the Puerto Rican Studies Association (PRSA) and a former chair of the Latin American Studies Association (LASA), Gender and Feminist Studies Section.

CHRISTINE E. BOSE is professor of sociology at the University at Albany, SUNY, with joint appointments in the departments of women's studies and Latino, Latin American, and Caribbean studies. She publishes in the areas of stratification and work, development issues, and gender studies. Her to-date six books include *Women in the Latin American Development Process*, Edna Acosta-Belén, co-ed. (see above), and *Women in 1900: Gateway to the Political Economy of the Twentieth Century* (Temple University Press, 2001). A scholar-activist focused on feminist and gender studies issues throughout her career, she was a founding member of the National Women's Studies Association, and the founding director of the University at Albany's Institute for Research on Women. She has served as chair of the Sex and Gender Section of the American Sociological Association, and is the editor of the journal *Gender & Society* (1999–2003). With Dr. Edna Acosta-Belén, she has co-directed several projects funded by The Ford Foundation, most recently *Gender Studies in Global Perspective*.

Suggested Further Reading

Acosta-Belén, Edna. *The Puerto Rican Woman: Perspectives on Culture, History, and Society.* New York: Praeger, 1979/1986.

Anzaldúa, Gloria, ed. *Making Face, Making Soul: Haciendo Caras: Creative and Cultural Perspectives by Women of Color.* San Francisco: Aunt Lute, 1990.

Garcia, Alma, ed. *Chicana Feminist Thought: The Basic Historical Writings.* New York: Routledge, 1997.

Moraga, Cherríe, and Gloria Anzaldúa, eds. 1981/1983. *This Bridge Called My Back: Writings by Radical Women of Color.* Watertown, Massachusetts: Persephone Press, 1981; second edition, New York: Kitchen Table Press, 1983.

Ramos, Juanita, ed. *Compañeras: Latina Lesbians.* New York: Latina Lesbian History Project, 1987.

Confessions of a Worrywart: Ruminations on a Lesbian Feminist Overview

KARLA JAY

I'M A FRET FETISHIST. Worrying is an exquisite habit, both painful and pleasurable, like picking at hangnails. I worry even in times of joy. On May 1, 1996, my partner, Karen, and I made our way to New York City's Municipal Building to get our Domestic Partnership. Our friends were mostly supportive. Others would have agreed with Sarah Vowell's assessment, when she wrote in a Seattle weekly, "I find it fascinating and heartbreaking that gays and lesbians must wage these ongoing legal battles to win the basic right to engage in activities (such as getting engaged) that I would cross international borders barefoot to avoid." Perhaps this is because as a young, straight, white woman, she takes her privileges for granted.

Only a third of a century ago, before the 1969 Stonewall uprisings in Greenwich Village started the modern lesbigay movement, no locale in the United States specifically granted gay rights. The most we could hope for was not to be persecuted or rounded up at election time as part of an overall "clean up" of sin. By 2001, thirteen states and dozens of municipalities prohibited discrimination based on sexual orientation. At this writing, fewer than ten states offer domestic partnership benefits, but private employers and some educational institutions offer equality to queer[1] employees and/or students. Domestic partnership sometimes ensures

---

1. The words "dyke" and "queer" are used positively throughout this essay. Just as the Civil Rights Movement reclaimed the once-negative word "black" and feminists

health benefits, eases the bequeathing of property, and may enable next-of-kin hospital visitation rights, as well as joint adoptions. There's also the right to be legally recognized as a grieving and injured party when a partner dies or is maimed. Yet in this regard, the United States is behind such countries as Denmark and the Netherlands, which allow same-sex partners to marry, or the Canadian province of Québec, which offers rights to partners (regardless of orientation) who live together for six months or more—e.g., lesbians don't have to file any special paperwork.

Still, sometimes I worry that the push for marriage, which started in Hawaii, has been machinated by lawyers eager for additional divorce clients. Gone are the days when the greatest difficulties for lesbians contemplating separation were custody and visiting-rights issues pertaining to the jointly adopted cats.

As I stood in the long line, other rights came to mind. Once, "sodomy" laws were almost universal. Homosexuality has been decriminalized in all but fifteen states, though some definitions of "indecent acts" excluded lesbians anyway. The founding patriarchs never envisioned women humping the sheep—or each other, for that matter. Few of us longtime activists imagined that lesbians would claim full erotic rights—or wrongs—depending on which side of the sexual-freedom debate you're on. My generation consisted of "in-your-face" activists; today, some young queers might prefer other parts of the anatomy.

But when Karen and I considered filing for domestic partnership, we didn't need any of these perks. I worried about my *single* friends—both homosexual and heterosexual—who wouldn't benefit from the alterations in marriage law that will surely come about in the next century. Though lesbians have long tended to merge households, pets, and even personalities after a week or so of dating, at some point we forgot about the rights of the single, the celibate, and the polyamorous. When did we decide that it was better to fight for the rights of the coupled rather than the rights of *everyone* to have decent health insurance, visit friends in the hospital, have society regard each person as a complete being—not as half of some entity? When did we buy the patriarchal logic that a single life is lonely and no life at all?

---

reclaimed "witch," lesbian women—primarily younger lesbians—have embraced uppity, in-your-face language.

The thought of betraying my single and adventurous friends made me want to turn back. "None of us is free until all of us are free" was a mantra of the 1960s. Karen and I did, however, want to make a statement, to claim whatever rights the patriarchy had finally been forced to offer, and to celebrate, not hide, our love. In theory, at least, gone were the days when activists kept relationships secret, just to make it harder for an already inept FBI to round us all up and put us into detention camps. But even in 1996, only one other couple we knew had registered for something like domestic partnership—that is, a benefit that would legally declare they were gay. Since then, only one other couple we know has registered. Many of my friends who considered themselves openly lesbian still aren't out to employers or certain relatives. Most of my students identify themselves as gay in essays that I alone read—but they let the rest of the class assume they're straight. Sadly, in terms of getting everyone to "come out," gay liberation hasn't succeeded in its first goal.

As the partnership line snaked its way toward the window of the civilly unioned—carefully separated by a few hundred feet from the "real" marriage office—I began sweating jelly beans. The male couple in front of us had best men, best women, champagne, rings. We'd brought each other, and that seemed sufficient. I was worried about jinxing our relationship. Would it be less fun once recognized by the state?

As the champagne corks popped in front of us, as women dressed as brides and grooms made their way to the cashier's window (a clever capitalist replacement for the altar), I wondered what they were there for. I fantasized that pasted over the exit sign was a handwritten notice: *"This way to the suburbs."* Were we the only ones claiming a *political* right? Were lesbians now running *from* difference? Had we abandoned equality in order to be the same as everyone else? Did lesbians really dream of a house with a white picket fence, a garden with a swing set, and some cheaply paid (undocumented) workers tending their homes, yards, and children? I feared that Martha Stewart had stealthily supplanted the politics of Audre Lorde, and Rosie O'Donnell had overtaken the popularity of Xena.

Surely, the struggles for the right to marry and raise children as a couple are among the foremost concerns of lesbians (and some gay men). It seems that almost everyone is doing it. If it's good enough for Melissa, it's good enough for us! (OK, her relationship didn't last—and I worry about that, too.) And when lesbians can't conceive through an alternative reproductive instrument (formerly, the turkey baster), via a sperm bank, or with intimate help from a male friend, then adoption for one or both mothers becomes the easiest alternative.

Adoption is still the stickiest issue prospective lesbian mothers have to face. Though media witch hunts about abusers in childcare centers have faded away, our politicians like to imagine they fear queers molesting children, as if this is a bigger threat than epidemic heterosexual child molestation or, for that matter, than some male legislators themselves groping everyone they can get their hands on. According to the National Center for Lesbian Rights, though only one state, Florida, specifically prohibits lesbian women and gay men from adopting, "in the past two years anti-gay adoption policies or legislation have been passed in Arkansas, Utah, and Mississippi. More states may soon follow." Many lesbian feminists feel that our heterosexual sisters have intentionally downplayed lesbian rights to parent a child in order to focus on a right to abortion that few homosexuals need to exercise (though we certainly understand its importance—and lesbian women can be rape victims of men, too). Perhaps priorities are backward. If lesbians were put forward as model parents—those who might raise children as ardent queer feminists—then abortion might suddenly appear holy to the Right wing. The patriarchs don't seem to care whether children are born into poverty or neglect, but the notion that kids might turn out both gay and happy horrifies them.

In the spring of 2001, a new study came out, claiming that the children of same-sex couples were more open to the possibility of homosexual relationships.[2] Well, *duh*. Fearing adversity, lesbian activists and/or parents play down the idea that we condition our children to be homosexual. Why not be honest? Shouldn't we celebrate, not cringe at the idea that our children want to emulate a positive model? Wouldn't we rather that our children turn out to be queers or militant straight feminists than Republicans? We should all have our limits. Having children

---

2. The authors of the April 2001 study, Judith Stacey and Timothy J. Biblarz, are professors of sociology at the University of South California.

could be a radical act if, as lesbian mother Jenifer Fennell so aptly put it, we choose to "parent 'queerly' or to 'queer' the job of parenting" rather than settling for being lesbian parents.

Despite Republican genes that can apparently sneak into the best amazonian bloodlines, we should celebrate our ability to raise children differently rather than assuming we should be able to make them just like everyone else. If Heather has two mommies, and the only difference in her life is that the family doesn't celebrate Father's Day, how is the world of our children going to be any different from the world we grew up in? Lots of children of single mothers don't celebrate Father's Day either, and they don't think of themselves as different. Is the nuclear family that worth emulating?

I would think that if lesbian feminists can't raise good sons, then no one can. Due to the fact that male sperm live longer when removed from a man's body, most of the young lesbians I know have sons. Lesbians have the best chance, I believe, of raising boys who have seen women running a household competently, boys who have had to listen to what women want, boys who put the toilet seat down when they're finished. For someone of my generation, children were a by-product of their heterosexual relationships, and they were often integrated into lesbian households with great difficulty. I admire young women today who believe they can have it all. They don't have to have a man to have children, give up children for a job, or choose between children and a job.

It's easier for everyone these days to adopt white, Asian, or Latino children abroad than go through state regulations. But I rarely hear lesbians discuss the politics of buying children from poor, developing nations as if they were bunches of bananas. What are the ramifications of removing children from their native culture, language, and relatives? There seems to be no feminist counterpart for "Save the Children" when we want the children for ourselves. We're not willing to fund better lives for these children *in* their homelands. Instead, we conjure up racist images of the barbaric slaughter and abandonment of girl children in countries like China,[3] without questioning who benefits from the spread of such news. And why is the plight of children who face infibu-

---

3. See "Reclaiming the Past, Redefining the Future: Asian American and Pacific Islander Women," by Helen Zia, p. 188.—Ed.

lation and clitoridectomies less compelling? There is no rush to adopt these girls, or the war orphans of Africa. Why doesn't our altruism extend to children of color and biracial children in North America? Is it less cruel to be shuttled from one temporary foster home to another?

I confess I am a bit surprised that so many lesbian women want children. Perhaps they haven't read the ads about how much a college education will cost twenty years from now. Perhaps they've seen the pitiful situation of some older activists, who are bankrupt and/or seriously ill, with no caregivers to help them. If lesbian feminists *have* failed in one thing, it's in providing communities and funds to take care of aging activists. Few of us made much money from the lesbian or feminist movements. I once calculated I made between a quarter and a dollar an hour from writing my most successful books. (I vowed never to do math again.) But at least I wasn't foolish enough to suppose that the movement would support me.

Of course, I worry all the time about retiring. Who will take care of us if Karen and I are both demented? Well, there are retirement communities for lesbians. Karen and I have visited two of them. One, in Arizona, was an enclave of politically savvy lesbians surrounded by a town of redneck guys packing shotguns in the cabs of their pickups. Another community, in the South, had younger retirees, mostly former military women who wanted to walk their dogs by day and play Scrabble by night, but "feminist" was not a bonus word. Growing numbers of lesbians are aging; many are failing in health. In the heyday of radicalism, an "older woman" was someone over thirty; that was the minimum age to get into Older Women's Liberation (OWL).[4] It's not surprising that so few of us made any plans for the future.

I'd be more likely to find die-hard feminists among retirees than among teens. Sure, some are political, but I worry about the F word. How did it happen—much to Betty Friedan's chagrin, I presume—that radical young women claim the terms "lesbian," "bisexual," and especially "queer," but cringe if someone suggests they might be "feminists"? Young adults who flaunt their difference—who are pierced, tattooed, hennaed, eco-minded, death-to-the-patriarchy feminists—

---

4. See "The Politics of Aging," by Barbara Macdonald with Cynthia Rich, p. 152.—Ed.

might be or do anything in bed. Yet they have no memory of war, of economic depression, of an era before reproductive choice, of the eons before the vote. It's easy to think the world has always been the way it is now.

I worry that we have left the young behind. Part of it, ironically, is our very success. The lesbian-feminist organizations that have survived run like well-oiled machines. No one would consider putting an eighteen- or even a twenty-year-old in charge. Middle-aged activists have forgotten that we managed to create and run organizations when many of us were in our early twenties. In our radicalism, we didn't dare condescend to anybody. Now, as activist Mattie Richardson has noted, "In the search for leaders for the next generation, the contemporary feminist movement has focused its attention on the college-bound and college-educated, again overlooking the voices of non-college-educated young women. Young women who have never been asked their opinions on anything, who are almost never called to be leaders, yet who have a great deal to contribute."

Educated or not, these young women are our future. But in thinking of the battles to be won, older feminists often think—in a patronizing way—that we are doing it *for* them. Rarely, do we consider that we should be working *with* them.

It's no surprise that there is an age divide. Older lesbian feminists have been portrayed as sexless, much the same way the suffragists were stereotyped as bitter spinsters. The world of dangers for today's young lesbians is very different from that of middle-aged or senior lesbians. The young confront a rise in fatal or debilitating sexually transmitted diseases. They see themselves as cool enough to sleep with their gay male friends, yet young lesbians are not educated to understand that they, too, are vulnerable to HIV/AIDS, which they perceive as a "guy thing."

They live in a world in which it will become increasingly difficult to know who is and is not a lesbian. It's no longer a matter of spotting flannel shirts and a pinky ring. Today's lesbian may be yesterday's man, who is in the process of taking estrogen and perhaps undergoing transformative surgery. In the future, femaleness may be more a matter of choice than of destiny. That affects all young women, but especially lesbians, since it is most of the lesbigay movement, not feminism, that has embraced transgender issues.[5]

The young are the generation of "sexual orientation," not "sexual preference." Despite the prevalence of "queer theory" in the academy positing the fluidity of sexuality, most young lesbians believe that their sexuality is fixed at birth. Their position is supported by lesbigay civil-rights organizations that claim sexual orientation is an essential category, like race or gender. As such, we should be entitled to civil rights like any other group. Indeed, genetic markers might shape a person's sexual identity—as might environmental factors in the womb (when in doubt, blame Mom). But appropriating "orientation" over "preference" is *not* a road to liberation. Feminism is based on the concept of choice and free will, and the push for the acceptance of an inherent orientation contradicts the notion that we can choose who we want to be. Moreover, the essentialist argument is flawed in that while one currently cannot choose race or gender, one *can* choose to be sexual or not. (A genetic tendency toward alcoholism, for instance, does not necessarily mean that a person cannot stop drinking.) In most periods of history throughout the world, left-handed individuals were forced to act as if they were right-handed and were persecuted if they persisted in their "sinister" ways. I worry that we have forgotten how people of color, despite the genetic bases of race, haven't had it so good.

I fret that white lesbians have turned away from the struggles of peo-

---

5. Transsexualism has been regarded by feminists as at best controversial and at worst misogynistic. The vast majority of "transgendered" persons are male-to-female—men who tend to come from repressive religious-fundamentalist backgrounds, cultures, and/or regions. In such a context, a young man feeling himself drawn to another male faces the belief that homosexuality is so horrifying it's preferable to assume that being attracted to another man must mean he's really a woman. Consequently, he invests huge sums of money and years of pain—to the profit of a cynical medical establishment—in drugs and surgeries aimed at attaining a stereotypical, extreme "femininity" (after which, in an alarmingly high number of cases, still sexually confused, he commits suicide). Radical feminists have noted that this process is inherently homophobic; that it *reinforces* gender stereotypes as opposed to weakening them; and that no surgeries, hormones, or apparel can compare with the experience of growing up and living lifelong *as* a woman in a patriarchy—in sum, that male attempts to mimic female experience are comparable to and as offensive as whites wearing blackface. See the scholarly analysis *The Transsexual Empire: The Making of the She-Male*, by Janice Raymond (Boston: Beacon Press, 1979).—Ed.

ple of color because we want to be just like straight, middle-class, white people and like our financially better-off gay brothers.[6] Just as the rest of the world has given lesser consideration to our priorities, we've now taken to looking out mainly for ourselves. The fact that a few lesbian women of color run some of our organizations allows us to think of ourselves as liberated, and to become complacent about the racism that affects *all* women of color. The success of a few lesbian corporate executives, politicians, athletes, and entertainers obscures the fact that lesbians still tend to make less than our heterosexual counterparts. A lesbian couple makes far less than a heterosexual couple—*or* two gay men.

We have learned to erase others as others have erased us. While individual lesbians are still on the forefront of international feminism and the struggle for a healthy and peaceful planet, our organizations look out only for our interests. Otherwise, how can we explain Elizabeth Birch of the lesbigay organization Human Rights Campaign having endorsed former Senator Alphonse D'Amato, hardly a friend of women or reproductive or sexual choice? The lesbian and gay movements, once rejected by feminism, now risk rejecting others to serve ourselves.

As Karen and I reach the front of the partnership line, I grapple with my fear of tunnel vision. Will I plummet into the rabbit hole of happily ever after? After we sign the documents, we kiss, and I realize that I didn't have to fret myself into a frenzy. Love hasn't made me into someone else. The state won't do that either. My partner and I are the same women at the end of the line as we were before. I'm the same radical curmudgeon I always was. Just a happier one.

KARLA JAY was a member of the New York–based radical-feminist group Redstockings, and also participated in Radicalesbians, and the Gay Liberation Front organizations in both New York and Los Angeles. She has to date written, edited, or translated ten books, the most recent of which is *Tales of the Lavender Menace: A Memoir of Liberation* (Basic Books). *Dyke Life* won the 1996 Lambda Literary Award in the category of Lesbian Studies. Jay has written for many publications, including

---

6. See "Traffic at the Crossroads; Multiple Oppressions," by Kimberlé Crenshaw, p. 43.—Ed.

Ms., The New York Times Book Review, the *Village Voice, Lambda Book Report,* and *The Gay and Lesbian Review.* Her short stories have appeared in the *Lesbian Polyamory Reader* and *Harrington Lesbian Fiction Quarterly.* She is distinguished professor of English at Pace University in New York City. She is currently at work on a mystery and on a collection of satires called *Migrant Laborers in the Fields of Academe.*

Suggested Further Reading

Jay, Karla, ed. *Dyke Life: From Growing Up to Growing Old—A Celebration of the Lesbian Experience.* New York: Basic Books, 1995.

Kleindienst, Kris, ed. *This Is What Lesbian Looks Like: Dyke Activists Take on the 21st Century.* Ithaca, N.Y.: Firebrand, 1999.

Smith, Barbara. *The Truth That Never Hurts: Writings on Race, Gender, and Freedom.* New Brunswick, N.J.: Rutgers University Press, 1998.

Stein, Edward. *The Mismeasure of Desire: The Science, Theory, and Ethics of Sexual Orientation.* New York: Oxford University Press, 1999.

Vaid, Urvashi. *Virtual Equality: The Mainstreaming of Gay and Lesbian Liberation.* New York: Anchor, 1996.

Poverty Wears a Female Face

THERESA FUNICIELLO

IN 1976 MY SMALL DAUGHTER and I were on welfare. I was a volunteer with the Downtown Welfare Advocate Center (DWAC), a small welfare-rights organization glued together by women's unpaid labor. Our workplace was a jumble of discarded furniture and supplies liberated from other people's offices, so cold in winter that we wore our coats inside. But somehow we gained recognition, and I got invited to a Washington, D.C., conference about then-President Jimmy Carter's proposed reform of welfare. I brought my daughter to stay with my mother, and went to D.C. The next day (surrounded by lawyers and social-welfare professionals, mostly men), I wondered why I'd come; they seemed not to have read the bill, pre-conference: the "reform" was loaded with forced-work provisions that would keep families poor and leave children barely cared for.

Then a woman's voice sang out from the back of the room. Everyone turned to see a magnificent black woman in her early fifties, wearing vibrantly colored African clothing. She spoke gently but with authority. If you didn't grasp her stylistic savvy, you might mistake what she was saying for naïveté. She claimed she didn't see much point going over things she "didn't understand." She said her children and her neighbors' children would have to live with the consequences of a law that failed to act on the real circumstances of poor, single-mother families. She wasn't interested in discussing such a law, but how to *stop* it. Her name was Johnnie Tillman.

Oooeeey, did she set off a firestorm.

Across the room, women stood to echo her concerns. Johnnie was still president of the once powerful National Welfare Rights Organization (NWRO), a movement of 100,000-plus members: poor, predominantly African American women. NWRO had been driven into the ground by the mostly white, male, upper-class professionals who once had staffed it—many of whom were present. They had tried for years to force the "ladies" to demand "work" in the form of "full employment." The women who *were* the movement took the position that mothering *was* important and *was* work.[1] They argued that income support independent of wages was the only way for poor women to make responsible choices (including whether and when to enter the waged labor market) in their children's best interests. Johnnie Tillman had put it this way in a 1972 *Ms.* article: "If I were president, I would solve this so-called welfare crisis in a minute and go a long way toward liberating every woman. I'd just issue a proclamation that women's work is *real* work. . . . No woman in the U.S. can feel dignified, no woman can be liberated, until all women get off their knees."

The professionals, however, always pushed their own agenda—as if the market would deliver decent wages for the asking, as if mothers weren't already working, as if care of small children wasn't relevant to the discussion. Unbeknownst to the women, the professionals held the purse strings; when they couldn't enforce their agenda, they left—taking the funding sources with them. NWRO never really recovered.

I knew nothing of the conflict between social-welfare professionals and welfare mothers. But I was about to learn; that night and over the years, we women would hold our own conferences *within* conferences, in our hotel rooms. As the new kid, I became the receptacle into whom accumulated NWRO wisdom was poured.

DWAC and other second-generation welfare-rights activist groups went on to do our own research, and further advance NWRO's theory of a "right to care." We found that what poor women were saying could be validated by data buried in government or other mainstream documents: *these*, not *our* stories, just might be taken seriously.

In the 1970s, it was novel to argue that welfare and poverty are "women's issues." It was obvious that nearly all adults on welfare (then known as Aid to Families with Dependent Children, AFDC) were single mothers. But U.S. political scientists seemed unable to ascribe

---

1. See "Parenting: A New Social Contract," by Suzanne Braun Levine, p. 85; and "*Just* a Housewife?!" by Helen Drusine, p. 342.—Ed.

meaning to that fact. Analysis of poor "people" was based almost entirely on male behavior patterns. Maybe poor men *would* have been well served with better access to wage-paying jobs—but men weren't on AFDC, or generally involved in giving practical, nurturing care to their children. "Unemployed" women, on the other hand, almost always revert to full-time caregivers. *More* work isn't what they need—*income* is.

Poring over obscure documents, we acquired proof that legitimized our experienced reality. For instance, Department of Health and Human Services (HHS) documents showed that in the 1970s, 94 percent of AFDC households were headed by single mothers who'd landed on welfare when fathers (to whom they were married or not) walked away from responsibility for children. In another example, among the teenage moms in our group, none had been impregnated by teen boys; sure enough, proof—often hidden in official documents demonstrating some other point—showed most "teen pregnancies" to be the consequence of sex with adult males; the younger the teen, the wider the age gap, e.g., sexually abusive situations.

But none of us could have imagined how hard it would be to get heard, given the vested interests who vied for ways to benefit themselves while claiming to represent our interests.

The Why

Some argue that women are more often and more deeply poor than men because we're less likely to be paid workers in the marketplace. True—in part. Others argue it's because women are more likely to be responsible for family caregiving. Also true—in part. But there's more.

As of 1999 (the most recent data available at this writing), single-mother families comprise about 23 percent of all families with children under age 18—yet represent *60 percent* of all such households in poverty.[2] Single-father families make up 5 percent of total families with children and 6 percent of those in poverty. Two-parent families constitute 70 percent of the total but only 32 percent of all those living in poverty. Their poverty rate (the percentage of people who are poor

---

2. U.S. Census Bureau, Current Population Reports, pp. 60–210 series, *Poverty in the United States 1999*, September 2000, Appendix B12.

within a given subgroup) is relatively low: 6.3 percent. The poverty rate of single-father families is higher: 16.2 percent. The poverty rate of single-*mother* families is 35.7 percent.[3] Why?

In the past, few fathers sought child custody, so reliable data was scarce: it was difficult to tell whether poverty among mothers and children was due to single parenthood, which does increase the chance of being poor. But being a single *mother* is dramatically worse. Single-mother families outnumber "male householders, no wife present" by four to one,[4] but the number of single-mother families below the poverty line is nearly *nine times* greater than father-only families. Why?

Two-parent families in which neither parent nor any other household member has a paying job have a predictably higher poverty rate than those with paid employment: 14.8 percent.[5] Yet the poverty rate of single mothers without paying work is 67.9 percent.[6] Poor mothers are not only more *often* poor but more *deeply* poor than other parents. Why?

Age doesn't improve matters for women relative to men, though Social Security benefits have improved income distribution to both sexes. For instance, 7.1 percent of men 65–74 live below the poverty line; as they age, their incomes actually improve, though fewer are alive to enjoy it. Over age 75, 6.6 percent of men live in poverty. Women 65–74 are poor at a rate of 10.3 percent. At age 75 and over, *women's* poverty rate increases to 13.4 percent.[7] One reason is the disparity in payments to women versus men, both from Social Security and other pensions. Why? Because the women didn't "work," of course.

If these patterns held only for low-income families, it could be argued that the problem was one of class: poor men skip out, poor women screw up. But going up the scale, median household income for single mothers in 1999 was $26,164 compared to single fathers' median of

---

3. Ibid.

4. Ibid.

5. Ibid., p. xi.

6. Ibid., p. xi.

7. Ibid., p. 2. [See also "The Politics of Aging," by Barbara Macdonald with Cynthia Rich, p. 152.—Ed.]

$41,838 and two-parent families of $56,827.[8] To boot, more education actually *widens* the gap for women compared to men. Why?

Controlling for race yields another surprise. As expected, income varies by race for both women and men. Non-Hispanic whites do better than non-Hispanic blacks and Hispanics, comparing same sex to each other. However, *women of all racial/ethnic groups are paid less than men of every race/ethnic group.*[9] If race were the dominant factor, then European American women would make more than men of other races/ethnicities. They don't.

In the marketplace, mothers (in single- *or* two-parent households) are paid less than men. *Single* women account for virtually all the (limited) closing of the gender wage gap. Oddly, male full-time year-round "workers" (as the Department of Commerce terms people paid for what they do) in families have higher median incomes than men who are single: $39,727 compared to $33,178.[10] The *opposite* is true for women. Single women have a median income of $30,469—several thousands higher than mothers in either two- or single-parent households.[11] At the same time, above the median, a majority of mothers are in the paid labor force; below the median, the majority are not. Families (unlike government) calculate that given the absence of comparable marketplace pay, mothers are often "worth" more at home.

---

8. U.S. Department of Commerce, Current Population Reports, pp. 60–209 series, *Money Income in the United States 1999*, September 2000, p. x.

9. Ibid. pp. 40–44. [See also "Traffic at the Crossroads: Multiple Oppressions," by Kimberlé Crenshaw, p. 43; "Native Americans: Restoring the Power of Thought Woman," by Clara Sue Kidwell, p. 165; "African American Women: The Legacy of Black Feminism," by Beverly Guy-Sheftall, p. 176; "Reclaiming the Past, Redefining the Future: Asian American and Pacific Islander Women," by Helen Zia, p. 188; and "U.S. Latinas: Active at the Intersections of Gender, Nationality, Race, and Class," by Edna Acosta-Belén and Christine E. Bose, p. 198.—Ed.]

10. These medians are lower than "household" incomes, which may have more than one paid person in them, or such other forms of income as interest, trust funds, etc.

11. *Money Income in the United States*, op.cit., pp. 30–31.

Who's Counting

The key is in the counting.

Worldwide, billions of people do the work of ensuring the survival of the species without pay or acknowledgment. In the USA, definitions of work and value remain the most crucially overlooked factors in debates on "welfare reform." Ignoring this, the political Right, Left, and Center were able to agree: forced work would end welfare.

The Right babbled "Family," that woman's place was in the home—unless she's poor.[12] The Centrist liberals and entrepreneurs offered to "train" and herd young mothers into open-market service jobs in exchange for generous government contracts. Meanwhile, most of the Left chanted, "jobs, jobs, jobs," turning welfare reform into another tool of corporatist/union-think. All agreed on one point: poor mothers could still be caregivers—just not for their *own* children. In the Left, Right, *and* Center, power was held primarily by people who were not women, mothers, or poor.

A minority of women's groups, chiefly such welfare-rights organizations as Justice Economic Dignity and Independence for Women (colloquially, JEDI Women) in Utah, the Coalition for Basic Human Needs in Massachusetts, Wisconsin Welfare Warriors, and others took welfare reform as an assault against women, as did the National Organization for Women (NOW) and Social Agenda. Most journalists settled for press-release propaganda, reporting any good news story on welfare mothers getting "jobs" but finessing the issue of childcare as if masses of quality care-workers were begging for this low-paid work. Few reported that decades of research, state after state, showed work programs designed for welfare recipients to be abject failures.

The government and The Ford Foundation funded many studies—mostly to the Manpower Demonstration Research Corporation

---

12. In their notorious book *The Bell Curve: Intelligence and Class Structure in American Life* (New York: The Free Press, 1994), Charles Murray and Richard Hernstein bemoaned the fact that eugenics have been politically unviable of late; they settled, in effect, on un-breeding through starvation welfare policy. Murray had written that welfare reform must be "so immediate and so punishing that even a young, poor, not very smart girl [must be] affected by it."

(MDRC)—disclosing (in fine print) that more people were harmed than helped. In 1986, unable to find actual positive effects but under pressure to report program success, MDRC argued that "Success may also become . . . deterrence. Some people may be sanctioned."[13] "Sanctions"—cutting children and their mothers from the welfare rolls *irrespective of financial need*—soon became welfare administrators' primary goal. By 1997, MDRC openly reported in the main body of a study that "Many welfare recipients . . . met a welfare obligation by virtue of *being sanctioned.*"[14] (Italics mine.) Success was defined as how far welfare-roll numbers dropped. Things looked different from the bottom.

Pat Gowens of Wisconsin Welfare Warriors noted, "Moms are living a nightmare of terror, fear, exhaustion, confusion, despair, bureaucratic battering. Kids are left with awful caregivers and alone." One Ohio woman, ordered to begin a forced-work program, offered to work shorter shifts for *more* total hours than required, so she could continue to nurse her two-month-old baby. No, she was forced to wean her infant, cold turkey. Unable to digest formula, the baby was hospitalized. Another mother, pressed into forced work before the welfare workers' authorized childcare, enlisted the only help she could find—the irresponsible alcoholic father she'd left. She returned after work to pick up her baby to find the father asleep, drunk, lying rolled over on top of a suffocated infant. In New York, homeless mothers with kids couldn't remain in a shelter unless they had open welfare cases. If they were cut off for "noncompliance" (such as having no babysitter for their kids), Child Protective Services instantly appeared and took the kids *away*. Is this sane social policy?

A widow with Social Security Survivors' benefits isn't terrorized into making rash decisions about "work" versus children. The average monthly payment to a widow (or widower) with two children in 2000 was $1,675 per month, not lavish but arguably liveable.[15] The average

---

13. Judith Gueron, *Work Initiatives for Welfare Recipients: Lessons from a Multistate Experiment*, Manpower Demonstration Research Corporation, 1986, p. 40.

14. MDRC, *Evaluating Two Welfare-to-Work Program Approaches: Two-Year Findings on the Labor Force Attachment and Human Capital in Three Sites*, December 1997.

15. Social Security Administration, "Draft Annual Statistical Supplement 2001," *Social Security Bulletin*, Table 5H, p. 212.

cash payment to welfare mothers with two children prior to "welfare reform" was less than $400. Since then, welfare "reform" expenditures have soared—but the increase is in "program" and administration, *not* income assistance to families. Why? Survivors' benefits aren't distributed because of a widow's paid work; millions of surviving mothers with minor children never were formally employed. And it's not because Social Security is an insurance program; it's an income-transfer program from currently paid workers to current beneficiaries. Widows (and widowers) are allowed to make *choices* linked to their families' best interests—like when/whether to enter (or leave) the labor market. Why aren't welfare mothers given such choices?

The Core of the Problem

The absence of fair income distribution to women has even more to do with long-term cultural bias than with the economy. To the extent that gender bias—sexism—is built into this equation, it's primarily one of *ownership.* Contemporary U.S. social programs were developed on the premise of women and children as *property.* What does one do with one's property? Uses it, until it's no longer useful or desired. One surely doesn't *pay* it, or ascribe "value" to it.

This is oversimplification, but it *is* the core of the problem. Official valuelessness fails mothers and children who have been rejected by fathers, and this gender apartheid of work also negatively affects the wages of women (and to a lesser extent men) who *have* paying jobs, in that *it helps keep market wages down.* Women are rarely underemployed, though many are *poorly* employed; sophisticated skills required to care for a dying adult or to produce the next generation—traditionally, female unpaid labor—are bought dirt cheap as market labor. In 1979, 53 percent of minimum-age workers were adult women; in 1999, *60 percent* (most of the rest are teenagers).

The vast bulk of jobs created in the past thirty years have been service (mother-replacement) jobs,[16] ironically proving that caregiving *always* had value (albeit unacknowledged) even when done gratis for one's fam-

---

16. Department of Labor, *Futurework: Trends and Challenges for Work in the 21st Century,* Part 4, *Workplace, Growth in Service Jobs,* 2000.

ily members. That value is now extracted from the economy, even producing profits in the market sector. The vast bulk of workers in service
jobs are women—and it's not hard to figure out why their pay is so low,
despite profits made on it by McDonald's and other corporate boys.[17] If
a woman's labor is worth zero in the home, how much can it be worth in
market terms? Unions may finally be trying to organize service workers,
but since they organize on an employer-by-employer (or even group)
basis, across-the-board gains are elusive.

One approach *would* make the difference: assessing the real dollar
value of caregiving and creating a rational distribution program to compensate women and men who take full responsibility for other humans.

Income support for unpaid caregiving was NWRO's primary goal.
Since then, DWAC, its spin-off Social Agenda, and others have continued to slip ideas about women and work into mainstream culture
through the limited means of communication at our disposal. Mostly,
we've had staying power. Today the discussion reaches beyond poor
women and welfare. Demographics worked to our advantage, since
more affluent people are discovering the financial downside of reduc-
ing/quitting market participation, as well as the physical/emotional
stress of unrelieved caregiving. Though men are giving more care than
before, *90 percent of all caregivers are still women.*

In 1999, Social Agenda, Inc. mounted a Caregiver Credit Campaign
to unify caregivers and those to whom care is given. This majaritarian
movement to acknowledge the value of unpaid labor through income
equity is intergenerational, cross race, ethnicities, and class, and is gender, ability, and sexuality inclusive. It is bipartisan, even multipartisan.
Its blueprint for action supports at-home caregivers *and* promotes comparable pay in the market. Its strategy predicates a visionary, humanist
movement offering practical remedies at state, local, and federal levels,
while seeking cultural transformation of work, value, and how we live
our lives.

In 1998, after many Internet discussions by mothers about caregiving, the Campaign's action phase was intensified by convincing an array
of other national advocacy groups to support making the child tax credit

---

17. See "Pink Collar Ghetto, Blue Collar Token," by Alice Kessler-Harris,
p. 358.—Ed.

refundable, so that lower-income families who don't pay taxes could still reap the benefit through a cash refund from the IRS. We added unique interactive functionality to our website *(www.caregivercredit.org)*, and people responded in force. In 2001, President George W. Bush signed a tax bill—with a hidden jewel in it: $8 billion in cash benefits for distribution to millions of low-income families. Though it doesn't cover all families, the *principle of refundability* is now a precedent.

The importance of this victory can hardly be overstated. It's the first time since NWRO days that a poor-women-based group conceived and moved their agenda at a national level; the first time a national effort for income support outside the "standard" tax structure was initiated and substantially won. Furthermore, it involves poor *and* non-poor people working together, and it's bipartisan—Senators Olympia Snowe (R., ME) and Christopher Dodd (D., CN) referred to child-tax-credit refundability as "the single greatest anti-poverty proposal in decades." [18]

Johnnie and I were roommates at that national conference almost thirty years ago. At bedtime she talked nonstop—while stripping, layer by remarkable layer, to slip into a big old nightgown and finally into bed. She talked about scrubbing floors on her hands and knees until a serious illness forced her onto welfare to feed her kids, about how she started a welfare-rights group just by giving her neighbors help. Her stories had a practical point: they always moved toward advice—including how to get the best price on vegetables. I didn't take her advice about vegetables. . . .

THERESA FUNICIELLO is the author of *Tyranny of Kindness: Dismantling the Welfare System to End Poverty in America* (The Atlantic Monthly Press, 1993), an examination of social policy from the perspective of poor mothers. Over the course of three decades, she went from being a homeless welfare mother to an organizer of poor women, a foundation officer, special assistant to the Commissioner of the New York State Department of Social Services, an advisor to the State Legislature, consultant, journalist, and policy analyst. She is now executive director of Social Agenda.

---

18. Quoted from a planned "Sense of the Senate" resolution.

Suggested Further Reading

Belenky, Mary Field, et al. *Women's Ways of Knowing the Development of Self, Voice, and Mind.* New York: Basic Books, 1986.

Katz, Michael B. *The Undeserving Poor: From the War on Poverty to the War on Welfare.* New York: Pantheon, 1989.

Morgan, Robin. *The Word of a Woman: Feminist Dispatches.* New York: W. W. Norton & Company, 1992; updated second edition, 1994.

Waring, Marilyn J. *If Women Counted: A New Feminist Economics.* San Francisco: Harper & Row, 1989.

Rights, Realities, and Issues of Women with Disabilities

LAURA HERSHEY

Dinner Conversation

IT WAS A typical conference banquet—mediocre food, long-winded speakers. Six women, some strangers and some friends, shared a table. Five of us had physical disabilities. Eventually, we began sharing personal memories, and suddenly, revelations lay on the table, clattering against the near-empty plates. Of five women with disabilities, three related memories of extreme abuse in medical settings. Not just the stuff nearly every disabled woman can describe, like being an eight-year-old nude model for medical students. These were deeper violations. Molestation. Rape.

One woman remembered a childhood interrupted by frequent hospitalizations. She had cerebral palsy, and had undergone several surgeries plus intensive physical therapy. These procedures, scary enough for a child, were accompanied by a series of sexual assaults by a staff member. This was her first recounting of the crimes, a disclosure that created a bond of sisterhood among six exhausted conference-goers.

If I stopped here, I'd be presenting a simplistic, disempowering picture of disabled women's experience. From news stories to horror movies, women with disabilities are falsely presented as natural victims—vulnerable, passive. In reality, the disabled women's community confronts its problems with the fierce creativity of a resistance movement.

While a majority of the women at that dinner table had been victimized as girls, none could now be described as passive victims. Each had grown into a strong disabled woman, conscious of injustice and equipped to fight it. One woman, institutionalized and assaulted during childhood, had become a lawyer, facing down the legal profession's sexist and disability prejudices. She related the power she felt when, several years earlier, she'd returned to the institution where she'd once lived—this time, to represent current inmates in their legal complaints against that institution. Another woman had become an advocate and researcher, exploring issues of disability, identity, and pride. Even the woman with the freshest disclosure was actively engaged in a project training medical students about the needs and rights of people with disabilities.

I think of that table as a metaphor for our community. We choose activism for our own survival, or in solidarity with our disabled sisters, or from an indistinguishable combination of the two.

Who We Are

There are about 26 million women with disabilities in the United States. Although the (rare) media images of disabled people tend to be white and male, the reality is different. More women than men have disabilities, and disability impacts women of color disproportionately. In African American and Native American communities, approximately 22 percent of women have disabilities; European American women have a disability rate of 20 percent.[1]

Our impairments run a gamut. Some affect the brain, some the body, some the senses; some involve a combination. Certain conditions are stable, others erratic; some originated at or before birth; others result from acquired diseases or injuries. Yet with all this diversity, we share many experiences: a proud assertion of difference, and survival against the odds; also systematic discrimination, crushing poverty, and social isolation. By most measures of social status, we find ourselves in last place. Yet we're also workers, students, artists, athletes, lovers, friends, mothers, grandmothers. We adapt to profound change, devising un-

---

1. Data from Survey of Income and Program Participation, quoted in *Chartbook on Women with Disabilities in the United States*, prepared by Lita Jans and Susan Stoddard (Berkeley, California: InfoUse, 1999).

usual, practical, elegant ways to accomplish what we cannot do through standard approaches. We pave the way for all women—any of whom might join our community at any moment.

We're also leaders, activists, organizers.[2] Every day, we resist society's compulsion to punish or banish us in encounters major and minor— from being called fire hazards and told to move our wheelchairs to the back of the theater, to being termed helpless, incompetent, or crazy, and sent to an institution. From this anger and pain, we wrench new visions of how society might respond to the inevitable, natural fact of disability. No single article can hope to detail every aspect of the disabled women's movement, but citing a few key issues and notable activists may illustrate our struggles and strategies.

Access to Safety

In addition to assaults on our bodily integrity due to the medicalization of our lives, disabled women (like all women) suffer violence at the hands of partners, spouses, family members. The same sexist factors— male rage and entitlement—fuel brutality toward women, regardless of disability.[3] Additional factors make escape more difficult for disabled women. They may feel less able to find jobs or housing, to build a life apart from their abusers. They may stay in such relationships from fear of going to a nursing home, preferring to endure abuse from one individual than from a whole staff. They may stay because they fear losing their children: judges have been known to award custody to an abusive parent rather than a disabled one. Police, service providers, and advocates rarely know how to communicate with deaf women in American Sign Language. Hotlines have no TTY access for deaf callers. Shelters often have stairs and inaccessible bathrooms, bans on necessary medica-

2. Women's historians and other feminists frequently cite U.S. nineteenth-century foremothers from the movements for abolition of slavery and women's suffrage. Yet it is rarely pointed out that at least two such major foremothers were disabled women: Harriet Tubman, a former slave and the leader of the Underground Railroad; and Elizabeth Blackwell, the first woman in the United States to become a doctor with a formal medical degree.—Ed.

3. See "Landscape of the Ordinary: Violence Against Women," by Andrea Dworkin p. 58.—Ed.

tions, or policies prohibiting attendants from visiting to provide needed assistance.

Women and girls with disabilities also experience abuse by service providers and/or authority figures: nursing-home aides, nurses, doctors, group-home supervisors, van drivers. (These perpetrators have effective weapons: they can deny privileges, withhold help, or use a victim's disability to discredit her.)

Activist disabled women have confronted these injustices. For example, the Domestic Violence Initiative for Women with Disabilities (DVI), was formed in Denver, Colorado, in 1985 as a grassroots response to the high incidence of battering of disabled women and the shelter system's inaccessibility to these women. Sharon Hickman, DVI's founder/director, has created a network of volunteers and staff to provide information to domestic-violence service providers.

Living in the Free World

Elaine Wilson and Lois Curtis were two women with mental disabilities who lived in institutions in Georgia. Both wanted to live more independently, in small group homes. The state refused, because there were no such "slots" available at the time. So Wilson and Curtis sued the state of Georgia under the Americans with Disabilities Act (ADA). In 1999, the U.S. Supreme Court ruled that states cannot unnecessarily institutionalize disabled people. Justice Ruth Bader Ginsburg's majority opinion stated, "[U]njustified isolation of individuals with disabilities is properly regarded as discrimination based on disability." The decision (*Olmstead v. Lois Curtis*) was regarded by the disability-rights community as a victory. Advocates like Lucy Gwin, Tia Nelis, and Stephanie Thomas then built on this triumph, fighting for noninstitutional living options. Gwin, who survived a brain injury, a coma, and a service system trying to control her life, now edits *The Mouth*, an in-your-face magazine that confronts patronizing, professional do-gooders. Terming *Olmstead* "a clear recall from exile,"[4] Gwin created the Freedom Clearinghouse *(www.freedomclearinghouse.org)*, an Internet-based project to

---

4. Quoted in "Tracking MiCASSA," by Josie Byzek, *New Mobility* magazine, April 2001 *(http://www.newmobility.com)*.

help connect advocates in different states and provide them with an advocacy tool kit.

Nelis adapted that tool kit for members of her group, People First. "Some of that stuff is hard for people to understand," says Nelis, who organizes her peers with cognitive disabilities. She's developed trainings and materials in easier language, and educated People First members—who then wear buttons reading: "Ask me about Olmstead"—in turn educating others about the importance of independent living options.[5]

Meanwhile, organizers like Stephanie Thomas of ADAPT (American Disabled for Attendant Programs Today) have been pushing federal legislation to ensure community support services to disabled people nationwide. About 9 million Americans with disabilities—at least half of them women—require personal assistance for everyday activities[6]: getting up, bathing, dressing, cooking, remembering routines, monitoring safety, and doing housework. The Medicaid Community Attendant Services and Supports Act (MiCASSA) would offer "real choice" to people who need such assistance and currently have no options but nursing homes. "Institutions are not our main way to go," Thomas insists. "We need to focus on the person, not the building."[7]

"The building" may be a nursing home, a long-term rehabilitation hospital, a state institution, or a psychiatric hospital. All these facilities thrive by confining people who need assistance of some kind and who, because of current policies, can't get it elsewhere. Disabled women are particularly susceptible to forced institutionalization. Although wives, daughters, sisters, and mothers provide most of the informal at-home assistance needed by disabled and older people, women are much *less* likely, when *we* need it, to have such assistance from husbands, sons, brothers, and fathers.[8] (It should be noted that low-income women, in-

---

5. "Interview with Tia Nelis: U.S. Self-Advocacy Leader," by Laura Hershey, *Disability World*, No. 8, May/June 2001 *(www.disabilityworld.org/050601/il/ nelisinterview.html)*.

6. John M. McNeil, analyst, "Disabilities Affect One-Fifth of All Americans," Census Brief, U.S. Census Bureau, Public Information Office, December 1997.

7. Interview with the author, October 2000.

8. "Disabled women living in the community may be particularly vulnerable to unmet needs because many of them live alone with limited resources. Even disabled

cluding many women of color, provide much of the cheap labor that makes institutions so profitable to those who own them.)

When dependable, responsive, high-quality assistance *is* available— e.g., through Medicaid-funded programs in some states—people with significant disabilities can be as independent as anyone. Without this assistance, many of us lose what most Americans take for granted: freedom.

Employment

Almost 100 years ago, social-justice campaigner Helen Keller, who was deaf-blind, offered a sophisticated analysis of the social construction of disabling poverty: "Facts show that it is not physical blindness but social blindness which cheats our hands of the right to toil."

Workplace barriers and the rule-bound U.S. benefit system combine to create deterrents to employment for disabled women. In a 1997 income survey, only about 30 percent of women with severe disabilities were employed, earning a median income of $12,030.[9] The reasons are complex, and include discrimination based on ableism and sexism, lack of retraining opportunities, and employers' failure to provide such rea-

---

women in married households may be vulnerable to unmet needs because they may be more likely than men to be in a caregiver role themselves. . . . Steven J. Katz, M.D., M.P.H., and colleagues from the University of Michigan (Ann Arbor), analyzed data from a nationally representative survey in the U.S. conducted at the University of Michigan in 1993 to determine sex differences in receipt of informal (generally unpaid) and formal (generally paid) home care. . . . [D]isabled elderly women were more likely to be living alone (45.4 percent, compared with men at 16.8 percent). Women were much less likely to be living with a spouse (27.8 percent, compared with men at 73.6 percent). The women were also older, reported less net worth than men, and received less informal care. . . . Overall, women received fewer hours of informal care per week than men (15.7 hours per week for women; 21.2 for men)," Katz et al., reported. "Married disabled women received many fewer hours per week of informal home care than married disabled men (14.8 hours per week for women; 26.2 for men)." Quoted in "Disabled Elderly Women Receive Less Home Care Than Men," *Women's Health Weekly*, 2000, via *NewsRx.com* & *NewsRx.net*. [See also "The Politics of Aging," by Barbara Macdonald with Cynthia Rich, p. 152; "Traffic at the Crossroads: Multiple Oppressions," by Kimberlé Crenshaw, p. 43; and (for more on caregiving) "Poverty Wears a Female Face," by Theresa Funiciello, p. 222.—Ed.]

9. Data from the Survey of Income and Program Participation (SIPP), U.S. Bureau of the Census, August–November 1997.

sonable accommodations as modified schedules, adaptive equipment, and on-the-job support. In addition, many women with disabilities decide, reluctantly but rationally, not to apply for jobs because of penalties for working that are built into disability-support programs like Social Security and Medicaid.

A number of disabled women have responded to these problems by starting their own small businesses. Barbara Knowlen fought an indifferent bureaucracy to get the necessary equipment and services to found Barrier Breakers. She succeeded because she learned the system's rules better than most of the people who work *for* the system. Now she helps others with disabilities win bureaucratic battles to obtain the necessary resources for going to work or starting a business.

Health Care

Women with disabilities worry about the same health issues as other women, but have less access to health care. We and our allies have begun taking control of this situation via several projects. One is the Health Resource Center for Women with Disabilities at the Rehabilitation Institute of Chicago. The Center began as a coalition of disabled women's health advocates and supportive medical professionals. It provides appropriate, accessible health-care services—including training for parents with disabilities, mentoring for teenage disabled girls, and clinical services. It also educates new health-care professionals (including some women with disabilities) in a supportive, disability-conscious environment, and advocates for improved state policies. Judy Panko Reis, director of the program and a disabled woman, says, "Our goal is to promote self-determination . . . which means physical and emotional wellness in teenage and adult women with disabilities." [10]

The women's health movement has largely failed to serve disabled women, who are denied necessary services because of "environmental, attitudinal and information barriers." [11] For example, many physically

---

10. Interview with the author, June 2000.

11. Margaret Nosek (Director of the Center for Research on Women with Disabilities at Baylor College of Medicine, Houston, Texas), quoted in "The Enemy Within, The Battle Without: Fighting for Accessible Services to Beat Breast Can-

disabled women can't access standard diagnostic equipment. We can't stand before scanners, climb onto high tables, or wrench our legs into stirrups. Consequently, we are less likely to have mammograms[12] and regular Pap tests.[13]

Projects organized by and for disabled women stand out as bold assertions that disabled women's lives are worth saving—that we have a right to expect good health *and* good health care.

Sexuality and Relationships

Our disabilities play a variety of roles in our erotic lives. A disability may cause awkwardness; and/or demand creative adaptation, cooperation, and communication between partners; and/or be a source of connection and excitement. All these experiences can be exciting, life-affirming, and pleasurable.

Yet women and girls with disabilities face significant barriers in trying to form romantic and sexual relationships. Myths abound that we are asexual, incapable of giving or receiving physical pleasure. This translates into more difficulty with dating, decreased likelihood of marriage, and higher divorce rates.[14] Bombarded by negative messages about our sexuality, many of us struggle for a sense of sexual identity. The media-morphed perfect female does not look like someone we can aspire to be.

---

cer," by Rachel Ross, a publication of the National Women's Health Information Center (NWHIC), a service of the Office on Women's Health in the Department of Health and Human Services, August 1999 *(http://www.4woman.gov/editor/aug99.htm)*.

12. *Centers for Disease Control and Prevention (CDC) Morbidity and Mortality Weekly Report,* 1998, quoted in *Services Denied: Why Women with Disabilities Aren't Screened for Cancer,* by Christine Haran, in National Women's Health Information Center (NWHIC), a service of the Office on Women's Health in the Department of Health and Human Services, December 2000 *(www.4woman.gov/editor/dec00/dec00.htm)*.

13. Ibid.

14. In a 1992 survey, only 44 percent of women with "severe activity limitations" were married, and these women had higher rates of divorce than women with less severe limitations: NHI Survey, quoted in *Chartbook on Women with Disabilities,* op. cit., p. 30.

But do we want that persona? Our distance from that gendered ideal is a double-edged sword, taunting some disabled women with impossible aspirations, releasing others from restrictive stereotypes. Corbett O'Toole, who uses a wheelchair and has been organizing in the disabled women's community for thirty years, recalls, "My disability gave me incredible freedom to break with gender stereotypes. When I didn't use makeup in high school, when I didn't date boys, when I wore gender-neutral clothing, there were knowing nods that it was because 'she's different.' "[15]

It takes time and a sometimes painful process of self-exploration to discover not only what we weren't, but what we could be; what we are. Only after that journey can we take the more rewarding step of realizing and claiming our true sexual identities. Even then, when we come out—whether as lesbian, bisexual, heterosexual, transgendered, sensuously chaste, or whatever—we may have to journey farther to find a community where we can be our full sexual selves.

With the leadership of women like O'Toole, we've developed our own networks for exploring issues of identity and community. Speaking frankly with each other and our partners, we affirm our sexiness in all kinds of ways.

Revolutionary Principles: Feminism and Disability Rights

I'm a feminist because I feel my own future and our collective human future depend on achieving real gender justice, and on ending patriarchal domination of culture and nature. I'm a disability-rights activist for very similar reasons: I want freedom and opportunity for myself, and I believe that acceptance of and accommodation to human variation are essential strategies for our human species' survival.

But despite my passionate commitment to both movements, I sometimes feel marginalized by both, as, I know, do many feminists with disabilities. Disability organizations often fail to consider gender issues. And urgent disability-related concerns rarely achieve a prominent place in feminist magazines or conferences.

And why should they? Aren't these the concerns of a small minority?

---

15. Personal correspondence with the author, March 2001.

I'd argue that disability rights and feminism directly serve two overlapping *majorities*. (More than half the human species is female, and a substantial percentage of people will, at some time in their lives, be affected by disability resulting from illness, injury, or old age.) Furthermore, both disability rights and feminism address compelling, universal, human needs.

Disabled women are working for change on fronts too numerous to explore here, given space limitations: educational equity; access to technology; media representations; artistic and cultural activities; reproductive rights—including both the right to abortion and the right to bear children; the right to raise children; body image, and identity development.

I believe deeply in the revolutionary principles expressed by the disability experience. For women like myself to deviate dramatically from prevailing norms yet expect the rights and privileges of any other citizen is radical. By demanding full participation in society and the accommodations to make that participation possible, the activist disabled women's community offers a liberating vision of human connectedness—for everyone.

Writer and activist LAURA HERSHEY works locally, nationally, and internationally for the rights of people with disabilities. As an independent consultant, Hershey lectures and conducts trainings on community organizing, disability rights and culture, and other topics. Her leadership positions have included Advocacy Editor at *CanDo.com* (2000); Interim Executive Director of the Denver Center for Independent Living (1998–1999); and Director of the Denver Commission for People with Disabilities (1989–1990). Her articles and poems have been published in numerous periodicals, including *POZ, New Mobility, Women's Studies Quarterly,* and *Ms.* She authored a report on disabled women's leadership strategies, based on interviews she conducted at the NGO Forum on Women at the 1995 UN World Conference on Women in China. Her work can be read online at her website, Crip Commentary (*http://www.cripcommentary.com*).

The above essay is dedicated
to the memories of
Barbara Waxman Fiduccia and Connie Panzarino.

Suggested Further Reading

Fine, M., and A. Asch, eds. *Women with Disabilities: Essays in Psychology, Culture, and Politics.* Philadelphia: Temple University, 1988.

Linton, Simi. *Claiming Disability: Knowledge and Identity.* New York: New York University Press, 1998.

Panzarino, Connie. *The Me in the Mirror.* Seattle: Seal Press, 1994.

Russell, Marta. *Beyond Ramps: Disability at the End of the Social Contract.* Monroe, Maine: Common Courage Press, 1998.

Willmuth, Mary, and Lillian Holcomb. *Women with Disabilities: Found Voices.* Binghamton, New York: Haworth Press Inc., 1994.

Alive Behind the Labels: Women in Prison

KATHY BOUDIN AND ROSLYN D. SMITH

IT IS 8 A.M. A green sea flows out past the barred gate opened by an officer. The sea streams down a corridor, out a door, along a walkway. We are a night-time ocean of dark green: dark green jackets, shirts, pants or jumpers. Officers line our path. We are not allowed to walk alone. We are always watched. These long lines flow between programs and prison cells. Like two rivers, our line divides. One group flows toward the laundry, commissary, reception center for new prisoners, and large vocational building. The other flows toward the academic school building, the Parenting Center, the Library, Pre-release, and the building holding the family-violence, AIDS/women's-health, and drug-treatment programs, plus the Nursery for mothers and babies. Bright faces shine above the green—mostly shades of brown-bronze, tan, cocoa, charcoal, with some pale pink or rose. We are women. We are women prisoners. We walk, part of the sea. But if you look closely, you can spot the irrepressible uniqueness of women's creative energy, the resistance to loss of self: a jacket's creases ironed into a design; hair in corn-rows; dreds with gold, red, and white beads; long blond hair; fingernails painted with a crescent moon and stars against a midnight background. We live in what is euphemistically called a "campus." But the rows and rows of razor wire catching the morning sun and glinting in every direction tell us where we are. We are prisoners in Bedford Hills Correctional Facility—New York State's maximum-security prison for women.

> I am the voice you locked away and do not want to hear. But
> I echo through your conscience. I am your average woman

244

prisoner: black, poor, with a history of family abuse. I came before your ice chamber, a 17-year-old girl, naive to the system, accused of two counts of murder. No, I'm not innocent in the legal sense, because I was *there:* I permitted an entry that caused two human lives to be halted suddenly in an unplanned violent act. I take full responsibility for everything I did. You gave me 50 years in a state penitentiary. Yet the story of my life is not so alien from yours. The abuse I survived might be abuse in your home. Like you, I've overcome obstacles. The love I feel for my child is as intense as yours for your child. Just like you, I want to make the world a better place. I am a statistic. But I am also a woman—a friend, a teacher, a creator of life. I am powerless and powerful. I am a human being.—Roslyn.

I am a woman. I have been in prison for 21 years, inhabiting multiple worlds. Here I am both different and the same. Different because I'm European American, white in a community where more than 80 percent are African American and Latina. I'm the oldest on my unit, almost 60; the average age is 34. I'm from a middle-class, liberal, professional background, and I arrived in prison with a history of social activism and a college degree when more than 51 percent of the women here arrive without a high-school diploma or GED.[1] I'm Jewish in a population of 800 with, on average, ten other Jewish women. Yet I am "we" as a mother among other mothers parenting from a distance—almost 80 percent of us. I am "we" when I cheer the bringing back of higher education to our community. I am "we" experiencing the devastation of families and friends in our community from HIV/AIDS. I am "we" as a longtermer who shares with other longtermers the many years in prison, the remorse, the keen urgency to go home. I am the same, I am different. But I am not an outsider. Here, in prison, no one is an insider. This

---

1. General Education Degree, a high-school-diploma equivalent.—Ed.

place is not any woman's home. Here we are all in exile.—
Kathy.

Between us, we have been in prison almost 45 years. The number of
women in Bedford Hills Correctional Facility has increased since
Roslyn arrived in 1980 from about 250 to almost 800. New buildings
have replaced old ones or occupied once grassy areas; new fences, new
rows of razor wire; a tower staffed by armed officers now overlooks the
prison entrance and exit. The changes at Bedford—which is not only
the state's maximum security prison for women but also the reception
prison for women entering the entire state prison system—mirror what
is happening across the country. The U.S. women's prison population
has risen 654 percent since 1980,[2] increasing at nearly double the rate of
men,[3] largely as a result of the nation's "war on drugs" and mandatory
drug-related sentencing."[4]

The increase of women in prison is part of a larger picture in which,
despite declining crime rates, incarceration has become a major tool for

---

2. "Gender and Justice" (Washington, D.C.: The Sentencing Project, 1999; *www.
sentencingproject.org*). [The number of women sentenced to a year or more in prison
has grown twelvefold since 1970; approximately 70 percent are nonviolent offenders and 75 percent have children; see "The Prison-Industrial Complex," by Eric
Schlosser, *The Atlantic Monthly*, December 1998; on-line at: *www.theatlantic.com/
issues/98dec/prisons.htm.*—Ed.]

3. A. J. Beck, *Prisoners in 1999* (Washington, D.C.: U.S. Department of Justice,
Bureau of Justice Statistics, 2000).

4. The so-called Rockefeller Drug Laws passed in New York State in 1973 (when
Nelson Rockefeller was governor) require harsh prison sentences for possession of
small amounts of illegal drugs—e.g., mandating a judge to hand down a sentence of
no less than 15 years to life on conviction of having sold two ounces or possessed
four ounces of a narcotic substance; whether this is a first-time or a repeat offender
is irrelevant. The Rockefeller Drug Laws soon became a model for similar dracon-
ian laws across the nation. Studies have exposed these as blatantly discriminatory.
For example, approximately 90 percent of crack cocaine arrests are of African Americans and 75 percent of powder cocaine arrests are of European Americans; under
federal law, it takes only five grams of crack cocaine to trigger a five-year mandatory
sentence—but it takes 500 grams of powder cocaine (100 times as much) to trigger
the same sentence. For more information on mandatory drug sentencing and the
various campaigns to repeal it—campaigns supported by state senators, clergy
members, human-rights organizations, etc.—see *www.droptherock.org.*—Ed.

addressing social problems: poverty; inequities in housing and education; physical and sexual abuse against women; racism. Prisons now warehouse people suffering from substance abuse or mental illness. More African Americans and Latinos are being held in New York State prisons than are attending the State University of New York (SUNY); nationally, five times as many African American men are currently in prison as are in four-year colleges and universities.[5] The U.S. prisoner population has risen from 250,000 before passage of the Rockefeller Drug Laws and other fixed-sentencing policies to almost two million, at this writing, in 2002.[6] The majority of Americans entering the prison system are *nonviolent* offenders: 52.7 percent in state prisons, 73.70 percent in jails, and 87.65 percent in federal prisons.[7] And women are easily overlooked in the world of corrections, where we comprise only 8.4 percent of 1.93 million prisoners.[8]

We arrive in prison labeled: "failure," "con artist," "violent," "crack addict." Labels are one-dimensional, leaving women—like Tillie Olsen's fictional shirt beneath the heavy, hot iron[9]—flattened. Once here, we're assigned another label—an ID, stamped onto each piece of our green state clothing—a further depersonalization, reducing a woman to a number. Then we label ourselves: "Bitch!" "Mental med!" "Baby killer!" "Niggah!" When you're told that you're nobody (but still,

---

5. V. Schiraldi, R. Gangi, and J. Ziedenberg, *New York State of Mind? Higher Education vs. Prison Funding in the Empire State, 1988–98* (Washington, D.C.: Justice Policy Institute, Correctional Association of New York, 1998); see also Marc Mauer, *Race to Incarcerate*, The Sentencing Project (New York: The New Press, 1999).

6. C. G. Camp and G. M. Camp, *The Corrections Yearbook 2000, Adult Corrections* (Middletown, Connecticut: Criminal Justice Institute); see also A. J. Beck, *Prisoners in 1999*, op. cit.

7. J. Irwin, V. Schiraldi, and J. Ziedenberg, *America's One Million Nonviolent Prisoners* (Washington, D.C.: Justice Policy Institute, 1999).

8. "Women Prisoners' Rights," by Ellen Barry, in *Social Justice, a Journal of Crime, Conflict, and World Order*, Vol. 27, No. 3, Issue: "Critical Resistance to the Prison Industrial Complex" (2000); see also Cynthia Cooper, "A Cancer Grows," *The Nation*, 6 May 2002.

9. See "I Stand Here Ironing" in the short-story collection *Tell Me a Riddle*, by Tillie Olsen (New York: Dell Publishing, 1956).—Ed.

somebody bad), it's hard not to treat other people the same way: that's the only thing you've got going to make you feel better.

But behind every label is a woman with a story. As women, we're good at talking—in our cells, in the yard; through tears, with anger or humor; while cooking, buffing the floor, braiding hair—women talk to each other, able to peel off the labels, to see each other and ourselves as whole people.

We sit in a circle in a parenting class. The wall is covered with photos of each woman with her children, framed inside colorful hearts home-made from construction paper. Although the word "sisterhood" is not part of our common language and women might even laugh cynically if someone said "sister," we slowly become that for one another. Women search their backgrounds, trying to understand how they came to rupture the bond with their children, to violate the responsibility of being a mother. They piece together the patterns of their lives as if they're working a quilt. Probably the most common patterns are violence and drugs. Tareema,[10] a small woman with the hands of an artist, energy coiled in her like a spring, remembers:

> As a child I was beat for things I didn't do. My mother broke my arm. I lived with violence between my parents. I was raped by my father from when I was age six to age thirteen and a half.

Iris, a lanky woman—so shy it took weeks for her to share her story—murmurs:

> During my pregnancy I got messed up—punches, black eyes, put in ice. I could see it coming in his face, so I'd put the kids in their room when I knew I'd get hit. My parents kept saying "Don't leave your husband." To outsiders, women are always the ones at fault.

Drugs became a way to numb pain. Women push one another to face the impact of their actions on their children. Wanda asks herself aloud:

---

10. The names of women quoted in this article, other than those of the coauthors, have been changed to protect their privacy.—Ed.

Where was I when my children needed me? I was with a man, working, drugging. Drugging became my total existence. When the kids called, "Mommy," I felt nothing.

Lack of education plus responsibility for children plus poverty[11] moves some women into illegal activities for money, often through relationships with men on whom they are dependent economically—which makes them more vulnerable to tolerating abuse. There are no big-time gangsters here, no serial killers, no Godmothers running drug empires, no Enron or WorldCom executives.

> A typical woman entering prison has at least two kids, most likely a drug-abuse problem, and is herself probably a product of welfare or workfare. She has no marketable skills for anything other than cleaning or minimum-wage jobs. TV ads bombard her with images: cars, jewelry, money as happiness, as the key to the finer things in life. Can such a woman possibly obtain the finer things in life? Hell, no. Not from a background of disaster.—Roslyn

Many women don't fit the typical description. Some were from "hard-working, God-fearing" families—U.S. born or immigrant—and got into illegal money-making because it was fun, fast, a challenge, a high. Others, suburban and college-educated, got caught up in drugs or an abusive relationship. But each woman's story is only one part of an entire life. When we listen to each other, we *see* each other. Yet women in prison want understanding not only from each other but from the broader society.

> When you are, as I am, incarcerated in a women's prison for the past 21 years, you crave a connection to the outside. A connection means someone understanding how you landed inside, understanding the *inside of you,* understanding that the inside of you is not so different from the inside of themselves. None of us want to be here. We carry with us every

---

11. See "Poverty Wears a Female Face," by Theresa Funiciello, p. 222.—Ed.

second the wish things had been different, the hope they still can be. But that's just the starting point for a journey we must take—into ourselves. How did we become who we are? How do we change into people we want to be? What do we hold on to, what do we discard? *How* do we do it? You know the world outside sees you, a prisoner, as a terrible person. You have to strain to embrace your own humanity—while remembering how easy it once was for you *not* to see the flesh and blood of another person, perhaps someone you harmed. You have to reach for the humanity in others—knowing they cannot see the good in you.—Kathy.

Outside, in the larger society, they cannot see many things. They don't see the sixteen- and seventeen-year-olds standing on our mess-hall line, some sucking their thumbs, others who ran away from homes where mothers on crack were never able to mother them. We old-timers cry out to each other as we pass by, "Oh my god, look at the babies." Those outside prison don't sit on our yard benches next to women who talk to the voices in their heads, who are among the more than 50 percent of women at Bedford with a history or diagnosis of mental illness—women who ended up here because mental institutions were deinstitutionalized but the promised community-based facilities never materialized adequately. And the broader society sometimes can't see us because race and class are prisms through which peoples' lives are understood or misunderstood and through which justice is refracted. African Americans constitute 12.3 percent of the U.S. population, Hispanics 12.8 percent.[12] Yet at Bedford, 52 percent of the women are African American and 29 percent are Latina; only 16 percent are European American, the remainder Native or Asian American.[13]

Tareema continues telling her story in the women's circle:

12. See "African American Women: The Legacy of Black Feminism," by Beverly Guy-Sheftall, p. 176, and "U.S. Latinas: Active at the Intersections of Gender, Nationality, Race, and Class," by Edna Acosta-Belén and Christine E. Bose, p. 198.— Ed.

13. See "Native Americans: Restoring the Power of Thought Woman," by Clara Sue Kidwell, p. 165, and "Reclaiming the Past, Redefining the Future: Asian American and Pacific Islander Women," by Helen Zia, p. 188.—Ed.

I still wear scars my father gave me, relive nightmares. When I started dating, it seems the only guys I attracted were abusive. I always thought it was me, my fault. I became afraid of men, passive. The impact of all this violence on my children is horrible. One died because I was trying to escape an abusive relationship: Carlos used my son against me, knowing he was my heart. Even before that, my children suffered because I constantly had a gun to my head, a knife to my throat, and was being beaten with extension cords while my oldest was forced to watch. Other times Carlos locked me in closets like my father used to. Talking here, with other women, I see I'm not alone. I see I'm a battered woman.

The headlines labeled her a "murderer." Her story is as tragic (and as comprehensible) as the news story of the white suburban teenager whose baby died because she was ashamed of having borne a child. That young girl received counseling and probation. But Tareema was from the inner city, poor, Puerto Rican. No one would hear her story until *after* she was sentenced. She is serving fifteen years to life.

Women try to tell their stories—to researchers, to Department of Justice volunteers collecting statistics. In some circles, women in prison are at least perceived as "victims" of social and economic conditions. Yet just as a label like "murderer" freezes a person—defining them by an act, and removing that from the whole person and the whole life—being defined as a "victim" also leaves out something: the role of a woman as *agent of her life*, with responsibility for past choices and possibilities for change. Women in prison are survivors of lives in which they made good *and* bad choices, and they're survivors in prison, too.

One way we survive here is by caring for each other—helping women in parenting programs be better mothers; becoming teachers' aides for women learning to read and write; counseling women about fibroids, hysterectomies, and HIV. Women tending each others' babies in the Infant Center; women making sure a birthday gets celebrated by baking a cake on top of a hot plate; a woman braiding another woman's hair for six hours; a woman holding another woman because she needs a hug. The mothering of each other is part of surviving, part of healing the ruptures in women who left children behind, or who cut themselves off from others (as well as from themselves) due to addiction, or who robbed and didn't care what happened to others when they did.

> The process of helping someone changes you. Others start seeing you as a good person. That acknowledgment keeps it going. We all want to be worthy, whether in a love relationship, a friendship, or helping someone less fortunate.[14] It's in the connection to others we find that sense of being worthy.—Roslyn.

Survival is also about creating space in prison, where it's so hard ever to be alone.

> You have to create space. Space inside yourself, space between you and other people; space *with* other people, space in a day to do something you *choose* to do—to remind yourself that you can make choices. But that space must be invisible, or it would not be allowed. You create and live this invisible life in order to survive; still, you must deny yourself a whole range of behavior and feelings that, though human, are not permitted. Maybe it's not until you get out that you realize the damage that's been done. For many, it's God who helps them feel connected to something that cannot be imprisoned. For me, it's nature—the sky, the wind, the birds, the cycle of seasons. They help me know that my world is not defined by these fences.—Kathy.

Survival is also about the lifeline to family and friends outside, "in the street," as we say. For some it's parents, a cousin, a sister, or surrogate family; for others, a boyfriend, even if just for a while. For only a few, there are husbands—unlike at men's prisons, where the visiting room is filled with women who remain committed. For those of us who are mothers, the connection with our kids is central: letters, visits, phone calls, dreams.

---

14. See "Sisterhood Is Pleasurable: A Quiet Revolution in Psychology," by Carol Gilligan, p. 94.—Ed.

Where do I go to find peace in a world so full of hate, confusion, broken lives, crimes of every magnitude? I go to you, my child—conceived in love, a blessing—sweet, yet strong as steel. I bask in your innocent beauty, not owning you but respecting the individuality of your life, glad to be part of it. "You're just the mommy," your little voice says to me—you, hands on hips, head cocked to the left, grinning. I laugh and tickle your lean little body. You're right. I'm just the mommy. Our conversations are like most mother-kid conversations: "You know you have to brush your teeth twice a day so they'll be strong and healthy." "Saying curse words is for people with limited vocabularies." We've had discussions on good touch, bad touch, what to do in case of fire, knowing emergency numbers to call if something bad happens. She knows to trust her teachers and local police, how bees pollinate, that homosexual people are just people, how flowers grow, why it's important to eat fruits and vegetables and not a lot of candy. Then there is the Number 1 conversation: why is Mommy in prison and is she bad. We are still working on that one and will probably talk about it for the rest of our lives.—Roslyn.

My visits with my son Chesa always give me an incredible energy. My whole relationship with him has been a life-force. As a child, he used to race across the visiting room and leap into my arms. Now he is twenty-two, and he leans down as I reach up to him when we hug. He was my window through which I faced the enormity of the tragedy I was a part of; he was the door through which I walked toward repair. I had to struggle with my unending guilt about abandoning him, and answer his hard questions at each age—but through his anger, he still wanted my love and gave me his. We often used to look at the moon at an agreed-on time—he from his house, me from prison—and feel our love and connection from a distance.—Kathy

Survival is about our health, too. Doctor's appointments. We wait. The long benches are filled with women. There are no backs on the benches. Sometimes we wait for two hours or longer. Spines curved, straining to sit straight; spines leaned against other spines for support. A VCR affixed high on the wall plays a medical-information video for a largely indifferent audience. Below, women pass their time reading, sitting alone, or enjoying gossip—little circles of hushed voices, giggles, lifted eyebrows, and a quick change of conversation if the wrong person sits down nearby. We're locked in a bullpen, separated from the officers by another barred metal gate controlled from behind a Plexiglas window. We sit in the Regional Medical Unit, the prison's newest, largest structure. Its construction destroyed two older buildings, a hill covered with wildflowers, and the skyline—an expanse that once carried our gaze beyond the razor wire. In women's prisons, health is a major issue. We have special problems men don't have[15]—gynecological problems; breast, cervical, and ovarian cancers; fibroids and hysterectomies; pre-natal care for pregnancies; menopause; long histories of sexual and physical abuse. Since the late 1980s, *between 16 and 20 percent of women coming into the state prison system have been HIV-positive*—an epidemic of staggering proportions, a toll parallel to the AIDS devastation in southern Africa.[16]

But women in Bedford are comparatively fortunate. In 1974, inmates here initiated a class-action lawsuit about medical conditions. In 1981, the judge appointed a monitor to oversee the prison's compliance with standards, and women were afforded a level of protection. As a result, there have been continual improvements in medical staff and procedures. There is also a health program—ACE (AIDS Counseling and Education)—which we women initiated to meet the AIDS crisis in our community, but which has since expanded into other areas of women's

---

15. See "Our Bodies, Our Future: Women's Health Activism Overview," by Judy Norsigian, et al., p. 269, and "Diagnosis and Prognosis: Women Physicians and Women's Health," by Wendy Chavkin, M.D., p. 378.—Ed.

16. Centers for Disease Control statistics indicate that the HIV/AIDS rate among all women has risen from 7 percent of total AIDS cases in 1985 to 23 percent of all cases in 1998. African Americans represent an estimated 12 percent of the U.S. population, yet comprise almost 37 percent of all reported AIDS cases; AIDS has resulted in more deaths among African American women than any other cause (e.g., heart disease and cancer), with injection drug usage accounting for 44 percent and heterosexual contact at present being the greatest risk factor/mode of transmission (National Black Women's Health Project: *www.blackwomenshealth.org.*). See also Guy-Sheftall, op. cit., and Norsigian, op. cit.—Ed.

health. Every unit has a copy of *Our Bodies Ourselves*[17]—an administrative decision. But none of this makes up for problems in prison health care in a society where health care costs spiral upward while spending on prisoners' needs declines. Women in prison lack access to different medical opinions, medications, and treatments. As sentences lengthen and parole is denied, there is a growing group of older women with special medical needs. All these problems—plus wearing shackles (that chafe and bruise) to outside hospital trips—make medical care, even at one of the best prisons, an ongoing issue.

Beyond the subject of health, physical survival is not an issue in Bedford. There are occasional fights—sometimes comical flailing fists that don't even make contact. A serious punch or cut occurs very rarely. As one officer was overheard to say to another whom he was orienting, "It's nothing, small stuff. With women you don't have to look over your shoulder all the time." We do not live with the threat or fear of violence here. Most of the women here were themselves victims of violence before prison: this place is *safer* for them.[18]

But like all women, we ache to do more than survive: to live, grow, repair. In prison philosophy this comes under the concept of "rehabilitation." (It's tied to our being called "inmates" in a "correctional facility" with "officers" and a "superintendent"; the words *prisoners, prison, guards,* and *warden* are not in current usage—formally.) Yet during this contemporary era of punishment and revenge, there is clearly conflict over whether "rehabilitation" is even relevant anymore in corrections.[19] The overriding concern of prisons is security. Absolute obedience is required and implemented with myriad rules and a system of rewards and punishment.

---

17. At this writing, the most recent edition of the multi-versioned *Our Bodies Ourselves*—the women's health movement classic first published in the early 1970s—is *Our Bodies Ourselves for the New Century,* by the Boston Women's Health Book Collective (New York: Simon & Schuster, 1998).—Ed.

18. See "Landscape of the Ordinary: Violence Against Women," by Andrea Dworkin, p. 58.—Ed.

19. In 1976, California Governor Jerry Brown endorsed and signed into law a state crime bill that, among other things, amended the section of the penal code that had pronounced rehabilitation the ultimate goal of imprisonment: "rehabilitation" was replaced with the word "punishment." See Schlosser, op. cit.—Ed.

We always hear, as inmates, that we're the scum of the earth. That's what they think of me? Then that's who I'll be. It's like with a child—teach them they're dumb and they'll behave like that. So much inside prison is like a parent-child relationship. We depend on the officers for everything. They regulate all that we do. Our movement is controlled; we're locked in, locked down, each day is fragmented by counts around the clock. When one of us is "drafted" to another prison, she must pack her whole life into four burlap bags.— Roslyn

In a recent study of the Texas prison system, women were given 1,322 citations for violations of written and posted rules, while only nine were given to men.[20] These included misbehavior reports for "trading shampoo in a shower, lighting another inmate's cigarette, having too many family photos on a wall." The warden of the male prison stated that his system effects an "accommodation" with male inmates, a tacit contract of noninterference in return for relative compliance with rules. But for the women there are rules regarding dress, placement of lockers and beds in cells, size of space on wall for photos, pat frisks, strip frisks, cell searches, lock-downs, lock-ins, counts, and illegality of love relationships (termed "degenerate acts"). This reinforces gender stereotypes of obedience and dependence.

Last summer at Bedford we lost the right to wear our own colored tops to work. Everything was green. All your buttons had to be buttoned except for the very top one or you'd get a misbehavior report. Despite 95-degree weather, we had to wear sneakers or boots—no sandals allowed: they didn't want our toes showing. If you took in your pants because they'd been made for male prisoners and were so wide you felt like a whale, you'd get a misbehavior report for "altering state

---

20. D. S. McClellan, "Disparity in the Discipline of Male and Female Inmates in Texas Prisons," *Women & Criminal Justice*, Vol. 5, No. 2 (1994); and D. S. McClellan, David Farabee, and Ben Crouch, "Early Victimization, Drug Use, and Criminality," *Criminal Justice and Behavior*, Vol. 24, No. 4 (1997).

property." Wherever you walked, your body was scrutinized by male officers—who were doing their job implementing the dress code in the guise of shrouding women's sexuality. This of course only increased the level of sexual tension.— Alvie (in a letter).

All people need to experience some sense of efficacy, individual potential, cooperative social activity—qualities in conflict with the goals of disempowerment and obedience that prisons require. Fortunately, more than most prisons (for men *or* women), Bedford during the 1980s and 1990s has been run by an administration that has supported women's role in creating and sustaining critical programs which, in turn, provide women in the prison with the possibility of change. The first, defining program was/is the Children's Center, which affects the 80 percent of us who are mothers. Formally initiated by Sister Elaine Roulet in 1980, it has blossomed into a Parenting Center, with parenting classes (facilitated by the women themselves), an advocacy program for children, and activities to help moms and kids connect: a nursery for mothers and babies, a children's playroom for visiting, pre-teen and teen programs, and a staff of more than forty-five women whose prison jobs are focused on helping mothers and kids build relationships. Consequently, we grow as mothers *and* as teachers, peer counselors, and advocates. Similar efforts have followed, inspired by an "inmate-centered" philosophy—including a family-violence program, an AIDS/women's health program, and recently a four-year college program. Though operating with civilian supervision, these efforts rely on the creativity, initiative, and day-to-day work of the imprisoned women, who, in turn, begin to see themselves no longer as bad—or even as victims—but as *women with real strengths who can make a difference.*

You come here, stripped of everything, alone, defeated. Gradually, you become part of things: a program for parenting, for domestic violence; an academic route—basic literacy or GED. Then pre-college. Finally, *college.* You see that you can change. Other people give you accolades. You start to feel better about yourself. You imagine a different life. Those of us who've been here a long time, we've reached a pinnacle. So where do we go from here? We try to bring what we've learned to others, so the circle of change keeps turning.— Roslyn.

The gym. Graduation. Celebrating each other's achievements: GEDs, college associate and bachelor's degrees, apprenticeships in printing, teachers' aides, peer counseling. Tables are set up for family guests. The bleachers are filled with inmates, poised to cheer. The superintendent and deputy superintendents take their seats onstage with the chaplains and guest speakers—two former inmates who made it in "the free world." A tape starts playing over the loudspeaker: "Pomp and Circumstance." The women file in. The bleachers erupt, whistle, shout out names: "Angie!" "Baby-Girl!" "Shuggie!" "Joanne!" "Wanda!" The women walk by in GED blue gowns, in college black gowns. Annie passed her GED after taking it eight times. Petie, who started at a basic literacy level, wears a cap and gown for her bachelor's degree. Determination. Perseverance. Support. The place goes wild. Tears flow. Gossip, negativity, put-downs—all gone. *For this moment, all we feel is the best in us.*

Here, as outside, college is about skills, knowledge, documentation for a future job. But in prison it is most profoundly a rite through which women pass, reinventing themselves. When the Clinton administration's 1994 Omnibus Crime Bill eliminated federal financing for college education in prisons, the states followed suit. Prisons across the country closed down such programs. That included Bedford's program, which had begun to develop in the wake of the 1971 Attica prison revolt when, for a moment, the nation saw prisoners as human. Here, the difference was instantly palpable, as if the door to hope had been slammed shut. Fights increased. In lower-level classes, demoralization set in. Rates of passing the GED dropped. Bedford, through joint efforts of the administration, inmates, community, and academic leaders, worked hard to create a new model for prison higher education, one based on private funding and the donation of professors' time by a consortium of colleges. The program is currently [2002] in its fifth year, its benefits borne out: *women who participated in the college program while in prison had a re-*

*turn rate of 7.7 percent over a three-year period after release; women who had
not participated in the college program had a return rate of 29.95 percent during the same period.*[21]

> Did you see *no* potential in me? You noted my high IQ, how
> "articulate" I was, how "mature." I'd run away from home
> because I refused to let my mother keep hurting me. You put
> me in a home for bad kids; my roommate wasn't even sane. I
> left there, too, so you put me in a group home. You call that
> help? No matter who I tried to tell, no one *got* it. So then you
> sentenced me, said no hope for rehabilitation, said I'm as
> good as dead. Just like my mother: kicks, flights of stairs,
> words that made me flinch. Well, you were both wrong. I
> have a life. I have a beautiful daughter, a college education. I
> teach parenting skills. I make a difference in people's lives.
> You never gave me a chance, so I made my own. My poverty,
> skin color, background, past—who at age seventeen can't
> change, won't grow? You robbed me of my youth, of my be-
> lief in justice. But from the graveyard, the barbed wire, and
> the cinderblock, I'm resurrected. I'm worthy. *I'm somebody.*—
> Roslyn.

Life moves forward. Dreams for the future are part of that movement. But in prison, we're always looking backward. Remorse, responsibility—these are part of the process of change. In a parenting class, a
woman who'd sold drugs watched the movie, *Basketball Diaries.* She saw
a teenager's life devastated by drugs, and she was shaken: the drugs she'd
sold might have done that to someone else's child. Others who'd sold
drugs and once might have shrugged, "It's their choice, nobody has to
buy it," have been confronted with the deaths of friends from AIDS,

---

21. *Changing Minds: The Impact of College in a Maximum-Security Prison: Effects on
Women in Prison, the Prison Environment, Reincarceration Rates, and Post-Release Out-
comes.* Collaborative research by The Graduate Center of the City University of
New York and Women in Prison at the Bedford Hills Correctional Facility, 2001;
Preface by Helena Huang, Open Society Institute. *Changing Minds* is available at
www.changingminds.ws.

sometimes contracted by sharing needles; they now feel very differently about their crimes. For those here because of a death—an ex-lover, a child, a stranger during a robbery—the consequences are ever-present. Each woman wrestles with this differently. In her own way, each expresses the desire to communicate her regret, her grief. Sometimes she does so in a letter written, but not delivered.

When someday I walk out the prison gate I will gently touch the air that surrounds me like a shawl. I will be with my child, with family and friends who've lived through these decades with me. I will step into the uncharted waters of freedom we all long for but no one really understands. Yet I have another journey to make. I must cross a river of sorrow into the past, where the flames burn with spirits. I must approach and search for your faces, find your eyes and look directly at you, go back to that day, kneel at the place where you lay on the ground, tell you that your ghosts haunt me. Wail with the flames, *Oh if I could replay that day. I would not have been there. I would not have gone. I would not have my hands in any way touch the tragedy of that day.* If I could remake the past! I would look into your faces the colors of flame and tell you how, when I've held the hands of friends dying of AIDS—in their youth, before their time—I've thought of you, and longed to bring you back, as if by holding their hands I could exchange souls. I would tell you how I've lived out these decades giving as much life as I can to people where I am, yet waiting for that time to face you, you to whose living and dying I am connected by a thread of humanity—whether we notice it or not. And I know now: *it is in the not noticing that we can do devastating things.* My journey cannot be taken without facing your eyes—and the eyes of those who loved you but had to go on living their lives without you. If only there were a place where the living and the dead could meet, tell their tales, and weep with rage, pain, mourning. I would reach for you—not so that you could forgive me, but so that you could know I have only the most profound regret for what I have done, and a wisdom that came too late.—Kathy.

Parole-board day. Angie waits, sitting on a plastic chair outside the "Board Room," used once a month for this occasion. She will sit opposite the board but not register their faces, just the blur of her own future that these all-powerful people will determine. Soon the door will open. A woman will emerge and twelve waiting women will watch to see if she has tears in her eyes or is smiling. Yet that won't reveal any decision, merely how she was treated. Angie waits. She has served nineteen years of her seventeen-to-life sentence, handed down when she herself was only seventeen. She went to her second board with a judge's court order saying she should have been released at her first board; that her growth, remorse, accomplishments, and future plans warranted release. But the board members, appointed by the governor, didn't care. Now, when this third board questions her, she will again go over the day of the crime, again describe who she was nineteen years earlier, again speak of her regret, of how she's changed. They will question her, perhaps harshly, perhaps disinterestedly, perhaps even kindly. None of it matters. In forty-eight hours she will get a letter announcing that she must spend another two years in prison—then appear at a fourth board hearing.

A cloud hangs over the prison after each parole board hearing: "All they do for women with violent crimes is re-sentence them." "It's like nothing we do *matters*—no change, no remorse, nothing." *The Shawshank Redemption* is one of the most popular movies among women here, for, among other reasons, the prisoner's multiple appearances before parole boards, all of whose members regard as irrelevant his life story or justice. On initial parole board appearances in New York State, for people (men and women) convicted of homicide, parole release dates went *down* from 30 percent in 1994 to 5 percent in 1999–2000—despite declined rates of murder.[22] Individual success at rehabilitation has no relevance. New York's policy is not unique: California's "Three Strikes" Law and the federal government's "Truth and Sentencing" Law, adopted by many states, are other examples. This is the result of several

---

22. New York State Division of Parole statistics show a significant drop since 1994 release rates. The release rate at 64 percent in fiscal year 1993–94 steadily decreased to approximately 33 percent for 2001. See also data from The Legal Aid Society (October 1999), and CURE NY Newsletters, Spring 2002 (p. 3) and Summer 2002 (p. 4); see the criminal justice reform website of CURE [Citizens United for the Rehabilitation of Errants]: *www.bestweb.net/~cureny.*

factors: a subculture of revenge and punishment, incarceration as a form of social control,[23] and the economic growth role of prisons.[24]

> Hope is the air we breathe—as prisoners, as human beings.
> We give it to one another as we change, repair, and give back.
> But hope from each other in here isn't enough. Society and
> the criminal justice system also have to offer hope that we

---

23. See *Lock-Down America: Police and Prisons in the Age of Crisis*, by Christian Parenti (New York and London: Verso Books, 2000); see also *Building Violence: How America's Rush to Incarcerate Creates More Violence*, John P. May and Khalid R. Pitts, eds. (Thousand Oaks, California: Sage Publications, 2000).

24. This has been termed the Prison-Industrial Complex—a confluence of bureaucratic, economic, and political interests that have made the U.S. prison system the largest and most expensive one in the world. Politicians gain votes using fear of crime as an issue; impoverished rural areas welcome prisons as economic development—for construction *and* jobs (prisons are recession-proof, labor-intensive institutions, offering year-round employment); private companies regard the $35 billion spent on corrections annually as a lucrative market. AT&T, Bell South, MCI, and other carriers vie for prison contracts: one prison pay-phone—an inmate's lifeline to the outside—can generate five times the revenues of a street pay-phone. As Eric Schlosser reported in *The Atlantic Monthly:* "The prison-industrial complex now includes some of the nation's largest architecture and construction firms, Wall Street investment banks that handle prison bond issues and invest in private prisons, plumbing-supply companies, food-service companies, health care companies, companies that sell everything from bullet-resistant security cameras to padded cells available in a 'vast color selection.' The *Corrections Yellow Pages* lists more than 1,000 vendors." Furthermore, private prisons—run for profit across state lines and now globalizing across national boundaries—are the fastest growing segment of the prison-industrial complex: the higher the occupancy rate, the higher the profit margin, with virtually no government oversight. The private companies transporting thousands of inmates across the U.S. each day face even less oversight than private prisons, and looser federal regulations than those concerning interstate shipment of cattle. Private-prison businesses are intensely competitive: in 1998, the Corrections Corporation of America (CCA, the country's largest private-prison company) participated in a buy-out of the U.S. Corrections Company—thus obtaining several thousand additional inmates. Among investors backing what has been called "the private-prison building spree" are American Express, General Electric, Allstate Insurance, Merrill Lynch, Smith Barney, and Shearson Lehman. Private prisons have taken the practice of cheap or free prisoner labor to high technological levels: now not only raising hogs, but doing data entry for Chevron, taking telephone reservations for TWA, sewing lingerie for Victoria's Secret, manufacturing products for Microsoft and Starbucks. See Schlosser, op. cit.; see also *The Prison Industrial Complex and the Global Economy*, by Linda Evans, Chrystos, and Eve Goldberg (Oakland, California: Regent Press, 1998); and *The Prison Industrial Complex*, by Angela Y. Davis (Oakland, California: AK Press, Multimedia CD-ROM).—Ed.

will return to our families and communities. One young woman told me, "What an irony, after so many years of wanting to die and not caring if my life was taken, here I am in prison—and finally I want to live." I think of another irony: all this potential being realized inside prison, when our families and communities desperately need what we can give them—and we can't get out.—Kathy.

The overwhelming majority of women *do* get out of prison: those with nonviolent offenses, many of whom are in for under five years (unless they're serving mandatory drug sentences). The irony is that *those who get out are the most likely to come back*, whereas those with longer sentences are highly *un*likely to come back: most are in prison for a one-time tragic violent act, and these are the women who've changed most, obtained more of an education, had time to develop some self-confidence. As one longtermer said, "I saw Jessie and didn't want to say hello to her—this is her third time back. Well, I relented—but I told her, 'Don't complain to me. Just give *me* the chance *you* had, to be free.' "

Even if a woman does manage to take something positive away from her prison time, she faces enormous obstacles if she returns to the same neighborhood, unaffordable housing, looking for a job and for childcare as a single mother with a GED while facing the stigma and legal limits on resources that felons face—such as denial of TAP grants to help with college tuition. *Prison is a place where many women actually feel safer than they do outside;* safer, for the first time in their lives, from abuse by and dependency on men, drugs, AIDS, peer pressure to do illegal, self-destructive things; it's a place to contemplate their lives; even a place where they say, "I'm a better mother to my kids from inside than I was at home; here I really pay attention to them." Prison: what an insane solution to the problems these women face! Though the number of long-termers is growing, in every state the vast majority of women in prison are serving shorter terms for nonviolent crimes, usually drug-related or property crimes. They too need support. When we ask ourselves, "Are we advocating for longer sentences?" the answer should be *No*. Yet it's also clear that prisons are not working for the women who become a statistic of recidivism.

What *does* work is no mystery. Educational opportunities; economic and social support systems that address the entirety of a woman's life—as mother, girlfriend, wife, worker; the chance to belong to a community; drug-treatment programs geared toward women's needs; parenting programs; family-violence programs. *Not* having such programs in prison is *more* expensive. And for the majority of incarcerated women, rehabilitation could be better accomplished outside, *and* be far less costly for society. So, do we put our efforts into advocating for better prisons? Or do we create real alternatives to incarceration? Do we tackle the roots of the problem: poverty, inequality, abuse? *And what do we, who are inside, want?*

The answer is all of the above.

When we were writing this essay, we asked women here, *"What do you hope such an article can accomplish?"*

And the almost universal answer was, *"To help people see us as human beings like themselves."*

From the classroom windows on the school building's second floor we can watch when women leave. It's the Waving Goodbye Ritual. Just before the visitors' parking lot sits a small building. They enter one door of it. Five minutes later they come out another door, free women. We watch our friends walk from the main entrance of the prison buildings into the small structure, then out into freedom. Today three women are leaving. They have lived with us for more than fifteen years each. We wave. They can't see our heads or bodies—just our hands sticking out. Waving our love and support. Waving our own dreams.

> Now, as I crane to catch a glimpse of my friends, I look into the sun's rays bouncing off the razor wire. Row on row, circle on circle, silver, gleaming. I wonder what happens to birds and butterflies—do they get caught in it? Do our dreams ultimately get caught in it? I can barely see my friends. Now I can't see them at all. My gaze is caught in the wire.—Kathy.

Can you recognize us yet? Can you *notice* us, phantom shapes shimmering behind you in your mirrors?

Women. Human. Like you.

KATHY BOUDIN is in her twenty-second year of prison at the Bedford Hills Correctional Facility for Women in Westchester, New York. She is a teacher active in prison-community efforts in parenting, basic literacy, higher education, and AIDS/women's health. She is also a poet and writer who is part of poetry and prose workshops at Bedford Hills, and has published work both as an individual and with other women in prison. Some of her writing appeared in "Net of Souls," performed as a benefit to support the college program at the prison. She has completed her master's degree in adult education and is pursuing additional graduate studies. Her sentence is twenty years to life, and she goes to her second parole board in August 2003. Her son Chesa continues to be her greatest joy, an inspiration for her commitment to her work with mothers and children, and the center of her love.

ROSLYN D. SMITH is an inmate/writer at the Bedford Hills Correctional Facility for Women in Westchester, New York. She is serving two consecutive twenty-five years to life sentences for a double homicide, and (as of 2002) has been incarcerated for the past twenty-four years. Her writings from "Net of Souls" have helped raise needed funds for the continuation of college programs at Bedford Hills Facility. She has taught "Parenting from a Distance" classes in the facility, and is currently involved in the writing workshop, as well as with "Puppies Behind Bars"—a program through which inmates raise guide dogs for the blind. She is raising her second pup, Quinn. She has a B.A. from Mercy College, Dobbs Ferry, New York, and is the proud mother of her daughter, Anastasha, who is the inspiration for her writing. This is her first published piece.

Suggested Further Reading

Baunach, Phyllis Jo. *Mothers in Prison*. New Brunswick, New Jersey: Transaction Publishers, 1985.

Changing Minds: The Impact of College in a Maximum-Security Prison: Effects on Women in Prison, the Prison Environment, Reincarceration Rates, and Post-Release Outcomes. Collaborative research by The Graduate Center of the City University of New York and Women in Prison at the Bedford Hills Correctional Facility, 2001; available at *www.changingminds.ws.* For further information, contact Research Director Maria Elena Torre, *mtorre@gc.cuny.edu.*

Chesney-Lind, Meda. *The Female Offender: Girls, Women, and Crime.* Thousand Oaks, California: Sage Publications, 1997.

Ritchie, Beth, E. *Compelled to Crime: The Gender Entrapment of Battered Black Women.* New York and London: Routledge, 1996.

The Prison Journal, Vol. 75, No. 2, June 1995 (the entire issue is devoted to women in prison); see *www.sagepub.co.uk/frame.html.*

PART IV.

Bodies Politic

Our Bodies, Our Future: Women's Health Activism Overview

JUDY NORSIGIAN

With Barbara Brenner, Lisa Paine, and Kiki Zeldes for
The Boston Women's Health Book Collective

EARLY IN THE CONTEMPORARY feminist wave, activists realized that women's health issues were a central component of our fight for justice and equality. Women in the late 1960s–early 1970s self-help groups fought to reclaim the processes of menstruation, childbearing, and menopause as natural life stages rather than ailments needing cures. As the women's health movement matured, we began examining an array of issues, from access to health and medical care to the politics of illness[1] through feminist perspectives. Since then, the number of groups focusing on the many crucial health concerns affecting women everywhere has grown steadily. Although the majority of these groups have minimal access to resources, they continue to work tirelessly.[2] This essay highlights only a few of these issues and U.S.-based initiatives.[3]

---

1. See, for example, "Rights, Realities, and Issues of Women with Disabilities," by Laura Hershey, p. 233.—Ed.

2. See, for example, the organizing done by women prisoners regarding health and medical care in "Alive Behind the Labels: Women in Prison," by Kathy Boudin and Roslyn Smith, p. 244.—Ed.

3. In addition to resources noted throughout and following this article, many more groups and projects are accessible through our website, Our Bodies, Ourselves (*www.ourbodiesourselves.org*), which offers links to hundreds of other websites with noncommercial, action-oriented information.

The Issues

Overall, women in the United States tend to have healthier lifestyles (regarding tobacco, alcohol, and illicit drug use) than men, as well as better health-insurance coverage and ongoing primary-care services,[4] and they are more likely than men to seek treatment for depression. But women tend to ignore their own needs while ministering to others.[5] In a sense, all health issues are "women's issues," ranging from rising U.S. rates of junk-food obesity through disability discrimination,[6] from alcoholism to the growing elderly population.[7] But because public policies in this country largely don't recognize circumstances unique to women, special campaigns to improve women's health include:

- Sexuality and reproductive-health education that focuses on power imbalances and gender differences, safer sex (including promotion of barrier contraceptive methods), and the right to sexual pleasure.
- Creating and maintaining safe and legal access to abortion.
- Making motherhood safer and healthier through better nutrition, pre-natal care, and post-partum support.
- Challenging harmful routine medical practices (e.g., unnecessary Caesarian-section births and hysterectomies, indiscriminate prescribing of mood-altering drugs).
- Exposing the tobacco industry's promotion of tobacco products to women and girls.
- Challenging unethical practices in the pharmaceutical industry.
- Establishing a national health program that responds to women's needs.

---

4. See "Diagnosis and Prognosis: Women Physicians and Women's Health," by Wendy Chavkin, M.D., p. 378.—Ed.

5. Reasons for this include the experience of discrimination, low self-esteem, and/or the simultaneous burdens of parenting/caregiving plus working both inside and outside the home.

6. See Hershey, op. cit.—Ed.

7. See "The Politics of Aging," by Barbara Macdonald with Cynthia Rich, p. 152.—Ed.

Three cultural forces have a major influence on our health: poverty, mass media, and violence. Poverty remains the primary cause of ill health and a key reason women may find ourselves and families with limited access to adequate food, shelter, primary health care, and environmentally safe, nonviolent circumstances in our homes, communities, and workplaces; poverty often results in a lower level of education and diminished status, making it harder to achieve good health.[8] The pervasive influence of mass media saturates popular culture with unhealthy, unrealistic images of women and with glorified images of violence, sexual and otherwise—a health issue, since violence is a leading cause of injury and mortality in U.S. women (see section below on childbirth).[9] Below is a sampling of issues that remain cornerstone concerns for women's health activists.

Abortion

Annually, approximately 20 million unsafe abortions are performed worldwide, resulting in the deaths of nearly 80,000 women. In the U.S., increased access to safe, legal abortion has reduced mortality rates to about 40 per year. Abortion remains a contentious issue, with anti-choice and Right-wing organizations escalating efforts to prohibit abortion worldwide; in many countries, religious fundamentalisms have intensified opposition to abortion-rights advocacy.[10] Restrictive laws

---

8. See "Poverty Wears a Female Face," by Theresa Funiciello, p. 222; see also Chavkin, op. cit.; for additional health data disaggregated by ethnicity, see "Native Americans: Restoring the Power of Thought Woman," by Clara Sue Kidwell, p. 165; "African American Women: The Legacy of Black Feminism," by Beverly Guy-Sheftall, p. 176; "Reclaiming the Past, Redefining the Future: Asian American and Pacific Islander Women," by Helen Zia, p. 188; and "U.S. Latinas: Active at the Intersections of Gender, Nationality, Race, and Class," by Edna Acosta-Belén and Christine E. Bose, p. 198.—Ed.

9. See "Landscape of the Ordinary: Violence Against Women," by Andrea Dworkin, p. 58; see also "From Fantasy to Reality: Unmasking the Pornography Industry," by Gail Dines, p. 306; "The Media and the Movement," by Gloria Steinem, p. 103; and "Standing By: Women in Broadcast Media," by Carol Jenkins, p. 418.—Ed.

10. See "Unfinished Agenda: Reproductive Rights," by Faye Wattleton, p. 17; and Chavkin, op. cit.; see also "Combating the Religious Right," by Cecile Richards, p. 464; and "Dancing Against the Vatican," by Frances Kissling, p. 474.—Ed.

and regulations plus attacks on abortion providers have created a climate of terror. In the U.S. alone, there were approximately 2,100 reported instances of violence against providers between 1977 and 1999; the years 1991 to 2001 witnessed multiple attacks, leaving eight dead and 33 seriously wounded, with 20 arsons and attempted arsons, 10 bombings and attempted bombings, and clinics in 23 states receiving threats of anthrax and chemical offensives.[11] Not surprisingly, there is currently [2002] a shortage of providers: 94 percent of rural areas, and 84 percent of *all* U.S. counties have *none*. Because half of all ob-gyns who provide abortions are 50 years of age or older, alternative groups are crucial—e.g., Medical Students for Choice *(www.msfc.org)*, and the Abortion Access Project *(www.repro-choice.org; www.abortionaccess.org)*, involved in training health care providers other than physicians in the latest abortion techniques.[12]

Women of all backgrounds seek abortions for many reasons: 43 percent of women in the U.S. will have had at least one abortion by age 45; annually, fewer than three out of 100 women between the age 15–44 have abortions. Abortion rates have generally been decreasing since 1990.[13] Since the late 1990s, U.S. women have had expanded access to nonsurgical ("medical") abortions using mifepristone (frequently called "RU-486") plus a prostaglandin drug; the method had long been used abroad, and abortion-rights activists worked hard for decades to secure this additional method for women in the U.S. Abortion services will al-

---

11. Feminist Majority Foundation's National Clinic Access Project *(www. feminist.org)*.

12. See Wattleton, op. cit., and Chavkin, op. cit.—Ed.

13. According to the Centers for Disease Control, this might reflect multiple factors, including "the decreasing number of unintended pregnancies; a shift in the age distribution of reproductive-age women toward the older and less fertile ages; reduced access to abortion services, including the passage of abortion laws that affect adolescents (e.g., parental consent or notification laws and mandatory waiting periods); and changes in contraceptive practices, including an increased use of contraception, particularly of condoms, and, among young women, of long-acting hormonal contraceptive methods that were introduced in the early 1990s" ("Abortion Surveillance—United States," Joy Herndon et al., Division of Reproductive Health, National Center for Chronic Disease Prevention and Health Promotion, Surveillance Summaries, June 2002, 51(SS03):1:32).

ways be a necessity, and we must commit ourselves to preserving and *expanding* the currently limited services for this basic human right.

Childbirth

Feminist and childbirth-preparation groups have long worked toward the judicious use of medical intervention during pregnancy and childbirth, as well as a greater emphasis on preventive approaches, focusing on good nutrition, breastfeeding, greater access to/use of midwifery services, and the development of support systems. Nonetheless, in recent years, some ground has been lost. Breastfeeding rates, on the rise until the late 1980s, have decreased—despite mounting evidence of breastfeeding's benefits to women *and* babies (including improvements in infant and child health, and the reduction of breast-cancer risk). Breastfeeding is much *less* expensive than bottle-feeding, yet low-income women tend to be most influenced by formula companies promoting "free" products: consistently, hospitals that give out free formula samples have lower breastfeeding rates.

Rates of Caesarian-section deliveries, declining for years, rose precipitously in the late 1990s. Between 1989 and 1999, the number of births involving induction of labor went from 8.2 percent to 19.6 percent—with no demonstrable connection to improved outcomes for mothers or babies. By 2000, nearly 23 percent of all births were by C-section, the highest percentage since 1989.

Safe motherhood initiatives, first designed in the late 1980s to address the high maternal mortality in "developing" countries, are now in place in the U.S.—for tragic reason.[14] Recent studies indicate that, when appropriately measured and accounted for, *homicide is emerging as the most common reason for maternal mortality.*[15] Links to domestic vio-

---

14. For more information, see the World Health Organization's Safe Motherhood website *(www.safemotherhood.org)*, and that of Safe Motherhood Initiatives USA *(www.smi-usa.org)*.

15. Krulewitch, C. J. et al., "Hidden from View: Violent Deaths among Pregnant Women in the District of Columbia, 1988–1996," *Journal of Midwifery and Women's Health*, 2001, vol. 46, #1, pp. 4–10 *(www.jmwh.org)*. See also The American College of Nurse-Midwives *(www.midwife.org)* press release (February 15, 2001) on the subject; and the ABC News story by Ephrat Livni, "Deadly Pregnancies Study,"

lence are becoming clearer (old news to activists and health profession-als). Racial/ethnic disparities continue to surface regarding safe mother-hood, as do issues affecting rural women (lack of access), and women with low incomes or limited education.

It won't be easy to sustain our efforts promoting women-centered midwifery care in a climate encouraging ever-greater medical interven-tion during pregnancy and birth.[16] Yet we need to do this—especially if we are to achieve government health care objectives, which call for all preventive services and public-health campaigns to be women centered and women friendly.[17] Although childbirth (and even sexuality) has be-come overly medicalized, we can reverse this trend. As much evidence-based research has shown, the unnecessary use of such technologies as epidurals, artificial induction of labor, episiotomies, and C-sections has a negative effect on birth outcomes, including the likelihood of experi-encing a welcome birth as the awe-inspiring event it can be.

Breast Cancer

Breast cancer is not one disease but a complicated group of diseases that occur in an environmentally complex world. The misinformation

---

(*http://more.abcnews.go.com/sections/ living/dailynews/pregnancy homicide*), for reports quoting the American College of Nurse-Midwives on violent death during preg-nancy being "a hidden epidemic." Because of death coding standards (it is not rou-tine for pregnancy to be recorded on death certificates), collecting accurate data has been difficult. The World Health Organization has begun compiling data on the links between homicide and pregnancy.

16. One innovative example is the Centering Pregnancy Program (*www. centeringpregnancy.com*), which brings women out of exam rooms into groups for pre-natal care, where they gain empowering knowledge and learn to be more capa-ble advocates for themselves and their families.

17. In January 2000, Clinton administration Secretary of Health and Human Ser-vices Donna Shalala launched Healthy People 2010—a comprehensive, nationwide health promotion and disease prevention agenda containing 467 objectives designed to serve as a road map for improving the health of all people in the U.S. during the twenty-first century's first decade. The objectives, organized in 28 pub-lic-health focus areas, are targeted for improvements to be achieved by 2010. See *www.cdc.gov* and *www.health.gov/healthypeople.*—Ed.

abounding about breast cancer reflects this complexity, as well as the politics of disease.[18]

As many as 70 percent of breast-cancer cases occur in women who have no identifiable risk factors other than age. Only 5 to 10 percent of breast cancers are the result of an inherited genetic predisposition, yet incidence of the disease is skyrocketing throughout both "developed" and "developing" nations. With the exception of ionizing radiation, we still know relatively little about what causes cancer (for more on the effects of hormone-replacement therapy [HRT] and tamoxifen, see the section on prescription-drug advertising below). Since the 1980s, activists have called for more research into possible environmental links to breast and other cancers. Groups like Breast Cancer Action (BCA) in San Francisco have urged a more cautious approach, whereby we would limit exposure to toxic substances based on available evidence rather than waiting for conclusive proof. Several excellent articles by BCA on suspected environmental links to cancer are available on-line at *www.bcaction.org.*

Since poorer communities—urban and rural—shoulder a heavier burden of exposure to toxic materials, many activists now focus efforts on reducing and eliminating exposure to identified environmental carcinogens through legislation, regulation, research, and education.[19] Other aspects of viewing breast cancer in a feminist framework include the need for more effective, less toxic treatments, and for health care systems guaranteeing all women access to quality health care. While large breast-cancer charities fall under increasing influence from pharmaceutical and related corporations that fund them, organizations like the BCA are urging citizens to become involved in effective preventive steps against the epidemic. Skyrocketing breast-cancer rates, the limited effectiveness of mammography as a screening tool (see *www. bcaction.org)*, and the absence of effective treatments for many cases of aggressive breast cancer underscore the need for true prevention.

---

18. See, for example, *Breast Cancer: Society Shapes an Epidemic,* Anne S. Kasper and Susan J. Ferguson, eds. (New York: St. Martin's Press, 2000).

19. See "Update: Feminism and the Environment," by Paula DiPerna, p. 503.—Ed.

Breast Implants

For over 20 years, the U.S. Food and Drug Administration (FDA) regulated neither silicone nor saline breast implants, despite pressure from women's health advocates. In 1992, the breast-implant industry and the American Society of Plastic and Reconstructive Surgeons (ASPRS) spent $4 million on a PR campaign to downplay potential risks of silicone implants and block FDA regulatory action to restrict access to them. Because of the insistence of such groups as Command Trust Network, the National Women's Health Network, and the Boston Women's Health Book Collective, as well as the principled stance taken by then-FDA Commissioner David Kessler, silicone implants were limited to clinical-trial use, with mechanisms in place to collect meaningful safety data.

When saline implants came under closer scrutiny in August 2000 at FDA hearings, it was noted that more than 190,000 problems from all breast implants had been officially reported to the FDA—including 123 deaths.[20] These complaints represent potentially more than 10 percent of the estimated 1.5 million women who now have breast implants. Particularly disturbing was that more than one-third of the reports were for *saline* implants. Much of this information is now available in an FDA consumer booklet *(www.fda.gov/cdrh/breastimplants)*.

Since cosmetic surgery and breast-implant procedures are heavily advertised, it isn't surprising that augmentation is on the rise, despite mounting evidence of harm. About 150,000 women received implants in 2000, most of which were saline.[21]

---

20. Unfortunately, the types of symptoms experienced by women with silicone implants don't lend themselves to a clear clinical diagnosis, and this difficulty with nomenclature has made it easier to discredit women who have suffered from implants and physicians who recognize that implants *are* causing serious problems. Some recent studies have shown that women who suffered silicone leakage were at higher risk of developing the syndrome referred to as fibromyalgia.

21. For additional information on breast implants, see the website of the National Center for Policy Research for Women and Families: *www.cpr4womenandfamilies. org*.

Prescription Drug Advertising

Pharmaceutical advertising, often directed at women, presents itself as "educational," though its primary purpose is to increase company profits. Today, we see frequent campaigns shilling prescription medications for arthritis, allergies, and PMS—but the marketing of hormone therapy, geared both to women and their doctors, represents one of the most successful and misleading promotional efforts over the past decades. Although hormones offered some clear benefits (e.g., relief from debilitating hot flashes and vaginal dryness), many women's health advocates called for a cautious approach until well-designed, large-scale studies could be completed. In 2002, after preliminary results of the largest prevention trial ever funded by the U.S. government demonstrated more harm than benefit from the study's section involving combined (estrogen plus progestin) HRT, the National Institutes of Health *halted* the study. Most experts immediately recommended that women avoid long-term use of HRT, noting the increases in breast cancer, stroke, blood clots, and heart attacks associated with extended use. That close to half of post-menopausal women had used hormone therapy *before* these data were made available suggests how effectively (and misleadingly) hormones had been marketed.

The "direct-to-consumer-advertising" (DTCA) phenomenon—where prescription drugs are marketed directly to consumers rather than doctors—has burgeoned into a multimillion-dollar effort since the late 1990s. In 2000 alone, the pharmaceutical industry spent over $2.5 billion on DTCA; the amount spent on promotions directed at physicians was twenty-fold greater.

Growing concerns about DTCA's destructive impact united a group of women's and consumer-health organizations seeking to raise public awareness. Called Prevention First, the coalition began with a critique of ads touting tamoxifen to reduce breast-cancer risk—promoting potentially dangerous pills to *healthy* women, as breast-cancer "prevention" (see *www.bcaction.org* for details). A longer-term goal of Prevention First is to foster new understandings of health and disease prevention that will support ultimate implementation of the Precautionary Principle of Public Health (see *www.sehn.org/precaution.html*) as the basis of regulatory and health policy.[22]

Tobacco

Tobacco use is the leading cause of preventable mortality in the United States, responsible for more than 400,000 deaths each year—more than caused by AIDS, alcohol, drug abuse, car crashes, murders, suicides, and fires *combined*. Nearly one in four people in the U.S. currently [2002] smoke; half of all long-term smokers die of smoking-caused diseases. Since 1987, lung cancer has been the leading cancer killer among women. Heart disease is the overall leading cause of death among women, and smoking accounts for one of every five deaths from heart disease. In addition, smoking can cause complications during pregnancy and birth.

Tobacco use among women goes with our cultural obsession with thinness (see the body image section below), and pervasive tobacco use in TV and films. Data from the National Health Interview Survey of more than 102,600 women showed an abrupt increase in smoking initiation in girls under age 18 around 1967, when tobacco advertising introduced cigarette brands for women; from 1991 to 1999, smoking among high-school girls increased from 27 to 34.9 percent. Outraged activists responded to the promotion of tobacco to girls,[23] but recent trends are not encouraging. Smoking is often a means of dealing

---

22. The coalition also hopes to challenge an emerging double standard in the cancer establishment where, for example, tamoxifen is described as "not perfect but a step on the way to the kind of pill we want," while the imperfections and uncertainties inherent in environmental prevention become the basis for dismissing the environmental-prevention approach altogether. In order to avoid possible conflicts of interest, no coalition organization accepts grants from pharmaceutical companies. See *www.ourbodiesourselves.org* for more information.

23. Campaign for Tobacco-Free Kids has an extensive website *(www.tobaccofreekids. org)* with reports about the tobacco industry, efficacy of stop-smoking programs, politics of tobacco farming, legislative efforts to hold tobacco companies accountable for the damage their product causes, and the tobacco industry's history of creating ads aimed at women. "Pack of Lies," a video featuring consumer-rights activist Jean Kilbourne, exposes the seductive advertising gimmicks geared especially to women; in particular, how tobacco ads exploit the cultural obsession with thinness *(www.mediaed.org/videos)*.

with stress at work or school, and women have a harder time quitting than men.

More recently, the tobacco industry has cynically targeted both women of color in the U.S. and overseas with ads that link empowerment, individuality, and rebellion to smoking. Tobacco-control activists and public-health officials are fighting back, among them the American Legacy Foundation's Women and Smoking Initiative *(www.americanlegacy.org)*, the World Health Organization's Tobacco Free Initiative *(www.who.int/tobacco)*, and the "Virginia SLAM!" campaign *(www.members.tripod.com/slammusic/article.htm)*.

Body Image

The pressure on women to look a certain way is so ingrained that it's easy to overlook the impact mass culture has on how we feel about our bodies. Feminists have been working on body-image issues for three decades. Still, TV and movies, magazines and newspapers, and now the Internet bombard us with airbrushed images of beauty and thinness. Inevitably, we absorb the message: this is the norm, and is achievable—*if* we use this makeup, remove that hair, reshape that body part.

Feminists are challenging these culturally imposed standards of beauty, pointing out health risks involved in a never-ending struggle toward nonexistent perfection, whether from breast implants (see above) or weight-loss diets that can result in illness or serious eating disorders. "Redefining Liberation," an inexpensive video by the National NOW Foundation *(www.nowfoundation.org)*, critiques tobacco, alcohol, and fashion-industry messages, and is a consciousness-raising tool for young women, who are particularly vulnerable to such eating disorders as anorexia and bulimia.[24]

HIV/AIDS and Other Sexually Transmitted Infections (STIs)

As of late 2001, more than 21 million people had died from HIV/AIDS worldwide, while more than 40 million others were living with the in-

---

24. See "Girls: 'We Are the Ones Who Can Make a Change!' " by Ana Grossman and Emma Peters-Axtell, p. 121, for more on body-image activism; and "Generation 'Why?': A Call to Arms," by Jasmine Victoria, p. 126, for more on eating disorders.—Ed.

fection.[25] AIDS is the fourth leading cause of death worldwide and the leading cause of death on the African continent. About one-fourth of individuals estimated to be living with HIV in the U.S. are women.[26] More than 90 percent of new infections are spread through unprotected sex, and heterosexual contact represents the primary source of risk for women. (Among African American women, injection drug usage accounts for 44 percent of all AIDS cases, with 37 percent due to heterosexual contact; AIDS has resulted in more deaths among African American women than any other cause, and black women represent the highest percentage—62 percent—of all reported AIDS cases among U.S. women.[27]) Because women are biologically and socio-economically more vulnerable than men—and frequently face violence when they try to control where, when, and how intercourse will occur—women need alternatives to dependence on the male condom as the sole source of protection against STIs, including HIV/AIDS. Other common STIs include chlamydia, gonorrhea, and HPV (human papilloma virus) infections—often referred to as genital warts. About one in five people in the U.S. has an STI, with more than 15 million new infections occurring each year—causing infertility, cervical cancer, pelvic inflammatory disease, ectopic pregnancy, and even death.

The female condom has offered an important means of protection from STIs, and studies show them to be more acceptable (to both women and men) than predicted. However, there are still women who can't or won't use them, and many men don't use male condoms. The diaphragm has demonstrated some protective benefits, but provides only a partial barrier. In the 1990s, women's health activists began campaigning for more research and development of microbicides—chemical entities which, when applied to the vagina or rectum, can prevent or reduce transmission of certain STIs. With about 25 percent of new STI infections (including HIV) occurring in people ages 15–19, this new form of protection could help prevent much pain and suffering. Several

25. UNAIDS, AIDS Epidemic Update, December 2001 *(www.unaids.org)*.

26. National Institute of Allergy and Infectious Diseases (NIAID), "HIV Infection and Women," May 2001 *(www.niaid.nih.gov/factsheets/womenhiv.htm)*.

27. National Black Women's Health Project *(www.blackwomenshealth.org)*. Also see Boudin and Smith, op. cit.—Ed.

promising microbicide products may come to market by the middle of the twenty-first century's first decade.

New Reproductive Technologies: From IVF to Cloning

Assisted reproductive technologies such as in-vitro fertilization (IVF) generated considerable controversy through the 1980s and '90s—with low IVF success rates, limited access for poorer women, and risks to women's health among the concerns cited. Contract motherhood ("surrogacy") arrangements raised questions about the commodification of children, especially when women were paid to carry a baby to term and surrender it for adoption, with reduced payments in cases that didn't result in healthy babies.

In the early 1960s, the "father" of IVF—Robert G. Edwards, Ph.D., of Great Britain—discovered that the inner cell mass of the blastocyst could be used to obtain stem cells that could multiply. At the time, no molecular technology techniques were available to enable further investigation. But soon after, one of Edwards's students injected stem cells into the tail vein of a mouse; these cells began to migrate, colonized in the liver, and multiplied in bone marrow, demonstrating how stem cells might someday be used to cure injured organs in humans. Despite more than 20 years of stem-cell research in mice, however, no successful cures for diseases have yet been demonstrated. But recently, the development of somatic cell nuclear transfer and the successful cloning of several types of animals [28] have introduced scenaria that could profoundly alter human relationships, thus making cloning research a major debate. The majority of people are opposed to human cloning that produces a genetic duplicate human being, but much disagreement exists regarding allowing human embryo cloning for research purposes. Some in the biotechnology industry promise miracle medical advances from cloning embryos and extracting embryonic stem cells for research purposes; others remain doubtful that certain technical/safety hurdles can be overcome so therapies for humans would be safe and effective. One concern receiving minimal attention in public debates on embryo cloning is

---

28. See "Bitch, Chick, Cow: Women's and (Other) Animals' Rights," by Carol J. Adams, p. 494.—Ed.

the lack of adequate, long-term, safety data on the super-ovulating drugs *women* must take in order to *provide* multiple eggs for embryo cloning.

Most disturbing is the prospect that newer genetic technologies could be used to produce "designer babies."[29] Once developed, the availability of such techniques could pressure parents to use them or allow a child to be born less than "ideal." Pre-natal Genetic Diagnosis (PGD)—praised as the most significant recent advance in reproductive technology—has evolved to where scientists can now test IVF embryos for genetic disorders prior to their transfer to the uterus. PGD does allow couples or individuals with serious inherited disorders to decrease the risk of having a child affected by the same problem. However, it also makes possible sex selection and other types of genetic engineering that raise ethical concerns. (India's experience with sex selection—primarily using amniocentesis—has created a grave sex imbalance in the population, due to preferences for male children.)

We're still at the early stages of understanding the consequences of genetic technologies, some of which might ultimately benefit people with access to them. Many activists point to their potential for widening the gap between rich and poor, creating a new caste system where the genetically well-endowed would dominate others. Sometimes labeled "anti-science" or "anti-choice," these critics nonetheless deserve consideration; they ask us to scrutinize the dark side of a "post-human" future that might have little to do with biotech hype.[30]

Health Care Reform

Health care reform has long been a feminist issue, since women are both the majority of the uninsured and the under-insured, as well as the majority of health care providers. For decades, advocates have called for a medical system with better primary, low-tech, and preventive care, while offering interventionist, hi-tech care in more appropriate fashion.

---

29. See *The Clone Age: Adventures in the New World of Reproductive Technology,* by Lori Andrews (New York: Henry Holt & Company, 1999).

30. See "What Human Genetic Modification Means for Women," in *World-Watch,* July/August 2002.

Although health care reform in the U.S. was attempted many times during the twentieth century, our biggest successes came in 1965 with the creation of the Medicaid and Medicare programs, which have provided medical services to millions of poor, underserved, and older persons. Universal health coverage and the notion of *health care as a right* remain elusive goals. Furthermore, services essential to women, including long-term care, are often not covered by insurance plans.[31] *The United States remains the only industrialized country in the world without a universal health care program.* Access to services, however, will not be sufficient: the health care system must be evidence-based, responsive to women's needs, less profit-driven, and more equitable.

Finally, it is not primarily health and medical services that have the greatest impact on our well-being. It is, rather, the food we eat, water we drink, air we breathe, physical activity, and environments in which we live.[32] Finding and sharing quality information, supporting one another to make sensible personal choices, and working together to create communities with minimal violence, poverty, and pollution—these remain our most basic means of achieving good health for all.

JUDY NORSIGIAN is co-founder of the Boston Women's Health Book Collective (now called "Our Bodies, Ourselves"), and coauthor of *Our Bodies Ourselves for the New Century* (New York: Simon & Schuster, 1998). Barbara Brenner is executive director of Breast Cancer Action, San Francisco. Lisa Paine, Dr.PH, is principal of The Hutchinson Dyer Group, senior advisor to *Our Bodies, Ourselves,* professor of Maternal and Child Health and Obstetrics and Gynecology, Boston University Schools of Public Health and Medicine, and certified nurse-midwife. Kiki Zeldes is the Boston Women's Health Book Collective website manager.

Suggested Further Reading

Kaschak, Ellyn, and Leonore Tiefer, eds. *A New View of Women's Sexual Problems.* West Hazleton, Pennsylvania: Haworth Press, 2002.

---

31. See Chavkin, op. cit.—Ed.

32. See DiPerna, op. cit.—Ed.

The National Women's Health Network. *The Truth About Hormone Replacement Therapy*. New York: Prima Publishing, 2002.

Null, Gary, and Barbara Seaman. *For Women Only: Your Guide to Health Empowerment*. New York: Seven Stories Press, 1999.

Ruzek, Sheryl Burt, Virginia L. Olesen, and Adele Clarke, eds. *Women's Health: Complexities and Differences*. Columbus: Ohio State University Press, 1997.

Weisman, Carol Sachs. *Women's Health Care: Activist Traditions and Institutional Change*. Baltimore, Maryland: Johns Hopkins University Press, 1998.

On-line resources: The Boston Women's Health Book Collective *(www.ourbodiesourselves.org)*, The National Women's Health Network *(www.womenshealthnetwork.org)*, The National Black Women's Health Project *(www.blackwomenshealth.org)*, The National Women's Health Information Center *(www.4women.gov)*, and The International Women's Health Coalition *(www.iwhc.org)*.

Women in Sports:
What's the Score?

BARBARA FINDLEN

ONCE UPON A TIME, there was Billie Jean King.

King was an outspoken feminist and a champion athlete when the U.S. Women's Movement was growing in size and influence and women athletes were gaining new visibility and opportunities. She brought an unprecedented feminist consciousness to sports, bravely putting both reputation and career on the line by speaking out, organizing other players to boycott tournaments where pay inequities were most egregious, and traveling around the country promoting the value of women as professional athletes.

Then there was the Battle of the Sexes—the 1973 match between King (reigning Wimbledon champion) and Bobby Riggs (a fifty-five-year-old tennis pro who boasted that females were so inferior to males that no woman could defeat a man). The winner would receive $100,000, but more was at stake. Riggs fashioned himself a proud "male chauvinist pig," challenging King as an explicit provocation against feminism. The title "Battle of the Sexes" was conceived for maximum hype; they played at the Houston Astrodome before a live audience of 30,000, the largest ever for a tennis match.

I had just turned nine years old, and my antennae were starting to tune in to feminist ideas. As Billie Jean was borne into the arena on a Cleopatra-style gold litter by five toga-clad men, I sat among the world-wide TV audience of 60 million. The Battle of the Sexes felt monumentally important to me. My status as an aspiring girl athlete was on the line. If Billie Jean won, it would vindicate my quest for legitimacy on the playing fields and be a triumph for womankind in our efforts to compete on—or in—any field. If she lost, I anticipated humiliation on the playground: I'd be a target for all the boys as well as, sadly, for adult women and men who were looking for excuses to keep me and my girlfriends benched.

She won. *I* won. *We* won.

King's trouncing of Riggs provided a memorable lesson about the power and potential of women, and strengthened her quest to achieve parity for women athletes. In 1971, there was $250,000 in prize money to be won by women tennis players. By the time King retired thirteen years later, women tennis pros were collectively grossing $11 million.

The struggle for equity in sports is important for *all* women. Why? Because seeing the female face of athletic excellence helps us imagine new possibilities for ourselves in other areas. Because restricting women's physical freedom is a fundamental means of controlling women. Because sports are a way for a lot of girls and women to discover their own power. Because girls can learn to work with other girls on a team. Because women can discover and build their own physical strength, as well as other kinds of strength. Because we can experience ourselves—and other women and girls—as capable, as leaders, as achievers. Because by creating new models of what womanhood means, we also inspire new models for manhood.

The great myth of sports is that it's a meritocracy, that those who win games and championships are the greatest athletes. But sports are part of society, and reflect society's biases and inequities when it comes to access and opportunity. You can't win if you don't play, and you can't play if you're not allowed on the field. This has been one of the greatest challenges for girls and women.

In the Beginning

In the nineteenth century, conventional wisdom was that excessive physical activity was unhealthy for women (that is, for *white* women), and that women were in any case incapable of true athletic excellence. In 1897, for example, sociologist William I. Thomas wrote that a woman "resembles the child and the lower races, i.e., the less developed forms," and that the size and shape of women's bodies relative to men's constituted "a very striking evidence of the ineptitude of woman for the expenditure of physiological energy through motor action."[1]

His astute opinion notwithstanding, around the turn of the century women educators at elite private high schools and colleges in the United States began to incorporate moderate physical activity as part of an overall student program of health and education. Young women were allowed participation in a limited number of games and sports— archery, basketball, rowing, track, field hockey, and tennis—though they played in restrictive clothing and according to modified rules that minimized action and physical contact. In women's basketball, for instance, players had to remain in their assigned section of the court and weren't allowed to hold the ball longer than three seconds or bounce it more than three consecutive times. In tennis, women would play to two of three sets instead of three of five, a modification that survives to this day.

But after World War I, there was a backlash to even this limited version of competitive sports. Physical educators, many of them women, worried that excessive competitiveness and growing athleticism were contrary to women's and girls' true "nature" and might even be harming them. A little noncompetitive game-playing was all right, but these advocates fought hard against county, district, national, and intercollegiate competition, and strenuously protested the introduction of women's track and field events at the 1928 Olympic Games. As one male writer worried in a 1929 article, "Intense forms of physical and psychic conflicts . . . tend to destroy girls' physical and psychic charm and adaptability for motherhood."[2]

Women took advantage of all the opportunities available. In the 1920s and 1930s a number of U.S. companies started recreation clubs for employees and eventually formed industrial leagues. Mildred "Babe" Didrikson Zaharias, one of the greatest athletes in history, was

---

1. William I. Thomas, "On a Difference in the Metabolism of the Sexes," *American Journal of Sociology* 3 (1897): 41.

2. Frederick R. Rogers, "Olympics for Girls?" *School and Society* 30 (August 10, 1929): 193–94, cited in Allen Guttmann, *Women's Sports: A History* (New York: Columbia University Press, 1991), 139–40.

hired by Employers Casualty Company in Dallas—as a typist—so she could compete on the company's basketball and track and field teams. She won three gold medals in track and field in the 1932 Olympics. But when she took up golf, there was no women's professional league, and she spent years touring the country playing men in exhibition matches. So in 1949 Zaharias cofounded the Ladies Professional Golf Association (LPGA), then went on to win thirty-one of its tournaments.

During World War II, the door to professional team sports opened briefly for women. The All-American Girls' Professional Baseball League thrived in the Midwest from 1943 to 1954, attendance reaching nearly one million a year. Tennis great Althea Gibson smashed barriers throughout the 1950s, becoming the first African American to win both Wimbledon and the U.S. Open; she too had a second career as a professional golfer. But such chances were few and far between, and bigotry persisted. It took federal legislation to win women and girls real access.

A Turning Point: Title IX

On July 1, 1972, President Richard Nixon signed into law Title IX of the Education Amendments of 1972, outlawing sex discrimination at educational institutions that receive federal funds. Almost all schools and colleges receive some federal money, so Title IX's impact would be broad. Originally conceived as a remedy to sex discrimination against women professors, Title IX's implications for athletic programs wasn't reckoned until two years later, when the National Collegiate Athletic Association (NCAA) devised guidelines for colleges' compliance: having the number of female athletes be "substantially proportional" to the number of female undergraduates; establishing a "history and continuing practice" of expanding opportunities for women in sports; *or* having a program that "effectively accommodates the interests and abilities" of women athletes. Suddenly, virtually every school in the country had to reevaluate its athletic programs and start creating new teams for girls and women.

It's hard to overstate the impact of Title IX. The numbers speak for themselves. In 1971, about 294,000 girls in the United States were participating in high-school interscholastic athletics. In 2000, that figure was 2,675,874—an increase of 810 percent. (Boys' high-school sports participation increased by 4.5 percent over the same period.) On the college level, before Title IX, there were about 300,000 U.S. women playing intercollegiate sports. As of 1997, there were about 2.25 million.

In one generation, we've seen Title IX's legacy bear fruit. Consider women's sports in the late 1990s. In 1996, the U.S. won gold medals in Olympic women's basketball, softball, and soccer. In 1997, two professional women's basketball leagues began: the American Basketball League (ABL) and the Women's National Basketball Association (WNBA). In 1998, the first U.S. women's Olympic ice-hockey team won the gold medal. The following year, 40 million U.S. households watched on TV as the U.S. women's soccer team won the Women's World Cup. The Women's Professional Football League started in 2000, and a professional women's soccer league launched in the spring of 2001. And the real revolution is that ordinary women—about 40 million—are tackling virtually every kind of sport: mountain climbing, soccer, dogsledding, kayaking, marathon, boxing, football, in-line skating, jogging, weightlifting, crew, lacrosse, ice hockey, judo, volleyball, rugby, fencing, triathlon, wrestling, speed skating, skiing, skateboarding, snowboarding.

Still, it's crucial to remember that opportunities afforded by Title IX have come about almost entirely because of the persistent activism by advocates for women athletes. Almost as soon as it passed, Title IX was resisted by schools, attacked by politicians, and flouted by athletic directors. The 1980s witnessed continual efforts in Congress to repeal or gut Title IX. Some colleges have spent millions of dollars in lawsuits to try to avoid compliance. There are still ongoing lawsuits by women athletes, to force schools to comply with the law.

Any time there's been a major advance—new Olympic events for women; girls playing Little League baseball; increased prizes for professional golfers and tennis players; women's memberships in community health clubs—it's been the result of women and girls pushing, speaking, suing, standing up for ourselves and for each other.

In Search of a Level Playing Field

The concept of finding a "level playing field" is sometimes quite literal for female athletes. Title IX applies only to educational institutions, not municipal or private leagues or associations. Girls and women all over the country still must fight for teams and programs in their communities[3]; access to decent fields, courts, and rinks; reasonable game scheduling; career opportunities in coaching, sports administration, and sports journalism.[4] Federal law doesn't touch those areas.

While the number of women's programs has grown tremendously, by 2002, on the college level women still got only 38 percent of all athletic scholarship money, 27 percent of recruiting money, and 23 percent of overall athletic budgets. One unforeseen consequence of Title IX is that many schools merged their men's and women's athletic departments— and men run the combined departments. Consequently, while in 1972 more than 90 percent of women's athletic programs were directed by women, in 2002 women are athletic directors at only 9 percent of NCAA Division I schools. The percentage of women coaching women's college teams declined from more than 90 percent in 1972 to 48 percent in 2000. African American women constitute only 2 percent of all women's teams' coaches; *all* women of color comprise only 2.7 percent. Of the more than 1,000 NCAA schools, only 5 have women of color as athletic directors.

Furthermore, despite the enormous growth in women's sports participation, according to research by the Women's Sports Foundation, female athletes receive approximately 6 to 8 percent of total media sports coverage.[5]

The Image Problem

Billie Jean King once observed that women athletes wanted "recognition as athletes, pros, not for our looks. Do the reporters care if a football player is ugly as long as he can block, tackle, and do his job? An athlete has to perform. Measure us that way; not on sex."[6]

---

3. See "Girls: 'We Are the Ones Who Can Make a Change!'" by Ana Grossman and Emma Peters-Axtell, p. 121.—Ed.

4. See "Standing By: Women in Broadcast Media," by Carol Jenkins, p. 418.—Ed.

5. Ibid.

6. "Billie Jean King Evens the Score," by Bud Collins, *Ms.*, July 1973.

What sports requires of athletes—being competitive, wanting to win, sweating, developing muscles—is contrary to almost everything required of "femininity," so sports writers and commentators, league and program officials, coaches, and sometimes athletes themselves bend over backward to prove that these women are still "feminine," *even though* they're athletes. It may not be surprising that players in the All-American Girls' Professional Baseball League of the 1940s were required to keep their hair long, wear dresses in public, and wear makeup at all times— even on the field. But as late as 1987 the LPGA reportedly had an "image consultant" traveling with the tour.[7] In 1996, members of the U.S. Olympic softball team appeared on the *Oprah* Winfrey show after having undergone a "makeover."[8] And in 2001, basketball pro Jamila Wideman wrote, "You think that we've come so far . . . but I guarantee that in three out of four interviews I get asked, 'How can you still be feminine if you're an athlete?' What does it mean to be feminine? Does it mean I go to the locker room and change into my prom dress after a game?"[9]

Mary Jo Kane, director of the Tucker Center for Research on Girls & Women in Sport at the University of Minnesota, has observed that in media reports, women athletes "are routinely shown off court, out of uniform, and in highly sexualized poses," with a great emphasis on sexiness and beauty.[10] Many features on professional women athletes focus on their husbands and children, an approach virtually unthinkable in coverage of male athletes.

What's everyone so nervous about? For one thing, if the definition of femininity is shaken up, rigid definitions of masculinity are threatened. For another, they're afraid of women athletes being seen as—or actually being—lesbians.[11] "Femininity," according to sports scholar Pat Grif-

---

7. Pat Griffin, *Strong Women, Deep Closets: Lesbians and Homophobia in Sport* (Champaign, Illinois: Human Kinetics, 1998), p. 71.

8. Ibid., p. 73.

9. Jane Gottesman, *Game Face: What Does a Female Athlete Look Like?* (New York: Random House, 2001).

10. Glenda Crank Holste, "Women Athletes Often Debased by Media Images," *Women's E-News*, 17 October 2000.

11. See "Confessions of a Worrywart: Ruminations on a Lesbian Feminist Overview," by Karla Jay, p. 212.—Ed.

fin, "is a code word for heterosexuality."[12] Griffin continues, "One of the most effective means of controlling women in sport is to challenge the femininity and heterosexuality of women athletes. When a woman is called 'masculine,' 'unfeminine,' or 'dyke,' she knows she has crossed a gender boundary or challenged male privilege. In this way, homophobia serves as glue that holds traditional gender role expectations in place."[13]

Women's figure skating imposes perhaps the most intense constraints around image and femininity. As Kate Rounds observed in *Ms.*, in figure skating, women's "athleticism is to be hidden, not flaunted." It's a performance, one judged by subjective criteria, and the athletes understand that part of what they will be judged by is how they look, how graceful they are, even their public image *off* the ice.[14] French Olympian Surya Bonaly's athletic back flips earned her resentment in the mid-1990s. Tennis titan Martina Navratilova offered an interesting hypothesis on what would have happened had tennis been a judged sport: "I'm not the girl next door. The judge would have said, 'Maybe you hit the ball harder, but Chris [Evert] is a good Catholic girl, she goes to church, we like her family, she doesn't complain about anything, she wears mascara, we like her dress, her forehand's very pretty—and she's heterosexual.' "[15]

Imagine what women athletes might accomplish if they didn't have to worry about appearing sufficiently "feminine."

Marketing the Female Athlete

The use of women's bodies to sell products is nothing new. But if you watch women's games on TV, these days you see a new presentation of a

---

12. Griffin, op. cit., p. 68.

13. Griffin, op. cit., pp. 18–20.

14. Kate Rounds, "Ice Follies: Reflections on a Sport Out of Whack," *Ms.* (May/June 1994), 26–33. See also *Little Girls in Pretty Boxes: The Making and Breaking of Elite Gymnasts and Figure Skaters,* by Joan Ryan (Doubleday, 1995; Warner Books, 1996).

15. Rounds, op. cit.

woman athlete. Images of strong, fast, muscled women champions are used to sell everything from tampons to cars, hair coloring to sneakers. These images show girls and women of color as positive role models (a rarity in media overall), and reflect greater visibility of women achieving and excelling at sports, not to mention greater availability of sports equipment for girls and women. But it's important to remember that the impetus is not women's empowerment, but selling a product. This is a rich question for feminists, because such ads are based on the assumption that the *idea* of women's power is so appealing that it can be used to *sell* us things. Some of these ads seem to sell women's empowerment itself. A famous Nike ad that aired during the late 1990s showed girls in different athletic settings, with girls' voice-overs saying: "If you let me play sports, I will like myself more. I will have more self confidence. . . . I will be 60 percent less likely to get breast cancer. I will suffer less depression. If you let me play sports, I will be more likely to leave a man who beats me. I will be less likely to get pregnant before I want to. I will learn . . . what it means to be strong. If you let me play sports."

This ad was both an eloquent statement about the power of sports for girls and a plea for opportunities for girls' participation. But was this an act of conscience? This is Nike, the same company that later ran—and stopped, because of feminist protests—an ad featuring distance runner Suzy Favor Hamilton being chased by a chainsaw-wielding stalker; the same company that is, at this writing, still subject to a long-running boycott by feminists and other activists outraged at its use of sweatshop labor.

A Golden Age

In September 2001, *Time* magazine writer Robert Sullivan declared this era a Golden Age of women's sports, pointing to the explosive growth in participation, the creation of myriad new pro leagues, and the high general quality of play. The money's not there yet, he conceded, "but it will be."[16]

We have, in fact, come a long way from a time when bloomer-clad

---

16. Robert Sullivan, "For Women, a Golden Age," *Time*, 3 September 2001.

women athletes were considered scandalous and male spectators were barred from women's matches. We've created new opportunities and changed expectations of women's capabilities. We enjoy unprecedented participation and visibility while still confronting barriers and stereotypes. We're starting to see serious money pumped into women's programs and leagues.

So we must take advantage of this Golden Age by *creating more opportunities* and *envisioning new models* of competition based on respect rather than obliteration. We can develop professional leagues that promote people as well as profit. The WNBA, for example, has been financially profitable while engendering the loyalty of fans because of its reasonable ticket prices and accessible, community-involved players.

We also have a chance—and an imperative—to continue challenging sexist, homophobic, and racist assumptions in the sports establishment and the media, in order to free women athletes to be our true best selves. History has shown that the gains women athletes make come from activism and advocacy off the field as well as hard work and excellence on it. Working for equality, both in athletic institutions and in the broader society, remains our best defense.

BARBARA FINDLEN is coauthor of *Remarkable Women of the Twentieth Century: 100 Portraits of Achievement* (Friedman/Fairfax, 1998) and editor of the anthology *Listen Up: Voices from the Next Feminist Generation* (Seal Press, 1995; Avalon paperback, 2001). She worked at *Ms.* magazine for thirteen years, the last five as executive editor, and is currently managing editor of *Family Fun* magazine. She lives in Amherst, Massachusetts, with her partner, Kristen Golden, and their two children.

Suggested Further Reading

Gottesman, Jane. *Game Face: What Does a Female Athlete Look Like?* New York: Random House, 2001.

Griffin, Pat. *Strong Women, Deep Closets: Lesbians and Homophobia in Sport.* Champaign, Illinois: Human Kinetics, 1998.

Nelson, Mariah Burton. *The Stronger Women Get, the More Men Love*

Football: Sexism and the American Culture of Sports. New York: Harcourt Brace, 1994.

Smith, Lissa, ed. *Nike Is a Goddess: The History of Women in Sports.* New York: Atlantic Monthly Press, 1998.

Twin, Stephanie, ed. *Out of the Bleachers: Writings on Women and Sport.* New York: The Feminist Press at CUNY, 1979.

The Nature of the Beast:
Sexual Harassment

ANITA HILL

QUITE A FEW YEARS have passed since October 1991, when my world would be forever changed by the events that culminated in the "Hill-Thomas hearing." I am no longer an anonymous, private individual; my name has become synonymous with sexual harassment.[1] To my supporters I represent the courage to come forward and disclose a painful truth—a courage which thousands of others have found since the hearing.[2] To my detractors I represent the debasement of a public forum, at best a pawn, at worst a perjurer. Living with these conflicting perceptions has been difficult, sometimes overwhelming. The event known as

---

1. In 1991, Anita Hill was a law professor at the University of Oklahoma. She had previously been an assistant to the chairman of the U.S. Equal Employment Opportunity Commission, Clarence Thomas, later a George Bush nominee to the Supreme Court. Hill's book, *Speaking Truth to Power* (Bantam Doubleday Dell, 1997), is the account of her testimony at Thomas's Senate Judiciary confirmation hearing, to which she had been called as a witness and during which she charged him with sexual harassment. Thomas's confirmation managed to squeak through the Senate, while Hill was targeted for personal invective and even death threats. Some of the vicious slander was carefully politically orchestrated as, years later, David Brock, one of her attackers, would confess (*Blinded by the Right: The Conscience of an Ex-Conservative*, Crown, 2002). Nevertheless, long before such validation, Hill's integrity at the time, her quiet dignity, and her courageous testimony—as well as the blatant, virulent sexism evidenced by some male members of the Senate Judiciary Committee—galvanized women in Congress, across the United States, and internationally.—Ed.

2. According to the National Organization for Women, in the wake of Hill's testimony bringing the issue into mainstream public consciousness, between the years 1990 and 1995, sexual-harassment cases reported to the Equal Employment Opportunity Commission rose by 153 percent.—Ed.

the Hill-Thomas hearing has been described variously as a watershed in U.S. politics, a turning point in the awareness of sexual harassment, and a wake-up call for women. For me it was a bane that I have worked hard to transform into a blessing for myself and for others—especially because it brought to bear for the average public issues of sexual harassment, issues of race, gender, and politics. I have not lived one day since the hearing without feeling its significance or the immeasurable weight of responsibility it has left with me. During her testimony before the Judiciary Committee, Judge Susan Hoerchner commented that I did not choose the issue of sexual harassment; rather, it chose me. Having been chosen, I have come to believe that it is up to me to try to help give meaning to it all.

Sometimes I fear that my writing will not communicate the power of the experience effectively. Sometimes I fear that it might, thus provoking further attacks on me. But it is as important today as it was in 1991 that I feel free to speak. If I let my fears silence me now, I will have betrayed all those who supported me in 1991 and those who have come forward since. More than anything else, the Hill-Thomas hearing of October 1991 was about finding our voices and breaking the silence forever.[3]

The response to my Senate Judiciary Committee testimony was at once heartwarming and heart-wrenching. In learning that I was not alone in having experienced harassment, I also learned that there are far too many women who have experienced a range of inexcusable and illegal activities—from sexist jokes to sexual assault—on the job.

My reaction has been to try to learn more. As an educator, I always begin to study an issue by examining the scientific data: the articles, the books, the studies. But perhaps the most compelling lesson lies in the stories told by women who have written to me over the years. I have learned much; I am continuing to learn.

"The Nature of the Beast" describes the existence of sexual harassment, which is alive and well: a harmful, dangerous thing that can confront a woman at any time.

What we know about harassment, sizing up the beast:

---

3. This essay is based in part on an article by Anita Hill—her first on the subject—that originally appeared in *Ms.* in January/February 1992.—Ed.

Sexual Harassment Is Pervasive

1. *It still occurs at an alarming rate.* Statistics show that anywhere from 42 to 90 percent of women will experience some form of harassment during their employed lives.[4] At least 1 percent experience sexual assault.[5] But no statistics can fully reveal the story of the anguish of women who have been told in various ways on the first day of a job that sexual favors are expected. Or the story of women who were sexually assaulted by men with whom they had to continue to work.

2. *It has been occurring for decades and decades.* In letters, women told me of incidents that occurred fifty years ago when they were first entering the workplace—incidents they have been unable to speak about for all those years.[6]

3. *Harassment crosses lines of race and class.* In some ways, it is a creature that practices "equal opportunity" where women are concerned. In other ways it exhibits predictable prejudices and reflects stereotypical myths held by our society.

---

4. Statistics vary—but all are alarmingly high. The National Organization for Women reports that 50 to 75 percent of employed women will experience sexual harassment on the job. Some surveys are job/career-specific: a 1995 Pentagon study revealed that 78 percent of all military women have been sexually harassed; despite zero-tolerance rhetoric from military leadership, harassment and assaults continue (see "Redefining the Warrior Mentality: Women in the Military," by Claudia J. Kennedy p. 409). Academia-based harassment is also prevalent: according to a 1993 survey cosponsored by the NOW Legal Defense and Education Fund, 89 percent of girls and women had been sexually harassed in school, and 39 percent had been harassed on a daily basis during the prior year. The U.S. Department of Labor—usually conservative in its assessments—estimates that 50 to 80 percent of women in the United States experience some form of sexual harassment during their academic or work lives. See the "Workplaces" section, p. 323.—Ed.

5. See "Landscape of the Ordinary: Violence Against Women," by Andrea Dworkin, p. 58.—Ed.

6. Numerous women's groups held speak-outs and teach-ins on sexual harassment in the early 1970s, at the start of the contemporary feminist wave—but it was not until Hill's testimony and the subsequent furor in the early 1990s that the issue went mainstream in public consciousness.—Ed.

Harassment All Too Often Goes Unreported

This happens for a variety of reasons:

1. Unwillingness (for good reason) to deal with the expected consequences;[7]
2. Self-blame;
3. Threats or blackmail by co-workers or employers;
4. In many cases, it boils down to a sense of powerlessness women experience in the workplace, and our acceptance of a certain level of inability to control our careers and professional destinies. This sense of powerlessness is particularly troubling given some research findings that individuals with graduate degrees experience more harassment than do persons with less than a high-school diploma. The message: when you try to obtain power through education, the beast harassment responds by striking even more often and more vehemently.

Harassment Is Still Treated as a Woman's "Dirty Secret"

We know what happens when we "tell." We know that when harassment is reported, the common reaction is still disbelief or worse.

1. Women who "tell" lose their jobs. A typical response described in letters to me was: "I not only lost my job for reporting harassment, but I was accused of stealing and charges were brought against me."
2. Women who "tell" become emotionally wasted. One writer noted that "it was fully eight months after the suit was concluded that I began to see myself as alive again."
3. Women who "tell" are, sadly, not always supported by other women. Perhaps the most disheartening stories are of mothers not believing daughters. In my kindest moments, I believe that

---

7. Court cases have established that it is the complainant's burden to prove that the alleged harassment was unwelcome. Although Congress extended the federal rape shield law (which prohibits lawyers' abusive questions) to include sexual harassment cases, women still find themselves under attack in the courtroom.—Ed.

this reaction represents attempts to distance ourselves from the pain of the harassment experience; the internal response is "This didn't happen to *me*. This *couldn't* happen to *me*. In order to believe that *I* am protected, I must believe that it didn't happen to *her*." The external response becomes "What did you do to provoke that kind of behavior?"[8] Yet at the same time that I have learned about hurtful and unproductive reactions, I have also heard stories of mothers and daughters sharing their experiences. In some cases the sharing allows for a closer bonding. In others a slight but recognizable mending of a previously damaged relationship can occur. What we are learning about harassment requires recognizing this beast when we encounter it. And more. It requires looking the beast in the eye.

We are learning, painfully, that simply having laws against harassment on the books is not enough. The law, as it was conceived, was to provide a shield of protection for us.[9] Yet that shield is failing us: many fear reporting, others feel it would do no good.[10] The result is that an estimated less than 5 percent of women victims file claims of harassment. Moreover, the law focuses on quid pro quo, but this makes up considerably less than 5 percent of the cases. The law needs to be more responsive to the reality of our experiences.

---

8. See Dworkin, op. cit., on both internal self-blame and the "blame the victim" phenomenon in situations of violence against women.—Ed.

9. See "Women and Law: The Power to Change," by Catharine A. MacKinnon, p. 447, for an explanation of how Title VII's prohibition on sex discrimination in employment was used by feminists during the 1970s to forge the first civil rights created by women—the prohibition on sexual harassment—and how, by 1980, Title IX of the Education Amendments of 1972 (which guaranteed women equal access to the benefits of an education) was authoritatively interpreted to prohibit sexual harassment in education—Ed.

10. The law does not protect all women. Women working for employers with fewer than fifteen employees are not protected by federal laws (although state laws may apply). Women of color are especially vulnerable; they are the majority of employees in low-paying jobs with little job security. Undocumented immigrant women have no legal recourse when harassed. And lesbian workers have many reasons for not reporting harassment. Data from the NOW Legal Defense and Education Fund *(www.nowldef.org)*.—Ed.

As we have learned, enforcing the law alone won't terminate the problem. What we are seeking is equality of treatment in the workplace. Equality requires an expansion of our attitudes toward workers. Sexual harassment denies our treatment as equals and replaces it with treatment of women as objects of ego or power gratification. We have learned that sexual harassment is more about power and fear than about sex.

Yet research suggests two troublesome responses exhibited both by workers and by courts. Both respond by:

1. Downplaying the seriousness of the behavior (seeing it as "normal sexual attraction" between people) or commenting on the "oversensitivity" of the victim.
2. Exaggerating the ease with which victims are expected to handle the behavior. (But the letters make clear that unwanted advances do *not* cease—and that the message was power, not genuine interest.)

We have learned that women are angry. The reasons for the anger are various and perhaps all too obvious:

1. We are angry because this awful thing called harassment exists in terribly harsh, ugly, demeaning, and even debilitating ways. Many believe it is criminal and should be punished as such. It is a form of violence against women as well as a form of economic coercion—and our experiences teach us that it won't just go away.
2. We are angry because for a brief moment we believed that if the law allowed women to be hired in the workplace, and if we worked hard for our educations and on the job, equality would be achieved. We believed we would be respected as equals. Now we are realizing this is still not true. We have been betrayed. The reality is that this powerful beast is used as a means of social control, to perpetuate a sense of inequality, to keep women in their place notwithstanding our increasing presence in the workplace.

What we have yet to explore about harassment is vast. But it is what will enable us to slay the beast.

Research is helpful, and I hope that the results of surveys now being conducted with regularity by unions and women's groups will be required reading for all legislators. Yet research has what I see as one shortcoming: it focuses on our reaction to harassment, not on the harasser. How do we enlighten men who are currently in the workplace about behavior that is beneath our (and their) dignity? Men tend to have a narrower definition of what constitutes harassment than do women. How do we expand their body of knowledge? How do we raise a generation of men who won't need to be reeducated as adults?

And there are other questions. What are the broader effects of sexual harassment on women? Has our potential in the workplace been greatly damaged by this beast? Has this form of economic coercion succeeded? If so, how do we begin to reverse its effects? We must begin to use what we know to move to the next step. What will we do to change this? How do we capture our rage and turn it into positive energy?

We manage such a transformation through the power of women working together, whether it be in the political arena, or in the context of a lawsuit, or in community service. This issue goes beyond partisan politics. Making the workplace a safer, more productive place for ourselves and our daughters should be on the agenda for each citizen. It is a tribute, as well, to our mothers—and it is something we can do for ourselves. Out of our pain we can forge consciousness and action, and in so doing make a contribution to the entire population.

Epilogue

Since 1991, I've learned many things about sexual harassment. Perhaps the most surprising is how little we knew then about this age-old problem, and how firmly our thinking was shaped by myths and misinformation. Since the Thomas confirmation hearings, so much has been written that at first it may appear there is *too* much information about the subject. While there is no such thing as "too much" accurate information, wading through the various titles to find the best sources may feel overwhelming. As an educator, I'm committed to the idea that knowledge is empowering. The best way for us to end sexual harassment on both personal and societal levels is to be well-informed, and willing and able to *act* out of our knowledge. There are many well-researched, well-written books in print. The following list is only a sample, ranging from the practical to the theoretical, and reflecting the depth and breadth of the problem not only as a compelling legal issue, but as a social, psychological, and cultural problem as well.

- *Celia, a Slave*, by Melton A. Mclaurin (University of Georgia Press, 1991) presents the tragic story of a young slave girl in antebellum Missouri whose sexual abuse at the hand of her owner ultimately ends in her trial, conviction, and hanging for his murder. It reminds us that the problem of sexual exploitation of women at work has a long history and has taken brutal forms. Celia's is a heartbreaking story, but I hope that its harshness does not cause the reader to see it as anomalous. Rather, I hope it encourages the reader to see the parallel between modern sexual harassment and reactions to it, and the physical, psychological, and economic exploitation suffered by Celia.

- *No Safe Haven: Male Violence Against Women at Home, at Work, and in the Community*, by Mary P. Koss, Lisa A. Goodman, Angela Browne, Louise F. Fitzgerald, Gwendolyn Puryea Keita, and Nancy Felipe Russo (American Psychological Association, 1994). This is a compilation of social-science information on assorted forms of violence against women. As part of the discussion about gendered violence, this book documents various forms of sexual harassment as well as the frequency of its occurrence among different groups of women. It also chronicles responses to harassment, forms of intervention, and methods of prevention and treatment. I include it here in an effort to contextualize sexual harassment as one manifestation of the violence in women's lives, violence that can be expressed at work, but that also occurs in the home, the school, and the community.

- *Sexual Harassment of Working Women: A Case of Sex Discrimination*, by Catharine A. MacKinnon (Yale University Press, 1979),[11] is a pioneering theoretical work that framed the legal

---

11. This book, originally published in 1979, is out of print in hardcover. The reader may have to make a trip to an academic library in order to find it.

discourse about the problem. In the 1970s, MacKinnon's work was critical in changing lawyers' and judges' perception of sexual harassment, moving it from the realm of socially acceptable behavior to the domain of equal-rights violation.[12]

The final two books are guides suitable for anyone wanting to understand and put an end to sexual harassment, whether they are personally victimized by the problem, or in charge of others who may be, or are witness to it among co-workers.

- *Sexual Harassment on the Job: What It Is and How to Stop It,* by William Petrocelli and Barbara Kate Repa (Nolo Press, 2000), addresses the origins of sexual harassment and defines the current legal rights of women and men seeking to work in environments free of the problem.
- *The 9 to 5 Guide to Combating Sexual Harassment: Candid Advice from 9 to 5, National Association of Working Women,* by Ellen Bravo[13] and Ellen Cassedy (9 to 5 Working Women Education Fund, 1999), uses facts, figures, and anecdotes to illustrate the face of sexual harassment today, and outlines measures that can be taken to stop it.

Each of these books has added to my understanding of the "nature of the beast" that is this problem, as have many other books, articles, cases, and personal letters. Yet with each new report, I realize there is much more to know. I remain committed to learning more, and hopeful that through knowledge and action we can put an end to sexual harassment.

ANITA HILL has had a long-standing interest in civil rights, and served as special counsel to the assistant secretary of the Department of Education's Office for Civil Rights in 1981. She lectures frequently on issues of race and gender, and is a Professor of Social Policy, Law, and Women's Studies at Brandeis University. Her books include *Speaking*

12. See MacKinnon, op. cit., p. 447.—Ed.

13. See "The Clerical Proletariat," by Ellen Bravo, p. 349.—Ed.

Truth to Power (Bantam Doubleday Dell, 1997) and (with Emma C. Jordan) *Race, Gender, and Power in America: The Legacy of the Hill-Thomas Hearings* (Oxford University Press, 1995).

Suggested Further Reading

See author's Epilogue, above.

From Fantasy to Reality: Unmasking the Pornography Industry

GAIL DINES

I'VE BEEN ACCUSED of censorship, of being in bed with the Right wing, and of being a member of the sex police.

This must mean I'm an anti-pornography radical feminist.

One expects such insults from pornographers with billions of dollars at stake, but sexual libertarians (with some *faux*-feminist token women) have also vehemently defended pornography.[1] Yet the issue is simple. The radical feminist critique of pornography grew out of the larger struggle to confront men's violence against women. Feminists exposed rape, battery, child sexual assault, and sexual harassment as forms of sexual terrorism, social controls that maintain male power in a patriarchal system.[2] Rather than being defined as "deviant," men's violence against women was analyzed and understood as *predictable* in a women-hating culture.

Refusing to accept male violence as natural, certain feminists began

---

1. Pornography is defined here as any product produced for the primary purpose of facilitating male arousal and masturbation. While there may be other uses for the product (for example, *Playboy* magazine as an advertising conduit teaching men how to live "a playboy lifestyle"), pornography's main selling feature—for the producer, distributor, and consumer—is sexual arousal. *Note:* Since this article focuses on mainstream, mass-distributed pornography, I have not included lesbian or gay pornography in this particular analysis.

2. See "The Nature of the Beast: Sexual Harassment," by Anita Hill, p. 296, and "Landscape of the Ordinary: Violence Against Women," by Andrea Dworkin, p. 58.—Ed.

exploring how the culture *teaches* men to become violent. Such writers as Alice Walker,[3] Robin Morgan,[4] Andrea Dworkin, and Diana Russell (see Suggested Further Reading below) argued that one such teaching tool was pornography—veritable how-to manuals objectifying women as "fuck objects," legitimizing violence against women by sexualizing it, thus rendering the violence *per se* invisible. These critics argued that analyses of pornography needed to go beyond discussions of morality (the religious Right's crusade) or free speech (the liberals' defense), and focus on pornography's real impact on real lives. For the first time, questions were raised about the *nature of harm* done to women by pornography production and consumption.

Feminists have now been organizing on this issue for more than three decades. We've picketed, given thousands of educational presentations, attempted to pass legislation,[5] lobbied international organizations, de-

3. "Coming Apart," in *Take Back the Night: Women on Pornography*, Laura Lederer, ed. (New York: William Morrow, 1980).

4. "Theory and Practice: Pornography and Rape," 1974 essay first published in *Going Too Far* by Robin Morgan (New York: Random House/Vintage 1977); later collected in *The Word of A Woman: Feminist Dispatches* by Robin Morgan (New York: W. W. Norton, 1992; second expanded edition 1994).

5. Andrea Dworkin and Catharine MacKinnon pioneered draft legislation in the form of a local ordinance permitting civil—not criminal—action toward obtaining relief from pornography's violent effects. The ordinance was attacked and ultimately defeated, despite its potential to afford legal recourse for defending one's civil rights, which is, as Laurence Tribe and a number of other distinguished constitutional scholars have noted, *not* "censorship." The Dworkin/MacKinnon ordinance defines pornography as the graphic, sexually explicit subordination of women through pictures and/or words that also includes one or more of the following: (a) women are presented dehumanized as sexual objects, things, or commodities; (b) women are presented as sexual objects who enjoy humiliation or pain; (c) women are presented as sexual objects experiencing sexual pleasure in rape, incest, or other sexual assaults; (d) women are presented as sexual objects tied up or cut up or mutilated or bruised or physically hurt; (e) women are presented in postures or positions of sexual submission or servility, (f) women's body parts—including but not limited to vaginas, breasts, or buttocks—are exhibited so that women are reduced to these parts; (g) women are presented being penetrated by objects or animals; (h) women are presented in scenarios of degradation, humiliation, injury, or torture; shown as filthy or inferior, bleeding, bruised, or hurt, in a context that makes these conditions sexual. From *Pornography and Civil Rights: A New Day for Women's Equality*, by Andrea Dworkin and Catharine A. MacKinnon (Minneapolis: Organizing Against Pornography, 1988).

veloped global activist networks, and documented the connections between the pornography and prostitution industries and the global sex traffick in women and girls.[6] This has led us to conclude that, if we take women's lives seriously, pornography is not an industry that can be "saved" by unionizing or legitimization.

One industry defense is that pornography is "just fantasy."[7] Other apologists argue that we've always had pornography (cave images are usually the examples given),[8] so ours is a losing battle. Our responses should include an exposé of *how pornography actually became the industry it is today.* If we examine the history and economics of the business, we destroy the excuse that it's a "natural" part of male sexuality and unmask it for what it *is:* the result of a carefully crafted marketing strategy—a global industry founded on capitalism, racism, and patriarchy.

Magazines were the genre that brought pornography out of the back streets and into the mainstream. Specifically, it was the success of *Playboy,* followed by *Penthouse* and *Hustler,* that laid the groundwork for the current almost $60-billion-dollar-a-year industry. Today's porn videos, DVDs, and computer websites are the outcome of the legal, economic, and cultural spaces that the pornography magazines of the 1950s, '60s, and '70s created through marketing techniques they developed. Prior to *Playboy,* most pornography was under-the-counter, poorly produced, with minimal distribution channels. This changed

---

6. See Kathleen Barry's definitive work, *The Prostitution of Sexuality* (New York: New York University Press, 1995).

7. Thirty years of studies on pornography's effects have demonstrated the links between viewing pornography and men's increased levels of violence against women. For an overview of these studies see, for example: Edna Einsieel (1992), "The Experimental Research Evidence: Effects of Pornography on the 'Average' Individual," in *Pornography, Women, Violence and Civil Liberties: A Radical New View* (pp. 248–283), Catherine Itzin, ed. (Oxford: Oxford University Press). See also Dolf Zillman and Jennings Bryant (1989), *Pornography: Research Advances and Policy Considerations* (Hillsdale, New Jersey: Lawrence Erlbaum Associates).

8. This example deliberately ignores three basic aspects of cave paintings: first, that representations of the female are *equal* to those of the male both in frequency and, more important, in power and agency; second, that such images are not violent; and third, that, according to most scholars, such paintings were created for and used in religious rites. All three aspects are certainly a far cry from *Hustler* magazine.

in 1953, with the publication of *Playboy*'s first issue: its founder/publisher, Hugh Hefner, was transformed from a failed cartoonist into a multimillionaire.

While *Playboy* (circulation 3.4 million a month) and *Hustler* (1.4 million a month) are often lumped together, they played different yet connected roles in the industry's development. In the continuum from soft-core to hard-core—the latter distinguished by sexually explicit activity and images of penises and of internal female genitalia (termed "pink" in the magazines)—*Playboy* was the premier publication of the soft-core end of the market; *Hustler* of the hard-core. *Hustler*'s aim to be the "first nationally distributed magazine to show pink"[9] could never have been realized without Hefner's having developed a mass-circulation soft-core periodical. He did this by cloaking *Playboy* in upper-middle-class respectability; a "quality magazine" carrying airbrushed, soft-focus, pinup-style pictorials of women. Encouraging men to see themselves as playboys (not porn-users), Hefner wrote in the April 1956 issue, "What is a playboy? He can be a sharp-minded young business executive, a worker in the arts, a university professor, an architect or an engineer . . . a man of taste."

Flynt was equally clear about the *Hustler* reader. In 1974, in the first issue, he wrote, "Anyone can be a playboy and have a penthouse, but it takes a man to be a Hustler." Flynt repeatedly identifies his target audience as "the average American"[10] whose income makes it impossible to identify with the high-consumption lifestyle associated with *Playboy* and *Penthouse*. Criticizing those magazines for masquerading "pornography as art by wrapping it in articles purporting to have socially redeeming value,"[11] *Hustler* contrasted itself as a no-holds-barred publication. For twenty-one years, *Playboy* had "seasoned" men to accept and want more pornography, thus providing cultural space for the mass distribution of a more hard-core magazine. By positioning itself as a "no-frills" periodical unashamedly aimed at the lower-working-class white male ("trailer

9. Larry Flynt, *Hustler* magazine, July 1984.

10. *Hustler,* July 1984.

11. Larry Flynt, *Hustler,* November 1983.

trash" in *Hustler* terms), *Hustler* promotes itself as targeting a specific audience to which few see themselves belonging. Most whites view themselves as middle class, since, in a racist society, "class differences become racial differences." [12] Herein lies *Hustler's* brilliant marketing strategy: no man is *meant* to see himself as the implied reader; this allows a man (of any class) to buy *Hustler* while keeping safe denial-distance from its images of semen, feces, child molesters, degraded women. While reading and masturbating, he can slum in a "white trash" world, a mere observer.

This strategy helped pave the way for men to buy hard-core porn by allowing them to separate themselves from what was the (supposed) audience. Now, the Armani-clad businessman, fraternity jock, or suburban father can buy or download pornography secure in his knowledge that *he's* not really a *user,* just a man visiting a different world. When finished, he can zip his pants and return to his own reality. Unfortunately for women, the worlds collide, and we must deal with men whose notions of sexuality and manhood and womanhood are constructed via such cultural images. Furthermore, the majority of these representations are now prevalent in mainstream media, filtering out from pornography into everyday images, albeit subtler ones: billboards, bus ads, MTV videos, pages in *Esquire, GQ, Cosmopolitan, Vogue,* etc., combine to create an omnipresent, increasingly pornographic, visual landscape. This further normalizes violence against women, and opens a cultural space for actual pornography to become even more explicit and violent.

Playboy's soft-focus pictures have been replaced by videos competing to abuse the female body. Hefner's marketing strategy—sexualizing commodities while commodifying sexuality—promised the consumer that by buying the right products he'd win women who were like the airbrushed centerfold. Thus the woman had to be sold as the "girl next door," not as an unattainable actress or model. Today, her image has changed: pornography features the "insatiable fuck object" who "craves" bondage, beatings, anal sex, and multiple penetration. A recent

---

12. Sut Jhally and Justin Lewis, *Enlightened Racism: The Cosby Show, Audiences, and the Myth of the American Dream* (Boulder, Colorado: Westview Press, 1992). [See also "Traffic at the Crossroads: Multiple Oppressions," by Kimberlé Crenshaw, p. 43.—Ed.]

content analysis [13] of popular pornographic videos found that violent sex was almost routine—for example, brutally forced anal penetration and gang-rape. In the androcentric definitions of the porn world, these images are not classified as violent; pornography's lie is that this is what women "want." Such videos have now overtaken the magazine sales, while *Playboy, Penthouse,* and *Hustler* have migrated to local newsstands, mainstream chain-bookstores—and the Internet. The sleaze shop is becoming a thing of the past: the Internet has brought porn home. [14]

In fact, pornography has helped *develop* the Internet and has been a leading innovator in Internet technology—pioneering streaming audio and visual, flash and chat, the click-through ad banner, the pop-up window, high-speed Internet connections, security improvements, and a new form of a la carte pay services. [15] At a recent panel of entertainment executives from TV, film, and the Internet, Larry Kasanoff, chair and CEO of the Los Angeles-based Threshold Entertainment, noted that porn has flourished where other dot-coms failed: "[Porn was first] in cable TV, it was first in home video, and [is first] on the Internet—so you know what? Porn is great for all of us. We should all study it." [16]

This isn't the only time pornography has been a leading innovator in developing new technologies. It's been credited with helping to drive the evolution of the camera, the home-video business, cable TV, and DVDs. [17] As the operator of a bondage website boasts, "Technology is driven by adult entertainment . . . because sex then sells the technol-

13. Robert Jensen and Gail Dines, "The Content of Mass-Marketed Pornography," in *Pornography: The Production and Consumption of Inequality,* Gail Dines, Robert Jensen, and Ann Russo, eds. (New York: Routledge, 1998).

14. In an interview with *The New York Times* in 2002, Bob Guccione, publisher of *Penthouse,* acknowledged that the magazine's run was at an end, declaring that there is "no future for adult business in mass market magazines" because "the future has definitely migrated to electronic media." He announced that he expects to be a part of that future. "Cybersmut and Debt Undermine Penthouse," by David Carr, *The New York Times,* 8 April 2002.—Ed.

15. *The New York Times,* 23 October 2000, p. 1; *American Heritage,* September 2000, v51, p. 19; *National Journal,* 2 January 1999.

16. *Brandweek,* October 2000, v41, p 1Q48.

17. *Video Age International,* November 2000, v20, p. 3.

ogy."[18] Businesses that fail to follow this strategy pay a price; entertainment analysts maintain that Sony, by refusing to license its Betamax technology to pornographers, allowed VHS to monopolize the market by the early 1980s.[19]

Studies of on-line pornography demonstrate that the money to be made is staggering. Datamonitor, a New York- and London-based research company, found that in 1998 nearly $1 billion was spent by users accessing at an estimated 50,000 porn-specific sites worldwide—an amount expected to *triple* by 2003.[20] According to a March 2000 study conducted for *US News & World Report*, off-line porn accounts for 69 percent of the current $1.4 billion domestic cable TV pay-per-view market, compared to 4 percent for video games and 2 percent for sports.[21] According to the June 14, 1999 issue of *Forbes* business magazine, the contemporary legal porn business is a $56 billion global industry. As Andrew Edmond, president and CEO of Flying Crocodile, a $20 million pornography Internet business, has noted, "We operate just like any Fortune 500 company."[22]

Indeed, many Fortune 500 companies have links to the pornography industry. General Motors, the world's largest company, now sells more pornography films than Larry Flynt. According to an October 23, 2000 front-page story in *The New York Times*, "the 8.7 million Americans who subscribe to DirecTV, a General Motors subsidiary, buy nearly $200 million a year in pay-per-view sex films via satellite." The article also reported that AT&T, the nation's biggest communication company, offers subscribers to its broadband cable service a hard-core porn channel, Hot Network, and owns a company that sells porn videos to nearly one million hotel rooms. The *Times* story notes that the second largest satellite provider, EchoStar Communications Corporation, makes more

---

18. *PC/Computing*, 24 January 2000, p. 64.

19. See "Changing a Masculinist Culture: Women in Science, Engineering, and Technology," by Donna M. Hughes, p. 393.—Ed.

20. *PC/Computing*, op. cit.

21. Ibid.

22. Ibid.

money selling hard-core films through its satellite subsidiary than all of the Playboy holdings *combined.* The chief financial backer is Rupert Murdoch, CEO of News Corp. Murdoch's holdings include *The New York Post,* the Fox Television Network,[23] Twentieth Century-Fox, and the Los Angeles Dodgers. Frontier Media, one of the most popular Internet properties, features links to porn sites and does business with In Demand, the nation's largest pay-per-view distributor—which is owned in part by AT&T, Time Warner, Advance-Newhouse, Cox Communications, and Comcast. The financial connections between mainstream companies and pornography highlight the degree to which pornography is no longer a marginalized industry but a major player in the development of sophisticated, multibillion-dollar, media technologies.[24]

Today, a porn-buyer can regard himself as a computer-savvy Internet-user who knows his way around cutting-edge media. While pornography has glorified technology, technology now glorifies pornography. Meanwhile, newer technologies will use porn to make themselves even more user-friendly: virtual reality is around the corner, and pornographers are already investing in its development.

But there's a flip side. A previously untapped, powerful form of activism against the porn industry would be to *target the mainstream corporations who make money off pornography.* General Motors, AT&T, Time Warner, and News Corp. are vulnerable to *consumer pressure.* Exposing these hidden connections, educating the public, and mounting boycotts, letter-writing and e-mail campaigns, and protests are the last things corporations want—thus the first things we should do.[25] We can

---

23. In an interesting display of having-it-both-ways hypocrisy, the intense Right-wing slant of both *The New York Post* and the Fox TV Network regularly denounces pornography—from a "family values" anti-sex posture, which is very different from a feminist anti-sex*ist* analysis.—Ed.

24. For example, the $4 billion that Americans spend on video porn alone is more than the annual revenue accrued by either the NFL, the NBA, or major league baseball, and more money is spent on pornography in the U.S. each year than on movie tickets plus all the performing arts combined. For further information on the mainstreaming of porn via the new technologies, see "Naked Capitalists," by Frank Rich, *The New York Times Magazine,* 20 May 2002.—Ed.

25. See "Cyberfeminism: Networking the Net," by Amy Richards and Marianne Schnall, p. 517.—Ed.

also refuse to stay in hotels offering cable pornography, refuse to rent videos or buy books from stores carrying pornography, change our phone companies and Internet servers, and (especially) pressure stockholders of corporations linked to pornography. We can *embarrass* corporations, and hit them where they hurt.

We must also fight against the harm done to women abused *in* pornography. No woman was put on this earth to be hurt or humiliated in order to facilitate male masturbation. Feminism is about sisterhood—which means refusing to believe that some women are meant to serve as men's "whores" in order to save other women from that fate. Our *collective* well-being is our agenda, and liberation is our goal. That might seem like a fantasy on my part. But as we've learned, fantasy does *not* just reside in the mind. It has social implications in the real world.

GAIL DINES is an associate professor of sociology and women's studies at Wheelock College in Boston. She is co-editor (with Jean M. Humez) of *Gender, Race and Class in Media* (Sage Publications, 2002) and coauthor (with Bob Jensen and Ann Russo) of *Pornography: The Production and Consumption of Inequality* (Routledge, 1998). Dines is an antipornography activist who lectures across the country on pornography, the media, and images of violence against women. She is a featured presenter in the documentary *Beyond Killing Us Softly: The Strength to Resist* (Cambridge Documentary Films, 2000).

Suggested Further Reading

Dines, Gail, Robert Jensen, and Ann Russo. *Pornography: The Production and Consumption of Inequality.* New York: Routledge, 1998.

Dworkin, Andrea. *Pornography: Men Possessing Women.* Reissued with a new introduction, New York: Dutton, 1981.

Itzin, Catherine, ed. *Pornography: Women, Violence and Civil Liberties.* Oxford: Oxford University Press, 1992.

MacKinnon, Catharine A. *Only Words.* Cambridge: Harvard University Press, 1993.

Russell, Diana, ed. *Making Violence Sexy: Feminist Views on Pornography.* New York: Teacher's College Press, 1993.

Prostitution = Slavery

VEDNITA CARTER

IN 2001, I was invited to be a participant in a symposium held at the New York City College of Law. The topic of the debate was legalization of prostitution. Fortunately, I was one of the last presenters. The more I listened, the more stunned I became—at the general tone of the discourse, and at the staggering lack of concern for the women being discussed by these pro-prostitution activists.[1] Listening, I felt as if—though my body remained in the twenty-first century—I had somehow been transported to the 1800s, where I was overhearing a conversation on a slave plantation. Here we were, seriously considering the legality of buying and selling human beings. Incredible. Debate regarding the purchase, sale, and trading of women and girls should not be part of *any* discussion in our society, and we as a nation should condemn any country that would allow such a conversation or such a practice.

It is very important to define what prostitution *is*.

Prostitution is about power and control, expressed through sexual violence. Prostitution is about men using women to satisfy their sexual desires, no matter how perverted, degrading, or humiliating. Contrary to the assumptions of some speakers at that panel, prostitution is *not* "sex work." It is *not* "groovy" or "liberating," not "unforced" or "victimless." *It is never, ever, really "a woman's choice."* Prostitution is based on acute economic inequality: being driven to "choose" prostitution because of poverty *is* force, *is* coercion. The damage that this sex act can—

---

1. By "pro-prostitution activists" I do not mean pimps—though they would certainly fit that definition. I mean the supposedly well-meaning liberals and libertarians who fiercely defend prostitution. This even includes some women who call themselves feminists, yet who take a pro-prostitution stand—in opposition to the vast majority of genuine feminists in the Women's Movement.

and will—do to the body, mind, and soul of the prostituted woman is permanent. In order for a woman to complete the act of sex in prostitution, she must learn to separate her consciousness from the act, learn to separate her body from her own sexual identity. So she depersonalizes; she mentally goes away—like most rape victims do. This act of disengagement is conscious and intentional—a survival mechanism. Through depersonalization, she is able to set limits. She deliberately puts parts of herself aside so that she doesn't lose her entire self while performing sex acts on demand. In order to cope with the psychological fallout of prostitution, many women dissociate through drug and alcohol abuse. Dissociation is crucial. It's what keeps that woman alive. It erases the face of each man who has used and abused her.

Let's examine the demographics of prostitution:

- The average age of entry into prostitution in the United States is 14.
- 75 percent of women involved in prostitution are survivors of child molestation, child rape, and/or other child sexual and physical abuse.
- 60 to 75 percent of these women were sexually abused before the age of 18.
- 95 percent suffer from drug and/or alcohol addiction.
- 80 percent are victims of rape 8 to 10 times every year.
- 66 percent are victims of physical and/or sexual abuse by pimp "boyfriends."
- 55 percent are victims of kidnapping.
- 83 percent are victims of assault with a weapon.[2]

---

2. Statistics assembled from studies by: M. H. Silbert and A. M. Pines, "Victimization of Street Prostitutes," *Victimology: An International Journal*, #7, 1982; D. Kelly Weisberg, *Children of the Night: A Study of Adolescent Prostitution* (Toronto: Lexington Books, 1985); the Council on Prostitution Alternatives *Annual Reports* (Portland, Oregon, 1991, 1994); Melissa Farley and Howard Barkin, "Prostitution, Violence, and Post-Traumatic Stress Disorder," *Women and Health*, 1998; Melissa Farley, Isin Baral, Merib Kiremire, Ufuk Sezgin, "Prostitution in Five Countries: Violence and Post-Traumatic Stress Disorder," *Feminism and Psychology* #8, 1998. See especially "Prostitution: Factsheet on Human Rights Violations," by Melissa Farley, Ph.D., Prostitution Research and Education, *www.prostitutionresearch.com*.

This "victimless crime" leaves a devastating impact on its victims. Prostituted women express feelings of humiliation, degradation, dirtiness, even defilement—sometimes for years. They experience difficulty establishing intimate relationships with men; they feel extreme mistrust, caution, disdain, or outright hatred for men; some want to have no contact whatsoever with men. Prostituted women also suffer physical trauma—from beatings and rape, and from complications due to chronic bladder infections, chronic pelvic inflammatory disease, vaginal tearing, infertility, sexually transmitted diseases (STDs) including HIV infection, and death from AIDS. On August 18, 1998, *The New York Times* reported a new study of Vietnam veterans and post-traumatic-stress disorder (PTSD). It found that PTSD was diagnosed in 20 to 30 percent of the Vietnam vets, approximately half of whom suffer long-time psychiatric problems. The article also reported that PTSD is found in less than 5 percent of the general population—but is found in *two-thirds* of prostituted women.[3]

All of these factors have a disproportionately harsher impact on African American women and other women of color; African American women are 7 percent of the U.S. population, yet comprise more than 50 percent of the women used in prostitution. Other women of color—especially Native Americans and Latinas—are also overrepresented as prostituted women.[4] Racism not only makes black women and girls particularly vulnerable to sexual exploitation; it also *keeps* them trapped in the sex industry—a process reinforced by limiting the educational and career opportunities for African Americans, and doubly so for black women. In general, African American women must deal with the dual oppression that comes from being black in a white-supremacist culture *and* female in a male-supremacist culture.[5] The double jeopardy is intensified and sustained by a welfare system that divides and destroys

---

3. Farley, et al., op. cit.

4. See "Native Americans: Restoring the Power of Thought Woman," by Clara Sue Kidwell, p. 165; and "U.S. Latinas: Active at the Intersections of Gender, Nationality, Race, and Class," by Edna Acosta-Belén and Christine E. Bose, p. 198.—Ed.

5. See "African American Women: The Legacy of Black Feminism," by Beverly Guy-Sheftall, p. 176.—Ed.

African American families: if a mother is formally employed, or if her children's father contributes to their support, her check and food stamps are cut by that amount; consequently, these women are left trying to fend for themselves and raise their kids on grossly inadequate grants.[6] Prostitution, a hidden-economy industry, recruits such desperate women, who have nowhere else to turn.

Racist stereotypes in mainstream media as well as in pornography[7] portray black women as wild animals ready for any kind of sex, any time, with anyone. Furthermore, strip joints and massage parlors are typically zoned in African American neighborhoods, which sends the message to European American men that it's OK to solicit African American women and girls for sex, implying that "they're all prostitutes, anyway." On almost any night, you can see white men cruising through black neighborhoods, rolling down car windows, calling to women and girls as if our communities were their private plantations. The contempt these men feel for women is palpable.

And that contempt expresses itself. Concretely. Dramatically.

Prostituted women are the Number One target of serial killers. In 1992, in Detroit, Michigan, eleven poor African American women were murdered and mutilated, their bodies thrown away like so much trash. That year, when one black man—Rodney King—was beaten by four white police officers, every African American activist in the country, in-cluding the Reverend Jesse Jackson, cried out against racism and the culture of poverty that precipitated the Los Angeles "riots." But after the Detroit murders of eleven women, the only sound we heard, beside a deafening silence, was a comment by a local Baptist minister that these women were "already among the walking dead." In 1996, in Minneapo-lis, Minnesota, eight African American women were found dead—pieces of their bodies dredged from the river, limbs discovered under bridges. The only news story about their murders was a short article in the *Minneapolis Star Tribune* titled, *"Another prostitute found dead; public at large not in danger."* During my thirteen years as an anti-prostitution

---

6. See "Poverty Wears a Female Face," by Theresa Funiciello, p. 222; and "Traffic at the Crossroads: Multiple Oppressions," by Kimberlé Crenshaw, p. 43.—Ed.

7. See "From Fantasy to Reality: Unmasking the Pornography Industry," by Gail Dines, p. 306; see also Crenshaw, op. cit.—Ed.

activist, I've heard of many such incidents. Every time I hear about a new murder, I ask myself, *Why isn't the community up in arms? Isn't it clear that all of these women were poor, all of them black, all of them abused in prostitution? Where are the cries of outrage?*

Some have claimed that prostitution is tolerated in the black community; they are *wrong;* we do *not* tolerate prostitution. It has been imposed on us since the days of slavery, when the master would come out to the field and choose whichever women he wanted for sex; light-skinned slaves, known as "fancy girls," were sold in the marketplace at high prices, and later rented out, or sold to brothels. In the eighteenth and nineteenth centuries, the system was called slavery. In the twentieth and twenty-first centuries, it's called prostitution.

Much of the discussion during the law symposium at which I spoke echoed arguments from 300 years ago: buying, selling, and trading— *human beings.* There had been a lot of controversy prior to the slaves being freed in the nineteenth century. Many heated discussions had taken place, with some white individuals managing to convince themselves that Africans were "better off" being enslaved, that slaves had no right or capacity to enjoy freedom, that slaves were closer to animals than to human beings. There were even some slaves who claimed to feel that slavery was a good thing; usually they worked in the master's house, so their situation was (seemingly) better than that of people toiling in the fields. Some house slaves felt satisfied at eating scraps the master left; they could envision no condition other than slavery. Meanwhile, the field slaves had to endure a deeper level of mistreatment: constant abuse. *They* wanted to *leave* the bondage and torment of slavery. They wanted freedom.

As I sat listening to various apologists for prostitution—mostly people who had never worked in the industry, been abused by it, suffered in it, yet dared "speak for" prostituted women—I found myself wondering why we were repeating history. Yes, there *are* some pro-prostitution women who have worked or are still working in the industry, who claim that being prostituted is a fine thing, or that it's "just a job like any job," or even that it's "empowering" to women. Such a woman—an elite call girl, perhaps, or a madam—may insist that her experiences are different from women who work the streets (who live, in her estimate, at the bottom of the bottom). Yet this is an *imaginary hierarchy,* just as it was in slavery—house slaves vs. field slaves. The harsh truth is that they are *all* slaves, in bondage to the same master. Before such women can begin to comprehend their level of bondage, they too must first be set free. Only then will they be able to grasp and analyze the truth about prostitution.

There is a sexual war against women and children in this world.[8] It has been going on for a long time. This war has managed to disguise itself as "the oldest profession" when, in reality, it is the oldest *oppression*, one against women and children. Women are dying, and will continue to die on this battlefield of sexual slavery, until drastic measures are taken to end this inhumane treatment of female people.

As women trying to survive in this new century, we face a great challenge—but at the same time we encounter a promising opportunity for *all* women: *to change the course of human history.*

We women must build a united front, regardless of race, ethnicity, class, religion, age, sexual preference, ability, and any other barriers—whether or not we have been used in prostitution. It is time to take a stand and ask some questions. How long are we going to allow a certain portion of our women and children to be made available for men's sexual satisfaction? How long are we going to allow slavery in the twenty-first century? It is time to take a stand and *say* it: *prostitution is not only a crime against all women and children, it is a crime against humanity.*

VEDNITA CARTER, founder and executive director of the St. Paul, Minnesota-based Breaking Free, Inc. organization, previously developed and directed the Women's Services Program at WHISPER (Women Hurt in Systems of Prostitution Engaged in Revolt), and had counseled incarcerated women for five years. Her articles on the connections between prostitution and racism have appeared in such publications as *The Michigan Journal of Gender and Law,* the *Hastings Women's Law Journal,* and numerous feminist periodicals, and she has appeared on local and national media, addressing prostitution as a form of violence against women and girls. She serves on the Ramsey County Sexual Assault Protocol Development Advisory Board, and is a consultant to

---

8. See "Landscape of the Ordinary: Violence Against Women," by Andrea Dworkin, p. 58; and "The Nature of the Beast: Sexual Harassment," by Anita Hill, p. 296.—Ed.

the U.S. Department of Justice and the Coalition Against Trafficking in Women. She has spoken out against prostitution and sex trafficking in national forums and also internationally—in Bangladesh, in South Africa, and at the United Nations.

Suggested Further Reading

Barry, Kathleen. *The Prostitution of Sexuality*. New York: New York University Press, 1995.

Dworkin, Andrea. *Intercourse*. New York: Free Press, 1987.

Penn State Report, International Meeting of Experts on Sexual Exploitation, Violence, and Prostitution (State College, Pennsylvania, April 1991). Report published by UNESCO and the Coalition Against Trafficking in Women *(www.catw.org)*.

Russell, Diana E. H. *Sexual Exploitation: Rape, Child Sexual Abuse, and Workplace Harassment*. Beverly Hills, California: Sage, 1984.

Wyatt, Gail Elizabeth. *Stolen Women: Reclaiming Our Sexuality, Taking Back Our Lives*. New York: John Wiley & Sons, Inc., 1998.

PART V.

Workplaces

Transforming Traditions
and Breaking Barriers:
Six Personal Testimonies

The following six voices—three women working in jobs considered traditional women's employment, and three women working in jobs considered nontraditional for females—are based on interviews conducted on special assignment for Sisterhood Is Forever *by Mary Thom.*

Transforming Traditions

NURSES

Mary Foley, President, American Nurses Association

Nursing was the perfect combination of my interests: science and people. In rural New Hampshire in the late 1960s, studying medicine would have been a financial stretch for a single-mom family like ours. But I was a smart kid, and I got the opportunity to enter nursing training with all expenses paid. It was the best decision of my life. In fact, that's something we're still working on: increasing access to a great profession.

Early on, while working night shifts at a Boston hospital, I became president of the National Student Nursing Association, which exposed me to health policy issues. In 1980, I moved to California, where I've been ever since. In nursing, you're mobile and you don't have to be bored. For instance, when I was a hospital staff nurse in the evenings, during the day I studied health and safety policy issues, to get my master's degree. For a while, I combined clinical teaching with my practice. There are stereotypes about nurses wearing white caps and taking doctor's orders—but you see very few caps these days; we really work as a team with physicians to implement good care. Nursing is also a versatile field. You can be a clinical scientist. If you want to be a flight nurse, you can hop into a helicopter. If you want to work independently, you can be a nurse practitioner in a rural setting.

Our profession falls victim to the eternal economics of health care. We upgrade salaries to recruit and retain staff during a shortage, as in the 1970s and again in the late '80s. But in what we call the "Nasty Nineties," hospitals and managed-care systems cut back on nurses, supposedly to save money—losing the very people who *could* save money by preventing complications. Now we're back in another shortage. *Sustained* value for the skilled contributions nurses make, that's the goal— and it makes sense, whether we're facing a natural disaster, a possible crisis of bioterrorism, or just on a regular basis. National polls show that nurses have great credibility; people say we're the backbone of the health system. But most don't notice their backbone until it hurts. You can't under-invest in the professionals who give really complex care; if you do, the safety net for patients deteriorates. It takes prepared people to catch medication errors, surgical mistakes. You might have all the great medicines in the world, but if you don't have people who can deliver them safely, they're worthless.[1]

These days, demographics tell us we should gear up both for more senior and more pediatric care. That's not necessarily high tech; that's high *touch*. But student bodies for nursing are down by 30 percent.

---

1. In 2002, a largely U.S.-government-funded study was published in the *New England Journal of Medicine;* the study, whose lead author was Dr. Jack Needleman of the Harvard School of Public Health, found a direct correlation between the number of registered nurses and the quality of patient safety—estimating that hundreds, perhaps thousands of deaths each year are due to decreased nursing staffing. The new study validated research data put forth by the American Nurses Association in the mid-1990s ("Shortage of Nurses Hurts Patient Care, Study Finds: 'Eyes and Ears of the Hospital' for Problems," by Denise Grady, *The New York Times*, 30 May 2002). Furthermore, a nationwide study, issued in August 2002 by the Joint Commission on Accreditation of Healthcare Organizations, found additional evidence linking the national shortage of nurses to ill health and to patient death ("Patient Deaths Tied to Lack of Nurses: Hospital Study Finds Nationwide Problem," by Sheryl Gay Stolberg, *The New York Times*, 8 August 2002). In July 2002, Congress passed the Nurse Reinvestment Act, authorizing financial aid programs for nursing students to the tune of $30 million during 2003–2007, a commitment that the above-cited commission labeled as not going anywhere near far enough. For further information, visit the website of the American Nurses Association: *www.ANA.org.*—Ed.

Women today can choose any profession, so many have dismissed nursing, as have a lot of men. We want to put nursing back onto the menu of choice. It should be a profession that offers you an incredible sense of satisfaction[2] and also rewards you financially. Given the chance to provide good care—with enough staff and reasonable hours—nursing is not the drudgery it's depicted to be.

We talk about recruiting nurses from around the world, but the group I'm excited about is comprised of minority students from right here in the USA. Great recruitment projects are going on—in Texas border towns, for example—and we need to make sure kids have enough math and science through grade school and junior high. And what about those laid-off airline employees turning to nursing?[3] Nurses for a Healthier Tomorrow—a new coalition of organizations—is focusing on recruiting, with national ad campaigns. It's all quite exciting. Nursing could remain stereotyped and traditional—or it could really take off. Today, as a career, nursing is right on the edge.

TEACHERS

Patricia Silverthorn, High School Social Studies Teacher

I started teaching when I was thirty-four years old. I'd been a union organizer—garment workers, transit workers—and I'd worked as a train cleaner, then in a mattress factory. That was hideous. So I got myself to college (at age thirty), then started teaching. Even as a first-year teacher, I earned more money than I'd ever made before. Nobody in my family had gone to college. For me, teaching was an educated job that paid well. I didn't think of it as a traditional job for women.

I teach social studies (what else would a good union organizer teach?) to students who haven't done well in large high schools. Ours is an alternate school, with about 350 students. A lot of them have had bad attitudes, but I can relate to that; they make it more challenging. Our campus is open; students come and go; many have jobs; some are older

2. See "Unfinished Agenda: Reproductive Rights," by Faye Wattleton, p. 17.—Ed.

3. See Patricia Friend on Flight Attendants, below.—Ed.

students. We have a lot of special-ed students—mostly with learning disabilities—and a lot of students who speak English as a second language. There's a fair amount of parenting teens, and I really respect the ones who stick it out and graduate.

Most of my colleagues are women who seem to have worked their way up to teaching, as I did. Numbers are important: our principal is female, and luckily, we have a lot of female administrators here in Fairfax County, Virginia—though I may be judging that more on assistant principals than principals.[4] But the administrators are overwhelmingly white. Men here are fairly enlightened about women, though there's the occasional old-guard male. But in education it seems the values of women come through more—like patience and nurturing, like being a lifelong learner. In other jobs I've held, the values were more like those of the business world, the patriarchal system. Education is a not-for-profit world, for the most part.

One aspect that drew me to teaching is that it's almost like owning your own business: you're by yourself in your classroom, which gives you a certain freedom. Of course, we're more and more bound to teach what's in the standards. But I don't have a huge problem with that. I can take a subject—say, the paradox of socialism versus capitalism—and make it fit within the curriculum. But I *don't* like standardized testing. It's not an accurate reflection of a kid's knowledge, and there's no leeway for intelligence or creativity. Then again, I'm lucky: I have autonomy and our faculty is cohesive. Though now we are getting backlash, because regular schools are worried about their fail-rate numbers, so they dump unsuccessful kids into alternative schools.

There's little input from parents. On the other hand, that means I don't have the parent pressure that my partner—who teaches at a regu-

---

4. In "Gender Equity: A Critical Democratic Component of America's High Schools," an article by Patricia A. Schmuck and Richard A. Schmuck in the January 1994 issue of *The Bulletin of the National Association of Secondary School Principals*, recent studies were cited as having reported that approximately 90 percent of U.S. high school principals were men. *The Digest of Education Studies 2000* noted that by the mid 1990s—their latest reported period—women constituted 73 percent of high school teachers but only 35 percent of high school principals. See also *How Schools Shortchange Girls*, a study on high schools as places designed by men for boys, jointly sponsored by the National Education Association and the American Association of University Women, 1992. Also see the "Hard Hats" section, below, for data on gender tracking in vocational courses and schools.—Ed.

lar school—has to endure from conservative book-banning groups. In the regular schools, if you ask your students to read *The Washington Post*, some parents are going to jump on you. It's ridiculous.

I've remained good friends with my former students. One is a kid who came here an emotional wreck after failing three years of high school. He would literally bang his head against the wall. It was so neat to watch him learn about himself and grow into a self-confident young man. Many who were expelled from their regular schools for fighting succeed here, rising to the challenge of being treated with respect, as an adult. And teachers here feel they get a lot of respect *from* the students.

It's great to witness change—like watching young men who don't think it's at all odd for a young woman in class to say she's going to be a doctor. It's one of the things I like about education. You get to see generations actually making progress, *living* the changes we've fought to bring about.

FLIGHT ATTENDANTS

Patricia A. Friend, International President, Association of Flight Attendants

If you interviewed ten flight attendants today, you'd probably find eight of them have an additional career. The work encourages it, because the hours are compressed and eventually you find yourself looking for something to fill the time-off stretches. People start businesses or go back to school or spend time raising kids. I got involved with the union, filing grievances; I must have been a frustrated lawyer. I moved from there into a leadership position.

That was back in the early 1970s. We were not allowed to fly while pregnant. The first male flight attendant had been hired only in 1972. We still had to suffer through demeaning appearance checks, and had to weigh in once a month to meet what someone decided was the arbitrary standard. There were a lot of gender issues. We were trying to implement a court decision that United Airlines had to offer jobs back to the women who had been forced to resign when they got married. It had been a long legal struggle, and those women were very pleased to return.

When I started flying, we viewed it as something to do while you finished growing up. Still, there's something about the work and camaraderie that gets in your blood; you're part of a team, a crew. But the whole wage and benefit package was structured for someone who wasn't going to stay, so we began to focus on changes needed to make it into a career.

When aviation began as a transportation industry, you had to have a nursing degree to a be a flight attendant.[5] They wanted to send a message that it was safe to fly: if these young women weren't afraid to get on an airplane, why should you be? That got dropped during World War II (many of the RNs were at war) but flight attendants were then turned into a marketing strategy to appeal to male travelers: "all these young, single, available women" was implied. That's an image we continue to fight to this day.[6] Only recently, I had a debate with a United manager who was adamant that we must wait until the flight took off before changing from high heels into flats. I tried to explain that takeoff and landing were the most likely times you might have to evacuate the aircraft and we should wear flat, practical shoes, but he wasn't listening. To him it was all about image. We try to explain to management that the traveler who is a *customer* when buying a ticket becomes a *passenger* on boarding the plane. Customers have an expectation of certain rights, but passengers should have an expectation of certain responsibilities as well. We can all have a good time, but first we must make sure we're as safe as possible.

Flight attendants walk a tightrope between acting as enforcers for the FAA (Federal Aviation Administration) and as the persons who make the flight experience enjoyable. It's difficult. There's always been a need for a certain level of physical fitness to do our job—removing window exits that can weigh sixty pounds, for example, or doing firefighting exercises. These days we're pushing for basic self-defense training. For years we've had to deal with unruly passengers, but now we must prepare to respond mentally and physically to possible situations like those of September 11, 2001. I sat on the Secretary of Transportation's Rapid Response Team for Aircraft Security, and I'm involved with groups

---

5. See Mary Foley on Nurses, above.—Ed.

6. For further information, visit the website of the Association of Flight Attendants, AFL/CIO: *www.AFANET.org.*—Ed.

continuing to work on implementing the recommendations our team made.

In a way, the job of being a flight attendant is shifting from a very traditional [woman's] job to a nontraditional one. Global safety issues are involved. For instance, we're concerned that in the wake of 9/11 and some subsequent airlines folding, some companies will try to take advantage of the situation to change laws that currently prevent cross-national-borders mergers. That's a possible safety threat to our passengers. In a global airline, whose safety regulations apply? Who staffs? What are the training standards, the language standards? Flight attendants want to be in on those discussions. We stood in front of airline deregulation in the U.S. with our arms folded and told them repeatedly that it was a bad idea—yet we got run over. This time, especially if the industry is going to be restructured, we intend to have a seat at the table.

Breaking Barriers

FIREFIGHTERS

Brenda Berkman, Lieutenant, New York City Fire Department
Ladder Company 12

The overwhelming impetus for me to become a firefighter was exactly what the whole world witnessed the day of the 9/11 attacks: the opportunity to help somebody in the direst hour of need. After practicing law for five years, I became the named plaintiff in a 1978 lawsuit challenging the physical abilities exam for firefighters as being discriminatory and not job-related. When we finally won (1982), there was a lot of money riding on the notion that I'd just wanted to make some sort of "women's lib" statement, that I was a lawyer and wouldn't even take the job. I wish I'd been able to lay some money on those bets.[7]

About forty of us went into the Fire Academy at the same time. There

---

7. Women have been volunteer firefighters in the U.S. since the early nineteenth century. The first known woman firefighter was Molly Williams, an African American who, held in slavery, worked in New York City on Oceanus Engine Company #11, in 1818. The first woman *career* firefighter in the U.S. was Judith Livers Brewer, who was hired in 1974 in Arlington County, Virginia, and who retired in 1999 at battalion chief rank. Information from Women in the Fire Service, Inc. (see below).—Ed.

was a great deal of questioning about women's physical abilities, about "watering down" physical standards—even though we'd taken a test based on standards being met by men already *on* the job who set the performance level. Then they proceeded to *re*-test us, using it as a field day for harassment. About a dozen of us were allowed to graduate on time; the rest were held over for "re-training," since they kept changing the requirements. We were in danger of being picked off one by one. So we formed an organization, the United Women Firefighters. The only support we got was from the Vulcan Society, the organization of African American firefighters. The Firefighters' Union had stood with the city, defending against our lawsuit; in fact, after we'd won, the city surrendered at district court—but the union appealed to the second circuit.

Meanwhile, as they were trying to kick women out of the Academy one by one, some of us graduates went into the field as probationary firefighters. But nothing was done to prepare firefighters in the field for the fact that women were on the way. The women were going out, one per firehouse, with no accommodations in terms of bathrooms or changing areas. No one bothered to make the guys aware that they shouldn't be walking around naked in front of us. During this period, some women never changed or went to the bathroom in the firehouse—and I'm convinced that their reaction to this lack of privacy actually damaged their health, because they weren't performing normal bodily functions and also were unable to shower, so dangerous materials and chemicals stayed on their skin.

I was the spokeswoman, since I'd been the named plaintiff. At the end of our probationary period, they tried to fire me and another high-profile woman (Vida Gongolez, who had been the subject of a *New York* magazine profile), claiming grounds of physical incapacity. But in every test, we'd been among the three or four fittest women; furthermore, we were able to prove they were really trying to terminate the most visible spokeswomen. A judge ruled that they had to take us back, and that the city must provide anti-harassment training. Unfortunately, the judge wasn't in the firehouses to *enforce* the guidelines he established. So there were some years of total misery, from minor incidents (guys put feces in women's boots and nasty things in our beds) to major ones (women's firefighting equipment was tampered with; women weren't backed up in firefighting situations). Because I was a spokesperson, I got extra treatment: the men refused to eat with me or talk to me—incredibly danger-ous in an occupation where your lives depend on one another. I also re-ceived mailed and phoned death threats—but the police weren't sympathetic since the NYPD had recently gone through their own re-sistance to women police officers.

Eventually, I decided to get a change of scenery and started teaching at the Fire Academy, where I encountered a group of older guys who for the most part were pretty accepting. That's when I realized for the first time that I could have a semi-normal experience in the department. Later, I went to a different firehouse in Brooklyn, working with people who had a much more professional attitude toward the job. I was doing pretty well—until I was sexually assaulted by a fire-department doctor during a routine medical exam. I had to take it to court. Three other women he'd molested also came forward, and we organized demonstra-tions and held press conferences, but the department waited until the last minute to bring charges against him; ultimately, he was fired.

A few years later, I got promoted to lieutenant, and returned to Man-hattan. It's certainly been a challenge. The Fire Department is an or-ganization that regards itself as paramilitary—which I actually don't mind, because rank can work in minorities' favor, since once you merit rank you supposedly gain authority—but it's also a culture of boss fight-ers, drawn from a very traditional group of men. There's a sort of back-to-the-1950s *Father Knows Best* atmosphere. That's ironic, since a lot of these guys are Mr. Mom because of their schedules—but that's *not* the image they want portrayed. Maybe instead of studying law, I should have studied cultural anthropology—because women in the New York fire service are required to be bicultural: we're supposed to learn and conform to the cultural life of Irish/Italian white males. As of 2002, we have only three percent African Americans in the New York City Fire Department, and three percent Hispanics/Latinos. And 25 women—among 1,100 firefighters.[8]

---

8. Between 1982 and 2002, the New York City Fire Department hired only seven women; the most recent class after 9/11/01 produced 308 male hires and not a sin-gle woman hire. Nationwide, as of 2002, approximately 5,600 women are full-time career firefighters and officers; approximately 35,000 women are in volunteer fire service. For further national statistics, history, and related issues, visit the website of the national organization of women firefighters, Women in the Fire Service, Inc.: *www.WFSI.org.*—Ed.

If you talk to the women on the job, they become firefighters for exactly the same reasons as men. There's the service aspect, plus the hours are good, and there's a halfway decent salary with pension and health benefits. The job is interesting, too: we never know what's going to happen when we go into work for the tour. Furthermore, women have changed the job for the better: parental leave, increased professionalism, more emphasis on training, more attention to human relations. Women now are blamed or credited with getting rid of the height requirements for New York firefighters, but in fact it was Hispanic men who pushed for that change. Firefighters were never all six feet one inch tall and 250 pounds; in reality, men of all sizes have been firefighters.

I've had to look outside my department for my own professional survival. Through Women in the Fire Service, Inc., I can watch women in some departments achieving great success in their careers. But we're deeply concerned that little girls are seeing only the faces of men as heroes of September 11. That's totally out of touch with reality, because women were there. That we weren't there in large numbers is the result of a history of discrimination in the Fire Department and many other emergency services. Still, *women were there*. And we're going to *go on* being there.

Hard Hats

Mary Baird, Telephone Repair Worker, Co-founder of Hard Hatted Women

I had a career in education in the mid-1970s, when the phone company started running television ads picturing a woman in a hard hat up a telephone pole. AT&T had signed an affirmative-action consent decree that required it to begin hiring in those categories.[9] Well, I'd been a tree climber as a kid, and I was a feminist, and I thought it would be great to work outdoors in a union job. So a friend and I applied; she went first. They said she had too much education and gave her a management application—so I deliberately left out a few things on my form.

I took an entry-level job as an order typist in 1975, in Louisville, Ken-

---

9. Jobs for women in U.S. tradeswork began to open up during the 1970s, following a successful National Women's Law Center suit against the Department of Labor that demanded goals and timetables for hiring women in construction.—Ed.

tucky, at South Central Bell. Later I moved to Cleveland, Ohio, and got promoted into customer service. But I had my eye on the prize: what they called a craft job, outside. I was working for the Bell system in Cleveland when I finally got my job as an outside service technician, the only woman on my crew. I installed and repaired phone lines for seventeen years until I retired, and I really loved it. There's nothing about the job that someone can't do because she's a woman. First I worked with pay phones, then with small businesses and in residential repair.

Following my years at Ameritech, I returned to education with a focus on nontraditional career development: it was time to introduce this option systematically to schoolgirls. So I helped design and manage several educational outreach and mentoring projects at Hard Hatted Women,[10] the organization I co-founded in 1979 with one friend who worked in the steel mills and another who was a truck driver—over twenty years and we're still going strong. We'd heard of a similar group in Pittsburgh, so we put an article in the local feminist newspaper and started meeting as a support group. Now we offer pre-apprenticeship training and a mentoring program at a local trade school, where girls enrolled in nontraditional shop (metalwork welding, for instance) previously didn't get placed in internships.[11] We're also part of a national network of tradeswomen's groups.[12]

---

10. For more organizational information, job opportunities, pre-apprenticeship training, school recruitment programs, and updates, etc., visit their website: *www.hardhattedwomen.org.*—Ed.

11. A report released on June 6, 2002 by the National Women's Law Center found that, nationally, vocational and technical courses remain heavily gender segregated, with girls often being steered away from any but traditionally female jobs. For example, cosmetology students were 96 percent female, and childcare and health-aide students 85 percent female. Contrarily, plumbing and electrical work students were 94 percent male, welding and carpentry students 93 percent male, and auto mechanics students 92 percent male. The report further noted that federal wage figures showed workers in the heavily female service fields earning only a fraction of what workers earned in, for instance, building trades or computer support. (See "Pink Collar Ghetto, Blue Collar Token," by Alice Kessler-Harris, p. 358.) The National Women's Law Center filed a dozen complaints—one for every regional office of the Federal Education Department's Office of Civil Rights—demanding investigations into whether public schools with such gender-segregation training were in violation of Title IX.—Ed.

12. One such national group was founded on March 8 (International Women's Day), 2002, in New York City: Tradeswomen Now and Tomorrow (TNT). The

I was also able to connect with other women at the phone company, though they had us pretty much spread out. It's rare even today to find more than one woman working in any given location. At first I didn't get much acceptance from my male co-workers. Some became friends, but other guys I worked with for ten or fifteen years never did accept me. And company policy could be interestingly skewed. For instance, pay-phone coin collectors were traditionally men, but the company gave that job to women because it was basically unskilled work; it had been a highly paid job, but once women were doing it, the wage level was frozen over the next several contracts. I think that if you looked at the records of, say, Ameritech, you might *think* you see a good gender balance, because they have a lot of technical jobs that are indoors and women are hired for these faster than for the outside jobs. There's still paternalistic pressure to move women back inside. They tried with me, but I refused. Thank goodness for the union (Communications Workers of America) at that point, because I filed grievances and held my own. Still, that was also hard, because I was in a predominantly male local, and I had a difficult time getting accepted. Once I became active and outspoken in union affairs, I wound up being labeled and ostracized. Apparently, the leadership felt threatened. Their attitude was "Well, we like women coming to union meetings but we don't want to *hear* from them." I had to knock heads with some of those guys. Eventually I did become a union steward, and I edited my local's newsletter.

All in all, my situation wasn't nearly as difficult as that of women who work construction. They work with changing groups of men and have to prove themselves over and over. Even if guys in their own trades—say, carpenters—accept them, there's still the electricians' gang and the plant-maintenance gang and all the others in the workplace they have to deal with. Ironworkers feel like they're the last stronghold: the tough guys' job women have no business even trying.

Our progress creeps at a snail's pace as we try to move a critical mass of women into getting—and keeping—these jobs; in fact, job retention is a big issue. A nontraditional job for women is usually defined as one in

---

network is committed to addressing such issues as sexual harassment, family-friendly work policies, and expanded training and pre-apprenticeship opportunities (see *Ms.*, Summer 2002). Their website is *www.tradeswomennow.org.*—Ed.

which 25 percent or less of the workforce is female. In our case, since women still represent only 2.4 percent of tradesworkers in the United States, having even 15 percent would be wonderful.

COMPUTER PROGRAMMERS

Sandy Lerner, Co-founder, Cisco Systems, Inc.

I started programming for hire in the mid-1970s. I had an undergraduate degree in comparative communist theory, but there were very few jobs for political science graduates. So I decided if I couldn't do what I wanted to do, I would do something people would pay me to do: I began contract programming for people doing research in sociology or political science or economics. They were silly projects—quantitative methods in the social sciences were pretty primitive thirty years ago—but I got paid $25 an hour, even back then, and for that I could put up with a lot of silly.

The concept of the router [a device to allow communications among computer networks] began with the Defense Department in the late 1960s. I was at Stanford University, which had one of the first viable internets using layer-3 (router) technology. Len (my husband and colleague, Leonard Bosack) worked in a different part of the campus. We were all just collaborative players trying to convince our respective managements that this new technology was the way to build a large, diverse network.[13] When Stanford wouldn't allow us to transfer the technology to other universities—the University of Texas at Austin and the University of Washington had been major players, among others, in router development and testing—Len and I said, "That's not fair. It's anti-academic, and all these people helped to develop this technology. Besides, you need to make this work in different network situations." But we couldn't get them to listen.

---

13. Although Lerner and Bosack have repeatedly acknowledged numerous other contributors in their collaborative work, the media—ranging from a PBS documentary even to some Stanford websites—has tended to give Lerner and Bosack sole or predominant credit for inventing the multiprotocol router. Cisco Systems was the first company to develop a commercially viable multiprotocol, multimedia, multilayer internetworking system.—Ed.

Finally we said, "We'll just commercialize it ourselves." There was no economic motive. We weren't blazing capitalists. But we knew the technology *had* to get *out*. There were literally dozens of venture capitalists telling us we couldn't possibly make any money on an *open* protocol (at this time, every computer company had its own proprietary network technology), but we knew that this was how internetworking technology had to move forward. It was an uphill battle to convince people that *(a)* a proprietary technology wouldn't work because no one was going to have a completely pure network of only company X machines, and *(b)* none of the proprietary protocols had the properties necessary to allow for an infinitely extensible internetwork, so from a fundamentally mathematical point of view, the open protocol was the only way to construct a worldwide Internet. That all turned out to be true. It was like Lister's battle for sterile procedures against infection in the nineteenth century—trying to convince people to do things the way he knew they had to be done in order to make progress.

No one could even understand why you would want to build the Internet. But you can believe in a technology for its own sake, like some people believe in a religion. We were harebrained academic scientists, but we had a few forward-thinking customers—at Hewlett-Packard and later at Boeing. Basically, we were trying to stay out of the way of the big players like IBM. It really wasn't that deliberate or planned, we just got carried along by events. That's how we founded our company, Cisco Systems, in 1984—in our living room—to commercialize Internet routing technology.

Len and I were equal players in starting the company, but as soon as it got venture funding, I was taken off the board and eventually fired. It was *my* company, but I had to watch as women on the executive staff got replaced by men; then had to hear the company get criticized for not hiring women. It was just a brutal place. I watched an executive in the sales department tell a woman, "I'll lose my job before I'll allow a woman on the sales force." This was *a woman's company!* But once you have venture financing, it's *their* company.

I've got a girlfriend in biotech, and it's part of the same thing. One day we sat down over coffee and found thirty-seven words—a punitive vocabulary for women—that has no male counterpart in the language: shrew, harpy, harridan, and so forth. If a woman stands up for what she believes in, she's called "difficult to work with" and "not a team player." If a man does the same thing, he's seen as "committed to his beliefs," and a leader. If a man is vocal about something he feels is wrong, he's regarded as courageous. If a woman is vocal, she's a mouthy bitch who doesn't know how to conduct herself in business.

At Cisco, if a woman tried to exercise an authority that rightfully went with the position she nominally held in the company, they replaced her. I was fired in 1990. We went public that February and I was fired in August. In an act of supreme loyalty, love, friendship, and all the rest of it, Len walked out with me. We both stood to lose half of our stock in the company that we had funded on our own for three years and worked at for seven years. Only because Len walked out with me, were we able to bring enough pressure by saying, basically, "It's one thing if you're going to fire a founder, but if you fire *both* founders, it doesn't look good, guys." They eventually gave us our stock.

Now I own almost a thousand acres in Virginia that I farm organically, and a restaurant in the nearby town. I'm also excited about starting a long-term critical-care facility for animals, and I have a patent for a pet carrier. We've got some interesting biotech stuff we're working on that Len and Richard Troiano, another of the Cisco founders, are into; the core group has stuck together. Len and I started an audio recording studio, too, doing some really cool stuff with surround sound. For my fortieth birthday, I wrote *The Dilettante's Dictionary*, a 400-page dictionary on audio engineering *(www.dilettantesdictionary.com)*. Instead of a midlife crisis, I had a midlife opus.

In technical fields, either you can do the work or you can't, so women can make progress on their merit. Today most technical departments are headed by men of my generation who would really *like* to work with women. They're less threatened by women than men in the business world seem to be.

But the younger women perceive this out of context. A few years ago I spoke at the first conference for women in computing, and I talked with a lot of young women. I was in my early forties at that point, and I was on a panel with women in their fifties. The younger women couldn't understand why we were dissatisfied with the status quo,[14] when actually all we were saying was, "Hey, when you get out there, some men are not going to be nice to you." The younger women said that we must be lesbians or man-haters or something, that the men *are* nice to them. Well, they haven't yet tried to take a man's job. They're still cute. I don't mean physically; I mean their actions. They're perceived as being cute, not threatening. They haven't yet risen to a place in the organization or in their own careers where it's going to come down between them and some man for a job, or where they'll *have* a job but must then decide whether some man gets one. Eventually they'll get to that level—and then it'll be an eye-opener. Their treatment in the workplace will be radically changed. We wanted them to see it coming.

Basically, I believe things won't progress much until parents change the way they raise their kids. If you're working in computer science or engineering, you need to be encouraged to develop a long attention span, and you need to have a belief that your work is important. Many things in science are just *hard*, and all children need confidence and encouragement to persevere and succeed. I watch my friends with their children. Sons are left alone. Their time is regarded as valuable, so little boys develop an attention span plus confidence in the belief that whatever they do is important; they know they're *expected to succeed*. Daughters are interrupted, taught constantly to watch for and respond to the needs of other people. Little girls who play by themselves are called antisocial and are criticized, or at least redirected to group activity. If girls fail at something, they're told it's OK. Only when little girls are taught to take a proprietary, positive view of their own time, will women be able to compete, fully and successfully, especially in science and engineering.[15]

---

14. Women working in the Internet economy earn 24 percent less than men, and they receive 50 percent less in bonuses than do men (*The Standard*, 25 December 2000; *www.thestandard.com*).—Ed.

15. See "Changing a Masculinist Culture: Women in Science, Engineering, and Technology," by Donna M. Hughes, p. 393; "Sisterhood Is Pleasurable: A Quiet Revolution in Psychology," by Carol Gilligan, p. 94; and "Girls: 'We Are the Ones Who Can Make a Change!' " by Ana Grossman and Emma Peters-Axtell, p. 121.—Ed.

MARY THOM, who interviewed the above six women on assignment for *Sisterhood Is Forever,* is a former executive editor of *Ms.* magazine. She edited *Letters to Ms.: 1972–1987* (Henry Holt, 1987) and authored *Inside Ms.: 25 Years of the Magazine and the Feminist Movement* (Henry Holt, 1997), as well as *Balancing the Equation: Where Are Women and Girls in Science, Engineering, and Technology?* (Prentice Hall, 2001) for the National Council for Research on Women.

"*Just* a Housewife?!"

HELEN DRUSINE

I WAS ONE of many women who grew up in the 1950s and 1960s daring to believe I didn't have to be "just a housewife." I wasn't going to marry, stay home, have children, take care of a husband and household, and do "nothing" like most of the older women around me. These feelings were reinforced by my attending the then all-girls Hunter College High School in New York City, a school for the so-called intellectually gifted. Hunter girls were supposedly too smart to become housewives; it was assumed we would go on to college and "make something" of ourselves. This feeling was so instilled in us that at our fortieth reunion, a number of women admitted they'd been afraid to attend prior reunions because of a fear they hadn't "measured up": they were fulltime housewives and mothers.

Politicians have always spouted rhetoric about family values and the glories of wifely devotion and motherhood—"the most important jobs in society." Yet that same society denigrates, demeans, devalues, and dismisses these jobs as "woman's work." Justifications range from basic misogyny (whatever women do is less important than whatever men do) to the fuzzy-minded "natural division of labor" argument (women are biologically built for childbearing, therefore we are also meant to scrub floors).[1] But a crucial component in the trivializing of "woman's work" is that it is done at home, is unsalaried, and stands outside the formal labor force and market economy.[2]

---

1. See "Biologically Correct," by Natalie Angier, p. 3.—Ed.

2. For more on paid and unpaid caregiving, see "Poverty Wears a Female Face," by Theresa Funiciello, p. 222; and "Pink Collar Ghetto, Blue Collar Token," by Alice Kessler-Harris, p. 358.—Ed.

Feminist economists like Boserup and Waring (see Suggested Further Reading below) have pointed out that the worldwide system of economic measurement known as the United Nations System of National Accounts (UNSNA) is a major culprit. The UNSNA was developed in 1953 and has been adopted by virtually all nation-states, as well as by such powerful international institutions as the World Bank and the International Monetary Fund. It legitimized and enshrined the practice that women who work as housewives should *not* be taken into account by governments—not in assessing need (even for childcare facilities), not for development assistance, not for future planning, not as contributors to society. The result is that housewifery and mothering are not factored into a country's Gross Domestic Product; in other words, homemakers suffer from what feminists have termed "GDP invisibility." This accounting system, used globally to determine basic public policy, has classified housewives as "nonproducers," "inactive," and "unoccupied." Such nonproductivity includes a woman's work of *re*production, without which no *production* could take place, since she births workers for any labor force. But in a market economy, only waged labor is visible and only those in the formal labor force are "productive."[3]

A middle-class North American housewife, therefore, is considered unoccupied and economically inactive, since she earns no salary for her minimum-fourteen-hour workdays. This is a woman who spends her time shopping for food, preparing it, cooking it, washing dishes, washing clothes (which also means sorting laundry, separating laundry, folding finished laundry, *and* putting it away), ironing, cleaning, dusting, polishing, scrubbing, scouring, vacuuming, mopping, gardening, picking up after others, dressing and undressing the kids, getting them ready for school, taking them to school, arranging the social lives of her husband and herself as well as of their kids, picking up hubby's suit at the cleaner's, picking up the kids from school (and sports and extra classes and playdates), doing the household accounts, getting to the bank on time, shopping for kids' clothes, making appointments, taking kids to the doctor or dentist . . . you get the point. Just when she thinks *maybe* her day is over at around 9:00 P.M., the kids need help with homework.

---

3. See "Poverty Wears a Female Face," by Theresa Funiciello, p. 222, and the Introduction, p. *xv*.

Not to speak of who—the woman—is the one usually up all night taking care of a sick child. Even if there are no children, it's still the wife who keeps the husband going: clean, fed, clothed, ego-stroked, and off on time to his job—which *is* visible. Yet her labor, which enables his, remains "disappeared."

This woman can never call in sick. She never has a day (or night, or weekend) off. She reaps no pay, no vacation time, no benefits, no health insurance, no sick leave, no retirement. The demands of her "nonproductive, unoccupied" job never stop.

But isn't the New Man doing more of this work? Yes, some have started to share the load—not merely "help her" with what's assumed to be her purpose in life, but actually *share* the load.[4] (Which means *noticing*—that the socks are still lying in the middle of the floor for the third day now, *noticing* we're about to run out of milk instead of waiting for her to tell him to please go to the store, *noticing* the underwear drawer is getting low so it's time to do a laundry . . . again, you get the point.) Even so, those few men who actually carry their fair share of the burden hardly constitute a critical mass. And what if there *is* no man in the picture? Single mothers endure the housewife crisis tenfold. (Of course, there's that myth about labor-saving devices, as if errands and other imperatives don't abhor any vacuum—pun intended—in a homemaker's time; such time will instantly be filled, if by nothing more than her having to locate, call, wait for, and deal with various repairpersons when those labor-saving devices dependably break down.)

If she happens also to be formally employed in a waged job, she still does most of the work at home—the now-familiar two-job burden. Employed mothers (I don't write "working mothers" because, as the 1970s feminist button proclaimed, "*All* mothers are working mothers") log longer hours than almost anyone in the economy. According to one nationwide study of European American married couples in the United States, a mother's average workweek ranged from 76 to 89 hours.[5] Author Ann Crittenden writes that "as women enter the workplace, they

---

4. See "Parenting: A New Social Contract," by Suzanne Braun Levine, p. 85.—Ed.

5. Juliet B. Schor, *The Overworked American* (New York: Basic Books, 1992).

take on the equivalent of two fulltime jobs, forcing them to cut back on everything in their lives but paid work and children."[6]

Added to this is the unpaid work a woman does (also contributing to the economy!) at her children's schools, her church/synagogue/mosque, community social functions, and other volunteer work. If this unpaid labor *were* taken into account, the GDP of European and North American countries would increase *by 40 percent*.[7]

No wonder women get tired. *And* feel guilty that we're somehow not Doing It All. Many of us growing up in the 1960s postponed having children (so we could have careers), sometimes until it was too late. Of ten women friends my age, I'm the only mother—and I waited until I was age thirty-six for my first child and age forty for my second.

When I finally decided to have a baby, I was sure *I* could Do It All, be Superwoman, juggle career and family, *and* be Earth Mother: I would do everything *naturally*; I wouldn't give *my* baby a bottle. Yet somehow I thought I'd nurse her only at mealtimes. The incongruities were ridiculous. Babies know nothing about schedules and they don't give a damn whether you have a job or not.

Believing I could Do It All, I had taken a two-month maternity leave. But how could I forsake my baby after two months? I was in agony. The night before I was to return to work I developed a fever of 102 degrees. The next morning I called the office, offering to work at home for a while (I had worked at home during the last months of my pregnancy), half hoping they would say no. They did.

So I became a fulltime homemaker, someone I thought I never would be. Like many other women, I also became an economic dependent overnight. And I became not only financially invisible but socially invisible. A few months after the birth of my first child, I attended a book-launching party. When another guest asked me what I did, I replied (somewhat facetiously, suspecting what the response might be) that I

---

6. Ann Crittenden, *The Price of Motherhood* (New York: Henry Holt & Company, 2000).

7. Robin Morgan, ed., *Sisterhood Is Global: The International Women's Movement Anthology* (New York: Doubleday/Anchor, 1984; updated edition The Feminist Press at CUNY, 1996).

took care of babies. She responded with a condescending "Oh!" and walked away. After that, no one at the party had any interest in talking with me.

That myth of "housewife worthlessness" gets internalized by a lot of women—though probably less so now, after more than four decades of the contemporary Women's Movement raising these issues. For me, it was a constant conflict. I thought I had to prove (more to myself than those around me) that I was doing something "meaningful." I went back to school to get a master's degree, while my mother babysat. Then, almost immediately after my second daughter was born, I started looking for a job. But you can't put "housewife and mother" on your résumé. What had I "done" during the preceding four years? It took nine months to find a job—one that paid less and was less interesting than my previous one. Furthermore, I regretted every moment that took me away from my kids. So in less than two years I was home again—but this time with a job I could do *at* home while still being there for my kids (I had became a licensed neuromuscular massage therapist). But I was now a single mom, too, so I couldn't even have done *this* job if it weren't for my mother—another unpaid homemaker—on whom I became completely dependent for childcare. And so today, because I chose to work at home, like millions of U.S. homemakers, I have no health insurance, pension, or retirement benefits.

Yet it doesn't have to be this way. There can be sane, practical, humane policies addressing this issue.[8] In Sweden, parents can work a six-hour day until their children are age eight; in France, the legal workweek was reduced from 39 to 35 hours in 2000. Mothers in France and Sweden have the right to a one-year *paid* maternity leave, and can work an 80 percent schedule while a preschool child is at home.[9] By 1986, in Sweden, "some 90 percent of mothers of children under age sixteen were working outside the home," more than anywhere else in

---

8. As of mid-2002, the United States was one of only five countries—along with Australia, Lesotho, Papua New Guinea, and Swaziland—that had no paid maternity leave; Australia was expected to enact such legislation in the near future.—Ed.

9. Crittenden, op. cit.

the world—*and* less than 10 percent quit their jobs after childbirth.[10] In France, every mother receives free health care and a cash allowance for each child; other benefits include approximately $6,000 worth of annual housing subsidies. These are reduced when the child reaches age three—when public nursery school is available. Largely due to these benefits, the child poverty rate in France is 6 percent—compared with 17 percent in the USA.[11]

When we devalue women who work as mothers, we devalue not only women but children—and the future. When we devalue women who work as homemakers, we consign that crucially important job to literal feudal status: labor that's invisible yet critical to society's functioning. That's one description of serfdom.

No wonder Patricia Mainardi's hilarious (and deadly serious) article "The Politics of Housework," written in 1969,[12] became a feminist classic, along with Jane O'Reilly's deadly serious (and hilarious) article "The Housewife's Moment of Truth," which was the cover story of *Ms.* magazine's premier (December 1971) issue. No wonder Judy Syfer's now famous satire from that same *Ms.*, "Why I Want a Wife," ends with the plaintive question, "My god, who *wouldn't* want a wife?"

HELEN DRUSINE has a B.A. in French and comparative literature and masters' degrees in journalism and international affairs, all from Columbia University. She's worked as a ballet dancer, freelance journalist, neuromuscular massage therapist, housewife, and single mom. Her articles have appeared in *Omni*, the *International Herald Tribune*, and *The New York Times*. She has done extensive volunteer work with such international grassroots women's organizations as GROOTS.

---

10. Suzanne A. Stoiber, *Parental Leave and Woman's Place* (Washington, D.C.: Women's Research and Education Institute, 1989).

11. Crittenden, op. cit.

12. In Robin Morgan, ed. *Sisterhood Is Powerful: An Anthology of Writings from the Women's Liberation Movement* (New York: Random House/Vintage Books, 1970).

Suggested Further Reading

Boserup, Ester. *Women's Role in Economic Development.* New York: St. Martin's Press, 1970.

Chodorow, Nancy. *The Reproduction of Mothering: Psychoanalysis and the Sociology of Gender.* Berkeley: University of California Press, 1978.

Crittenden, Ann. *The Price of Motherhood.* New York: Henry Holt & Company, 2000.

Leghorn, Lisa, and Katherine Parker. *Women's Worth: Sexual Economics and the World of Women.* Boston/London/Henley: Routledge & Kegan Paul, 1981.

Waring, Marilyn J. *If Women Counted: A New Feminist Economics.* San Francisco: Harper & Row, 1989.

The Clerical Proletariat

ELLEN BRAVO

THE LAST TWO DECADES of the twentieth century have seen phenomenal change in the secretarial—now clerical—proletariat: what these workers do, how they do it, when, where and for whom they do it, even what the job is called. We at 9 to 5, National Association of Working Women, have kept track—and noticed that the only thing that hasn't changed substantially is how the job is valued. Fortunately, office workers today are more likely to demand greater pay and respect, but they face significant challenges in doing so.

Who Administrative Support Staff Are

Non-management administrative support remains the largest occupational category for women, employing 18.5 million people, 79 percent of them female—nearly one in four of all employed women. At this writing, in 2002, more of these workers are people of color than ever before: 18 percent, up from 11.7 percent in 1983. And yet the very technology that spurred the growth of administrative support jobs by expanding business and financial services has also resulted in job loss for many women workers.

Today, those performing clerical tasks are called by various names: secretary, support staff, word processor, office manager, administrative assistant, administrative professional. But whatever they're called—and although the office could not run without them—they remain at the bottom of the heap in status, treatment, and pay.

What They Do

In many ways, secretaries and other clericals are still expected to function as the office wife. "We are expected to smooth out difficult situations, put on a good face for the clients, create a clean and pleasant workspace (but not *too* personal), stay late if needed, make our bosses look good, and sometimes even babysit or get coffee."[1] Running personal errands for the boss is still not out of bounds. At 9 to 5 we've heard it all, from waxing a boss's unsightly back hair to taking his stool specimen to the lab, planning his dog's funeral—and spending Saturday nights in a bar scanning for suitable women,[2] then beeping him so he won't have to waste time doing the scouting himself.[3] Like burnt pot roast, the work of clericals is often noticed only when a mistake is made.

Yet the clerical's job description has otherwise undergone enormous change. In addition to typing, filing, copying, answering the phone, ordering supplies, handling communication, paying bills, scheduling, and general trouble-shooting, the job may now include a wide array of desktop publishing, graphic design, and database management. What's more surprising, office workers commonly find themselves morphed into sales clerks: telephone workers selling caller ID, bank workers hawking credit cards, airline-reservation clerks promoting rental cars.

Just as support staff have taken on functions formerly performed by designated professionals, parts of their job can now be done by the executives, who may type their own memos, check messages on voice-mail, and e-mail their own correspondence. This might have been a delightful turn of events—had it not been accompanied by a loss in jobs. Secretaries, for example—a job category that remains more than 97 percent female—decreased from 3.9 million employed in 1983 to 2.4 million in 2001. Other positions, such as information clerk, increased during this

---

1. Ann Eyerman, *Women in the Office: Transitions in a Global Economy* (Toronto, Canada: Sumach Press, 2000), p. 87.

2. See "The Nature of the Beast: Sexual Harassment," by Anita Hill, p. 296.—Ed.

3. Winners over the years of various 9 to 5 contests, including "The Pettiest Office Procedure" and "Nominate Your Boss: The Good, the Bad, and the Downright Unbelievable."

time—but are paid much less. And disappearing jobs didn't stop with secretarial positions. Several categories where people of color made up more than 20 percent of the workforce—keypunch operators, mailroom clerks, and file clerks—were among the first to be cut.[4]

A variety of technical courses and even associate-degree programs have sprung up to provide training for the new office technology. But along with requirements for greater skills comes a greater burden on the worker to acquire these skills on her own time—and her own dime.

How They Do Their Jobs

Technology has transformed the office in more fundamental ways than ever before. The electronic revolution didn't just allow greater speed and quantity; it facilitated change in the *nature* of what work could be done and *how* that work is managed. Although technology seemed to promise far greater independence, many office workers have experienced a loss of control as well as a loss of security.

Supervisors today can peer over dozens of shoulders at once, via electronic surveillance. "Your call may be monitored for quality purposes" has become a common refrain. Spying on workers has brought increased reliance on scripts and quotas. At 9 to 5 we've talked with word processors whose computer screen might flash a message reading, *You're not working as fast as the person next to you.* Airline reservationists are graded on how many minutes they spend in "unplugged time" (time in the bathroom). A customer-service rep quit her job when management decreed that no more than one person at a time could be in the bathroom, posting a checkered flag on the door to let workers know when the room was occupied. "They treat you like a machine," one woman said, explaining she got more grades in a month than her kids did at school in a year, "I feel violated."[5] Some offices resemble what Barbara

---

4. See Joan Greenbaum, *Windows on the Workplace* (New York: Monthly Review Press, 1995) for more discussion on job loss and the relationship to de-skilling of office work.

5. "Stories of Mistrust and Manipulation: Electronic Monitoring of the American Workforce" (Cleveland, Ohio: 9 to 5 Working Women Education Fund, 1990).

Garson labeled the "electronic sweatshop," where pay is determined by keystroke.[6]

The speed and stress have ushered a new set of health hazards into the office, a workplace commonly rated "zero" on compensation analyses in the area of risk. In addition to repetitive-strain injuries and stress-related ailments, many workers suffer from "sick building syndrome," as stale air circulates various bugs and pollutants. Magazines run ads for the three most popular computer accessories: Tylenol, Ben-Gay, and Visine.

When an expert on work and family[7] asked children what they most wanted for their parents, she expected them to say "more time." Instead, their answer was "less stress."[8] Work problems score higher on stress lists than financial or family problems.

Where They Do Their Jobs—and for Whom

The new office might be anywhere. Many workers who had been personal secretaries have found themselves working in a "pool" for multiple managers. Others have landed in a call center, where scores of workers who are stationed in one large room handle calls and manage information. Some are able to work at home or in a branch office. While this can be a useful option, telecommuters often find themselves with unanticipated costs for equipment and electricity and lament the loss of social contact and networking opportunities.[9]

In this era of globalization, you may work in a call center far from company headquarters, or you may perform work for many companies,

---

6. Barbara Garson, *The Electronic Sweatshop: How Computers Are Transforming the Office of the Future into the Factory of the Past* (New York: Penguin Books, 1998).

7. Ellen Galinsky, *Ask the Children: The Breakthrough Study that Reveals How to Succeed at Work and Parenting* (New York: William Morrow, 1999; Quill paperback, 2000).

8. See "Parenting: A New Social Contract," by Suzanne Braun Levine, p. 85.—Ed.

9. The Communications Workers of America formulated eight principles for telecommuters to limit both financial and career costs to workers. See Ellen Bravo, *The Job/Family Challenge: A 9 to 5 Guide (Not for Women Only)* (New York: John Wiley and Sons, 1995), pp. 123–124.

none of which you know. The job you used to do may now be "out-sourced." New York police tickets are processed in Ghana, New Jersey food-stamp questions are answered from India, airline reservations may be processed by prisoners in Tennessee. In addition to the loss of local jobs and revenue, such restructuring intensifies the removal of management from the impact of working conditions on workers or customers.[10]

When They Do Their Jobs

Some have hailed the increase in flexibility for women workers. Indeed, the 1980s and 1990s have seen significant growth in nonstandard jobs: part-time (including job sharing), temporary, and contract employment. The real question is, *flexibility on whose terms?* For many women workers, reduced hours or temporary status are involuntary, reflecting the lack of fulltime permanent jobs, or of suitable childcare.[11] And nonstandard workers typically receive less pay and fewer or no benefits than their fulltime, permanent counterparts. No law says they must be treated equitably, even if they do exactly the same job for the same employer.[12]

The growth in call centers has meant a shift from 9-to-5 to 24/7. More parents are working evenings and weekend hours, with significant negative impact on their children's emotional well-being and school performance.[13] Furthermore, working hours for many are increasing. A

---

10. See "Globalization: A Strategic Advance for Feminism?" by Jessica Neuwirth, p. 526.—Ed.

11. Of the more than two million people working for temp agencies at the end of 1998, 80 percent said they were doing so involuntarily because they couldn't find permanent work (Carol Kleiman, "Flexible Temp Work Preferable for Some," *The Chicago Sun-Times*, December 1998). Involuntary part-time status is especially a problem for the working poor; approximately 20 percent of these workers are employed involuntarily part-time. See "Problems Facing the Working Poor," by Marlene Kim, in *Balancing Acts: Easing the Burdens and Improving the Options for Working Families*, Eileen Appelbaum, ed. (Washington, D.C.: Economic Policy Institute, 2000).

12. For more on the problem of nonstandard workers, see North American Alliance for Fair Employment, "Contingent Workers Fight for Fairness" (Boston: NAAFE, 2000).

13. Jody Heymann, et al., *Work-Family Issues and Low-Income Families* (New York: The Ford Foundation, 2002).

California legal secretary described the almost daily routine of being asked to stay late to help prepare documents. She received no overtime, but the lawyers told her she could take comp time. Yet whenever she asked for time off to be with her kids, she was told the firm was "too busy."

"Flexibility" for employers has also meant replacing "nonessential" workers (e.g., clericals) with leased or temporary employees. Sometimes a firm will hire back the same employees in this new category—only at lower compensation and with no seniority. With labor costs down, stock prices go up; instead of being included in payroll, the workers are listed under a category like "supplies." And instead of being overseen by Human Resources, decisions for these workers are made by Procurement.[14] One company calls these workers the "LOs" for "Low Overheads."[15]

How Clericals Are Valued

Nor have the new skills and responsibilities necessarily brought higher pay. A 2000 poll by the International Association of Administrative Professionals showed 94.7 percent of respondents said their responsibilities increased in several areas, including accounting and supervising others, yet only 39.3 percent said they saw the increase reflected in their pay.

Some organizations have consciously transformed themselves into high-performance operations where workers at all levels receive training on multiple tasks and see a corresponding increase in compensation. An executive secretary at Harley Davidson, for example, used to take notes for the group deciding corporate giving; now she runs the program.[16] But for most office staff, being "just a secretary" carries low status and relatively low pay.[17] Unlike numerous male-dominated

---

14. Greenbaum, op. cit.

15. Eyerman, op. cit.

16. 9 to 5 Working Women Education Fund, "High Performance Office Work: Improving Jobs and Productivity" (Cleveland, Ohio: 9 to 5 Working Women Education Fund, 1993).

17. See *"Just a Housewife?!"* by Helen Drusine, p. 342; "Up the Down Labyrinth: Ins and Outs of Women's Corporate and Campus Careers," by Ellen Appel-

occupations, where productivity gains brought on by technology were accompanied by increased earnings, office work was described as "easier" because of technology, hence no more valuable.

Being a secretary once meant being the trusted advisor of the chief executives, a high-status, highly compensated profession, stepping-stone to the top—and virtually all male. When females were allowed in to replace men fighting in the Civil War, their pay was set at half to two-thirds that of men. Not surprisingly, women did a fine job, and employers hired more and more of them—at a legally lower rate. Soon the field became female-dominated, the discriminatory pay became the market rate, and the road to advancement faded. A barrage of literature in the early and mid-1920s was aimed at persuading women that secretarial work was a satisfactory goal in itself.[18] Today, what advancement opportunities once existed have narrowed with the loss of middle-management positions.

What Support Staff Can Do About It

"My consciousness is fine—it's my pay that needs raising."—9 to 5 button.

Low pay and lack of respect add up to high stress levels. A whole industry has sprung into being to help workers deal with work-related stress. You can dial up Dr. Bob and choose remedies from a menu of options, throw a "stress ball" (it emits the sound of a plate-glass window breaking), or put on a "scream muffler" to holler without being noticed.

Yet as an early 9 to 5 study—one of the first ever to focus on employed women—pointed out, the best way to deal with stress is to deal with its *cause*. The worst combination for women workers was found to be a high level of responsibility matched with a low level of control—the job description for most administrative support staff.

A number of public policy measures are needed to help change this situation. Groups like 9 to 5 help organize women to work for such changes as pay equity (revaluing jobs based on skill, effort, and responsibility rather than on a legacy of discrimination), more affordable and

---

Bronstein, p. 387; and "Poverty Wears a Female Face," by Theresa Funiciello, p. 222.—Ed.

18. Alice Kessler-Harris, *Out to Work* (New York: Oxford University Press, 1982).

accessible family leave and childcare,[19] paid sick leave, and equal treatment for part-time and temporary workers.

Another important route to change is unionization. Women now account for two-fifths of all union members (although that proportional gain also reflects the loss of union jobs for men). Much of the growth has come in the public sector, where women of color made inroads in employment. But even such private institutions as Harvard have seen clericals turn to collective bargaining.[20] Union women on average earn 31 percent more than non-union women, and are more likely to have family-flexible policies and a say in determining workplace policies. Still, women's unionization rate remains low: only 11.4 percent of all women in the workforce. Penalties for anti-union activity are ridiculously weak, and pursuing unfair labor charges can take years. Labor law reform is urgently needed.

You don't always win when you stand up for yourself—but you never win if you don't. Working together on changes such as these will bring us closer to achieving 9 to 5's original goals: raises, rights, and respect—goals so sensible they ought to be shared by everyone.

ELLEN BRAVO is Director of 9 to 5, National Association of Working Women *(www.9to5.org)*, a grassroots organization founded in 1973 that strengthens women's ability to win economic justice. She is the coauthor (with Ellen Cassedy) of *The 9 to 5 Guide to Combating Sexual Harassment* (Milwaukee, Wisconsin: 9 to 5 Working Women Education Fund, 1999) and author of *The Job/Family Challenge: A 9 to 5 Guide (Not for Women Only)* (New York: John Wiley & Sons, 1995), along with numerous reports and articles.

Suggested Further Reading:

Albeda, Randy, and Chris Tilly. *Glass Ceilings and Bottomless Pits: Women's Work, Women's Poverty.* Boston: South End Press, 1997.

Duffy, Ann, et al., eds. *Good Jobs, Bad Jobs, No Jobs: The Transformation of*

---

19. See Levine, Drusine, and Funiciello articles, op. cit.—Ed.

20. For a detailed description of the organizing drive, see John Hoerr, *We Can't EAT Prestige* (Philadelphia: Temple University Press, 1997).

Work in the Twenty-first Century. New York: Harcourt Brace and Company, 1997.

Mott, Jo Ann. *Not Your Father's Union Movement: Inside the AFL-CIO.* New York: Verso, 1998.

Rogers, Jackie Krasas. *Temps: The Many Faces of the Changing Workplace.* Ithaca, New York: ILR Press, 2000.

Pink Collar Ghetto, Blue Collar Token

ALICE KESSLER-HARRIS

MOST WOMEN WORK in places where other women work, and most women hold the kinds of jobs other women hold. Social scientists call this "occupational segregation by sex"—in popular jargon, a "pink collar ghetto"—but they pay less attention to its sources and consequences than we as women should pay. Because women work in pink collar ghettos, they earn less, amass fewer benefits (vacation days, sick time, pensions), and have less opportunity for advancement than most comparably educated male workers. Why? Why did women end up in these jobs? Why do the jobs continue to be relatively poorly paid, even when, in fields like nursing, there's a shortage of workers?[1] Why, years after the enactment of legislation ending formal discrimination, do women still work in jobs with limited pay and potential? How can women change the terms of the pink collar ghetto—or break down its walls? Does the new global economy offer an opportunity for change?[2]

The first answer to these questions lies in the sheer *size* of the ghetto. As of 2000, there were about 132 million jobs in the United States, 62 million (47 percent) of them held by women. These women work in every conceivable sort of occupation. But many kinds of jobs boast relatively few female workers; in others, women constitute the overwhelming majority of the workforce. On one side of the equation, skilled blue

---

1. See the nurses section in the Transforming Traditions part of "Transforming Traditions and Breaking Barriers: Six Personal Testimonies," p. 325.—Ed.

2. See "Globalization: A Strategic Advance for Feminism?" by Jessica Neuwirth, p. 526.—Ed.

collar and high-level managerial jobs, the physical sciences and engineering, and politics and policy-making are among the areas where women's faces are scarce.³ On the other side, 70 percent of all wage-earning women (nearly 44 million souls) work in the service industries or in wholesale and retail trade. Some work in clerical and office jobs as receptionists, data processors, and customer-service representatives.⁴ But huge numbers are elementary-school teachers, librarians, and childcare providers. They are health care workers, home-health aides, and beauticians. They are waitresses and fast-food cooks, laundry workers, hotel maids, office and household cleaners. They work as cashiers and saleswomen in supermarkets, chain stores, and department stores. These are the women in the pink collar ghetto. They are, by and large, the women who work in caregiving jobs: they staff our schools, libraries, hospitals, and homes, with and without pay;⁵ they process and dispense our food; manufacture, stock, and sell our clothing; supply our households with goods and our institutions with social services. Yet they remain largely invisible.⁶

The pink collar ghetto is a residue of a nineteenth-century ideal: the male-breadwinner family. Its continuation speaks to the power of ideas about sex differences. At the onset of industrialization, when wage-work demanded ten to twelve hours of hard physical labor six days a week, the desire of both men and women for someone to maintain a home consigned one family member (generally the wife or oldest daughter), to

---

3. See the Breaking Barriers section (especially the segments on firefighting and hard-hat tradeswork) in "Transforming Traditions and Breaking Barriers: Six Personal Testimonies," p. 325; see also "Up the Down Labyrinth: Ins and Outs of Women's Corporate and Campus Careers," by Ellen Appel-Bronstein, p. 387, "Changing a Masculinist Culture: Women in Science, Engineering, and Technology," by Donna M. Hughes, p. 393, and "Running for Our Lives: Electoral Politics," by Pat Schroeder, p. 28.—Ed.

4. See "The Clerical Proletariat," by Ellen Bravo, p. 349.—Ed.

5. For more on the economics of caregiving, see "Poverty Wears a Female Face," by Theresa Funiciello, p. 222; see also "*Just* a Housewife?!" by Helen Drusine, p. 342, and the sections on nursing and teaching in "Transforming Traditions and Breaking Barriers: Six Personal Testimonies," op. cit.—Ed.

6. For more on structural invisibility, see "Traffic at the Crossroads: Multiple Oppressions," by Kimberlé Crenshaw, p. 43.—Ed.

the home. The division made sense in a time when the production of food and clothing was still based largely in the household. No one person could work effectively inside and outside the home. Conceiving of household labor as real work enabled men and women to fight for a family wage—a single male wage that would sustain an entire family. To rationalize their work in the home, women were depicted as being more nurturing, moral, selfless, and docile. And, in a self-confirming prophecy, women's work inside the home appeared "natural." Men, by contrast, learned to become providers in a mobile labor force; they had to take risks, forge opportunity, take advantage of education and training. These qualities, also thought of as "natural" or "manly," would place men at an advantage in a competitive labor market and enable them to earn sufficient incomes to define their homes as sanctuaries.

But most working men never earned a family wage, and most wives (to say nothing of self-supporting women) couldn't get along without bringing in some income. Still, the idea that women could or should remain attached to the home influenced women's education and training, and limited their access to many jobs. Employers sought them out for jobs to which they were "naturally" suited—those that required little training, no initiative, and steady supervision—while reserving other jobs for men. In such ways, gender helped structure the labor force and provide it with a modicum of social order.

As women moved into jobs considered appropriate to their characters, so the jobs reflected tasks and qualities associated with the home. Probably two-thirds of all wage-earning women in the nineteenth century earned their livings in one form or another of domestic service. They worked in other women's homes, as house-cleaners, cooks, laundresses, and personal maids. Married women and those with children took work into their own homes: boarders, laundry, and sewing becoming staples of every poor and immigrant household. More fortunate women ran their own enterprises, providing food and lodging; and became "she-merchants" in their own small shops, selling cloth, household supplies, and clothing. When it became inefficient for women to do every aspect of housekeeping in their own homes, younger women sought jobs in factories to earn the income a cash economy required. Translating spinning and weaving skills into home-based manufacturers and then to the factory, they became the backbone of the industrial revolution's textile industries. When they entered offices in the late nineteenth century, they did so as helpers: typists (or typewriters in nineteenth-century jargon), bookkeepers, and clerks. And when affluent ladies began to shop in large department stores, young women stood behind the counters to guide their purchases and ensure their comfort.

Because the skills involved in many of these jobs were associated with the household or seemed extensions of women's natural roles, they were widely available or readily acquired—and often demeaned.[7] The phrase "women's work" conjured up nurturing activities that every woman was expected to perform naturally,[8] and because women were not expected to support families from their wages, they remained poorly paid. The mid-nineteenth-century skilled weaver, for example, earned a fairly decent living, and the young women who learned the trade in Lowell, Massachusetts, and other mill towns took pride in their high wages. But as employers tried to increase profits by simplifying the work process and speeding up the pace of work, they sought to turn immigrant women into cheaper sources of labor, or they moved their mills to areas in the South where women had few other job choices. Employers justified low pay with generally false assumptions about women as temporary workers destined to quit work when they married. By the late nineteenth century, low pay and women's work were inextricably linked.

Residues of these attitudes remain embedded in our conceptions of jobs and what they are worth. They account for women's firmly fixed places in certain kinds of jobs. Of the nearly one million people who work in private households as cleaners and nannies, 90 percent are female. Of the five million who work in hospitals, 76 percent of the total and 90 percent of the nursing aides are female.[9] Of the six million who work in public and private clinics, nursing homes, and doctors' offices, 80 percent are female. So are 80 percent of childcare workers, 84 per-

---

7. See Bravo, op. cit., for more background on how women's entry into secretarial work was considered as "devaluing" the job.—Ed.

8. See Funiciello, op. cit.—Ed.

9. These and the following figures are from the U.S. Department of Labor, Bureau of Labor Statistics, *Bulletin of the Women's Bureau*, May 2000.

cent of elementary-school teachers, and 90 percent of hairdressers.[10] In fact, in 12 of the 20 leading occupations in which women earn wages, women constitute more than three-quarters of all workers.

Even in these jobs, women earn less than men. Reflecting women's low status *inside* the pink collar ghetto, those few men who work in domestic service or as nurses and cashiers earn more than women do, generally by a factor of 10 to 15 percent. And when we compare the pay for jobs in which women dominate with those in which men dominate, women's pay is generally only about two-thirds that of men.[11] Health aides, for example, earn $11.06 an hour; beauticians $8.49. Electricians, by contrast, make $19.29 an hour; computer-support specialists $17.26.

Low pay isn't the only problem. Women who work in the pink collar ghetto complain of the lack of respect associated with routine work. They often must clock in and out for lunch and coffee breaks, as well as every morning and night. They lack such amenities as decent places to stow belongings, change clothes, eat lunch, or rest during the day. Retail-sales workers and hospital employees are frequently subject to random searches; some workers have suffered the indignities of urine-testing to detect possible drug use.[12] While unpaid maternity leaves are now mandated by law for many workers, women in the pink collar ghetto rarely benefit from the paid leaves that enable women in more prestigious jobs to take time off from work in order to care for babies and other family members.

Despite the poor pay and problematic working conditions, the walls of the pink collar ghetto are proving difficult to surmount. Training in high schools is still offered mostly along gendered lines. A 2002 study by

---

10. For additional data on racial, ethnic, and class factors among women in these employment sectors, see, for example, "U.S. Latinas: Active at the Intersections of Gender, Nationality, Race, and Class," by Edna Acosta-Belén and Christine E. Bose, p. 198; "Reclaiming the Past, Redefining the Future: Asian American and Pacific Islander Women," by Helen Zia, p. 188; and "African American Women: The Legacy of Black Feminism," by Beverly Guy-Sheftall, p. 176; see also Funiciello, op. cit., and Crenshaw, op. cit.—Ed.

11. U.S. Department of Labor, Fair Pay Clearinghouse, "Wage and Occupational Data on Working Women," *www.dol.gov/dol/wb/public/programs/lw&occ.htm*.

12. For illustrations of these sorts of behavior, see Barbara Ehrenreich's book *Nickel and Dimed* (see Suggested Further Reading, below).

the National Women's Law Center discovered that 96 percent of students in high-school cosmetology courses were female, as were 85 percent of students in childcare and health care courses. Males constituted 94 percent of students in plumbing and electrical work, 93 percent of those in welding and carpentry, and 92 percent in auto mechanics.[13] The result is that few women are prepared, psychologically or by training, to enter the labor force in jobs held mostly by men. But the question of whether this remains personal preference or a product of long-standing attitudes and practices has not yet been resolved.

There are many reasons why women move into women's jobs in large numbers. Motherhood is one. Jobs in the pink collar ghetto are far more often offered on a contingent or part-time basis, making them accessible to women who still bear the major responsibility for childrearing. Persistent ideas about appropriate gender roles, in turn, account for the absence of support systems for women's family labor as well as for the male sensibility that working with women undermines masculinity and denigrates the job.[14] Thus, any serious effort to break down the walls of the pink collar ghetto challenges masculinity—both at home and in the workplace.

Economic pressures contribute to the continuing pink collar ghetto, weighing women's increasing need to contribute to family income against the male provider role. Faced with both a declining male wage and rising standards of living, more and more women have chosen to become secondary wage earners. About a third of all women workers work part-time—a figure that reflects women's continuing family responsibilities, but that also suggests some reasons for the persistence of the pink collar ghetto. Despite the need for most families to bring in two adult incomes to pay the bills, men with the least attractive jobs feel most uncomfortable when their wives earn wages—so women tend to choose unthreatening jobs, to pacify male egos.[15]

---

13. "Group Says Course Training Still Breaks Along Sex Lines," by Diana Jean Schemo, *New York Times*, 7 June 2002. See also the tradeswork segment in "Transforming Traditions and Breaking Barriers: Six Personal Testimonies," op. cit.—Ed.

14. See, for example, the firefighters' segment of "Transforming Traditions and Breaking Barriers: Six Personal Testimonies," op. cit.—Ed.

15. See *Working Hard and Making Do: Surviving in Small Town America*, by Margaret K. Nelson and Joan Smith (Berkeley, California: University of California Press, 1999).

A mixed workforce has not always appealed to men *or* women. The idea of women working with other women still has a wide attraction. Many women find the companionability, sociability, and shared culture useful and supportive. The atmosphere contrasts sharply with that in most male workplaces, where workers continue to resist the incursion of women by sexual harassment, refusal to cooperate with women, and failure to provide appropriate equipment.[16]

The degree of occupational segregation has not retreated much, despite more than three decades of contemporary feminist activism. To be sure, some jobs at top levels have opened up in ways never before imagined: a few top managerial and financial jobs are now open to women;[17] and the presidencies of prestigious academic institutions have followed suit.[18] But for most ordinary women, the best place to find jobs is still in the pink collar ghetto.

One result has been that women in these jobs are increasingly focusing on improving their working conditions through unionization. They have joined unions in large numbers, especially where they work in the public sector. In the 1990s, women constituted the majority of newly organized workers, winning major battles for union recognition among the cleaners and janitors in Los Angeles, and among nursing-home attendants and home-health aides in northern California. This has not been easy. Women in blue collar jobs—textile operators in the South, for instance—struggled for ten years to have their union recognized, because employers expected them to be tractable and accommodating. In garment-manufacturing sweatshops scattered throughout New York and Los Angeles, women's unionization has been hindered by the fear that their jobs will be moved abroad.[19]

---

16. See "The Nature of the Beast: Sexual Harassment," by Anita Hill, p. 296; the Breaking Barriers section of "Transforming Traditions and Breaking Barriers: Six Personal Testimonies," op. cit., and "Redefining the Warrior Mentality: Women in the Military," by Claudia J. Kennedy, p. 409.—Ed.

17. See "Standing By: Women in Broadcast Media," by Carol Jenkins, p. 418, and Appel-Bronstein, op. cit.—Ed.

18. See "Climbing the Ivory Walls: Women in Academia," by Jane Roland Martin, p. 401.—Ed.

19. See Bravo, op. cit., and Neuwirth, op. cit. For data on the increasing use of cheap (or free) prison labor, see "Alive Behind the Labels: Women in Prison," by Kathy Boudin and Roslyn D. Smith, p. 244.—Ed.

How then should we think about the future? Two competing positions, both equally feminist, vie for attention.

The first is to continue to make heroic efforts to get women out of those jobs and into "men's" jobs. By means of affirmative action, and with stringent judicial enforcement, men can be induced to open privileged jobs to women, and women can be encouraged to become electricians, plumbers, and carpenters. This strategy confronts both women and men with the need for fundamental changes in how they perceive themselves and each other, and with the demand for major transformations in how families are formed, supported, and nurtured. In a world of high unemployment, uncertain jobs, and global marketing, this strategy creates inevitable tensions over who is entitled to which jobs and at what price. It holds a promise of new opportunities for women, and a capacity for economic independence not available in the pink collar ghetto.

But caregiving is a valuable function, and a second position holds that the world would be a poorer place if we tempted women away from jobs as caregivers. Advocates of this position have sought incentives to make such jobs attractive to men as well as women: better pay, more benefits (including health insurance and pensions), greater job security, more flexible working hours, more humane working conditions. For a while, the comparable-worth approach sought to achieve pay equity, by demanding equal pay for jobs that demanded comparable skill, effort, responsibility, and education, regardless of whether the jobs were the same. But efforts to assess jobs carry with them the burdens of long-standing ideological mindsets. When Minnesota's firemen discovered that they had been evaluated at the same level as nurses, they protested.[20] Yet pay alone is not enough. Though the pay of registered nurses nearly doubled during the 1990s, the hard work, enormous responsibility, and lack of respect accorded nurses has discouraged an influx of new workers into the field. The shortage continues, and hospitals are making up the difference by placing more responsibility on practical nurses and health aides, who have taken up the slack.[21]

---

20. *Wage Justice: Comparable Worth and the Paradox of Technocratic Reform*, by Sara M. Evans and Barbara J. Nelson (Chicago, Illinois: University of Chicago Press, 1989).

21. See the nurses section of "Transforming Traditions and Breaking Barriers: Six Personal Testimonies," op. cit.—Ed.

Just as problems associated with the creation of a pink collar ghetto and its perpetuation lie in deeply rooted gendered attitudes, so its solution will emerge from a shift in how we imagine gender. That's a slow process. But continuing pressures on women already in the workforce, plus the demands of families for attention,[22] suggest the need to forge a new compromise—one that will encourage employers in the pink collar ghetto to raise wages and re-evaluate the demands of workers, even as women seek jobs in a greater variety of occupations so far closed to them.

ALICE KESSLER-HARRIS is the R. Gordon Hoxie Professor of American History at Columbia University, where she also teaches in the Institute for Research on Women and Gender. Her books include *In Pursuit of Equity: Women, Men, and the Quest for Economic Citizenship in Twentieth-Century America* (Oxford University Press, 2001), *Out to Work: A History of Wage-Earning Women in the United States* (see Suggested Further Reading, below), *A Woman's Wage: Historical Meanings and Social Consequences* (University Press of Kentucky, 1994), and *Women Have Always Worked: A Historical Overview* (The Feminist Press at CUNY, 1981). In collaboration with others, she has edited *Protecting Women: Labor Legislation in Europe, Australia, and the United States, 1880–1920* (University of Illinois Press, 1995), *U.S. History as Women's History* (University of North Carolina Press, 1995), and *Perspectives on American Labor History: The Problem of Synthesis* (Northern Illinois University Press, 1990).

Suggested Further Reading

Costello, Cynthia B., Shari Miles, and Anne J. Stone, eds., *The American Woman, 1999–2000.* New York: W. W. Norton and Company, 1998.

Ehrenreich, Barbara. *Nickel and Dimed: On Not Getting By in America.* New York: Metropolitan Books, 2001.

Kapp Howe, Louise. *Pink Collar Workers: Inside the World of Women's Work.* New York: Avon, 1977.

---

22. See "Parenting: A New Social Contract," by Suzanne Braun Levine, p. 85, and Drusine, op. cit.—Ed.

Kessler-Harris, Alice. *Out to Work: A History of Wage-Earning Women in the United States.* New York: Oxford, 1982.

Mishel, Lawrence, Jared Bernstein, and John Schmitt, *The State of Working America, 2000–2001.* Ithaca, New York: Cornell ILR Press, 2001.

Rural Women: Sustaining Farms, Feeding People

CAROLYN SACHS

INTERNATIONALLY, women provide more than 50 percent of the labor in producing, harvesting, and processing the planet's food.[1] Nevertheless, women's contribution to agriculture is often underestimated and undervalued in the United States and elsewhere. Although women contribute substantially to feeding their own (and everyone else's) families, they frequently have limited access to land, credit, and technologies—a disadvantage regarding resources that can intensify when factoring in their race, ethnicity, class, and nationality.

Historically, agriculture in the U.S. has been organized around family farms, which, characterized by patriarchal relationships, set the context for gender relations. Women have contributed vast amounts of labor, but this has not necessarily brought control over income, ownership of land, or equal participation in decision-making.[2] Men have often owned the land, controlled farming decisions, and been recognized as farmers—while women have been seen as farm wives or helpers. An agrarian ideology has prevailed in rural areas in the U.S., which has con-

---

1. In some regions, e.g., on the African continent, women perform 60 to 80 percent of all agricultural work, 50 percent of all animal husbandry, and 100 percent of all food processing; women produce 60 percent of all food grown in Asia, and between 30 and 40 percent of all food grown in Latin America and "Western" countries. Women also own only two percent of all land, and receive one percent of all agricultural credit. See *Sisterhood Is Global: The International Women's Movement Anthology*, Robin Morgan ed. (New York: Doubleday/Anchor, 1984; updated edition The Feminist Press at CUNY, 1996).—Ed.

2. See Carolyn Sachs, *Gendered Fields: Rural Women, Agriculture, and Environment* (Boulder, Colorado: Westview Press, 1996).

tributed to women's subordination.[3] Agrarian ideologies romanticize rural life and idealize families, thus concealing women's oppression and their lack of power on family farms. But today, with changes in family farms and the world outside the farm, the grip of agrarian patriarchal authority is loosening—and shifting.

Women are becoming more involved in farming, both as independent operators of their farms and as partners with their spouses. The U.S. Department of Agriculture (USDA) reports that in 1997, women comprised 9 percent of farmers—a number that may seem low, but one representing a substantial increase since 1987, when only 6 percent of farm operators were women.[4] The number of female independent farmers increased from 131,641 in 1987 to 165,102 in 1997—at the same time the number of male farmers decreased.[5] Many female farmers are widows who continue operating the farm after their husbands die. However, others are single and farming on their own, or married but assuming the primary responsibility for running the farm. Women farmers tend to have smaller farms and specialized operations: horse farms, sheep and goats, greenhouse operations, or fruit and vegetable farms. Interestingly, when women are the principal decision-makers on their farms, they're less likely to use pesticides, chemical fertilizers, and genetically modified seeds.[6]

While some women farm on their own, the majority of U.S. women involved in farming do so with their husbands. A recent study of 2,661 women on U.S. farms found that 53 percent of farm women reported they were major operators of their farms,[7] providing a significant amount of the management and decision-making, plus labor across a wide range of tasks. They are most likely to be involved in running er-

3. Deborah Fink, *Agrarian Women: Wives and Mothers in Rural Nebraska, 1880–1940* (Buffalo, New York: State University of New York Press, 1992).

4. USDA Census of Agriculture, 1997. Washington, DC: USDA. See the USDA National Agricultural Statistics Service: *www.usda.gov/nass.*

5. USDA, 2002.

6. See "Update: Feminism and the Environment," by Paula DiPerna, p. 503.—Ed.

7. Jill Findeis, "U.S. Farm Women: Leaders in Rural Prosperity," paper presented at the Agricultural Outlook Forum, Arlington, Virginia, 2002.

rands (86 percent), book-keeping (78 percent), caring for farm animals (69 percent), and harvesting crops (59 percent). At least a third perform other tasks—plowing, planting, and doing field work without machinery—though they're least likely to be involved in applying fertilizer or pesticides. Our 2002 study[8] shows that the majority of women on farms participate in major decisions relating to the farm's operation: 73 percent are involved in decisions about buying or selling land, 58 percent in deciding whether to buy major farm equipment, and 53 percent in deciding whether to produce a new product or try a new production technology.

However, despite women's increasing involvement on family farms, all is not rosy in the countryside. With prices of agricultural commodities stagnant and costs of production increasing, farms are struggling to survive—and many are going under. In this process, farms are increasing in size and becoming more specialized, with production decisions shifting from farm families to large-scale, corporate agribusiness firms. The smaller farms that remain in operation have been forced to find creative ways to survive—the most common strategy being reliance on off-farm jobs for additional income. In fact, the majority of women living on farms in 2000 (52 percent) had off-farm jobs. Women's off-farm income provides reliable income for the household; in addition, many women report that a major reason for working off the farm is to obtain health insurance for their families.[9]

But lack of health insurance is only one risk faced by farmers. Farming is risky business, due to fluctuations in prices, weather, government policies, and, of course, the increasing power and concentration of the global agrifood system. In this risky business, women historically have contributed to farm and household survival through different means. Until recently, women's gardens and livestock production provided a significant amount of the food and subsistence needs of their house-

---

8. Carolyn Sachs, Atsuko Nonoyama, and Amy Trauger, "Women's Involvement on Farms and the Use of Sustainable and Chemical-Intensive Practices," paper presented at the Rural Sociological Society Meeting, Chicago, Illinois, 2002.

9. See "Our Bodies, Our Future: Women's Health Activism Overview," by Judy Norsigian, et al., for The Boston Women's Health Book Collective, p. 269, and "Diagnosis and Prognosis: Women Physicians and Women's Health," by Wendy Chavkin, M.D., p. 378.—Ed.

holds.[10] Women have had major responsibility for raising, harvesting, and processing vegetables and fruits for farm families. However, their work has rarely been *limited* to subsistence production.

One clear example of how women's role in agriculture has changed over time is their involvement in poultry and egg production. During the early twentieth century, women were major producers of poultry and eggs, and until the 1940s, they raised chickens *and* marketed both chickens and eggs. They could enter the poultry and egg business with limited capital investment, credit, or the assistance of men. While their earnings from such enterprises were referred to as "pin money," their poultry operations actually often brought substantial income to farm households. In fact, during such difficult economic times as the Depression, women's "egg money" saved many farms, while commodities that men were producing provided little income.[11] After World War II, large-scale commercial egg and broiler production pushed women out of chicken production. Today, in the U.S., chickens are produced in large-scale confinement operations that contract with poultry agribusiness firms. In response to consumer concerns about antibiotics in meat and about animal welfare[12] at these poultry farms, an increasing number of people—especially women—are beginning to operate small, "free-range" chicken enterprises.

Chicken raising is not the only enterprise that has shifted from small-scale family production to vertically integrated agribusiness operations. Unfortunately, as food and agricultural production increasingly shift to global systems that rely on large-scale, nonfamily-managed farms, women do not necessarily benefit. Control of agriculture and food production is being increasingly consolidated by a few multinational corporations, such as ConAgra and Monsanto. Farmers are caught in the middle, faced with selling their products to fewer companies *and* often buying seeds, chemicals, and other inputs from the same companies. In

10. For more information about agribusiness pressure on poorer farmers, especially in the global South, to shift from subsistence farming to (sometimes newly introduced) cash crops, see *Sisterhood Is Global,* op. cit.—Ed.

11. Fink, op. cit.

12. See "Bitch, Chick, Cow: Women's and (Other) Animals' Rights," by Carol J. Adams, p. 494.—Ed.

some commodities, especially animal production, agribusiness firms have vertically integrated contract operations in which the farmer signs a contract to sell products to such a firm as IBP or Cargill.[13] The processor specifies the conditions of production, the farmer takes the risk, and control of the farm operation shifts from the farmer to the company. The majority of chickens in the U.S. are produced under contract, and hog production is quickly following suit; in 1998, the USDA estimated that 35 percent of all agricultural products were produced under contract. These contracts are developed under conditions where farmers have very little power and limited legal protection: both women and men on farms lose control over food-production decisions. Although family farms were formerly characterized by patriarchal authority— such that women had limited power in farm households—women have not *gained* power as the control over the food system by these new agri-food industries increases. Women seldom gain power when farms expand—and few women hold positions of power in agrifood industries. Furthermore, large-scale agricultural production and processing exacerbates class, ethnic, and racial differences in rural areas, through reliance on cheap labor, often performed by racial and ethnic minorities.

In addition to issues of labor and control, the expanding global food system is characterized by environmental problems resulting from large-scale, chemical-intensive agriculture. Soil erosion, pesticide run-off, water contamination, and declining biodiversity threaten the long-term productivity of our soils as well as the health of people in both rural and urban areas.[14]

In response to environmental problems and lack of control over the food system, the sustainable agricultural movement has emerged to push for an agricultural system that protects the environment, is economically profitable for farmers, and is socially just. Women have been involved in efforts for more local control over the food system and for

---

13. IBP (Iowa Beef Packers, Inc.), originally founded in Iowa in 1961, became part of the giant corporation Tyson Foods in 2001; IBP International is the largest U.S. exporter of red meat and allied products to the rest of the world. Cargill is another gigantic agribusiness corporation, producing and marketing a range of commodities from cereals, beverages, and candies to dairy foods, meat and poultry products, and pharmaceuticals.—Ed.

14. See DiPerna and Norsigian essays, op. cit.—Ed.

limited use of pesticides and genetically modified seeds, as well as for better treatment of animals on farms.[15] Many women have been involved, at the grassroots level and on their farms, as leaders of the sustainable agricultural movement. Our study[16] found that farms where women were the principal operators were less likely than other farms to use pesticides, chemical fertilizers, and genetically modified seeds. The sustainable agricultural movement also emphasizes the connection between farmers and consumers, and attempts to create access to locally produced food. Compared to conventional agriculture, women are more involved in these local, environmentally friendly, production systems.[17] Men and women often work together to create farmers' markets, organic farms and cooperatives, and community supported agriculture. For example, women have been key participants in the creation of community-supported agriculture (CSA), an alternative to the global agrifood system that attempts to provide local alternatives that simultaneously support farmers and provide high-quality food. CSAs are partnerships between a farm and a community of supporters; they provide a direct connection between the production and consumption of food. Members pay a fee to join a CSA, and the farmer provides the members with food on a weekly basis. Thus, the farmer is supported in raising crops and animals, and the members have access to high-quality, locally grown food throughout the season; some CSAs also provide memberships and food for poor families in their communities. Women have been key players in CSAs, both as farmers and consumers. While the number of CSAs grew substantially during the 1990s, the majority of farmers continue to produce for the global system, and the majority of consumers eat food that is not produced locally.

Consequently, in addition to pushing for alternatives, women in rural areas are also organizing to maintain their farm operations and to have an impact on farm policy. Historically, men have dominated such major agricultural organizations as commodity associations and the Farm

---

15. See Adams, op. cit.—Ed.

16. Sachs, et al., op. cit.—Ed.

17. Amy Trauger, *Getting Back to Our Roots: Work, Space, and Representation: Women Farmers and Sustainable Agriculture*. Master's Thesis (University Park, Pennsylvania: Penn State University, 2001).

Bureau, though the latter now has a women's committee that encourages women to serve in leadership positions. More progressive farm associations—for example, the Grange and the National Farmers' Union—long ago integrated women into their organizations. Such commodity groups as the National Cattleman's Association, the National Pork Producers Association, and the Wheat Producers Organization all at one time had "auxiliaries" for women. But the names (and goals) of these auxiliaries—the Cowbelles, the Porkettes, the Wheathearts—hardly emphasized women's power. In the 1990s, many of the national auxiliaries were folded into the commodity associations. Nevertheless, in some areas these organizations still thrive. American National Cattlewomen support the cattle industry and provide education about beef through promoting beef to consumers. In some states, women involved in the cattle industry belong to local and state Cowbelle organizations; for example, in 2002 there were 12 local chapters of Cowbelles in Arizona and 24 in New Mexico. In Kansas, the Wheathearts promote awareness and usage of wheat and wheat products, and encourage farm safety and other educational programs that enhance the quality of rural life. Few of these women's organizations take stands to promote women's rights. Rather, their primary work is to save family farms, provide education about agriculture, and promote commodities. Still, although these organizations don't explicitly work to promote feminist issues, they often provide support networks for women.

Other organizations explicitly recognize the centrality of women on farms and attempt to increase their visibility and improve their lives. The Women's Agricultural Network in Vermont provides a series of educational programs and technical assistance aimed at increasing the number of women owning and operating profitable farms and agriculture-related businesses.[18] The Farm Women's Network of West Central Minnesota provides explicit support networks for women and helps

---

18. See the website of the Women's Agricultural Network (*www.uvm.edu/~wagn/*); see also the websites of American Agri-Women (*www.americanagriwomen.com*), and the Association of Women in Agriculture (*www.sit.wisc.edu/~awa/*). For resources and annotated hyperlinks to smaller, local, and sometimes openly feminist groups (such as "Wild Wolf Women of the Web"), also see the website of Rural Women Online: *www.ruralwomyn.net/us.html.*—Ed.

them deal with problems on their farms ranging from financial crises to domestic violence.[19]

While most of these organizations attempt to support farm women, many U.S. women involved in agriculture—especially women of racial and ethnic minorities—have limited access to land or other resources. Many work as agricultural laborers or have left agriculture because their land has been appropriated. However, some women have led organizations to provide access to land for African American, Latino, or Native American women and men. One example is the Land Recovery Project on the White Earth Indian Reservation in Northern Minnesota. Winona LaDuke has been instrumental in organizing this project to recover land, practice land stewardship, encourage community development, and strengthen spiritual and cultural heritage.[20] The project offers Native produced goods—including wild rice, maple products, native coffee, hominy corn, and quilts—with the goal of providing nutritious food to elders and young people on the reservation and also selling to the organic and gourmet market in order to support families on the reservation. White Earth also has a Young Women's Leadership project that promotes self-esteem, provides opportunities to learn cultural survival tools from elders, and teaches young women to survive in both worlds, as well as how to combat violence against women at global and local levels.[21]

At the global level, the Third World Congress of Rural Women met

---

19. Despite the persistent stereotype about domestic violence being a phenomenon primarily found in poor, urban areas, as early as the 1970s scholars discovered that the greatest concentration of U.S. domestic violence and abuse was in the "buckle of the Bible Belt," isolated Midwest and Southern farming community states. See *Family Violence*, by Richard Gelles (Thousand Oaks, California: Sage Publications, 1979); *The Violent Home: A Study of Physical Aggression Between Husbands and Wives*, by Richard Gelles (Sage, 1972); and *Behind Closed Doors: Violence in the American Family*, by Murray Straus and Richard Gelles (Garden City, New Jersey: Doubleday, 1981). See also *Rural Women Battering and the Justice System: An Ethnography*, by Neil Websdale (Sage, 1998).—Ed.

20. See *Last Standing Woman*, by Winona LaDuke (Stillwater, Minnesota: Voyager Press, 1997).

21. See "Native Americans: Restoring the Power of Thought Woman," by Clara Sue Kidwell, p. 165.—Ed.

in October 2002, focusing on structural problems that affect rural women's lives. Approximately 1,500 women from five continents attended the meeting to address ways of increasing rural women's participation in policy-making, and ways to improve conditions in poorer countries where women are feeding households and producing food under increasing poverty with limited access to technology, credit, or land.[22]

The future of our global, national, and local food systems is unclear. At the same time that the global agrifood system is thriving, women in the U.S. and internationally are working to create safer food supplies and more environmentally sustainable, socially just, agricultural production systems. Clearly, what happens on farms here, in the United States, is tied to policies at the global level. Consequently, U.S. women, with women from all regions of the world, will continue to organize, pushing for changes that will insure their sisters in poorer countries have access to land as well as the capacity to feed themselves and their children. Such efforts—like those of small farmers to sustain their farms, protect the environment, and challenge the global agrifood system—all point to the centrality of activism by rural and farm women in the United States.

CAROLYN SACHS is professor of rural sociology and women's studies at Penn State University, where she is also director of women's studies. Her research focuses on women, agriculture, environment, and sustainable agriculture. Her books include *The Invisible Farmers: Women in Agricultural Production* (Lanham, Maryland: Rowan & Allenheld Publishers, 1983), *Women Working in the Environment: Resourceful Natures* (London and Philadelphia: Taylor & Francis, Inc., 1997), and *Gendered Fields: Rural Women, Agriculture, and Environment* (Boulder, Colorado: Westview Press, 1996). She has also worked on international issues related to women in agriculture in Bangladesh, Zimbabwe, Swaziland,

---

22. World Rural Women's Day is October 15, annually. See the website of World Rural Women *(www.-rural-womens-day.org)*. For more on the intersecting issues of rural women, agriculture, sustainability of resources, health, environment, and the global Women's Movement, see the website of the Women's Environment and Development Organization (WEDO): *www.wedo.org.*—Ed.

Kenya, and Peru. Her current research involves a national study of farm women in the United States.

Suggested Further Reading

Hassanein, Neva. *Changing the Way America Farms: Knowledge and Community in the Sustainable Agriculture Movement*. Lincoln, Nebraska: University of Nebraska Press, 1999.

Rosenfeld, Rachel. *Farm Women: Work, Farm, and Family in the United States*. Chapel Hill, North Carolina: University of North Carolina Press, 1985.

Shiva, Vandana. *Stolen Harvest: The Hijacking of the Global Food Supply*. Cambridge, Massachusetts: South End Press, 2000.

Shortall, Sally. *Women and Farming: Property and Power*. New York: St. Martin's Press, 1999.

Whatmore, Sarah. *Farming Women: Gender, Work, and Family Enterprise*. London: Macmillan, 1991.

Diagnosis and Prognosis: Women Physicians and Women's Health

WENDY CHAVKIN, M.D., M.P.H.

I HAD NEVER GIVEN a thought to medical school until I was almost finished with college. Two factors shifted my attention toward medicine. The major factor was involvement with the women's health movement of the early 1970s,[1] particularly the focus on contraception and abortion. Control of one's reproductive life seemed so pivotal for every woman, and the constraints so outraged me that I began to think becoming an obstetrician-gynecologist would be a useful political contribution. The second motivator was, frankly, that I liked the thought of doing something women weren't expected to do.

Thirty years have passed. Contraception and abortion rights are still critical flashpoints around the world, including here in the United States. It is, however, pretty mainstream to be an American woman in medicine, or—let me be more precise—to be a white, middle-class woman in *certain* fields of medicine.

There have been dramatic changes in the gender composition of U.S. medical students over these past three decades. At the time I got my wild idea, in the early '70s, women constituted about 10 percent of the medical-student body; by the time I graduated, more than 25 percent; nowadays, almost half: 48 percent. Whereas 80 percent of female medical students were white in my day, that majority has declined to less

---

1. See "Our Bodies, Our Future: Women's Health Activism Overview," by Judy Norsigian, et al., for the Boston Women's Health Book Collective, p. 269.—Ed.

than two thirds (61 percent in 2001). This decline in European American medical students has not come about because of an increase in African American or Latina students—whose proportions have unfortunately remained at low plateaus over these years. It is due, rather, to an influx of Asian American and Pacific Islander students into medicine (from 4 percent in 1978 up to 20 percent in 2001).[2]

While I may have experienced my own personal decision as unusual, I was part of a larger trend. Spurred by the Civil Rights Movement, the Women's Movement, and subsequent federal legislation barring discrimination in education and employment on account of race or sex,[3] medical schools increased both female and minority enrollment. This change regarding inclusion of minorities was short-lived as the anti-affirmative action backlash of the '70s slowed black and Hispanic enrollment while medical schools continued to welcome white and Asian American women. From the mid-1970s to 1990, the African American and Latino populations in the U.S. grew at a faster pace than did proportional medical-school enrollment, resulting in these groups being *more* underrepresented in 1990 than in 1975. In the 1990s, the only groups to increase were Asian American men and Asian American women.

One of the major arguments made on behalf of affirmative action has been that of equity—in this case, equal opportunity to become a member of a gratifying, respected, well-paid profession. Another justification for diversity in medicine has been to ensure that *all* the U.S. public receives care—as it has been documented that minority-group doctors are more likely to work in minority neighborhoods. A California study showed that black and Hispanic physicians were more likely than white and Asian physicians to practice in underserved areas, care for poor patients, and care for patients of their own racial/ethnic background.[4]

---

2. See Association of American Medical Colleges data: *www.aamc.org*. Their data's terminology used "white" and "Asian and Pacific Islander," but the latter category was listed as distinct from the category "Foreign"—thus the use here of "Asian American and Pacific Islander."

3. See "Women and Law: The Power to Change," by Catharine A. MacKinnon, p. 447.—Ed.

4. Komaromy, M., Grumbach, K., Drake, M., et al., "The Role of Black and Hispanic Physicians in Providing Health Care for Underserved Populations," *New England Journal of Medicine*, 1996; 334: 1305–1310.

Since serious disparities in health status between racial/ethnic groups of women continue to plague the nation, effective care for those needing it remains critically important.[5]

Geographical distribution is one measure of the population's access to care; another is specialty distribution. Here, we continue to see stark patterns by gender, even as we've seen shifts over the past 30 years. Women still gravitate toward the primary-care fields, comprising almost half of all residents in both internal medicine and family practice, and about two thirds of all pediatric residents. Women are still very much in the minority in the surgical specialties, making up about 20 percent of all general surgery residents and even less for such surgical subspecialties as thoracic surgery and neurological surgery. The lone exception indicates that I was not unique in my choice, because women are now the majority in obstetrics and gynecology residency programs and it is one of their top choices of all residencies. Women also make up almost half of preventive medicine and psychiatry trainees and are highly represented in pathology, dermatology, allergy-immunology, and medical genetics as well—but, contrary to rumor, we make up only about a quarter of radiology or anesthesiology residents.

Women continue to be underrepresented in academic medicine altogether,[6] as well as in the higher ranks and leadership positions.[7] The salary gap between female and male physicians in clinical practice is wider than between women and men workers in general in the U.S.: women physicians average 60 percent of male physicians' earnings,[8] whereas the average employed woman earns about 75 percent of what her male counterpart earns.[9] Some of this discrepancy is attributed to

---

5. Satcher, D. "American Women and Health Disparities," *Journal of the American Medical Women's Association (JAMWA)*. 2001; 56(4): 131–132.

6. See "Climbing the Ivory Walls: Women in Academia," by Jane Roland Martin, p. 401, and "Changing a Masculinist Culture: Women in Science, Engineering, and Technology," by Donna M. Hughes, p. 393.—Ed.

7. Bickel, J. "Women in Academic Medicine," *JAMWA*. 2000; 55(1): 10–12.

8. Scherzer, E., Freedman, J. "Physician Unions: Organizing Women in the Year 2000," *JAMWA*. 2000; 55(1): 16–19.

9. U.S. Census Bureau. "Money Income in the United States: 2000." September 2001.

pregnancy and to prevailing gender divisions regarding childrearing and household responsibilities. Yet certain developments in medicine during the same decades witnessing the entry of women may both exacerbate these differentials and offer possibilities for change.

The most dramatic of these developments is the growth in health care costs and the resulting shift in emphasis to outpatient care and managed care, with the concomitant rise in salaried physicians. Women are more likely to be salaried than men because they are younger, newer entrants to the health care field. Additionally, they are more likely to provide primary care rather than specialty care; and they may hope that salaried arrangements offer the prospect of greater flexibility, which in turn might better enable them to simultaneously handle family responsibilities, the bulk of which still fall to women. Thus, we are currently in the middle of a transformation from the prestige and autonomy associated with the *private-practice model* of medicine into *salaried circumstances* typical of other fields. This transformation coincides with the entry of women, as well as with dramatic rises in the cost of medical care, consequent declines in health-insurance coverage, and a host of cost-containment measures.

While in the short term, women physicians have not affected the financial underpinnings of the U.S. medical enterprise, they and women's health activists have had an impact on the *content* of clinical medicine and research. During these same past three decades, the concept of women's health emerged with a concurrent awareness of the paucity of gender-specific research.[10] This lack of research reflected both protectionism and the failure to consider gender as a significant determinant of health. The protectionist impulse had some positive, understandable beginnings: regulation to protect human-research subjects originated in response to revelations of previous abuse—from Nazi-conducted experiments on concentration-camp inmates to the decades-long observational study of untreated syphilis in African American men in Tuskegee, which continued even after the discovery of antibiotics. Extension of this protective concern to pregnant women followed discovery of the impact of thalidomide and diethylstilbestrol on children born after in-utero exposure as a result of their mothers' treatment. Although

---

10. See Norsigian, op. cit., and the Introduction, p. *xv*.—Ed.

these latter two instances reflected clinical practice and not research, the regulatory response was to exclude both pregnant women and women of childbearing potential from early phases of drug trials.[11]

Women's health advocates, however, called for more research on women's health, and decried the discriminatory downside of protectionism. They argued that women had to be included in clinical trials in order for scientists to learn whether the course of disease and treatment success varied by gender. They stressed that failure to include pregnant women in clinical trials paradoxically left physicians in ignorance as to whether a medication had adverse consequences for fetal development or whether pregnancy-induced physiologic changes might necessitate different dosages. Finally, they argued that women were competent, when properly informed, to weigh risks and benefits and make complex decisions about participating in clinical research. The 1980s then witnessed a host of federal and professional organizational statements calling for more research on women's health; the establishment of the National Institutes of Health Office of Research on Women's Health in 1990, as well as subsequent requirements that researchers demonstrate adequate inclusion of women and racial/ethnic minorities in study design; and the Food and Drug Administration's revision of its earlier restrictions on the inclusion of fertile women in early phases of clinical trials.

As I wrote above, a major reason I wanted to become a doctor was so that I could provide abortions, since control of their own fertility seemed to me a prerequisite for women to have expanded opportunities. Those of us who entered medicine in order to assist women to control their reproductive lives were walking into a firestorm. Our ability to provide such care to individual patients has been constrained by one after another political intrusion into clinical practice.[12]

After the legalization of abortion in 1973, feminists advocated for a model of abortion services that stressed counseling and a supportive environment, thought best achieved in a free-standing clinic. As the backlash against abortion set in rapidly after *Roe*, hospitals and residency

---

11. Chavkin, W. "Women and Clinical Research," *JAMWA*. 1994; 49(4): 99–100.

12. See "Unfinished Agenda: Reproductive Rights," by Faye Wattleton, p. 17, and Norsigian, op. cit.—Ed.

training programs were able to sidestep the controversy by acceding to this model. Ironically, abortion then remained marginalized within mainstream medicine and medical training, despite the safety, efficiency, and low costs of the free-standing abortion clinic providing a successful model for the transition to outpatient surgical care in *other* fields, described above.

Studies in the 1980s revealed that the majority of obstetrics and gynecology residents were not being trained to provide abortions.[13] In the mid-1970s, about a quarter of ob-gyn residencies mandated training in first-trimester procedures and two thirds made it optional. These numbers *halved* by the early 1990s, despite evidence from the Centers for Disease Control that safety increased directly with operator experience, and that certain techniques requiring specific training were safer than others. In the 1990s, a group of medical students organized as Medical Students for Choice (MSFC), to change this. Through peer education and pressure on medical schools, residency programs, and medical associations, plus a host of sophisticated activities, they have had an impressive impact. They have worked with students at many medical schools to revise curricula to include abortion, and have developed a Reproductive Health Externship Program and resource materials.[14] Also in the 1990s, a group of physicians—many of them older men who had been among the earliest abortion providers—organized as Physicians for Reproductive Choice and Health (PRCH). This group, today comprising about 5,000 members, is involved with trying to reintegrate training about all aspects of reproductive health into the medical school and residency curricula, and with providing scientific expertise to policymakers and the press. PRCH maintains seats on its board of directors specifically for MSFC, and is also committed to documenting the history of abortion provision prior to *Roe*.[15]

The schism between women's impact on health care content and financing in the context of the political battles over reproductive auton-

---

13. Westhoff, C. "Abortion Training in Residency Programs," *JAMWA*. 1994; 49(5): 150–152.

14. See their website: *www.ms4c.org*.

15. See their website: *www.prch.org*.

omy is exemplified by the long-term struggle to get health insurance to cover contraception. While most employment-related insurance policies in the United States cover prescription drugs and outpatient medical care, the majority do *not* cover contraceptive drugs and devices, nor do they cover the care to provide these. Efforts had been well under way to remedy this when Viagra, a medication to treat erectile dysfunction, was introduced to the U.S. market in 1998. Within two months, more than half of prescriptions for Viagra had received insurance coverage. This glaring inequity further fueled efforts to mandate contraceptive coverage legislatively on both the state and federal levels, and legally on the grounds of sex discrimination. But while significant partial victories have been achieved, at this writing in mid-2002, the Equity in Prescription Insurance and Contraceptive Coverage Act has not yet been passed.[16]

During the 1990s, many health care-providing institutions merged, in order to solidify their relative market positions. Religious and secular institutions have merged—with the religious proscriptions on reproductive health care services (as well as on certain end-of-life care options) trumping the secular.[17] The forbidden services extend beyond abortion to contraception—including provision of emergency contraception to women who have been raped—and sterilization, infertility, and participation in certain clinical research.[18] This has led to significant loss of access to such care in many communities and to drastic constraints on physicians' abilities to practice medicine according to scientific standards. A national initiative known as Merger Watch has developed to track these consolidations and to assist local providers and communities in resisting the constriction of service.

In sum, the last three decades of the twentieth century in the United States witnessed dramatic changes regarding the physician workforce. European American and Asian American women gained entry in significant numbers, while African American and Hispanic women and men

16. See *www.covermypills.org*.

17. See "Combating the Religious Right," by Cecile Richards, p. 464, and "Dancing Against the Vatican," by Frances Kissling, p. 474.—Ed.

18. See the website of Merger Watch, the national initiative to track this trend: *www.mergerwatch.org*.

remained marginalized. Women assumed roles as primary-care practitioners and in certain specialties but, with the exception of obstetrics and gynecology, didn't become surgeons. Nor did women ascend the ladder of academic medicine, and as academics and clinicians women are paid poorly relative to male physicians. Medicine began the transformation from the paradigm of the autonomous private practitioner to that of the salaried employee. It remains to be seen whether this coincides with lowering of status or with successful demands for improved working conditions (including those conducive to childrearing). The construct of women's health became recognized, as did the importance of related research and women's capacity for deciding on participation. However, the terrain of reproductive health remains embattled, with a cascade of restrictions on physicians' abilities to be adequately trained and to practice scientifically based reproductive medicine. These restrictions, as well as those resulting from health care system mergers and insurance inequities, continue to impede access to reproductive health care for U.S. women. There remain deep structural problems in the United States, leading to disparities in health between groups, gender and racial/ethnic inequities for both patients and providers, and limitations and deformation of the health care system itself.

Much has changed—and much has changed not nearly enough.

WENDY CHAVKIN, M.D., M.P.H. is professor of Clinical Public Health and Obstetrics and Gynecology at Columbia University's Mailman School of Public Health and College of Physicians and Surgeons. From 1994 to 2002, she was editor in chief of *The Journal of the American Medical Women's Association*, and is an associate contributing editor for women's health for *The American Journal of Public Health*. She chairs the board of directors of Physicians for Reproductive Choice and Health and has written extensively about women's reproductive health issues for more than two decades. Her research has focused on policy and treatment issues regarding perinatal transmission of HIV and drug use; abortion in medical education; surveillance, planning, and assessment of services for maternal and child health; and, most recently, the consequences of welfare reform for the health of women and children. She wishes to "acknowledge gratefully the thoughtful assistance of Michelle Mulbauer with research and manuscript preparation."

Suggested Further Reading

Addressing Health Disparities: The National Institutes of Health (NIH) Program of Action: *http://healthdisparities.nih.gov.*

More, Ellen S. *Restoring the Balance: Women Physicians and the Profession of Medicine, 1850–1995.* Cambridge, Massachusetts: Harvard University Press, 2001.

Leavitt, J., ed. *Women and Health in America: Historical Readings.* Madison, Wisconsin: University of Wisconsin Press, 1999.

Joffe, C. *Doctors of Conscience: The Struggle to Provide Abortion Before and After Roe v. Wade.* Boston: Beacon Press, 1996.

Journal of the American Medical Women's Association (www.jamwa.org).

Up the Down Labyrinth: Ins and Outs of Women's Corporate and Campus Careers

ELLEN APPEL-BRONSTEIN

WHEN I WAS AN undergraduate majoring in chemistry, my favorite cartoon showed one chemist asking another, "Suppose you do invent powdered water, what will you mix it with?" Like powdered water, career change is a hard concept to grasp. Recently I heard a physics teacher announce that he'd changed careers: he's now teaching a different kind of physics. On the other hand, when a friend went from being a professor of Japanese to being a receptionist in an accountant's office (to "buy" time for her family and her art), she merely changed *jobs*.

"Career" is a white-collar, upward-mobility word. I define a career as a series of job changes within the same profession, each job a stepping-stone to the next, with net gain in rank, prestige, power, experience, or income. Applying this definition to my circle of friends, only one or two women—but most of the men—have had "careers." After thirty years of hard work, almost all the men have achieved some pinnacle of recognition (vice presidents, CEOs, college professors, senior managers) and substantial financial success, which, at a minimum, is sufficient to fund a comfortable retirement. Most of my women friends, however, have simply had a series of jobs—sometimes in different professions—which have taken them sideways or even down as often as up, and left them despairing of any hope of retirement, comfortable or otherwise.

Unlike powdered water, data on career change—albeit limited and indirect—can be found. It can be encapsulated in two facts. First, women went from 33.9 percent of all managerial and professional jobs in 1983 to 49.5 percent in 2000. Second, the number of women in the ranks of institutional leadership is minuscule: in 2000, only two CEOs of Fortune 500 companies were women (though that was a 100 percent increase over 1999) and only 12.5 percent of all corporate officers were female.[1]

In short, the growing numbers of women getting in on the ground floor can't seem to board an elevator that goes all the way to the top. Instead, they reel through a maze bounded by sticky floors, glass ceilings, and the glass walls of such female job ghettos as "human resources" and "public relations."

No field is an exception. Pipelines leak everywhere:[2] government, labor unions, law, medicine, finance, management, the military, academia. Except where they hemorrhage: science, engineering, manufacturing, and production.[3] Women received 31 percent of Ph.D.s awarded in chemistry in 1998, yet by 2000, only 15 percent of tenure-track faculty positions in chemistry were held by women at Ph.D.-granting institutions.[4] Women chemists fare no better in industry: a survey of forty-eight top chemical companies found "corporate management teams that look like the industry's version of a football team—all men. Women occupy 7.3 percent of the 709 top management positions. At the companies where women are on the management team, they are found primarily in legal, human resources, public affairs, and other administrative positions."[5]

---

1. Catalyst Census of Women Corporate Officers and Top Earners of the Fortune 500 (2000).

2. See, for example, "Standing By: Women in Broadcasting," by Carol Jenkins, p. 418; and "Redefining the Warrior Mentality: Women in the Military," by Claudia Kennedy, p. 409.—Ed.

3. See "Changing a Masculinist Culture: Women in Science, Engineering, and Technology," by Donna M. Hughes, p. 393.—Ed.

4. *Chemical & Engineering News, Perspective*, September 25, 2000, Volume 78, Number 39, "Women Chemists Still Rare in Academia: Survey of Top 50 universities finds only 10% of tenure-track positions are held by women." September 21, 1998, Volume 76, Number 38, "Challenges Await Women Chemists in the New Millennium: A 'web of hidden processes' leads to nontrivial barriers to workplace success," by Madeleine Jacobs.

5. *Chemical & Engineering News, Perspective*, 8 May 2000, Vol. 78, N. 19, "Women in Industry Still Hit Glass Ceiling," by Madeleine Jacobs and William Storck.

Enough already. Clearly these data show that intelligent, motivated, highly qualified women somehow do not arrive at the destinations for which they're trained. Where *do* they go? Down and out.

The *downs*, hoping to find lower stress and greater flexibility, move to lesser positions with the same employer, or to part-time positions instead of full-time, or to smaller or less prestigious employers. The *outs* start their own businesses.[6] Their major reason for leaving the corporate fold, according to one survey, is also a desire for more flexibility. But their other key reasons read like a litany of glass-ceiling concussions: they weren't recognized or valued, weren't taken seriously, or felt isolated as one of a few women or minorities.[7]

Case in point: Mary Schiavo, former Inspector General of the Department of Transportation. I first learned of Schiavo's existence when she appeared amidst the talking heads on TV after September 11, 2001. She was saying, in effect, *I told you so*. She had indeed been sounding alarums on airline security—on precisely the deficiencies the hijackers had exploited—as far back as the early 1990s. Yet despite her credentials (lawyer *and* pilot) and position as Inspector General (whose job it is to surface unpleasant truths political appointees can't and career bureaucrats won't), her recommendations were repeatedly ignored by agency officials.[8] Would she have been ignored if she were a man? Schiavo resigned her position in protest in 1996, and founded her own consulting firm—which makes her one among a staggering number of *outs*.[9] More than 9 million women-owned businesses were operating in 1999, up from 0.7 million in 1977 and 4.1 million in 1987.[10] The growth rate of

---

6. See "Owning the Future: Women Entrepreneurs," by Sara K. Gould, p. 456.—Ed.

7. *Women Entrepreneurs: Why Companies Lose Female Talent and What They Can Do About It*, Catalyst, 1998.

8. In 2002, the "woman whistleblower" became a recognized phenomenon in the wake of corporate financial scandals at such major corporations as Enron and WorldCom—when mid- and executive-level women (so-called insiders with outsider values) tried to warn their bosses of illegal practices and malfeasance, but were ignored or silenced.—Ed.

9. *Flying Blind, Flying Safe*, by Mary Schiavo with Sabra Chartrand (New York: Avon Books, 1997).

10. National Foundation for Women Business Owners, 1999, as quoted in *Catalyst Fact Sheet: The Glass Ceiling in 2000: Where Are Women Now? Labor Day Fact Sheet*.

such businesses outpaces the growth rate for all businesses by a factor of three to one.[11]

Clearly, women accommodate to or abandon, rather than change, workplaces inimical to them. The few who make it to the top are, as researchers Dana Britton and Christine Williams put it, "generally very similar to the men in possessing personal attributes that are highly rewarded by work organizations (e.g., few domestic responsibilities, uninterrupted career trajectories)."[12] Not only do they show little interest in creating an environment less hostile to women, they also behave, once they've "arrived," like eager first-generation immigrants repudiating their relatives. They suffer from what I call the Fiorina Effect, after Carleton S. (Carly) Fiorina, CEO of Hewlett-Packard (and one of the rare women leaders of Fortune 500 companies), who said of her own promotion, "There is not a glass ceiling. . . . My gender is interesting, but really not the subject of the story here."[13]

In defense of the Fiorinas, a girl growing up in the pre-Women's Movement U.S., dreaming beyond boys and babies—a girl who wanted, say, to be a chemist—was ostracized by other girls. She might have felt she was not a "real" girl, and would have coveted the freedom and fellowship of boys. This conditioning (female aversion, male identification) takes years to outgrow, if it *is* ever outgrown. In the late 1960s and early 1970s, as contemporary feminism was gathering steam, the best I could do was sit on the sidelines feeling conflicted, like a Christian Scientist with appendicitis. I was nearly thirty before I was able to make close friends among women. Still, I always hired and mentored women. Along the way, I learned that without a peer group you can't see the patterns in your own life.

The irony, of course, is that today's alpha females had male mentors. Fiorina's was H-P chairman Lew Platt, whose experience as a widower with two young children enabled him to "get" what Fiorina still doesn't:

---

11. National Women's Business Council, Release Number 01–03, April 2001.

12. *Gender & Society*, December 2000, "Response to Baxter and Wright," Dana M. Britton and Christine L. Williams.

13. "Hitting the Gold Ceiling: Why aren't young female entrepreneurs making it into the upper echelons of Silicon Valley wealth?" by Janelle Brown, *Salon*, *Salon.com*, 9 September 1999.

that the model of a successful career is implicitly male. As Arlie Russell Hochschild explained back in 1973, a career "subcontracts work to the family—work women perform. Without changing the structure of this career, and its imperial relation to the family, it will be impossible for mothers to move far up in careers and for fathers to share at home."[14]

Encouragingly, a survey conducted in 2000 found that "Younger men and women have more in common when it comes to job priorities than younger men do with older men. For men in their twenties and thirties, and for women in their twenties, thirties, and forties, the most important job characteristic is having a work schedule that allows them to spend time with their families."[15] This seeming re-education of men in the span of one generation is heartening.[16] It may well become the most far-reaching and enduring legacy of contemporary feminism.

ELLEN APPEL-BRONSTEIN entered MIT with 36 other women and 900 men in the class of 1967. After graduating, she successively: worked as a research chemist at DuPont while simultaneously a graduate student in physics at the University of Pennsylvania; got married; worked at American Science and Engineering, and then Arthur D. Little, doing mathematical modeling and computer programming; moved to Chicago as a "trailing spouse"; worked for Standard Oil of Indiana doing operations research and then for G. D. Searle developing medical electronics; "trailed" back to New York and analyzed clinical trials of new pharmaceuticals at Pfizer; got divorced; accepted a political appointment as Associate Commissioner for Policy Coordination (lone woman at the top) of the Food and Drug Administration during the Carter administration; remarried; had a baby; tried writing; moved—without husband and with toddler—to work at ITT as an editor; got di-

14. "Inside the Clockwork of Male Careers," by Arlie Russell Hochschild, in *Women and the Power to Change: Essays Sponsored by the Carnegie Commission*, Florence Howe, ed. (New York: McGraw Hill, 1975).

15. "Life's Work: Generational Attitudes toward Work and Life Integration," a national survey conducted by The Radcliffe Public Policy Center with Harris Interactive, Inc., 2000.

16. See "Parenting: A New Social Contract," by Suzanne Braun Levine, p. 85.—Ed.

vorced again; quit ITT to start her own writing consultancy; and finally, tired after twelve years of self-employment and single-parent isolation, became executive director of a research center at MIT, then executive director of MIT's Gender Equity Project. She feels sure that both job *and* career changes are represented here, but leaves it to the reader to decide which is which. Someday she hopes to write a novel.

Suggested Further Reading

(A number of these works are "classics." It's a measure of the persistence of the problems that they are as current now as when written.—E. A-B.)

Bailyn, Lotte. *Breaking the Mold: Women, Men and Time in the New Corporate World*. New York: Free Press, 1993.

McCracken, Douglas M. "Winning the Talent War for Women: Sometimes It Takes a Revolution." Boston: *Harvard Business Review*, November–December 2000.

Meyerson, Debra E., and Joyce K. Fletcher. "A Modest Manifesto for Shattering the Glass Ceiling." Boston: *Harvard Business Review*, January–February 2000.

Rich, Adrienne. "Toward a Woman-Centered University," "The Antifeminist Woman," and "Taking Women Students Seriously," in Rich's *On Lies, Secrets, and Silence: Selected Prose 1966–1978*. New York: W. W. Norton & Company, 1979.

Valian, Virginia. *Why So Slow? The Advancement of Women*. Cambridge, Massachusetts: MIT Press, 1998.

Changing a Masculinist Culture: Women in Science, Engineering, and Technology

DONNA M. HUGHES

As long as science and technology have existed, women have been scientists, engineers, and inventors. The resurgence of the Women's Movement in the United States during the last third of the twentieth century inspired many historians to research and write about the foremothers of science, mathematics, and technology.[1] So many had been erased and/or forgotten that most people regarded the entrance of women into these fields as a relatively new phenomenon.

As science and technology studies and industries have grown, the numbers of women participating in them has increased, though the proportion of women to men has varied. A significant influence on this proportion is the strength of the Women's Movement, since female

---

1. A sampling: Phaenarete (midwife, mathematician, and, incidentally, Socrates' mother); Hypatia of Alexandria (the most revered woman mathematician and scientist of the ancient world, 385–415 C.E.); Trotula (medical doctor and lecturer at the University of Salerno, considered to be the mother of gynecology, circa 1050); astronomer Caroline Herschel; Ellen Swallow (who founded the scientific discipline of ecology and was the first woman admitted to the Massachusetts Institute of Technology); Emily Roebling (who took over design and construction of the Brooklyn Bridge when her husband was incapacitated); Marie Curie and her daughter Irene; Grace Murray Hopper (inventor of COBOL, an early major computer language); Rosalind Franklin (molecular biologist and co-discoverer of the DNA helix), etc., etc. More comprehensive lists appear in *Taking Hold of Technology* (Washington, D.C.: American Association of University Women, 1983), and in Elise Boulding's classic work, *The Underside of History: A View of Women Through Time* (Boulder, Colorado: Westview Press, 1976).

participation in male-dominated fields reflects women's status in society as a whole. Female access to male-dominated fields depends on men's willingness to include (or exclude) women. At this writing, at the beginning of the twenty-first century, legal discrimination has been largely eliminated in education and employment, but men still construct and control the *culture* of fields of study, and the *climate* of learning and of workspaces. Women have the greatest access to male-dominated fields when we gain power to force open doors, challenge hostile behavior and discriminatory practices, and garner equal respect and rewards. Such progress for women as a group has always resulted from organized feminist activism.

Women's gains and losses in science, engineering, and technology have run parallel to the rise or fall of feminism's strength as a social force. Women were active in science and engineering in the late 1800s and early 1900s: their numbers rose with the suffrage wave of the Women's Movement. But after achieving suffrage, the movement waned, men reasserted their domination, and the proportion of women in these fields fell. Women's participation rose again during World War II, when men were called to military service—but after the men returned, women were demoted or dismissed. The proportion of women in science, engineering, and technology then remained at a low level until the resurgence of feminist activism in the late 1960s/early 1970s, when women, working in ignorance of the buried history of their foremothers, thought they were breaking new ground.[2]

Today, the participation of women in the fields of science, engineering, and technology varies widely. We've made the greatest advances in the biological sciences, where we comprise approximately half of all undergraduate students—though later, in graduate school and university positions, our representation decreases.[3] In mathematics and the physical sciences, our numbers have improved but are still well below men's. Women's participation remains lowest in engineering fields. In all fields, the number of women declines in proportion to a rise through the institutional hierarchies of academia and industry—that is, women are most

2. See "The Art of Building Feminist Institutions to Last," by Eleanor Smeal, p. 541.—Ed.

3. See "Biologically Correct," by Natalie Angier, p. 3.—Ed.

likely to be found in the lower ranks; our numbers dwindle where there is power, prestige, and decision- and policy-making.[4]

Computer science is a special case, warranting closer examination. Here the proportion of women has *declined*. Although computing has been done for decades, the *field* of computer science came into being parallel with the start of the current Women's Movement. Initially, women entered the field in almost the same numbers as men. For a while, some thought the creation of a new field—especially at a time when increasing numbers of women were entering male-dominated realms—would result in computer science being the first field where women reached parity with men. Yet the proportion of women in computer science has stagnated, and even declined.[5]

Computer and high-tech culture plays a large role in this: it dissuades girls and women from entering the field. Most computer games are male oriented and often violent, geared to attract more boys than girls. In classrooms, girls frequently give up the aggressive competition with boys to use computers. The workplace culture of the high-tech industry is also highly competitive: young men proudly work all night, subsist on pizza and soft drinks, and sleep under their desks, in a quest for riches. While some women may fit into this lifestyle, most don't. Furthermore, the high-tech world has an ultra-libertarian culture, with pornography and the sex industry playing a central role; it was the sex industry that *led* the commercial development of the Internet. Sex industry sites are actually featured as *business models* in mainstream computer magazines, and—though it isn't widely admitted—the Internet industry is financially dependent on the sex industry for revenue, especially now that the boom years of the 1990s are over. As of this writing, on-line pornography and sex shows are a multibillion-dollar industry, responsible for *approximately 70 percent of all Internet on-line content sales*. Globally, new information technologies are being used to traffick women and children

---

4. See "Climbing the Ivory Walls: Women in Academia," by Jane Roland Martin, p. 401, and "Up the Down Labyrinth: Ins and Outs of Women's Corporate and Campus Careers," by Ellen Appel-Bronstein, p. 387.—Ed.

5. The December 25, 2000 on-line issue of *The Standard* reported that women in the Internet economy earn 24 percent less than men and receive 50 percent less in bonuses than men *(www.thestandard.com)*; also see Sandy Lerner on women in computer technology, in "Transforming Traditions and Breaking Barriers," p. 325.—Ed.

for sexual exploitation.[6] Women who don't support this high-tech industry sexist culture are unwelcome. As the number of women in engineering plateaus and the number in computer science plummets, advocates for women in science and engineering wring their hands and wonder why. Yet most resist examining precisely such issues—pornography or sexist libertarian culture—that make them uncomfortable by seeming "too feminist."

In their scientific training, women are taught that good scientists remain objective, never mixing science and politics or their science will be compromised. (This appears to be less of a problem for the men, who seem to regard their attitudes and preferences as norms, not "politics.") Women have learned to preserve their detachment and distance from the politics of the *use* of scientific and technological knowledge, and this belief causes many women to fear taking a political stand on *any* issues. Moreover, at some level, women know their participation in male-dominated fields is conditional on men's approval, and this knowledge fosters a kind of self-censoring. One can tell how hostile the climate is to women by the survival strategies they adopt—for instance, not drawing attention to themselves *as* women: "I don't want to be seen as a woman. I want to be seen as a scientist (or engineer)." Such women reassure men that *they* aren't like "those *other* women" who notice discrimination or harassment. Often, they don't support other women or even associate with them, and don't risk openly supporting women's rights. In universities, they keep their distance from women's studies. They often align themselves with men against women who *do* complain about sexual harassment, pornography in labs, unequal lab space, salary discrepancies, and unequal tenure or promotion. Sadly, too few women in science and technology appreciate that the feminists from whom they disassociate themselves are the same group that enabled them to participate in those fields in the first place. Of course, there are women scientists and engineers who do speak up for themselves, and become advocates for women colleagues and students. Over the years, there have been many

---

6. See the following articles in this anthology for related details: "From Fantasy to Reality: Unmasking the Pornography Industry," by Gail Dines, p. 306; "Prostitution = Slavery," by Vednita Carter, p. 315; "Cyberfeminism: Networking the Net," by Amy Richards and Marianne Schnall, p. 517; and "Traffic at the Crossroads: Multiple Oppressions," by Kimberlé Crenshaw, p. 43.—Ed.

who filed lawsuits and helped research and write reports documenting unfair practices.

Over the past few decades, there have been numerous programs to encourage girls' and women's participation in science and engineering.[7] The government funds quite a few, possibly less from a commitment to women's participation than from concern that the lack of a scientifically and technologically qualified workforce might threaten U.S. global competitiveness. Evaluations show that these programs are in fact successful in generating and sustaining girls' and women's participation in these fields. However, probably due to conservative sources of funding for most of these programs, they do so out of context, failing to connect the progress of women in science and engineering with the success of women's rights movements—past, present, or future. Furthermore, few programs have been aimed at *institutional* or *cultural change* in male-dominated fields. The result: more girls and women interested in science, engineering, and technology, but little change in the unfriendly culture or climate of the fields themselves and the institutions that define them.

Women's studies has played an important role in trying to make science and engineering more woman-friendly. Women's studies created the curriculum transformation movement to get more topics on women and gender into the male-centered curriculum, in all subjects.[8] Curriculum transformation projects aim to have science and engineering subjects taught with more social context, so that students understand the benefits and risks of scientific knowledge and technological developments. They also promote multidisciplinary approaches, links connecting the humanities and social sciences with engineering and the sciences. Women's studies provides a home for scholars to write feminist critiques of medicine, science, and technology that in turn provide analyses for activists, and eventually have an impact on policies and practices in those fields. And more than a few women in scientific and technological disciplines have found support for their struggles against discrimination among women's studies colleagues.

---

7. See "Outer Space: The Worldly Frontier," by Mae C. Jemison, p. 560.—Ed.

8. See "The Proper Study of Womankind: Women's Studies," by Florence Howe, p. 70.—Ed.

In general, feminism's promotion of diversity and opposition to discrimination based on gender, race, class, ethnicity, sexuality, age, or disability has brought about many changes in society, schools, campuses, and the workforce. People from diverse backgrounds with different experiences, cultures, and perspectives offer new insights to fields that have been previously dominated by a single group: white men.[9] They enrich such fields, asking different questions, setting different goals.

Beyond women's participation in the professional fields of science, engineering, and technology, the Women's Movement needs science and technology literacy for *all* women. The women's health movement has been an essential part of the contemporary feminist wave.[10] Women realized the need to know our bodies, to gain knowledge necessary to criticize sexist medical practices and myths about our health. Beyond that, such scientific undertakings as the Human Genome Project offer new information about our individual and collective make-up as humans—but how is that information going to be used? Who will set the policies and write the laws? Who will own the knowledge? Women activists need a solid understanding of science, mathematics, and technology in order to analyze the wide range of issues related to health, the environment, biotechnology, information technology, food security, industry, and economics—to name only a few.

We have made large gains in our status and rights. With rights comes responsibility: to *keep the pressure on for more change*. Despite individual exceptions, women in science and technology have not been in the vanguard of the Women's Movement. One of the goals of feminists, inside *and* outside scientific and technological fields, should be to *connect* the success of women in these fields *to* the success of the feminist activism. They are intricately linked. The waning of feminism as a societal force allows men to reassert their sense of entitlement to jobs (and entire fields), to keep women out or marginalized in the lower ranks. This is what happened in computer science, when men seized the opportunities of that high-tech industry in the 1900s: they built a masculinist culture that excluded and dissuaded girls and women from entering; this even-

---

9. See Crenshaw, op. cit.—Ed.

10. See "Our Bodies, Our Future: Women's Health Activism Overview," by Judy Norsigian, et al., p. 269.—Ed.

tually created a climate in which the new industry could be misused to promote the sexual trafficking and exploitation of women and girls; that in turn has brought about a serious global women's rights crisis. This is a cautionary lesson about what happens when women are excluded from participating in the technological and commercial development of a new field.

Feminists are learning that we need to understand, critique, and act on issues that didn't yet exist or seem relevant at the beginning of this feminist wave—issues like genetic engineering, agribusiness, and food security. Furthermore, feminists are just beginning to grasp fully the impact that new communication and information technologies have on women and children. Globalization has brought new issues to the fore that require analysis and action on local, national, regional, and global levels.[11]

To respond to these challenges, the Women's Movement needs more women in science, engineering, and technology—women who can help mold the research questions, as well as help determine the uses to which scientific and technological findings are put. We need more women and girls taking courses in science, engineering, technology, *and* women's studies,[12] so that they can learn, understand, and strengthen the connections between these fields and women's rights and status—in the lab, *and* in the world.

DONNA M. HUGHES has a B.S. and M.S. in Animal Science and a Ph.D. in Genetics. She is a professor, holding the Eleanor M. and Oscar M. Carlson Endowed Chair in Women's Studies at the University of Rhode Island. As a Lecturer in Women's Studies at the University of Bradford in England, she was the degree coordinator of an innovative B.A. degree: Women's Studies, Technology, and Management. She does research, teaching, and writing on women, science, and technology, and has promoted curricular transformation in science, engineering, and Women's Studies for many years.

---

11. See "Globalization: A Strategic Advance for Feminism?" by Jessica Neuwirth, p. 526.—Ed.

12. See Howe, op. cit.—Ed.

Suggested Further Reading

Mies, Maria, and Vandana Shiva. *Ecofeminism.* London: Zed Books, 1993.

Rosser, Sue. V. "Building Inclusive Science," *Women's Studies Quarterly,* 2000.

———. *Women, Science and Society—The Crucial Union.* New York: Teachers College Press, 2000.

Rossiter, Margaret W. *Women Scientists in America—Struggles and Strategies to 1940.* Baltimore, Maryland: Johns Hopkins University Press, 1982.

———. *Women Scientists in America—Before Affirmative Action, 1940–1972.* Baltimore, Maryland: Johns Hopkins University Press, 1995.

Climbing the Ivory Walls:
Women in Academia

JANE ROLAND MARTIN

IT TOOK A LONG TIME— approximately three and a half centuries—and it took the concerted effort of generations of women and men! Still, we women prevailed. Gender equality in higher education, the goal that so many of our foremothers (and fathers) worked hard for, has finally been achieved.

Or so it seems.

Higher education took root in the United States back in 1636—as a man's prerogative. Today, female students have attained numerical parity with men, and coeducation has become an accepted way of life. In addition, academic women now compete, often successfully, for the highest honors: research grants, journal editorships, endowed chairs, distinguished professorships. As if these were not sufficient gains, women's studies has become a flourishing field,[1] and feminist scholars have been accepted (sometimes actually even welcomed) in traditional academic departments.

But here's the rub.

In the nineteenth century, the United States boasted a two-track, gender-based educational system that required girls and boys, and men and women, to attend separate institutions where they studied different curricula designed to fit them for their different gender roles and responsibilities. Almost everyone who considered this situation unjust believed coeducation was the remedy. No one expected that when the

---

1. See "The Proper Study of Womankind: Women's Studies," by Florence Howe, p. 70.—Ed.

twentieth century abandoned this official tracking system, a de facto gender tracking system in coeducation would develop to replace it. But one did. Statistically speaking, men and women in coeducational environments are today on two separate curriculum tracks: far more men than women study the physical sciences, mathematics, engineering, and economics[2]; many more women than men study languages and literature, the arts, teaching, nursing, social work.

The new gender tracking shatters the illusion of women's equality in higher education. The problem is not so much that men and women congregate in different academic areas as that the different fields of study are differentially *valued* and *rewarded* by U.S. society. The subjects in which men predominate are traditionally viewed as male occupations, and are accorded high status. Many areas in which women predominate—for instance, teaching, nursing, social work—represent what were once unpaid activities performed at home by women. Although these occupations have moved into the larger world where they have been dubbed "caring professions," they continue to be devalued.[3]

Because the new gender tracking is facilitated by higher education's elective system, discussions of it customarily employ the language of "choice." But choice rhetoric masks the degree to which the self-selection into different kinds of study—and ultimately into different areas of work—is influenced by social pressures, cultural expectations, economic realities, and the higher-education experience itself.

Research shows that males and females are treated differently at all levels of education in the United States, and that in coeducational settings this differential treatment tends to create a chilly classroom climate for women. Studies remain to be done on pinpointing such a chilly climate's contributions to the new gender tracking. But common sense

---

2. See "Changing a Masculinist Culture: Women in Science, Engineering, and Technology," by Donna M. Hughes, p. 393.—Ed.

3. For further information on devaluing of the "caring professions," see "Parenting: A New Social Contract," by Suzanne Braun Levine, p. 85; "Poverty Wears a Female Face," by Theresa Funiciello, p. 222; "*Just* a Housewife?!" by Helen Drusine, p. 342; "Pink Collar Ghetto, Blue Collar Token," by Alice Kessler-Harris, p. 358; "Rights, Realities, and Issues of Women with Disabilities," by Laura Hershey, p. 233; and the Tradition Transformers section in "Transforming Traditions and Breaking Barriers: Six Personal Testimonies," p. 325.—Ed.

wonders: How likely is it that a high-school girl whose teacher calls her "airhead" and "ditz" will choose to major in mathematics or the physical sciences in college? What are the odds that a young college woman will concentrate in physics when on the first day of class her professor seriously asks her, "Don't you feel out of place?" How many female students will stay the course when beginning science classes for majors represent what even a physics professor perceives to be "a very macho environment"?

Research is also needed on how the dearth of women in the highest faculty ranks influences the new gender tracking. Once again, the academy's claim to gender equality is illusory: although women do now participate in its reward system, men account for the greater *portion* of the professoriate.[4] The United States may appear to have a better record on this score than some other countries, but women are overrepresented in the *lower* grades. At the highest levels (everywhere) there are many more men than women,[5] and, across the board, a persisting salary differential remains, one that still favors men. In addition, women are clustered in such non-tenured positions as adjuncts, part-timers, and instructors or lecturers. We are also concentrated in two-year institutions, are more likely to be teachers than researchers, and tend to be heavily represented in low-status fields.

---

4. As of 2002, women across the U.S. have been entering the lowest faculty ranks in numbers almost equal to men (about 45 percent of assistant professors are women)—but representation remains low at the top: only 20 percent of full professors are women ("More Women Taking Leadership Roles at Colleges," by Karen W. Arenson, *New York Times*, 4 July 2002).—Ed.

5. On the rare occasion when this is not the case, it makes headlines. For example, in 2001, Shirley M. Tilghman became the first woman to be president of Princeton University. Since then, she has appointed Amy Gutmann as provost, Anne-Marie Slaughter as dean of the Woodrow Wilson School, and Maria Klawe as dean of the School of Engineering and Applied Science, and reappointed Nancy Weiss Malkiel as dean of the undergraduate college. These moves have put Princeton—which only three decades earlier did not even admit women as undergraduates—well ahead of all other major research universities in placing women in top jobs. Nevertheless, women constitute only about 27 percent of the Princeton faculty, and only 14 percent of full professors. Dr. Tilghman claims that the key to closing the gender gap in higher education is to appoint more women administrators. Only three of the eight Ivy League college presidents and about 22 percent of all college presidents are women, according to a survey by the American Council on Education; these figures more than double the 9.5 percent proportion in 1986 and quadruple the 5 percent in 1975 (Arenson, op. cit.).—Ed.

Does this lack of a genuine "co-professoriate" matter? In terms of fairness and equality it certainly makes a difference. Moreover, it stands to reason that when women achieve numerical parity with men across faculty ranks, women students will benefit. It is too much to expect parity by itself to make coeducational classrooms more hospitable to women. But parity will at least put women students in touch with a wide range of mentors and role models who represent diverse strategies for living as women in what is still relatively "a man's world." And with parity, men students will find it increasingly difficult to label successful women students "femi-Nazis," or to patronize, even tyrannize, women professors.

The scarcity of women in higher faculty ranks (in other words, the absence of a genuine "co-professoriate") signifies the lack of gender equality in higher education today—and so does the existence of a real "co-curriculum." Instead, we have a curriculum that continues to give far more space and attention to the study of men than women. In the 1970s, scholars began to document the ways in which various subjects in the liberal curriculum were male biased, and to bring women's lives, works, and experiences into the disciplines of knowledge. Yet despite the establishment of women's studies[6] programs in colleges and universities across the U.S., and notwithstanding the numerous attempts at mainstreaming what came to be called "the new scholarship on women," a genuine "co-curriculum" has not yet been achieved. Nor will it ever be, if defenders of the status quo have their way.

The scorn and derision they have showered on women's studies programs has shocked many. Yet in hindsight it was to be expected. Reinforcing the cultural stereotype that women are incapable of making meaningful contributions to society (let alone doing significant scholarly research), the curricular gender gap deprives women students of historical role models who prove the contrary. One can only speculate about the extent to which a genuine co-curriculum would improve the chilly undergraduate classroom climate. One can only wonder how many women would be inspired to undertake academic pursuits of their own, were they able to see themselves and their realities reflected in their course materials.

---

6. See Howe, op. cit.—Ed.

Even as Women's Studies programs have been the objects of hostility, feminist scholars have been the targets of anti-feminist intellectual harassment. Who would have thought that our analyses of canonical knowledge would earn us hate mail, threatening phone calls, jeers, jokes, and large doses of homophobia? Who could have foreseen the defacement of feminist journals in university libraries, and the heckling of feminist scholars? The intensity of the backlash is a measure of how threatening the feminist dream—of transforming knowledge and transfiguring the world—is to some members of academe.[7]

Whatever the effects of the backlash against feminist scholars, many of us ourselves began for other reasons to lose sight of our own mothers, daughters, sisters, half sisters, female cousins, and aunts. In the late 1980s, rightly responsive to charges of racism and classism, feminist scholars undertook much-needed research focusing on the differences among women. Yet in the course of so doing and without really realizing it, they became alienated from one another. Creating a chilly research climate for *themselves,* they condemned recent landmark studies of women for being "essentialist," and went so far as to denounce *all* use of the categories of *women, gender identity,* and even *mothering* that had only just been introduced into academic circles by the new scholarship.

When feminist scholars adopted the academy's practices as their own, they became estranged from women in the "outside world." Tacitly agreeing that scholarship requires an aerial distance from one's subject matter, many lost sight of the problems being confronted daily by

---

7. One form such backlash takes is tenure denial to women professors. In 2002, the proportion of women holding fulltime tenured positions was only 52 percent, compared with about 70 percent for men—almost unchanged from what it was 20 years earlier. A new form of backlash has been identified as "collegiality," a slippery category recently being added to the three previous ones on which tenure evaluation had for decades been based: teaching, research, and service to the institution. "Collegiality" has been defined as "not fitting in," "being pushy or aggressive," or "acting uppity"—and in recent years several women who were denied tenure partly on this basis have filed lawsuits charging discrimination. In 1999, the American Association of University Professors adopted a statement urging colleges to cease using collegiality as a tenure-evaluation category, stating that "Collegiality has not infrequently been associated with ensuring homogeneity, and hence with practices that exclude persons on the basis of their difference from a perceived norm. . . . An absence of collegiality ought never, by itself, to constitute a basis for nonreappointment, denial of tenure, or dismissal for cause" (" 'Collegiality' as a Tenure Battleground," by Tamar Lewin, *New York Times,* 12 July 2002).—Ed.

women of all classes, races, sexualities, and states of being. Readily accepting the academy's dogma that genuine knowledge must be expressed in esoteric language only they themselves could comprehend, they separated themselves from feminist activists. And implicitly endorsing the academy's devaluation of whatsoever the culture associates with women and the private home, they turned their backs on any study of the traditional female professions and their practitioners.

As it happens, the study of academic women provides a window onto the world of academe: the estrangement from women that feminist scholars began to experience is a basic *tenet* of the academy as we know it. From the beginning, Western culture has defined the function of formal education as preparation for life in the public "world" of work, politics, and the professions. The culture has also long considered this "world" to be men's turf and the private "world" women's place—and it also regards the two "spheres" as polar opposites, so preparation for the one has been assumed to involve rejection of the other. Accordingly, *estrangement from women*—and from the knowledge, skills, duties, responsibilities, virtues, and values associated with women—*has been a basic tenet of schooling in general and of the academy in particular.* True, higher education has opened its doors to teaching, nursing, social work, and other "female occupations." From inside, however, these fields are systematically denigrated.

So long as the academy is predicated on dissociation from women, gender equality would seem an impossible goal. But cultural definitions of education are not writ in stone. Remembering the feminist dream of transforming knowledge and radically revising the academy, women (and men too) can reject the outdated gender ideology that divides our society into two spheres and defines girls and boys, women and men, as polar opposites.

To many people, the academy's implementation of the ideal of gender equality seems so simple a proposition, so moderate a desire as to require no deliberate plan of action other than an occasional reminder to women's supposedly well-meaning hosts. Yet, like women's suffrage, women's entrance into the academy as the *equals* of men is a world historic event. The suffrage case teaches patience, and patience we must have, for though our struggle has already lasted much longer than we would like to admit, it will surely take even more time before it is won.

But history also teaches us to hope, for though the struggle for the vote took well over a century, it *did*, at long last, succeed. And perhaps most important, the suffrage case teaches that to effect a world historic change, it is necessary to call upon the whole *range* of political action.

In the beginning, the very thought of women having the vote made some men laugh and others cringe—yet the sons of those naysayers now take women's suffrage for granted. In the beginning, many women were made uneasy by the suffrage movement's "excesses," yet their daughters and granddaughters don't think twice about their right to vote. The suffrage movement offers hope of a future in which the idea of an academy that welcomes feminist scholarship, a genuine co-professoriate, a true co-curriculum, and women-friendly classrooms, will be taken for granted.

Rather, I should specify that the example of the suffrage movement gives confidence that all this will happen *provided* women decide that the academy's full acceptance of gender equality is a cause worth fighting for. True, ours is a systemic problem, and one of grand proportions: practically everything about higher education is subtly or blatantly gendered. This is why the moment one inequality concerning women is eradicated, another crops up.

It will require concerted actions great *and* small, moderate *and* radical, by women *and* men working within the academy *and* without, to create and sustain an academy genuinely free from androcentric biases against women. But when we think of how outdated and dysfunctional are the academy's gendered practices and ideology today, and when we recall the stubbornness and eventual success of the suffrage movement, then our dismay at academia's current distance from any goal of parity surrenders to the firm conviction that we simply must—and we *will*—eventually succeed.

JANE ROLAND MARTIN is a pioneer in the study of gender and education and the author of many books and essays on the philosophy of education; she is professor of philosophy emerita at the University of Massachusetts, Boston. The holder of honorary degrees from universities in Sweden and the United States, and a past president of the Philosophy of Education Society, she is the recipient of numerous awards, among them fellowships [sic] from the John Simon Guggenheim

Memorial Foundation, the National Science Foundation, and the Japan Society for the Promotion of Science. Her most recent books include *Changing the Educational Landscape: Philosophy, Women, and Curriculum* (Routledge, 1993); *The Schoolhome: Rethinking Schools for Changing Families* (Harvard University Press, 1992); and *Cultural Miseducation* (Teachers College Press John Dewey Lecture Series, 2002)—a work that develops a new "cultural wealth" framework for thinking about education.

Suggested Further Reading

Martin, Jane Roland. *Reclaiming a Conversation: The Ideal of the Educated Woman*. New Haven: Yale University Press, 1985.

————. *Coming of Age in Academe: Rekindling Women's Hopes and Reforming the Academy*. New York: Routledge, 2000.

Sandler, Bernice Resnick, Lisa A. Silverberg, and Roberta M. Hall. *The Chilly Classroom Climate: A Guide to Improve the Education of Women*. Washington, D.C.: National Association for Women in Education, 1996.

Solomon, Barbara M. *In the Company of Educated Women*. New Haven: Yale University Press, 1985.

Woolf, Virginia. *Three Guineas*. New York: Harcourt Brace Jovanovitch, 1938.

Redefining the Warrior Mentality: Women in the Military

CLAUDIA J. KENNEDY (LT. GEN., RET.)

WHY WOULD ANY WOMAN want to join her country's armed services? I didn't hear that question very often while I was in the army (it might have seemed rude to ask it to my face), but I often saw it in the eyes of new acquaintances, especially men, sometimes even military men. *What kind of woman are you, to want to be a soldier?* the eyes asked. *Are you a "real woman" under that uniform?*

The question reflects not only a male-dominated society's conflict over gender roles but also the persistence of a largely outdated "warrior" stereotype of military life. Together, they have created a climate in which the armed services have welcomed women with one hand and pushed them away with the other.

Sadly, this situation shows few signs of change. Today's military reality for women is a culture of official silence: silence when women's rights should be defended, and silence when men's abuses should be corrected. Yet the situation of women in the U.S. military should be examined as a barometer of women's status in the larger society, because the armed forces have historically constituted the epitome of a man's world, and women everywhere are putting that world—to use a military metaphor—under siege.

Women have joined armies as far back as chronicles go. At first, they did so in secret, disguised as men. They joined then and still join for the same reasons men volunteer: to test themselves, get away from home, look around before choosing a life direction, have an adventure, learn a career skill, serve their country, feel a sense of belonging. The army was the first U.S. service to welcome women, as nurses, in 1901. Women began serving in separate services during World War II, and were integrated with the men's services at the end of the Vietnam draft in the 1970s, when plummeting voluntary enlistments created shortfalls and pragmatic leaders realized that women could fill up the ranks.

Today's armed forces offer salaried work and good benefits—plus food, housing, medical and dental care, clothing, education, technical training, and travel.[1] Furthermore, you share in a patriotic cause, and the system does reward hard work and talent. If you might also kill or be killed, well, that's less prominent in many young minds than are the benefits. Young women are just as patriotic and idealistic as young men—and just as prone to disillusionment and sober reassessment when faced with hard reality.

More complicated is the military gender gap. Military service has always been a rite of passage for boys into manhood, one viewed as a cure for teenage laziness, self-absorption, or rebellion; military service is also perceived as obligatory for aspiring politicians, and as necessary in time of national emergency. The "brotherhood of war" created "foxhole buddies" with shared experiences (beyond the understanding of those who weren't there): an inner circle of powerful warriors. Honorable discharge from the armed services was a valuable credential of a man's responsibility, patriotism, leadership ability, group loyalty, and survival skills.

Girls have no comparable rite of passage. Beauty pageants? Cooking contests? Weddings? A "real woman" was until recently stereotyped as the opposite of a warrior: flighty, irresponsible, unreliable, incompetent, weak, and in need of a man to cope with the world on her behalf. A woman's value resided first in her sexuality, then in her fertility—in marriage and children, and in demonstrating "family values." Because of the Women's Movement, these attitudes are now considered laughable—except in the last bastions of conservatism where, unfortunately, a number of military leaders are proud to be found. Yet when they were

---

1. The U.S. Department of Defense was once the second-largest centrally planned economy anywhere, topped only by the Soviet Union. Now, given the state of Russia's finances and politics, the DOD could claim to be the largest socialist economy in the world.—Ed.

ordered to integrate women into the armed services, these men, who are trained to follow orders, did *try* to comply—sort of.

The armed services are top-down command hierarchies, but silent resistance keeps women in the military at second-class status. Where African American men have been thoroughly integrated, women of all ethnicities and races have not.[2] In the army, for example, about 16 percent of all soldiers in 2002 were women, and they served in every sector *except* the infantry and armor (tanks). These exclusions result from the explicit decision that women are not "warriors." But women fly fighters and engage in air combat; women fly the airplanes that drop bombs and the jets that escort them; women drive the trucks that transport troops to the front lines and the ambulances that carry out the wounded; women are nurses and doctors on the battlefield. Women *are* in combat, in all but name. Why can't women join the ground combat branches?

The argument is that this would "disrupt the cohesion and discipline of the fighting unit." It is feared that men would be slowed down, feel a need to protect the women, carry their field packs, compete for sex with them, and be otherwise distracted from the military mission; and that women's lesser upper-body strength would keep them from carrying out a wounded comrade, scaling a wall, or shouldering heavy guns. The presence of women, the argument goes, creates awkward health needs and hazards; rape and pregnancy are constant dangers. These views have persuaded generations of decision-makers that women cannot join the "fraternity of warriors."

Left unsaid is the fact of simple *distrust*. The assumption is that men bond with men into teams for joint struggle, watching each other's backs—but that women and men can bond only sexually, and those alliances are shifting and unreliable, disruptive to cohesion. In other words, women cannot be trusted to be "true warriors." This general dis-

---

2. Since the end of the draft and the beginning of the "volunteer army," the U.S. armed forces have been increasingly comprised of men and women of color, primarily African American, in numbers disproportionate to their percentage of the overall U.S. population. (In a society still racked by sexism and racism, the economically disadvantaged segments of the population are in even greater need of a merit-based promotion system offering free education, medical care, etc.: this appears to be why, for example, almost a third of the U.S. forces fighting the Gulf War—and nearly half of the 27,000 women—were African American.) See "African American Women: The Legacy of Black Feminism," by Beverly Guy-Sheftall, p. 176.—Ed.

trust of women goes further, to the heart of the status of women in the armed services and in the larger society.

Consider the issue of promotion. Merit-based promotion is the bedrock of the armed services. In a distinct improvement over civilian workplaces, promotion criteria in the armed forces are spelled out in print. Every soldier is evaluated frequently, in writing, and then counseled on the results. A promotion board for each rank reports regularly to the Army Secretary on the ratio of minority soldiers and women soldiers being selected for promotion, as compared to white (European American) males. But some areas of every branch are closed to women, usually because such areas are closely related to ground combat. Yet experience in combat units is among the criteria deemed essential for promotion to many elite positions. This is a classic Catch-22.[3]

Another area where women are distrusted is in the handling of charges of sexual harassment and abuse.[4] A 1995 Pentagon study revealed that 78 percent of all military women have been sexually harassed. Yet despite the zero-tolerance rhetoric from military leadership, harassment and assaults continue. Complaints are officially kept secret and the man or woman involved retains normal responsibilities during the investigation, usually being transferred from the area of conflict. Word always gets around, however. If the water-cooler chat leads to media involvement, officers' interviews tend to stress that an accused male officer's "many other contributions will surely dwarf this charge," and to mention (not for attribution, of course) a woman's possible "motives for trying to ruin the man's reputation." When it is the *woman* under fire, however, spokesmen tend to discuss only her reasons for "failing to be a credit to her uniform." In either case, the woman is isolated. She has betrayed the club of warriors, proving once again that women cannot be trusted. Women who appeal to the stated military

---

3. For more on the pipeline-promotion phenomenon, see "Standing By: Women in Broadcast Media," by Carol Jenkins, p. 418; see also Brenda Berkman on purported merit-based paramilitary-structure promotion among firefighters, in "Transforming Traditions and Breaking Barriers: Six Personal Testimonies," p. 325.—Ed.

4. See "The Nature of the Beast: Sexual Harassment," by Anita Hill, p. 296, and "Landscape of the Ordinary: Violence Against Women," by Andrea Dworkin, p. 58.—Ed.

principles of justice and equality are missing the point: men's loyalty to each other, not to the institution, seems to be the primary requirement.

Therefore, official silence works against women *doubly:* to protect men charged with abuse *and* to sully the reputation of women who dare to complain. Aware of this, women in the military tend to hesitate for a long time and to suffer repeated, often escalating abuse before filing complaints. The principle that military women deserve justice loses credibility where harassment, abuse, and rape go unpunished.[5]

Again, the situation reflects the larger society. Women's reluctance to speak up was anticipated. As part of the initial integration of women into the armed services after World War II, the Pentagon set up a Defense Advisory Committee on Women in the Service (DACOWITS), that monitored the changeover, received complaints, and suggested solutions. In the early 1980s, when the momentum of the broader Women's Movement appeared to have been slowed by backlash, DACOWITS was the most reliable advocate military women had.

DACOWITS and its functions have come under fire in the early twenty-first century as being no longer necessary—but that is far from the truth.[6] A strong advocate for women within the military system remains a vital need if women are ever to reach their potential as military assets. Women's rights groups have not commonly adopted military women's issues as a cause, perhaps because only a small number of women wear military uniforms, or perhaps because military women are still seen as atypical.[7] President Clinton opened more than 90,000 new military jobs to women in the army, but at this writing, George W. Bush's administration has sought to roll back many of those gains.

---

5. General Kennedy gained national recognition for successfully blocking the promotion of another general on grounds of his having sexually harassed her.—Ed.

6. In February 2002, Bush administration Secretary of Defense Donald Rumsfeld allowed the DACOWITS charter to lapse and dismissed all the members. Later, he "reorganized" the committee under a new charter. As of late 2002, DACOWITS, which traditionally holds both spring and fall meetings, had not met since spring of 2001, e.g., not since the Bush II administration took office. ("Women in Military at Crossroads Without Signposts," by Nancy Cook Lauer, 11 August 2002, Women's E-News, *www.womensenews.org*).—Ed.

7. See "Why Peace Is (More than Ever) a Feminist Issue," by Grace Paley, p. 537.—Ed.

Bush's critical "transformation" of the armed forces for a new kind of combat warfare may gradually exclude women from areas where we have long served, such as engineering, as well as from nuclear, biological, and chemical specialties.

Yet in the post-9/11/2001 world, upper-body strength is less relevant in the armed forces than it ever was. The classic masculine "warrior" definition might be viewed as appropriate for males between the ages of 17 and 22, when raging hormones mean that both sexes are sorting out gender roles and seeking self-definition, partly through job descriptions. But new weaponry, communications advances, and battlefield techniques now have far more to do with training and technology than with muscle.

The U.S. armed services face several crucial tasks in achieving women's further integration (if, in fact, they actually *want* that).

The first, most pressing need—for women *and* men—is for childcare. Fully 84 percent of soldiers are men, and in today's army two-thirds are married, most with young children and wives who must hold down jobs in the waged labor force in order to keep the family above the poverty line. An estimated 65 percent of all recruits need childcare services in order to leave home. This is a need that must be met, and soon.

Next, modern sexual reality means that women in uniform, like other women, occasionally become unintentionally pregnant. No contraceptive is 100 percent reliable. Yet military hospitals deny to military women a legal option available to all other U.S. women: the right to an abortion as part of the medical care that comes with the job.[8] Federal assistance for military personnel and dependents to obtain abortions was outlawed in 1979, and in 1988 the Reagan administration banned all abortions at U.S. military facilities, except in cases of rape, incest, or danger to the woman's life. President Clinton lifted the ban on privately funded abortions at military facilities in 1993—but in 1995 the ban was reinstated when Republicans gained control of Congress. In 1996, the

---

8. See "Unfinished Agenda: Reproductive Rights," by Faye Wattleton, p. 17. See also "Our Bodies, Our Future: Women's Health Activism Overview," by Judy Norsigian, et al., p. 269; and "Diagnosis and Prognosis: Women Physicians and Women's Health," by Wendy Chavkin, M.D., p. 378.—Ed.

Senate voted to drop the ban, but the House refused to compromise.[9] This situation must be reversed, *permanently*—so that the constitutionally protected reproductive rights of women in the military are not continually being treated as a proverbial political football.

Finally, and most fundamentally, job exclusions should no more be based on gender than on race or on sexual preference/orientation[10]; they should be based on individual capacities and goals. Gender cannot be the first filter or an automatic one for placement within the vast spectrum of the military workload, neither on the battlefield nor in peacetime operations. The warrior mentality must be confronted, analyzed rationally, and redefined *inclusively*, as "patriot" or "public defender," with every field open to women and men alike. Discrimination, discipline, and promotions must be based on talent and behavior.

Even these reforms, however, will not necessarily deal with the fundamental problem of trust. If soldiers do not trust their colleagues (men *or* women), no matter how physically strong, the fighting unit is indeed compromised. But for that dilemma, the only solutions may, again, be the same as those emerging in the larger society: experience, practice, and time. As more young girls come to play team sports, they learn

---

9. In June 2002, the Democratic-controlled Senate again voted to lift the ban on privately funded abortions at U.S. military hospitals; the decision was approved 52–40, as part of a $393 billion defense authorization bill. But the same month, the Republican majority in the House of Representatives again rejected a similar plan, and at this writing, the House is expected to maintain its anti-abortion stance during conference negotiations with the Senate.—Ed.

10. The problem of homophobia in the military, supposedly settled by the "don't ask don't tell" approach codified by Congress in 1993, persists and may even be increasing. According to the Servicemembers' Legal Defense Network, a legal aid group, the number of military discharges of lesbian women and gay men rose to its highest number in 14 years between 2000 and 2001, and reported incidents of harassment climbed by 23 percent during that same period. This, despite the 13-point plan approved in 1999 by then-Defense Secretary William S. Cohen, in the Clinton administration, to curb anti-gay harassment. The Servicemembers' Legal Defense Network findings show that *women have been disproportionately affected by the current "don't ask don't tell" policy: 30 percent of all discharges on homosexual grounds in 2001 were women—even though overall women constitute only about 14 percent of the armed forces population* ("Military Discharges of Gays Rise, and So Do Bias Incidents," by Christopher Marquis, *New York Times*, 14 March 2002).—Ed.

group cohesion earlier in life.[11] Co-ed dormitories are healing college students' psyches of sexual mystification and behavioral anxiety. As young men and women increasingly study, play, and work together throughout the society in brother-sister relationships of mutual respect and friendship, these new habits and attitudes will more often survive the donning of a uniform.

The military is an institution where an order must be obeyed. Indeed, lives can depend on an order being obeyed. This basic fact of military life makes it fundamentally different from civilian existence, and the resulting erasure of individual quirks can blind observers to the larger truth: *the system can also be moved.*[12] Orders to change, *if* leaders are serious at the top, will in fact *mean* change—in those leaders' lives, in the lives of the rawest new recruits, and for every soldier, sailor, and airman [sic] in between. If the armed forces are serious about wanting to integrate women, it will happen. To find out, all we have to do is watch.

And, of course—strategically—help move things along.

CLAUDIA J. KENNEDY, Lieutenant General (retired), is the first and only woman to achieve the rank of three-star general in the U.S. Army, taking her from the Women's Army Corps in the late 1960s to the position of Deputy Chief of Staff for Army Intelligence from 1997 to

---

11. See "Women in Sports: What's the Score?" by Barbara Findlen, p. 285; and "Girls: 'We Are the Ones Who Can Make a Change!' " by Ana Grossman and Emma Peters-Axtell, p. 121.—Ed.

12. As an example of the system moving: in January 2002, the U.S. military quietly lifted an order originating during the Gulf War era, requiring servicewomen based in Saudi Arabia to wear head scarves and black robes *(abbayas)* when off base. *The New York Times* reported on a classified directive that made clear the wearing of the *abbaya* would no longer be mandatory, though it was still "strongly encouraged." The policy change followed a lengthy review initiated by complaints the previous year from Lt. Col. Martha McSally, the highest-ranking female fighter pilot in the U.S. Air Force. McSally had filed a lawsuit contending the dress code was unconstitutional and that it improperly forced U.S. women to conform to others' religious and social customs. The Pentagon reportedly regarded the suit as frivolous, until Col. McSally went public with her cause in the media, post 9/11—at which point the Pentagon reversed course. Col. McSally, no longer based in Saudi Arabia, is, however, still fighting regulations requiring military women to be accompanied by men and to ride in the backseats of cars when off base in Saudi Arabia. ("Servicewomen Win, Doffing Their Veils in Saudi Arabia," by Elaine Sciolino, *New York Times,* 25 January 2002.)—Ed.

2000. She oversaw policies and operations affecting 45,000 people stationed worldwide, with a budget of nearly $1 billion. During her career, she commanded a company, an intelligence battalion, a recruiting battalion, and an intelligence brigade; she served as the senior intelligence officer for the U.S. Forces Command, and Deputy Commanding General for the Army Intelligence Center and School. Her military honors include the National Intelligence Distinguished Service Medal, the Army Distinguished Service Medal, and four Legions of Merit (awarded for "exceptionally meritorious conduct in the performance of outstanding services and achievements"); her civilian awards include honors from the National Women's Law Center, the National Center for Women and Policy, and Business and Professional Women (USA). She lives in Virginia, and works to help children by chairing First Star, a nonprofit corporation, and serving as advisor to Every Child Matters and to Education Through Leadership. A past member of the Board of Governors of the Army and Navy Club and a military consultant for NBC, she authored a memoir, *Generally Speaking* (Warner Books, 2001).

Suggested Further Reading

Germer, Fawn. *Hard-Won Wisdom: More than 50 Extraordinary Women Mentor You to Find Self-Awareness, Perspective, and Balance.* New York: Berkley Books/Penguin Putnam, 2001.

Holm, Jeanne (Maj. Gen., USAF, Ret.). *Women in the Military: An Unfinished Revolution.* Novato, California: Presidio Press, 1982; revised edition 1992.

Kerber, Linda K. *No Constitutional Right to Be Ladies: Women and the Obligations of Citizenship.* New York: Hill & Wang, 1998.

Morden, Bettie J. *The Women's Army Corps, 1945–1978.* Washington, D.C.: The U.S. Government Printing Office, 1989.

Wheatley, Margaret J. *Leadership and the New Science.* San Francisco: Berrett-Koehler Publishers, 1993.

On-line resources: National Women's Law Center–Women in the Military *(www.nwlc.org/display.cfm?section-military)*; The Defense Advisory Committee on Women in the Services *(www.dtic.mil/dacowits/)*.

Standing By: Women in Broadcast Media

CAROL JENKINS

IN 2001, after years of suffering declining credibility, broadcast journalists won some respect. In polls taken after the 9/11 attacks, the U.S. viewing public overwhelmingly approved of how they were doing their jobs.

Well, not *all* of them. In several notorious instances, women broadcast journalists were singled out for ridicule, reminding us that hostility to the serious woman reporter is alive and well. The most bizarre example was a column in the tabloid *New York Post* calling CNN senior correspondent Christiane Amanpour—arguably the premier foreign correspondent of recent times—a "war slut." When an apology was demanded, *Post* owner Rupert Murdoch gave one, reluctantly. Then there was a *Wall Street Journal* column comparing women reporters covering Afghanistan: Amanpour again was attacked for, among other things, her choice of clothes; the new MSNBC-TV reporter, Ashleigh Banfield, who had dyed her blond hair dark to better blend into Afghan society, was described as "fine boned"—as if that were relevant to reporting skills. The columnist decided a British reporter was "best in show," later bragging about the controversy he'd caused with his beauty contest. Earlier, *The Wall Street Journal* had given CNN's Paula Zahn—who logged the most airtime of any woman during the crisis, solo anchoring for hours—a harsh critique, partly blaming her haircut. Imagine Edward R. Murrow, who invented modern broadcast war reporting, having to cope with scrutiny of his signature upturned collar.[1]

---

1. Zahn was subjected to friendly fire from within her own company, too. CNN aired, then quickly yanked, a promo it admitted was a "major blunder." The promo

Such tactics have been used against women broadcasters before, most infamously against those trying to sit at the network evening news desk. We've all been watching TV news for more than half a century, with women working in it almost as long, so the persistent absence of a primary woman anchor at any of the networks is alarming. Both Barbara Walters (at ABC in 1973) and Connie Chung (at CBS twenty years later) had the temerity to sit in the anchor chair next to, respectively, Harry Reasoner and Dan Rather. Subjected to assaults on their competence—and more importantly, low *ratings*—Walters and Chung were relegated to anywhere else in the schedule *except* the evening news. Even Jessica Savitch's tragic story is spun as a cautionary tale about women being unable to handle pressure. The troubled Savitch, said to be in line for the evening news spot at NBC in the mid-1980s, had an on-air meltdown and later died in an accidental car crash. Some interpreted that as a warning of what might happen if you dared aspire to the evening news anchor chair.[2]

The stories are legion. One news director told me he wanted my male co-anchor on the 6:00 P.M. New York news to read the lead story every evening because his voice "had authority," bolstering his decision by research indicating viewers trusted men more. This was in 1995, twenty-five years into my career as a reporter and anchor. Pauline Frederick, the first woman to do network news, had been told essentially the same thing, by Murrow himself at CBS in 1946, by executives at NBC in 1950, and by other bosses for the rest of her prestigious career. Yet when you listen to her tapes, you hear the essence of what we've come to re-

---

called Zahn "a morning newsanchor who's provocative, super-smart, oh yeah, and just a little bit sexy"—and the sound that accompanied "sexy" was remarkably like that of a zipper being unzipped.

2. In June 2002, NBC News named Brian Williams, the NBC cable anchor, to succeed Tom Brokaw on his impending retirement from anchoring the NBC network news. "The three anchor chairs are the last all-male preserve in all of television," noted Bonnie J. Dow, associate professor of communication at the University of Georgia and author of *Prime-Time Feminism: Television, Media Culture, and the Women's Movement Since 1970* (Philadelphia: University of Pennsylvania Press, 1996), while Greta Van Susteren, the Fox cable news anchor, commented "There are 280 million people in this country—surely they can find one smart woman to deliver the news" ("News Anchors and the Cathode-Ray Ceiling," by Jim Ruttenberg, *New York Times*, 3 June 2002.)—Ed.

gard as the serious, confident voice of authority. Mine wasn't bad either—and after some lively debate, the news director's proposal was dropped. In that instance, my boss (not a bad guy otherwise) summed up the unspoken sentiments about TV newswomen. He referred to the other woman anchor at the station, a popular presence in New York news, as the "hood ornament on the male anchor's Rolls Royce" (e.g., her popularity generated millions of dollars and helped pay our salaries). That image explains many anchor pairings.

In her social history of women in broadcasting, *Invisible Stars* (see Suggested Further Reading below), Donna Halper reports that even the estimable Walter Cronkite was once quoted as saying women's voices were too high-pitched to be understood. Today the voice of authority remains male, white, older, and well-off (on air *and* in the executive suites)—even in an age when we might assume news management to be enlightened, especially regarding the threat of lawsuits about discrimination.

In the old days, a newsroom was expected to be a temple of cigar-chewing, high-decibel machismo. More than one of my news directors wore a gun to work, and more than a few TV executives were notorious for making unwanted sexual advances; one was suspected of having his own corporate-sponsored hush fund to try to pay off women who protested. We newswomen have had to put up with a lot. We still do.

We also need to remember that it has taken the insistence of feminists, demanding that women reporters be assigned to serious stories, to advance women through the ranks.[3] Yet recently I've worked with young women producers who sputter "feminist" with disdain, as if women proudly identifying with the word have misspent our lives. One such producer aired a swimsuit-modeling segment in the middle of a news program. Some younger women now on the rise in broadcasting seem to have little understanding of the very struggle from which they've benefited.

For example, when Norma Quarles started at NBC in the 1960s, she was the first African American woman to file reports for a network. Women reporters weren't allowed to wear pants then, so she covered

---

3. See "The Media and the Movement: A User's Guide," by Gloria Steinem, p. 103.—Ed.

breaking stories squeezed into a girdle and skirt, tottering on high heels; furthermore, getting her story filed involved negotiating with her own all male, all white, often resentful crews. In the late '60s, she expressed interest at filling in for Barbara Walters on the *Today* show, but was told that "the Committee of Seven" who made such determinations had decided her presence would offend viewers in the South and also west of the Mississippi; the answer was No.

In the early 1970s, as I was starting in television news, the U.S. Civil Rights Commission issued a report concluding that in this field minority men and all women were "window dressing on the set." It took the full force of the Women's Movement, lawsuits by women employees, and several affirmative-action laws to change the view that news was a white man's burden.

As part of that new wave of hires meant to repair the industry's reputation, I was among the first women reporters admitted to the Yankees' locker room. Today, there are many terrific women sportscasters—some high profile, like Robin Roberts of ESPN and ABC. But according to a survey[4] of 126 local newscasts in 1993, less than 5 percent of sports newstime was devoted to women's events, and as late as 1999, more than 90 percent of sports coverage was still dedicated to men's events.[5]

Financial and business news also has numerous women reporters, many of them analysts, experts, and economists. Pamela Thomas Graham, an African American with three Harvard degrees, currently heads up NBC's cable business channel, CNBC. Nevertheless, the best-known on-air female business-news presence, Maria Bartiromo, is absurdly referred to as "the money honey."

Once, such Sunday morning interview programs as *Meet the Press* were an exclusive club of male reporters and politicians; now, you find women on both sides of the table—though only (soon to be retiring) Cokie Roberts at ABC holds a permanent position. In a 2001 study, The White House Project found that women constituted only 10 percent of the guests, spoke 10 percent less than their male counterparts, were relegated to less desirable segments, and were less likely to be invited back.

---

4. The Amateur Athletic Foundation of Los Angeles, *Gender in Televised Sports*, 1989, 1993, 1999, 2000.

5. See "Women in Sports: What's the Score?" by Barbara Findlen, p. 285.—Ed.

After the 9/11 attacks, the presence of U.S. women experts *dropped nearly 40 percent*. When national concerns are being discussed, women are still barely present.

Overall, women represent about one third of the television news workforce, but only one quarter of the country's newsrooms are headed by female news directors. Unquestionably, the perspective of these journalists has given weight to stories important to women. For example, it's doubtful that Anita Hill's sexual harassment charges would have gone far without the women who insisted on airing them. These reporters said their bosses—like the panel of senators exonerating Supreme Court Justice nominee Clarence Thomas—just didn't "get it."[6]

In the new century and new millennium, we should expect—and demand—more.

Marlene Sanders—author of *Waiting for Prime Time: The Women of Television News* (see below)—believes broadcasting women *are* making progress, but in a profession declining in credibility and influence. Sanders's pioneering career includes being the first woman to anchor an evening newscast, filling in on ABC in 1966, and the first to file features from a war zone, Vietnam. In 1964, she had been one of only six women network reporters. She and I spoke during coverage of the World Trade Center collapse, and we noted the extraordinary number of women correspondents reporting from around the world. But Marlene's enthusiasm was measured. The sober, responsible coverage underscored what serious journalists had been saying for years: while more women were employed and succeeding in television, there was less to be proud of. After years of dumbing down the news and juicing up entertainment values, the news suffers.

Americans were so engaged in amusing ourselves that on 9/11 networks had to scramble to get reporters on the ground. The previous summer, a friend of my daughter's—a Fulbright scholar fluent in several Middle Eastern languages—applied for an internship at one of the networks. When she expressed interest in international reporting, she was told the networks "weren't in that business anymore"; they'd left world coverage to CNN. CBS anchor Dan Rather admitted after 9/11 that ignoring foreign news had been a mistake, even if viewer ratings and polls

---

6. See "The Nature of the Beast: Sexual Harassment," by Anita Hill, p. 296.—Ed.

indicated disinterest. We were an ill-prepared nation who paid dearly for our ignorance. Men and women in journalism must answer for our inattention.

By other indicators, however, 2001 was a watershed year for women in television. Katie Couric, the popular "girl next door" co-anchor of the *Today* show, was offered the richest contract in the history of TV news: a four-year package worth $60 million. Other network news stars, including the male anchors of the evening newscasts, were reported to earn $8 to $12 million per year. The president of NBC news articulated Katie's value in having-it-all terms: "She is able to be the serious news interviewer in one segment, talking to senators or the president, and be Peter Pan in the next segment." Since we're not used to women pulling their worth in compensation, there was much questioning about whether this made the girl next door a more threatening presence. Yet hardly an eyebrow was raised when Rush Limbaugh, who built a lucrative career out of bashing feminists, scooped up $285 million for his multi-year radio contract.

Meanwhile, Barbara Walters turned seventy in 2001, still an on-air personality as well as a producer for ABC network. For those who wondered if television women would be allowed to age gracefully, growing in experience and wisdom—the Cronkite effect—the answer seems to be a (qualified) yes.

Such newswomen as Diane Sawyer, Jane Pauley, Connie Chung, and Carole Simpson, all in their fifties, continue working at top level. Yet even Walters isn't invulnerable: her Friday night magazine show, *20/20*, a ratings powerhouse, was summarily moved to make room for *Once and Again*, a family series starring Sela Ward. (The move was cast in the press as an older/younger women's catfight. Ironically, Sela Ward reportedly felt the sting of ageism herself, when she heard casting directors asking for "a young Sela Ward.")

Meanwhile, Lifetime Television for Women scored impressively in the cable universe, becoming the most watched prime-time cable channel. It's not a complete victory, since Lifetime doesn't deliver what the industry regards as the most desired TV audience: young males. Still, Lifetime was an industry joke for years, a way of insulting women programmers and viewers; if executives termed a program "too woman" (meaning, to them, soft-headed or mushy), they labeled it "a Lifetime project." Owned jointly by ABC/Disney and Hearst, Lifetime, initially headed by a man, has a new CEO, Carole Black, who has developed the channel and herself into major industry players.

Creating segregated media, or narrowcasting, for women, is debatable. The tendency so far has been to treat women as tall children with compromised intellects, primarily interested in buying things. Many women responded to women's Internet sites negatively for that reason, claiming they could find everything they wanted to know on mainstream sites. Yet it's true that women also feel the broadcast networks are not responsive to their viewing interests—while women working in television continue to wage battles on the fronts of gender, age, weight, looks, and skin color.

In the TV entertainment industry, women—while representing a quarter of the workforce—comprise only 7 percent of directors and 2 percent of cinematographers, according to Martha Lauzin of San Diego State University, who has tracked women's participation in media for several years. And while more women are working, their *own* projects are not getting made.[7]

One of the more interesting experiments testing the power of women in television has been the creation of a woman-owned, woman-run cable network for women, Oxygen. In 1998, preparing for my transition from news anchoring to forming my own production company, I wrangled a press seat at one of the media power conferences held in a swank New York hotel. These are sessions kept exclusive by charging $1,000 for one day of speeches and panels by leaders in media and technology—in this case, Microsoft's Bill Gates, Time Warner's Gerald Levin, and CBS's Mel Karmazin. In an entire day of discussions there was only one woman

---

7. Nancy Miller, writer/producer of *Any Day Now*, a thoughtful series about two girlhood friends—one black, one white—in the South, spent eight years trying to get the show on the air. All the networks passed on the project when she refused to make it a series about two boys. This series is now pivotal to Lifetime's successful programming lineup. Lee Grant, after a successful career as an actor, has become perhaps the most consistently engaged woman director/producer in television. While she does projects for the networks, she says it is in cable, at Lifetime in particular, that she feels most free. Being young, cute, and thin—on camera *and* behind it—is less of an issue there.

panelist, Geraldine Laybourne, and one person of color, Bill Kennard (then head of the Federal Communications Commission).

Laybourne, a former teacher, had acquired an aura of invincibility by steering the children's network, Nickelodeon, to the top. Now she had turned her attention to women's programming, and in 1998 was assembling Oxygen Media. It would include a cable channel and Internet sites—and offer competition to Lifetime. Laybourne chose as her partners two of the savviest women in the business: Oprah Winfrey and Marcy Carsey, whose independent production company, Carsey Warner, has had unrivaled success with TV comedies starring Bill Cosby and Roseanne. For many women in the business (and viewers), Oxygen represented hope. Oxygen represented *ownership*. If these three women couldn't pull it off, no women could.

Three years after the posh media conference I attended, by the autumn of 2001, Gerald Levin had brokered a deal with Steve Case of AOL to form AOL Time Warner, the largest communications company in the world. Mel Karmazin had paired CBS with Sumner Redstone's Viacom to form a powerhouse of broadcast, cable, and film properties. The much-anticipated Oxygen had arrived—but had yet to register a presence, hampered by failure to get cable berths in some major cities (the all-important New York City market wouldn't be available for another two years). Initial critical response was not positive: Oxygen had yet to define its real audience; an early warning appeared on an Oxygen website displaying photos of Laybourne's evolving hairstyles.

While we had hoped for women's partnership—Thelma and Louise, but with a happy ending—we were still stuck with the same old "buddy plots": Sumner and Mel (see above), Steve and Gerry (later, when Levin announced his retirement, he handed the reins to Dick Parsons and Bob Pittman[8]), *and*: Mike and Bob (Eisner and Iger, at Disney/ABC), Andy and Jeff (Andy Lack, helped by his pal Jeff Zucker, to assume the GE/NBC presidency), and Rupert and Lachlan (Murdoch, turning the

---

8. Interestingly, a 2002 power shift at AOL Time Warner lifted Ann Moore, the force behind *People* magazine's success, to chair and CEO of Time Inc. Bob Pittman was forced out and replaced by two male company executives. This meant that *if* succession precedent were followed, Moore was just one management layer away from the top of the world's biggest communications company.

reins of NewsCorp—with all its Fox TV stations, cable networks, movie studios, and newspapers—over to his son, Lachlan).[9]

Not only were there no women at the top in broadcasting, but the pipeline was getting narrower and longer. The 1996 Telecom Act green-lighted a series of mega-mergers that saw the number of broadcasting companies dwindle. Such consolidation affected women executives negatively—by adding new layers to the corporate structure above them. The glass ceiling was still impermeable; furthermore, it had been *lowered.*

That's a story Sheila Wellington knows all too well. She heads up Catalyst, which tracks women in the corporate world. One day, my production office received a fax from her that heralded a 200 percent jump in women CEOs at Fortune 500 companies. Yet all that meant was that there were now *four* such women. Catalyst is wonderful at demystifying the problems of women stuck in the corporate pipeline, including a lack of mentors and exclusion from informal gatherings with the boss. But here's what Wellington sees as key: women who do not hold *line positions*—positions responsible for *budgets and personnel*—have no chance to ascend in the corporate structure; *93 percent of line jobs in corporate America—jobs that lead to the top—are held by men.*[10]

But even when on-track, it's easy to get derailed. Paula Walker Madison was the first African American woman to become news director in the number one market, at WNBC-TV in New York, and later general manager of KNBC in Los Angeles. Yet she'd been passed over twice before winning the news director slot, and only now will admit to the frustration she endured. Many corporate women opt out after such rejection, but she stayed put. Once she became news director, *and* took all three news programs to number one in the ratings, she was offered the high-profile position of vice president of diversity for the NBC net-

9. For information about NewsCorp, AOL Time Warner, and other major corporations as background owners of pornography businesses, see "From Fantasy to Reality: Unmasking the Pornography Industry," by Gail Dines, p. 306.—Ed.

10. For parallel Catch-22 pipeline predicaments, see "Redefining the Warrior Mentality: Women in the Military," by Claudia J. Kennedy, p. 409; "Climbing the Ivory Walls: Women in Academia," by Jane Roland Martin, p. 401; and "Up the Down Labyrinth: Ins and Outs of Women's Corporate and Campus Careers," by Ellen Appel-Bronstein, p. 387.—Ed.

work. But Madison knew that such a network post would take her out of a *line* position. She counter-offered by being willing to assume the diversity job if she could keep the news director position. Fortunately, the surprised executives agreed—so she was eligible when the job of KNBC general manager opened up. Which is how Paula Madison wound up on "the list," one of only seven women of color with significant clout in entertainment media.[11]

In December 2001, *The Hollywood Reporter* issued its controversial issue that lists the most powerful women in entertainment—yes, unfortunately, TV news does come under that category, a function of the medium. Some women had lobbied for discontinuing this segregated vertical ranking (claiming "We're executives, not *women* executives"), but the publisher defended the process, noting, "Most of the highest positions of power are not currently occupied by women. When they are, there will be no reason to publish this issue." His concession was to expand the list for the first time, doubling the 50 names to 100, a statement of progress. The list is skewed toward the movie business, where three studios (Paramount, Universal, and Columbia) have women chairs. Among the top ten, the women who toil in television include the CBS, Fox, and MTV presidents of entertainment (Susan Lyne would subsequently be appointed entertainment head at ABC). But almost all of these "most powerful women" report to male bosses.[12]

In her study of women in broadcasting, Donna Halper summed it up: despite progress, all the important decisions are still being made by a small group of men, just as they were—here's the chilling part—in the 1930s. The underlying reason is *money*. True power in media is *ownership*, which is still a male domain.

---

11. The other six are Oprah Winfrey (chair, Harpo Entertainment Group), Sylvia Rhone (CEO, Elektra), Tracey Edmonds (president, CEO, Edmonds Entertainment), Debra L. Lee (president, CEO, BET Networks), Debra Martin Chase (producer, *Princess Diaries*), and Tanya York (president, CEO, York Entertainment).

12. At this writing, the Annenberg Public Policy Center of the University of Pennsylvania has just weighed in with its 2002 report, "Glass Ceiling in the Executive Suite," an analysis of women leaders in communications. It examined the leadership in the 10 biggest entertainment conglomerates, and the results are not surprising: women comprise merely 13 percent of the powerful boards of directors and 14 percent of top executives. Only one woman could be said to be in the very top echelons: Elsie Ma Leung, co-president and CFO of Gemstar-TV Guide.

I remember hearing in the mid-1980s that a former street reporter, a then-little-known talk-show host who had bested Phil Donahue in her market, was demanding ownership of her show. It was inconceivable to me, a local reporter who felt nothing but powerlessness in the system, that this woman would actually get her way. The result, we know now, is the Oprah Winfrey empire. It has made her not only the richest woman in broadcasting (on her way to becoming probably the first woman street reporter to earn a billion dollars), but an influential figure in the book-publishing, magazine, and film industries as well. Her true power lies neither in ratings nor salary, but in participation in the *profits*.

As a contrary example, Kay Koplovitz, the early cable pioneer who for twenty-one years nursed the USA network to robust health as its *hired* executive, found herself promptly unemployed when Barry Diller bought USA network and installed himself at the helm. It wasn't that she didn't try. In her book *Bold Women, Big Ideas* (see below), she recounts the previous owners' resistance in the boardroom; without a second thought, they turned down the $100 million she had raised and the $350 million more she could raise. When the company sold in 1999, says Koplovitz, "Logically, a piece of that $5.5 billion should have been mine. But it wasn't. The issue was ownership. And I wasn't in that game."

Martha Stewart, the second most powerful entrepreneurial media woman, has shown the world what a half-hour syndicated TV cooking show can become: a marketing tool beyond the wildest predictions. Stewart's power also comes less from a paycheck than from ringing the bell at the opening of the Stock Exchange the day shares of *her company* went public.[13]

---

13. There is danger in playing with the big boys, as Stewart learned in 2002. As this book went to press, Stewart was embroiled in insider-trading and obstruction-of-justice questions from the U.S. House of Representatives Energy and Commerce Committee. At issue was her sale of 4,000 shares of the biotech company ImClone, one day before the FDA refused to consider the company's application for its colon cancer drug. Her friend Sam Waksal, head of ImClone, had been arrested and indicted on securities fraud, perjury, bank fraud, and obstruction of justice. Stewart maintained her innocence, but the scandal decimated shares of Martha Stewart OmniMedia through much of 2002 and cast a pall over her "squeaky clean" image. On September 10, 2002, her case was referred to the U.S. Department of Justice. Her celebrity status and gender ensured that she garnered the lion's share of headlines, outstripping coverage of major corporate implosions that involved many more billions of dollars of investors' money.

The future of women in television lies in our ability not only to rise to the top of existing media giants, but to create companies, and to be willing to merge them. I dream about what might be possible if Oprah and Martha, for instance, decided to become Thelma and Louise, after all— only this time giving us our long-delayed, happy ending.

And a woman *network* evening news anchor *would* still be nice. . . .

CAROL JENKINS heads her own New York-based company, producing documentaries and television films. For nearly thirty years, she reported and anchored the news and hosted her own talk show for television stations, primarily NBC, in New York City. On international assignment, she reported from South Africa on apartheid and Nelson Mandela's release from prison. Winner of the Emmy among numerous other awards for her work, she was honored with the Lifetime Achievement Award by the New York Association of Black Journalists.

Suggested Further Reading

Douglas, Susan J. *Where the Girls Are: Growing Up Female with the Mass Media*. New York: Times Books, 1994.

Halper, Donna L. *Invisible Stars: A Social History of Women in American Broadcasting*. Armonk, N.Y.: M.E. Sharpe, 2001.

Koplovitz, Kay. *Bold Women, Big Ideas: Learning to Play the High Risk Entrepreneurial Game*. New York: Public Affairs Books, 2002.

Postman, Neil. *Amusing Ourselves to Death: Public Discourse in the Age of Show Business*. New York: Viking, 1985.

Sanders, Marlene, and Marcia Rock. *Waiting for Prime Time: The Women of Television News*. Chicago: University of Illinois Press, 1988, reissued 1994.

Zevnik, Jean, ed., for American Women in Radio and Television. *Making Waves: The 50 Greatest Women in Radio and Television*. New York: Andrew McMeel Publishing, 2001.

Theater: A Sacred Home
for Women

EVE ENSLER

FROM ANCIENT GREECE through Elizabethan England, until only a few centuries ago, women were virtually barred from theater. Men performed women's roles. Only in the past century or so have (token) women playwrights been (grudgingly) admitted to the boys' club. For most of recorded history, women have not been allowed to participate in theater—public, shared, communal, and cathartic space—at all. Not as playwrights, not as actors, often not even as audience. I know why.

I've been a playwright for more than twenty years, and have written plays about nuclear war, homeless women, incest, death, S&M, refugees. I've written about these subjects because these were issues I feared most, having learned early on that whatever secretly terrifies me ultimately controls me—determines how I feel, think, and behave. I believe this holds true for society at large: sometimes what is right in front of us is what we most adamantly avoid. Confronting such realities head-on has often rescued me from paralyzing depression and a sense of malignant helplessness. While whole areas of women's lives still remain unspoken in public discourse, the theater—which brings people together and gives us the opportunity to confront concerns as a community—has the potential to be women's great ally. Through theater, the invisible can be made visible, paradigms can shift, the world can change.

Let's begin with vaginas.

It was an accidental possession. Vaginas snuck up on me, slowly consuming me, cell by cell.

I started talking to a few women friends in 1994. By 1998, I'd interviewed over 200 women and performed their stories all over the world—from Oklahoma to Connecticut, Texas to Baltimore; in Zagreb at the anti-fascist theater and in Jerusalem (where there is no Hebrew word for vagina); in colleges, recital halls, back rooms, and private homes. After a run at a small theater downtown in New York City, *The Vagina Monologues* moved Off-Broadway. That led to commercial productions all over the world, which in turn gave birth to V-Day, a global drive to end violence against women and girls.[1] In V-Day's first year, there was one production in New York City where actresses—including Glenn Close, Whoopi Goldberg, Rosie Perez, and Susan Sarandon—performed the play; the second year, benefit productions were staged in three major cities and at 55 colleges, raising money for local groups to stop violence against women.

As I write this, the show has premiered in 45 countries and been translated into 23 languages. In 2002, V-Day was performed in 800 cities, 550 colleges, and 250 towns and villages around the world, including in an Anglican church in Nova Scotia, a stadium seating 8,000 in Manila, the Folies Bergère in Paris, a pool patio in Tucson, a girls' boarding school in Zaire, and the Royal Albert Hall in London. This year (2002), V-Day will have raised close to $10 million for local, national, and grassroots groups around the world—to stop sexual slavery, rape, battery, and female genital mutilation.

In thinking about this in the context of women in theater, I wind up asking myself, *How did all this happen?* How did a few interviews with women about their vulvas and clitorises become an international phenomenon?

I did not realize the full potential and viability of the theater when I began *The Vagina Monologues*. I had certainly experienced theater's magic and power, but I had yet to understand its truly sacred nature, its ability to explode trauma, create public discourse, empower people on the deepest political and spiritual levels, and ultimately move them to action. I certainly had never understood what a significant role theater could play in the lives of women, who often came to see the show in groups. I did not know that the theater could be a forum for holding and

1. See "Landscape of the Ordinary: Violence Against Women," by Andrea Dworkin, p. 58; "The Nature of the Beast: Sexual Harassment," by Anita Hill, p. 296; "From Fantasy to Reality: Unmasking the Pornography Industry," by Gail Dines, p. 306; and "Prostitution = Slavery," by Vednita Carter, p. 315.—Ed.

exploding the depth of women's outrage, humor, and joy. I had not realized that the theater—its nature being personal, intimate, and community-based—was a perfect home for women.

It all began on a western mountaintop overlooking a polluted view of a corrupted city, the smell of gardenias wafting through the haze. I was engaged in a conversation with a brilliant woman when she stumbled onto the subject of sex and menopause. Out of nowhere, she began to talk about her vagina. "It's dead," she said. "Dried up, ugly, finished." She went on in detail. It was the bitterness of her tone, her self-contempt, that spun me into an altered state, one I often enter when my fantasy version of reality is fragmenting in front of me, when I'm being propelled out of denial. This was an insightful woman, a self-proclaimed feminist, a wonderful artist, a smart businessperson, an icon of sorts, at the top of her form. And there she was, sitting on a mountaintop, hating her vagina.

I clung to my denial. I decided she was aberrant, not like other women. There was the Women's Movement, after all. We have all been Down There with our hand mirrors and speculums. We have come to love our bodies. Yet in spite of my denial, some wicked thought had broken loose, and I had to explore it further. I began to talk to women. Each conversation exploded my notions of who I thought women were and what they should be feeling. Each interview detonated more questions and dilemmas, knocked down more doors around my denial.

When I first began to perform these monologues, I realized that just saying the word "*vagina*" caused enormous controversy, because *vagina* is in fact the most isolated, reviled word in the English language. The words *anthrax* or *plutonium* never caused anywhere near such a stir. The taboo on this word is no accident—for as long as we cannot *say* vagina, vaginas do not exist. They remain isolated and unprotected.

This is where theater comes in—making what's right in front of us truly visible. Theater insists that we inhabit the present tense, and by being there *together*, we are somehow able to confront the impossible. We are able to feel what we fear might destroy us—and then to be educated, and thus transformed.

It's the playwright's task to entice the audience into journeying where they may have been reluctant to go alone—but what happens when the playwright finds herself so moved by the emotional intensity of the material she's exploring that the creative process itself is threatened? This was nearly the case while I was writing *Necessary Targets* in 2001. This play addresses what happens when an American psychiatrist and a human-rights worker go to "help" a group of Bosnian women refugees during the early 1990s war in the former Yugoslavia. It is based on interviews I did with Bosnian refugees in 1993 and 1994. I spoke with women in cafés, abandoned hotels, and refugee camps—old women, modern women, traditional women, young, glamorous, rural, and professional women. Stories they told of the atrocities they'd endured almost destroyed me; being isolated with that information overwhelmed me, made me feel helpless.

Once I started to transform the stories into art, I felt them begin to have energy and vitality. By placing them in the context of a theatrical structure, the stories themselves become part of a larger community. That experience taught me that the theater is sacred, because it allows— encourages—us as a community of strangers to face *together* realities that may be too difficult to confront alone. Theater translates personal issues into social and political concerns (and responsibilities), ultimately giving us reasons for being with each other in that room.

For several years, I have had the privilege of working with a writing group at a women's prison in upstate New York. There are fifteen women in the group, and they come from many different racial, educational, and economic backgrounds. Most of these women have been sentenced for murder. There are also political prisoners in the group, and women who have been raped and subsequently killed their rapists. One day, we were struggling with a big issue. I had asked each woman to write a letter to the person she loved most profoundly, explaining why she's in prison. The women struggled over this for weeks, and the work got deeper, and the truth got deeper. Every personal detail they wrote and talked about reinforced the feminist adage that "the personal is political." Some had grown up in environments where they had little food, where people beat them and raped them, where no one ever told them that they were worth anything. Some had never been educated. Some were there because they had once believed violent revolution was necessary. All of this was political. In that sense, they were *all* "political prisoners."

If artists don't see and portray the links between art and politics, we wind up creating work that asks an audience only to be entertained, to escape for a few hours, enjoy the disassociation, and be let off the hook. I think people need to be *on* the hook.

When I performed *The Vagina Monologues* in Oklahoma, a young woman fainted and fell to the ground after the Bosnia rape section. We stopped the show, turned on the lights, brought cold water. It turned out that she had been raped by her stepfather and was overcome with memories. In the context of the theater that night, her suffering became our suffering. Audience members held her and spoke gently to her. Her abuse found a context and her suffering became legitimized, as her personal history became part of a larger social order that oppressed all women.

There is a notion that if we really let ourselves think about all the terrible things in the world, we'll get depressed. True, thinking from a detached position *can* be paralyzing: we can become undone by the overwhelming mass of horrifying, objective facts. But theater is not objective. It invites us *in*, into the subjective, invites us to inhabit others' experiences and emotions, to experience compassion. We enter the joy and pain of the characters, but this is not a pain that paralyzes; it expands us, makes us more than ourselves.

Of course, in an industry that tends to underestimate its audience's desire for plays that have the potential to transform, heal, and perhaps radicalize, none of this is easy—especially for a woman. It took me years to learn that writing the play is never enough. Like having a child, you can't just give birth to it and trust others to feed it or raise it. The success of *The Vagina Monologues* was due to a larger community that nurtured the play, and nourished me in the process. That community was able to survive and deflect bad reviews, able to laugh off attacks from vagina-fearing forces. It was able to stay focused on the intentions of the play—one of which was to empower and pleasure vaginas, the other to stop violence against women. There was an energy to this community, and a determination without which V-Day could never have happened.

I read once in a review that "only women" came to see my show. The insult of this "only women" explains why many female playwrights (myself included) have been so afraid to be marginalized or ghettoized as "women playwrights" *per se*. Almost every time I'm interviewed, the same questions are asked: How many *men* are now coming to see the show? How do you feel that so few *men* come to see the show? What do *men* feel about the show? The not-so-hidden assumption is that the show is not valid because thousands of men don't flock to it, that it's not "a real play," not "worthy," the way other things women do are not considered "real" or "worthy." Surviving in the theater as a woman writer means that you finally and forever break from this paradigm, that you hold women worthy because you hold *yourself* worthy, that you cherish your female audience and feel gratitude to them. You do not keep waiting for the "real" validation (or love) to show up.

I've come to see our culture as if all of it were that brilliant, talented woman on the mountaintop. Everything's in place: the picture, the success, the view. The only problem was that she felt dead inside, dried up, finished. My experience has led me to believe that only by wholly entering, wholly feeling, wholly *inhabiting* who we are can we discover happiness or fulfillment—and only by allowing ourselves to see what is already in front of us can we be freed from depression and inaction.

This is possible, especially in the theater—*if* we are willing to strip away the layers and risk making ourselves uncomfortable for a while. *If* we are willing to risk saying the word *vagina*, when that's what needs to be said.

EVE ENSLER has received a Guggenheim Fellowship [sic] Award in playwriting, the Berrilla-Kerr Award for playwriting, the Elliot Norton Award for Outstanding Solo Performance, and the Jury Award for Theater at the U.S. Comedy Arts Festival, as well as the 2002 Amnesty International Media Spotlight Award for Leadership, and The Matrix Award (2002). Her performance in her own Obie award–winning play, *The Vagina Monologues*, was made into an HBO film that has been released on DVD. Her play *Necessary Targets*, set in a Bosnian refugee camp, opened Off-Broadway in 2002; other plays include *Conviction, Lemonade, The Depot, Floating Rhoda and the Glue Man*, and *Extraordinary Measures. The Vagina Monologues* and *Necessary Targets* have been published by Villard/Random House, as will be Ensler's new play, *The Good Body*. Ensler's work, including that of being the founder and artistic director of V-Day *(www.vday.org)*, grows out of her own personal experiences with violence.

Suggested Further Reading

Brown, Janet. *Taking Center Stage: Feminism in Contemporary U.S. Drama*. Lanham, Maryland: Scarecrow Press, Inc., 1991.

Fraden, Rena, with a foreword by Angela Y. Davis. *Imagining Medea: Rhodessa Jones and Theater for Incarcerated Women*. Chapel Hill: University of North Carolina Press, 2001.

Steadman, Susan M. *Dramatic Revisions: An Annotated Bibliography of Feminism and Theatre, 1972–1988*. Washington, D.C.: American Library Association, 1991.

Woodman, Marion. *Addiction to Perfection: The Still Unravished Bride*. Toronto, Canada: Inner City Books, 1985; and Sharp, Daryl, ed. *Conscious Femininity: Interviews with Marion Woodman*. Toronto, Canada: Inner City Books, 1993.

Wynne-Davies, Marion. *Renaissance Drama by Women: Texts and Documents*. New York: Routledge, 1996.

Women and the Art World: Diary of the Feminist Masked Avengers

KÄTHE KOLLWITZ AND FRIDA KAHLO,
FOUNDING MEMBERS
OF THE GUERRILLA GIRLS

1984–85: Something Is Wrong with This Picture

KÄTHE AND FRIDA go to a demonstration at the Museum of Modern Art in New York to protest "An International Survey of Painting and Sculpture"—a show of 183 artists with only 17 women. The demo is totally ineffective. We want to educate the public, show them that sexism and racism, conscious and unconscious, keep (all) women artists and (male) artists of color out, but we end up arguing with museum-goers who truly believe curators make the best choices because . . . they're curators.

There's gotta be a way to prove that the art world is *not* a meritocracy where the cream *always* rises to the top. Something more contemporary, more media-savvy? How about "selling" our message, using advertising techniques? How about pointing fingers and naming names to get everybody talking about the issue? We decide to use ridicule, shame, and humor to make the liberal art world feel uncomfortable with itself. We dub ourselves "The Conscience of the Art World."

We begin meeting with a small group of women artists. We put up posters at night around New York City, spelling out the names and records of artists, dealers, critics, curators, and collectors who participate in a system that discriminates against us. As freedom fighters in the world of culture, we call ourselves "Guerrillas." To reclaim a word used for years to belittle and trivialize women, we call ourselves "Girls." To keep the focus on the issues, not our identities, we remain anonymous and appear in public wearing gorilla masks. To keep their memory alive, we take on the names of dead women artists. To make the "F" word (*feminism*) sexy and fashionable, we mug for photos in miniskirts and fishnet stockings. Everyone's talking about the issues we've raised. It worked!

1987: The Advantages of Being a Woman Artist

By now do we have a rep! But word on the street is the Guerrilla Girls are way too negative. We decide to do a poster to make women feel better: "The Advantages of Being a Woman Artist." We work on it for a long time. When we put it up, it's a big hit. It gets translated into at least ten other languages. A supporter buys a page in *Art in America* to send it around the world. Journalists threaten to "out" us, although when they

THE ADVANTAGES OF BEING A WOMAN ARTIST:

Working without the pressure of success.
Not having to be in shows with men.
Having an escape from the art world in your 4 free-lance jobs.
Knowing your career might pick up after you're eighty.
Being reassured that whatever kind of art you make it will be labeled feminine.
Not being stuck in a tenured teaching position.
Seeing your ideas live on in the work of others.
Having the opportunity to choose between career and motherhood.
Not having to choke on those big cigars or paint in Italian suits.
Having more time to work when your mate dumps you for someone younger.
Being included in revised versions of art history.
Not having to undergo the embarrassment of being called a genius.
Getting your picture in the art magazines wearing a gorilla suit.

A PUBLIC SERVICE MESSAGE FROM **GUERRILLA GIRLS** CONSCIENCE OF THE ART WORLD
532 LaGUARDIA PLACE, #237· NY,NY 10012
www.guerrillagirls.com

venture some names, they're usually wrong. We tell them we have so many supporters that an exposé would be the last article they'd ever be asked to write.

Art critics and curators send us apologies. Women artists send us money. A New York gallery asks us to do a Salon des Refusés concurrent with the Whitney Biennial. Instead, we do a show of information about the declining status of women artists at the museum. We use information culled from the museum's own publications, and we find a Deep Throat in the development office who smuggles out sensitive information about the museum trustees. We discover that one trustee, Alfred Taubman, is chief stockholder of Sotheby's *and* chair of the painting and sculpture committee that approves exhibitions. We call this insider trading and conflict of interest. Taubman later goes to prison for price-fixing.

What started as a lark now takes up more and more of our lives. But who's complaining? Instead, we look for new ways to extend and deepen our critique.

1989: Get Naked

The Public Art Fund (PAF) asks us to propose a billboard. We go to the Metropolitan Museum on a "weenie count" to tally the number of naked males versus naked females in the museum's permanent collection. Our findings? Greek and Roman: mostly male; Early Christian: everyone's covered up; Renaissance and Baroque: only exposed body is the Baby Jesus; Nineteenth Century and Modern: religion is out the window and naked women take its place. We find our statistic and our poster idea: "Do Women Have to Be Naked to Get Into the Met Museum?" Certain that all those trapped nude females in paintings are Guerrilla Girls, we put a mask on one by Ingres. The PAF is now afraid to sponsor the project—so we run it as an ad on New York City buses. It's a runaway success, and becomes our most popular, best-selling poster.

Do women have to be naked to get into the Met. Museum?

Less than 5% of the artists in the Modern Art sections are women, but 85% of the nudes are female.

GUERRILLA GIRLS CONSCIENCE OF THE ART WORLD
www.guerrillagirls.com

1993–95: Token Times

Multiculturalism in full swing.[1] Things are getting better for women and artists of color, but the art world still lags way behind the rest of society. It's not avant-garde, it's derriere. We decide to start a watchdog newsletter, *Hot Flashes*,[2] so that we can cover issues more fully than we do with our quick-shot, individual posters. We receive a National Endowment for the Arts grant to publish it—but the first Bush administration tries to take the grant away, claiming that our posters deface private property. Some influential art-world friends and a few outspoken journalists help us prevail. We take a look at museums all over the country and discover this interesting fact: the farther you get from New York, the *better* it is for women and for artists of color!

But there's a problem—the *same* women and artists of color get shown over and over. Tokenism in full bloom. Is this a solution to discrimination or a continuation of it? We do several posters, including "Token Times," where we look behind the multicultural agendas of cultural institutions to see if there isn't hypocrisy lurking there. We get letters from poets, journalists, musicians, veterinarians, and meteorologists who tell us tokenism is the story of their professional lives.

In 1995, we tell our story—and reproduce our first 60 posters—in

---

1. See, for example, Lucy R. Lippard, *Mixed Blessings: New Art in a Multicultural America* (New York: Pantheon, 1990).—Ed.

2. For *Hot Flashes*—and for all the Guerrilla Girls' posters, including those mentioned but not shown here—see their website: *www.guerrillagirls.com.*—Ed.

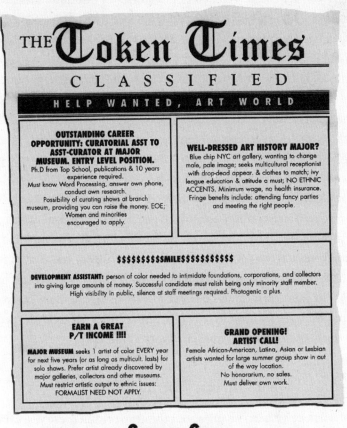

our memoir, *Confessions of the Guerrilla Girls* (New York: Harper Perennial). It goes out of print in about 16 months.

1996–2000: Today the Art World, Tomorrow the World

By now, we've branched out with posters about politics, rape, and abortion rights,[3] in addition to keeping up the pressure on the art world. We start a website, *guerrillagirls.com*, where we receive thousands of letters

---

3. See "Running for Our Lives: Electoral Politics," by Pat Schroeder, p. 28; "Landscape of the Ordinary: Violence Against Women," by Andrea Dworkin, p. 58; and "Unfinished Agenda: Reproductive Rights," by Faye Wattleton, p. 17.—Ed.

from all over the globe. Women tell us stories of discrimination. Many letters ask for advice. Lots of love letters. Some hate letters, too.

Ever since the poster "When Racism and Sexism Are No Longer Fashionable, What Will Your Art Collection Be Worth?" we've been thinking about how art history gets written and what gets put into the canon. (For that poster, we showed how $17 million—the same amount that had been spent on a single Jasper Johns painting—could buy enough work by every prominent woman artist and artist of color throughout history, to fill an entire museum!) In 1998, we finally got a chance to write our own version of art herstory, *The Guerrilla Girls' Bedside Companion to the History of Western Art* (Penguin). We research the lives of women artists who were able to get around all the rules designed to keep them out. Using research by feminist art historians[4] and our own crazy visuals, we prove that standard art history has it all wrong: there have *always* been great women artists! Either they weren't taken seriously in their own times or sexist historians wrote them out of the record. The book is used as a text at universities all over the world. We're thrilled! It even gets translated into Chinese!

2000–2002: Lights, Camera, Discrimination!

A lot of what we've been saying about the art world all these years finally comes to light. Auction houses are accused (and later convicted) of price-fixing. Museum directors and collectors get caught fibbing and exchanging favors and influence. Our early poster, "Guerrilla Girls' Code of Ethics for Art Museums," seems eerily prophetic.

We do "Historic Brooklyn Landmark for Sale," to make fun of New York Mayor Rudy Giuliani's attempts to censor the "Sensation" show at the Brooklyn Museum. We do "Intercepted by the Guerrilla Girls," a parody of a letter sent from Charles Saatchi, the art collector who owns a lot of the work in the show, to Giuliani, thanking him for all the negative publicity since it drove up the prices of his collection.

We discover there's someplace as bad as, or worse than, the art world: the film industry. Women in movies are usually young, white, and half-

---

4. See, for example, Ann Sutherland Harris and Linda Nochlin, *Women Artists 1550–1950* (New York: Knopf, 1976).—Ed.

naked. Behind the scenes, at the production level, it's an all white, all boys' club that gives millions to liberal causes to create the impression it's progressive. Supporters help us "Send a Message to Those Body Obsessed Guys in Hollywood" by sneaking our stickers into movie theater bathrooms. With a group of women filmmakers who call themselves Alice Locas,[5] we do stickers for the Sundance Film Festival and the Oscars. Sample: "The U.S. Senate Is More Progressive than Hollywood. Female Senators: 9%. Female directors: 4%." Our 2002 billboard in Hollywood, "The Anatomically Correct Oscar," showing the golden boy looking like the middle-aged white guys who usually win, puts Tinsel Town in a titter. We do endless press interviews and get letters from as far away as Australia and Japan. When two African American actors win awards we feel we may have helped a little. Our "The Birth of Feminism Movie Poster" addresses the history of feminism, some of our feminist heroes, and Hollywood, all at the same time (it stars, for example, Catherine Zeta-Jones as Bella Abzug). The tag line reads, "They made women's rights look good. Really good." It's a poster for a film we hope *never* gets made the Hollywood way.

2002–03: Still Crazy After All These Years

Eighteen years and we can't stop now! Our third book, *Bitches, Bimbos and Ballbreakers, the Guerrilla Girls' Illustrated Guide to Female Stereotypes* (Penguin, 2003), traces the evolution of female imagery in popular culture. In it, we propose a series of ethnic stereotype dolls guaranteed to make every ethnic group feel superior. In the final chapter, we invent new stereotypes to help women, not limit them: *Rockette Scientist*, girls who are smart, and make sure they get credit for it; *Lesbeanythings*, girls who get It wherever they want; *Fab Flabs*, girls who don't want to look like fashion models; *Elder Stateswomen*, girls who get better with age; and *Anti Types*, girls who make up their own rules and refuse to be put into any category.

---

5. The group's name comes from two sources: "Alice" is intended as homage to Alice Guy Blache, an early twentieth-century filmmaker who is credited as being the first narrative (e.g., storytelling) filmmaker as well as the first to found a movie studio; "Locas" is based on the Spanish word for "crazy"—in this case, meant affirmatively.—Ed.

We can't imagine our lives without the Guerrilla Girls. Lots of fun. Lots of work. Travel around the world, speaking at schools and universities about our anonymous activism, encouraging women (and men) to invent their own outrageous identities and tactics to fight discrimination in their own lives. We hope you won't forget to eat your bananas— and go ape with us in the twenty-first century! The best is yet to come!

Love and kisses,
The Guerrilla Girls

The original KÄTHE KOLLWITZ (1867–1945) was a German painter, lithographer, and sculptor who issued intensely dramatic prints and posters about war and poverty. The original FRIDA KAHLO (1907–1954) was a Mexican painter known for her impassioned, autobiographical, surrealist works. THE GUERRILLA GIRLS (also known as The Feminist Masked Avengers) are anonymous, as explained above. For more on their herstory, activism, posters, books, appearances, slide shows, etc., visit *www.guerrillagirls.com*.

Suggested Further Reading

Chadwick, Whitney. *Women, Art and Society*. London and New York: Thames & Hudson, Third Edition, 2002.

hooks, bell. *Outlaw Culture: Resisting Representations*. New York and London: Routledge, 1994.

Nochlin, Linda. *Women, Art, and Power*. New York: HarperCollins, 1989.

Pollock, Griselda. *Differencing the Canon: Feminist Desire and the Writing of Arts' Histories*. New York: Routledge, 1999.

On-line: *www.bitchmagazine.com*.

PART VI.

Tactics and Trends

Women and Law:
The Power to Change

CATHARINE A. MACKINNON

WOMEN MOVING TO END women's inequality to men have found law to be a wall as well as a tool for taking down walls. Sometimes they have made law a door.

Law, variously potent in all cultures, is particularly used in the United States to distribute and negotiate resources, rules, and power itself. Law in the United States is at once a powerful medium and a medium for power. Backed by force, it is also an avenue for demand, a vector of access, an arena for contention other than the physical, a forum for voice, a mechanism for accountability, a form of authority, and an expression of norms. Women seeking change for women have found that all these consequences and possibilities cannot be left to those elite men who have traditionally dominated in and through law, shaping its structures and animating attitudes to guarantee the supremacy of men as a group over women in social life. Women who work with law have learned that, while a legal change may not always make a social change, sometimes it helps, and law *un*changed can make social change impossible.

Historically, women have not been permitted the tool of law in our own hands. We had no voice in writing the U.S. Constitution. When, 100 years and a civil war later, an equality provision was added in 1868, it was without any expectation that the legal status of the sexes would be affected. Equality for women under the Constitution has been late, slow, and short. Severely undertexted, all that is there are the five words—"equal protection of the laws"—their application to women only by interpretation. In 1920, the Women's Movement of that period gained passage of the Nineteenth Amendment, formally institutionaliz-

447

ing women's equal citizenship: the right to vote, to decide who governs; the right to serve on juries, to decide what happens when people do not agree; and the right to practice law, to use this lever of power directly. Even with that, it took until 1971 for the U.S. Supreme Court to decide for the first time that different rights for women than for men could violate the constitutional equality principle.

The 1970s saw women moving into the legal profession in ever greater numbers, determined to end law's sexism, root and branch. The Women's Movement of the 1980s and 1990s applied equal protection doctrine to women where it fit and exposed its male bias where it did not. Women revealed that its main interpretive doctrine—while a big improvement on no constitutional sex-equality guarantee at all—works best for women's problems that arise least: where sex discrimination is explicit on its face, or where an elite individual woman meets male standards but is not treated as men are treated. But most laws that promote sex inequality do not discriminate on their face, even as most women in unequal societies do not have the advantages of being similarly situated to men. That is, the existing equality rule works best for problems, however important, that fewest women have.

Despite the shortfall in the Equal Protection Clause, a federal Equal Rights Amendment (ERA), originally proposed in 1923, narrowly failed ratification in 1982 after several attempts at passage.[1] Similarly, the international Convention on the Elimination of All Forms of Discrimination Against Women (CEDAW), which could help compensate for the lack of an explicit sex-equality guarantee in the U.S. Constitution, has, as of this writing, yet to be ratified by the U.S. Senate. As of 1973, most U.S. women who needed abortions were no longer criminals, but those who could not pay for abortions were still effectively deprived of access to them by lack of federal funding for this medical procedure.[2] At the beginning of the twenty-first century, no explicit words yet granted overarching legal equality to U.S. women.

---

1. The federal ERA as proposed in recent times reads simply: "Equality of rights under the law shall not be denied or abridged by the United States or any State on account of sex."—Ed.

2. See "Unfinished Agenda: Reproductive Rights," by Faye Wattleton, p. 17, and "Our Bodies, Our Future: Women's Health Activism Overview," by Judy Norsigian, et al., p. 269.—Ed.

Statutory law, passed by elected representatives of the people in a political system far from flawless at conveying the will of the governed, attempts to address some of the problems unremedied due to the absence of constitutional and international rights. In the late nineteenth century, married women secured the right to own property in their own name, so their material existence no longer had to be dependent on husbands by law. But a sex-unequal marketplace still did not necessarily provide them economic independence—and does not today.[3] In 1963, the Equal Pay Act guaranteed equal pay on the basis of sex for work that requires equal skill, effort, and responsibility. But most women have been and remain segregated into occupations that mostly women do—jobs that either are different or are seen as different from those men do and that are paid less. Title VII of the Civil Rights Act of 1964, propelled by the Civil Rights Movement, prohibited discrimination on the basis of sex in employment, although this amendment may have been introduced in Congress for racist reasons. Later Congresses did take sex discrimination seriously—for example, by prohibiting discrimination on the basis of pregnancy in employment in 1978 and extending Title VII to the federal labor force. Under the aegis of Title VII, sexual harassment and sex stereotyping as an employment standard were made actionable as violations of sex-equality rights, and discriminatory intersections between race and sex were increasingly recognized, inseparably, as a basis for legal action. But despite more than thirty years of legal guarantees of workplace sex equality—and some progress, mainly for elites—the workplace remains overwhelmingly gendered unequal to women's disadvantage.

Law functions also as a form of politics. On this level, law has required that women use its rules to be effective, even as part of women's political agenda has been to challenge and change those rules—rules women had no voice in making.[4] In its analysis of politics *as* sexual, the Women's Movement in our time has illuminated law's dynamics from beneath, casting new light on law as such. Before this movement, women, defined as the denizens of the private, were not thought of as a

---

3. See the "Workplaces" section, p. 323.—Ed.

4. See "Running for Our Lives: Electoral Politics," by Pat Schroeder, p. 28.—Ed.

political group at all. So law, embodying the rules by which public power is distributed, was thought inappropriate for addressing women's situation as members of a sex—certainly a convenience for male supremacy. Once women exposed the line between public and private as gendered—revealing that masculine is to public as feminine is to private—the male bias built into the definition of "the public" by law was also exposed. The public/private line that distinguished the properly legal from the legally exempt stood revealed as a barrier that excluded and marginalized women from law, and under and within it as well. Women thus began to claim a place in the public world of law, to redefine the legal as already involved in "the private" and as a determinant of women's status and treatment, top to bottom and society-wide. As women thus became subjects of law, the hidden and denied ways women had been subordinated to men prior to law and under law became revealed to public view, requiring accountability for the first time.

One example of this theory in action is the way Title VII's prohibition on sex discrimination in employment was used by women in the 1970s to forge the first civil right created by women: the prohibition on sexual harassment, a formerly subterranean practice considered a private privilege of powerful men.[5] By 1980, Title IX of the Education Amendments of 1972, which guaranteed women equal access to the benefits of an education, was authoritatively interpreted to prohibit sexual harassment in education, giving young women some legal rights against sexually exploitive teachers and coaches. Under Title IX, young women also routinely came to take part in organized athletics on a mass scale for the first time in U.S. history. Whether in so doing they reclaimed their bodies (becoming strong, self-possessed, and physically self-respecting) or whether their bodies were further claimed on male terms (competing to dominate rather than excel, striving to meet new sex-object standards, and having their victories co-opted as trophies for male triumphs), or whether some of both, remains to be seen.[6]

Also during the latter quarter of the twentieth century, some aspects of rape law were reformed in an attempt to make them more effective.

---

5. See "The Nature of the Beast: Sexual Harassment," by Anita Hill, p. 296.—Ed.

6. See "Women in Sports: What's the Score?" by Barbara Findlen, p. 285.—Ed.

The numbers of rapes reported soared for a time, but conviction rates rose barely, if at all. Pornography's harms were also legally confronted as a form of sex discrimination,[7] but the pornographers retained their First Amendment right to violate women's civil rights through pornography—at least for now.[8] Initiatives were taken to shelter women from battering in their homes, and to contain and educate the men who attacked them, but the rate of physical assault of women by men in intimate relationships did not measurably drop.[9] The Violence Against Women Act—a legal tool to empower the battered and raped by allowing direct accountability of batterers and rapists to their victims when their violence was sex-based—was passed by Congress in 1994, but was invalidated (as a violation of states' rights) in 2000 by a conservative majority of the U.S. Supreme Court. And while some statutes have begun to address international sex trafficking, little to nothing has been done by law for women in prostitution.[10]

All these issues will remain new questions for law until they are effectively addressed, even as other issues loom on law's horizon. Whose genetic material can be used how? How will "family" be created and defined?[11] As women participate in the armed forces, will aggression at home and abroad decrease or increase?[12] Will women and children be used and trafficked for sex in ever new technological forms and social configurations, or will the predators be stopped?[13] Will national and re-

---

7. See *In Harm's Way: The Pornography Civil Rights Hearings*, Catharine A. MacKinnon and Andrea Dworkin, eds. (Cambridge: Harvard University Press, 1997).

8. See "From Fantasy to Reality: Unmasking the Pornography Industry," by Gail Dines, p. 306.—Ed.

9. See "Landscape of the Ordinary: Violence Against Women," by Andrea Dworkin, p. 58.—Ed.

10. See "Prostitution = Slavery," by Vednita Carter, p. 315.—Ed.

11. See "Parenting: A New Social Contract," by Suzanne Braun Levine, p. 85.—Ed.

12. See "Redefining the Warrior Mentality: Women in the Military," by Claudia J. Kennedy, p. 409.—Ed.

13. See Dines, op. cit. See also "Changing a Masculinist Culture: Women in Science, Engineering, and Technology," by Donna M. Hughes, p. 393; and "Globalization: A Strategic Advance for Feminism?" by Jessica Neuwirth, p. 526.—Ed.

ligious strictures cease to subordinate women, so we can define our own cultures equally?[14] What new definitions and markers of gender will emerge? Will any truly fade? Will international law, uniting women globally in rights as they are currently united in inequality, prove capable of supporting changes in women's human rights that domestic laws have not? Will anything shift the unequal division of power between women and men?

In working with law, women have learned that the system of male supremacy is like a vampire: it thrives on women's blood but shrivels when exposed to the light of day. When subjected to law, male dominance is exposed in public. The private is a place, but it is also a mode; it is both where and how women are defined as women, a dimension of being as well as a location in space. Both are lawless sites to which women are relegated. This is what we have been tossed instead of having access to a whole life and a wider world. Law is the opposite, the quintessential public mode, private's antithesis.

When women claim and use law *as* women, women go public. This in itself challenges the hierarchy of men over women that has been built into law. For women to speak in a legal voice—especially to represent people effectively—requires something other than the ways in which women, socialized as private beings (as women, as feminine), are trained and allowed to speak: apologetic, soothing, imitative, pandering, approval-seeking, risk-averse, ineffective, deprived of consequence. But law is not only combat; it is also cooperation—and here women's training under inequality is a skill. Yet law also requires skills of contention—including standing one's ground—and persuasion—including touching and moving others onto one's ground—abilities that are still widely stigmatized, even demonized, in women.

As more and more women graduate from law schools,[15] legal culture will accommodate them. Perhaps it will respect them and women's sta-

---

14. See "Combating the Religious Right," by Cecile Richards, p. 464; "Dancing Against the Vatican," by Frances Kissling, p. 474; and "Inner Space: The Spiritual Frontier," by Margot Adler, p. 551.—Ed.

15. In 2000, for the first time, more women than men applied to law school. The American Bar Association estimates female enrollment in the law-school class of 2004 to be 49 percent. See "Law Schools' New Female Face," by Ted Gest, *U.S. News & World Report*, 9 April 2001.

tus will rise. Perhaps the status of the legal profession will sink as more women move into it, or women's legal ghettos will form within it. Possibly women in law—who will remain a small minority of all women—will become lawyers as men have, using its advantages as an elite profession over other women and men. In any case, women, once lawyers, will likely never have to sell themselves on street corners for sex to men by the thousands, or beg for an abortion from a back-alley butcher. They will either forget or remember the fact of their privilege, however earned, among women. But they will neither be insulated nor exempted from the rest of women's status, a fact they will either deny or else work with other women to change. Whether their practice of law reflects a consciousness of these facts of sisterhood under male dominance until it is finally ended will be—as it is now—up to them.

Most women think of law as alien, subject to influence they do not have, ignorant of the realities they live. Many conclude that law can do nothing for them, so they should stay as far away from it as possible. One result of this turning away, however realistic its reasons, is that male power can continue to own law unopposed. When law is abandoned to the powerful, corruption and physical force remain the real law, a fact ignored by those who urge abdicating this ground. It is hard to avoid the feeling that women are urged to think law can do nothing for them precisely because it can do so much.

Law means community: your people stand behind you, hear you, support you. It means reality: what you say happened is found to have happened, your knowledge is validated. It means vindication: it is wrong that you were wronged; someone took something that belongs to you; you count. It means hope: what happened to you might not happen to someone else, or to you, again.

Movement for women through law is not a marginal movement. It intends to change the mainstream, to make ordinary everyday rules work for ordinary everyday people—women included—and to give them tomorrow what they do not have today.[16] In whose interest is it for women to leave a power like this to men?

Women who use law for women in our time have tried to ensure ac-

---

16. See "Traffic at the Crossroads: Multiple Oppressions," by Kimberlé Crenshaw, p. 43.—Ed.

countability for the unspeakable: for sexual abuse, for torture, for genocide, for trafficking in human beings. Law *names* authoritatively. This is why survivors of abuse will take tremendous risks to say what happened to them only when law calls their abuse by its real name. Consider the almost-unbelieving ecstasy on the faces of the tortured when former Chilean dictator Augusto Pinochet was extradited in 1999. Recall the stoicism replaced by bitter uplift on the faces of surviving families when racist murderers in the U.S. South were brought to justice even decades later. Remember the crumpled blankness on the faces of raped women when their violators are exonerated, the look of hope vanquishing disbelief when their violators are convicted. It is this—not closure, not incarceration, not money—that law can mean. It can give people back a piece of the humanity that their violation took away. This is what gives law the power to change.

CATHARINE A. MACKINNON, Elizabeth A. Long Professor of Law at the University of Michigan and a long-term visitor at the University of Chicago, is a lawyer, teacher, writer, and activist on sex equality, domestically and transnationally. The analysis she pioneered of sexual harassment as sex discrimination was adopted by the U.S. Supreme Court (1986) and has spread worldwide. Together with Andrea Dworkin, she coauthored ordinances recognizing pornography as sex discrimination. The Supreme Court of Canada largely embraced her approach to equality (which has also been influential in South Africa), hate propaganda, and, in part, pornography. Her pro bono representation of Bosnian Croat and Muslim women resulted in the recognition of rape as a civil claim for genocide under the Alien Tort Act (1996) and has affected the jurisprudence and practice of international tribunals. Her publications include *Sexual Harassment of Working Women* (Yale University Press), *Toward a Feminist Theory of the State* (Harvard University Press), *Only Words* (Harvard University Press), and numerous articles, including "Disputing Male Sovereignty: On United States v. Morrison," 114 *Harvard Law Review* 135 (2000). Her work is among the most frequently cited in legal scholarship. She is co-director with Jessica Neuwirth of The Lawyers Alliance for Women (LAW) Project of Equality Now, which promotes women's equality under law globally.

Suggested Further Reading

Charlesworth, Hilary, and Christine Chinkin. *Boundaries of International Law*. Manchester, England: Juris Publishing, 2000.

Crenshaw, Kimberlé. "Demarginalizing the Intersection of Race and Sex: A Black Feminist Critique of Antidiscrimination Doctrine, Feminist Theory, and Antiracist Politics," 1989 University of Chicago Legal Forum 139 (1989).

MacKinnon, Catharine A. *Sex Equality*. New York: Foundation Press, a division of West Group, 2001.

Millett, Kate. *Sexual Politics*. New York: Simon & Schuster, 1969.

Rhode, Deborah L. *Justice and Gender*. Cambridge: Harvard University Press, 1989.

Owning the Future:
Women Entrepreneurs

SARA K. GOULD

MAREA WASHINGTON, a single mother with a three-year-old child, is a licensed family day-care provider in Lowell, Massachusetts. She learned how to start her home-based business through training offered by the nonprofit, Lowell-based, Acre Family Day Care Corporation. AcreFDCC offers women starting home-based family day-care businesses 96 hours of child development and business administration classes and 144 hours of direct experience in various childcare settings. The women also join Acre's network of family day-care providers, receiving a range of benefits that jump-start their businesses and help them grow. Marea was recently elected vice president of Acre's board of directors, and is applying to schools for in-depth training to equip her for working with special-needs children and their families. In 2000, she reported business revenue of $34,000, and she's saving for the down payment on a house through AcreFDCC's Individual Development Account (IDA) program, a subsidized savings plan that's the first of its kind in Massachusetts. Acre also led a coalition of organizations, represented by the providers themselves, that successfully advocated increasing state reimbursement rates, making licensed family day-care providers in Massachusetts among the highest paid in the country.

What related threads weave through Marea's story? *First,* women's economic security: every woman's ability to generate income at least sufficient to support herself and her family, and build savings that can fund investments and secure her retirement. *Second,* Marea Washington is not just a worker but an *owner:* she encounters an owner's level of authority, responsibility, risk, and benefit in her working life. *Third,* her story exemplifies the power of organizing and advocacy to change policy and practice in ways that spread benefits beyond the individual. Weaving together these three threads—*economic security, ownership,* and *advocacy*—empowers women through business development.

Women's Economic Security

Economic security is a basic key to every woman's ability to govern her own life and influence the world around her. Until recently, however, the United States addressed issues surrounding women's economic security only through a social-service framework. Economic policies/programs focused on protecting and improving the health of the *mainstream* economy, treating white men as the main players. A different set of policies—welfare, social services, and employment and training—offered (some) support to women and children, and to men of color. This created a separation that made it difficult to perceive anyone other than European American men as stakeholders in economic-development efforts.

After more than thirty years of U.S. feminist activism, the picture has changed. Local, regional, and national women's organizations operate innovative programs and advocate for responsive policy to help women gain access to productive, well-paying, stable work outside the home. Such efforts stress good pay, benefits, and the importance of childcare, transportation, and job training—and reflect a growing understanding that building security means more than increasing income. Families move out of poverty by building assets they can rely on in times of crisis and pass along to future generations: accumulating savings, buying a home, growing a business, acquiring advanced and specialized education.

Women as Workers and Owners

In the mid-1980s, local women's organizations involved in helping poor women train for jobs realized that many women were adding home-based business activity to their livelihood strategies. Groups began developing ways to aid these women, helping them obtain small loans, training them in how to price goods, write business plans, market products. Many such techniques were based on microenterprise programs in developing countries, like those of the originator of such programs, the Self Employed Women's Association (SEWA) in India, or, later, Bangladesh's Grameen Bank.

Microenterprises are very small businesses, usually owned and operated by one person, employing five or fewer workers and requiring less than $25,000 in start-up capital. From the beginning, women have been at the center of microenterprise work in the U.S., representing the majority of clients and leading innovators. At this writing, there are more than 500 programs providing business training and credit services to at least 100,000 people a year.[1] Funding from federal and state government agencies, while still insufficient, has greatly increased, following the lead of private foundations and banks.

Because of the sophistication of the U.S. economy, microenterprise programs often find that entrepreneurs need training and business counseling as much or more than loans. So programs assist women on a myriad of issues: finding a profitable market niche, marketing over the Internet, mastering government regulations, keeping their books. They also work with entrepreneurs in groups to create peer support, and involve program alumni and experienced business owners in mentoring.

Women-owned businesses of all sizes—from one-woman microenterprises to businesses employing 100 or more people—are now a vital, expanding part of the mainstream U.S. economy. As recently as 1976, the Small Business Administration (SBA) did not yet disaggregate its data by gender. By 1999, according to research sponsored by the National Foundation for Women Business Owners (NFWBO), the number of women-owned firms had more than *doubled* between 1987 and 1999. In 1999, there were 9.1 million women-owned businesses in the U.S., representing 38 percent of all businesses, employing 27.5 million people, generating over $3.6 trillion in sales annually. *Women-owned businesses are growing faster than any other small business sector, and they participate in every industry.* They're continuing to diversify into many industries considered "nontraditional" for women. For example, though

---

1. John Else, "An Overview of the Microenterprise Development Field in the U.S.," in John Else, et al., *The Role of Microenterprise Development in the United States* (Geneva, Switzerland: International Labour Organisation, 2001).

the largest share of women-owned firms is in the service sector, the greatest *growth* in the number of such firms is, according to NFWBO, in construction, wholesale trade, agriculture, transportation/communications, and manufacturing.

The Office of Advocacy of the SBA estimates that some 4.7 million women will be self-employed by 2005: an increase of 77 percent since 1983, compared with a 6 percent increase in the number of self-employed men. As of 1996, a woman of color owned one in 8 women-owned firms in the U.S.; the number of these firms increased *three* times faster than the overall rate of business growth between 1987 and 1996.

Change is evident not only in the almost exponential growth but also in *content* and *style*. A 1994 NFWBO study showed that women business owners are more likely than men to offer flextime, tuition reimbursement, and job sharing. They also tend to share their business's profits with employees at a much earlier stage: nearly twice as many woman-owned firms employing fewer than 25 employees have set up such programs, compared with all small firms employing 20 or fewer employees. The same study found that women business owners with 50 or fewer employees are almost two thirds more likely than other businesses of the same size to use computer technology.

Why do so many women become owners of their own businesses? Many are tired of climbing a corporate ladder, or have bashed into a glass ceiling, or don't want to spend more energy fighting to reach the top.[2] Some never considered working for anyone else. If a local economy is flagging or a woman lives in a rural area, she may have no other choice than to engage in business activity to generate some or all of her household's income. Women from different racial, ethnic, and class backgrounds, and women who are lesbians, disabled, or older often start businesses for reasons related to the specifics of their having experienced multiple discriminations in the workplace.[3]

Starting and building a business transforms more than a woman's economic circumstances. It can change the way she sees herself and her

---

2. See "Up the Down Labyrinth: Ins and Outs of Women's Corporate and Campus Careers," by Ellen Appel-Bronstein, p. 387.—Ed.

3. See the "Juggling Jeopardies" section, p. 163, and "Traffic at the Crossroads: Multiple Oppressions," by Kimberlé Crenshaw, p. 43.—Ed.

role in the community. As an owner, she gains greater autonomy over her working life; enjoys a new level of authority and responsibility; and may be in a position to create a fair, productive work environment for others. She gains confidence as she overcomes challenges, and develops a stake in the way business rules and practices are created and exercised. Her business becomes an asset she can pass on to her children. She derives satisfaction from being her own boss and doing work she *chooses* to do, instead of *has* to do.

Extending such benefits to groups of women working together is the prime motivation for the many women's cooperative businesses organized over recent decades. Experience in cooperative development by and for women is extremely varied—small sewing and quilting co-ops in the South; co-ops marketing the products of artisans; co-ops in traditionally low-wage industries (like childcare[4]), where ownership structure allows return of a greater portion of revenue to workers/owners in the form of both wages and dividends.

New York–based Cooperative Home Care Associates (CHCA) is an example of this last type. Serving the South Bronx and upper Manhattan since 1985, CHCA employs some 600 home health aides and an administrative staff of 25. Approximately 70 percent of its workers are also owners of the company, and workers/owners elected by their peers constitute the majority of the board of directors. An elected 25-person worker council advises the board on operational issues. Many administrative staff members were promoted from the position of home health aide, and approximately 70 percent of the company's workers formerly received public assistance. CHCA is a yardstick business (one demonstrating new, effective ways of enterprise) in the home health-care industry, because of its work with health-care paraprofessionals. The company's belief—that good jobs for frontline, paraprofessional workers will result in higher quality care for clients—directs its actions. CHCA's wages and benefits are among the highest in the New York City area. To deal with the short duration of many home-care cases, the company pioneered a guaranteed-hours policy through which every three-

---

4. See the discussion of caregiving in "Poverty Wears a Female Face," by Theresa Funiciello, p. 222; and in "Pink Collar Ghetto, Blue Collar Token," by Alice Kessler-Harris, p. 358.—Ed.

year employee receives 30 hours of pay a week, as long as they are available for work. CHCA's workers/owners understand their company's beliefs and strategies, as well as their own role in industry change. When the Home Care Association of New York State sponsors a lobbying day in Albany, CHCA workers are the only paraprofessionals walking the halls of the legislature to push for higher reimbursement rates that will reach workers in improved wages and benefits.

A younger nonprofit organization engaged in developing women's cooperatives is WAGES—Women's Action to Gain Economic Security. In 2001, WAGES was supporting two nontoxic house-cleaning co-ops owned and operated by twenty Latina women in northern California. The co-ops provide a healthier work environment plus wages above the industry average. WAGES works with co-op members to build their business skills, and offers them leadership-development opportunities, such as public-speaking and group-communication skills, or designing/providing environmental education in their communities.

Changing Systems and Practices

Many programs that assist women business owners also organize to bring about progressive public policies and changes in industry-wide practices—to improve the circumstances of many women at once. This kind of advocacy is driven by both vision and opportunity. For example, when the Temporary Assistance for Needy Families (TANF) program debuted at the federal level in 1996, local and state organizers knew that the window of opportunity for influencing the design of state-level programs was small. Organizations like the Good Faith Fund in Pine Bluff, Arkansas, the Women's Self-Employment Project (WSEP) in Chicago, Illinois, and the Appalachian Center for Economic Networks (AceNET) in Athens, Ohio, went to work.

The Good Faith Fund assembled a coalition of groups as the Welfare Reform Working Group to influence the legislature in Little Rock, and won several successes: state welfare law recognized microenterprise as an allowable work activity, introduced individual development accounts with no financial cap, and included a one-year delay in the two-year time limit for cash benefits. Also working in coalition, WSEP successfully advocated for Illinois to adopt additional self-employment exemptions, individual-development account and self-employment disregards, and changes of TANF rules to permit microenterprises to grow. In Ohio, at the urging of the Community Development Corporation Association's IDA Task Force, the state authorized Individual Development Account programs, and a statewide coalition successfully inserted into state law key provisions, including increased monthly TANF payments to the neediest families and childcare support for the working poor.

Toward the Future

Women-owned businesses are recognized today as a major, growing contributor to the U.S. economy. There's little doubt now that entrepreneurship is a viable option for many women. But in the United States, where much is made of "pulling yourself up by your own bootstraps," it's worth reflecting on the daily context for most women entrepreneurs. They, like their wage-earning sisters (*and* their unwaged yet working homemaker sisters), are striving to gain greater economic security. If successful, their business activity moves them into economic self-sufficiency, not into great (or even modest) wealth. In fact, many move back and forth between self-employment and waged employment, depending on the economy and business conditions. Still others combine self-employment *and* a waged job to make ends meet.[5]

These realities mean we must not lose sight—or grasp—of the first thread: economic security. Ownership will be the path to such security for a relatively small number of women. In the coming decades, we must delve more deeply into what works in assisting women from a wide *range* of circumstances, in a variety of industries and ownership structures, to become successful business owners.

Perhaps our most compelling challenge lies in learning how to harness the growing economic, political, and social power of women business owners for effective advocacy: the third thread. Today's women business owners are a diverse group from different identities, backgrounds, ages, and situations. Leaders in their communities and role

---

5. See Funiciello, op. cit., and Appel-Bronstein, op. cit.; also see "*Just* a Housewife?!" by Helen Drusine, p. 342.—Ed.

models in their families, they know the challenges (and compromises) women face on the job and at home. Many feel highly motivated to help other women from similar circumstances. Their stories attract media and public interest, and their voices on economic and social issues are growing stronger. Working in alliance with other women's organizations, they are well positioned to engage in advocacy aimed at changing economic conditions for *all* women.

SARA K. GOULD is the executive director of the Ms. Foundation for Women. She joined the foundation in 1986 as the founding director of the economic development program, and led the design of the program's flagship activities, including the Institute on Women and Economic Development and the Collaborative Fund for Women's Economic Development. She has authored, coauthored, and edited several publications in the field of microenterprise, and is a frequent speaker on women's economic security. She received a master's degree in City and Regional Planning from Harvard University in 1977, and has held professional positions with the Corporation for Enterprise Development, the Women's Action Alliance, and the Massachusetts Community Economic Development Assistance Corporation.

Suggested Further Reading

Dawson, Steven L., and Sherman L. Kreiner. *Cooperative Home Care Associates: History and Lessons.* New York: Paraprofessional Healthcare Institute, 1993.

Edgcomb, Elaine, Joyce Klein, and Peggy Clark. *The Practice of Microenterprise in the U.S.* Washington, D.C.: The Aspen Institute, 1996.

Else, John et al. *The Role of Microenterprise Development in the United States.* Geneva, Switzerland: International Labour Organisation, 2001.

Krimerman, Len, and Frank Lindenfeld, eds. *When Workers Decide: Workplace Democracy Takes Root in North America.* Philadelphia, Pennsylvania: New Society Publishers, 1992.

Combating the Religious Right

CECILE RICHARDS

RIGHT-WING FUNDAMENTALISM is nothing new to American culture.

For years, such televangelists as the Reverend Jerry Falwell and Jimmy Swaggert developed an enormous religious following, preaching over the airwaves to millions of viewers. However, in the late 1980s, Right-wing fundamentalists turned their attention to the political arena. Many of their leaders believed the United States had been founded as a Christian nation and should be governed by Christians sympathetic to the Right-wing political perspective. In 1989, with the formation of the Christian Coalition, the religious Right movement launched an effort to change U.S. politics fundamentally. Founder Pat Robertson explained their mission: "to mobilize Christians—one precinct at a time, one community at a time—until once again we are the head and not the tail, and at the top rather than the bottom of our political system."[1] The Christian Coalition realized their plan through old-fashioned political organizing. They identified their voter base (primarily fundamentalist Christians), trained them in political action, ran them for office—and turned them out to vote.

Under the politically savvy leadership of then-executive director Ralph Reed, the Christian Coalition was the most effective national group of the lot, but they were hardly operating on their own. Several significant religious Right organizations became politically active in the 1990s and remain so today. The American Family Association, obsessed with sex and pornography, organized national boycotts of TV programs

---

1. Institute for First Amendment Studies website (*www.ifas.org*), Profile on the Christian Coalition.

and companies; Focus on the Family, led by Dr. James Dobson in Colorado Springs, Colorado, communicated the religious Right political message to millions of Americans through their daily radio program and ten monthly magazines; Phyllis Schlafly's Eagle Forum organized to censor school texts and library books; and Beverly LaHaye's Concerned Women for America led the fight against sex education and against civil rights for lesbian and gay people. Each of these multimillion-dollar-budget national organizations carried out their own particular agenda, and the combined political power of the Right grew exponentially.

They organized their supporters around the traditional hot-button social issues of abortion and sex, and also launched a full-scale assault on public institutions. They attacked public libraries, public television, and the arts, but saved most of their energies for public education. Falwell, founder of The Moral Majority, proclaimed, "I hope I live to see the day when . . . we don't have any public schools. The churches will have taken them over again and Christians will be running them. What a happy day that will be!"[2] They portrayed government as dangerous and subversive; they made elected officeholders the enemy; they used sophisticated tactics to gain media attention.[3]

It didn't take long to make an impact. In the 1994 elections, candidates across the country faced an onslaught from religious Right organizations—one they never saw coming. The Christian Coalition alone claims to have distributed 33 million election voters' guides in churches across the country that fall, and they mobilized an enormous fundamentalist Christian voting bloc.[4] As a result, they totally reshaped Congress (for which, at this writing, the nation is still suffering); they took control of many state Republican parties; and they delivered the extra 5 to 10 percent of the vote that made the difference between victory and defeat in many local races.

Ralph Reed infamously admitted his political strategy: "I want to be

2. Jerry Falwell, "America Can Be Saved," 1979.

3. See "The Media and the Movement: A User's Guide," by Gloria Steinem, p. 103.—Ed.

4. *Norfolk Virginian-Pilot*, 9 November 1991; People for the American Way (*www.pfaw.org*) website.

invisible. I do guerrilla warfare. I paint my face and travel at night. You don't know it's over until you're in a body bag."[5]

That year, many politicians didn't know until election night—when the Christian Coalition and others turned them out of office. And moderate Republicans discovered that there was no room left for them in their own party.

In the aftermath of 1994 (the election that launched George W. Bush's political career), the U.S. public began to learn more about the religious Right's political activities and agenda. Seeing the dramatic impact they made on my own state, I decided to quit my job and form a state-wide organization to counter this movement. One of the religious Right's more expansive spokespersons, the Reverend Pat Robertson, certainly provided enough inspiration for anyone to become active. His view of the fight for women's equality is described as follows: "The feminist agenda is not about equal rights for women. It is about a socialist, anti-family, political movement that encourages women to leave their husbands, kill their children, practice witchcraft, destroy capitalism, and become lesbians."[6] It's tempting to laugh at this statement. But Robertson was arguably responsible for electing many members of Congress who took office in 1995. This was a situation that was hard to ignore.

So, in January of 1995, we formed the Texas Freedom Network (TFN), to bring together mainstream parents, religious leaders, and community leaders, to fight back. Our mission is to monitor the religious Right, train leadership, alert the media to religious Right activities, and advocate for public education and for civil and religious liberties.

What we've found over the past years is that although the religious Right has assembled a formidable grassroots organization nationwide, only a small minority of voters supports their movement. They have not been able significantly to convince Americans to embrace their agenda. *But.* When the majority of voters don't vote, and when most of the public isn't paying attention, a small minority can do a lot of damage. The real danger is when no one takes them on. So whether in defense of a

5. PFAW website: Who's Who on the Religious Right.

6. Rev. Pat Robertson, direct mail, Summer 1992.

local public-school reading list or a bill before Congress, we have to mobilize *our* side.

In the process we've learned some important lessons. The most critical is that *the religious Right movement has nothing to do with religion*: it's a far-Right political movement that exploits and misuses religion in order to promote its political agenda. Although many of the supporters may be religious, *the agenda is to gain political power.* The Christian Coalition is not trying to get more people to go to church; it's organizing Right-wing voters to go to the *polls*, precinct by precinct, just like a political party.

Their success is largely based on their commitment to grassroots organizing. Every major religious Right organization has an enormous, committed following. Ralph Reed brought to the Christian Coalition—and the overall movement—an appreciation for turning these members into political activists. He built the political infrastructure around local elections and issues where his troops could gain experience, groom candidates, and build local political operations. Reed said, "The real battles of concern to Christians are in neighborhoods, school boards, city councils, and state legislatures."[7] He understood that all politics is ultimately local, and *that* is where to gain a foothold.

The religious Right also mastered the use of fear-based politics, seeking to divide the country on issues of race, gender, sexuality, and religion. The Christian Coalition and others rely on slanderous electoral campaigning, using bedrock anti-gay, anti-abortion rhetoric that fires up their followers. They don't need to build *majority* support for these issues; they simply need them to be able to *mobilize their own voters*. Even in races for state boards of education, the Christian Coalition would often score candidates on the irrelevant but defining issues of abortion, the death penalty, or lesbian and gay rights. Ironically, in many targeted elections both candidates are Christians, but the voters' guides promise to help distinguish the "true" Christian candidates. Some guides even helpfully printed a pink triangle next to candidates who supported civil rights for lesbian women and gay men.

The religious Right movement heavily fueled the backlash against women's rights during the 1990s. The Right has always considered the

---

7. *The Washington Post*, 14 March 1990.

Women's Movement as fodder, starting in the 1970s with Phyllis Schlafly's dire forecast of "unisex toilets" during their attack on the Equal Rights Amendment. But the threat of women's economic equality has especially inflamed the Right: in their opinion, women have usurped the traditional, appropriate role of men as providers and leaders of the family, and have disrupted the supposed previously harmonious gender balance in society. Promise Keepers, the religious movement of men started in the 1990s, hoped to reestablish men's "rightful place" as leaders at home and in society. Their leadership articulated most clearly the inherently misogynistic nature of the religious Right. Promise Keepers' founder, former football coach Bill McCartney, warned of revenge: "There's coming a day when the strongest voice in America will be that of a Christian male."[8] Falwell praised Promise Keepers, saying, "It appears that America's anti-Biblical feminist movement is at last dying, thank God, and is possibly being replaced by a Christ-centered men's movement."[9]

From electoral politics to public policy, the religious Right continues to exert a tremendous impact in the United States. Their political influence culminated with the 2000 election of George W. Bush and his enthusiastic support of the Right-wing agenda. Still, hard times provide historic opportunities. There are many things that can be done by people who support reproductive rights and civil rights, clean air and water, public schools, separation of church and state, etc.

The first thing is to *know the opposition*, so that you can effectively organize your supporters and educate the press. Whatever the issue—an electoral campaign, a ballot initiative, hate-crimes legislation, a book challenge at the local school—get on religious-Right mailing lists, attend their meetings, read their literature, check their websites, and become familiar with the national organizations with which they are affiliated.

In 1995, out of nowhere, religious Right candidates suddenly took over a suburban school board in Round Rock, Texas. They began banning books by such authors as Maya Angelou; they ended counseling

---

8. Institute for First Amendment Studies website: "Promise Keepers: Seven Reasons to Watch Out," by Amy Neiberger.

9. Jerry Falwell, *National Liberty Journal*, March 1995.

programs and fired the superintendent. Research showed that the candidates were affiliated with Citizens for Excellence in Education, a national religious Right organization formed to take over school boards across the USA.[10] Once the organization's agenda was exposed to the community and the press, religious Right board members were voted *out*. But it took organizing, research, and education to turn the school board around.

Effective research and monitoring can also forestall the religious Right's ability to forge bad public policy when no one is looking. School textbook adoptions are an area where the religious Right is active (but often nobody else is), and textbook hearings don't usually attract much media interest. Still, when the Eagle Forum in Texas proposed taking Langston Hughes out of literature textbooks because of his "communist sympathies," and filed complaints that social-studies books contained an "overly negative portrayal of slavery in the South," we notified the press—and had standing-room-only hearings. The proposed changes were defeated.

The second key to success is to *build your own grassroots network*. Whether it's an issue before Congress or the local school board, the religious Right succeeds when they can generate hundreds (or thousands) of calls overnight. Politicians usually don't vote with them because they *agree*; they vote with them because they're *afraid* of the constituency they can mobilize.[11] *We must be able to do the same.* Whether battling a Supreme Court nomination or a bill before the state legislature, we have to demonstrate that our side *cares* as much as theirs does. On any given issue, Pat Robertson can deliver half a million paid phone calls to Congress from Christian Coalition supporters.[12] The American Family Association, Focus on the Family, Concerned Women for America, and others join forces in support. But *we can be equally as effective:* women's,

10. According to Dr. Robert Simonds, President of CEE: "There are 15,700 school districts in America. When we get an active Christian parents' committee (CEE) in operation in all districts, we can take complete control of all local school boards." Citizens for Excellence in Education, Direct Mail; PFAW website.

11. See "Running for Our Lives: Electoral Politics," by Pat Schroeder, p. 28; see also "Dancing Against the Vatican," by Frances Kissling, p. 474.—Ed.

12. PFAW website.

labor, civil rights, and other organizations can generate hundreds of thousands of calls, letters, and e-mails. This effort of progressive allies must become routine, collaborative, and disciplined, demonstrating our widespread engagement on issues of concern.

Perhaps the most important task anyone can undertake locally is to *organize the clergy*. We need to have religious leaders on our side. They're busy, and they must be organized one by one. But they're influential in the community—and they're living proof that the religious Right does *not* speak for all people of faith. We organized the Texas Faith Network, composed of clergy from various denominations that share a politics of community and compassion not represented by the religious Right.[13] Faith Network members have testified before the legislature, city councils, and the State Board of Education, have spoken to countless state and local organizations, and have held press conferences on issues ranging from domestic violence to school vouchers. They are courageous, articulate, thoughtful speakers, and our most important allies.

At this writing, the religious Right wields enormous influence through George W. Bush, their ally in the Oval Office. Pat Robertson recently crowed on his TV show, *The 700 Club*, that, now back in control of the White House, the "conservative operatives are making the most of their opportunity."[14] The religious Right has been amply rewarded for delivering their electoral troops, and is openly elated that the Bush cabinet is "chock-full of free enterprisers and social conservatives."[15] Less than two years into this administration, we've already been flooded with Right-wing appointments, restrictions on international family planning and abortion services, abandonment of air- and water-pollution standards, and efforts to breach the constitutional separation of church and state.[16]

---

13. Texas Freedom Network *(www.tfn.org)* website.

14. Robertson speaking on *The 700 Club*, May 2, 2002; Americans United for Separation of Church and State website, *www.au.org*.

15. Larry Kudlow, *National Review* On-line; PFAW website.

16. In July 2002, over the objections of Bush-appointed Secretary of State Colin Powell, the Bush administration withdrew all previously approved U.S. funding from the United Nations Population Fund. See the Introduction, p. *xv*.—Ed.

As I write this, it's been less than a year since the world witnessed the horrifying attacks on the World Trade Center and Pentagon. These acts of terrorism seem to have been fueled in large part by fears of the perceived threat ostensibly posed by other cultures and religious beliefs—the same kind of fear-based divisiveness we must guard against here in our own country. Soon after the attacks, in a now notorious TV exchange with Pat Robertson, Jerry Falwell declared that civil libertarians, along with "the pagans, and the abortionists, and the feminists, and the gays and lesbians" had so enraged God that he "lifted the curtain of protection" and allowed the terrorists to "give us probably what we deserve."[17] At least in this instance, the lessons Americans have learned about the dangers of intolerance seem to have escaped the religious Right. It is this type of incendiary rhetoric we must guard against—especially now, when people are legitimately afraid and thus most susceptible to the politics of fear, whether it be anti-woman, anti-immigrant, anti-gay, or any other divisive political agenda the religious Right so vigorously promotes.[18] It is more important than ever that we respond, actively, at all levels of our society, in order to learn and teach the correct lessons from this tragedy: that we need to champion our pluralistic society, celebrate and further the progress made for women and minorities, and promote a growing appreciation for our diversity of religion, sexual preference/orientation, ethnicity, and race—which are precisely the qualities that make this country unique. The political

17. Falwell, September 13, 2001, on Robertson's *The 700 Club*, Fox Family Channel (a subsidiary of the Walt Disney Company).

18. A sobering study released in September 2002 noted that "socially conservative churches" have grown in membership faster than any other religious denominations during the 1990s. The study—"Religious Congregations and Membership: 2000," by the Glenmary Research Center, sponsored by the Association of Statisticians of American Religious Bodies—reported that the Church of Jesus Christ of Latter-Day Saints (the Mormons) was the fastest-growing denomination (increasing by 19.3 percent), followed by the conservative Christian Churches and Churches of Christ (18.6 percent), the Pentecostal Assemblies of God (18.5 percent), and the Roman Catholic Church (16.2 percent). The study noted that denominations with *declining* memberships were the "more moderate or liberal" churches (e.g., the Presbyterian Church USA). The study's authors acknowledged imprecision, since the data are based on self-reporting by the religious groups, and the groups can inflate their numbers. ("Conservative Churches Grew Fastest in 1990s, Report Says," by Laurie Goodstein, *New York Times*, 18 September 2002).—Ed.

impact of September 11, 2001 is still to be realized fully, but the need for people of good conscience to organize and speak out has never been more acute.

The great civil-rights activist Fannie Lou Hamer said that you can get sick and tired of being sick and tired. But there's no time for that. *It's time to quit despairing over the political success of the religious Right—and learn from them instead.*

We need to stand up and be counted.

We need to organize politically at the grassroots level, train our supporters to run for office, to work their precincts, to get folks to the polls.

We need to show up at hearings, to call, write, fax, and e-mail our legislators.

We need to organize religious leaders to support us in these crucial causes.

The future is at stake, in the U.S. and around the world. If we truly believe in civil rights, reproductive rights, public schools, and clean air and water, then we'll be in the Congress *and* in the streets, fighting for them—or have no one but ourselves to blame.

We know what to do. It's time to get busy.

CECILE RICHARDS spent fifteen years as a labor and political activist in Texas, Louisiana, and California, organizing women working for the minimum wage in the health care, hotel, and janitorial industries. In 1995, she founded the Texas Freedom Network (TFN), a grassroots, nonpartisan organization of religious and community leaders working to support public education and individual and religious liberties, and provide a balance to counter Christian-Right influence in Texas electoral politics. She served as Executive Director for more than three years, during which time TFN became a resource on the issue of the religious Right for state and national press as well as for activists across the country. Richards has also worked on reproductive rights and family planning issues for the Turner Foundation, in Atlanta, Georgia. She serves as a member of the Board of Directors of Progressive Majority, the National Abortion and Reproductive Rights Action League (NARAL), the National Planned Parenthood Action Fund, and the Texas Freedom Network; she is also the President of Pro Choice Vote, a political action committee that educates voters about reproductive rights. Richards and her husband, Kirk Adams, live in Washington, D.C., and have three children: Lily, 14, and Hannah and Daniel, 10.

Suggested Further Reading

Boston, Rob. *The Most Dangerous Man In America?: Pat Robertson and the Rise of the Christian Coalition.* Amherst, New York: Prometheus Books, 1996.

Hardisty, Jean. *Mobilizing Resentment: Conservative Resurgence from the John Birch Society to the Promise Keepers.* Boston: Beacon Press, 1999.

Dancing Against the Vatican

FRANCES KISSLING

I WAS WORKING in my Washington, D.C., office when my friend Goeffrey Knox, then communications consultant for the International Women's Health Coalition, phoned from the United Nations' observers' gallery. It was spring, 1995; the UN was in the midst of a planning meeting for the Fourth World Congress on Women, to be held that year in Beijing. The accrediting committee had presented its report to the plenary session, requesting that over 1,800 women's organizations all over the world be granted the right to participate in the conference. The Vatican, using its status as a non-member state in the UN, had spoken from the floor, challenging the credentials of my organization, Catholics for a Free Choice (CFFC).[1] The Vatican claimed we weren't Catholic enough, and urged the UN to reject us.

I boarded the next plane to New York.

For centuries, the Vatican has suppressed dissent within the Church,

---

1. There are only two non-member states in the UN: the Vatican and Switzerland. Because it issues stamps and owns its own radio station, the Vatican belonged to international associations whose members were invited to participate in early meetings of the UN. Active in these meetings, the Vatican began unilaterally increasing its participation, and eventually established a mission to the UN in New York, claiming the status of a "non-member state permanent observer." Most likely recognizing that it could not meet the criteria and obligations of full membership, it simply notified then-Secretary General U Thant that, claiming statehood, it had established a mission to the UN. *This went unchallenged.* Although non-member states do not vote in the General Assembly, they have both voice *and* vote in UN conferences and regarding some agencies—and their presence gives them major lobbying power with full member states. Over time, as UN meetings have become more focused on women's rights, reproductive health, and recently, sexual rights, the Vatican has led efforts to unite countries where conservative religious forces have the power to oppose international governmental consensus and to block progressive international policy.

especially when women are the dissenters and the subjects are women's, sexual, or reproductive rights. Where the church has succeeded in silencing Catholics, it has usually acted in secret, with the complicity of those sanctioned. With CFFC this strategy has never worked. We always "go public." So we immediately held a press conference, pointing out that the word "Catholic" was not morally or legally owned by the institutional church. If the Vatican had a problem with our claiming our spiritual and institutional identity, then the place to go was court, not the UN.

The UN should have dismissed the Vatican's objection out of hand, but like most of the world's secular institutions struggling with the global rise of religious fundamentalisms, it was unsure how to react. Thus a committee of ten countries was convened; they met twice before confirming that CFFC met the criteria for participation as an international non-governmental organization (INGO). Chalk up another victory for feminists of faith, in the continuing struggle to limit the power of conservative religious institutions over our bodies and lives.

Roman Catholicism is certainly not the only religion seeking to control women. Buddhism, Hinduism, Islam, Judaism, and other branches of Christianity (among others) also discriminate against women.[2] And while the claim is frequently made by religious apologists that it isn't religions that degrade women but misinterpretations of religious teachings that lead to discrimination, it's hard to distinguish between teachings and interpretations, given the long history of religious texts *and* acts that punish women.

In Roman Catholicism, the scriptures and writings of early leaders of the church—men—laid the foundation for today's hatred and fear of women, of our sexuality, and of our ability to have children, attitudes that still permeate church positions. When St. Jerome told a widow who was contemplating remarriage that she was like a "dog returning to its own vomit"; when St. Odo of Cluny compared women to "a sack of manure"; when St. Paul advised women to be silent and obey their husbands; when women were continually told they were temptresses to blame for men's sexual sins, the message was clear: women are worth-

---

2. See "Combating the Religious Right," by Cecile Richards p. 464, and "Inner Space: The Spiritual Frontier," by Margot Adler, p. 551.—Ed.

less; sex is bad. From early childhood, girls are given a model of saint-hood physically impossible to emulate: Mary, the virgin mother. Who among us can be biological virgin and biological mother at the same time?

Sometimes I've worried that I'm too hard on the church, interpreting present behavior on the basis of past offenses. Perhaps these ideas about women had died out? After all, this pope—John Paul II—has publicly called himself "the feminist pope," claiming to promote women's equal-ity in all spheres of life except the priesthood. But recently reaffirmed church positions on women sadly reassure me that my suspicions are valid.

Is there anyone who doesn't know that the Vatican is officially op-posed to all abortions, even those that would save women's lives? Actu-ally, the church's opposition to abortion was *not* always so absolute. Most people don't realize that it was only in 1869 that abortion at any stage was made subject to automatic excommunication. This had much more to do with the church's position on sexuality than with respect for fetal life.[3] In fact, church opposition to sex for reasons other than pro-creation means it forbids both contraception for married couples and the use of condoms to prevent the spread of HIV/AIDS. The Vatican

---

3. Most people assume the church's position on abortion has been based on a "right to life" and has remained unchanged for 2,000 years. In fact, it has varied continually over the course of history, with no unanimous opinion on the subject at any one time. In 400 C.E., St. Augustine expressed the mainstream view that early abortion required penance only for the *sexual* aspect of the sin, *not* as homicide; 800 years later, St. Thomas Aquinas substantially agreed. Between 1198 and 1216, Pope Inno-cent III ruled abortion as "not irregular" if the fetus was not "vivified" or "ani-mated"; animation was considered 80 days for a female and 40 days for a male (though it was not explained how anyone could tell the difference in the womb). Pope Sixtus V forbade all abortions in 1588, but in 1591 Pope Gregory XIV re-scinded that order, reestablishing permission to abort up to 40 days for both a male or female fetus. St. Antoninus, Archbishop of Florence, a fifteenth-century Domini-can who wrote a major treatise on abortion, taught that early abortion to save a woman's life was *moral*. Thomas Sanchez, a seventeenth-century Jesuit, noted that all his Catholic theologian contemporaries justified abortion to save the life of the woman. It was only in 1869 that Pope Pius IX ruled all abortion murder and defined it as an excommunicable sin—possibly under pressure from Napoleon III, who was concerned that the birth rate had been dropping and France might face a serious de-pletion of soldiers for fighting wars and for colonization. Furthermore, and also contrary to popular belief, *the prohibition of abortion is not governed by claims of papal infallibility*—which leaves more room for discussion than is usually assumed.

also considers homosexual acts evil, and all heterosexual sexuality outside of lifelong, monogamous, church-sanctioned marriage evil as well. The church forbids any discussion of women priests, claiming women cannot be priests because we do not look like Jesus. Married Catholic men cannot be priests—but Lutheran and Episcopalian married priests who oppose women priests in their *own* churches *are* welcome to become Catholic priests, *and* to bring their wives along. Most of the world is so numbed by these positions that it doesn't even think about their effect on women's actual lives.

Women are so poorly regarded by the church that within the last decade the pope beatified[4] a nineteenth-century Italian woman whose sanctity was based on her having remained in a marriage where her husband constantly physically abused her. She was not considered saintly because she was beaten, but because she did not leave her husband. This veneration of marriage above women's lives was reinforced recently when the Vatican was asked to render an opinion on a particular case: could a husband who had contracted HIV/AIDS from a blood transfusion be permitted to use condoms to prevent his wife from becoming infected? The Vatican's advice was clear and harsh: the couple was called by God to a celibate marriage; however, should celibacy so strain the marriage that divorce was contemplated, then the couple should have sex—but *not* use a condom. The marriage sacrament was considered more important than the woman's life.

While these positions are deeply disturbing, the fact is that they are rejected universally by Catholics. Opinion polls throughout the world demonstrate that Catholics simply ignore the church when it comes to making decisions about sexuality and reproduction. In the United States, Catholic women use contraception to the same extent as other women—but U.S. Catholic women have 30 percent *more* abortions than Protestants and Jews in the U.S. What is disturbing is that the Vatican, unable to convince Catholics to follow its teachings voluntarily, has appealed to the UN and parliaments worldwide to act as its police force. *The Vatican seeks laws that would deny sexual and reproductive rights to Catholics and non-Catholics alike.*

For example, at UN conferences on population, on AIDS preven-

---

4. Beatification is a step on the way to sanctification (sainthood).

tion, and on women, the Vatican has consistently fought against including in UN documents such issues as condom education and provision. The leading bishop in Kenya publicly burned a supply of condoms in protest of government policy that provided condoms and information about safer sex. The Vatican has also been a frequent, vocal opponent of early abortion and emergency contraception for victims of rape, even when rape has been used as an instrument of war. During the 1993 war in Bosnia, the pope wrote to Muslim women rape survivors, asking them to turn their rape into an "act of love" and "accept the enemy within them," making the fetus "flesh of their flesh." Unfortunately, the Vatican has the power to turn such horrendous statements into public policy—by refusing to provide emergency contraception or early abortion in the many refugee camps it controls, even though the *funding* for such camps is provided by national governments and the UN. The Vatican has often threatened poor countries with the closure of Catholic hospitals if a country adopts policies that differ from church teachings. In Poland, the church supported government efforts to close down nursery schools and after-school programs, claiming it was better for women to stay home and care for children and the elderly. The Polish church called for an increase in men's salaries so that one salary would support the whole family. The position of this "feminist pope" is clear: the same "biology is destiny" line plus the one about motherhood being women's natural, most important role.

Of course, there are women in the church who support this view of "papal feminism," proclaiming themselves prophets of a "new feminism"—which applauds women only as mothers and opposes abortion because it's "bad for women" in that it "lets men off the hook" (as if all men took care of children they father whenever abortion *is* illegal). These women ignore feminist groups in developing countries, claiming feminism is a northern, U.S./European phenomenon forced on women of the global South—who are, we're told, innocently interested *not* in themselves but only in their families. And of course the "new feminism" rejects the new biology—women must not conceive babies without men (preferably husbands), and pregnancies must never be prevented, even after rape.

This conservative pope has conservative allies. He has fostered "new movements" in the church. Opus Dei answers to him personally, and its members are sent to cities where liberal bishops have not enforced the pope's line sufficiently.[5] New groups like the Catholic Family and Human Rights Institute prowl the halls of the UN, seeking to intimidate governments and NGOs. Their language is belligerent, racist, and sexist. They say aloud what the Vatican only whispers: feminists are evil. The executive director of this new arm of the Vatican publicly bragged that a priest in the Vatican's UN delegation promised him "absolution" if he "took out" Hillary Rodham Clinton—and he made it clear that "taking out" did not mean "on a date" but was intended in the gangster or military sense. Conservative Catholic women sit in on feminist meetings (sporting self-designed habits no self-respecting nun would ever wear) silently mouthing the rosary. Lesbian women participating in UN meetings in New York report being surrounded by these activists and forcibly "prayed over"; other women have reported being sprinkled with holy water in mock exorcisms to drive out the "evil spirits that dwell in feminists."

What *does* dwell in feminist and lesbian activists is a passion for justice and the courage to take on powerful global institutions: governments, corporations, religions. And in spite of the privileged place religion still enjoys in most countries, feminists—both religious and secular—have played a major role in limiting the impact of religion on public policy. Because of a highly developed feminist movement in Latin America, the Vatican has found that Mexico, Brazil, and Colombia, among others, have refused to support conservative positions on women and reproductive rights in the UN.

Taking on the Vatican—*and* the Taliban *and* the Muslim Brotherhood *and* the ultra-Orthodox rabbinate, *and* even the sexism of the Dalai Lama—*works*. Religious feminists have learned from secular feminists,

---

5. Though Opus Dei is the best known of the conservative groups, its workings are controversial and secretive. Founded in Generalissimo Franco's Spain but now a worldwide phenomenon, its members are drawn from the most powerful sectors of society, including industrialists, military leaders, and government officials. It has its own parishes, schools, and houses on college campuses from Stanford to Princeton. Men and women members are segregated, and ultra-traditional sex roles are encouraged and enforced. The women's program also emphasizes training poorer women to serve as housekeepers for Opus Dei's male centers. See *Beyond the Threshold: A Life in Opus Dei*, by Maria del Carmen Tapia (New York: Continuum Publishing Company, 1997).

and from each other. In 1999, Buddhist nuns followed the example of Episcopalian women priests and held an international ordination in India where sympathetic Buddhist monks transmitted the full ordination (normally received only by men) to qualified women. Muslim women in Malaysia are reinterpreting the Koran to reflect women's experience and rights, similar to work done by Christian and Jewish feminists in reinterpreting the Bible and the Talmud.[6]

Roman Catholic feminists have launched a particularly strong international movement designed to counter the political power of the church, and to change church teachings that are hostile and damaging to women. Perhaps the extreme centralization of male power in the church has contributed to the strength of the feminist movement within Catholicism. The absence of *any* concessions to women plus the harshness of church teachings actually inspires and contributes to activism. After all, Judaism has ordained women rabbis, and other branches of Christianity have ordained women priests and ministers; Sufis have women heads of temples; even evangelical fundamentalist Jerry Falwell approves of contraception (for married couples), and abortion (*if* a woman's life is at stake).

Feminist Catholics have found no such safety valves, so have had to fight for even the smallest advances. Our long-term goal is nothing less than total transformation of the church into a discipleship of equals where women share power and positions with men, where decisions are democratically based on the experience and needs of women as well as men. Our short-term goal is to break the power of the church in political life and ensure that public policy is based on what's good for women, not on what bishops need to stay in power.

In the U.S., Catholics for a Free Choice acts on the Catholic social-justice value of solidarity with the poor and works for the restoration of government funds for low-income women who choose abortion. In Brazil, CFFC lobbied the parliament and prevented the passage of an amendment to the constitution that would have declared the fetus a person from the moment of conception. In Europe, we work to ensure that the Charter of Rights promulgated by the European Union does not contain exceptions that allow the church to discriminate against homo-

---

6. See Adler, op. cit.—Ed.

sexuals in employment—and to ensure that it does not call Europe a "Christian nation." The media is often our friend: by publicizing church positions and injustices against women, press coverage adds to our legitimacy and exposes the Vatican's hypocrisy.[7] For example, press throughout the world has covered CFFC's international campaign to change the Vatican's UN status to the same status held by every other religion. Most people didn't know that the small space in Rome housing church offices, museums, and other tourist attractions has the same UN rights and privileges as the nation of Switzerland. After two years of our "See Change" campaign, they now know—and they don't like it.

In early 2001, *The National Catholic Reporter,* a liberal U.S. weekly newspaper, published accounts of official reports on the sexual exploitation of Catholic nuns by priests in 23 countries. The first report was issued in 1994, a follow-up in 1998. The Vatican did nothing. In 2001, a coalition of feminist religious, secular, and human-rights groups, mobilized by CFFC and the Feminist Majority, organized to put pressure on *civil* authority to punish these crimes. If the church wants to act like a secular power, it must answer to secular powers *and* to its members.

This has never been clearer than it is now, in the year 2002, when the church is in the throes of perhaps the greatest crisis of moral credibility it has faced in centuries. Thousands of articles in the worldwide press have reported on thousands of cases of sexual molestation of children and teens[8] by Roman Catholic priests, including some bishops—not only in the U.S., but in countries around the world. Some priests sexually assaulted once, others repeatedly; many predatory priests were reassigned to other parishes where they continued to abuse minors. And—despite the fact that the church has to date paid up to $1 billion in settlements and hush money—cardinals, bishops, and their lawyers still follow an aggressive blame-the-victim strategy.[9] The bishops who have

---

7. See "The Media and the Movement: A User's Guide," by Gloria Steinem, p. 103.—Ed.

8. See "Landscape of the Ordinary: Violence Against Women," by Andrea Dworkin, p. 58.—Ed.

9. Again, the Roman Catholic Church isn't alone in such abusive behavior and criminal cover-up. An August 2002 *New York Times* article broke the story of major sexual abuse in the Jehovah's Witnesses—a denomination claiming one million

covered up priestly pedophilia are the same bishops who have lied to us about birth control, saying it was intrinsically evil although they know full well there is no theological basis for banning it. Meanwhile, church leaders and Right-wing Catholics have latched on to the pedophile scandal to further their homophobic agendas, pushing to purge all homosexual men from the priesthood and blaming the worldwide scandal on "American licentiousness." What *is* it they don't *get?* The roots of the problem lie in the sins of elitism and sexism. Priests who abuse and bishops who defend them believe that preserving male power and privilege is more important than respecting the bodies and dignity of children and women. Priests who are, the church admits, often psychosexually immature are bound to seek out those they can dominate sexually. Celibacy [10] does not cause pedophilia, nor does homosexuality. But a diverse, mature priesthood that included women and men, gay and straight, married and single people, would go a long way toward creating a community in which domination of the defenseless was unacceptable. Encouragingly, as a silver lining in the cloud of the current scandal, more and more average Catholics are now beginning to question, and to say what Catholic feminists have been saying all along.

Working to change the church is exhilarating. The power of the church in the political arena *can* be diminished, and women's voices *can* make themselves heard. But three decades of modern Catholic feminist movement activism has raised questions about whether the church can be renewed or must be destroyed. Many religious feminists have worked

---

members in the U.S. and six million globally—as well as the same attempted cover-ups and intimidation tactics, in this case by church elders (themselves not infrequently accused abusers); church databases reportedly contain more than 23,000 names of church members and associates accused of, or found culpable in, such abuse. In the Jehovah's Witnesses cases, the majority of victims stepping forward are mostly girls and young women, which follows the pattern of what happened in the Roman Catholic Church, although there it was not until the victimization of young *boys* became public that the issue was taken seriously ("Ousted Members Say Jehovah's Witnesses' Policy on Abuse Hides Offenses," by Laurie Goodstein, *New York Times*, 11 August 2002).—Ed.

10. Church rules regarding chastity are as varying and recent as rulings regarding abortion (see above). Chastity—these days defended as always having been necessary for spiritual reasons—was actually made a clerical requirement by the Vatican as late as the twelfth century, out of monetary concerns about the clergy bequeathing their property to their own children and not to the church.

to reinterpret scripture and church history in a way that highlights values of democracy and equality. These scholars seek to use what's positive in these traditions, to effect change. At the same time, the religious texts of most if not all of the world's religions are so toxic with misogyny that some women question the value of a positivist approach. Buddhist Christian feminist Chung Hyun Kung has asked whether it is time simply to reject these texts and create new ones. Catholic women who have worked to invent new forms of worship and community experience within the church have for years created house churches, rituals, and liturgies that don't depend even on friendly priests, but simply ignore the priesthood as an irredeemable form of male power. These groups, like Sisters Against Sexism, meet as women-only worship groups in the safe space of homes; they need no priest to turn bread and wine into flesh and blood. Like secular feminists twenty-five years ago, we are focused on the question of whether we just want our piece of the pie—or whether the pie needs re-baking.

Interestingly, secular feminists have begun to ask questions about religion. The historic approach of feminism has been near total rejection of religion, as well as some suspicion of women who are religious. Both ultra-conservative Catholics *and* feminists have been among the first to say, "You can't be Catholic and feminist." Yet growing interest in feminist spirituality, positive examples of religious feminist activism, and solidarity with women—combined with the recognition that conservative, patriarchal religion is best countered by liberating, feminist approaches to faith—have opened the door for real collaboration between secular and religious feminists. The bonds of sisterhood celebrated between these groups are what will further the Women's Movement—a joyful movement with the courage, passion, and strength to dance our way to justice.

FRANCES KISSLING has been an activist and feminist leader for twenty-five years. In the 1970s, she directed one of the first family-planning clinics to provide legal abortions in the United States. In the 1980s, she became director of Catholics for a Free Choice *(www. catholicsforchoice.org)*. Today, as president of CFFC, Kissling is known around the world as a leader in the international reproductive health and feminist religious movements. She has given formal presentations to Britain's House of Lords, debated the U.S. Catholic Bishops spokesperson on abortion, and addressed the United Nations 1995 Fourth World Conference on Women in Beijing. She has also demonstrated (and been arrested) at the Vatican embassy in Washington, D.C., providing a dissident's commentary during bishops' conferences and papal visits, helped develop the skills of activists in Eastern Europe, and worked with Roman Catholic feminists throughout Latin America.

Suggested Further Reading

Daly, Mary. *Beyond God the Father: Toward a Philosophy of Women's Liberation.* Boston: Beacon Press, 1973.

Fiorenza, Elisabeth Schussler. *In Memory of Her: A Feminist Theological Reconstruction of Christian Origins.* New York: Crossroads Publishing Company, 1984.

Milhaven, Annie Lally, ed. *Sermons Seldom Heard: Women Proclaim Their Lives.* New York: Crossroad Publishing Company, 1991.

Reuther, Rosemary Radford. *Women and Redemption: A Theological History.* Minneapolis: Fortress Press, 1998.

Weaver, Mary Jo. *New Catholic Women: A Contemporary Challenge to Traditional Religious Authority.* San Francisco: Harper, 1986; Indiana University Press, 1995.

Front Line:
The Funding Struggle

MARIE WILSON

ASK ANY ACTIVIST what's the hardest part of her work and you'll hear the same answer: raising *money*. The scramble for cash is a hidden cause of burn-out for even the most talented visionaries. Although we who do fundraising think of it as another form of organizing, it can often feel frustrating. The best fundraisers are committed, passionate, and serious about their work, but they still say they feel like beggars. Feminists have named fundraising "the second oldest profession."

It's not that raising money doesn't offer a sense of accomplishment. Getting that check feels like the end of a mission, one on which people's lives and salaries often depend. But that mission can feel demoralizing when the money doesn't come.

Unfortunately, some aspects of fundraising haven't changed since the early days of women's causes: if what you're doing is the least bit controversial or doesn't seem to benefit *both* sexes, you will have to self-fund. Historically, women of all classes and ethnicities have held bake sales, raised dues from members, charged for speeches, tapped into church groups, and otherwise done whatever worked to raise money they needed for schools, settlement houses, anti-slavery movements, antiwar movements, and the cause of suffrage. It was guerrilla fund-raising. A few women, like Alma Belmont, broke ranks in the early part of the twentieth century, using their personal fortunes to support the women's suffrage movement. Today, there are many more women of wealth willing to focus their resources for the good of all women.

In the 1970s, the birth of contemporary feminism brought new waves of money and new ways to acquire it, as national women's institutions were formed and as feminist efforts pushed through legislative successes. Government-funded programs helped women enter (or re-enter) the workforce in nontraditional employment. The term "displaced home-maker" was coined, and government funds helped some of these women replace money they'd lost (through divorce or widowhood) with their own wages. Department of Labor grants began to address the job-training needs of poor women and women on public assistance.[1] Local funding helped women with day care and transportation.

Colleges across the U.S. vied for the new Women's Educational Eq-uity Act grants, which provided resources for continuing education as well as funding for research on barriers to women attaining higher edu-cation. There were grants and loans to send women to vocational train-ing schools and to private colleges, many of which, at the urging of women students and faculty, created women's programs.

When the 1980s arrived, government money vanished as swiftly as it had appeared, though the programs remained in place. Abandoned by the public sector, women's organizations looked to the foundation com-munity for funding. As early as 1972, the founders of *Ms.* magazine had had such difficulty raising money that they vowed to ease the pain of fundraising for women's causes by donating the magazine's profits to the movement. As they were foundation shopping to seed their new women's fund, they learned there was not even a *category* of funds in foundations that was designated for women. So the Ms. Foundation for Women was begun with funds from the John Hay Whitney Foundation; ironically, women who wanted to empower women got their first fund-ing via a program category designated for "powerlessness."

A group of program officers in the foundation community conducted a survey in the early '70s, documenting the pennies available to women: *0.5 percent of total foundation giving.* The shocking results of this survey sparked the creation of a new organization, Women and Founda-tions/Corporate Philanthropy (renamed Women and Philanthropy in 1995), with a mission to increase the philanthropic dollars available to women and girls. For a few years, it worked. In the late '70s, foundations created categories for funding women. Some of the largest founda-tions—among them Ford, Rockefeller, and Carnegie—took up the

---

1. See "Poverty Wears a Female Face," by Theresa Funiciello, p. 222.—Ed.

challenge. Program officers like Susan Berresford (now president of The Ford Foundation), together with some male allies, pushed for these changes.

New women's foundations were also created. Modeled on two existing national women's funds—the Ms. Foundation for Women, and Astraea—a host of state and local women's funds sprang up, from San Francisco to Minnesota to New York City. Women donors and activists worked side by side to create these new institutions, which embodied innovative ways to raise and distribute money. In 1985, they formed the National Network of Women's Funds in order to make their collective power felt.

Soon afterward came money for women and electoral politics. Ellen Malcolm, a donor who originally gave money to women's groups through her own foundation, the Windham Fund, traveled the country to involve people in Emily's List (Emily being an acronym for "early money is like yeast," e.g., it makes dough rise). It caught on, and created what has become a major Political Action Committee in the United States.

For a few happy years in the early 1980s, it looked like a wellspring had been tapped. Despite the lack of government funds, the foundation pot dedicated to women and girls grew from 0.5 percent to 3.4 percent of total foundation giving. (At this writing, in 2002, the figure is now close to 5 percent of total foundation giving—that's progress, but still shocking, since women comprise over 50 percent of the U.S. population.) Then this financial stream slowed to a trickle, much to everyone's surprise. Female philanthropists conducted a survey to determine why. The responses can be summarized in one memorable quote: "We *did* women." Foundations apparently felt that the agenda for over half the country's population had been adequately funded in a few short years. We were back at square one, having to think creatively about how to scrounge the money we needed for our under-funded causes.

Corporate philanthropy also changed around that time. No longer were those foundations providing money on the basis of the cause being good; now the cause also had to fit with their *marketing* aim. A central funding question became: "Will this grant help us to build loyalty among women customers?" With funding at a crisis point, the women's community revisited its ongoing debate over "clean money." Could we ever defend taking money from *Playboy?* From Phillip Morris or other cigarette manufacturers? Some organizations refused to do so; some made compromises, especially if their money filtered to poor women and women of color; others questioned whether any money is truly clean, if traced to its roots. The late 1980s also saw an alarmingly effective Right-wing assault on corporations that funded specific women's issues: for instance, strategic letters from Right-wing anti-choice groups could dissipate funding for Planned Parenthood, an organization that served millions of women on various reproductive health issues.[2]

A headline for the story of women's funding in the 1990s could well have been *Women's Funds Spread and Grow Across the U.S.* Having experienced the fickleness of funding sources and the instability of year-to-year fundraising, these women's funds began to build their capital. Following in the footsteps of pioneers like Helen Hunt and Lucia Woods Lindley, new individual women donors began to found their own private funds or create local funds. The Women's Funding Network made a plan to grow, strengthen, and increase the joint power of such funds. By 2000, over 90 women's funds had given away $25 million.

"Leveraging" became the strategy. In collaboratives and donor circles, participants were asked to give from $25,000 to $50,000 a year to learn about and to fund such cutting-edge issues as fighting the Right-wing agenda domestically and fighting sex-trafficking globally. This strategy provided donors with an education and gave the participating foundations a way to take on new issues at reduced risk. The Ms. Foundation for Women had begun building donor collaboratives and circles in the late '80s, born of necessity as new issues arose that seemed riskier to foundations and to individual donors. The Ms. Foundation's first economic-development collaborative, established in 1991, took on microenterprise for low-income women. Donors pooled and leveraged their money while evaluating the effectiveness of microenterprise as a strategy. This collaborative on women's economic development is, at this writing, in its tenth year; it has involved forty donors and put

---

2. See "Combating the Religious Right," by Cecile Richards, p. 464; "Dancing Against the Vatican," by Frances Kissling, p. 474; and "Unfinished Agenda: Reproductive Rights," by Faye Wattleton, p. 17.—Ed.

$10.5 million into the field of women's microenterprise,[3] plus it has leveraged millions more as the ripple effect of the collaborative has grown.

The past three decades of the contemporary feminist wave have been characterized by enormous creativity, by entrepreneurship in building institutions and programs, and by gathering resources to carry the work forward. In the years ahead, the challenge will be to continue and expand what works, and to keep adding new funding—in an environment where many potential sources view the work of helping women as already completed.

Wilma Mankiller, activist and former paramount chief of the Cherokee Nation, says that when tackling a problem, begin at the beginning. So here is a shortened alphabet of new millennium strategies for a movement that remains rich with vision but short on cash.

A. *Alumnae.* Private schools and colleges have prospered from their ever-growing, built-in source of funds—the loyal, grateful educated. Women's organizations have also educated several generations for a new world beyond patriarchy and have done so without classrooms and textbooks. These institutions should ask alums to consider this "living education," and to provide funding to keep building these "universities of democracy" for the next generation.

B. *Business.* Many companies have found that serving women means business. Most of this service has been non-controversial—mentoring programs and breast cancer awareness, for instance. But older, trickier issues (once even unmentionable), like family violence, have now been named and understood, and are becoming part of the mainstream corporate give-back to women. Many smaller companies (for example, Ben & Jerry's, The Body Shop, Tom's of Maine, Stonybrook Yogurt) have integrated social responsibility into their businesses. Part of their corporate profits go to funding, and they also partner with organizations offering employment to residents of low-income neighborhoods, employment in the manufacturing and sales of their products. For instance,

---

3. See "Owning the Future: Women Entrepreneurs," by Sara K. Gould, p. 456.—Ed.

Esprit's clothing division has contracted with Appalachian women's groups for knitting and buttons—groups they located through foundations that originally funded the microenterprise.

C. *Collaboration.* Women who find themselves with money to give are often stumped by how to give it. Research and practice show that women want to give smartly and strategically; they want their gift to count. Donor circles and collaboratives set up by foundations allow women to pool their money and learn about issues in depth. The leverage and loyalty this builds are worth the effort for everyone involved.[4]

D. *Donate* (monthly!). The most successful charities in the United States—religious institutions—require tithing. About 85 percent of all giving in the United States happens when people gather in religious groups. Protestant churches have a history of asking people to give up to 10 percent of their annual income, and they collect these pledges weekly or monthly. Women's organizations have much to learn from organized religions (which are often supported on the backs of women).[5] We should be as aggressive as they are, collecting for what is surely our own divine cause. Donating regularly over time is also a way that people with lower incomes—historically the most generous among us—can contribute.

E. *Endowments.* We need money of our *own.* Endowments give organizations a cushion in hard times; they also communicate a sense of permanence, and lend reality to the time it will take to truly accomplish our goals.[6] They also provide a source of funds for general support (the most difficult money to raise), and can provide seed money for issues considered edgy or controversial. The oldest women's funds have endowments, but they're not as large as they must be to sustain the institutions over time. The good news is that these endowments are growing, and their growth makes it safer for our allies to bequeath us money.

---

4. See Julie Peterson, "The Collaborative Fund Model: Effective Strategies for Grantmaking," New York: The Ms. Foundation for Women, 2002.

5. See "Inner Space: The Spiritual Frontier," by Margot Adler, p. 551.—Ed.

6. See "The Art of Building Feminist Institutions to Last," by Eleanor Smeal, p. 541.—Ed.

F. *Family Foundations.* These foundations are now replacing community foundations as the fastest growing segment in the foundation world, giving away $9 billion in 1999. Women are often the overseers of family foundations—the "softer side of wealth"—and find themselves learning about philanthropy as well as managing relational issues between family members. Women have tremendous potential power to use this money and to teach the next generation about philanthropy. This is where local women's funds can help, providing the training, staff, and infrastructure that's often lacking. In some instances, the family foundation may choose to become a permanent part of the local women's fund.

G. *Generational and planned giving.* More and more, donors are involving their children in their philanthropy, not only planning through bequests, but also bringing the next generation of funders into the circle. The baby-boomer wave of feminists is aging, and these women are starting to make bequests to the organizations that changed their lives. We can work with this constituency, helping them to will legacies toward completing the work so valued in their own personal experience.

I could continue this alphabet, but space and time limitations necessitate jumping directly to the letter "I"—for *Imperative.*

Since its founding, the United States has been consumed with national security, building armies and the machinery and weapons needed to protect and defend our country. In the wake of September 11, 2001, the definition of national security has broadened. Each day Americans witness how little poor nations and poor people feel they have to lose; how dire poverty and hatred drive people to strike out. Little by little, we are coming to understand how futile armed defense is without human security at home and abroad.

The case for human security—security for self, family, home, community and country—is what women have articulated for years. Ironically, in a time when our nation looks to the places that have been the province of men, war and weapons, it is the part of our world traditionally assigned to women that is key. Women have a unique, crucial role to play in uniting the citizens of this country—of whom we are the major-ity—but we will have to accelerate people's understanding that the agenda of empowering women *is* our best defense. And the capacity to both frame and build the necessity for human security will only happen if we raise money—lots of money.

When I first began fundraising, I quickly discovered that it was per-haps the most effective kind of consciousness-raising. Not only were you able to give people information that changed their views of women and women's ability to influence the world around us, but you gained the resources to spread these changed views. It's a powerful tool, made more powerful because our very existence now depends on it.

MARIE WILSON became president of the Ms. Foundation for Women in 1984, raising millions of dollars for programs and organiza-tions serving women and girls, including the Ms. Foundation's $16 mil-lion endowment fund. She co-founded The White House Project in 1998, to get more women elected to office, including the presidency; and in 1999, she founded the Women's Leadership Fund, a public edu-cation initiative dedicated to changing perceptions about and biases against women's leadership abilities. She also co-created Take Our Daughters to Work Day, and coauthored (with Elizabeth Debold and Idelisse Malave) *Mother Daughter Revolution: From Good Girls to Great Women* (Bantam Books, 1993).

Suggested Further Reading

Capek, M. S. *Women and Philanthropy: Old Stereotypes, New Challenges.* A Monograph Series. Battle Creek, Michigan: The W. K. Kellogg Foundation, 1998 (available on-line at *www.wfnet.org*).

Mead, Molly. *Gender Matters: Funding Effective Programs for Women and Girls.* Battle Creek, Michigan: The W. K. Kellogg Foundation, 2001 (available on-line from *www.wfnet.org*).

Saville, Anita, and the Feminist Majority Foundation. *Empowering Women in Philanthropy.* Arlington, Virginia: The Feminist Majority Foundation, 1991.

"Women and Philanthropy: Sharing the Wealth," a study released in May 1999 by the PBS television series *To the Contrary*.

On-line resources: Foundation Center *www.fdncenter.org;* Women and Philanthropy, *www.womenphil.org;* Ms. Foundation for Women, *www.ms.foundation.org;* Women's Philanthropy Institute, *www. women-philanthropy.org;* Women's Funding Network, *www.wfnet.org.*

Bitch, Chick, Cow: Women's and (Other) Animals' Rights

CAROL J. ADAMS

FEMINISTS DON'T SEE different things than other people see; feminists see the same thing differently. One same thing that some feminists see differently is animals. What we see differently is, in effect, animals' *absence*. We see the animal whose existence enabled a meal, or a coat, or a pair of boots. We see that what's absent (and thus what's present) is burdened with ethical, practical, and environmental imperatives: "Our culture kills animals with impunity; what is our responsibility?" And we animal-rights[1] feminists, we animal-liberation ecofeminists, we vegan-feminists (I know, I know, *what* should we call ourselves?) reply: "Our responsibility is to stop using and abusing animals." Consciousness has led us here.

Sandra Bartky, the feminist philosopher whose insights form the basis for the opening sentence of this article, notes that "Feminist consciousness . . . turns a 'fact' into a 'contradiction.' "[2] *Fact:* people

---

1. "Animal rights" has become the generic term for the movement for the liberation of other animals. However, there is an ongoing debate both inside and outside of the AR movement about the appropriateness of "rights" language. For many feminists, rights discourse is problematic. Some of us have proposed that arguments on behalf of animals be placed within ethics of care theory—nurturance, sympathy, and love are values that need not be directed solely toward human beings. In this article, however, for ease of comprehension and because this is the popular term, I will use "animal rights" in the generic sense. For more information on a caring approach to animal issues, see *Beyond Animal Rights: A Feminist Caring Ethic for the Treatment of Animals*, Josephine Donovan and Carol J. Adams, eds. (New York: Continuum, 1996).

2. Sandra Lee Bartky, "Toward a Phenomenology of Feminist Consciousness," in *Feminism and Philosophy*, Mary Vetterling-Braggin, Frederick A. Elliston, and Jane English, eds. (Totowa, New Jersey: Littlefield, Adams & Co.).

(including feminists) use animals for food, sport, clothing, and other commodities. *Contradiction:* such exploitation of animals continues, although animals are unique individual beings who enjoy social relations and possess a range of capabilities, including the ability to suffer pain.

How can people, especially feminists, use animals? Because of individual mental compartmentalization, and because of societal compartmentalization—which permits one person's contradiction to remain another person's fact. It is both the burden and the gift of life-changing consciousness to try to create conditions for others to experience the dissolution of fact into contradiction.

In feminist style, I offer my personal experience as an example. I remember the precise moment when a fact erupted into contradiction. I was about to take another bite of a hamburger. Earlier that day I had run to the pasture where our two ponies had been grazing. Jimmy, a beloved pony, was lying dead—either shot by hunters or dead by a heart attack after hearing the nearby guns. That evening, biting into that hamburger, I suddenly remembered Jimmy's dead body and asked myself, "Why am I eating a dead cow when I wouldn't eat my dead pony?" I encountered my own hypocrisy. The *fact* of the hamburger became a *contradiction:* "How can I, a feminist committed to stopping violence and working for liberation, eat slaughtered animals?"

A friend tells a different story. She was being choked to death by her husband. Suddenly she thought, *My husband says he loves me yet he is trying to kill me; I say I love animals yet I eat them.* In the midst of a murderous attempt on her life, she experienced life-changing contradictions. She was able to escape the attack, the husband, the marriage, *and* her own complicity in animals' deaths; she became an animal-rights activist.

It isn't surprising that women aware of how sexist violence inhabits our lives can extend this understanding to include other beings. Violence against animals is often an aspect of sexual and domestic violence.[3] An abuser—a rapist, an incest perpetrator, a batterer—may threaten to

---

3. See "From Fantasy to Reality: Unmasking the Pornography Industry," by Gail Dines, p. 306, and "Landscape of the Ordinary: Violence Against Women," by Andrea Dworkin, p. 58.—Ed.

kill (or *actually* kill) a beloved pet to terrify and control his victim.[4] Sexual predators and serial killers often began their violent activities by torturing and killing animals. Numerous tragic incidents of high-school violence usually involve boys and young men who had hunted, shot, and/or tortured animals first.

Ironically, the low status of animals that results in their usability forms the basis for a circular-logic argument *against* considering animals; e.g., how can I talk about *animals* when *women* are being beaten, raped, sexually abused and exploited and harassed, and further pauperized while being misrepresented as unworthy "welfare queens"?[5]

Because they are connected.[6] Animals are feminized and sexualized; women are animalized.

Falsely generic words (*mankind*) that elevate men to full human status must be analyzed in tandem with animal pejoratives for women (*catty, bitch, sow, shrew, dog, chick, cow*). Joan Dunayer, author of *Animal Equality: Language and Liberation* (Derwood, Maryland: Ryce Publishing, 2001), demonstrates that "Applying images of denigrated nonhuman species to women labels women inferior and available for abuse; attaching images of the aggrandized human species to men designates them superior and entitled to exploit."

This is nothing new. Historically, the ideological justification for women's alleged inferiority was made by associating us with children, animals, nature, and the body—which was devalued, if not repudiated outright. Most Western theorists construed rationality as the defining requirement for membership in the moral community.[7] And since all

---

4. See Carol J. Adams, "Woman-Battering and Harm to Animals," in *Animals and Women: Feminist Theoretical Explorations*, Adams and Josephine Donovan, eds. (Durham, North Carolina: Duke University Press, 1995); see also "Bringing Peace Home: A Feminist Philosophical Perspective on the Abuse of Women, Children, and Pet Animals," in Carol J. Adams, *Neither Man nor Beast: Feminism and the Defense of Animals* (New York: Continuum, 1995).

5. See Dworkin, and Dines, cited above. See also "The Nature of the Beast: Sexual Harassment," by Anita Hill, p. 296, and "Poverty Wears a Female Face," by Theresa Funiciello, p. 222.—Ed.

6. See "Traffic at the Crossroads: Multiple Oppressions," by Kimberlé Crenshaw, p. 43.—Ed.

7. See "Inner Space: The Spiritual Frontier," by Margot Adler, p. 551.—Ed.

women—along with men of color and with animals—were seen as less able to "transcend" our bodies, we were excluded from that membership, and from political participation. Women's claims on behalf of themselves were ridiculed by re-equating women with animals; philosopher Mary Wollstonecraft's eighteenth century classic, *A Vindication of the Rights of Woman*, was dismissively parodied in *Vindication of the Rights of Brutes.*[8]

Quite a few theorists associate women's oppression with animal exploitation. Anthropologist Peggy Sanday correlates male domination with animal-based economies and concludes that gatherer societies were more egalitarian.[9] Pro-feminist attorney and journalist Jim Mason proposes that the original model for oppression was the domestication of animals, and that based on information about reproduction gained from that, women's oppression evolved.[10] Theologian Rosemary Radford Ruether identifies "the male ideology of transcendent dualism" as being at the root of the connection between the domestication of animals, the development of urban centers, the creation of slavery, and the creation of sexual inequality.[11] In *Beyond Power: On Women, Men, and Morals* (Simon & Schuster, 1985), Marilyn French identifies the domination of women as a result of Western masculine denial of the human-animal connection. "Patriarchy," she argues, "is an ideology founded on the assumption that man is distinct from the animals and superior to [them]. . . . [because of] man's contact with a higher power/knowledge called god, reason, or control. The reason for man's existence is to shed all animal residue and realize his 'divine' nature, the part that seems unlike any part owned by animals." Marti Kheel, founder of the organization Feminists for Animal Rights *(www.farinc.org)*, argues that the

---

8. Thomas Taylor, *A Vindication of the Rights of Brutes* (London: Jeffrey, 1792).

9. Peggy Sanday, *Female Power and Male Dominance: On the Origins of Sexual Inequality* (Cambridge and New York: Cambridge University Press, 1981).

10. Jim Mason, *An Unnatural Order: Why We Are Destroying the Planet and Each Other* (New York: Continuum, 1997).

11. Rosemary Radford Ruether, "Men, Women, and Beasts: Relations to Animals in Western Culture," in *Good News for Animals? Christian Approaches to Animal Well-Being* (Maryknoll, New York: Orbis Books, 1993).

reason hunting has been defended in some environmental writings is because it is associated with male self-identity.[12]

One feminist response to the historical alignment of women and animals has been to sever all woman-animal identification, declaring instead that women are intellects and have rational minds—*like* men and *unlike* animals. Perhaps this response was a necessary phase in the transformation of cultural ideology about women. Associated with this response is one that asserts feminist theory has nothing to do with animals whatsoever.

Admittedly, the animal-rights movement lends the above approaches momentum. Feminists who have challenged street sexual harassment have encountered a new expression of it in the verbal (and sometimes physical) harassment of women wearing fur. Anti-fur-campaign advertisements, posters, and billboards have displayed scantily clad models and actresses, with the ad legend coyly announcing "I'd rather go naked than wear fur." PETA (People for the Ethical Treatment of Animals), recognizing that pornography sells products—even a "product" like animal rights—has made alliances with Hugh Hefner, used *Playboy*-identified women, and depicted violence against women in their campaigns on behalf of animals. While some AR activists believe that their position extends to opposing abortion rights for women, feminist animal defenders oppose the forced pregnancies or forced sterilizations of *any* female—human or nonhuman. Basic animal-rights arguments of the 1970s and the 1980s went something like: "We've '*done*' Civil Rights and Women's Rights. Now it's time for Animal Rights." This argument, while appealing to ethical grounds for considering animals, is highly problematic. An advocate fighting racism or sexism understands how fragile is any forward movement on these issues, and may not be ready to widen such advocacy to include different species. Moreover, *the use of animals is addressed as though it weren't related to the oppression of nondominant humans.* And because it has not theoretically linked the status of animals, all women, and men of color, the animal-rights movement has sometimes egregiously *exploited* the sexualized status of women, as well

---

12. See Marti Kheel, "License to Kill: An Ecofeminist Critique of Hunters' Discourse" in *Animals and Women: Feminist Theoretical Explorations*, op. cit.

as maintaining male dominance in organizations while benefiting from the fact that the vast majority of AR activists are women.

Much is lost when these movements are kept disconnected.[13] For instance, as feminist animal-rights lawyer Maria Cominou notes, while U.S. feminists who use their First Amendment rights to educate about pornography's harms are accused of being against freedom of speech, animal-rights activists in the 1990s had their speech curbed by the passage of "hunter harassment laws."[14] What a contradiction! Pornography remains so-called "protected speech," but talking to hunters while they hunt, or warning the animals hunters are stalking as prey, is not!

As the work of numerous feminist animal-rights activists and scholars suggests, many feminists *are* involved in bringing together an understanding of the interconnections between feminism, veganism, and animal activism. We believe that feminism is a transformative philosophy embracing the betterment of existence for all life forms. We believe that no one creature will be free until all creatures are free, and until the mentality of domination is ended in *all* its forms.

As feminists, we try to envision an alternative to the current oppressive culture. In 1976, I posed this question in a feminist magazine: "If it is our goal to live in a world without oppression, where does meat-eating fit into this vision?" Meat-eating becomes a central concern because of its many overlapping exploitative practices—including the oppression of workers who must kill, process, and package the slaughtered animals. These workers are mostly people of color, immigrants, and poor European American women, and they suffer the highest incidence of worker injury in any occupation.[15] Raising and then killing animals also involves the extensive exploitation of the natural world—water, fossil fuels, land use, deforestation for pastureland,[16] etc.—as well as requiring the deaths of close to 10 billion land animals per year in the

---

13. See Crenshaw, op. cit.—Ed.

14. Maria Cominou, "Speech, Pornography, and Hunting," in *Animals and Women: Feminist Theoretical Explorations*, op. cit. See also Dines, op. cit.

15. See *Fast Food Nation: The Dark Side of the All-American Meal*, by Eric Schlosser (New York: HarperCollins, 2001).

16. See "Update: Feminism and the Environment," by Paula DiPerna, p. 503.—Ed.

United States alone. I have argued that opposition to vegetarianism in patriarchal cultures occurs because of the *sexual politics of meat*: meat-eating is associated with virility, seen as symbolic of masculinity (meat advertisements now position animals in classic pornographic poses so that men can indirectly enjoy the exploitation of women without even being honest about it). With the proliferation of U.S.-owned corporations in other parts of the world (especially fast-food restaurants specializing in burgers), many issues raised by Western feminist animal defenders—especially those concerning animal agriculture—increasingly apply to other cultures.

Feminist critiques of science include analyses of assumptions about animals, assumptions that undergird justifications for animal experimentation. Lynda Birke and Barbara Noske argue that while feminist analyses of patriarchal science reject biological determinism for women, they do so by relying on overgeneralized and inaccurate ideas—fostered by patriarchal science—of "animals," as well as "humans."[17]

You might ask, "Is sisterhood here, too?" And I would say, "Yes, it is." After all, most animals are being exploited *because they are female*, e.g., breeders, as well as producers of milk and ova (eggs). Cows, milked until physically debilitated, may become "downers," unable to walk into the slaughterhouse. The first reproductive technologies, such as embryo transplants, were developed as part of the cattle industry—then transferred to women. Chickens are kept captive in small cages to produce eggs. The sheep, pig, and cattle cloning experiments now ongoing are all female-based.

Facts dissolving into contradictions. . . . An anti-war activist collecting blood from a slaughterhouse for a protest, suddenly wondering how she could continue to eat animals; a feminist academic watching eggs being harvested from a female sturgeon; a woman who stopped wearing leather after seeing the movie *Silence of the Lambs*. Feminist consciousness prepares us for such moments. And then what do we *do* with this amazing insight that transforms the way we perceive our lives? In her novel *Break of Day*, Colette describes looking at "the broken joints of the

---

17. See Barbara Noske, *Beyond Boundaries: Humans and Animals* (Montreal: Black Rose Books, 1997); see also Lynda Birke, *Feminism, Animals and Science: The Naming of the Shrew* (Philadelphia: Open University Press, 1994).

plucked and mutilated chickens, and you could see the shape of the wings, and the young scales covering the little legs that had only this morning enjoyed running and scratching." Then she poses a question. "Why not cook a child, too?" But soon Colette's narrator smells the "aroma of the delicate flesh, dripping on the charcoal, and concludes, 'I think I may soon give up eating the flesh of animals, but not today.' Do we, like Colette's narrator, become tempted by the smells of meat, the sights of the zoo or the circus, the feel of leather, the "necessity" for animal products or animal research, and think "but not today"? Or do we let that contradiction glow inside us and move us forward, one life-changing realization after another?

When I meet them on campuses, young feminists give me hope. Many have been vegans since, say, age twelve; they organized their first animal-rights protest at, probably, age fourteen; and they have arrived at college determined to ensure that these two forms of consciousness remain in dialogue with each other. These young people are ready to take on the implicit sexism of the dairy industry's Madison Avenue "Got Milk?" ad campaign. They are working at battered women's shelters while setting up resources for the animals that battered women don't want to leave behind. They are sponsoring vegan fundraisers for rape-crisis centers, creating senior-class projects that address the exploitation of women as meat, educating their professors about animal experimentation based on feminist critiques of patriarchally controlled science. They are part of the feminist process of envisioning and reconstructing human nature, and they are beginning at a basic level, the level we would all do well to consider: *Why must we define human as opposed to animal? After all, we are animals too.*

CAROL J. ADAMS is the author of *The Sexual Politics of Meat: A Feminist-Vegetarian Critical Theory*, now in a tenth anniversary edition (Continuum, 2000); *Living Among Meat Eaters: The Vegetarians' Survival Handbook* (New York: Crown, 2001); and a series of books on *The Inner Art of Vegetarianism: Spiritual Practices for Body and Soul* (Lantern Books, 2000). She edited *Ecofeminism and the Sacred*, the first multicultural ecofeminist anthology (Continuum, 1993); authored *Woman-Battering*, a book for ministers and pastoral counselors (Fortress Press, 1994); and, with Marie Fortune, coedited an anthology, *Violence Against Women and*

Children: A Christian Theological Sourcebook (Continuum, 1995). An anti-violence activist since the 1970s, Adams received her Master of Divinity degree from Yale University Divinity School. She and her partner started a hotline for battered women in upstate New York and she also worked at the grassroots level addressing issues of poverty, racism, and sexism. She is a frequent speaker at colleges and universities, showing her Sexual Politics of Meat Slide Show, and can be reached through her website: *www.caroljadams.com.*

Suggested Further Reading

Bloodroot Collective. *The Perennial Political Palate: The Third Feminist Vegetarian Cookbook.* Bridgeport, Connecticut: Sanguinaria Publishing, 1993.

Coe, Sue. *Dead Meat.* New York and London: Four Walls Eight Windows, 1995.

Gaard, Greta, ed. *Ecofeminism: Women, Animals, Nature.* Philadelphia: Temple University Press, 1993.

Ozeki, Ruth L. *My Year of Meats.* New York: Viking Penguin, 1999.

Williams, Howard. *The Ethics of Diet: A Catena of Authorities Deprecatory of Flesh Eating.* London: 1883. New edition, with an introduction by Carol J. Adams. Chicago: University of Illinois Press, 2003.

Update: Feminism and the Environment

PAULA DIPERNA

ANNE ANDERSON OF WOBURN, Massachusetts, sat in the school cafeteria. It was 1984 and she was hearing scientists agree that, as she had long insisted, contaminated water likely played a role in the town's high incidence of leukemia, birth defects, and other illnesses. But the vindication was not sweet. Her son, Jimmy, had died in 1981 at age thirteen, one of twelve children diagnosed with the same type of leukemia between 1968 and 1979. Each house had received drinking, cooking, and bathing water from the same municipal wells—wells drawing on underground water that had become contaminated by seeping toxic chemicals, thanks to decades of industrial pollution.

A foolproof link between the Woburn illnesses and deaths and environmental contamination was never found, and possibly never will be. Contaminants appear in the environment and reach the human body through water, air, and other routes, where they can cause disease directly or trigger latent genetic dispositions or vulnerabilities—often long after the footprint of contamination can be traced. Epidemiology has not yet developed methods to nail down cause-and-effect when complex, multiple, environmental variables come into play. But that doesn't mean answers don't exist or policies can't be changed. The Woburn case became a twentieth-century environmental touchstone because it demonstrated that environmentalism is *more* than what science can demonstrate. Environmentalism crosses all sciences and touches all dimensions of contemporary life: biology and sociology, economics, employment, politics, etc. The truth of environmentalism is more than facts.

Feminist environmentalism expresses precisely this holistic approach, since feminism resists compartments and segregation of ideas.[1] Moreover, it is women who are on the front lines. The female reproductive system is especially vulnerable to environmental insult; the health of women is, in general, an early warning system for society at large.[2] Women are also first to notice when illness strikes their children, and are usually the most astute, persistent, and vocal citizens in confronting corporate or political bureaucracies. Women constitute 60 to 80 percent of the membership of mainstream and grassroots environmental organizations in the U.S. (although—and not for lack of women's trying—most large organizations, such as Greenpeace and The Sierra Club, remain headed by men). "Women are at the very grassroots of everything," says Florence Robinson, the Southern University biology professor who in 1989 founded the North Baton Rouge Environmental Association in Louisiana, to combat air pollution and hazardous waste caused by petrochemical plants in mainly African American communities.

Women's contemporary environmental activism has ranged from the 1970s Chipko Movement in India and the Green Belt Movement founded by Wangari Maatai in Kenya,[3] to the common-sense, kitchen-table science of mothers like Anne Anderson and Lois Gibbs,[4] to individual actions like that of Julia "Butterfly" Hill, who in 1997 took up

---

1. See "Sisterhood Is Pleasurable: A Quiet Revolution in Psychology," by Carol Gilligan, p. 94; "Traffic at the Crossroads: Multiple Oppressions," by Kimberlé Crenshaw, p. 43; "Bitch, Chick, Cow: Women's and (Other) Animals' Rights," by Carol J. Adams, p. 494; and "Inner Space: The Spiritual Frontier," by Margot Adler, p. 551.—Ed.

2. Toxic pesticides and herbicides, chemical warfare, leakage from nuclear wastes, industrial pollutants, acid rain, etc., take their first toll as a rise in cancers of the female reproductive system, and in miscarriages, stillbirths, and congenital deformities. See also "Our Bodies, Our Future: Women's Health Activism Overview," by Judy Norsigian, et al., p. 269.—Ed.

3. See *Sisterhood Is Global: The International Women's Movement Anthology*, Robin Morgan, ed. (updated edition, New York: The Feminist Press at CUNY, 1996).

4. Lois Gibbs was a housewife and mother who, with other neighborhood women in the 1970s, organized their community toward successful relocation from a neighborhood bordering on Love Canal, a mile-long industrial-waste-filled trench.—Ed.

residence in the branches of a 600-year-old redwood and stayed there for 738 days to protest logging of these ancient trees.

Globally, regionally, nationally, and locally, women's role in environmentalism will become even more vital as environmental issues become more complex and divisive. It's still easy for some to argue that environmental protection and resource management carry economic costs outweighing their benefits: in 2001, the new administration of George W. Bush spurned the Kyoto Protocol, which had been negotiated by the world's nations to set explicit goals for reduction of greenhouse gas emissions believed to be causing climate change. The renunciation was all the more insulting because the United States had been a lead party to the international consensus to reduce emissions at the 1992 UN Conference on Environment and Development, the "Earth Summit" in Rio de Janeiro. Against Kyoto, Bush offered a retread argument: the demand to reduce emissions would stifle growth of the U.S. economy and cost Americans jobs. In fact, the opposite is true. Yes, the U.S. is the lone superpower, the ultra-developed country. But the U.S. economy has become dangerously dependent on superfluous consumption of goods and services to maintain economic growth, as well as dependent on resource waste, especially low energy prices that discourage energy conservation.[5]

Indeed, the relevance of environmental issues to economics, public health, job creation, foreign policy, labor, democratic processes, and true national security are rarely articulated in politics. Yet renewable, accessible, sustainably usable natural resources underpin all economic activity and human well-being. Therefore, environmental issues must become central to U.S. political and economic life, and accomplishing this is the task of twenty-first-century environmental activism. This can't and won't happen without women's leadership.

Women have been stereotyped as being especially connected with the earth from time immemorial—in part derived from myths, cave paintings, oral traditions, and practices of the earliest cultures.[6] To the

---

5. According to the World Watch Institute, in 2001, the U.S. accounted for roughly 5 percent of the world's population, but produced roughly 25 percent of its carbon-dioxide emissions.

6. This association of women with nature has, demonstrably, not always been good for women—whose bodies have been "mined" as natural resources for patriarchally

extent that the earth has been defined as "feminine" ("Mother Nature"), it has been as subjugated as women themselves, a premise at the heart of ecofeminism.[7] In *Staying Alive* (London, Zed Press, 1988), Indian ecologist Vandana Shiva wrote, "The reductionist categories of modern western scientific thought . . . were intrinsically violent and destructive to nature as a producer, and to women as knowers."

American environmentalist Ellen Swallow preceded the term "ecofeminist" by a century, but she created the first environmental science curriculum in the world at the Massachusetts Institute of Technology, where she taught from 1876 to 1911—until she was dismissed, having been termed "the mother of Home Economics." In the 1950s and '60s, Rachel Carson's breakthrough study, *The Sea Around Us*, and later work *Silent Spring* (see Suggested Further Reading, below) on the dangers of pesticides, are credited with launching the U.S. environmental movement. A biologist, Carson was also a visionary. She grasped the broad implications of ecological facts. These facts remain daunting. According to the 2000 Global Environmental Outlook of the United Nations Environment Program (UNEP):

- *Global warming.* In the late 1990s, annual emissions of carbon dioxide were almost four times the 1950 levels. Expected results include a shifting of climatic zones, changes in species composition and ecosystems' productivity, an increase in extreme weather events, and impacts on human health.
- *Ozone depletion.* The abundance of ozone-depleting substances in the lower atmosphere peaked around 1994 and is now declining, which is expected to bring about a recovery of the ozone

---

defined sexual and reproductive purposes. In the late 1960s, early in the contemporary feminist wave, a proliferation of hippie communes and back-to-the-earth campaigns provoked healthy feminist reactions against women being regarded (and sentimentally patronized) as passive, mystical "Earth Mothers," instead of being recognized as rational, intellectual beings.—Ed.

7. French theorist Françoise d'Eaubonne has been credited with coining the word "ecofeminism" in 1974. In 1980, more than 1,000 women attended the first conference calling itself "Women and Life on Earth: Ecofeminism in the 1980s," in Amherst, Massachusetts.—Ed.

layer to pre-1980 levels by around 2050. But ozone-depleting substances are still being smuggled across national borders.

- *Nitrogen loading.* Huge additional quantities of nitrogen being used [to fertilize crops, etc.] are exacerbating acidification, causing changes in the species composition of ecosystems, and raising nitrate levels in freshwater supplies above acceptable limits for human consumption.
- *Chemical risks.* Exposure to pesticides, heavy metals, small particulates, and other substances poses an increasing threat to the health of humans and their environment.
- *Lands, forests, biodiversity.* Woodlands and grasslands are being degraded or destroyed, marginal lands turned into deserts, and natural ecosystems reduced or fragmented.
- *Freshwater.* Rapid population growth combined with industrialization, urbanization, agricultural intensification, and water-intensive lifestyles is resulting in a global water crisis. About 20 percent of the world's population lacks access to safe drinking water, and 50 percent lacks access to safe sanitation systems.
- *Marine and coastal areas.* The world's fisheries have reached a crisis point; about 60 percent are at or near the point at which yields decline.
- *Atmosphere.* Urban air pollution is reaching crisis dimensions in most large cities of the developing world. Some 50 percent of chronic respiratory illness is now thought to be associated with air pollution.

The U.S. is not immune. There is a dead zone in the Gulf of Mexico due to run-off of agricultural pesticides; roughly 60 percent of lake surface is impaired by agricultural runoff; more than half the nation's wetlands have been drained, dredged, or modified.

UNEP's overall assessment is that "the global system of environmental policy and management is moving in the right direction but much too slowly." This, a decade after the Earth Summit, which stamped environmental issues as affairs of state—credit for which goes to non-governmental organizations (NGOs) who insisted on negotiating as peers of the national delegates. The NGO presence was largely due to the efforts of women—primarily the Women's Caucus, spearheaded by former U.S. Congresswoman Bella Abzug through her NGO, the Women's Environment and Development Organization (WEDO).[8]

Women are still working to rekindle the promise of Rio. But the operative terrain should now be economics. We need to challenge the prevailing economic model and infuse this debate with a new "eco-morality," yet retain a strategic pragmatism. This means going beyond "greening" manufacturing and production[9] to forge a system that values healthy ecosystems and acknowledges local, national, and global stakes therein.

One early proponent of such a perspective was futurist/economist Hazel Henderson, an originator of the Green GNP—a national meas-ure to take into account environmental values as *assets* of an economy. In *The Politics of the Solar Age* (see below), Henderson wrote: "The nation-state, like all patriarchal systems, is hierarchically structured . . . on rigid division of labor (as well as polarization of sex roles) . . . [a] formal, monetized GNP economy. At the other end of the scale are the under-valued manual tasks, rural and agricultural life, and the unpaid work of the nonmonetized, 'informal' economy of household production and all the cooperative activities that permit the overrewarded competitive ac-tivities to appear 'successful.' " This analysis was developed further by political economist and former member of the New Zealand Parlia-ment, Marilyn J. Waring, in *If Women Counted: A New Feminist Econom-ics* (see below). The traditional economic model would, for example, represent the Woburn leukemia cluster in terms of growth and prosper-ity: the costs of cleaning up contaminated water meant that work was done, money changed hands, profit was made. But *the value of having kept the groundwater clean in the first place*—thus *avoiding* clean-up costs and medical costs, let alone heartbreaking illness and death—*goes un-noted and unaccounted for.*

The UN and a few countries have begun to review accounting prac-

---

8. For months leading up to the Earth Summit, WEDO facilitated the workings of the Caucus, which brought together women from around the world. WEDO's work continues: its website is *www.wedo.org*.

9. For ironies regarding the negative impact of certain "green" manufacturing on poor women of color, see "Reclaiming the Past, Redefining the Future: Asian Amer-ican and Pacific Islander Women," by Helen Zia, p. 188.—Ed.

tices along these feminist-inspired lines—though without the feminist label, to be sure. However, some efforts can produce a contradictory *de*valuation: a well-intentioned group tried to calculate the "value" of Lake Michigan in 2001, coming up with roughly $5 billion—small change compared to the importance of a Great Lake providing drinking water for most lakeside communities, including the city of Chicago, now and in perpetuity. *The elemental task is to assign measurable value, while acknowledging that the environment is essentially invaluable.*

Another emerging contradiction is the privatization of public policy. Environmental stewardship requires some form of subsidy and planning, both *non grata* concepts in a world that trumpets the private sector over government oversight. Without a third way, the trend toward privatization of public-service delivery (water distribution, road maintenance, school management, prison operations) pits private market incentives against public good. Protecting natural resources is incompatible with a privatized concept of public services.

Balancing such contradictory ideas requires the synthesizing approach of feminist thought—thus the key involvement of women.

A feminist approach might also catalyze the emergence of "post-cash" policies and transactions, to create new forms of valuing. Today, nations can turn debt into an asset through debt-for-nature swaps.[10] Bartering of services and commodities also transcends cash, and communities are experimenting with local currencies based on time-for-labor credits, which can be redeemed, "spent," or traded for other community services or goods. We could adapt these ideas and create "time banks" to promote sound environmental practices. Communities that value the open space, water-retention services, and filtering services provided by farmland could "pay" struggling farmers for those environmental services, by providing debt reduction and tax abatement. Or a farmer might be compensated for environmental benefits by other services she/he might not have cash for—house maintenance, legal services, childcare—paid by the time bank in time donated by others.

A new millennium Action Agenda could be organized in different

---

10. Indebted nations can achieve the forgiveness of hard-currency debt in return for committing an equivalent sum in local currency to environmental investment, thus using the debt for national needs that would not otherwise be met.

ways. One strategic start would be what I call the Three W's: *work*, *water*, and *women*. Every environmental decision should be viewed through these lenses: (1) Does a project create or protect jobs and income among the most directly affected population? (2) What are the implications for water use, abuse, and long-term quality? (3) Do women constitute at least half of the decision-makers involved?

1. *Work*. Fear that environmental management will stifle or eliminate jobs continues to undermine advances.[11] In the public trade-off between environmental protection and economic growth, job creation is the sole reconciling agent. Why not, therefore, create a Women's Institute for Jobs and Environment, to *make* the reconciliation? It could generate new economic research; publicize cases where jobs and income have been created/saved/enhanced by environmental investments; lead debate in key policy arenas; and mentor a new generation of women leaders in environmentalism.

2. *Water*. The substance on which all life depends also presents a strategic focus. Water quality can be tracked on a regular basis; the average person constantly interacts with water. Despite the knowledge that water is limited in quantity, its quality is on the decline virtually everywhere, including in the United States. The affluent may delude themselves by buying bottled water, but even that must come from clean sources: contaminated water is almost impossible to clean, especially if wetlands (natural filters) are disrupted and displaced. Putting water at the top of the agenda for protection would, by definition, elevate the health of other resources, since protecting water means protecting soil, trees, and air.[12] Furthermore, water is one of the few

---

11. In the U.S., the most obvious example is the barrage of misinformation used to suggest that U.S. participation in the Kyoto Protocol would cost thousands of jobs—when energy conservation is actually a permanent economic *plus:* more jobs could be created if energy costs were to decline, freeing dollars for reinvestment and expansion.

12. Healthy forests hold water, stable soil holds water, and polluted air deposits pollution on and in water—so if water receives priority status, all resources acquire its mantle of protection.

commodities states have socialized. Pipes that carry water to people *link the interests* of those people. To keep water clean requires holistic trans-border collaboration.

3. *Women.* Quite simply, if a process is going forward that does not include *at least* 50 percent women as decision-makers, neither the process nor its outcome can be credible.[13] *Since women suffer the first impact of environmental pollution and are the sentinels of environmental awareness, we cannot continue to be the last consulted.* Women who don't want to run for office should redouble efforts to elect feminist environmentalist women at every level—especially in community offices where decision-making begins. Women should press toward leadership of mainstream environmentalist NGOs. As for grassroots activists—though such women are too numerous to list—two in particular exemplify holistic thinking in pragmatic terms.

Peggy Shepard, executive director of West Harlem Environmental Action in New York City (WEACT), has developed WEACT into a leading national advocacy organization since its inception in 1988. She understands the centrality of water and its potential for policy leverage, including linkage of rural-urban constituents: "People call us all the time about their water—it's brown, etcetera.—and it's not hard to galvanize people around those clearly present concerns," she notes. WEACT was the first environmental organization to focus attention on the Human Genome Project (if tests identify individuals as genetically predisposed to certain illnesses, the simplistic case can be made that removing pollutants from the environment is superfluous, as "these diseases might appear anyway"; this would mean exploiting the complex triggering role of genetic disposition in order to delay or eliminate environmental regulation).

Denise Giardina, a West Virginia State College professor, went from being a concerned citizen to running for governor in West Virginia, in 2000—focusing on the declining fortunes of the coal industry in a state

---

13. This would be proportionally just, since women constitute the numerical majority of the human species, as well as the majority population of most nations, including the U.S.

where coal had long been king, stating, "Clean coal is an oxymoron. It's time for West Virginia to accept that the coal economy is doomed." She exposed the weakness of the economic argument: "The coal industry has notoriously underpaid workers. It's not like Alaska, which at least set aside a citizens' fund to pay the people of the state royalties from oil." Giardina ran on the new Mountain Party ballot, but her victory was unlikely from the start, and she won only 2 percent of the vote. Still, she attracted national attention, and says, "Other people can run on the Mountain Party, because now it exists." In the tradition of feminist activism, Giardina gave voice to ideas previously silenced.

In 1999, Hollywood made a film of the Woburn events. In the movie, a male lawyer became the central character; Anne Anderson and the other mothers—who had identified and publicized the problem in the first place—were portrayed as woeful, weak women relying on men to make their case. Hollywood got away with writing women out of that story. The real-life future of environmental activism cannot afford to do the same.

PAULA DIPERNA is an author and public-policy analyst. She was vice-president for international affairs for The Cousteau Society, and served as president of the Joyce Foundation, a major U.S. philanthropy focused on social policy and environmental issues. Chief editorial writer for *The Earth Times*, an international environmental newspaper, from 1996 to 1999, she was previously editor of *The Cousteau Watch*, a weekly column of environmental news syndicated by the *Los Angeles Times*, from 1990 to 1993. She is the author of several books, including *Cluster Mystery* (C. V. Mosby, 1984) about the leukemia cluster in Woburn, Massachusetts, developed from her article on the subject published by *The New York Times Magazine*, the first national treatment of those events. She has also written and co-produced a dozen documentary television films, including an examination of the Exxon Valdez oilspill and aftermath, nominated by the Writer's Guild for Excellence in Current Affairs documentary writing. She ran for the U.S. House of Representatives in 1992 in the 23rd Congressional District of New York and received a third of the vote cast.

Suggested Further Reading

Carson, Rachel. *The Sea Around Us.* New York: Oxford University Press, 1951, and *Silent Spring.* New York: Houghton Mifflin, 1962.

Henderson, Hazel. *The Politics of the Solar Age: Alternatives to Economics.* New York: Doubleday/Anchor Press, 1981.

King, Ynestra, and Jael Miriam Sullivan, eds. *Dangerous Intersections: Feminist Perspectives on Population, Environment, and Development.* Cambridge, Massachusetts: South End Press, 1999.

Mies, Maria, and Vandana Shiva. *Ecofeminism: Reconnecting a Divided World.* United Kingdom: Zed Press, 1993.

Waring, Marilyn J. *If Women Counted: A New Feminist Economics.* San Francisco: Harper & Row, 1989.

PART VII.

Politics for the
New Millennium

Cyberfeminism:
Networking the Net

AMY RICHARDS AND MARIANNE SCHNALL

IMAGINE IN ONE ROOM: a forty-year-old female truck driver struggling with childcare issues, a teenage boy worrying girls won't like him because he has acne, a bride deliberating how to address wedding invitations, an insurance broker in Canada concerned that obstetrical cases have a higher amount of claims than motor-vehicle accidents, and the director of a rape crisis center in South Africa. It's hard to imagine these people in one room—less because of diversity than simple logistics. Yet this room exists—though only virtually—and illustrates the potential cyberspace offers for mainstreaming feminist issues and linking them to solutions.

As we go on-line to check e-mail or surf favorite sites, it's easy to forget we're part of a social transformation affecting how we live our lives. But as we appreciate the Internet making our day-to-day existence easier—how we shop, communicate, search for information—we need to recognize and take advantage of its enormous potential to facilitate social change.

When Internet communications technologies were in their infancy, they were described as "new media," obscuring Internet capability for being more than just a new way to access news and events.[1] The Internet does provide some media unique to it, but its real power lies in its ability to interconnect people and ideas, as its name implies. Misunderstanding it merely as "new media" means we've missed its capacity to be a dy-

---

1. See "Standing By: Women in Broadcast Media," by Carol Jenkins, p. 418; and "The Media and the Movement: A User's Guide," by Gloria Steinem, p. 103.—Ed.

namic source for networking and activism. It might be more appropriate to call it a new *medium*, a new *means* toward feminism's goals.

An initial feminist Internet aim was simply to *get* women on-line. In 1995, only 15 percent of Internet users were women, but by early 2000, women comprised 50 percent of users (a 32 percent increase since 1999). Yet patriarchy has never been absent. Men controlled the content, men earned the profit.[2] Similarly, a gender gap emerged in how women and men *accessed* the Internet: men surfed, hopping from site to site; women went directly to certain sites or searched for information on specific topics. Making the Internet more women-friendly required easing the process of associating women with each other and the information they sought. Once "arrived," they'd connect with women's organizations, announcements, and resources, as well as with each other. Linking sites through hyperlinks (plus web rings, list serves, etc.) has become the ultimate in virtual sisterhood: we can steer one another to like-minded sites and organizations in order to better educate ourselves. The nature of the Internet makes being on-line a natural for women: expressing ourselves through words—as we do now in e-mail, list serves, or websites—is an extension of our own tendencies to communicate.

At first, there were relatively few women's sites on-line, the National Organization for Women (NOW) and the Feminist Majority Foundation among them. In time, *Feminist.com*[3] would offer a free web presence to those women's organizations not yet on the web. Meanwhile, less politically progressive women's sites (*iVillage, Oxygen, Women.com*) were only a glimmer in capitalists' eyes. In a few years, they went from

---

2. For details on Internet origins and on male-dominated Internet culture and economics, see "Changing a Masculinist Culture: Women in Science, Engineering, and Technology," by Donna M. Hughes, p. 393, and Sandy Lerner's report on the computer industry in "Transforming Traditions and Breaking Barriers: Six Personal Testimonies," p. 331.—Ed.

3. One of the first feminists to recognize the absence of feminism in cyberspace was Marianne Schnall (coauthor of this article), who became fluent in cyberspace through her experience in 1994 co-founding, with her husband Tom Kay, *EcoMall.com*, a portal for environmental information and resources. Marianne realized feminism needed this same type of one-stop central location, registered the domain name "Feminist.com," and contacted friends and colleagues—in feminist activism, law, television, journalism, music, marketing, and communications—to elicit their input about what *Feminist.com* should be.—Ed.

raising millions of dollars—by imitating the content and advertising-based model already entrenched in conventional women's magazines—to verging on bankruptcy.

Soon after *Feminist.com* launched in 1995, it began receiving e-mail queries from visitors on a variety of topics.[4] These e-mails reveal who's going on-line and why. Many are from people looking for ways to become activists, so it's useful to offer suggestions based on each person's interest, location, age, and background. (The single most asked question at *Feminist.com* is: "What *is* feminism?") Some e-mails are from raped or abused women, so a sensitive response is necessary, with suggestions for books, organizations, and other resources of comfort and support. E-mails from women experiencing such workplace problems as pay inequity or job discrimination require advice on concrete actions they can take. *Feminist.com* also gets e-mails from men, asking how they can help support women's causes or comfort a family member or girl-friend who's a survivor of sexual violence, so the site now has a "Pro-Feminist Men's Groups" section. The Internet encourages reaching out in ways people might not traditionally be inclined to do: they can write in anonymously. Over time, "Ask Amy" has become an information *exchange:* visitors discover feminist resources, and *Feminist.com* learns from visitors what issues feminism should be highlighting.

In this process, we also learn *who* is going on-line and what she/he is hoping to gain there. From e-mails, as well as logs that record some of our visitors' vital statistics (such as country of origin), we know that *Feminist.com*'s constituency is as diverse as the Women's Movement itself. Teenage girls visit from Pakistan, adult men write from Texas, women seek out resources to help themselves and others. They represent a range of ages, ethnicities, classes, abilities, sexual preferences, and cultures. Many are working-class people living in isolated places around the U.S. (*and* the world), seeking advice and support; for them, the Internet is a lifeline. Some go on-line from work, some from home, some from public venues like their local library. Because the Internet is a young medium, it's popular among younger people (although the fastest

---

4. Amy Richards (coauthor of this article), a feminist activist with contacts and resources, began answering the questions; questions and answers were then posted and formalized under the heading "Ask Amy."—Ed.

growing group of on-line users are now women over the age of 35).[5] The majority of women who visit *Feminist.com* are 18–25. Feminist content arriving via e-mail gets a warmer welcome by them precisely because it's in a newer medium. Result: the Internet helps attract younger women to feminism.[6]

The Internet's international scope means it can help women feel part of a global sisterhood.[7] Approximately 20 percent of visitors and e-mails to *Feminist.com* are from outside the United States. This is a natural opportunity for activism: to learn about and act on issues affecting women around the world. International atrocities sometimes anger people more than what happens in their own backyards; these exchanges provide a means to alert them to both.

Subjects people address are indicative of issues feminism needs to address, issues sometimes outside the parameters of a focus as dictated by major foundations and advocacy organizations. For example, after numerous job-discrimination e-mails complaining that federal legislation doesn't apply to companies with less than fifty employees, it becomes clear that feminist institutions should create alternative watchdog groups. Previously, many of these people experienced their situation in isolation, not realizing how common discrimination is, or despairing of any recourse. Now, we can share—and shake up—things without leav-

---

5. Demographics data from the May 2001 study by Jupiter Media Metrix. The same study found that women were continuing to surpass men in terms of their numbers on-line: in May 2001, women over age 18 constituted 40.9 percent of all on-line users—an increase from 40.3 percent in May 2000 and 39.3 percent in May 1999. Men age 18 and older, on the other hand, accounted for 39.8 percent of all on-line users in 2001, a decrease from 40.1 percent in May 2000 and 45.7 percent in May 1999. See "Women Maintain Lead in Internet Use" by Michael Pastore, INT Media Group, *http://CyberAtlas.Internet.com/big picture/demographics.*

6. See also "Girls: 'We Are the Ones Who Can Make a Change!' " by Ana Grossman and Emma Peters-Axtell, p. 121; "Generation 'Why?': A Call to Arms," by Jasmine Victoria, p. 126; "Gen X Survivor: From Riot Grrrl Rock Star to Feminist Artist," by Kathleen Hanna, p. 131; and "Stealth Feminists: The Thirtysomething Revolution," by Debra Michals, p. 138.—Ed.

7. See "Globalization: A Strategic Advance for Feminism?" by Jessica Neuwirth, p. 526; and "Update: Feminism and the Environment," by Paula DiPerna, p. 503.—Ed.

ing our desks. People searching for "custody" or "unequal pay" or even "female roadsters" can be virtually introduced to feminist resources without having realized that feminism is what they needed, after all. *They get the chance to grasp their connection to feminism without first having to confront and overcome their biases against it.* The process itself demystifies feminism. It puts the focus on the issue and the solution, not on semantics—which continue to deter too many people. Moreover, it's hard to tackle these issues piecemeal, but the safety in numbers—provided by feminism and realized through the Internet—means that people are able to challenge obstacles previously perceived as insurmountable.

Not only does the Internet offer space to voice concerns and share injustices, like consciousness raising (CR) groups did for feminists in the 1960s and 1970s, but—also like CR groups—it helps people devise solutions. When a woman writes to *Feminist.com*, furious that her health-insurance company covers Viagra, but not Clomid, she can immediately be referred to Planned Parenthood Federation of America and their prescription-drug-coverage campaign. Such networking existed pre-Internet, but was more difficult to find, and too few people knew how to make such connections.

Similarly, rather than reading in a newspaper about legislation that passed yesterday, we can be notified about *upcoming* legislation through action alerts on websites or e-mail lists. We can take instant, effective action: signing on-line petitions, or calling or e-mailing legislative representatives. The Internet makes it easy to become informed, active, *heard*, to feel part of the political process rather than passive victims of it. (But—at this writing—politicians haven't yet caught up with on-line activists, so we should remember that while e-mail petitions have impact, politicians don't value them as much as handwritten letters. Just as the political world had to evolve from mail to fax, it will eventually recognize that e-mails must be given serious consideration.)

Such changes will be—already are—of major impact. While formerly women and girls were steered away from computer technology, the Internet encourages us to overcome techno-fears. Today, girls and boys are introduced to computers at age two, through educational CD-ROMs. Anita Borg created the Institute for Women in Technology to network these new generations of computer-friendly women. Women involved in the founding of Cisco Systems, like Sandy Lerner[8] and Cate Muther, have created other feminist networks for women in technology. In 1995, when *Feminist.com* was developed, there were no web-design tools like those available today; women had to learn html programming. Fortunately, the technology has evolved and now offers tools for designing websites, so thousands of sites are being created by women, allowing us to express ourselves in a whole new interactive manner. Aliza Sherman of Cybergrrl was one of the first feminist "geeks" to link feminism and the Internet; her work and that of others was captured in the anthology *Surfer Grrrls: Look Ethel! An Internet Guide for Us!* (see Suggested Further Reading, below), thus proving that women and technology *are* compatible.

The Internet plays a major role in still another feminist trend—as a means for many women to work from home and not be forced to choose between employment and raising their children. More and more employers allow women (and men) to work from home either on a part-time or fulltime basis—and that's not even counting all the mother-owned, home-based businesses now on-line. In fact, the majority of women-owned businesses in *Feminist.com*'s "Women Owned Business Directory" are sites run from homes by women who have babies or small children. These entrepreneurs usually sell products with which they have first-hand experience (explaining why so many women-owned companies sell products for babies and children). Interestingly, when women have the opportunity, they often develop companies more in tune with their own values, like working with *other* women-owned companies or offering "natural" products (nearly half of the earth-friendly companies listed at the EcoMall are women-owned).[9]

With more businesses allowing employees to work from home, more fathers can share parenting and household responsibilities.[10] At Marianne's house—where she and her husband both work running Internet sites—Tom has been there to bond with and care for their two daughters

8. See Lerner, op. cit.—Ed.

9. See "Owning the Future: Women Entrepreneurs," by Sara K. Gould, p. 456.—Ed.

10. See "Parenting: A New Social Contract," by Suzanne Braun Levine, p. 85.—Ed.

from birth, as much as Marianne; he's available to take the kids to school, the park, and on playdates, as well as to share household duties. Such steps bring us closer to the goal of equality.

The Internet certainly isn't immune to sexism, and hatred of women and feminism has definitely replicated itself in cyberspace—a raw hatred, with little self-censoring. Moreover, in addition to furthering feminism, the Internet advances the causes of anti-woman, pornographic, and also ultra-conservative, Right-wing groups.[11] There are many degrading, hateful sites which, protected by the First Amendment, have no restraints to prevent them from expressing violent misogyny in deeply disturbing ways.

Still, there are recourses. For example, *Feminist.com* received an outraged e-mail about a site promoting date rape—with content ranging from posting glorified date-rape stories to recipes for drugging a woman's drink: a date-rape how-to primer. That week, Marianne was interviewed by *Wired On-line* and mentioned this site, so the story spread rapidly through on- and off-line news media. Unfortunately, one repercussion of the publicity was that traffic to the date-rape site skyrocketed. When *Feminist.com* took action, tracing the domain name to some college students in Florida and contacting the local police department, we discovered there was nothing anyone could do until a crime was committed. Then, Washington Feminist Faxnet (a widely circulated activist newsletter) joined *Feminist.com* in urging people to e-mail and phone protests to the site's Internet provider; this resulted in driving the site from provider to provider until it had to be hosted outside the United States, and eventually disappeared. An old lesson from this story: one person's action (the original complaint to *Feminist.com*) can have a ripple effect. A new lesson: the effect is *magnified* in cyberspace.[12]

---

11. See "From Fantasy to Reality: Unmasking the Pornography Industry," by Gail Dines, p. 306; and "Combating the Religious Right," by Cecile Richards, p. 464.—Ed.

12. The practice now known as "hacktivism" is being employed by many socially conscious groups in differing ways: to update information continually, to send emergency alerts for e-mail blitz campaigns, and even to stage "virtual sit-ins," which can immobilize and deactivate a website by targeting it and flooding it with hits requesting information. For more examples of creative cyber-networking, see "Native Americans: Restoring the Power of Thought Woman," by Clara Sue Kidwell, p. 165, and "Our Bodies, Our Future: Women's Health Activism Overview," by Judy Norsigian, et al., p. 269.—Ed.

The technology revolution is only beginning. We approach a wireless future, where all our technologies—Internet, television, telecommunications—will merge. As these technologies become more commonplace, we'll see a decrease in their cost, meaning that computers and the benefits the Internet brings will become more accessible to poor people (the majority of whom are women)—and will also spotlight the profiles and contributions of women as well as of racial and ethnic minorities.[13] As we enter chatrooms or e-mail each other, we often don't know the gender, age, or race of those with whom we interact, communicating free from the judgments and stereotypes that labels bring. Such revolutionary concepts are central to fighting sexism and other oppressions. Our human species is being prodded by the Internet to travel an evolutionary road toward becoming more unified, enlightened, and democratic. In cyberspace, we can learn from each other's experiences, alleviate suffering, banish injustices, and discover how to love and support one another. Those are virtual reality skills we need to bring into *full* reality.

AMY RICHARDS is a co-founder of the Third Wave Foundation, the only national activist organization for women between the ages of sixteen and thirty. She is also the voice behind "Ask Amy," and coauthor of *Manifesta: Young Women, Feminism & the Future* (Farrar, Straus and Giroux, 2000). She was named one of "21 Young Leaders for the 21st Century" by *Ms.* magazine.

MARIANNE SCHNALL is co-founder and president of the women's website *Feminist.com*, responsible for managing the editorial content as well as all aspects of programming and site maintenance. She's also co-founder and vice president of Ecology America Inc., parent company of *EcoMall.com*, an environmental portal on the Internet. A graduate of Cornell University, she was previously a contributing writer to *In Style* magazine and a reporter for *Us: The Entertainment Magazine*.

---

13. See "Poverty Wears a Female Face," by Theresa Funiciello, p. 222, and the "Juggling Jeopardies" section, p. 163.—Ed.

Suggested Further Reading

Gilbert, Laurel, and Crystal Kile, eds. *Surfer Grrrls: Look Ethel! An Internet Guide for Us!* Seattle, Washington: Seal Press, 1996.

McCorduck, Pamela, and Nancy Ramsey. *The Futures of Women: Scenarios for the 21st Century.* New York: Warner Books (reprint edition), 1997.

Sherman, Aliza. *Cybergrrl! A Woman's Guide to the World Wide Web.* New York: Ballantine Books, 1998.

Schiebinger, Londa. *Has Feminism Changed Science?* Cambridge, Massachusetts: Harvard University Press, 2001.

Stanley, Autumn. *Mothers and Daughters of Invention: Notes for a Revised History of Technology.* New Brunswick, New Jersey: Rutgers University Press, 1995.

Globalization: A Strategic Advance for Feminism?

JESSICA NEUWIRTH

YOU WALK INTO The Gap and spy a great pair of jeans. The price is right, but you notice the label saying *Made in Guatemala*, or *Made in Indonesia*. Your conscience kicks in and you feel a little queasy, thinking of the inhuman conditions of sweatshop labor you're likely supporting when you buy the jeans.

That's a globalization moment.

You go home, log on to the computer, and find an e-mail about the latest woman sentenced to death by stoning for adultery in Pakistan or Nigeria. At the *www.Feminist.com* website,[1] you find a petition of protest signed by individuals and organizations in countries around the world—Brazil to Norway, Singapore to Zimbabwe—all in the past twenty-four hours. You add your name to the petition and forward it to everyone on your address list.

That, too, is globalization.

In a corporate context, "globalization" is a positive word because it has meant more profits and more power. In a political context, "globalization" is a challenging word because it has been difficult to control in the context of traditional political power structures. In the international Women's Movement, "globalization" is a negative word because it has brought great harm to many women—by facilitating the systematic exploitation of women as a source of cheap domestic and migrant labor, for example, and accelerating the international operation of organized

---

1. See "Cyberfeminism: Networking the Net," by Amy Richards and Marianne Schnall, p. 517.—Ed.

crime, drastically increasing the trade in women and girls for various forms of commercial sexual exploitation. For these reasons, globalization has been largely demonized by the Women's Movement and perceived as a force only to be opposed.

At the core of globalization is a communications-technology revolution that has tremendous power and potential. This revolution is neither inherently good nor bad. It's a powerful catalyst that magnifies both good *and* bad, depending on *how* it is used, by *whom*, and to what *end*. To oppose globalization is an exercise in futility. This is a force moving inexorably forward; it will not be stopped. To denounce it categorically is a miscalculation in political judgment, in part but not only because such a denunciation is a strategic dead-end. Although to date globalization has magnified the power differentials that subordinate women,[2] it also creates an urgent need for fundamental political reform, and thus represents an opportunity to reorder the world in a way that serves humanity—and particularly the female majority of humanity—better.

By stealth, globalization has already changed the balance and distribution of power. Governments still struggle to get their bureaucracies on-line, while heavily resourced transnational corporations are using the same technology to run circles around controls that have been in place (at least theoretically) for regulating corporate conduct and curbing abuses. Governments can't keep up with the Internet. Everything from hate speech to bodily organs is being sold through the worldwide web, despite prohibitive laws in various countries. Like the Internet, globalization knows no boundaries—and any controls, to be effective, must likewise transcend the national boundaries that have historically marked the exercise of sovereign state power.

If, though, the nation-state as a fundamental building block of political power has been so quickly outmoded, there is no alternative political structure to take its place. Treaties and other international legal mecha-

---

2. A World Bank survey released in March 2002, on the eve of the globalization summit in Monterrey, Mexico, confirmed that the fast-paced growth of trade and cross-border investment has done far less to raise the incomes of the world's poorest people than to benefit a huge inflow of capital to the U.S.; after growing rapidly in the early 1990s, annual private capital flows to the developing world fell drastically, leaving populations in Africa, Latin America, Central Asia, and the Middle East no better off than they were in 1989 ("Losing Faith: Globalization Proves Disappointing," by Joseph Kahn, *New York Times*, 21 March 2002).

nisms rely largely on such inter-governmental structures as the United Nations or the World Trade Organization. These structures are as clumsy in the new age of globalization as the governments that comprise and underlie them. The steadfast refusal by governments to relinquish or allow derogation from national sovereignty has left international institutions bereft of power, so that even the most compelling joint public initiatives—to, for instance, reduce arms, protect the environment, or regulate transnational corporate conduct—lack effective enforcement mechanisms. Meanwhile, through the forces of globalization, the power of national sovereignty is increasingly illusory, and governments are less able to control corporations because, unlike corporations, their powers end at the border.

Operating largely outside the scope of international law, corporations have their own code of conduct. Unlike governments—which are at least in theory based on popular will and purportedly representative of public interest—corporations don't represent anyone other than themselves. They are accountable only to shareholders. The measure of their value and success is in numbers: net worth and gross profits. There is no place for the common good to be factored into decisions, even theoretically, since the shareholder structure is designed for a narrow economic purpose that doesn't encompass social and political goals. As the impact of corporate conduct on a global level becomes greater and also less subject to external control, the real danger is that the growing influence of transnational money and power in all aspects of life will be regulated only by the corporate mandate to maximize profits. While some companies have adopted their own rules and regulations in the rhetorical framework of social responsibility, ultimate control over these rules and regulations is *not* in the public domain. A cost-benefit analysis of policies relating to such lucrative endeavors as the sale of kidneys for transplant, or women for sexual exploitation, might come out very differently in a corporate boardroom than in a legislative process.

If globalization is a magnifier, what it has magnified to date is the status quo, including much good as well as much harm. For the Women's Movement, globalization has brought to life a previously unimaginable capacity to organize across continents and mobilize international solidarity on a moment's notice. Connections made and strengthened among women and organizations at the UN Fourth World Conference on Women in 1995 in Beijing have continued since that conference, and the Internet has created a more effective and more permanent networking capacity.[3] Action alert campaigns to protect women from being stoned, flogged, and mutilated have been exponentially amplified through the use of e-mail, as have interventions demanding justice for women who have been raped, beaten, or killed with impunity. On-line campaigns—protesting the systematic destruction of women through gender apartheid in Afghanistan, the failure of the Vatican to address the sexual violation of nuns by priests, and the detrimental role played by UN peacekeeping missions in promoting prostitution and trafficking—have raised awareness of these issues and generated public pressure to stop human-rights violations against women.

Women have also, via the Internet, had an increasingly active voice in such international fora as the United Nations. Amplified calls from across the globe for greater representation of women have led to an active exchange of ideas: for affirmative action at national levels, and for concerted international campaigns toward including women at the highest tiers of decision-making in inter-governmental organizations. These efforts have resulted in concrete positive results.[4] It's not a coincidence that the two most significant judgments on sexual violence of the *ad hoc* international criminal tribunals (established by the UN for the former Yugoslavia and for Rwanda) were delivered, respectively, by trial chambers that included a woman judge—in the case of the Rwanda Tribunal the only woman judge, and in the case of the Tribunal for the former Yugoslavia one of two women judges, the other of whom was subsequently replaced by a man. As a result of effective advocacy by the Women's Movement, the formative documents for the newly created International Criminal Court explicitly call for gender representation in the judiciary, and explicitly include crimes of sexual violence.

---

3. For background on the international Women's Movement, see *Sisterhood Is Global: The International Women's Movement Anthology*, Robin Morgan, ed. (New York, Doubleday/Anchor, 1984; updated edition, New York: The Feminist Press at CUNY, 1996).

4. As Mark Malloch Brown, administrator of the United Nations Development Programme (UNDP), wrote: "The most striking single social, political, and economic transformation of the past century has been the emergence of women as leaders in nearly every country and walk of life" (UNDP: *Choices*, March 2002).

Globalization has also furthered the concept of international and transnational criminal justice, so that ruthless dictators and genocidal maniacs can be held accountable. In August of 2000, a jury of citizens in the United States found Radovan Karadzic civilly liable for the genocidal rape of women in the former Yugoslavia. In June of 2001, a jury in Belgium found two Rwandans criminally guilty of genocide for their complicity in the killing of thousands of Tutsis—a milestone in international law, since this was the first time that a jury of ordinary citizens of one country had been asked to judge people accused of war crimes committed in another country. These are historic decisions that affirm human rights as transcendent of national boundaries. In this new vision of justice without borders, women have been able to raise (if not yet ensure) the importance of including sexual violence among other human-rights violations to be addressed. Similarly, domestic violence, female genital mutilation, forced marriage, and denial of reproductive rights[5] are increasingly being recognized by national legal systems as gender-based forms of persecution that fall within the scope of refugee protection.[6]

Globalization has also focused world attention more systematically on efforts to end armed conflict. Not only national and regional conflicts but internal warfare has become a legitimate subject of international concern and often intervention. In this context, the potential for women to play significant roles in peace negotiations looms on the horizon.[7] In October of 2000, the UN held an unprecedented session of the Security Council to listen to women from such war-torn countries as Somalia and Guatemala, and to consider the contribution women have

---

5. See "Landscape of the Ordinary: Violence Against Women," by Andrea Dworkin, p. 58; "The Nature of the Beast: Sexual Harassment," by Anita Hill, p. 296; "Prostitution = Slavery," by Vednita Carter, p. 315; "Unfinished Agenda: Reproductive Rights," by Faye Wattleton, p. 17; and "Women and Law: The Power to Change," by Catharine A. MacKinnon, p. 447.—Ed.

6. For a moving personal history of the precedent-setting case that established female genital mutilation as a recognized basis for political asylum in the U.S., see *Do They Hear You When You Cry?* by Fauziya Kassindja (New York: Delacorte Press, 1998).

7. See "Why Peace Is (More Than Ever) a Feminist Issue," by Grace Paley, p. 537; see also the Introduction, p. *xv*.—Ed.

been trying to make to the pursuit of world peace. This process resulted
in the adoption of Security Council Resolution 1325 on Women and
Peace and Security, calling for the inclusion of more women in peace
negotiations and peacekeeping forces. The power or potential power of
women is also being increasingly recognized in traditional mainstream
structures like the World Bank, which has finally been forced to acknowledge the central role of women in the promotion of sustainable
development.

However, the communications technology that has fueled this
progress and helped the Women's Movement get the message across to
these powerful institutions has not been equally accessible to all. Far
from it. And just as globalization on a larger scale has made the powerful relatively more powerful, within the universe of movements for social change, it has also in some ways widened the gap—of differential
access to resources—between groups and individuals in the global
North and those in the global South. In countries where telephone service and electricity are unreliable, or in villages where neither is even
available, the new power of globalization is ruthlessly leaving some
women behind while rapidly propelling others forward. Computers are
expensive, as is access to the Internet in many countries. Moreover, literacy must precede computer training, and efforts to ensure women and
girls access to basic education are massively underfunded. Two-thirds of
the world's illiterate population are women; almost 300 million women
cannot read or write.[8] Still, for those who do have access to electronic
communication, globalization has played a positive role. Women of the
South now have a greater voice in the Women's Movement, in part due
to greater access to information and a considerably enhanced ability to
participate in a global dialogue less hostage to distance. This technology
makes genuine equality within the global Women's Movement a more
readily achievable goal.

The immediate challenge for the international Women's Movement
is to mobilize and take the lead in building a new political order better
suited to a world already being reshaped by globalization. New institutions—*if* they result from a process in which women are integrally in-

---

8. *World's Women 2000: Trends and Statistics*, United Nations Publications, May
2000.

volved—are likely to serve the cause of equality and other fundamental human rights much more effectively than the current institutions of political power. Despite tremendous efforts and steady gains, women are still largely unrepresented in government institutions. There are just a few countries in which women hold the highest political office, and only a few in which women have more than 30 percent representation in the legislature. At this writing, women in Kuwait are still denied the right to vote on the grounds of their sex. The pressure that globalization exerts on traditional structures offers an external catalyst for possible sweeping reform, one that would not otherwise be within the short-term scope of possibility. Rather than watch the status quo transfer established patriarchal dynamics to new (even less democratic) methods of control, the global Women's Movement can provide an alternative vision of power, offer a response to globalization that draws on its strengths, and welcome a world without borders.

Such international solidarity may be the only force capable of heading off the harms of globalization. Rather than suffer the manipulation of capital flight, for example—the threat of which is used to keep wages in sweatshops around the world to below subsistence levels—a new political order could institute *a global minimum wage*. Such action is impossible in the current structure because political power as exercised through the nation-state system is sufficiently controlled by undemocratic forces; such forces suppress the galvanizing of political will necessary to forge fundamental social change. To date, international solidarity has, ironically, done more for the private sector than the public good. Negotiations on sovereign indebtedness, for instance, are held country by country, in each case with an international consortium of the commercial bank creditors. The bankers *know* they're more powerful as a united bloc, and they act accordingly. The governments—because they are unable to organize collectively and unable to divide and conquer the banks individually—are themselves divided and conquered in this process, all at the expense of the people they represent.

Like "democracy," "globalization" is a slippery word, wearing different meanings in theory and in reality. The current reality of globalization is dangerous, yet the theory is alive with promise. The political uncertainties of transition sparked by globalization provide a moment of opportunity: *to take and redefine power.* Channels of mass communication are more international, more accessible, and more democratic than ever before.[9] They can be used to replace transnational exploitation with global cooperation, to effect the redistribution of resources rather than further the concentration of wealth. Mobilizing transnational solidarity among like-minded citizens of the world is both an expression of the power to create *and* the ultimate protection from the power to control.

Just imagine:

- Women in Peru send out word that structural adjustment is driving them deeper into poverty and destroying all community support structures. Media coverage of the impact of intervention by international financial institutions is followed by mass transnational tax withholding in countries governing these institutions. The International Monetary Fund suspends the market-driven conditionality of its lending policies.

- After every woman (and maybe some men) in every parliament of every country threatens to go on strike if democracy is not restored in Burma, Daw Aung San Suu Kyi takes her rightful place as duly elected head of state.

- A clothing company in Texas starts a line of T-shirts for men imprinted "Wife Beater," including styles for young boys imprinted "Li'l Wife Beater." The shirts are advertised on *www. wife-beaters.com* for half price with proof of a wife-beating conviction and can be customized with a bloodstain or cigarette burn. A bulletin goes out on *www.womensenews.org*, and the wife-beaters' site is spontaneously bombarded by millions of hits from women's rights "hacktivists." The site folds.[10]

---

9. For example, the "Stop Esso Campaign" *(www.stopesso.com)* spreading across Europe—mounting a massive, successful boycott of Exxon Mobil gas stations there (Exxon goes by the name Esso in Europe); the campaign began to protest Exxon's being a key backer of the Bush II administration's decision to pull out of the Kyoto Protocol (see "Update: Feminism and the Environment," by Paula DiPerna, p. 503).—Ed.

10. You needn't imagine this one because (at this writing) the site actually exists and was reported on Women's Enews, a project of the NOW Legal Defense and Education Fund. The only part we need imagine is the site going down. For other important stories, see *www.womensenews.org*.

The Universal Declaration of Human Rights (UDHR), adopted by the United Nations in 1948, set forth a vision of life in which health, education, housing, employment, and respect for the dignity of all persons are fundamental human rights to which everyone is entitled without distinction.[11] The UN hasn't done justice to this vision, allowing it instead to degenerate to the lowest common denominator of political discourse. Globalization could be the new force replacing that lowest common denominator with a concept of collective action greater, rather than less, than the sum of its parts. Globalization could be the force capable of doing justice to the vision of the UDHR—or it could be the force capable of the entire destruction of the planet. It's up to us.

This has been made even clearer (and more urgent) since the events of September 11, 2001, which dramatically illustrated the political transformation caused by globalization, and which accelerated the need for radical reform. The world war currently underway at this writing began with the Taliban providing some semblance of a state target in Afghanistan. But with the removal of the Taliban from power, there is no state left on the other side of this war—a war alternately against Al Qaeda (a nongovernmental entity), or more generically against "terrorism," which has no defined or recognizable sovereign structure. Geographical boundaries bear little if any relation to this new kind of war, which is potentially more dangerous and destructive than any of its predecessors. The stakes are higher than ever, and the need for a new collective concept of security is urgent. What's more, the hunger for information and active agency among ordinary people is growing. That many Americans took a greater interest in foreign affairs post-9/11 did not surprise foreign-policy experts—but such experts were shocked that this interest persisted more than nine months later.[12] As a direct result of citizen action, a rapid exchange of private cell-phone calls on 9/11 led to the diversion of one hijacked plane from its intended target of destruction—citizen action that

---

11. See *A World Made New: Eleanor Roosevelt and the Universal Declaration of Human Rights*, by Mary Ann Glendon (New York: Random House, 2001).

12. The Carnegie Endowment for International Peace, the Council on Foreign Relations, the UN Association of the United States, and other such organizations report that their websites have continued to attract millions of more hits than usual ("American Web Browsers Continue a Global Turn," by Barbara Crossette, *New York Times*, 2 June 2002).

was much faster and more efficient than the multi-trillion-dollar defense industry. A few weeks later, a concerned passenger, sitting in an airplane seat near a shoe-bomber, was willing to take action on a moment's notice, thus saving lives. Such citizen activism is worth a lot more security than the X-ray screening of every traveler's shoes, or the proposed mass suspension (or subtler erosion) of civil liberties.

Saving the planet—and ourselves—really *is* up to us.

JESSICA NEUWIRTH is a founder and current president of the board of directors of Equality Now, an international women's rights organization based in New York and Nairobi. She holds a Juris Doctor from Harvard Law School and a B.A. in Medieval History from Yale. From 1985–1990, she worked for Amnesty International, eventually serving as the first Chair of AI-USA's Women and Human Rights Task Force, and has practiced international law, specializing in international finance for developing countries. She has also served as a legal officer for the UN Administrative Tribunal and as a consultant to the UN International Criminal Tribunal for Rwanda on sexual-violence charges in several cases—including the landmark case of *Akayesu*, which set forth a definition of rape in international law and a finding that rape constitutes a form of genocide.

Suggested Further Reading

Askin, Kelly D., & Dorean M. Koenig, eds. *Women and International Human Rights Law.* New York: Transnational Publishers, 2000.

French, Hilary F. *Vanishing Borders: Protecting the Planet in the Age of Globalization.* Washington, D.C.: Worldwatch, 2000.

Hancock, Graham. *Lords of Poverty: The Power, Prestige, and Corruption of the International Aid Business.* New York: Atlantic Monthly Press, 1992.

Wallach, Lori, and Michelle Sforz. *Whose Trade Organization? Corporate Globalization and the Erosion of Democracy.* Washington, D.C.: Public Citizen, 1999.

Sources for information on the international Women's Movement and for global feminist activism: Equality Now *(www.equalitynow.org);* Coalition

Against Trafficking in Women *(www.catwinternational.org);* The Feminist Majority Foundation *(www.feminist.org);* The Sisterhood Is Global Institute *(www.sigi.org);* V-Day *(www.vday.org);* Women's Environment and Development Organization *(www.wedo.org);* Women Living Under Muslim Laws *(www.wluml.org).*

Why Peace Is (More Than Ever) a Feminist Issue

GRACE PALEY

I. Words

I have received a couple of letters from people who reminded me that I am now an older person and what do I think I am leaving to the next generation? They explained that the world is in worse shape than it was when I was an energetic middle-aged person. What would be my—well, if I were a man, it would be patrimony. So I came to these two interesting words: patrimony and matrimony.

Patrimony and matrimony do not say what they mean. Patriarchy and matriarchy do. Patrimony, as any reader probably knows, is what you inherit from your father. Matrimony is the state of being in a marriage. Now men live in it—marriage—as well as women and it is therefore a little joke for men that this word is used about a condition in which women and families have often suffered the strongest patriarchal oppression. Matrimony is not what you inherit from your mother, probably because in history she didn't own much of anything. This was true at least 500 years ago, sounding a little more French. It was true in France and England and pretty much everywhere else. So you see, it's been a long time since we say that matrimony or marriage is women's inheritance. There are probably other words that disregard their etymological roots in order to be transformed into the gender-ridden history of men and women.

If marriage and its historic condition has been what women leave to their daughters and sons, what is it that men leave, have left, and continue to leave?

War, of course.

To their sons, its excitement, creativity, mutilation, and death.

To their daughters, rape, torture, widowhood, famine, and death.

II. A Story: Inherit the War

The father has been preparing a war for his son's birthday. He started long ago. You have to, you know. People who decide on a war and expect it to happen the minute or week or month they want it to are often disappointed. You also cannot do it alone. The father has a few friends from his war who are willing to help out. They have sons, too. There are quite simple ways to begin—probably in childhood. For instance, help the boy develop an easy dislike for your neighbor's daughter. Mild prejudice will then rest contentedly in his little breast. As time goes on, it can appear as nothing worse than sleepy contempt for the girl next door.

The father remembers his war, how long it took for *his* father to get it right. He was almost too old. (The father and his friends are now called The Great Generation. This isn't exactly fair. *Their* fathers had fought in an equally famous war, and luckily had survived to provide a war in turn for this father and his friends.)

This father does need more preparation, and quickly. His son is growing beautifully, but he's reading too much. Some of his ideas seem to come from Leftish media. The schools are also bad, even treacherous. But the father is sure he can find the old newspapers he's kept or the right pages of the history book, which are very clever about enumerating insults to our national soul and natural hegemony. The recollection of historical insult is as important in the life of great nations as their stunning victories.

The father would like his son to be an airman. Of course, anxiety about civilian deaths—women and children—always undercuts the enthusiasm of sentimental citizens and tender-hearted boys.

He's talked to many other fathers. They're nearly ready. They've begun their letters to newspapers, their attacks on the wimps in Congress and the administration. Most important, they've selected the enemy and are very clear about it.

The father has only one year left—before his son's eighteenth birthday.

His son is not unaware of what is coming. He has that boyish excitement, that intensifying patriotism—his own war at last.

III. Is There a Difference Between Men and Women

The arms trade. The slave trade. The trade in women's bodies.

IV. What Now

Today's wars are about oil. But alternate energies exist now—solar, wind—for every important energy-using activity in our lives. The only human work that cannot be done without oil is war.

So men lead us to war for enough oil to continue to go to war for oil.

I'm now sure that these men can't stop themselves anymore—even those who say they want to. There are too many interesting weapons. Besides, theirs is a habit of centuries, eons. They will not break that habit themselves.

For *our*selves, for our girl and boy children, women will have to organize as we have done before—and also as we have never done before—to break that habit for them, once and for all.

GRACE PALEY, one of the most beloved writers working in the English language, was born in the Bronx, New York, in 1922. A long-time activist in the anti-war, anti-nuclear, and feminist movements, she still regards herself as a "somewhat combative pacifist and cooperative anarchist." Her books of short fiction, essays, and poetry include *The Little Disturbances of Man* (1959, Viking Penguin 1968); *Enormous Changes at the Last Minute* (Random House, 1974; Farrar, Straus paperback 1985); (with Vera B. Williams) *Long Walks and Intimate Talks: Poems and Prose* (New York: The Feminist Press at CUNY, 1994); and *Just as I Thought* (Farrar, Straus and Giroux, 1998)—a collection of articles, reports, and talks "representing about 30 years of political and literary activity with a couple of occasional glances over my shoulder into disappearing family and childhood." Farrar, Straus and Giroux published her *Collected Stories* in 1994 and *Begin Again: Collected Poems* in 2000. She taught for 18 years at Sarah Lawrence College. Among her numerous honors is a Guggenheim fellowship [sic], an award from the

National Institute of Arts and Letters, a Senior Fellowship [sic] awarded by the National Endowment for the Arts in recognition of her lifelong contribution to literature, the 1992 REA Award for Short Stories, the first Edith Wharton Citation of Merit, and being named the first official New York State Writer.

Suggested Further Reading

Cambridge Women's Peace Collective. *My Country Is the Whole World: An Anthology of Women's Work on Peace and War.* Boston: Pandora Press, 1984.

Lerner, Gerda. *The Creation of Patriarchy.* New York: Oxford University Press, 1986.

Miller, Alice. *For Your Own Good: Hidden Cruelty in Child-Rearing and the Roots of Violence.* New York: Farrar, Straus and Giroux, 1983.

Morgan, Robin. *The Demon Lover: The Roots of Terrorism.* New York: W. W. Norton, 1989; revised, updated edition New York: Washington Square Press, 2001.

Woolf, Virginia. *Three Guineas.* New York: Harcourt, Brace and Company, 1938.

The Art of Building Feminist Institutions to Last

ELEANOR SMEAL

IN MARCH OF 2000, the Feminist Majority Foundation sponsored Feminist Expo 2000, to showcase the power of the Feminist Movement, its ideas for the twenty-first century, and the range of its work, constituencies, and accomplishments. With over 575 organizational co-sponsors, an attendance of 7,000 people, and delegations from every state in the USA, 176 campuses, and 45 countries, Feminist Expo 2000 was a magnificent display of the strength, diversity, and vision of feminism in the United States and throughout the world. Expo 2000 brought together feminists from the media, law, arts, politics, health care, business, education, labor, social services, advocacy, sports, entertainment, philanthropy, and religion. In each of these sectors, feminists have been creating new institutions and securing positions of influence within existing structures. Yet, successful as it was, Feminist Expo 2000—which deliberately accepted no government or corporate funding—could provide only a snapshot of the massive Women's Movement at the turn of the century. Today no sphere of society remains untouched by feminism.

But how can we make sure this movement lasts? What ingredients are necessary to build and sustain feminist institutions and the Feminist Movement itself?

Until I was in my twenties, I—like most Americans in the early 1960s—had never heard of feminism. When I learned of the heroic struggles waged for women's rights over past centuries, I was enraged. How can we be truly educated if we lack knowledge of the historical work of feminists here and worldwide? How can this knowledge be so effectively buried?

For several years, I've been haunted by the work of Gerda Lerner, especially her book, *The Creation of Feminist Consciousness* (Oxford University Press, 1993). She describes how the transmission of knowledge from one generation of women to another—knowledge about women's resistance to patriarchy—broke down. For centuries, women would repeat three stages: challenging the patriarchy for about thirty years, enduring a backlash for the next thirty or so years, then being erased utterly over the final thirty years. Feminist history has been destroyed so thoroughly that by the time a new feminist generation begins, the work of the prior wave has been obliterated; instead of being able to build on the accomplishments of previous generations, the new wave is forced to reinvent them.

Lerner's analysis haunts me because, despite our current strength, I can too clearly see it happening again. Many local and state women's liberation groups of the 1960s and 1970s have expired. Some national groups, like the Women's Equity Action League (WEAL), also disappeared, despite years of accomplishment. Ask the current generation of young (or even some older) feminists: they know very little about these groups—their ideas, work, contributions.

For over thirty years, I've been working in the activist wing of the movement, trying to create, stimulate, and grow feminist organizations and ideas that will last. I've had the opportunity to work with many organizations that approach this challenge from different perspectives. No single group has created the consummate "institution to last," but the collective efforts can teach us much about how it might be done.

Organizing for feminism is an art. There is no blueprint of how to get to equality. But we do know some principles that work and some that don't.

At its core, feminism is a multi-issue movement committed to extremely long-term goals: the ending of patriarchy; the achievement of economic, political, and social equality for all women; and the creation of a world free from sexism, racism, homophobia, classism, ageism, ableism, violence, and environmental exploitation.

For much of our history, however, we've been working to accomplish short-term goals we thought could be won. No better example of this phenomenon exists than the single-issue groups that emerged in the

1960s and early 1970s, focused on legalizing abortion.[1] The Pennsylvania Abortion Justice Association (AJA) had 16,000 members statewide when the U.S. Supreme Court legalized abortion with the historic *Roe v. Wade* decision. Shortly thereafter, the AJA board voted to go out of existence because their mission was accomplished—or so they thought. Fortunately, the National Association for the Repeal of Abortion Laws (NARAL) changed its name and continues to be a leader in the fight to this day.

I've learned over the years never to let down our guard or think we have won a final victory.

One ingredient is essential for building feminist institutions: ideas. Wherever feminists were in the 1960s and 1970s, we questioned the underlying assumptions of male supremacy. Many a night a group of us gathered in the basement of Drs. JoAnn Evansgardner and Gerry Gardner's home in Pittsburgh. We would offset, print, and collate research papers authored by feminist scholars from every discipline. This operation, known as KNOW press, had as its motto, "Freedom of the press belongs to those who own the press." Few publishing houses would print feminist analyses, research, or studies, so KNOW did, as did The Feminist Press in New York City.

We spread the feminist message not only with papers, but with symbols. As I became more active nationwide, I met Toni Carabillo and Judith Meuli, co-founders of the Los Angeles chapter of the National Organization for Women (NOW) and of Women's Graphics. They imprinted feminist slogans onto campaign buttons, t-shirts, and bumper stickers, and designed feminist jewelry. (I soon learned that the buttons and jewelry sold faster and scattered more widely than the papers, but both were necessary to spread ideas and build the movement.)

As the work of feminists grew in academia, especially through Women's Studies,[2] it also spread in pop culture via the media covering our local actions, speakers, press events, lawsuits, conferences, marches, picket lines. Our views and activities were often exaggerated or distorted by a media determined to ridicule us, but we soon learned that

1. See "Unfinished Agenda: Reproductive Rights," by Faye Wattleton, p. 17.—Ed.

2. See "The Proper Study of Womankind: Women's Studies," by Florence Howe, p. 70.—Ed.

the *slant* of media coverage mattered less than the coverage itself.[3] As we demonstrated, sued, and challenged the establishment, our ideas spread via local, state, and national media.

The generation of ideas and raising of consciousness are central to building a movement. More than money or resources, more than marching millions, first must come an understanding of what's wrong— better yet, a sense of outrage—and ideas for creating change. *Then* come resources: people, skills, in-kind services, materials, faxes, postage, phones, and now computers—and the money to make it happen.

Actually, nothing just "happens." Dedicated feminists *make* things happen. To build feminist institutions, both people and resources must be recruited. Too often we're led to believe that both will somehow just arrive—but in recruiting people, the "you all come" approach doesn't work. Everyone should feel welcome, but some must be *sought*, in order to achieve a diversity of skills, talent, and, frankly, *numbers*. Most of all, people must feel included and *needed*. They're used to being asked to participate, but they want to feel part of something unique, even historic— and they don't want their scarce resources of time and money wasted.

In the early days of this feminist wave, we didn't worry about money. We worked on the barter system, throwing in our own cash for stamps, phone calls, printing, etc. But as the movement grew, that became impossible. At some point, we became almost preoccupied with money, because everything *cost* so much. We worried about the source of the funds: would we be co-opted or, worse, sold out?

After years of struggles to fuel the movement, I still think that *those who pay for change must primarily be those who want it*. We can't expect our opposition to fund us. For that reason, money and resources must come mostly from feminists who believe and want the same goals as the group being funded—better yet, are a part of the group itself, or even the core. Too often, feminists and other reformers appeal for funding to the very institutions they want to change. Worse, they go to sexist institutions that want to ensure they won't be sued or that seek to co-opt the group as cheaply as possible.[4]

---

3. See "The Media and the Movement: A User's Guide," by Gloria Steinem, p. 103, and the Introduction, p. *xv*.—Ed.

4. See "Front Line: The Funding Struggle," by Marie Wilson, p. 485.—Ed.

I used to worry about the notion that those who want the revolution must pay for it. Then Dolores Huerta—a dear friend, co-founder of the United Farm Workers, and later co-founder of the Feminist Majority—told me that Cesar Chavez would go to the low-paid farmworkers and say, in effect, you can pay dues for the union or live at the mercy of the growers forever.

In building feminist institutions to last, we have to embrace class issues. Everyone can give something according to her own means; no one should be belittled or made to think they have nothing to contribute. Fees/dues can be on a sliding scale, and no one should be barred from participating because of inability to pay. At the same time, all should share in fundraising responsibilities. Too often women are taught that money and budgets are mysteries "beyond" them. Under-funded work is too frequently falsely valued as "noble" work, and fundraising thought of as "dirty." Let's face it: *under-funded work can't get the job done.* We must learn about budgets, especially government budgets, get our fair share, and prevent our opponents from getting *more* than their share. We must understand our own budgets *and* those of our opponents. What we value, we must make sure others value, too.

Peg Yorkin, who made the largest gift for the development of a feminist institution to date, decided not to give anonymously (as women often do). She felt it her duty, by example, to encourage others who could do more to do so. Giving is empowering, *if* we are giving for *ourselves*, our freedom.

I'll never forget one fundraiser in 1981. As national NOW president, I was encouraging NOW members at our annual conference to donate more to the Equal Rights Amendments (ERA) Countdown Campaign. Molly Yard, then political director of the campaign, grabbed the microphone. She thought I was being too timid. She said she would mortgage her house and match each person who gave $100 or more. It turned into an orgy of giving. People gave whatever they had: cash, jewelry, IOUs, promises of fundraising house parties, pledges. I was a bit embarrassed by it all—but after it was over, I walked through the audience of some two thousand women. A tearful woman grabbed me and *thanked* me for the opportunity to give; she said it was the first time in her life she'd ever written a sizable check, without asking her husband for permission, for something she wanted and believed in, and it gave her joy and self-empowerment. In one hour, we'd raised over $90,000 to save the ERA campaign.

To endure, feminist institutions must continuously foster self-empowerment *and* group empowerment: a "Yes, we. *can* do it," rather than an "It can't be done" philosophy. To accomplish great tasks, the first step must be to think you *can*. In doing so, one must also not be too cautious. For years, I've had a Susan B. Anthony quote in my office:

> Cautious, careful people, always casting about to preserve their reputation and social standing, never can bring about reform. . . . Those who are really in earnest must be willing to be anything or nothing in the world's estimation, and publicly and privately, in season and out, avow their sympathies with despised and persecuted ideas and their advocates, and bear the consequences.

Jennifer Jackman, a colleague for more than twenty years both in NOW and the Feminist Majority, began working with me when she was a junior in college; she and several feminist activists from Boston had the quote calligraphed and framed for me in 1985; they wanted me—us—never to forget it.

That leads me to the next principle: to last, feminist institutions must be *intergenerational*. Age must never be considered a prerequisite for function, value, or decision-making. Currently, at the Feminist Majority, our oldest fulltime workers are in their seventies and our youngest in their late teens. Our oldest staff member, Molly Yard, retired in her mid-eighties. Our supporters and volunteers range along the age continuum. To be intergenerational, the group must *recruit*. Young people's ideas must be valued, and they must play a part in decision-making.[5]

Leadership also must be valued and encouraged—nor can it be defined as singular. A group needs different leaders—preferably a team. Leaders should facilitate the group's decision-making and, most of all, *inspire*. Leadership shouldn't be a function of age or title; it must be won repeatedly, since it's often situational. Nor should we define leadership as innate behavior or a set of characteristics. Sometimes it's *learned* behavior, frequently *opportunity*, often a state of *mind*. A movement needs many lead-

---

5. See the sections "A Movement for All Seasons," p. 119, and "Personal Postscripts," p. 569.—Ed.

ers, and needs to invest in developing and nurturing them. Society continually tells women why we *can't* lead; we must empower *ourselves* to lead.

Shared goals and knowledge help both leaders and group members to function optimally. *Education and research*, as well as action, must be valued. No one is too old or too experienced for education, research, or study—and no one is too young. A *culture* of learning should be cultivated, and for knowledge to be widespread and not hoarded, everyone should take the responsibility to communicate. *Communication is essential to survival.*

Today, e-mail and teleconferencing are great tools. But face-to-face meetings are essential to build spirit. Nothing is possible with a demoralized team. What's a march or rally but a mass meeting, a spirit builder? What's a small group meeting but a more participatory spirit builder? Rather than enjoying esprit de corps, feminist (and other) organizations often face in-fighting that feels worse and more frequent than fighting the real opposition. In-fighting must be actively discouraged; once it becomes the culture of an organization, it takes on a life of its own. Debates over the future direction of the organization sometimes result in participants taking sides and believing, rightly or wrongly, that prevailing means life or death for the organization. Having been involved in such struggles, I now look back and think it might have been better to *split*, to establish two or more groups as allies in the struggle with different approaches.

Which brings us to another major principle in building feminist institutions to last. *Redundancy is good in anything important.* Just as we don't feel safe in a single-engine plane, neither should we feel safe with one organization for a movement as vital and important as ours. No one organization could be or should be all things to all people. More groups provide more opportunities for leadership, growth, diversity, issue-spread, and risk-taking. Some groups might fail, but others will prosper. And *failure is important.* We learn both from what succeeds *and* what doesn't.

Most important, to build a Feminist Movement that lasts, groups must be able to *seize an opportunity, be flexible, and remain relevant* to changing times, possibilities, and needs.

The easy part is getting feminists to agree on what's wrong. In the struggle of the day we seldom build in time to think about *what we really want*—as a group, a movement, a world. Too often, instead of envisioning a feminist future, we fall back on having been trained to consider only what we think we can get. We need to think big, think globally.

Ours is a diverse movement that is everywhere, and a global perspective is imperative for it to last and grow. A part of all institution/movement-building should be travel, exchange of ideas with other kindred souls. The exchange can be citywide, statewide, nationwide, or worldwide, but we must reach out. We cannot take on patriarchy—or even understand it—by thinking locally. Cross-cultural experiences provide an unparalleled understanding of the depth of patriarchy/male dominance, and the breadth of the exploitation of women and girls. This is vital knowledge.[6]

We cannot ignore our opposition. What will enable the movement to survive wave after wave of backlash is to *know the opposition*, what to expect from it, how to counter it. We can't be Pollyannas blithely building alternative institutions. Every inch of our struggle, we've had and *will* have opposition attempting to destroy us: infiltrate, defund, and attack us—intellectually and physically, even violently. We must be able to recognize the opposition—its sources, tricks, strengths, weaknesses—and deploy money, time, and resources to knowing and countering that opposition. This is essential for survival.

Feminist institutions also need *infrastructure*. If an administrative operation of an organization is working well, no one notices it—but at all times it should be valued. It raises, conserves, and spends resources. Nothing replaces effective financial accounting, and time must be taken to establish a reliable system with internal controls, so as to maintain honesty and integrity. As an institution grows, human-resource policies for staff, interns, and volunteers must be developed. I've tried every type of pay system—and in the long run, adequate and competitive pay is necessary, with vacation time, family medical leave, health insurance, and a pension plan in accordance with the best nonprofit principles.

Finally, to endure, *our institutions must have turf—we must build or buy places in which to reside*. Recent institutions of the contemporary feminist wave have been mostly renters. Many of the nineteenth- and early twentieth-century women's groups that survived were those that *owned their*

---

6. See "Traffic at the Crossroads: Multiple Oppressions," by Kimberlé Crenshaw, p. 43.—Ed.

own buildings, like the American Association of University Women (AAUW), the Federation of Business and Professional Women's Clubs (BPW), the YWCAs, and the National Women's Party. The ERA struggle survived from 1923 until now (and helped build feminist activism in the 1970s and 1980s) because the National Women's Party, its author, owned the Sewall-Belmont House next door to the Senate Hart Office Building in Washington, D.C. One reason religious institutions survive is because they own churches, synagogues, and mosques. We need a tangible "room of our own."

In fact, we need not only buildings but *monuments* to our ideas and our heroines. I never understood why men would fight to defend a monument until, in 1989, we erected a temporary monument to the "Courageous Women Who Had Died from Botched Illegal Abortions Because They Had No Choice."[7] The Feminist Majority had it built on the grounds of the Washington, D.C. Mall for the November march called by NOW. Peg Yorkin contracted with set designers to make it look as real as any other monument. Then, late one night before the march, word came that a gang of anti-choicers were approaching the monument to destroy it. Like madwomen, we all rushed from hotels, homes, the NOW Action Center, and all around town, to defend it. I'll never forget running to save it—nor will I forget overhearing a mother telling her children, "The Washington guidebook doesn't list this monument, but isn't this *nice!* About time! This monument is a tribute to women." She went on to explain to her kids that a long time ago, when abortion was illegal, many women died trying to obtain secret abortions; fortunately, she said, those days are over. I realized that our monument looked so real, she had no idea it was temporary. She taught me the value of monuments.

What we value we must enshrine—with symbols, books, our recorded history, buildings—edifices majestic enough to shelter our noble ideas, places for teaching, gathering, developing community. *We need all of the above* to help us to think, dream, organize, reach out, and connect with a global movement for feminism—forever.

ELEANOR SMEAL is the co-founder and president of the Feminist Majority Foundation (FMF) *(www.feminist.org)*. For more than three

---

7. See Wattleton, op. cit.—Ed.

decades, she has played a leading role in feminism, as political analyst, strategist, and grassroots organizer, working at the forefront of almost every major women's rights victory—from the integration of Little League baseball, newspaper help-wanted ads, and police departments to the passage of such landmark legislation as the Pregnancy Discrimination Act, Equal Credit Act, Civil Rights Restoration Act, Violence Against Women Act, Freedom of Access to Clinic Entrances Act, and Civil Rights Act of 1991. She has pushed to realign federal priorities by developing a feminist budget. As president of the National Organization for Women, Smeal spearheaded the drive to ratify the ERA, and led the first national abortion rights march, in 1986. When violence threatened to close women's health care clinics, she developed FMF's National Clinic Access Project, the largest program of its kind in the nation, and was chief architect of FMF's landmark 1994 U.S. Supreme Court case upholding the use of buffer zones to protect clinics. She initiated the Choices Campus Leadership Program on college campuses across the USA, and led a successful 12-year fight to bring mifepristone (formerly known as RU486) to U.S. women. Expanding her feminist activism to a global level, in 1997 Smeal launched the international Campaign to Stop Gender Apartheid in Afghanistan.

[The author would like to acknowledge the contributions of Sarah Boonin, Gaylynn Burroughs, and Jennifer Jackman to this essay.]

Suggested Further Reading

Carabillo, Toni, Judith Meuli, and June Bundy Csida. *Feminist Chronicles, 1953–1993*. Los Angeles, California: Women's Graphics, 1993.

Davis, Flora. *Moving the Mountain: The Women's Movement in America Since 1960*. New York: Simon & Schuster, 1991.

Delamotte, Eugenia, Natania Meeker, and Jean O'Barr, eds. *Women Imagine Change: A Global Anthology of Women's Resistance from 600 B.C.E. to the Present*. New York: Routledge, 1997.

Faludi, Susan. *Backlash: The Undeclared War Against American Women*. New York: Crown Publishers, 1981.

Gage, Matilda Joslyn. *Women, Church, and State*. (Original publication 1893.) Aberdeen, South Dakota: Pine Hill Press, Inc., 1998.

Inner Space:
The Spiritual Frontier

MARGOT ADLER

THE CONTEMPORARY WOMEN'S spirituality movement was born in the early 1970s, after women confronted an uncomfortable truth: "God" was male. The notion that "God" is considered male in the monotheistic religions dominating our present era "legitimates all earthly Godfathers," to quote feminist philosopher Mary Daly—or, as she summed it up, "If God is male, then the male is God."[1]

The Creative Force—God/Goddess, whatever we choose to call it—is, of course, beyond gender, perhaps beyond knowing. But though a thousand male and female deities populate the myths of Asian, African, and Native American cultures, and though powerful women, divine and mortal, figure in ancient legends from Egypt, India, Greece, Scandinavia, the British Isles, and virtually everywhere else,[2] most of us are burdened by the dominant image of god as male. This is particularly true for women who have grown up in the Abrahamic faiths or "religions of the book": Judaism, Christianity, and Islam. Women seeking a spiritual dimension to feminism have struggled, during the second half of the twentieth century, to locate or create female images of power. But they have also forged a spiritual movement emphasizing the sacredness of this world, the body, and the earth, one standing in stark contrast to

---

1. Mary Daly, *Beyond God the Father* (Boston: Beacon Press, 1973).

2. See, for example, *The New Book of Goddesses and Heroines*, by Patricia Monaghan (St. Paul, Minnesota: Llewellyn Publishers, 2000).

extremist, proselytizing religious views—especially fundamentalisms,[3] whether Christian, Hebrew, Islamic, or other.[4]

The women's spirituality movement originated, in part, from insights gained in consciousness-raising (CR) groups, in which women dared speak aloud their most intimate thoughts and feelings with no fear of being interrupted or silenced. They talked about work, motherhood, sexuality, menstruation, lesbianism, childhood, men; their discussions brought about a sharing of insights from which a new vision of power and politics emerged. A foundational insight of CR was that one's own experience should be trusted, so many women began forming small groups to discuss their dreams, intuitions, and spiritual odysseys, believing that these also contained truths. Some feminists studied ancient civilizations to see if women had different notions of power; others examined the history of their own religious traditions and created female-centered liturgies; still others, despairing that traditions so entangled with patriarchy could ever be a source of liberation, created new, women-centered religions outside the mainstream.

Meanwhile, some women felt a call to ministry and began to fight for their place in established faiths. At this writing [late 2002], Roman Catholic women still cannot become priests[5]; Orthodox Jewish women still cannot be rabbis; only recently have Conservative Jewish women been able to enter the rabbinate and have Episcopal women become priests and bishops. Women who chose to fight patriarchy within their own religions brought about serious reforms, at least in the more liberal branches: rewording of prayer books and hymnals to include female imagery; creation of new ceremonies (for example, women's seders in Judaism; alternate, lay masses in Catholicism; women's prayer groups in Islam).

Meanwhile, outside the mainstream religions, women's spirituality has flowered. There are thousands of small groups all across North America, embracing multiple forms of goddess and earth-centered

---

3. See, for example, "Combating the Religious Right," by Cecile Richards, p. 464.—Ed.

4. Hinduism, Shintoism, certain Buddhist traditions, and even some indigenous faith systems have generated fundamentalist sects and movements as well.—Ed.

5. See "Dancing Against the Vatican," by Frances Kissling, p. 474.—Ed.

belief systems. For women whose notion of the feminine had been shaped in the 1950s, images of Athena, Hecate, Artemis, Isis, Kali, and Spider Woman (to mention just a few) have been healthful medicine. Within a few years, the writings and practices of African and Native women had broadened a movement that at first was too Western and too white.[6] Not only were the original myths and legends of almost every indigenous culture vibrant with strong, active women—often the creators of civilization, the arts, agriculture, industry, politics, and social life—but non-Western cultures also taught North American and European women new ways of perceiving humanity's relationship to the natural world.

One example: during the 1970s, The Unitarian Universalist Association (UUA) created a study course in women and religion for their congregations—with books, a study guide, suggestions for rituals, even a film strip. Many women and quite a few men were changed radically by the course. They began to shift the direction of their churches, designing new liturgies and music, creating women's and men's circles, adding exuberant ritual to services that had previously been dry, often boring sessions. New tensions sprang up between humanists and rationalists on one hand, and those who embraced this new, more passionate, ceremonial direction. After much debate, the UUA included earth-centered spirituality as one of its official sources. The original course had emphasized Europe (ancient goddesses of Greece and the British Isles). A second study course brought goddesses of every continent into UUA congregations; new books and articles began to reflect women's experiences in a multitude of cultures, races, ethnic groups. But with the exception of the UUA example, most women's spirituality groups have grown outside of official religion: small groups of women creating meaningful religious life.

Starting in the late 1960s, certain feminist groups had begun to use the image of the witch as a metaphor for a powerful, self-reliant woman,[7] someone willing to rebel, to challenge the dominant culture's

---

6. See, for example, "Native Americans: Restoring the Power of Thought Woman," by Clara Sue Kidwell, p. 165.—Ed.

7. Groups such as W.I.T.C.H., begun in 1968, flourished and spun off into "daughter covens" across the country, but saw themselves more as secular and activist than

ideology. Barbara Ehrenreich and Dierdre English wrote a ground-breaking pamphlet, later a book, linking the persecution of women and witches with the rise of the medical profession.[8] The word "witch" is itself fraught with complex associations: Christians see evil and Satanism; Hollywood depicts seductresses casting spells; popular culture uses the word for someone, usually female, who tells fortunes or has psychic powers. Why would feminists identify with the word, given its negative connotations? "Witch" has associations with ancient knowledge, with women schooled in the arts of healing, herbology, midwifery. But it also evokes a person defined by herself, not by men. The word has a radical impact, resonating with a notion of spirituality based on the sacredness of nature and the life of this world, as opposed to a religion that denigrates earthly life and promotes only an abstract hereafter as valuable. Most major religions assume a hierarchy from a god on down through messiahs and prophets to gurus and disciples—with nature as a lowly servant. Because of association with childbirth, menstruation, and sexuality, women traditionally have been viewed as bound to the cycles of nature—and religions that denigrate the earthly plane tend to place women, too, at the bottom: spirit is exalted, flesh seen as inconsequential (or worse), and life regarded as something to pass through. The dichotomies characterizing our age—mind versus body, spirit versus material, sacred/secular, play/work, emotion/rationality, white/black, men/women—reflect religious and philosophical views mired in such dualisms and hierarchies.

What is truly revolutionary about feminist spirituality is that, at root, it posits a third way—and overthrows this hierarchy. Women's spirituality encourages a pluralism and egalitarianism worthy of democracy at its best.[9]

Human beings have evolved and lived successfully as a species on this planet for hundreds of thousands of years, yet we forget this because

---

theoretical, scholarly, or spiritual. See R. Morgan, *Saturday's Child: A Memoir* (New York: W. W. Norton, 2000) for details.—Ed.

8. *Witches, Midwives, and Nurses: A History of Women Healers* (New York: The Feminist Press at CUNY, 1970).

9. For parallel insights regarding feminist thought and democracy, see "Sisterhood Is Pleasurable: A Quiet Revolution in Psychology," by Carol Gilligan, p. 94.—Ed.

we're taught that the only valuable part of our heritage is the "historical part" recorded over the last 6,000 years. We may *believe* in evolution, but we *act* as if the world began with the myth of Adam and Eve. We forget that our ancestors, no matter where we're from, lived, hunted, gathered, procreated, established communities, questioned their relationship to the stars, acquired knowledge of seasons and flora and fauna, and created ceremonies that helped knit their lives into relationship with the lands on which they lived, the animals and plants they knew, and the communities they created.[10]

The so-called great religions, the monotheistic religions that dominate our time, are all quite recent in human history—and despite the beauty and profundity of many of their scriptures, they all contain foundational texts reeking with hatred of women and denigration of the body and the material world.[11] Whether it is the daily prayer of male Jews thanking God "for not making me a woman," or Paul's New Testament misogynistic contempt for women, or the concept in Islamic Shari'a jurisprudence that two female witnesses are needed to equal one male witness—Judaism, Christianity, and Islam all are based on texts deeply problematic for women. Alongside the poetry and wisdom in the *Torah*, the *Bible*, and the *Koran*, are texts justifying human sacrifice, religious war, martyrdom, and a preference for an abstract heaven over a tangible earth. The resulting history has been crusades, conquests, pogroms, jihads, inquisitions, witch burnings, rape, slavery, and murder—always justifiable if against the "unbeliever," the "infidel," the *other*. There has rarely been a better (or more bitter) moment for us to grasp the toxicity of these scriptural texts' impact than in the post-9/11/2001 reality.[12]

---

10. See "Bitch, Chick, Cow: Women's and (Other) Animals' Rights," by Carol Adams, p. 494; and "Update: Feminism and the Environment," by Paula DiPerna, p. 503.—Ed.

11. For many insights on the foundational texts of the "religions of the book," I am indebted to discussions with Caron Cadle, and in particular her excellent essay, "Haunted by the Afterlife, A Modest Proposal (To Dump the Whole Concept)," published in Fall 2001, issue of *Awakened Woman: The Journal of Women's Spirituality*, an on-line journal available at *www.awakenedwoman.com*.

12. In his last will and testament, the Al Qaeda hijacker Mohammed Atta stipulated that no woman should be permitted to visit his grave (because women are impure),

Unlike the "religions of the book," the old religions did not depend on literal texts, but on the doing and living that comprises experience. They were based on the rhythms of celestial bodies, the movement of herds, the turn of the seasons; they emphasized ceremonies of birth, life, death, regeneration. The earth religions were tied to *place*. Each people had its own sacred places, its own rivers and mountains, so there was no assumption that there was (or should be) a single truth. There was no missionary desire to proselytize, crusade, or convert because—though there was a sense of "oneness" in the experience of spiritual connection—different peoples had different cultures and therefore distinct sacred places, thus diverse divinities. Being based on oral tradition instead of literal text, there was no scripture to fight over. Furthermore, belief systems that perceive the world *metaphorically instead of literally* can adapt to new information and scientific findings. Earth-centered religions understand "god" or "gods" as immanent in nature, connected to all things, from rocks to trees to human creatures. The Sublime is not above, with humans below; *everything* is part of a vibrant, sacred reality.

It's perhaps no wonder that many women turned from beliefs that denigrated the body and the world, and looked to the earth-centered traditions for sustenance, sometimes recasting them in contemporary forms, seeking a metaphysics that might heal the split between material and spiritual. Nevertheless, it's important to note that large numbers of Jewish, Christian, and Muslim women are creating powerful forms of feminist spirituality *within* the monotheistic religions. Christian feminist writer Rosemary Radford Reuther has noted that hierarchy is not essential in the Christian tradition; God/dess is not merely mother and father but all roles and experience.[13] Jewish feminist writer Judith Plaskow has written about how women have often felt excluded from the central moments of Jewish history—yet over the past three decades

---

and that men who washed his body should wear gloves so as not to touch his genitals (*New York Times*, 4 October 2001). Such flesh-loathing and woman-hating is reminiscent of passages in the infamous handbook for witch hunters first published in 1486: *The Witches' Hammer*, by Dominican monks Heinrich Kramer and James Sprenger (New York: Dover, 1971).

13. Rosemary Radford Reuther, "Sexism and God Language," in *Weaving the Visions: New Patterns in Feminist Spirituality*, Judith Plaskow and Carol Christ, eds. (San Francisco: Harper & Row, 1989).

have demanded their right to pray at the Wailing Wall, and have become cantors and rabbis.[14] Moroccan sociologist Fatima Mernissi is one of numerous Muslim feminists who have done extensive studies reinterpreting Koranic and Shari'a texts and Hadiths to expose sexist, patriarchal interpretations and to encourage Muslim women to redefine Islam in more inclusive, humanist ways.[15]

As women's spirituality enters a new century and millennium (in Common Era terms, that is), there are issues this growing, changing movement needs to confront.

One is our scholarship. We need to be scrupulous. We need not exaggerate the number of witches killed under European persecutions, nor need we inflate the existence of real cultures where women held power (or women and men held equal power) into notions of an ancient, universal age of matriarchy.

We also need ethical clarity. Women have founded a range of support groups, from spiritual families to forms of therapy. These groups have been liberating, less patriarchal than traditional therapy/counseling. But there have been abuses (perhaps unavoidably, in a world dominated by capitalism, some women have charged money for "goddess circles," as if they were group-therapy sessions). Feminist spirituality may well have therapeutic results—but ultimately it is not therapy. Furthermore, although there's power in the idea that one's knowledge of reality springs from personal experience, in spiritual work reality is not always clear, and "trusting one's feelings" has led many a spiritual leader down the road to self-delusion. As the feminist spirituality community matures, we can admit that women, like all humans, occasionally lie or create fantasies.

We also need to remember our politics. Women's spirituality is not a "New Age" movement; it will always be deeply entwined with feminist analysis and a sense of the material world. It has a place for mystics—*and* for agnostics and atheists. One can feel a bond of community and a love

14. Judith Plaskow, "Jewish Memory from a Feminist Perspective," in Plaskow and Christ, op. cit.

15. Fatima Mernissi, *Beyond the Veil: Male-Female Dynamics in Modern Muslim Society* (Schenkman, 1975; revised edition Indiana University Press, 1987), and *The Veil and the Male Elite: A Feminist Interpretation of Women's Rights in Islam* (Addison-Wesley Publishing Company, 1991).

of ceremony without having to adhere to any particular creed. More-over, some "New Age" ideas are problematic for most feminists—e.g., we *didn't* all necessarily "choose to be here" or "choose our illnesses and oppressions." One of feminism's insights is that we are all more affected than we wish to believe by gender, race, class, age, disability, sexual pref-erence/orientation, etc.—*and* by the dominant ideologies around us.[16]

In the United States, whence much of the contemporary women's spirituality movement originated, both women and men must confront not only a liberation but also an impoverishment that comes with a lack of rooted traditions. No matter our ancestry, almost all of us live in a culture fairly barren regarding ceremonies, songs, stories, rituals—the juice and mystery that are part and parcel of indigenous religious expe-rience. If our ancestors were Native American peoples, our traditions were decimated through colonialism and forced conversion. If our ancestors were brought here as slaves or bonded labor, our traditions were brutally suppressed. If our ancestors came here as immigrants, fleeing authoritarianism, our traditions were lost in the desire to assim-ilate. All of us are missing elements that bind communities together. A crucial aspect of women's spirituality involves the discovery, re-creation, and creation of stories and ceremonies that foster that sense of commu-nity—but one with a contemporary sense of democracy and egalitarian-ism. This is a spirituality not based on literal scripture and fanatical belief, but on experience and pluralism; one at home with flexibility and new scientific knowledge, yet one that sees clearly the burden moder-nity has placed on the fragile earth. Allowing ecstasy and intellectual in-tegrity at the same time, the forms of such spirituality are many, but its coexistence with freedom and modern life is something that our whole world could use as a model.

The spiritual world is not unlike the natural world: only diversity will save it. Just as the health of a forest can be measured by the number of varied creatures who thrive there, so only by an abundance of spiritual and philosophical paths can human beings navigate a path through the murk of our epoch. Our culture has denigrated the female as evil or ir-relevant. Yet women and men who embrace a sacred female principle

---

16. See "Traffic at the Crossroads: Multiple Oppressions," by Kimberlé Crenshaw, p. 43, and the "Juggling Jeopardies" section, p. 163.—Ed.

can gain not only a new understanding of themselves as whole, sacred beings; they can envision a world complex enough to sustain—and evolve—humanity.

MARGOT ADLER has been a priestess of Wicca since 1973. She has worked for National Public Radio since 1979, and is a correspondent reporting for *All Things Considered, Morning Edition,* and *Weekend Edition.* A journalist, writer, and radio producer, she is the author of *Drawing Down the Moon: Witches, Druids, Goddess-Worshippers and Other Pagans in America Today* (first edition 1979, revised edition 1986; third edition, Penguin, 1997), and of *Heretic's Heart: A Journey Through Spirit and Revolution* (Beacon Press, 1997), a memoir of the 1960s. A graduate of the University of California (Berkeley) and Columbia University's Graduate School of Journalism, she was a 1982 Nieman Fellow [sic] at Harvard.

Suggested Further Reading

Christ, Carol, and Judith Plaskow, eds. *Womanspirit Rising: A Feminist Reader in Religion.* San Francisco: Harper & Row, 1979.

Gimbutas, Marija. *The Civilization of the Goddess.* San Francisco: HarperSanFrancisco, 1991.

Sjöö, Monica, and Barbara Mor. *The Great Cosmic Mother: Rediscovering the Religion of the Earth.* New York: Harper & Row, 1986; second edition New York: HarperCollins, 1991.

Spretnak, Charlene. *The Politics of Women's Spirituality.* New York: Anchor Press, 1982.

Starhawk. *The Spiral Dance, A Rebirth of the Ancient Religion of the Great Goddess.* San Francisco: Harper & Row, 1979.

Outer Space:
The Worldly Frontier

(By the Way, I Do Intend to Go and
to Make Something Out of It)

MAE C. JEMISON, M.D.

"THE STARS ARE REALLY SUNS, they're just millions of miles away. That's why they look so small. Right, Uncle Louis?"

My uncle smiled.

"That's right," he replied.

Summer nights in Chicago often found me lying on the ground, staring up at the stars. My Uncle Louis and I would discuss the universe and Einstein's theory of relativity. School days found me busy with science projects on how the earth was formed and the "Eras of Time." Growing up in the inner city in Chicago in the 1960s, I—like so many other six-, seven-, and eight-year-olds across the country—followed the Mercury, Gemini, and Apollo programs with almost zealous fervor. I knew line, stanza, and verse of how we humans would soon reach the moon. I knew which vehicles and probes were launched and what their missions were. I would begin watching a countdown at home and hurry to school to see the actual launch in Mrs. Connelly's (my third-grade teacher) classroom.

Alan Shepard, John Glenn, John Young, Pete Conrad, even Yuri Gargarin—I knew the human spacefarers' names. Unfortunately, they were all men—except for Valentina Tereshkova, a Russian cosmonaut and the first woman to go into space, in 1963 (and the only woman for many years afterward). This was a constant irritation to me, one I spoke of frequently: "There should be *women* in space!" I railed against adults who tried to "help" me understand why "women were not capable of going into space." I never believed it. I was born aware of my capabilities. Not only was this unfair *and* scientifically and socially unjustifiable, but I was also convinced that keeping women from space exploration was detrimental *to* space exploration. After all, what would the aliens think when they encountered only white males from the military as representatives of the planet Earth? Even as a child, I knew this would not make for a pretty picture.

I loved science fiction. Precocious for my age, I read books like *A for Andromeda* by the astronomer Fred Hoyle, *2001: A Space Odyssey* by Arthur C. Clark, *I, Robot* by Isaac Asimov. I never missed an episode of *Star Trek*. It pissed me off that I could only find women as the scientists and heroines in Madeleine L'Engle's *A Wrinkle in Time* and *The Arm of the Starfish*. Yet I was captivated by the mystery, the possibilities, and the promise. I somehow always knew that the failures were in society and that the authors' apparently limited imaginations had nothing to do with a woman's capacities, intellectual *or* physical. So it was critical that we got some other folks involved.

I intended to go into space, and I assumed I would. Furthermore, I was adamantly in favor of humankind expanding its presence in the universe.

Over the ensuing years I studied the fine arts, physical sciences, and social sciences. I went to Stanford University at age sixteen and made the decision not to become an astronomer, but to aim toward biomedical engineering. I was active in student politics, and I choreographed and produced modern and jazz dance shows—all the while learning how to solve partial differential equations, fluid flow, and heat transfer theory. By the time I entered medical school, NASA (the National Aeronautics and Space Administration) had admitted the first women, and the first African Americans, Asian Americans, and Hispanics, into the astronaut corps. As for me, nothing—not my having worked in Cambodian refugee camps in Thailand and not even my having been Area Peace Corps Medical Officer in Sierra Leone and Liberia in West Africa—had changed my love for space exploration and my intention to participate.

Sally Ride, the first European American woman to go into space, did so in 1983 while I was working in West Africa. Guy Bluford, the first African American man in space went up the same year (the first black man in space was a Cuban cosmonaut who had gone up with the Russians). By the time I entered the astronaut program in 1987, in the wake of the Challenger accident, the most critical issue confronting space exploration was not so much who could and should participate (though clearly we still had and have a long way to go).[1] The question was becoming "Why go up at all?"

In 1992, when I became the first woman of color in the world to go into space, I was still being asked *"Why?"* I found myself needing to an-

---

1. The current (2002) NASA website *(www.NASA.gov)* is at once educative, depressing, and hopeful when addressing the participation of men of color and any/all women. Acknowledged pressure from the Congressional Black Caucus has borne fruit in NASA having established serious outreach programs toward minority students, and having sought out minority businesses with which to contract. The website boasts that recently NASA doubled its number of African American senior executives—from 15 to 30—but fails to disaggregate by gender or tell us the total number of senior executives so that we might have a sense of scale. There is also a NASA women's outreach program, and women comprise over one third of NASA's overall workforce, employed in a range of skilled jobs—as aeronautical/astronautical design engineers, physicists doing laser research, pilots, research psychologists, oceanographers, geologists, and pilot crews performing high-altitude research and flying triple-sonic aircraft. But less than 25 percent of NASA's astronauts are women. (Only 6 percent of all aerospace engineers are women, as are only 1.2 percent of all civilian and commercial pilots and 2 percent of all military pilots.) As of September 1, 1998 (the most recent date listed by NASA), 40 women had been selected as astronauts and 29 women had flown Shuttle missions. Women were chosen as astronaut candidates for the first time in 1978; the first six included Sally K. Ride and Shannon W. Lucid, who holds the record for the most flight hours in space by any woman and the record for the longest time in space by any U.S. citizen. In 1999, Lt. Col. Eileen Collins became the first woman to command a space mission. And for the first time in the history of spaceflight, the ascent commentator, flight director, and Capcom (the voice astronauts hear from Mission Control) on the STS-95 team were all women. A hyperlink to Latina Women of NASA, however, lists a total of merely ten names, only one of whom—Ellen Ochoa—is an astronaut (there are seven Hispanic astronauts, with Ochoa the only woman). At another hyperlink, NASA's Marshall Space Flight Center Diversity News, African Americans in the U.S. space program have the longest reference list, with Hispanics coming in second and Asian Americans further down; the next-to-shortest list is for "Disabled Americans," followed by Native Americans, who come up last, with a single entry; "Age" as a category is replete with references to former senator and former astronaut John Glenn's second trip into space, in his seventies; Diversity News posts no category at all for "women." Yet the NASA site itself is canny enough to use the feminist coinage "Herstory" in describing the story of women in the U.S. space program.—Ed.

swer that question for others and to understand myself if indeed I was not just fulfilling an "adrenaline junkie dream" (not that there's anything wrong with that).

Why go at all?

As Ambassador to France, Benjamin Franklin had occasion to witness the first flights of hot-air balloons. When skeptics wondered to what use hot-air balloon exploration might possibly be put, Franklin is reported to have answered, "What is the use of a newborn baby?"

The exploration of space is as instinctive and natural a progression in human history as prehistoric humans leaving the security of the Rift Valley. Crossing the Sahara Desert in caravans. Building the pyramids. Delineating the laws of gravity. Elucidating the sequence of DNA replication. We have always tried to discover *why;* tried to understand the world and thus shape our own destinies. Through space exploration, we continue.

Definitions are important. *Webster's Dictionary* defines exploration as "to make a systematic search and to penetrate into or range over for purposes of geographical discovery." But exploration may take on different meanings in different contexts. I consider space exploration as being comprised of three realms, which I classify as the physical, the applied, and the imaginative.

- *The physical realm of exploration* is most immediately familiar and thus comfortable for us to consider. It is Matthew Henson and Commander Peary reaching the North Pole, and Marco Polo discovering that there *were* already people in China! Physical exploration puts us, body and soul, into a physical location—and thrills us viscerally.

- *Applied exploration* focuses our curiosity on solving a problem for which we have need of an immediate answer. In this context, exploration may produce a specific commercial, political, or technological reward during the subsequent five to ten years. It has to do with applicability in the immediate, foreseeable future.

- *Imaginative exploration* seeks knowledge just for the sake of knowing. It occurs as people yield to that irrepressible desire to know *why* something is or *what* it is. A child asks, "Why is there air?" We invent different means to gain this information. For all we know, the information obtained may or may not be practically applicable for generations to come—or ever. Yet a wonderful aspect of imaginative exploration is that many times the exploration has yielded tremendous gains in the most unlikely, unexpected ways.

History gives us examples of exploration in all of its forms, with many varied results. In a plague-ridden Europe of the sixteenth century, Sir Isaac Newton or his supporters would have been hard-pressed to justify research on the laws of motion as relevant to the circumstances and technology of that time. Similarly, it is difficult for me to explain the current utility of verification of time-space discontinuities in the nature of black holes, while HIV/AIDS threatens to sweep the world. Yet it's as a result of Newton's quest over 300 years ago for knowledge of the universe, *for the sake of pure knowledge,* that we are now able to peer through an electron microscope at the HIV virus in search of a cure. Newton's imaginative exploration has many times over proven itself a life saver and life enhancer.

One example of applied exploration that did *not* turn out to do what it was projected to do was the exploration undertaken by Christopher Columbus. He never did bring back the ginger he promised King Ferdinand or the red silk with gold weave he owed Queen Isabella. Yet in sailing west to get east, Columbus was not only looking for a more economical trade route, but was also in the process of proving a theory that the earth was round. Though Chris was clearly trying to gain economic advantage over the ensuing five to ten years (and he never did actually prove the world was round), his voyage fundamentally affected the course of world history over the past 500 years.

So as we ponder, "Why go? Why space exploration?" we should also realize that the twentieth century has afforded us quite a unique perspective of human history from which to view the choices. We are privileged. We have the advantage of years of knowledge, knowledge gained when the quest for understanding was important enough in itself, or cheap enough, to warrant the investment and the time. We can look back and be sure that our basic human desire to know *why* has the potential to lead to amazing inventions, comforts, and states of well-being that far outstrip any fantasy.

We have also seen that an insatiable desire to have dominion over nature sometimes brings us to the brink of global disaster.[1] What happens always depends on the life-long perspective of individuals doing the exploring: *who participates determines what opportunities are recognized, developed, and exploited.* The most enduring benefits will come from exploration when the opportunity for participation encompasses everyone. Our current dilemma is that the bounty of the past that we reap today has jaded us. Now we unceremoniously demand that our exploration yield rewards we can foresee in dollars and cents (not *sense*), preferably before the next election.

What possibilities does space exploration hold for today and tomorrow? Enhancement of life right here on earth through the use of the technologies that were designed to carry space vehicles aloft—the need to reduce the weight put into orbit and to monitor astronaut physiology—led to miniaturization of electronic parts and medical telemetry during the Apollo era; insulating materials developed for spacesuits provided roofing for the airport in Jeddah; the aerodynamics of an aircraft traveling 25 times faster than the speed of sound had to be understood in order to land the space shuttle. The vantage point of having equipment in space allows us to provide radio and television transmission to and from remote corners of the world; storm tracking by weather satellites helps to mitigate the impact of disasters; global positioning satellites (GPS) allow for pinpoint location accuracy; and remote sensing can even help with the prediction of disease prevalence. In addition, the platform of space can help us to understand basic physics, and chemical and even biological sciences, by removing factors of weight and atmospheric interference while helping us adapt to new environments.

Then there is *"just because."*

Space exploration, expanding human presence, can help us develop not only a sense of our place in the universe, but also a sense of self—who we are individually, and our relationship to one another on this planet.

When I went into space I carried with me, among other things: an Alvin Ailey Dance Company poster of Judith Jamison performing *Cry,* a Bundu statue from a women's society in Sierra Leone, and a Certificate

---

1. See "Update: Feminism and the Environment," by Paula DiPerna, p. 503, and the Introduction, p. *xv.*—Ed.

for the Chicago Public Schools students to work to improve their science and math. Folks asked me why I took these items. I did so because, to me, each represented the same thing: human creativity, human potential. The creativity it required to conceive, build, and launch the space shuttle springs from the same source as the imagination and analysis required to create the Bundu statue, the same ingenuity necessary to conceive and stage *Cry*. And I wanted to include cultures, ideas, and individuals not commonly thought of as involved in space exploration.

As we face the future, space exploration is now as much a part of the landscape of the whole world as it once was for the young girl I used to be, gazing at the stars over Chicago. It is part of our yesterday, today, and tomorrow. It is part of our human heritage—which is our responsibility not to forsake. That is a heritage some mistakenly see as harshly separating us from the rest of nature; yet our insatiable curiosity propels us to try to grasp, to understand, to know the secrets of the universe—and thereby once again belong. We should have learned this about ourselves by now.

Space. As we enter the twenty-first century, space continues to emerge as one of humankind's greatest challenges.

Space gives us another arena to explore physically—to touch, as woman first touched fire.

Space exploration permits us to experiment with materials—as when man first used gunpowder, or gazed at his image in a mirror.

Space compels us to peer billions of light years into the past, perhaps to see creation, just as the child who asks, "Where did I come from?"

The space age did not begin in 1957 with Sputnik. The space age has been part of us, part of humanity, since one of my ancestors more than a thousand generations before me looked skyward, saw the moon and a star-studded sky, reached out her hand but could not touch it, and so began to chart the movements of the heavens.

Space exploration is a human imperative as old as humanity itself.

MAE C. JEMISON blasted into orbit aboard the space shuttle Endeavour on September 12, 1992—the first woman of color on the planet to go into space. Science-mission specialist on the STS-47 Spacelab J flight, a U.S./Japan joint mission, she conducted experiments in life sciences and material sciences, and was a co-investigator of the Bone Cell Research experiment. She founded and is president of two technical companies: BioSentient Corporation, a medical technology company that develops and markets mobile equipment worn to monitor the body's vital signs and train people to respond favorably in stressful situations; and The Jemison Group, Inc., focusing on the beneficial integration of science and technology into everyday life—such as consulting on design/implementation of solar thermal electricity generation systems for developing countries, and satellite-based telecommunications to facilitate health care delivery in West Africa. Dr. Jemison also founded and chairs The Earth We Share (TEWS), an international science camp for students age 12–16 from around the world. Professor-at-large at Cornell University, Jemison was professor of environmental studies at Dartmouth, and is the author of *Find Where the Wind Goes: Moments from My Life*, autobiographical anecdotes written for teenagers (Scholastic, Inc., 2001). Dr. Jemison was elected into the National Academy of Sciences' Institute of Medicine, inducted into the National Women's Hall of Fame, and in 1999 selected as one of the top seven U.S. women leaders in a Presidential Ballot national straw poll conducted by The White House Project. She entered Stanford at age 16 on a scholarship, graduated with a B.S. in chemical engineering, and fulfilled the requirements for an A.B. in African and Afro-American studies; then earned her doctorate in medicine at Cornell. She loves cats, has appeared in an episode of *Star Trek: The Next Generation*, and lives in Houston, Texas.

Suggested Further Reading

At this writing, there are unfortunately no books about women and spacefaring that the contributor feels she can comfortably recommend. Hopefully, this will change, as greater numbers of women—who comprise more than half of humanity—participate in and help define the "human imperative" of space exploration.—Ed.

Personal Postscripts

To Vintage Feminists

FIRST OF ALL, *congratulations*. You've forged the largest, most diverse social justice movement in history—built it pretty much from scratch, since they'd buried about 10,000 years' evidence of women getting cranky under patriarchy. You've survived being red-baited, dyke-baited, straight-baited; being called a manhater, a ballbreaker, a commie *and* a fascist, bitchy, frigid (remember that one?), shrill, strident, divisive, ugly, crazy, and "not a *real* woman." More than 70 percent of your countrywomen acknowledge that the Women's Movement has vastly bettered their lives. *You did that.*

You've survived bitterness. You've watched flavors-of-the-month come and go, media-anointed stars who on the basis of one article or TV appearance suddenly "speak for all women"—then vanish while you're still circling the nearest abortion provider's offices, doing volunteer clinic defense. You've survived men yelling, "Nobody *else* feels this way, it's all in your head!"; survived women who built careers assaulting or misrepresenting feminism, thus making you wonder if sisterhood is suicide: the Phyllis Schlaflys and Camille Paglias, plus the latest conservative Bush Barbies: Condi Rice (who tragically seems to confuse herself with a rich white elderly male), and that long-blond-hair-tossing Stepford wife of the Right, Ann Coulter.[1] You've paid the personal cost.

You've ground your teeth at the "If it's good it can't possibly be feminist/If it's feminist it can't possibly be good" formula—e.g., the times you've been smeared for being "anti-children" though the only reason childcare is a national issue at all is because feminists *made* it one. You've spent years longing for the day when a record number of women run-

---

1. I used to fantasize about feminist abductions of such women: we would keep them sequestered in some nice country cabin, feed them homemade chicken soup and cups of tea, and de-program them as if they were cult victims, via consciousness-raising. They would then emerge, laughing and crying joyously, and proclaim having seen the light. I underestimated patriarchy's talent for rewarding its good girls, and overestimated feminist willingness to serve life sentences for kidnapping. But it *was* a nice fantasy. . . .

ning for office won't be newsworthy; when a nonsexist, nonracist, etc., world is the norm. You realize that you won't live to see it. In Elizabeth Cady Stanton's words, you are now "sowing winter wheat" for later springs to grow.

You've endured despair, when only the failures feel real, when feminist victories get conveniently dissociated from feminism—and when *we* don't brag: "Title IX was brought to you courtesy of the Women's Movement," or "We're the folks who won legalized abortion and RU486; rape-shield, sexual harassment, and no-fault divorce laws; laws prohibiting discrimination on the basis of sex, pregnancy, and marital status; third-party intervention in domestic violence cases; and lots—*lots*—more."

You may be from the generation that once warned "never trust anyone over thirty," but now you're not so sure you trust anyone *under* thirty. This isn't just ageism. It's because you got bashed both coming and going. Once, your elders denounced you as a sexual-revolution whore, just for being a feminist. Now you're dodging the condemnation of your juniors, who regard you as an anti-sex prude, just for being a feminist. *You* haven't changed, but somehow you've gone from slut to prig?[2]

Now, about those younger women. (Do glance at the personal postscript to them; it'll save all of us time.) If there's anything more maddening than being dissociated from victories you *have* won, it's being patronized or castigated for what you *didn't* do: for example, when some young women (drawing information from backlash in the media, not primary sources) declare that over the past thirty years the Women's Movement "didn't care about": fill in the blank—racism, homophobia, the environment, men. It's tempting to snarl, "What do *you* know, you twit?! You haven't a *clue!* You take it all for granted!" Unfortunately, that sounds as if you're channeling your grandfather, a feminist version of "*I* had to walk six miles in the snow to go to school!"

Although I know many individual vintage feminists who work beautifully with younger women, there's a too-common attitude we really need to watch out for: *preaching.* It's condescending at worst, patroniz-

---

2. See Gloria Steinem's article "The Media and the Movement: A User's Guide," p. 103, for more on this phenomenon.

ing at best.[3] After all, we were so busy "making the revolution" that we rarely spared time to train and develop in younger women organizing skills we ourselves were learning and inventing, so now we sometimes project onto them an ignorance we assume they must feel (surprise— they don't). But as Karla Jay writes,[4] older activists have forgotten that we managed to create and run organizations in our twenties. Young feminists deserve better than a guilt-trip. In fact, they deserve *thanks*, for ignoring all those pundits who told them that "young feminist" was an oxymoron.

The problem comes from the mother-daughter model. Even when meant affectionately, that model is based on a patriarchal, hierarchical family. If we must go to the family for a model, let's do it as sisters—approaching one another in all our flawed, frail, glorious humanity. But what if we took Barbara Macdonald's[5] advice and stepped *outside* the model? We want to redefine power; why not here? Surely there are ways to communicate with mutual esteem, balancing different strengths: age has the savvy of experience plus the confidence experience bestows; youth has the savvy of the future plus a splendidly arrogant sense of entitlement (which we wanted them to have, remember?). Cross-generational differences are like cross-cultural ones, and the basic element in international "feminist diplomacy" is *respect*—which means trying to *hear* each other. Interestingly, sometimes older women worry about the age divide more than younger ones. Without knowing one another, all the "Gen X, Y, and Z" and "thirtysomething" writers in these pages *reject* the generational labels as unrepresentative of their

---

3. There's another, less common attitude I've noticed in some older feminists that's equally unfortunate, though very different: trying desperately to be "with it." In this mode, an older feminist tends to avoid her contemporaries, seeks out younger women (ostensibly to mentor them—whether they like it or not), and dresses, embarrassingly, as if she were 20. (Remember when your parents tried to be "groovy" and you wanted to *die?*) Personally, I think this is the feminist version of Botox: a denial of aging—including a denial of the *power* that can accompany age.

4. See "Confessions of a Worrywart: Ruminations on a Lesbian Feminist Overview," p. 212; see also "The Art of Building Feminist Institutions to Last," by Eleanor Smeal, p. 541, on how and why it's vital that women's organizations include young feminists in their decision-making processes.

5. See "The Politics of Aging," p. 152.

complex realities. Should that surprise us? Those labels were created by advertisers to clump people into "targetable markets," and they are mostly an American obsession. They needn't be ours.[6]

A word on *our* future, as older women. If you were considering putting down or passing along your torch, uh-uh. Look around at all that's still *un*done. Besides, old women are the fastest growing demographic in the United States. With life expectancy rising, there's also an unprecedented number of old people in the world: more than 56 million between age 80 and 89, more than 6 million between 90 and 100, and 115,000 *over* age 100—numbers expected to multiply times *six* by the year 2050. Americans over age 50 (the majority of them female) account for half of all discretionary consumer spending; entire industries are developing to market new products to you. Think about your *clout*. You can redefine aging! (What would happen if feminists in droves joined and then *seized* the AARP, the largest, most effective lobbying group on age?) Back to Elizabeth Cady Stanton again, who vowed, "I shall not grow conservative with age." She didn't. At 87, she was critiquing sexism in the Bible. In fact, studies show that *men* grow more conservative with age, but women grow more *radical*.

When I was writing a memoir, I realized that failure *is* impossible, as Susan B. Anthony prophesied, and found myself writing about how historical perspective helps us tolerate the wait. But how boring to have to wait at all. Senators and congressmen who condemn progressives now are the same breed (in some cases the same *men*) who in the 1950s attacked Euripides, Christopher Marlowe, and Mark Twain as communists, and in the '60s predicted that racial segregation would endure forever. In the 1100s, when crusaders brought back to Europe table utensils adopted from the Saracens, the Catholic Church condemned them as obscene and heretical, claiming "God gave us fingers with

---

6. You don't find much generational tension between feminists internationally. Especially in the global South, women seem to understand that too much is at stake. For instance, I recall a march in the Philippines, led by three generations of women from one family. The grandmother had never learned to read, yet she fought off a batterer to raise her kids alone; the mother had managed to finish an eighth-grade education and enter the labor force as a hotel cleaner; the daughter was in medical school. They all called themselves feminists, marching arm in arm, tearfully beaming with mutual pride.

which to eat." And we're supposed to get politically *discouraged?* Oh, please. We're being opposed by people who denounced the *fork.*

So pick up your torch and let's get back to work. Age lends us more moral power—and, in one sense, more freedom—than we've ever known. Ursula K. Le Guin wrote it perfectly: "Old women are different from everybody else, *they say what they think.*"

In that case, I will.

I love you.

Robin

To Younger Women

FIRST OF ALL, *congratulations.* You've survived this far—in the book, in the Women's Movement (hopefully), and in gutsy curiosity, despite a barrage of hype telling you that because you're under forty you have no interest in your own freedom and power. You'll *need* both gutsiness and curiosity. You already know that—but remind yourself why. Cast a glance over the postscript to vintage feminists; it'll save all of us time. At the very least, you probably wouldn't be reading these words if you didn't see yourself in some way as sharing this inclusive, connective politics that's capable of saving sentient life on the small, fragile, blue planet we call home.

I wouldn't presume to go into your priorities: you know them better than I do. But since *we need each other* to save ourselves *and* each other, I have some tactical suggestions for getting along with older feminists. We/they might be driving you bonkers. Sometimes this is done when they try to act your age, not theirs; usually it's by preaching that you owe them gratitude and take hard-won freedoms for granted.

The problem comes from the mother-daughter model. Even when meant affectionately, that model is based on a patriarchal, hierarchical family. If we must go to the family for a model, let's do it as sisters—approaching one another in all our flawed, frail, glorious humanity. But what if we took Barbara Macdonald's[1] advice and stepped *outside* the model? We want to redefine power; why not here? Surely there are ways to communicate with mutual esteem, balancing different strengths: age has the savvy of experience plus the confidence experience bestows; youth has the savvy of the future plus a splendidly arrogant sense of entitlement (which older feminists wanted you to have, though they may forget that). Cross-generational differences are like cross-cultural ones, and the basic element in international "feminist diplomacy" is *respect*—which means *listening* to each other. Interestingly, sometimes the age di-

---

1. See "The Politics of Aging," p. 152.

vide is promulgated more by older women than by younger ones. Without knowing each other, all the "Gen X, Y, and Z" and "thirtysomething" writers in these pages *reject* generational labels as unrepresentative of their complex realities. Should that surprise us? Those labels were invented by advertisers to clump people into "targetable markets," and are mostly an American obsession. They needn't be ours.[2] *(Yes, a paragraph almost identical to this one is in "To Vintage Feminists"—on purpose.)*

Maybe, like Ana Grossman and Emma Peters-Axtell, you don't care about labels and just want to get stuff *done*. Maybe, like Jasmine Victoria, you chafe against "Gen" categories and want to flat-out disregard them. Maybe, like Kathleen Hanna, you're pissed because you're already being called old hat in your twenties, since marketers now define a generation as about five years long. Maybe, like "stealth feminist" Debra Michals, you find these categories arbitrary and want to define yourself.[3] (Whatever your bent, I hope you don't care which "wave" you are.[4] If you want to control your own life and body and help others do the same, you're riding a *tidal* wave.) "Identity politics" matter, but patriarchy's genius lies in emphasizing differences between people, so we may as well emphasize similarities wherever we can find them.

Anyway, the suggestions below might help move along a dialogue with older feminists.[5] (If you're already doing all the following, stop

---

2. You don't find much generational tension between feminists internationally. Especially in the global South, women seem to understand that too much is at stake. For instance, I recall a march in the Philippines, led by three generations of women from one family. The grandmother had never learned to read, yet she fought off a batterer to raise her kids alone; the mother had managed to finish an eighth-grade education and enter the labor force as a hotel cleaner; the daughter was in medical school. They all called themselves feminists, marching arm in arm, tearfully beaming with mutual pride.

3. See "Girls: 'We Are the Ones Who Can Make a Change!' " by Ana Grossman and Emma Peters-Axtell, p. 121; "Generation 'Why?': A Call to Arms," by Jasmine Victoria, p. 126; "Gen X Survivor: From Riot Grrrl Rock Star to Feminist Artist," by Kathleen Hanna, p. 131; and "Stealth Feminists: The Thirtysomething Revolution," by Debra Michals, p. 138.

4. See the Introduction for an explanation about why "first wave," "second wave," and "third wave" feminism are inaccurate misnomers with the unintended effect of collaborating in the erasure of women's history.

5. By older feminists I do not necessarily mean your mother, who is in a category by herself. Sometimes I meet mother-daughter feminist duos at a march or after a

reading and go be queen of the world.) It would be nice if you didn't believe most of what's been written about older feminists—or at least read
between the lines—and balance that by reading the work *of* the women
themselves. For instance, we're against pornography because we're
anti-*sexism*, not anti-sex (that's the Right-wing bad guys), and it's *because*
we love the delight of great sex that we oppose porn's message of domination and violence. (I was thirty before I got it together enough to stop
making fun of nineteenth-century suffragists for being—so I thought—
prudes. Then I actually read their work, and was mortified.)

Generally, younger women seem to adopt a variation of three types of
attitudes toward older feminists, none of which are really necessary.

One attitude implies envy or resentment: "I wish *I'd* been around in
the '60s! You had all the fun! You got to do it all!"—*or:* "Why *didn't* you
do it all? Why weren't you home making me cookies more? Why didn't
you *win* this fight already, so I wouldn't have to take it on?" Listen, jail is
not romantic. Tear gas stings like hell. Anyway, revolution is a renewable resource: picketing is fine exercise; who says buildings aren't still
there to be seized? And no, we weren't perfect. We screwed up a lot (see
the Introduction), but please don't buy into the myth that because we
did the cookie bit a little less, that meant we didn't adore the kids we
had, if we had them.[6] Don't waste energy envying *or* resenting us. Do
what *you* need to do.

The second attitude is the flip side of when older feminists get condescending (and if I'm doing that here, apologies). Younger women
often patronize older ones:[7] "How *cute* that you were all so *militant!*

---

speech; they gladden my heart, though they're rarer in the U.S. than elsewhere in
the world, where women speak proudly about being part of "a feminist dynasty."
Still, somewhere in my late twenties I realized that the hardest person in the world
to organize was your own mother. I'd suddenly seen her life through my newly feminist eyes. She was not just my mother! She was another woman! She was a sister!
That's when I learned that *you* may regard your mother as your sister—but *she* still
regards herself as your mother.

6. A footnote in defense of my generation as feminist mothers. We made mistakes,
yes—but far less damaging ones than *our* mothers made, in their powerlessness. In
any event, lots of us did revolution *and* the cookie bit. Overall, by god, we were fab-
ulous. You are evidence of that.

7. See Macdonald, op. cit.

Now, of course, you're *ancient*—so outta my way, gimme your torch." Speaking for myself, I'm hanging on to my torch, thank you. Get your own damned torch. It will take every torch possible to transform this system.

The third attitude is the most complicated. It's saturated with reverence and gratitude. The reverence can tend to make an older feminist feel like a walking artifact, a political pot-shard. (Sometimes it masks an unconsciously patronizing subtext like that just above, e.g., "Why, you're a living legend! So die already.") On the one hand, gratitude is lovely, simply because women at *any* age aren't celebrated much, while guys, who know how to do these things, busily bestow medals on each other. It's also pleasant because gratitude implies that the younger woman has done some homework and knows her own herstory.[8] Last, it's refreshing since most older feminists rarely got thanked for *any*-thing—much less for trying to affect a power structure that proceeded directly from predicting the Women's Movement would never get started to proclaiming it over, without once having passed through mere comprehension. So thanks now and then is a fine courtesy—*just as older feminists should express gratitude to younger ones*, for your gutsiness and curiosity (see above). But please don't put us on a pedestal, since then you can't look us in the eye. And never feel *obligated* to be grateful; if an older feminist tries to guilt-trip you into thanks, she's trapped in another turn of the mother-daughter screw.

It's assumed that when women act politically, we do so "for the sake of future generations" (the maternal model again). But here's the real truth, and may it set you free. *Older feminists didn't do it for you. We did it for ourselves*, each of us finding herself crushed against some moment of outrage so intense she could no longer *not* act. That's how we learned two essentials: *(1) we* have to hunger for our goals even more than the other side does, and *(2)* decisions get made by those who show up.

---

8. Such context is critical *to* younger women. Affirm or reject how we got this far, but *know* about it. As Kathleen Hanna writes, "Had I known more about the rich repertoire of tactical approaches used by feminists before me, I might have learned earlier how to apply strategies wisely instead of settling for a lazy, instant, one-size-fits-all approach" (Hanna, op. cit.).

So do it for yourself. Run for office, go into space, write songs, save the world. Make love, demands, policy, a fuss, miracles. Honor your own audacity. Act from *choice*, not obligation. *You owe us nothing.*

   You owe yourself everything.

In *(yesssss!)* sisterhood,
Robin